MISTER
X

MISTER

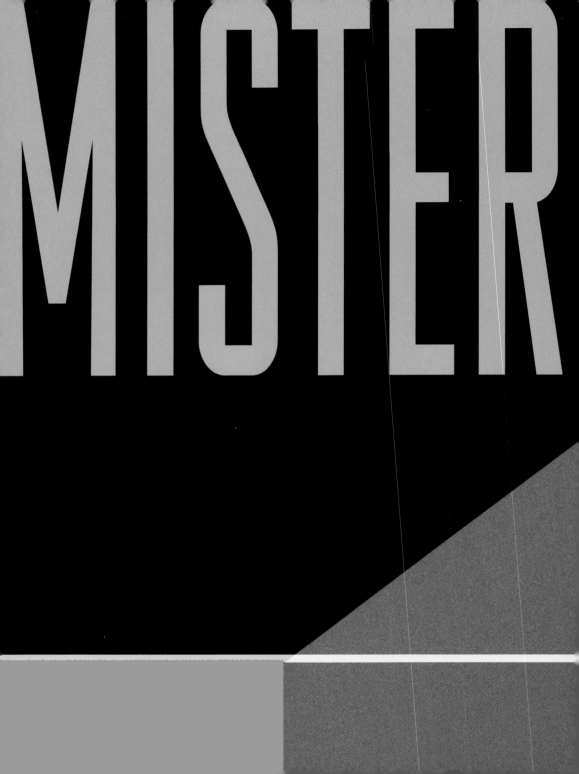

THE BRIDES OF MISTER X
AND OTHER STORIES

JEFFREY MORGAN · SHANE OAKLEY · D'ISRAELI
KEN HOLEWCZYNSKI · PETER MILLIGAN · BRETT EWINS

CREATED BY DEAN MOTTER

DARK HORSE BOOKS®

PUBLISHER **MIKE RICHARDSON**
ART DIRECTOR **LIA RIBACCHI**
BOOK DESIGNER **JUSTIN COUCH**
DIGITAL PRODUCTION **MATT DRYER**
ASSISTANT EDITOR **BRENDAN WRIGHT**
EDITOR **DAVE MARSHALL**
COVER ILLUSTRATION **DEAN MOTTER**

Published by Dark Horse Books
A division of Dark Horse Comics, Inc.
10956 SE Main Street
Milwaukie, OR 97222
DarkHorse.com

Library of Congress Cataloging-in-Publication Data

Morgan, Jeffrey, 1954-
 Dean Motter's Mister X : the brides of Mister X & other stories / created by Dean Motter ;
featuring Jeffrey Morgan, Shane Oakley, D'Israeli. -- 1st ed.
    p. cm.
 ISBN 978-1-59582-645-9
1. Graphic novels. I. Oakley, Shane. II. D'Israeli. III. Motter, Dean. IV. Title. V. Title: Brides of
Mister X.
 PN6728.M56M67 2011
 741.5973--dc22
                              2010051389

First edition: June 2011

10 9 8 7 6 5 4 3 2 1
Printed at 1010 Printing International, Ltd., Guangdong Province, China

This volume collects issues 1–12 of the Vortex comic-book series *Mister X* Volume 2, the Vortex
one-shot *Mister X Special*, and stories from issue 2 of the Atomeka comic-book series *A-1*, issue
6 of *Comic Book Artist* Volume 2, and issues 27 and 28 of *ArtReview*.

DEDICATED TO THE MEMORY OF BYRON PREISS,
HONORARY DEPUTY MAYOR OF RADIANT CITY.

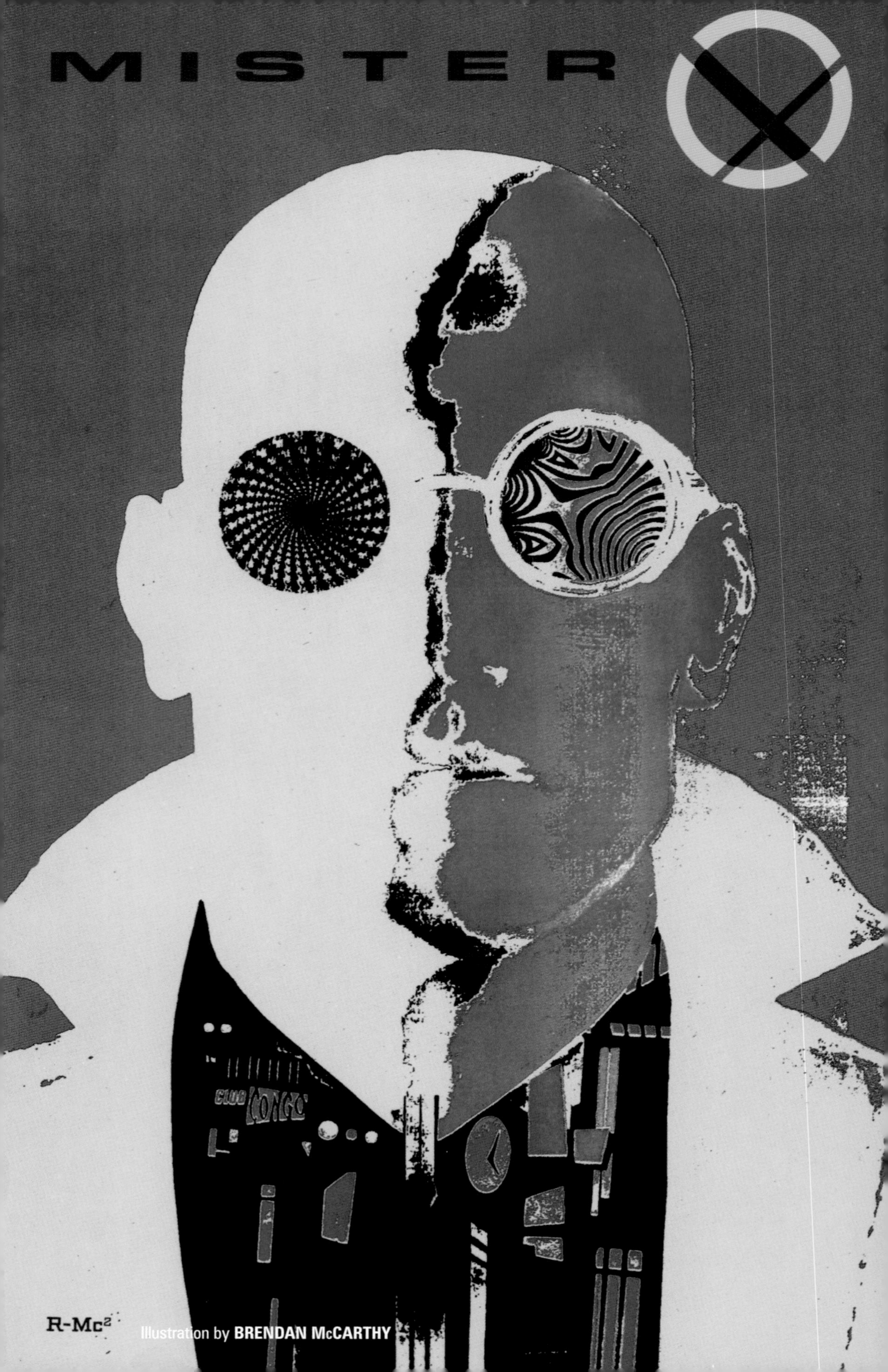
MISTER
CLUB CONGO
R-Mc²

Illustration by **BRENDAN McCARTHY**

CONTENTS

INTRODUCTION BY MARK WAID

Will Eisner came first, at least here in the States. Before Eisner brought us *The Spirit* in 1940, any of the buildings in any comic book in America could have been (and often were) drawn by a teenager with a T-square. Bus station? Box. Skyscraper? Tall box. House? Box with yard. To the artists who toiled in comic books, architecture on the page was like the bottle around their ink: something simple and bare minimum to contain the splashy stuff and give it context. Who cares what Metropolis looks like? Show us Superman.

Eisner found this unacceptable. Eisner, who realized that a character is defined not only by his actions but by his surroundings, lavished attention on the streets his heroes trod, on the tenements and sewers and rooftops where their battles took place. At his drawing board, Eisner invented worlds. His protagonists inhabited genuine real estate. In fact, it's been said of Eisner's *Spirit* comics that the city itself was a character. I'm not sure I buy that; it's a sweet thing to say and a romantic observation perfectly in keeping with Eisner's inventiveness, but (with all the respect in the world) I'd argue that his vistas were more about heightening verisimilitude than anything else. Still, without question, Will Eisner created cityscapes unique to his medium that remain points of reference to this day.

And then he stopped drawing comic books in 1952. The architect had stopped building, at least in this neighborhood.

It isn't like *nobody* kept pushing the geographic envelope in the years following. Steve Ditko's Spider-Man skittered through a highly atmospheric and authentic New York midtown, while conversely, Carmine Infantino's Flash sped along futuristic city streets that were at least a mile wide and looked like nothing on Earth. R. Crumb, in his classic twelve-panel "A Short History of America," brilliantly criticized urban creep by drawing a sixty-year time lapse of one street corner. But no one had gone the next step.

Jim Steranko came close. Steranko hit Marvel like a runaway train in the late 1960s and, briefly, the revolution was on again. Steranko was the Peter Max of funnybooks, folding pop-art graphics and psychedelic images into his storytelling. He pounded innovation into his pages with the energy of some crazy-ass John Henry, designing superspy Nick Fury's apartment to within an inch of its life with pop-art murals and a spiral staircase that defied gravity. He blew readers' minds (and budgets) with comics' first double double-page spread, a panoramic arch-villain's headquarters so sprawling and intricate that its image extended over four consecutive pages, requiring you to spring for a second copy of the book if you wanted to see it in all its glory.

Steranko drew twenty-nine comics and then, dusting off his hands, his job done, stopped. He'd melded the sensibilities of Eisner with his own take on modern design to once more reinvent comics' visual iconography in a way no one had ever seen, then moved on. And yet, as influential as his work was, as gripping as his skylines and underground lairs and spy HQs were, they—like Eisner's—still existed primarily to provide a framework for action. Yes, Steranko's cityscapes had character, but they weren't *a* character.

Dean Motter's and Paul Rivoche's *were*.

As impossible as it might be to envision in our modern, computer-driven, master-desktop-publishing-in-ten-easy-lessons era, in the early 1980s graphic design was almost completely absent from the comics medium. In a relentless attempt to grind the dominant tenor of illustration down into something as "realistic" and "adult" as possible, mainstream publishers had all but abandoned anything even remotely, shall we say, chimerical. Comics—still flinching from the censorship drives of the 1950s, still relying on unremarkable house styles so as to stay under the pop-culture radar—were ripe for a visual renaissance, and it took rebels like Frank Miller, Dave Stevens, and Howard Chaykin to reintroduce the audience of the early eighties to the power of the representational in lieu of the literal.

And it took Dean Motter to outdistance them all by blending art deco, Damon Runyon, the Bauhaus movement, Philip K. Dick, film noir, new-wave pop music, and Frank R. Paul into a series called *Mister X* that immediately and permanently changed the look of graphic storytelling throughout the Western Hemisphere. That's no exaggeration; Motter's creation was so provocative that thousands of readers, myself included, were ravenously hungry for it based simply on the initial promotional one-sheet tacked up in comics shops. With that one electric image, Mister X became the very first comics character to achieve icon status without yet having appeared in a single story.

And then, when the stories did come, Motter did the unthinkable: he outplayed Eisner and Steranko. The world of Mister X had a life even theirs never did, because it *literally had life*. Radiant City was Mister X's greatest and most terrifying creation because he built it using "psychetecture," a process known only to him that imbues the architecture with the ability to affect the very sanity of its inhabitants. In *Mister X*, the city—now known as Somnopolis, the City of Nightmare—really *is* a character. *It's the villain*.

That is the sound of ground breaking.

Visually, Somnopolis is remarkable because it doesn't build on existing familiarities. It is sui generis, wholly original, and among those films whose makers have gone on record as claiming *Mister X* as a direct influence are, unsurprisingly, *Brazil*, *Dark City*, and *The Matrix*. Neil Gaiman is a fan of the series, as are *Love and Rockets'* Hernandez brothers, who together helped Motter launch the series back in the eighties. Since then, as chronicled in this volume, many of comics' most talented writers and artists have paid a visit to Mister X's sinister city and lent him their own ingenuity as he struggles to free the citizens of Somnopolis from the tyranny of their surroundings. This collection particularly focuses on the tenure of Motter's friend and musical colleague, Jeffrey Morgan. It's not surprising that creators from far and wide are drawn to the world of *Mister X*; if there's anything artisans can universally relate to, it's the eternal yearning to fix the creations that didn't turn out the way we'd hoped.

Come to Somnopolis. Take the tour and see where comics history was made. You may never want to go home again.

Unless Mister X can save you.

MARK WAID
Fortress of Solitude, Los Angeles Annex
December 2010

Mark Waid has written for every major American comics publisher, including the landmark series Kingdom Come *for DC Comics, defining runs on* The Flash *for DC and* Fantastic Four *for Marvel, and work on countless more acclaimed titles. Waid recently served as editor-in-chief of BOOM! Studios, which publishes his creator-owned super-hero series* Irredeemable *and* Incorruptible.

MISTER X LIBRIS BY DEAN MOTTER

It's heartbreak to put one's child up for adoption. That's how I felt when I finished writing the tale of Mister X with issue 14. Business led me elsewhere, to a more profitable climate at DC Comics in 1988 at Richard Bruning's invitation. That led to *The Prisoner, Hellblazer, Terminal City*, and other work, including a stint on staff.

But my trench-coated, bald-headed, sunglassed offspring found a good foster home in the hands of longtime friend and collaborator Jeffrey Morgan. We had become colleagues as editor/writer/art-director team for Toronto's *Cheap Thrills/Stagelife* magazine in the seventies. We were always brothers under the skin. But very different kinds of people.

When Vortex relaunched *Mister X* (after my separation from the company in 1988), it hurt to think of my favorite creation going into other hands—but Vortex publisher William P. Marks put it into the hands of some comrades who did my baby right. Especially Herr Morgan, also my musical partner on the album *Thrilling Women*, a very Mister X–inspired work. He knew the material (and my muse/psyche), and, while moving to become the Canadian editor of *CREEM* magazine and doing Alice Cooper's liner notes, he managed to write a compelling sequel to my oeuvre.

But let's not omit Peter Milligan and the many groundbreaking artists who contributed their visions. They took up the effort and did a fine job of carrying the *Mister X* banner. This book represents their efforts, in addition to my reclamation of the shadowy phantom of Radiant City. And then there is the support of the whole Dark Horse outfit (especially Mike Richardson, Diana Schutz, and Dave Marshall). I'd also like to thank my Torontonian entourage—Paul Rivoche, Tom Robe, and Ken Steacy—once more. And then there's Karen Berger and Shelly Bond. There would be no *Mister X* books without any of them.

I hope you enjoy reading this as much I did when these issues were first published.

DEAN MOTTER
Last seen aboard the
Transatlantic Tunnel Express

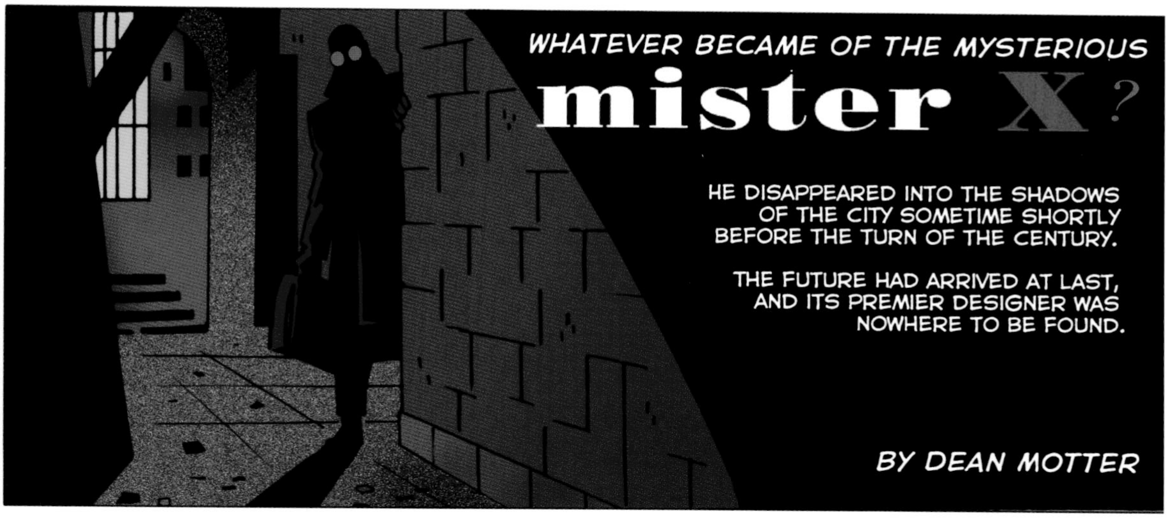
WHATEVER BECAME OF THE MYSTERIOUS
mister X?
HE DISAPPEARED INTO THE SHADOWS OF THE CITY SOMETIME SHORTLY BEFORE THE TURN OF THE CENTURY.
THE FUTURE HAD ARRIVED AT LAST, AND ITS PREMIER DESIGNER WAS NOWHERE TO BE FOUND.
BY DEAN MOTTER

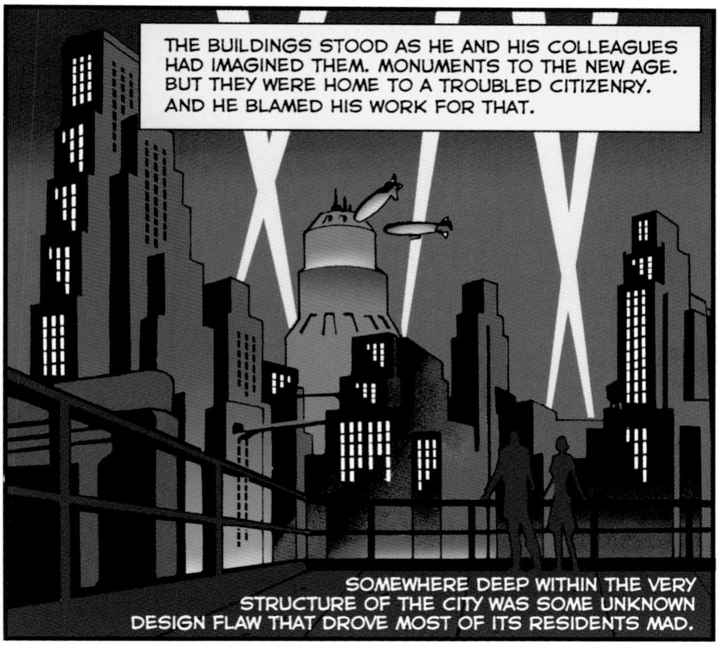
THE BUILDINGS STOOD AS HE AND HIS COLLEAGUES HAD IMAGINED THEM. MONUMENTS TO THE NEW AGE. BUT THEY WERE HOME TO A TROUBLED CITIZENRY. AND HE BLAMED HIS WORK FOR THAT.
SOMEWHERE DEEP WITHIN THE VERY STRUCTURE OF THE CITY WAS SOME UNKNOWN DESIGN FLAW THAT DROVE MOST OF ITS RESIDENTS MAD.

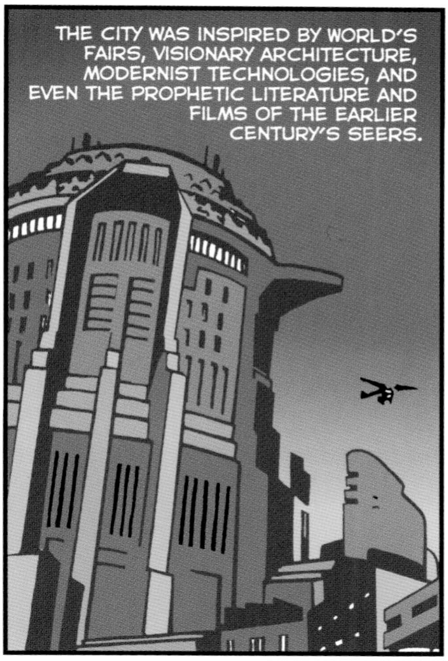
THE CITY WAS INSPIRED BY WORLD'S FAIRS, VISIONARY ARCHITECTURE, MODERNIST TECHNOLOGIES, AND EVEN THE PROPHETIC LITERATURE AND FILMS OF THE EARLIER CENTURY'S SEERS.

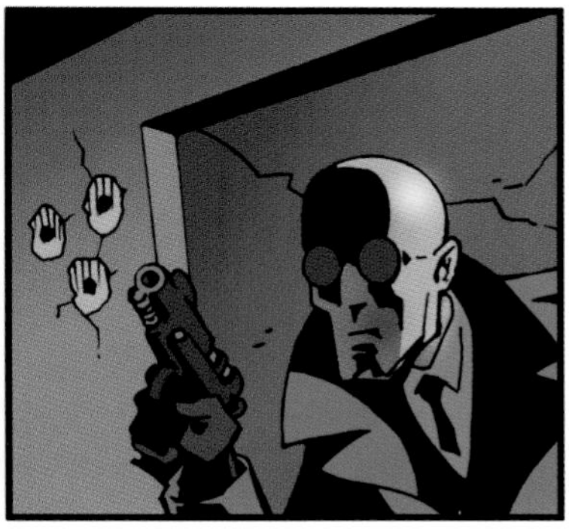

IN SPITE OF SUCH OPTIMISTIC ROOTS THE CITY'S POPULATION DEVELOPED A PLETHORA OF BEHAVIOURAL DISORDERS. AND THAT BECKONED ONE OF THE SURVIVING FOUNDERS TO RETURN FROM HIS EXILE TO ATTEMPT TO SET THINGS RIGHT. AN EFFORT THAT WAS MET BY VIOLENCE AND BLOODSHED. AN EFFORT HE HAD TO FIGHT TO MAINTAIN.

HIS LABOURS WERE THWARTED BY THE MASTERS OF CRIME AND CORRUPTION THAT PREYED ON TROUBLED INHABITANTS.

HIS ACTUAL IDENTITY WAS NEVER REALLY DETERMINED. HE MIGHT'VE BEEN ONE OF THE PRIMARY ARCHITECTS, OR A PUBLIC WORKS ENGINEER OR A PHARMACEUTICAL CHEMIST WORKING ON A CURE FOR THE RESIDENTS' MASS MENTAL CONDITIONS.

WHOEVER HE WAS, IT WAS CLEAR THAT OF ALL THE CITIZENS HE HAD BECOME THE MADDEST OF ALL, AND HIS VERY PERSONALITY HAD BEEN ERASED.

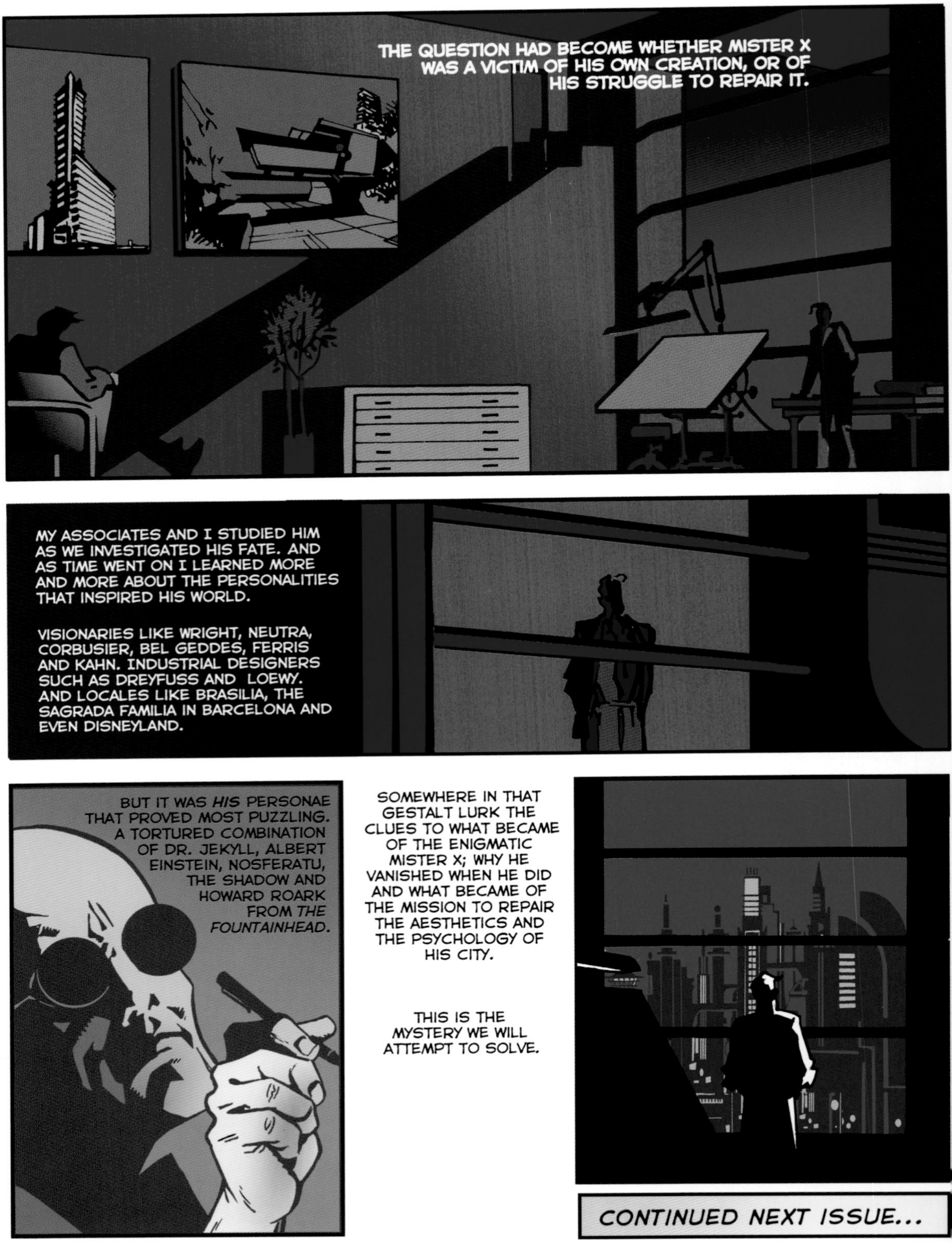
THE QUESTION HAD BECOME WHETHER MISTER X WAS A VICTIM OF HIS OWN CREATION, OR OF HIS STRUGGLE TO REPAIR IT.
MY ASSOCIATES AND I STUDIED HIM AS WE INVESTIGATED HIS FATE. AND AS TIME WENT ON I LEARNED MORE AND MORE ABOUT THE PERSONALITIES THAT INSPIRED HIS WORLD.
VISIONARIES LIKE WRIGHT, NEUTRA, CORBUSIER, BEL GEDDES, FERRIS AND KAHN. INDUSTRIAL DESIGNERS SUCH AS DREYFUSS AND LOEWY. AND LOCALES LIKE BRASILIA, THE SAGRADA FAMILIA IN BARCELONA AND EVEN DISNEYLAND.
BUT IT WAS *HIS* PERSONAE THAT PROVED MOST PUZZLING. A TORTURED COMBINATION OF DR. JEKYLL, ALBERT EINSTEIN, NOSFERATU, THE SHADOW AND HOWARD ROARK FROM *THE FOUNTAINHEAD*.
SOMEWHERE IN THAT GESTALT LURK THE CLUES TO WHAT BECAME OF THE ENIGMATIC MISTER X; WHY HE VANISHED WHEN HE DID AND WHAT BECAME OF THE MISSION TO REPAIR THE AESTHETICS AND THE PSYCHOLOGY OF HIS CITY.
THIS IS THE MYSTERY WE WILL ATTEMPT TO SOLVE.
CONTINUED NEXT ISSUE...

WHATEVER BECAME OF THE MYSTERIOUS

PART 2

mister X?

BY DEAN MOTTER

YOU!! WHAT THE *HELL* ARE YOU DOING HERE?!

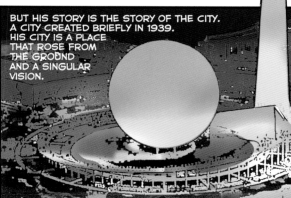

BUT HIS STORY IS THE STORY OF THE CITY. A CITY CREATED BRIEFLY IN 1939. HIS CITY IS A PLACE THAT ROSE FROM THE GROUND AND A SINGULAR VISION.

IT WAS A MAJESTIC CITY LIKE THAT ENVISIONED BY LECORBUSIER, NUETRA, WRIGHT AND EVEN ALBERT SPEER. AND BY ARTISANS LIKE WALT DISNEY, HUGH FERRIS AND THOSE OF THE BAUHAUS.

BUT IT BECAME MORE LIKE ONE ENVISIONED BY VON HARBROU, GEORGE ORWELL, OR H.G. WELLS. IT WAS THE VISION OF A VAST SCULPTURED AND MECHANICAL WORLD. BUT ONE IN WHICH THE CITIZENS WERE MERELY COMPONENTS. MAN, NEITHER THE INDIVIDUAL NOR THE COLLECTIVE, WAS NO LONGER THE MASTER.

AESTHETIC FUNCTIONALITY RULED.

ONE SUCH PLACE, BRASILIA, WAS BUILT IN 1960. A METROPOLIS THAT UNLIKE NEW YORK, LONDON OR TOKYO, WAS DESIGNED AND CONSTRUCTED, DISNEY-STYLE, FROM THE GROUND UP. IT DID NOT EVOLVE FROM SMALLER, OLDER COMMUNITIES LIKE OTHER COLOSSAL CITIES. IT TREATED ARCHITECTURE AS THE CENTRAL SOCIAL STRUCTURE. A BEAUTIFUL CITY-MACHINE.

BUT THE DREAMS OF MISTER X AND HIS FELLOW ARCHITECTS WERE MORE SPECTACULAR. MORE MONOLITHIC. MORE GARGANTUAN. ARCHITECTURE WOULD NOT ONLY SHAPE COMMERCE, TRAVEL AND LEISURE BUT HUMAN BEHAVIOR ITSELF AND THOSE DREAMS SOON BECAME NIGHTMARES FOR MISTER X AND RADIANT CITY.

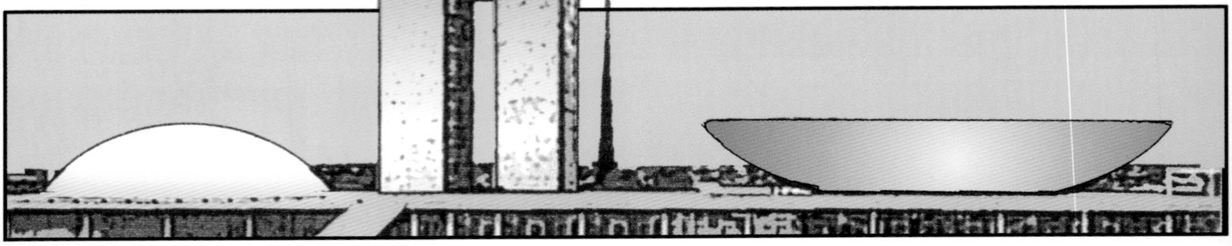

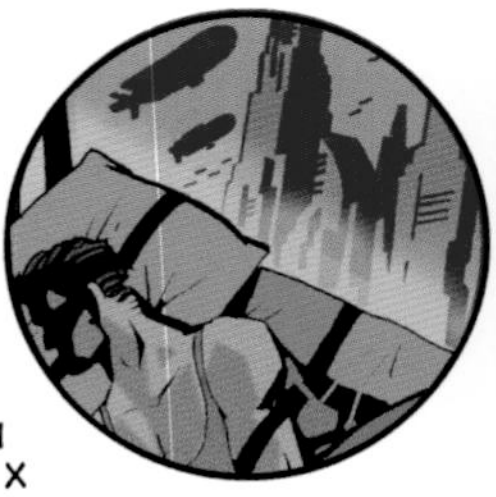

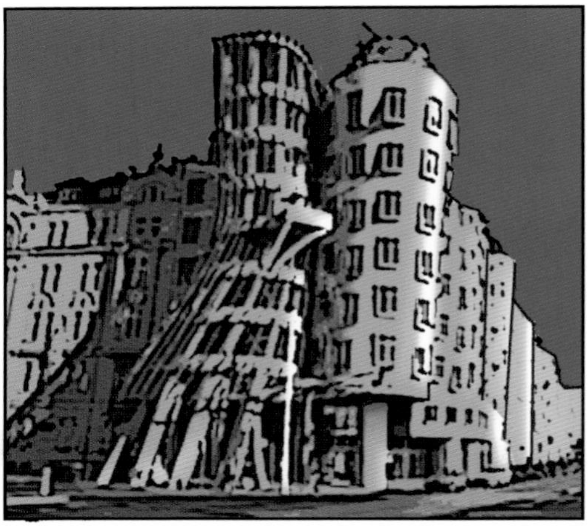

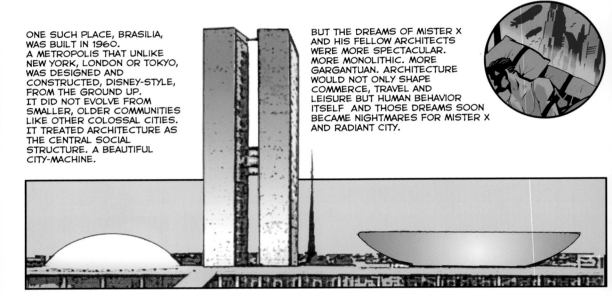

TODAY DE-CONSTRUCTIVISTS LIKE GEHRY, LIBESKIND AND THE COOP HIMMELB(L)AU DEMONSTRATE THE OVERT EFFECTS OF ARCHITECTURE ON THE PSYCHE. HENCE *"PSYCHETECTURE."*

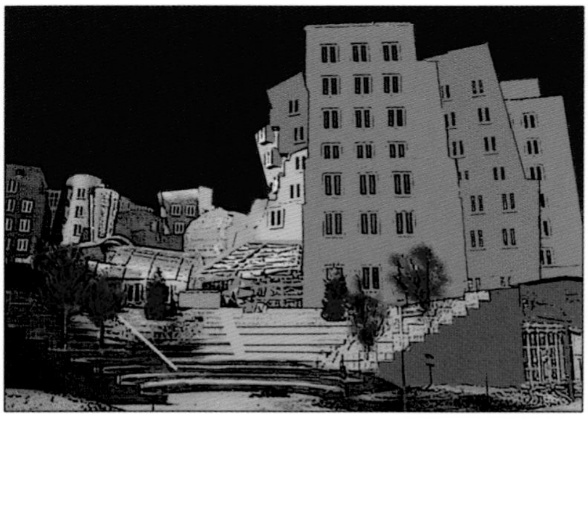

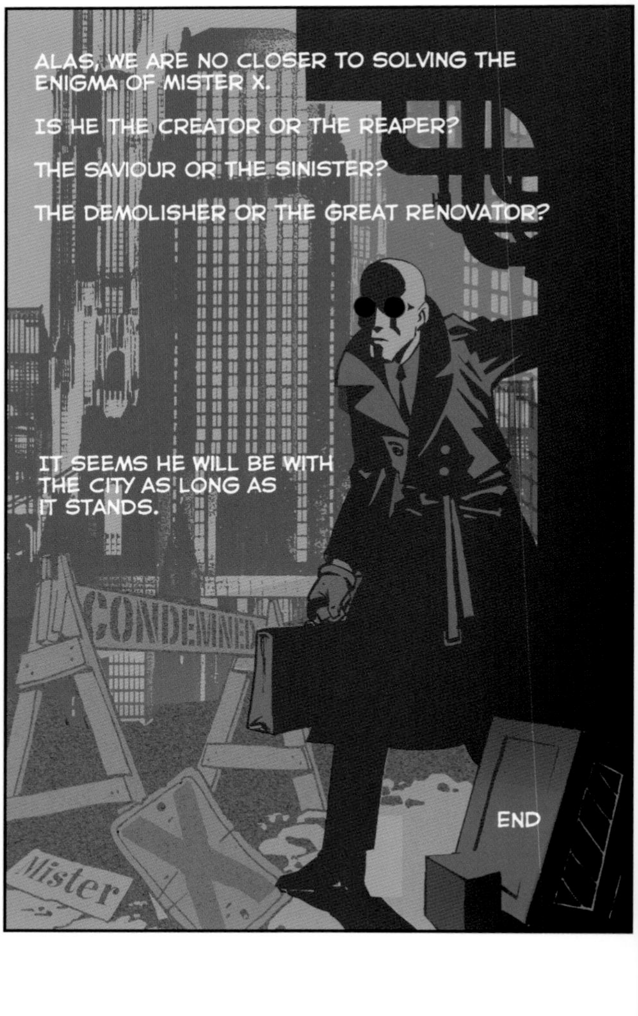
ALAS, WE ARE NO CLOSER TO SOLVING THE ENIGMA OF MISTER X.
IS HE THE CREATOR OR THE REAPER?
THE SAVIOUR OR THE SINISTER?
THE DEMOLISHER OR THE GREAT RENOVATOR?
IT SEEMS HE WILL BE WITH THE CITY AS LONG AS IT STANDS.
CONDEMNED
Mister
END

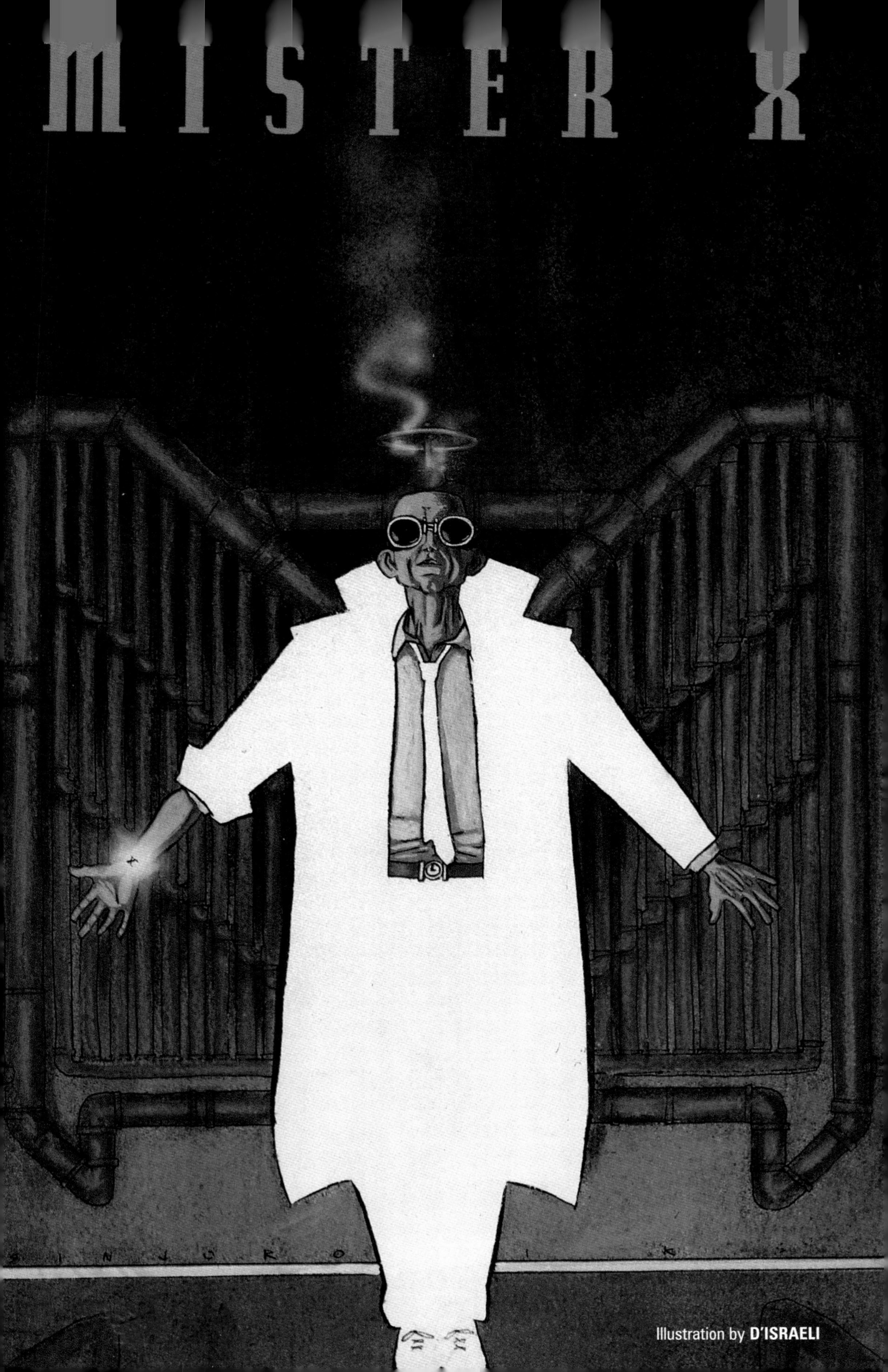
MISTER X

Illustration by **D'ISRAELI**

THE BRIDES OF MISTER X

WRITTEN BY **JEFFREY MORGAN**
PENCILED BY **SHANE OAKLEY**
INKED BY **KEN HOLEWCZYNSKI**
LETTERED BY **DEBORAH MARKS**

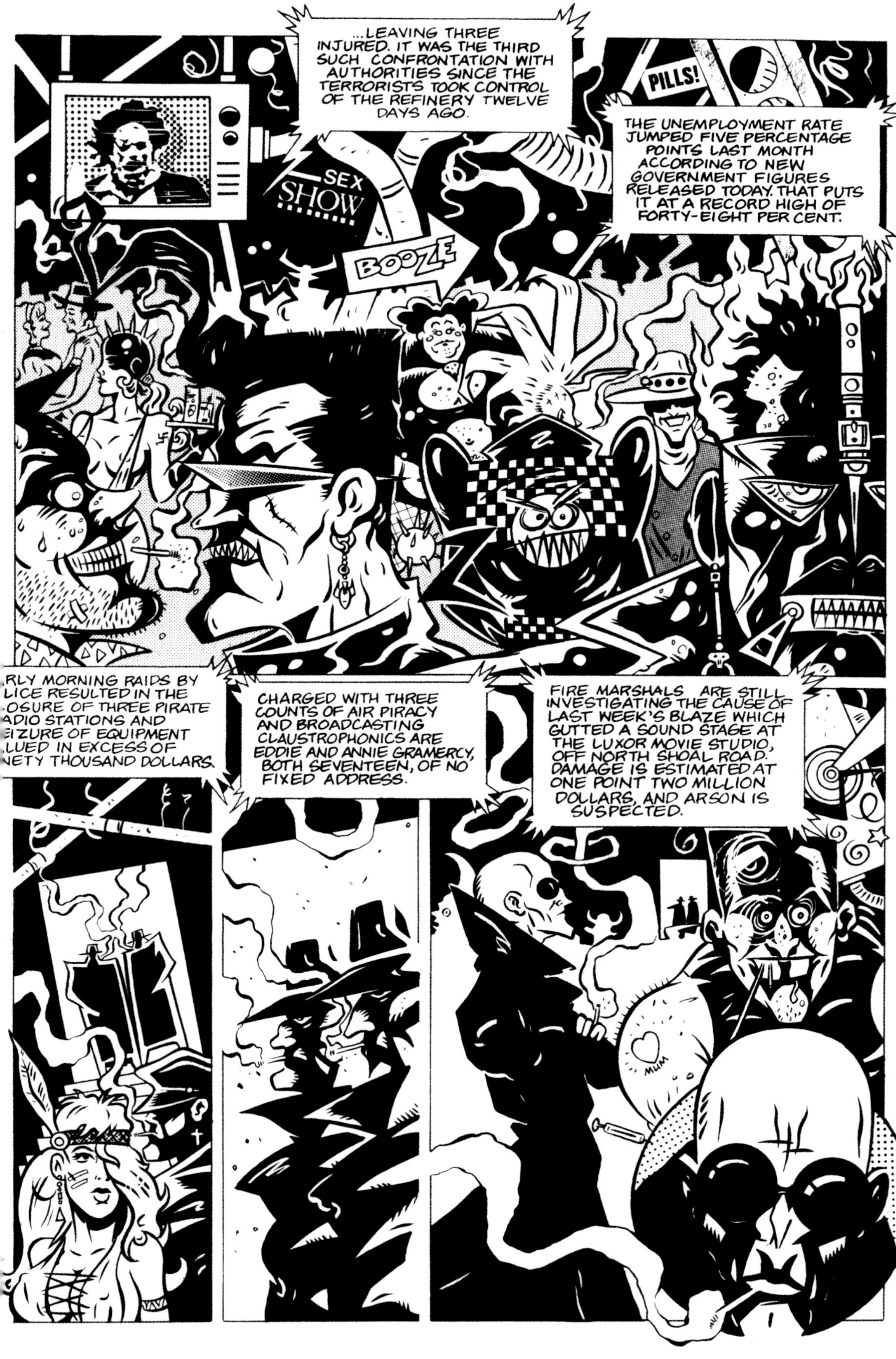
...LEAVING THREE INJURED. IT WAS THE THIRD SUCH CONFRONTATION WITH AUTHORITIES SINCE THE TERRORISTS TOOK CONTROL OF THE REFINERY TWELVE DAYS AGO.
PILLS!
THE UNEMPLOYMENT RATE JUMPED FIVE PERCENTAGE POINTS LAST MONTH ACCORDING TO NEW GOVERNMENT FIGURES RELEASED TODAY. THAT PUTS IT AT A RECORD HIGH OF FORTY-EIGHT PER CENT.
SEX SHOW
BOOZE
RLY MORNING RAIDS BY LICE RESULTED IN THE OSURE OF THREE PIRATE ADIO STATIONS AND EIZURE OF EQUIPMENT LUED IN EXCESS OF NETY THOUSAND DOLLARS.
CHARGED WITH THREE COUNTS OF AIR PIRACY AND BROADCASTING CLAUSTROPHONICS ARE EDDIE AND ANNIE GRAMERCY, BOTH SEVENTEEN, OF NO FIXED ADDRESS.
FIRE MARSHALS ARE STILL INVESTIGATING THE CAUSE OF LAST WEEK'S BLAZE WHICH GUTTED A SOUND STAGE AT THE LUXOR MOVIE STUDIO, OFF NORTH SHOAL ROAD. DAMAGE IS ESTIMATED AT ONE POINT TWO MILLION DOLLARS, AND ARSON IS SUSPECTED.
MUM

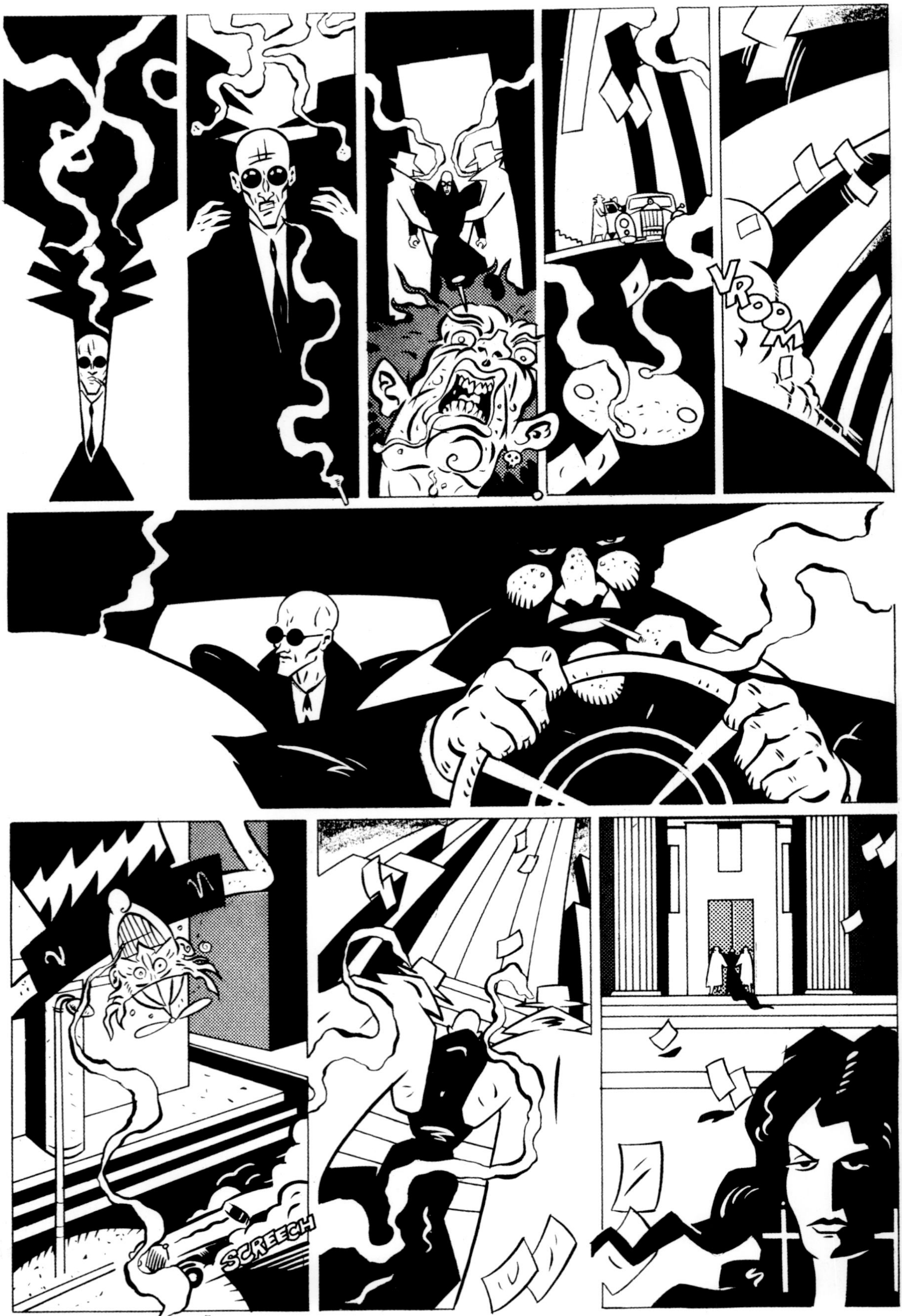
VROOM
SCREECH

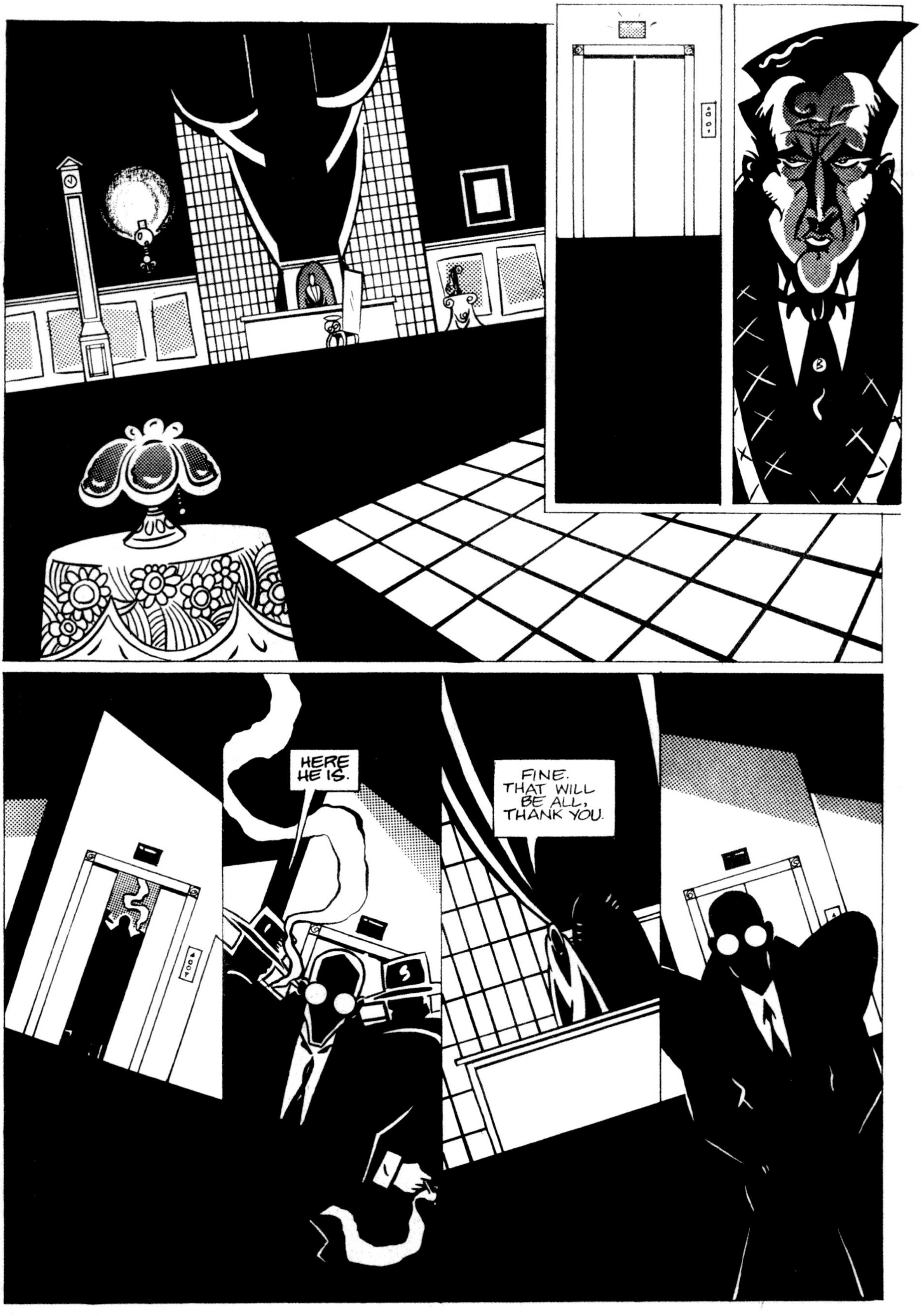
HERE HE IS.
FINE. THAT WILL BE ALL, THANK YOU.

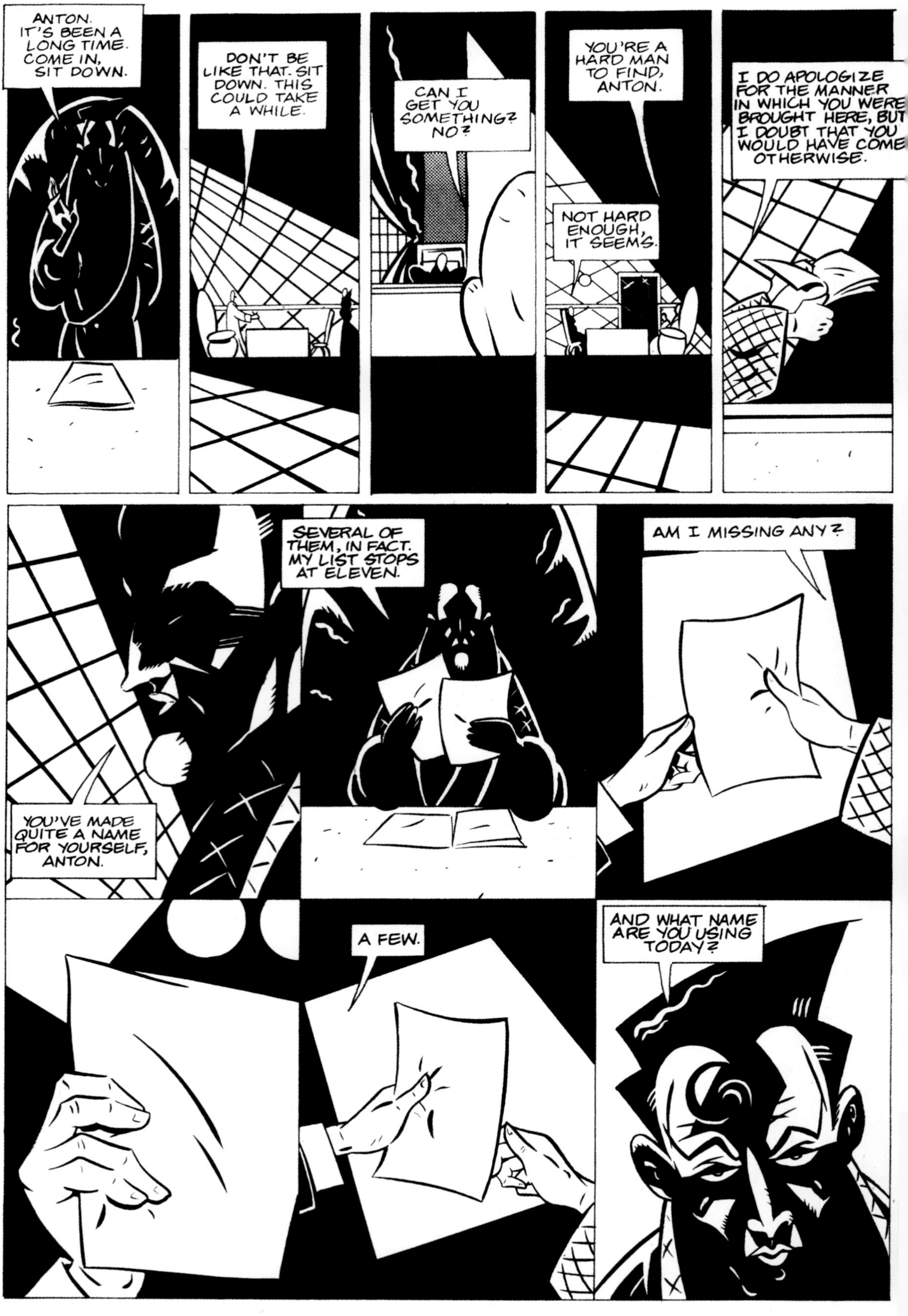
ANTON. IT'S BEEN A LONG TIME. COME IN, SIT DOWN.
DON'T BE LIKE THAT. SIT DOWN. THIS COULD TAKE A WHILE.
CAN I GET YOU SOMETHING? NO?
YOU'RE A HARD MAN TO FIND, ANTON.
NOT HARD ENOUGH, IT SEEMS.
I DO APOLOGIZE FOR THE MANNER IN WHICH YOU WERE BROUGHT HERE, BUT I DOUBT THAT YOU WOULD HAVE COME OTHERWISE.
YOU'VE MADE QUITE A NAME FOR YOURSELF, ANTON.
SEVERAL OF THEM, IN FACT. MY LIST STOPS AT ELEVEN.
AM I MISSING ANY?
A FEW.
AND WHAT NAME ARE YOU USING TODAY?

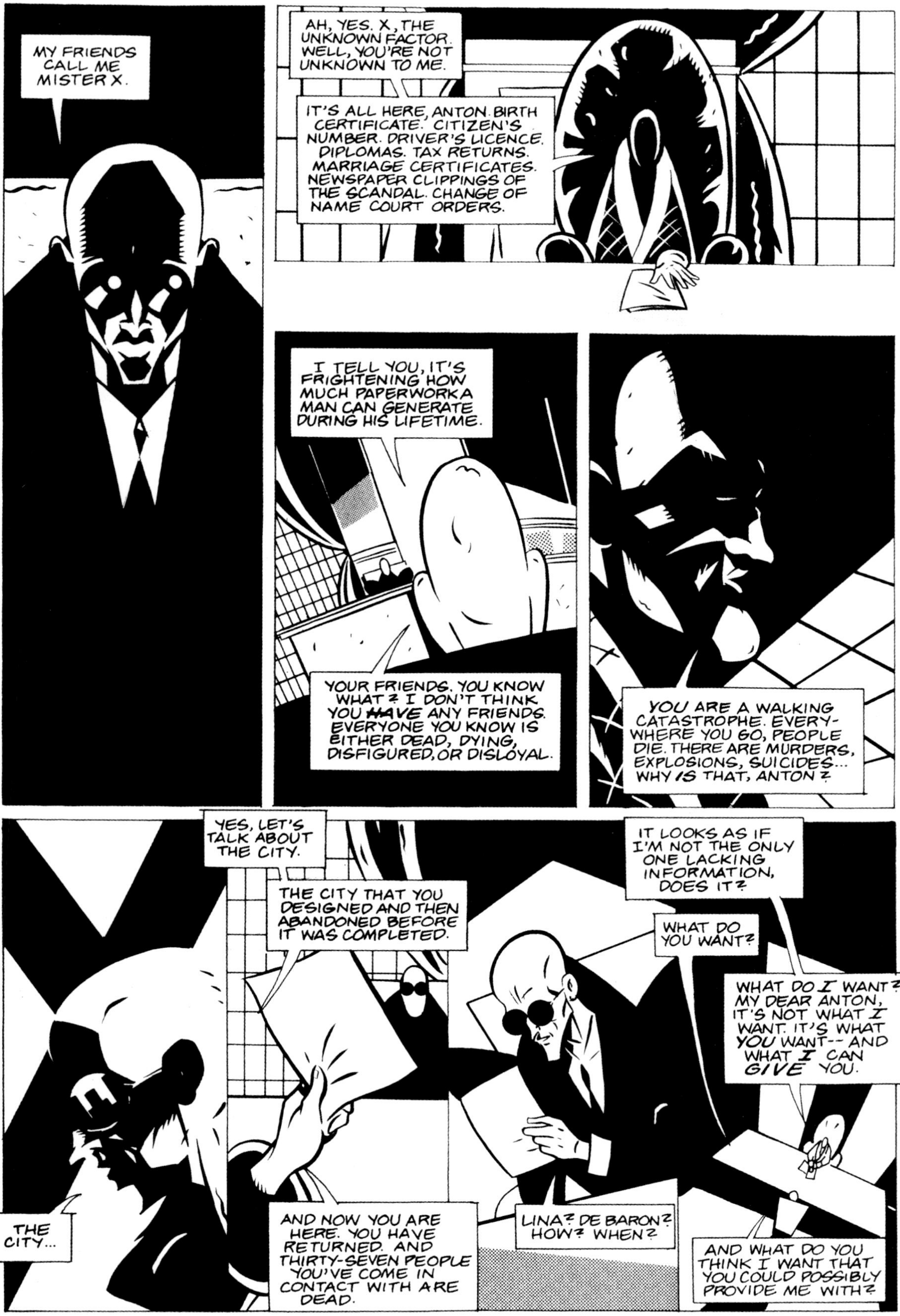
MY FRIENDS CALL ME MISTER X.
AH, YES. X, THE UNKNOWN FACTOR. WELL, YOU'RE NOT UNKNOWN TO ME.
IT'S ALL HERE, ANTON. BIRTH CERTIFICATE. CITIZEN'S NUMBER. DRIVER'S LICENCE. DIPLOMAS. TAX RETURNS. MARRIAGE CERTIFICATES. NEWSPAPER CLIPPINGS OF THE SCANDAL. CHANGE OF NAME COURT ORDERS.
I TELL YOU, IT'S FRIGHTENING HOW MUCH PAPERWORK A MAN CAN GENERATE DURING HIS LIFETIME.
YOUR FRIENDS. YOU KNOW WHAT? I DON'T THINK YOU HAVE ANY FRIENDS. EVERYONE YOU KNOW IS EITHER DEAD, DYING, DISFIGURED, OR DISLOYAL.
YOU ARE A WALKING CATASTROPHE. EVERYWHERE YOU GO, PEOPLE DIE. THERE ARE MURDERS, EXPLOSIONS, SUICIDES... WHY IS THAT, ANTON?
THE CITY...
YES, LET'S TALK ABOUT THE CITY.
THE CITY THAT YOU DESIGNED AND THEN ABANDONED BEFORE IT WAS COMPLETED.
AND NOW YOU ARE HERE. YOU HAVE RETURNED. AND THIRTY-SEVEN PEOPLE YOU'VE COME IN CONTACT WITH ARE DEAD.
LINA? DE BARON? HOW? WHEN?
IT LOOKS AS IF I'M NOT THE ONLY ONE LACKING INFORMATION, DOES IT?
WHAT DO YOU WANT?
WHAT DO I WANT? MY DEAR ANTON, IT'S NOT WHAT I WANT. IT'S WHAT YOU WANT-- AND WHAT I CAN GIVE YOU.
AND WHAT DO YOU THINK I WANT THAT YOU COULD POSSIBLY PROVIDE ME WITH?

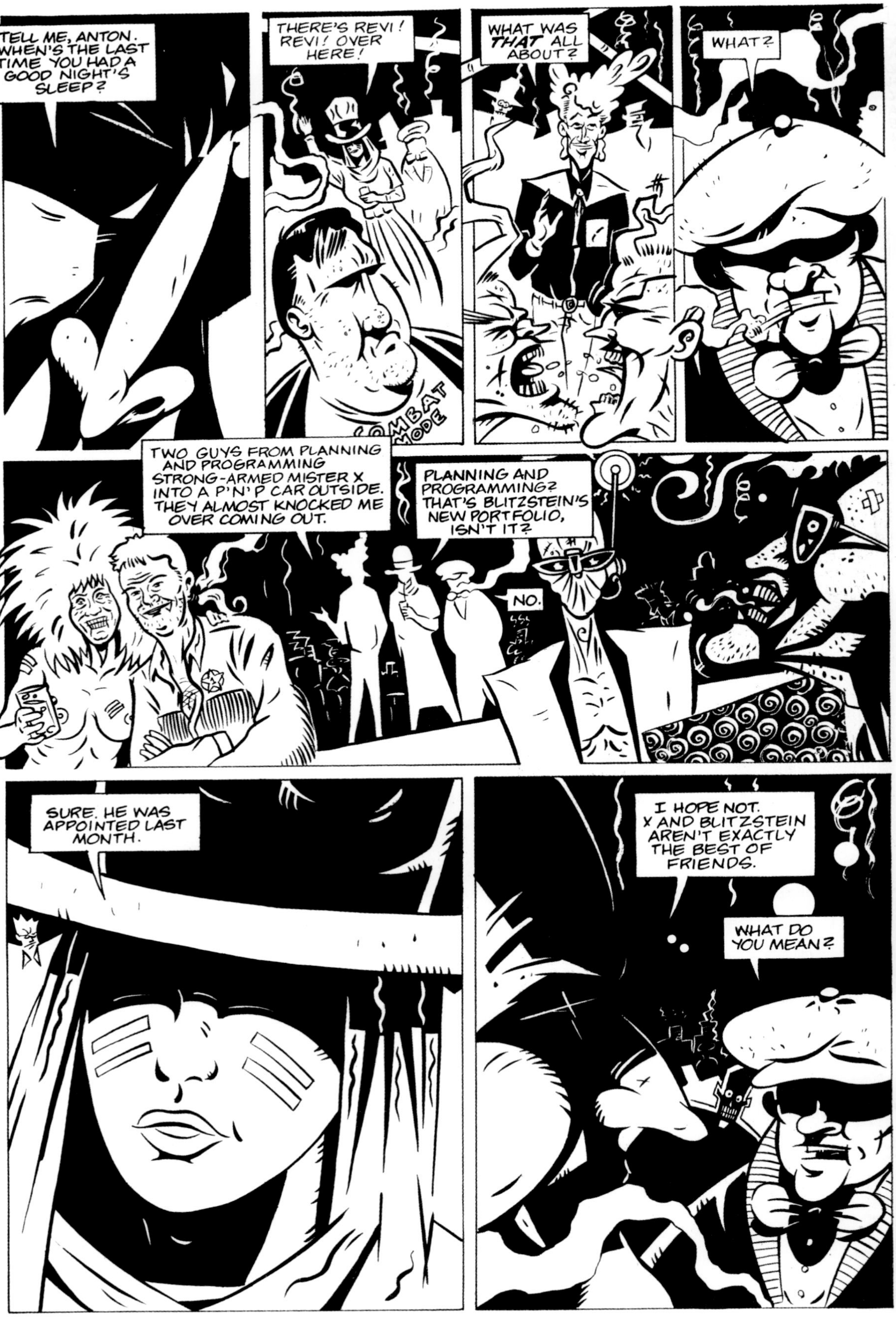
TELL ME, ANTON. WHEN'S THE LAST TIME YOU HAD A GOOD NIGHT'S SLEEP?
THERE'S REVI! REVI! OVER HERE!
COMBAT MODE
WHAT WAS *THAT* ALL ABOUT?
WHAT?
TWO GUYS FROM PLANNING AND PROGRAMMING STRONG-ARMED MISTER X INTO A P'N'P CAR OUTSIDE. THEY ALMOST KNOCKED ME OVER COMING OUT.
PLANNING AND PROGRAMMING? THAT'S BLITZSTEIN'S NEW PORTFOLIO, ISN'T IT?
NO.
SURE. HE WAS APPOINTED LAST MONTH.
I HOPE NOT. X AND BLITZSTEIN AREN'T EXACTLY THE BEST OF FRIENDS.
WHAT DO YOU MEAN?

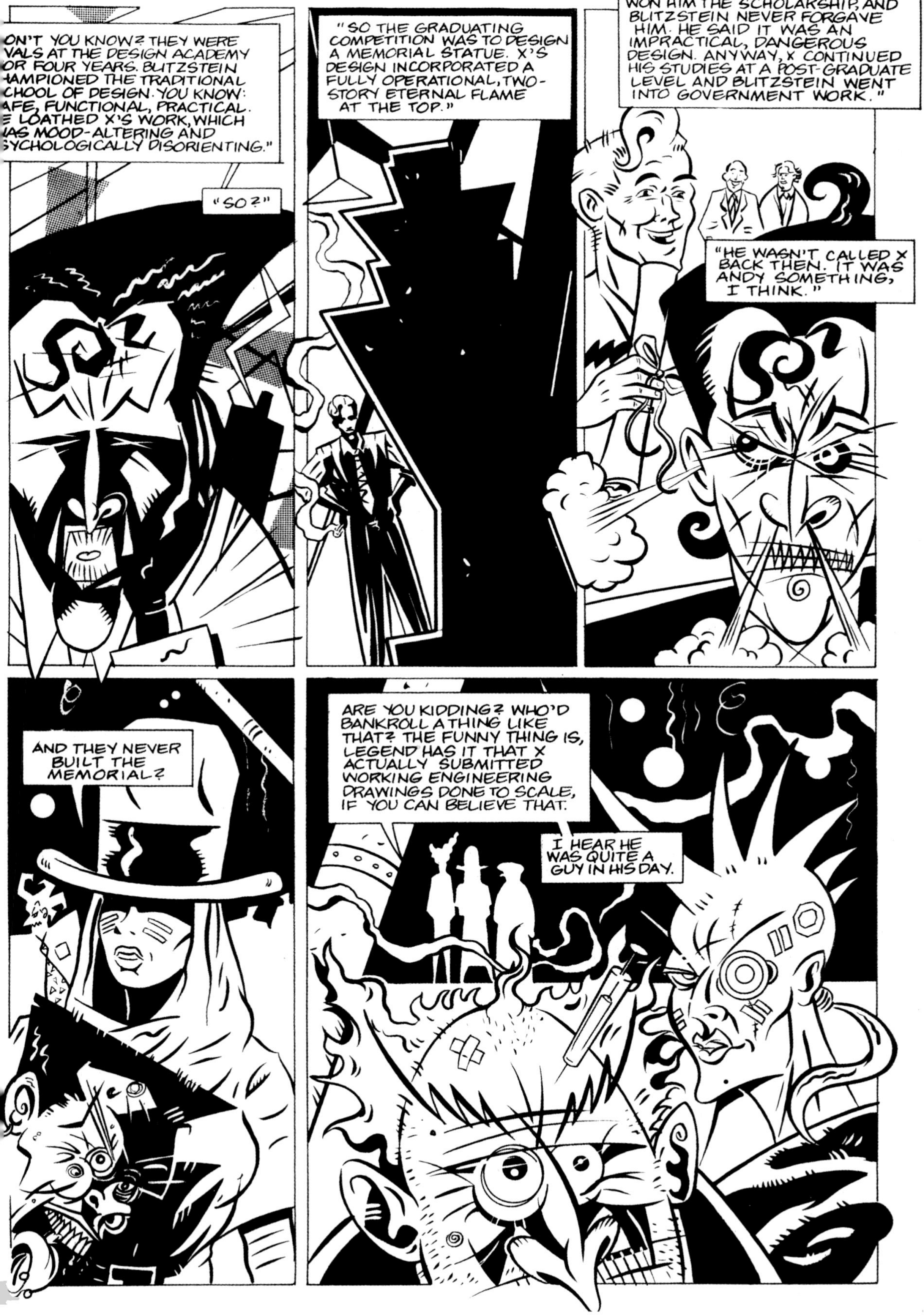
ON'T YOU KNOW? THEY WERE VALS AT THE DESIGN ACADEMY OR FOUR YEARS. BLITZSTEIN HAMPIONED THE TRADITIONAL CHOOL OF DESIGN. YOU KNOW: AFE, FUNCTIONAL, PRACTICAL. E LOATHED X'S WORK, WHICH AS MOOD-ALTERING AND SYCHOLOGICALLY DISORIENTING."
"SO?"
"SO THE GRADUATING COMPETITION WAS TO DESIGN A MEMORIAL STATUE. X'S DESIGN INCORPORATED A FULLY OPERATIONAL, TWO-STORY ETERNAL FLAME AT THE TOP."
"NEEDLESS TO SAY, HIS AUDACITY WON HIM THE SCHOLARSHIP, AND BLITZSTEIN NEVER FORGAVE HIM. HE SAID IT WAS AN IMPRACTICAL, DANGEROUS DESIGN. ANYWAY, X CONTINUED HIS STUDIES AT A POST-GRADUATE LEVEL AND BLITZSTEIN WENT INTO GOVERNMENT WORK."
"HE WASN'T CALLED X BACK THEN. IT WAS ANDY SOMETHING, I THINK."
AND THEY NEVER BUILT THE MEMORIAL?
ARE YOU KIDDING? WHO'D BANKROLL A THING LIKE THAT? THE FUNNY THING IS, LEGEND HAS IT THAT X ACTUALLY SUBMITTED WORKING ENGINEERING DRAWINGS DONE TO SCALE, IF YOU CAN BELIEVE THAT.
I HEAR HE WAS QUITE A GUY IN HIS DAY.

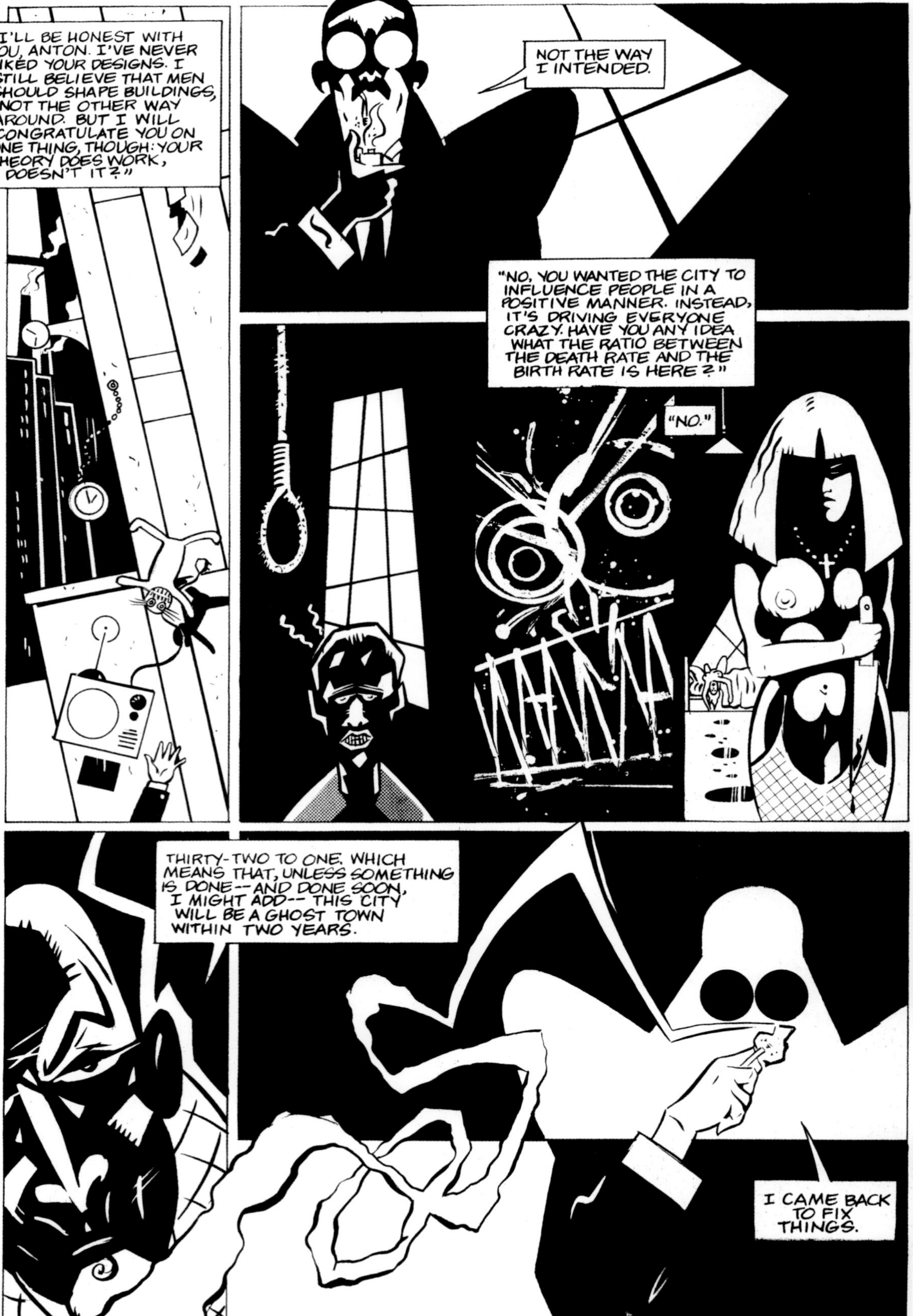
"I'LL BE HONEST WITH YOU, ANTON. I'VE NEVER LIKED YOUR DESIGNS. I STILL BELIEVE THAT MEN SHOULD SHAPE BUILDINGS, NOT THE OTHER WAY AROUND. BUT I WILL CONGRATULATE YOU ON ONE THING, THOUGH: YOUR THEORY DOES WORK, DOESN'T IT?"
NOT THE WAY I INTENDED.
"NO, YOU WANTED THE CITY TO INFLUENCE PEOPLE IN A POSITIVE MANNER. INSTEAD, IT'S DRIVING EVERYONE CRAZY. HAVE YOU ANY IDEA WHAT THE RATIO BETWEEN THE DEATH RATE AND THE BIRTH RATE IS HERE?"
"NO."
THIRTY-TWO TO ONE. WHICH MEANS THAT, UNLESS SOMETHING IS DONE--AND DONE SOON, I MIGHT ADD-- THIS CITY WILL BE A GHOST TOWN WITHIN TWO YEARS.
I CAME BACK TO FIX THINGS.

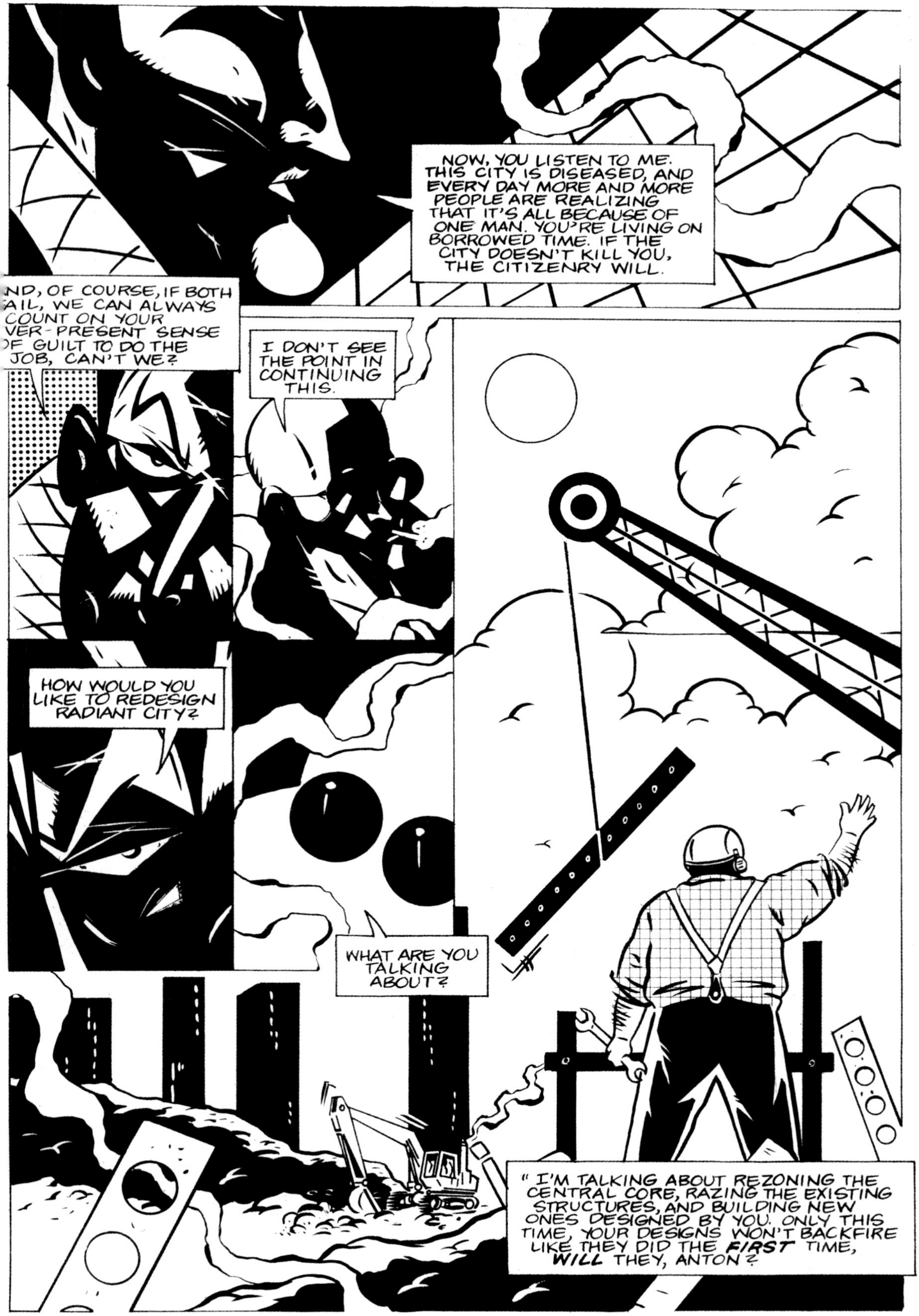
NOW, YOU LISTEN TO ME. THIS CITY IS DISEASED, AND EVERY DAY MORE AND MORE PEOPLE ARE REALIZING THAT IT'S ALL BECAUSE OF ONE MAN. YOU'RE LIVING ON BORROWED TIME. IF THE CITY DOESN'T KILL YOU, THE CITIZENRY WILL.
ND, OF COURSE, IF BOTH AIL, WE CAN ALWAYS COUNT ON YOUR VER-PRESENT SENSE OF GUILT TO DO THE JOB, CAN'T WE?
I DON'T SEE THE POINT IN CONTINUING THIS.
HOW WOULD YOU LIKE TO REDESIGN RADIANT CITY?
WHAT ARE YOU TALKING ABOUT?
"I'M TALKING ABOUT REZONING THE CENTRAL CORE, RAZING THE EXISTING STRUCTURES, AND BUILDING NEW ONES DESIGNED BY YOU. ONLY THIS TIME, YOUR DESIGNS WON'T BACKFIRE LIKE THEY DID THE FIRST TIME, WILL THEY, ANTON?

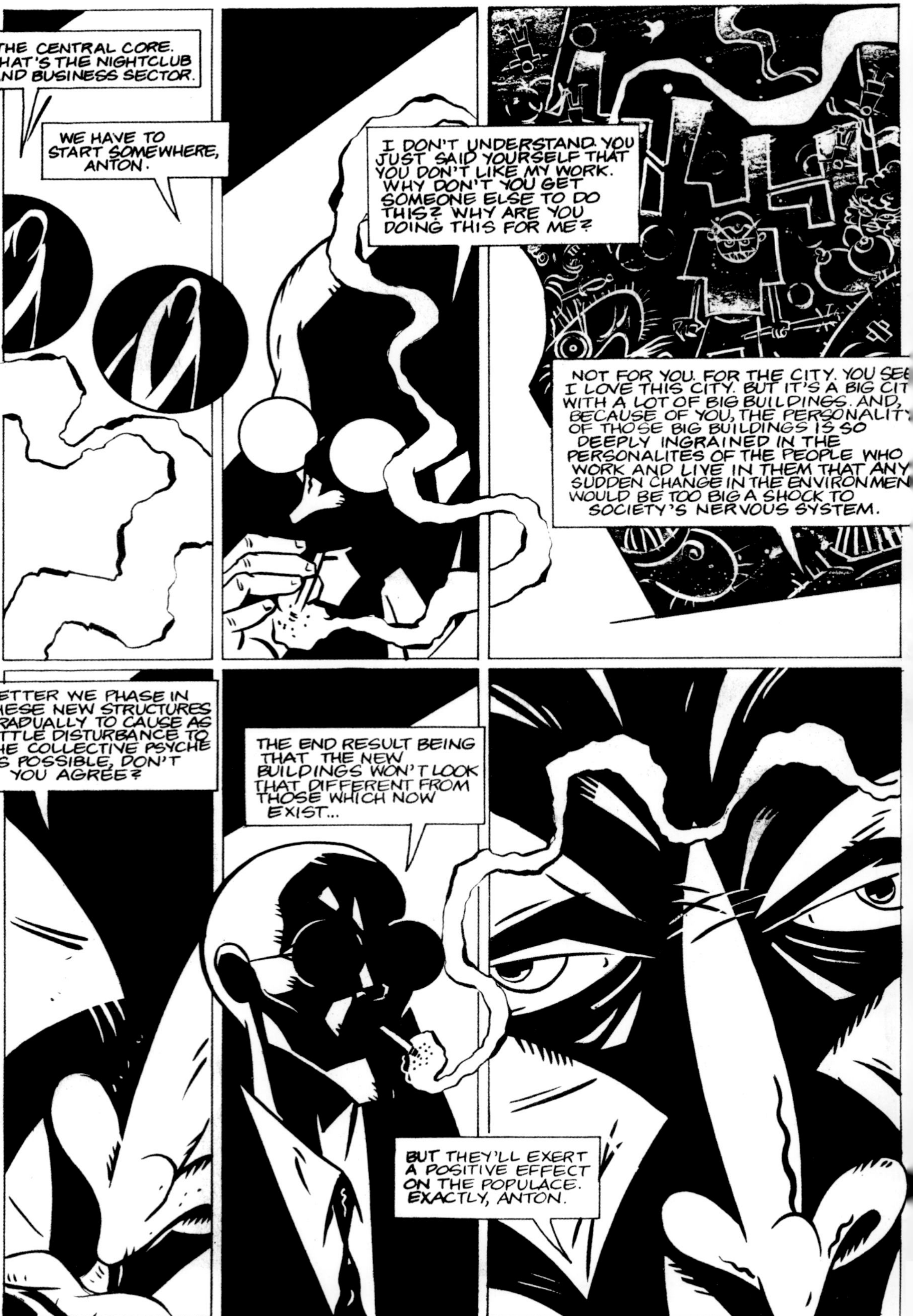
THE CENTRAL CORE. THAT'S THE NIGHTCLUB AND BUSINESS SECTOR.
WE HAVE TO START SOMEWHERE, ANTON.
I DON'T UNDERSTAND. YOU JUST SAID YOURSELF THAT YOU DON'T LIKE MY WORK. WHY DON'T YOU GET SOMEONE ELSE TO DO THIS? WHY ARE YOU DOING THIS FOR ME?
NOT FOR YOU. FOR THE CITY. YOU SEE I LOVE THIS CITY. BUT IT'S A BIG CIT WITH A LOT OF BIG BUILDINGS. AND, BECAUSE OF YOU, THE PERSONALITY OF THOSE BIG BUILDINGS IS SO DEEPLY INGRAINED IN THE PERSONALITES OF THE PEOPLE WHO WORK AND LIVE IN THEM THAT ANY SUDDEN CHANGE IN THE ENVIRONMEN WOULD BE TOO BIG A SHOCK TO SOCIETY'S NERVOUS SYSTEM.
BETTER WE PHASE IN THESE NEW STRUCTURES GRADUALLY TO CAUSE AS LITTLE DISTURBANCE TO THE COLLECTIVE PSYCHE AS POSSIBLE, DON'T YOU AGREE?
THE END RESULT BEING THAT THE NEW BUILDINGS WON'T LOOK THAT DIFFERENT FROM THOSE WHICH NOW EXIST...
BUT THEY'LL EXERT A POSITIVE EFFECT ON THE POPULACE. EXACTLY, ANTON.

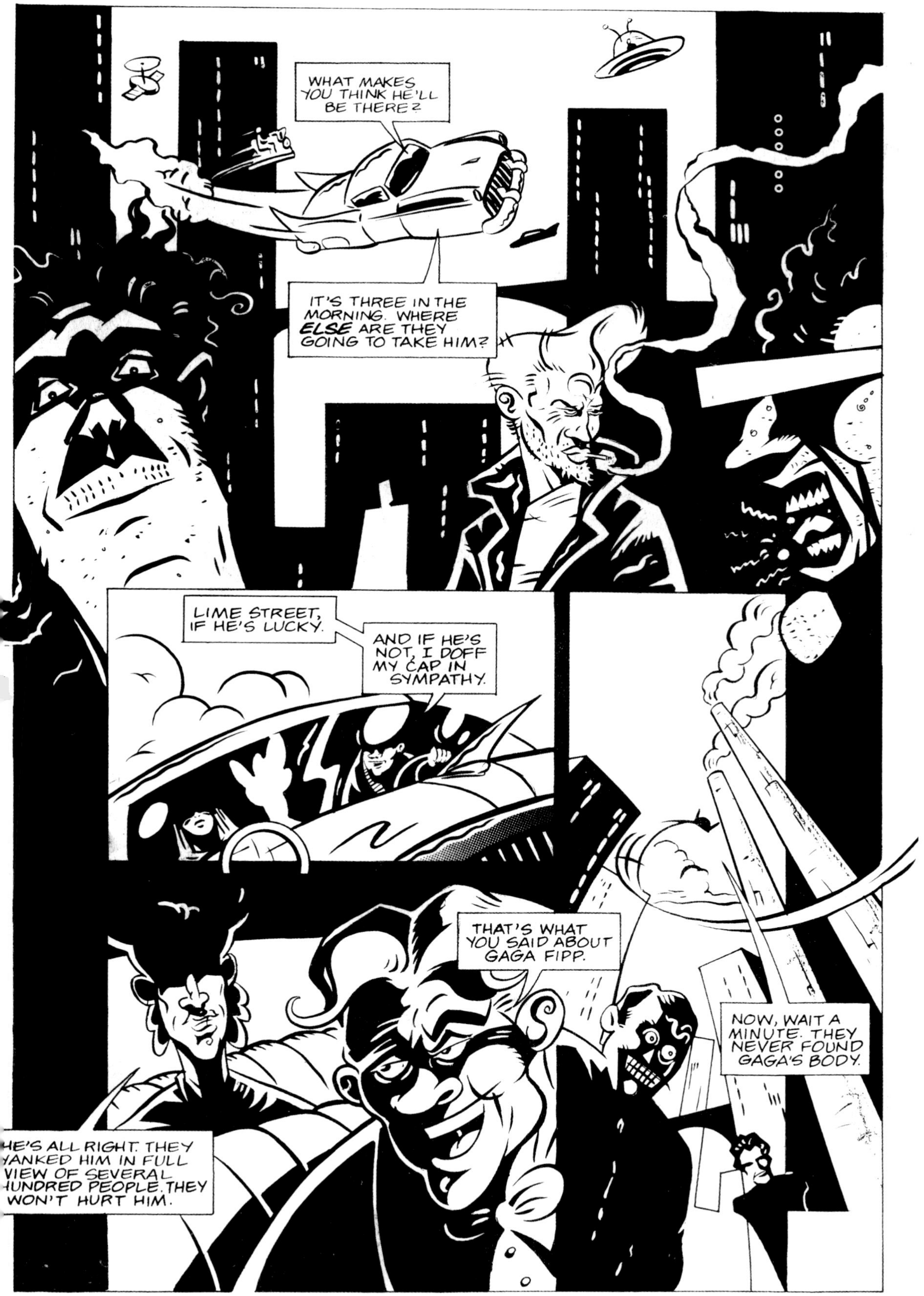
WHAT MAKES YOU THINK HE'LL BE THERE?
IT'S THREE IN THE MORNING. WHERE ELSE ARE THEY GOING TO TAKE HIM?
LIME STREET, IF HE'S LUCKY.
AND IF HE'S NOT, I DOFF MY CAP IN SYMPATHY.
HE'S ALL RIGHT. THEY YANKED HIM IN FULL VIEW OF SEVERAL HUNDRED PEOPLE. THEY WON'T HURT HIM.
THAT'S WHAT YOU SAID ABOUT GAGA FIPP.
NOW, WAIT A MINUTE. THEY NEVER FOUND GAGA'S BODY.

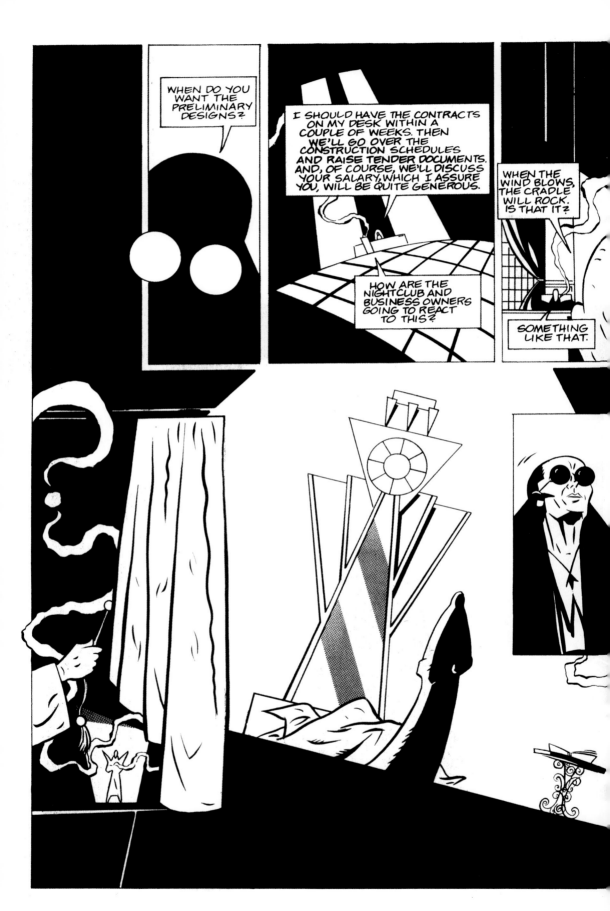

WHEN DO YOU WANT THE PRELIMINARY DESIGNS?

I SHOULD HAVE THE CONTRACTS ON MY DESK WITHIN A COUPLE OF WEEKS. THEN WE'LL GO OVER THE CONSTRUCTION SCHEDULES AND RAISE TENDER DOCUMENTS. AND, OF COURSE, WE'LL DISCUSS YOUR SALARY, WHICH I ASSURE YOU, WILL BE QUITE GENEROUS.

HOW ARE THE NIGHTCLUB AND BUSINESS OWNERS GOING TO REACT TO THIS?

WHEN THE WIND BLOWS, THE CRADLE WILL ROCK. IS THAT IT?

SOMETHING LIKE THAT.

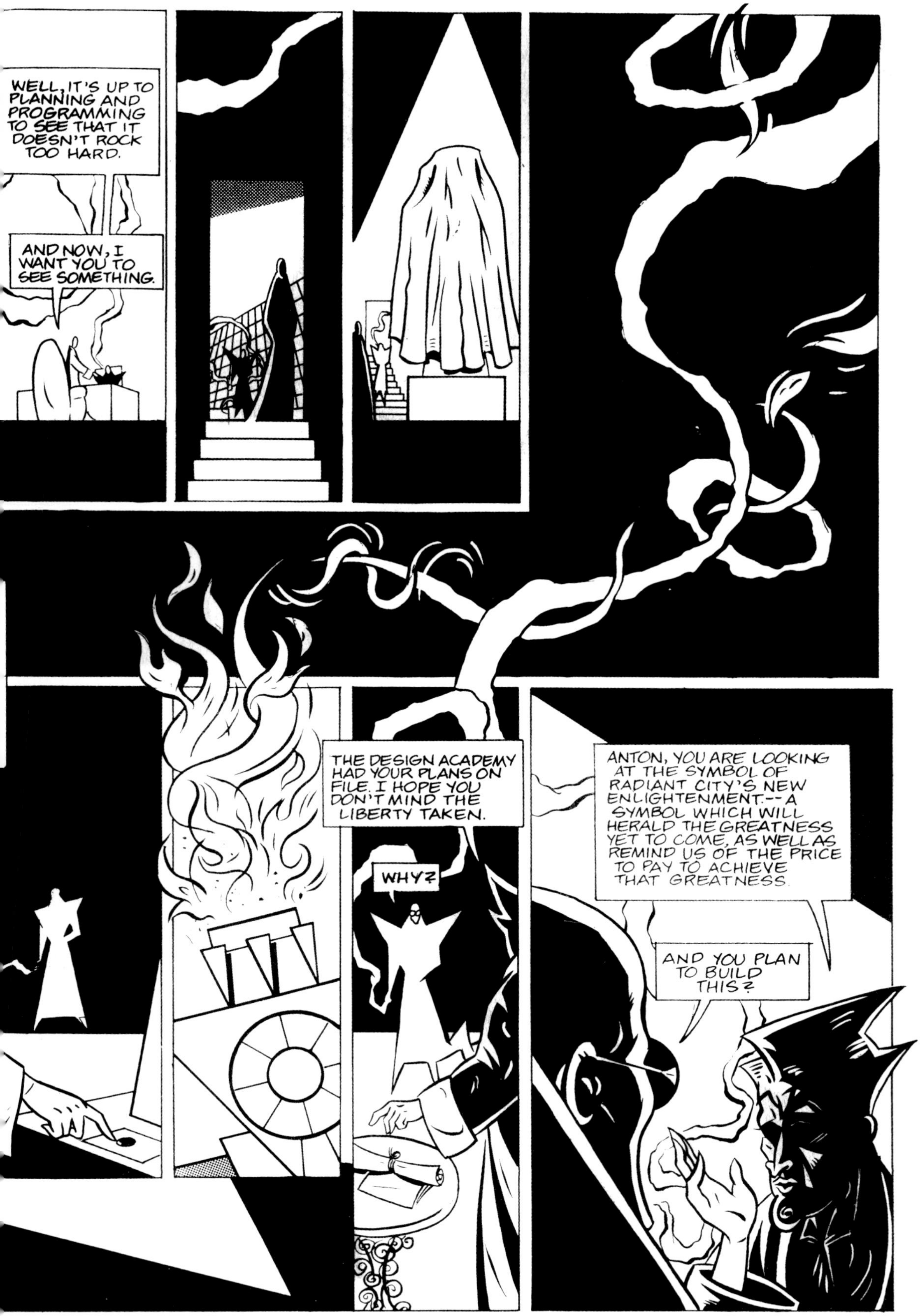
WELL, IT'S UP TO PLANNING AND PROGRAMMING TO SEE THAT IT DOESN'T ROCK TOO HARD.
AND NOW, I WANT YOU TO SEE SOMETHING.
THE DESIGN ACADEMY HAD YOUR PLANS ON FILE. I HOPE YOU DON'T MIND THE LIBERTY TAKEN.
WHY?
ANTON, YOU ARE LOOKING AT THE SYMBOL OF RADIANT CITY'S NEW ENLIGHTENMENT.-- A SYMBOL WHICH WILL HERALD THE GREATNESS YET TO COME, AS WELL AS REMIND US OF THE PRICE TO PAY TO ACHIEVE THAT GREATNESS.
AND YOU PLAN TO BUILD THIS?

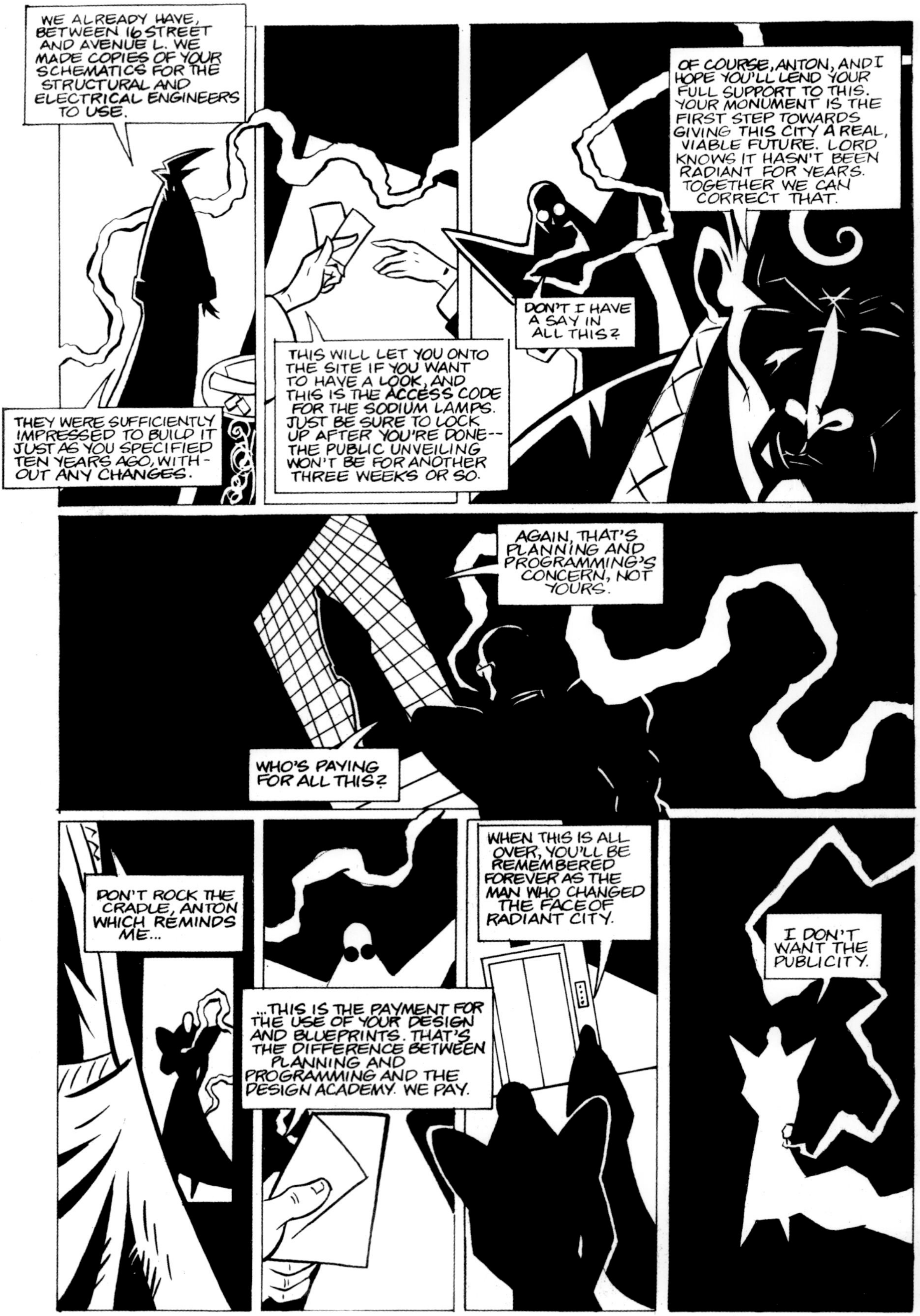
WE ALREADY HAVE, BETWEEN 16 STREET AND AVENUE L. WE MADE COPIES OF YOUR SCHEMATICS FOR THE STRUCTURAL AND ELECTRICAL ENGINEERS TO USE.
THEY WERE SUFFICIENTLY IMPRESSED TO BUILD IT JUST AS YOU SPECIFIED TEN YEARS AGO, WITH-OUT ANY CHANGES.
THIS WILL LET YOU ONTO THE SITE IF YOU WANT TO HAVE A LOOK, AND THIS IS THE ACCESS CODE FOR THE SODIUM LAMPS. JUST BE SURE TO LOCK UP AFTER YOU'RE DONE-- THE PUBLIC UNVEILING WON'T BE FOR ANOTHER THREE WEEKS OR SO.
DON'T I HAVE A SAY IN ALL THIS?
OF COURSE, ANTON, AND I HOPE YOU'LL LEND YOUR FULL SUPPORT TO THIS. YOUR MONUMENT IS THE FIRST STEP TOWARDS GIVING THIS CITY A REAL, VIABLE FUTURE. LORD KNOWS IT HASN'T BEEN RADIANT FOR YEARS. TOGETHER WE CAN CORRECT THAT.
WHO'S PAYING FOR ALL THIS?
AGAIN, THAT'S PLANNING AND PROGRAMMING'S CONCERN, NOT YOURS.
DON'T ROCK THE CRADLE, ANTON WHICH REMINDS ME...
...THIS IS THE PAYMENT FOR THE USE OF YOUR DESIGN AND BLUEPRINTS. THAT'S THE DIFFERENCE BETWEEN PLANNING AND PROGRAMMING AND THE DESIGN ACADEMY. WE PAY.
WHEN THIS IS ALL OVER, YOU'LL BE REMEMBERED FOREVER AS THE MAN WHO CHANGED THE FACE OF RADIANT CITY.
I DON'T WANT THE PUBLICITY.

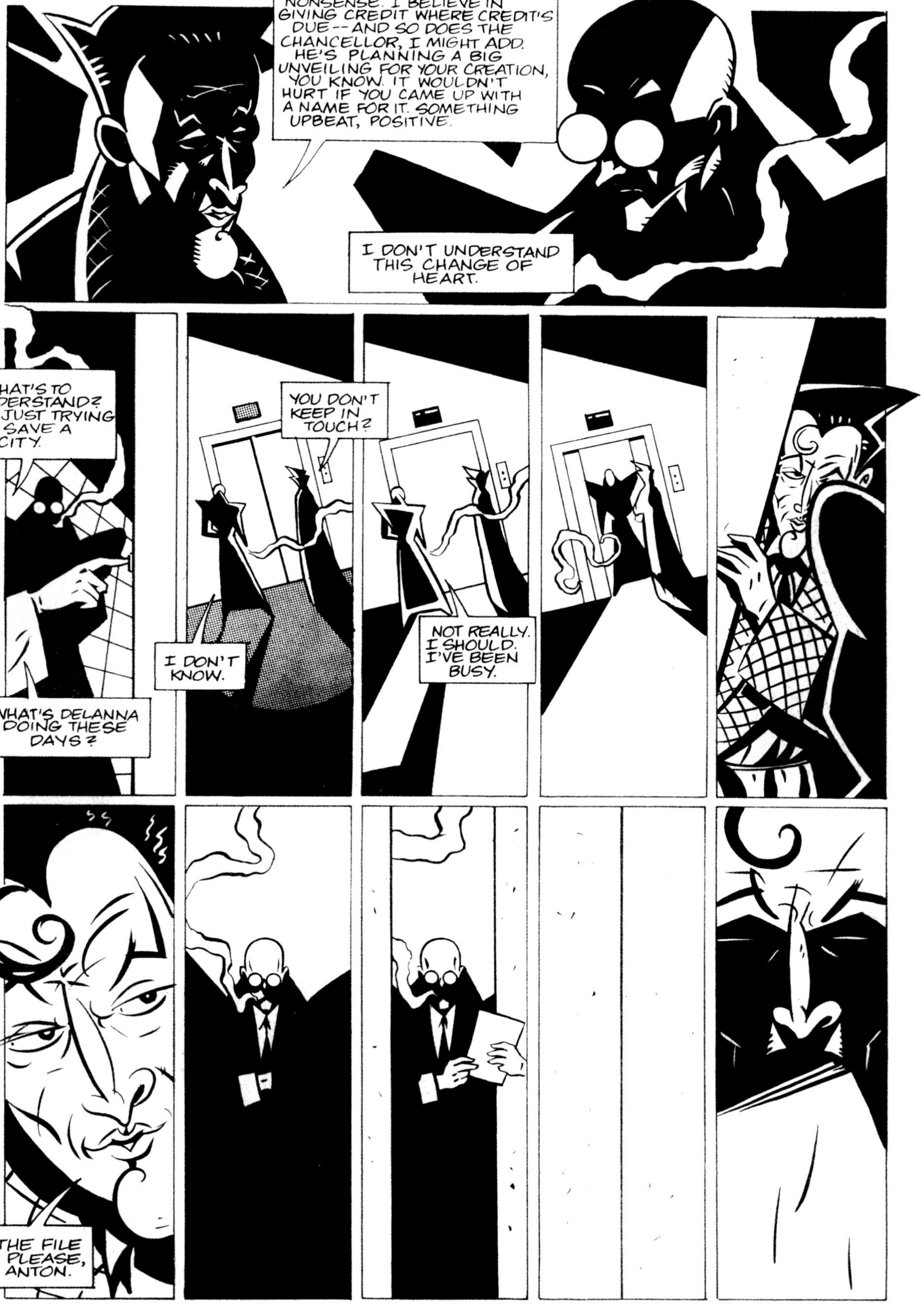
NONSENSE. I BELIEVE IN GIVING CREDIT WHERE CREDIT'S DUE-- AND SO DOES THE CHANCELLOR, I MIGHT ADD. HE'S PLANNING A BIG UNVEILING FOR YOUR CREATION, YOU KNOW. IT WOULDN'T HURT IF YOU CAME UP WITH A NAME FOR IT. SOMETHING UPBEAT, POSITIVE.
I DON'T UNDERSTAND THIS CHANGE OF HEART.
HAT'S TO DERSTAND? JUST TRYING SAVE A CITY.
WHAT'S DELANNA DOING THESE DAYS?
I DON'T KNOW.
YOU DON'T KEEP IN TOUCH?
NOT REALLY. I SHOULD. I'VE BEEN BUSY.
THE FILE PLEASE, ANTON.

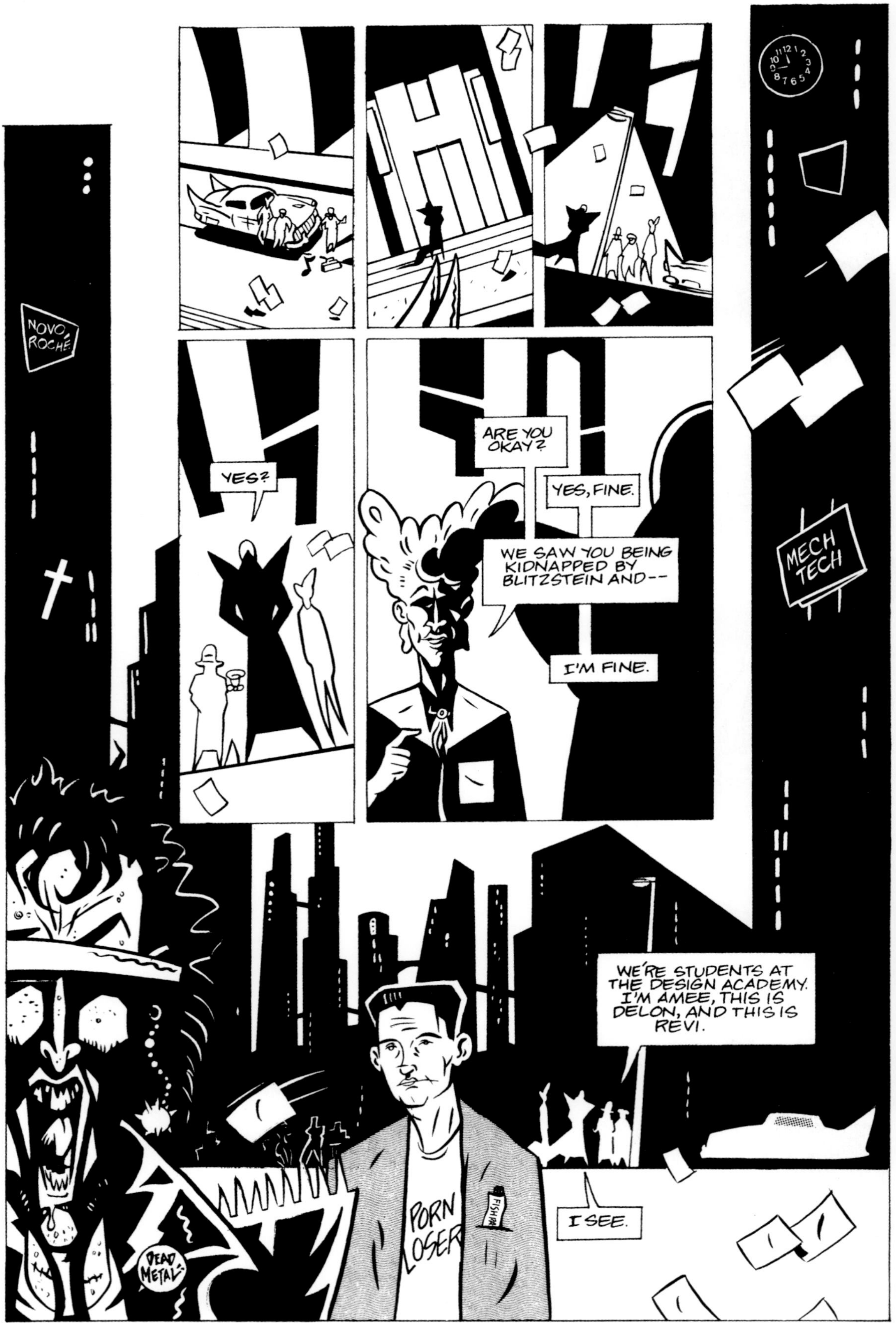
NOVO ROCHÉ
YES?
ARE YOU OKAY?
YES, FINE.
WE SAW YOU BEING KIDNAPPED BY BLITZSTEIN AND--
I'M FINE.
MECH TECH
WE'RE STUDENTS AT THE DESIGN ACADEMY. I'M AMEE, THIS IS DELON, AND THIS IS REVI.
I SEE.
DEAD METAL
PORN LOSER

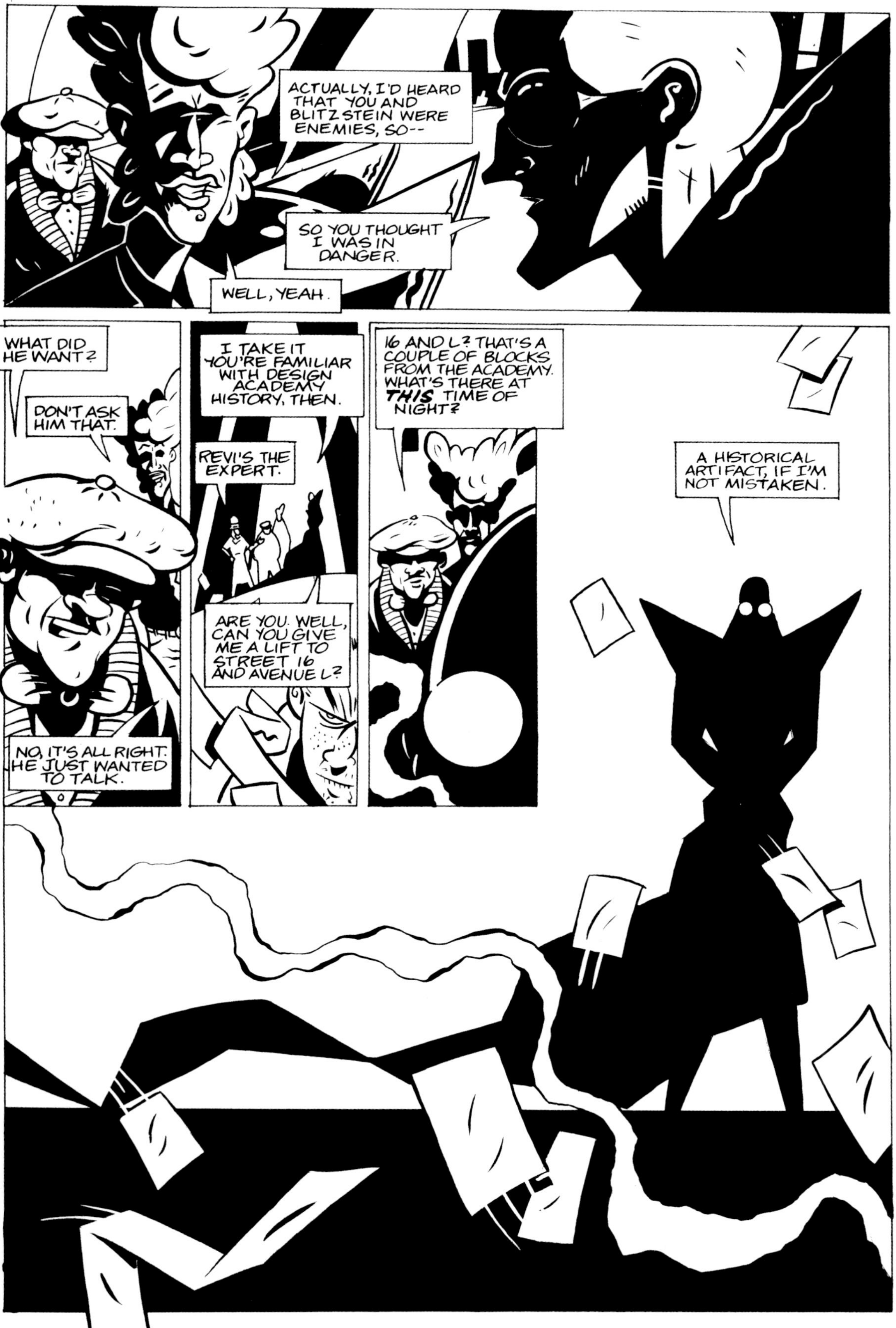

ACTUALLY, I'D HEARD THAT YOU AND BLITZSTEIN WERE ENEMIES, SO--
SO YOU THOUGHT I WAS IN DANGER.
WELL, YEAH.
WHAT DID HE WANT?
DON'T ASK HIM THAT.
NO, IT'S ALL RIGHT. HE JUST WANTED TO TALK.
I TAKE IT YOU'RE FAMILIAR WITH DESIGN ACADEMY HISTORY, THEN.
REVI'S THE EXPERT.
ARE YOU. WELL, CAN YOU GIVE ME A LIFT TO STREET 16 AND AVENUE L?
16 AND L? THAT'S A COUPLE OF BLOCKS FROM THE ACADEMY. WHAT'S THERE AT THIS TIME OF NIGHT?
A HISTORICAL ARTIFACT, IF I'M NOT MISTAKEN.

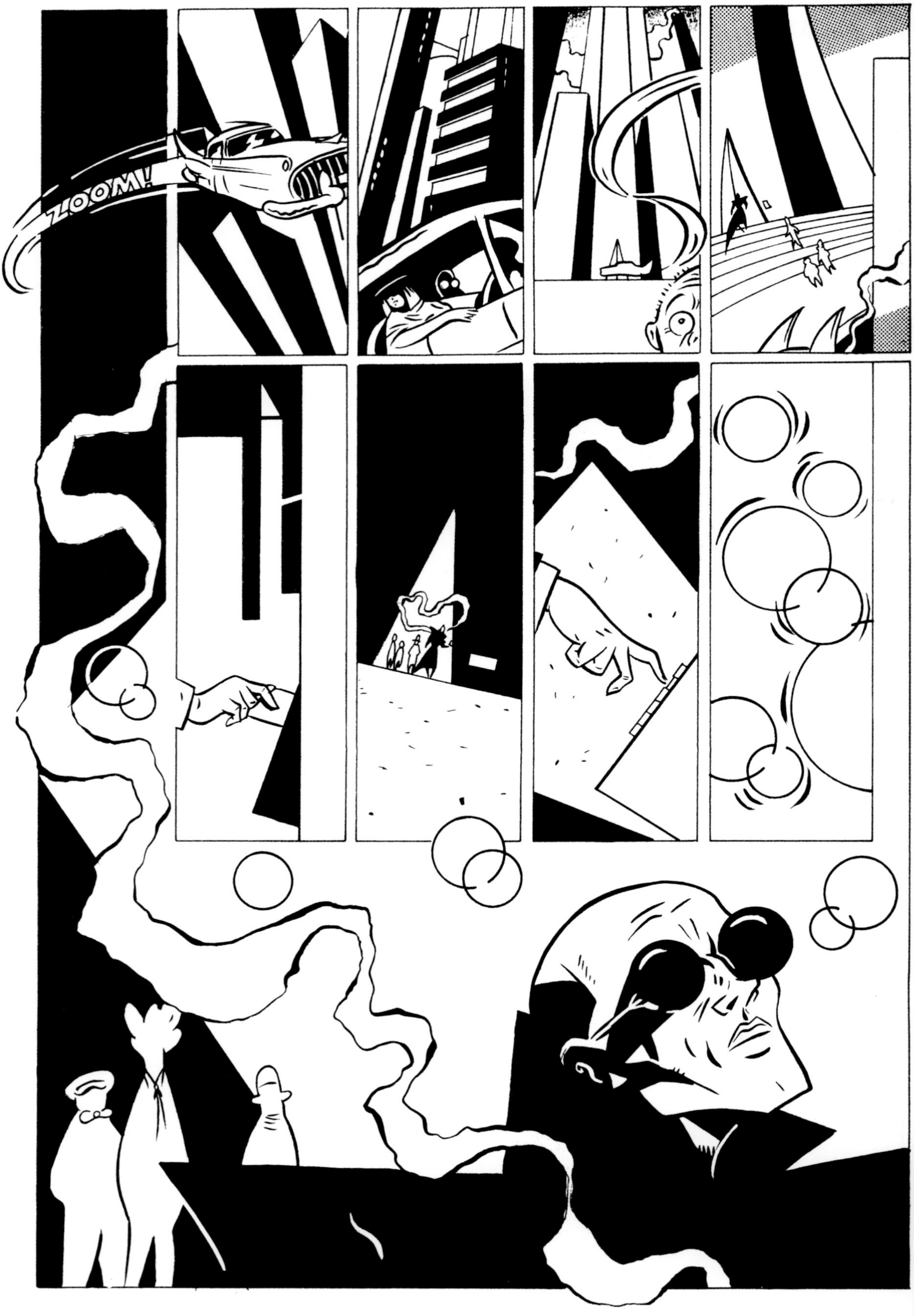
ZOOM!

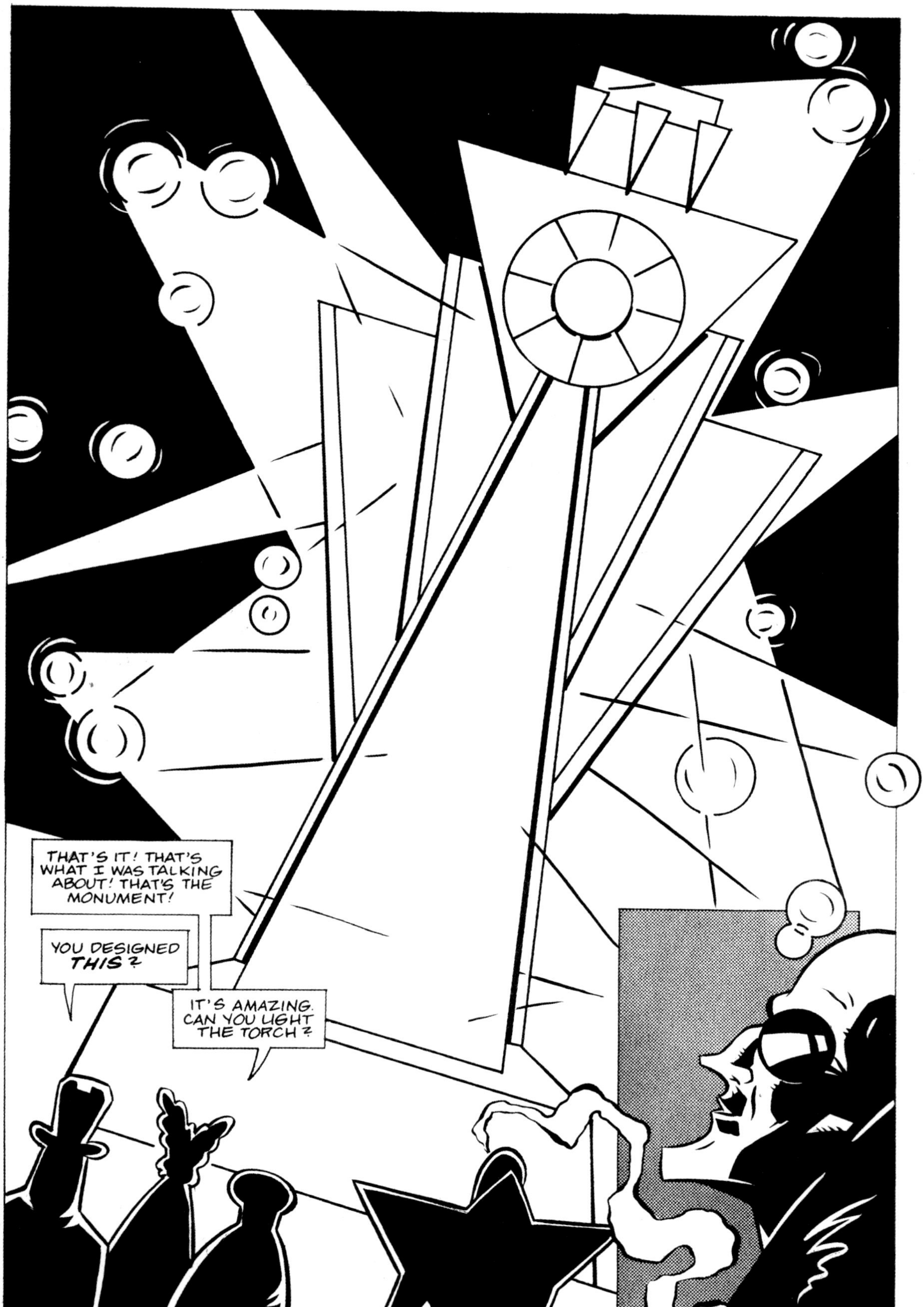
THAT'S IT! THAT'S WHAT I WAS TALKING ABOUT! THAT'S THE MONUMENT!
YOU DESIGNED THIS?
IT'S AMAZING. CAN YOU LIGHT THE TORCH?

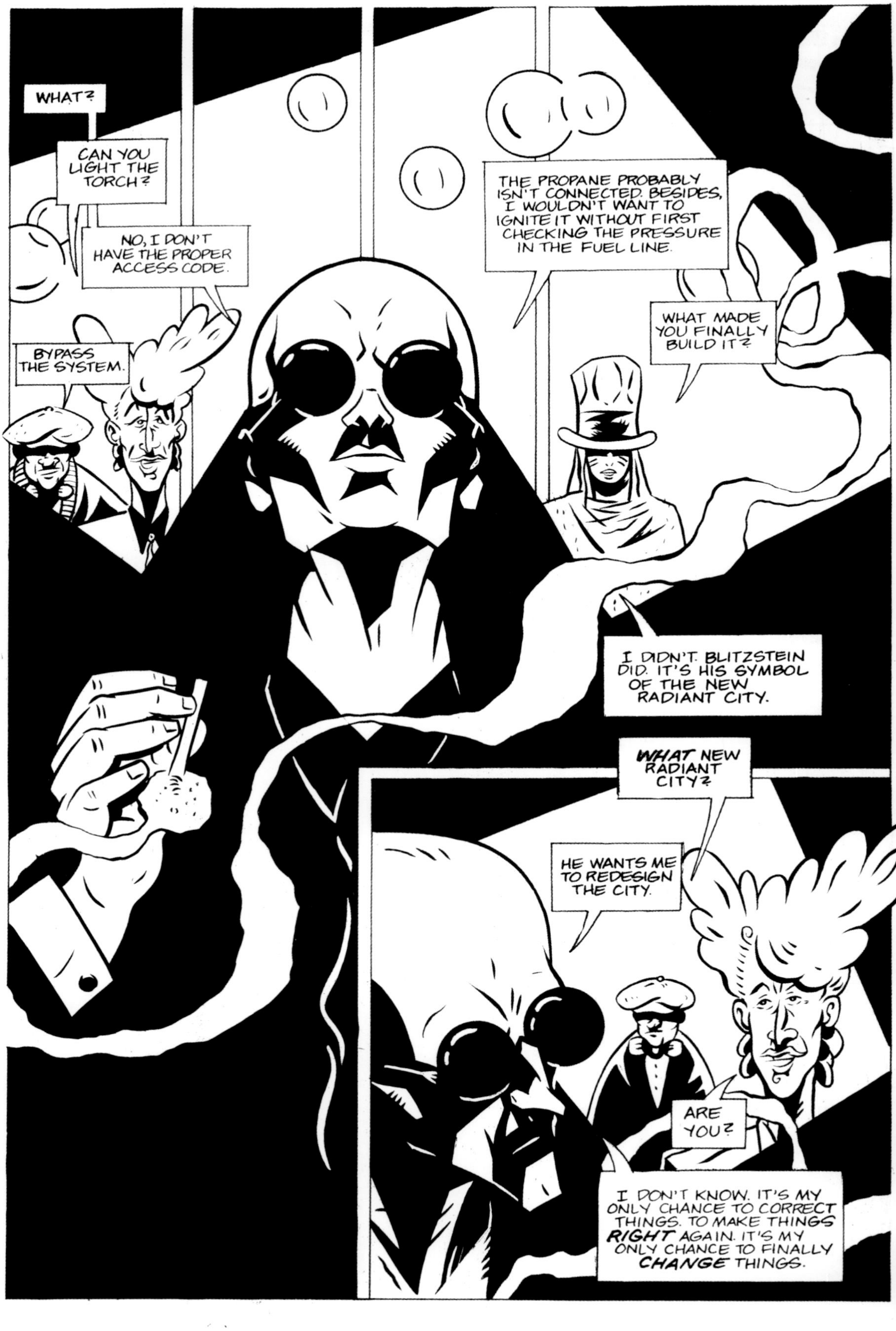
WHAT?
CAN YOU LIGHT THE TORCH?
NO, I DON'T HAVE THE PROPER ACCESS CODE.
BYPASS THE SYSTEM.
THE PROPANE PROBABLY ISN'T CONNECTED. BESIDES, I WOULDN'T WANT TO IGNITE IT WITHOUT FIRST CHECKING THE PRESSURE IN THE FUEL LINE.
WHAT MADE YOU FINALLY BUILD IT?
I DIDN'T. BLITZSTEIN DID. IT'S HIS SYMBOL OF THE NEW RADIANT CITY.
WHAT NEW RADIANT CITY?
HE WANTS ME TO REDESIGN THE CITY.
ARE YOU?
I DON'T KNOW. IT'S MY ONLY CHANCE TO CORRECT THINGS. TO MAKE THINGS RIGHT AGAIN. IT'S MY ONLY CHANCE TO FINALLY CHANGE THINGS.

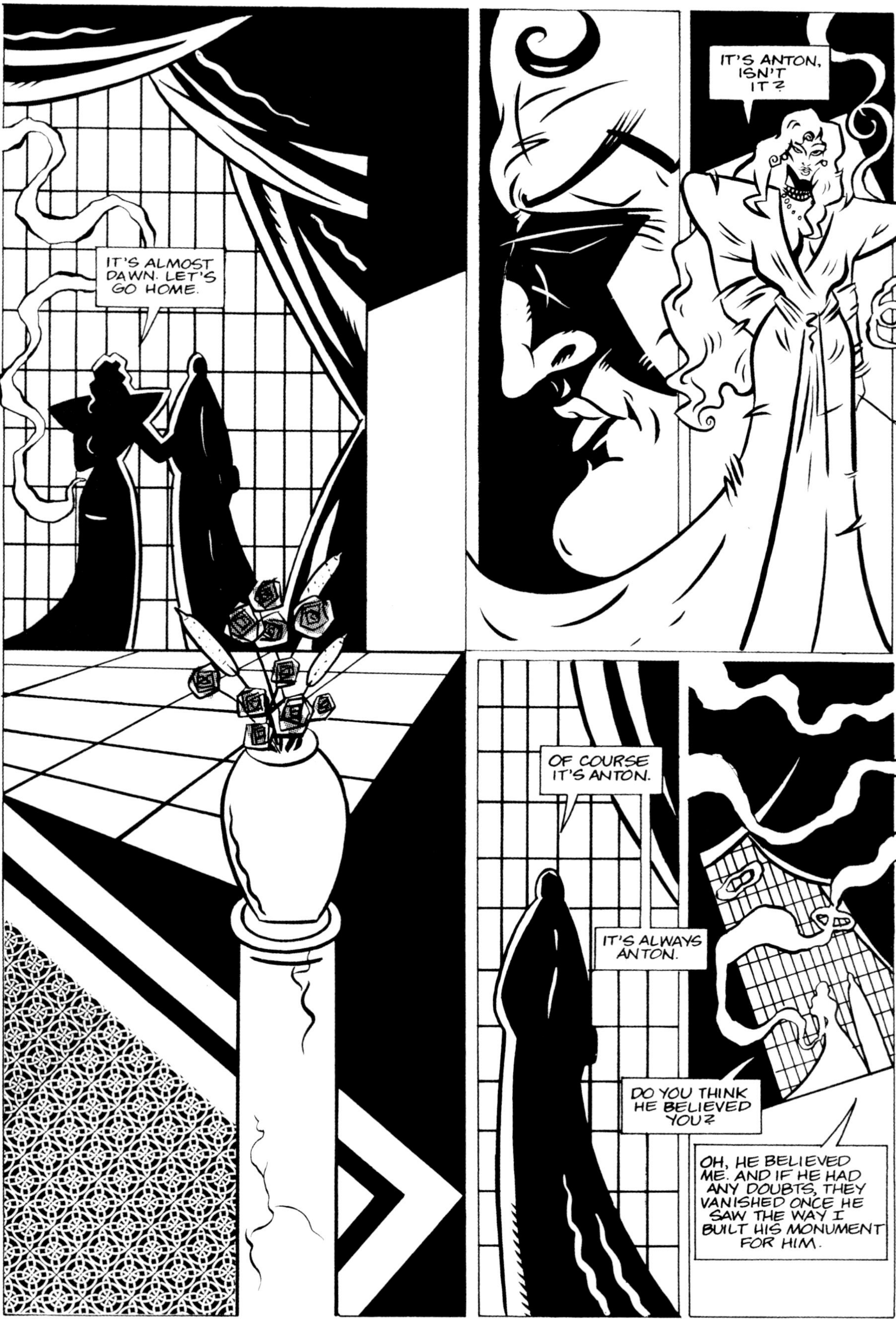
IT'S ALMOST DAWN. LET'S GO HOME.
IT'S ANTON, ISN'T IT?
OF COURSE IT'S ANTON.
IT'S ALWAYS ANTON.
DO YOU THINK HE BELIEVED YOU?
OH, HE BELIEVED ME. AND IF HE HAD ANY DOUBTS, THEY VANISHED ONCE HE SAW THE WAY I BUILT HIS MONUMENT FOR HIM.

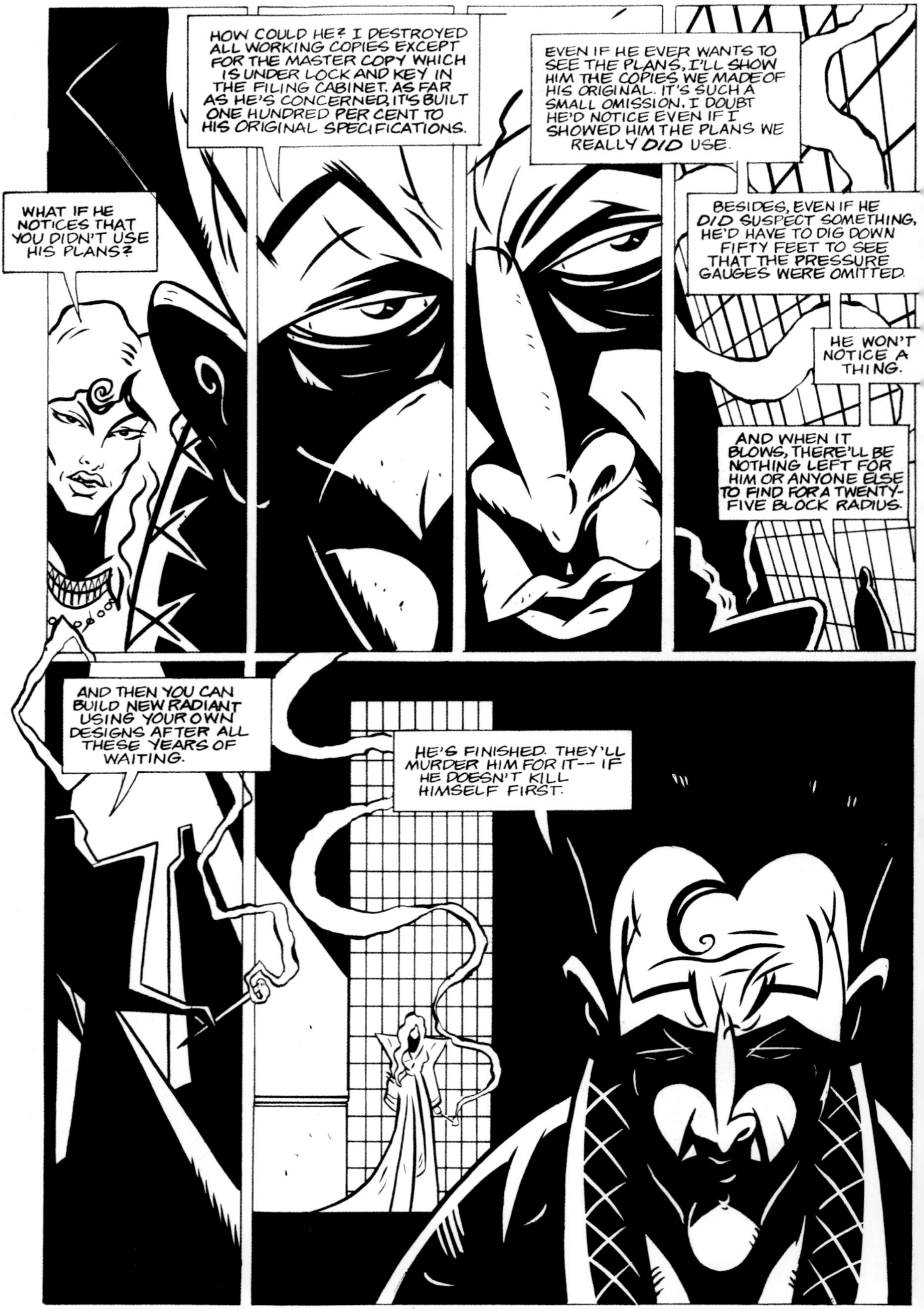
WHAT IF HE NOTICES THAT YOU DIDN'T USE HIS PLANS?
HOW COULD HE? I DESTROYED ALL WORKING COPIES EXCEPT FOR THE MASTER COPY WHICH IS UNDER LOCK AND KEY IN THE FILING CABINET. AS FAR AS HE'S CONCERNED, IT'S BUILT ONE HUNDRED PER CENT TO HIS ORIGINAL SPECIFICATIONS.
EVEN IF HE EVER WANTS TO SEE THE PLANS, I'LL SHOW HIM THE COPIES WE MADE OF HIS ORIGINAL. IT'S SUCH A SMALL OMISSION. I DOUBT HE'D NOTICE EVEN IF I SHOWED HIM THE PLANS WE REALLY DID USE.
BESIDES, EVEN IF HE DID SUSPECT SOMETHING, HE'D HAVE TO DIG DOWN FIFTY FEET TO SEE THAT THE PRESSURE GAUGES WERE OMITTED.
HE WON'T NOTICE A THING.
AND WHEN IT BLOWS, THERE'LL BE NOTHING LEFT FOR HIM OR ANYONE ELSE TO FIND FOR A TWENTY-FIVE BLOCK RADIUS.
AND THEN YOU CAN BUILD NEW RADIANT USING YOUR OWN DESIGNS AFTER ALL THESE YEARS OF WAITING.
HE'S FINISHED. THEY'LL MURDER HIM FOR IT-- IF HE DOESN'T KILL HIMSELF FIRST.

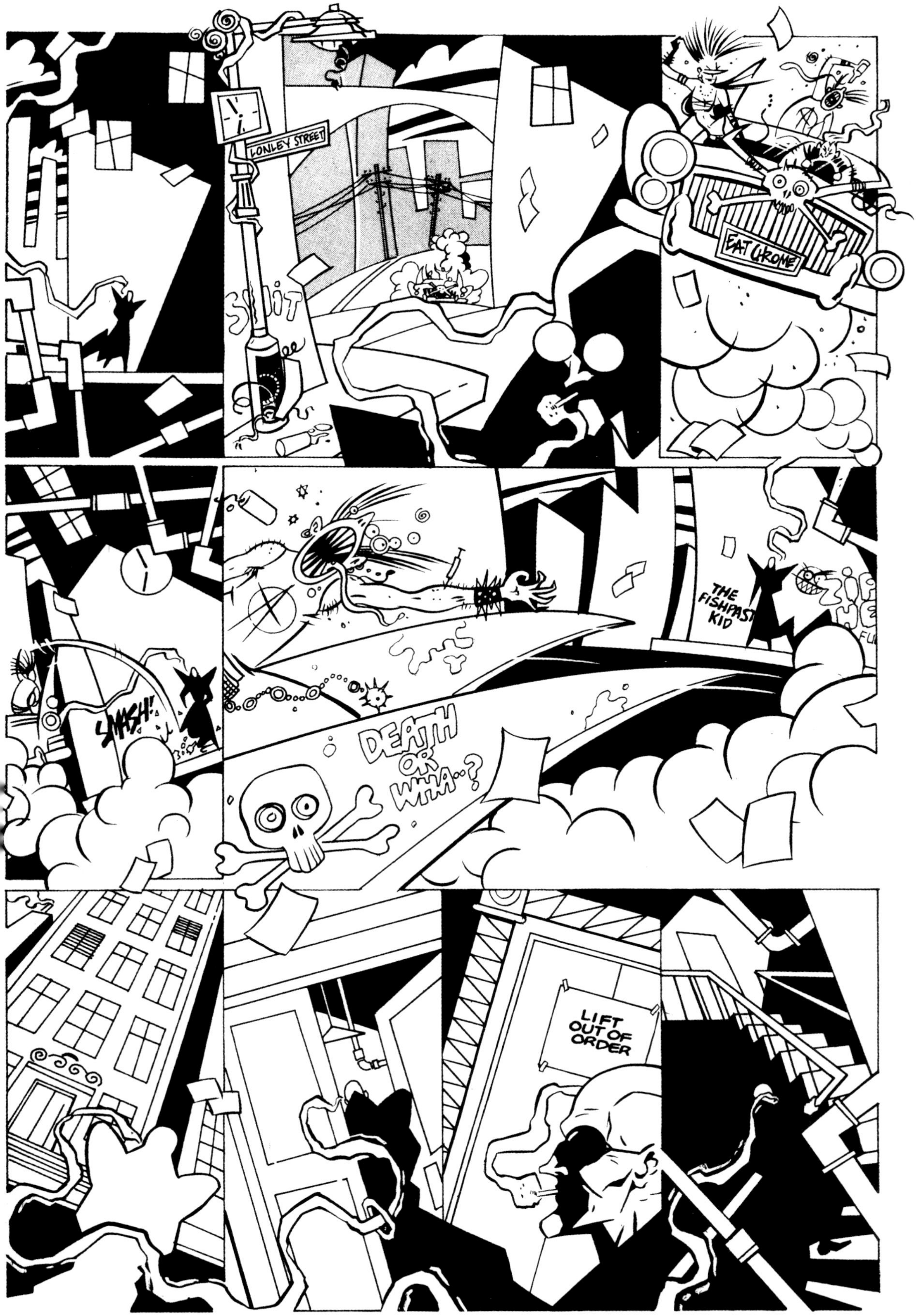
LONLEY STREET
SHIT
EAT CHROME
SMASH!
THE FISHPASTE KID
DEATH OR WHA..?
LIFT OUT OF ORDER

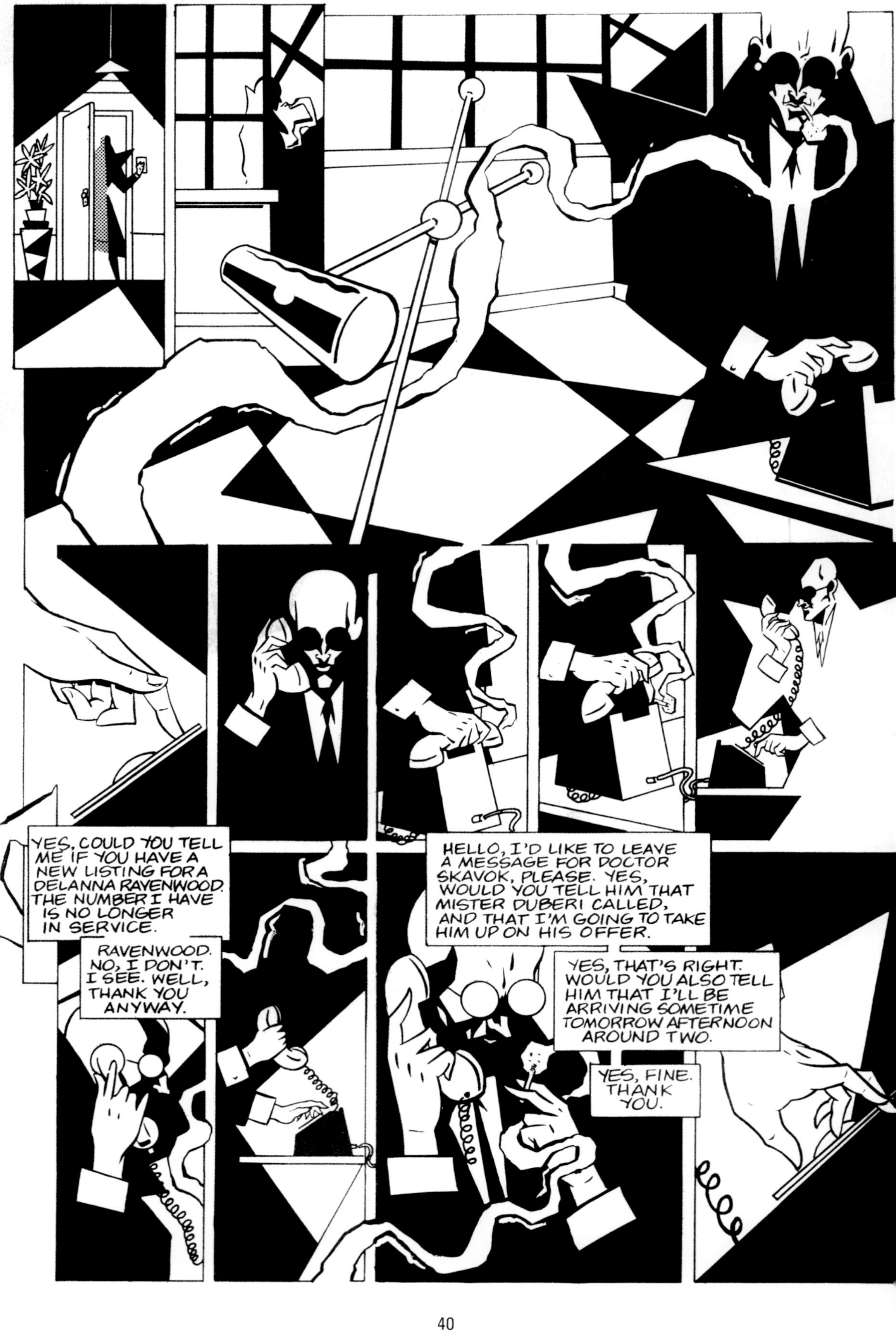
YES, COULD YOU TELL ME IF YOU HAVE A NEW LISTING FOR A DELANNA RAVENWOOD. THE NUMBER I HAVE IS NO LONGER IN SERVICE.
RAVENWOOD. NO, I DON'T. I SEE. WELL, THANK YOU ANYWAY.
HELLO, I'D LIKE TO LEAVE A MESSAGE FOR DOCTOR SKAVOK, PLEASE. YES, WOULD YOU TELL HIM THAT MISTER DUBERI CALLED, AND THAT I'M GOING TO TAKE HIM UP ON HIS OFFER.
YES, THAT'S RIGHT. WOULD YOU ALSO TELL HIM THAT I'LL BE ARRIVING SOMETIME TOMORROW AFTERNOON AROUND TWO.
YES, FINE. THANK YOU.

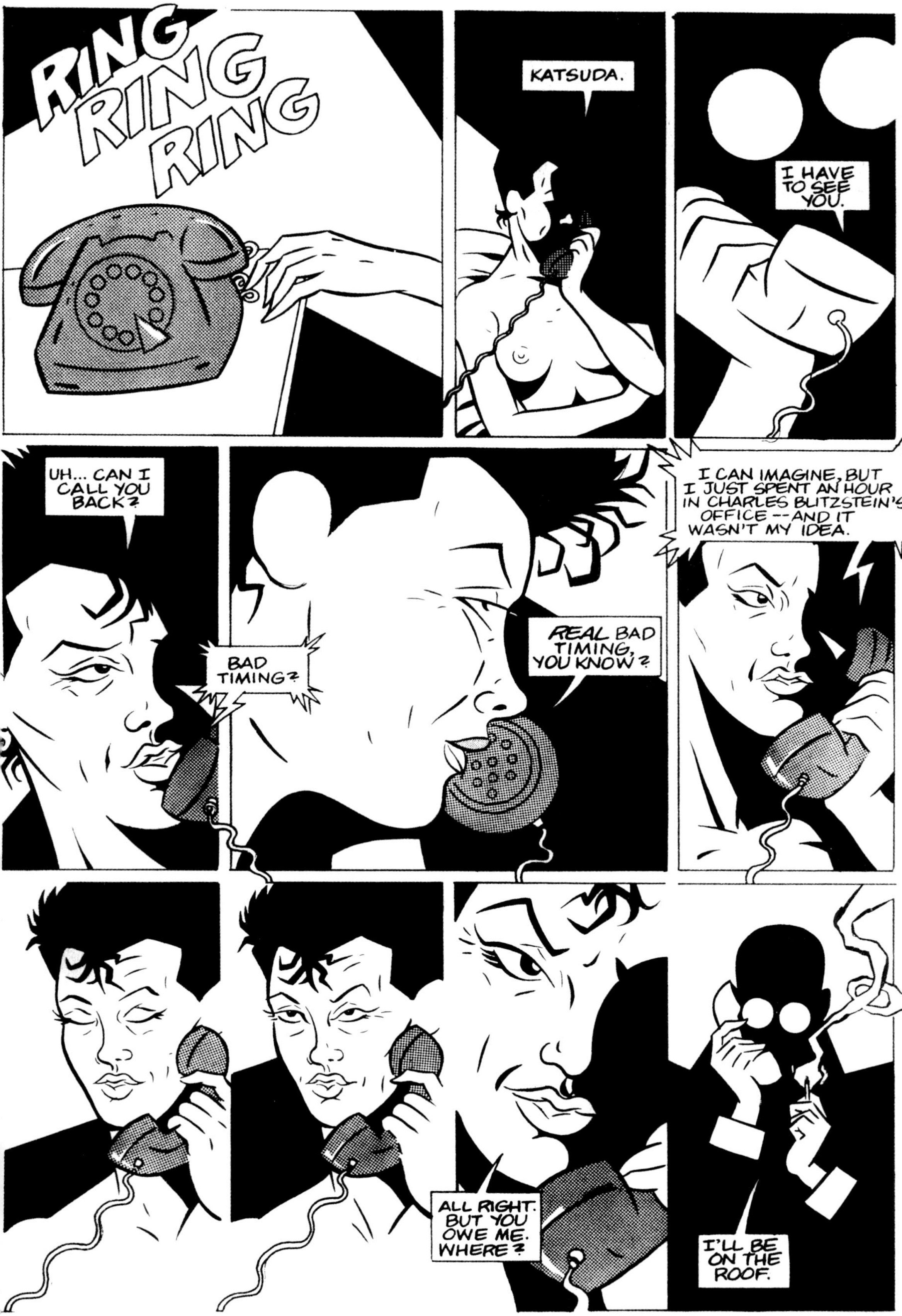
RING RING RING
KATSUDA.
I HAVE TO SEE YOU.
UH... CAN I CALL YOU BACK?
BAD TIMING?
REAL BAD TIMING, YOU KNOW?
I CAN IMAGINE, BUT I JUST SPENT AN HOUR IN CHARLES BLITZSTEIN'S OFFICE -- AND IT WASN'T MY IDEA.
ALL RIGHT. BUT YOU OWE ME. WHERE?
I'LL BE ON THE ROOF.

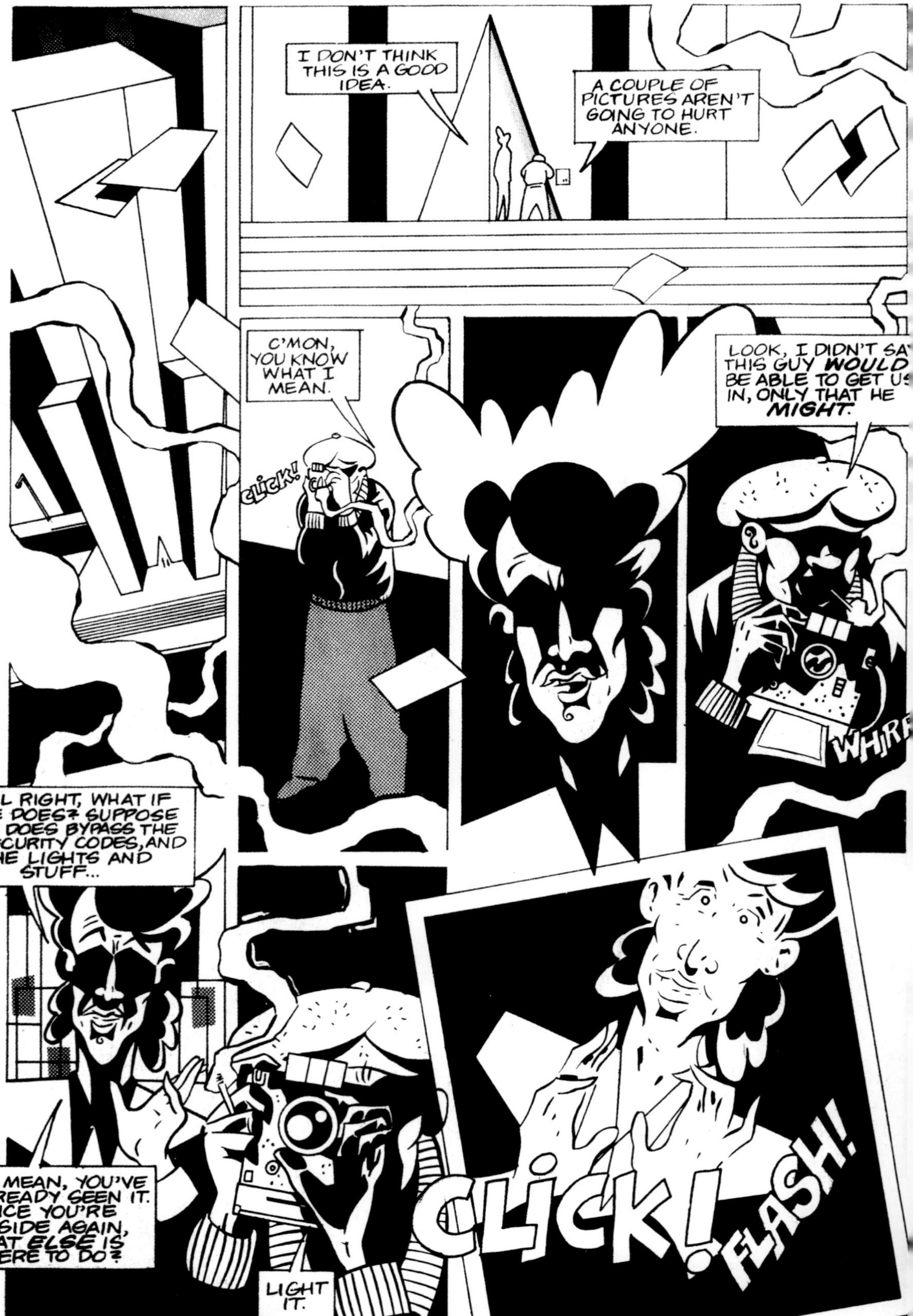
I DON'T THINK THIS IS A GOOD IDEA.
A COUPLE OF PICTURES AREN'T GOING TO HURT ANYONE.
C'MON, YOU KNOW WHAT I MEAN.
CLICK!
LOOK, I DIDN'T SA THIS GUY WOULD BE ABLE TO GET US IN, ONLY THAT HE MIGHT.
WHIRR
ALL RIGHT, WHAT IF HE DOES? SUPPOSE HE DOES BYPASS THE SECURITY CODES, AND THE LIGHTS AND STUFF...
...I MEAN, YOU'VE ALREADY SEEN IT. ONCE YOU'RE INSIDE AGAIN, WHAT ELSE IS THERE TO DO?
LIGHT IT.
CLICK!
FLASH!

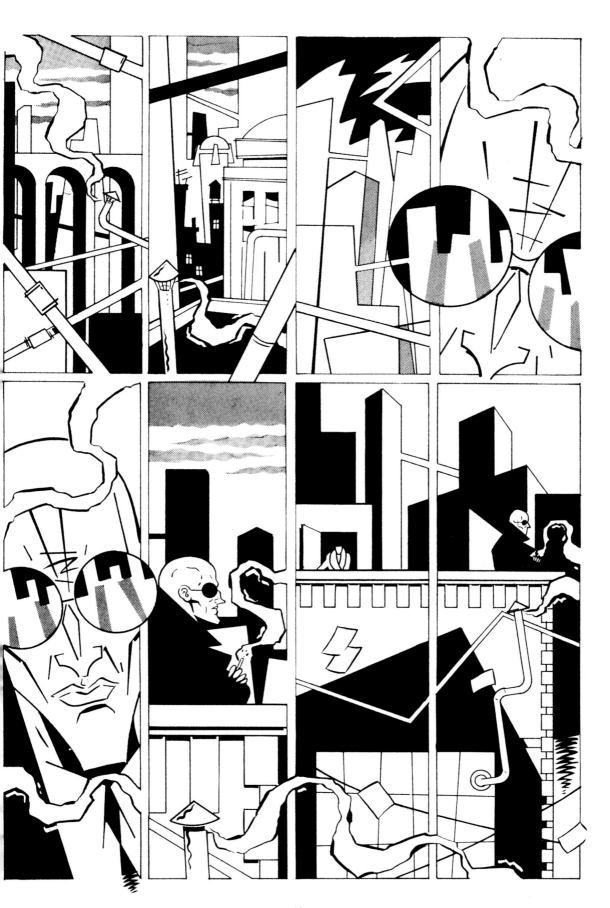

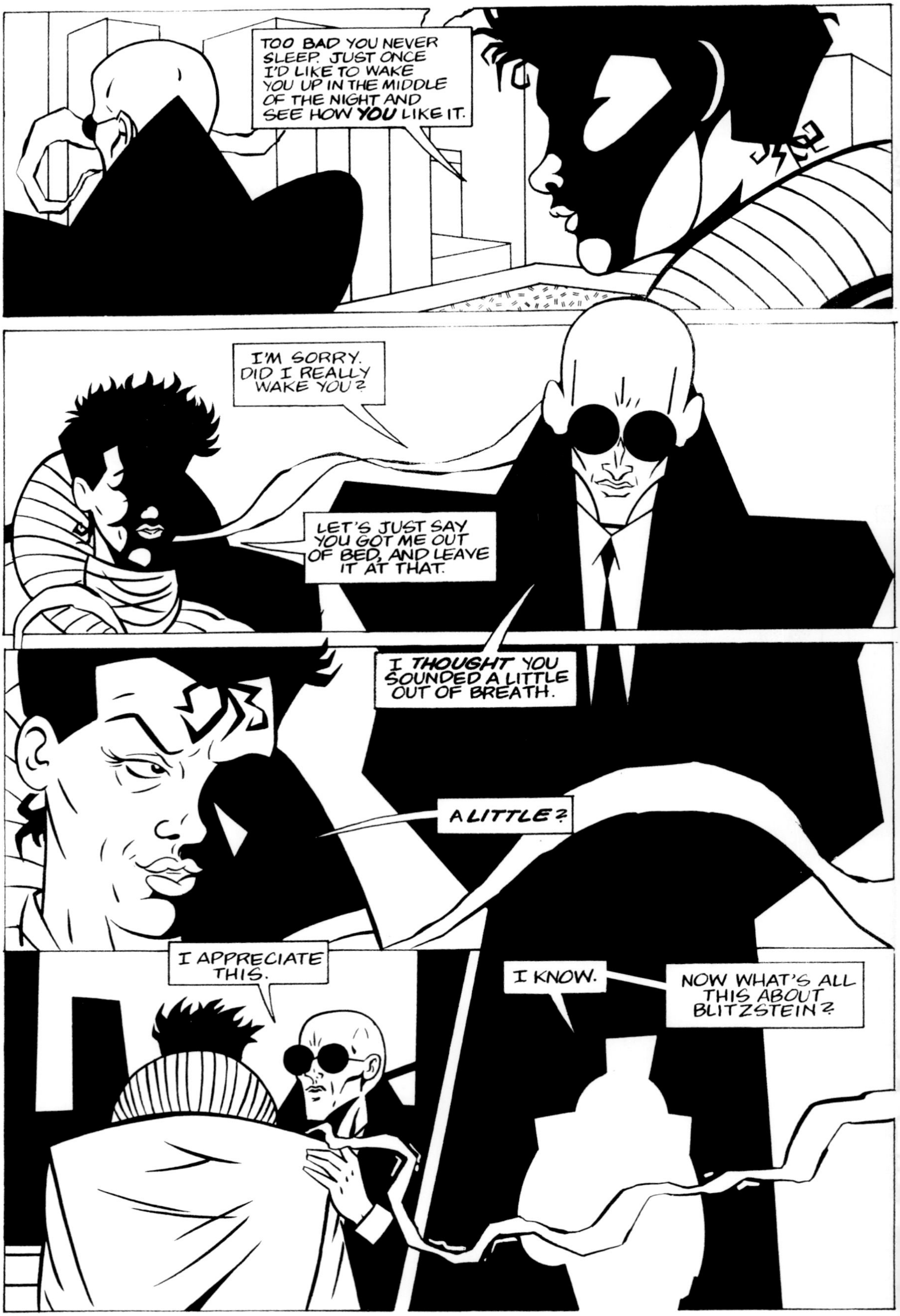
TOO BAD YOU NEVER SLEEP. JUST ONCE I'D LIKE TO WAKE YOU UP IN THE MIDDLE OF THE NIGHT AND SEE HOW YOU LIKE IT.
I'M SORRY. DID I REALLY WAKE YOU?
LET'S JUST SAY YOU GOT ME OUT OF BED, AND LEAVE IT AT THAT.
I THOUGHT YOU SOUNDED A LITTLE OUT OF BREATH.
A LITTLE?
I APPRECIATE THIS.
I KNOW.
NOW WHAT'S ALL THIS ABOUT BLITZSTEIN?

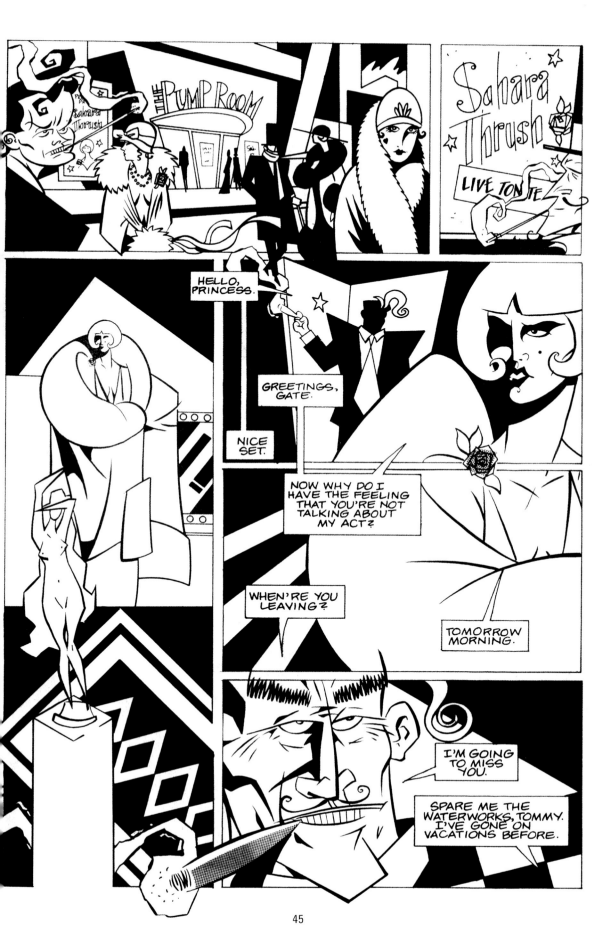

THE PUMP ROOM

Sahara Thrush

LIVE TON_TE

HELLO, PRINCESS.

GREETINGS, GATE.

NICE SET.

NOW WHY DO I HAVE THE FEELING THAT YOU'RE NOT TALKING ABOUT MY ACT?

WHEN'RE YOU LEAVING?

TOMORROW MORNING.

I'M GOING TO MISS YOU.

SPARE ME THE WATERWORKS, TOMMY. I'VE GONE ON VACATIONS BEFORE.

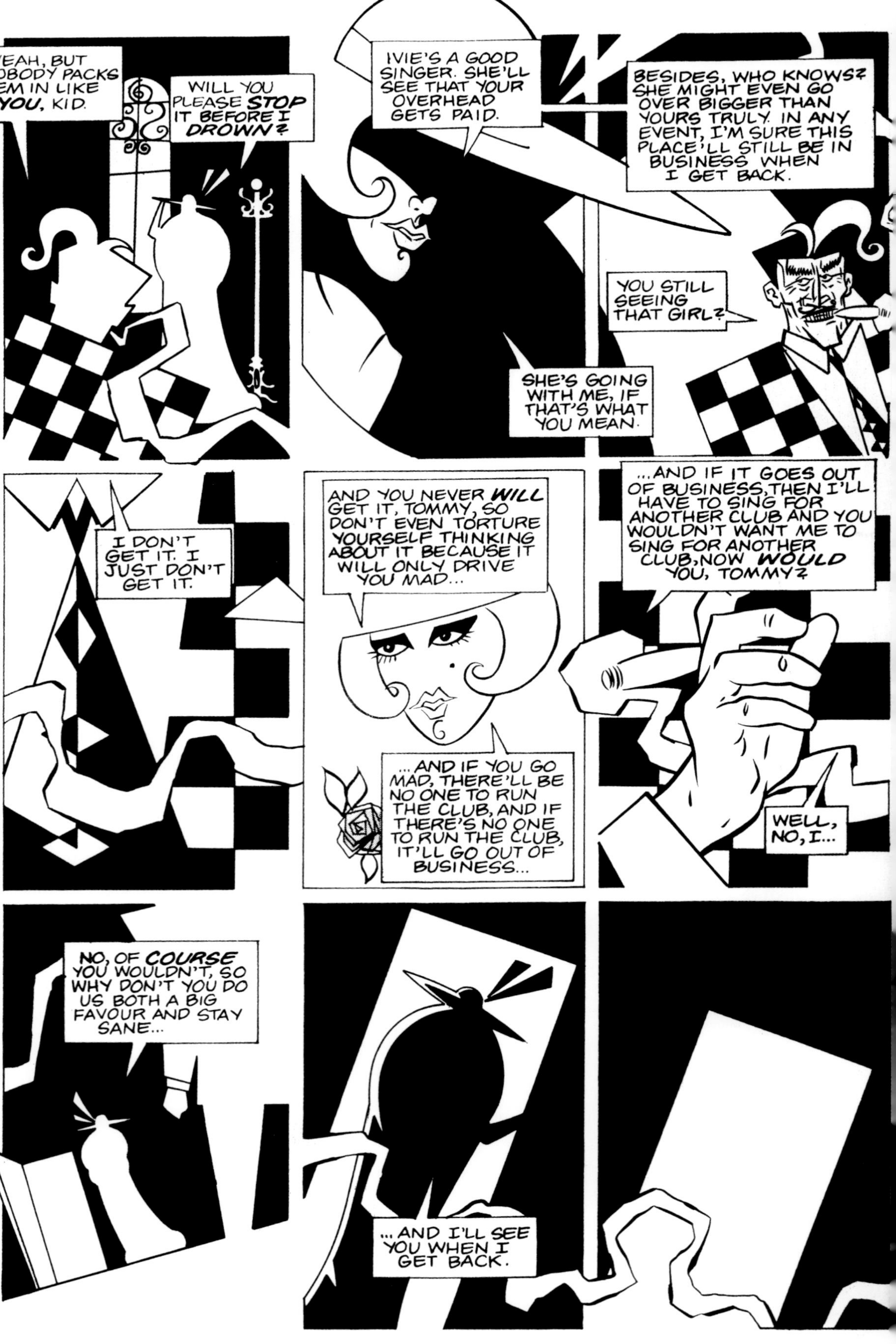
YEAH, BUT NOBODY PACKS 'EM IN LIKE YOU, KID.
WILL YOU PLEASE STOP IT BEFORE I DROWN?
IVIE'S A GOOD SINGER. SHE'LL SEE THAT YOUR OVERHEAD GETS PAID.
BESIDES, WHO KNOWS? SHE MIGHT EVEN GO OVER BIGGER THAN YOURS TRULY. IN ANY EVENT, I'M SURE THIS PLACE'LL STILL BE IN BUSINESS WHEN I GET BACK.
YOU STILL SEEING THAT GIRL?
SHE'S GOING WITH ME, IF THAT'S WHAT YOU MEAN.
I DON'T GET IT. I JUST DON'T GET IT.
AND YOU NEVER WILL GET IT, TOMMY, SO DON'T EVEN TORTURE YOURSELF THINKING ABOUT IT BECAUSE IT WILL ONLY DRIVE YOU MAD...
...AND IF YOU GO MAD, THERE'LL BE NO ONE TO RUN THE CLUB, AND IF THERE'S NO ONE TO RUN THE CLUB, IT'LL GO OUT OF BUSINESS...
...AND IF IT GOES OUT OF BUSINESS, THEN I'LL HAVE TO SING FOR ANOTHER CLUB AND YOU WOULDN'T WANT ME TO SING FOR ANOTHER CLUB, NOW WOULD YOU, TOMMY?
WELL, NO, I...
NO, OF COURSE YOU WOULDN'T, SO WHY DON'T YOU DO US BOTH A BIG FAVOUR AND STAY SANE...
...AND I'LL SEE YOU WHEN I GET BACK.

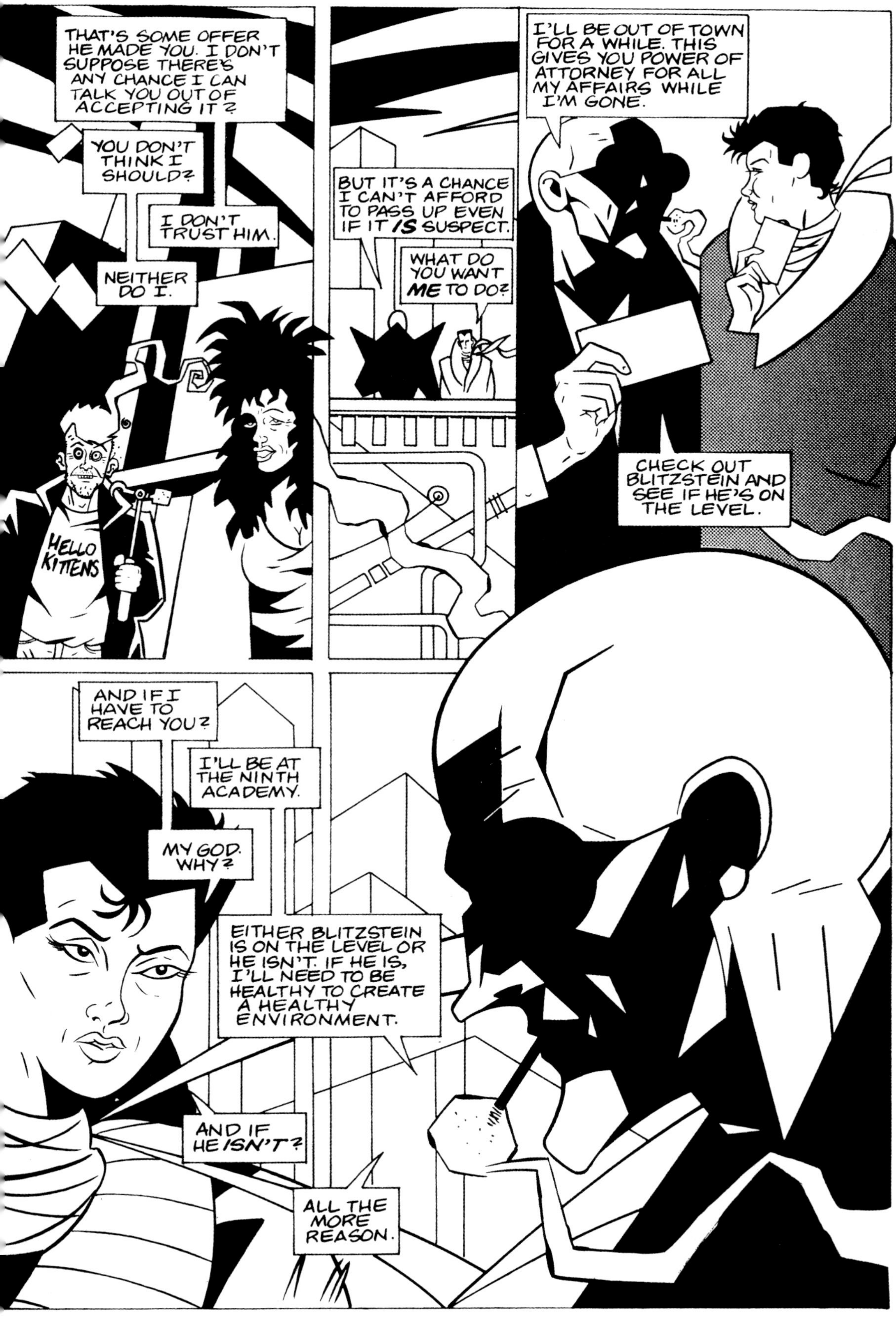
THAT'S SOME OFFER HE MADE YOU. I DON'T SUPPOSE THERE'S ANY CHANCE I CAN TALK YOU OUT OF ACCEPTING IT?
YOU DON'T THINK I SHOULD?
I DON'T TRUST HIM.
NEITHER DO I.
HELLO KITTENS
BUT IT'S A CHANCE I CAN'T AFFORD TO PASS UP EVEN IF IT *IS* SUSPECT.
WHAT DO YOU WANT *ME* TO DO?
I'LL BE OUT OF TOWN FOR A WHILE. THIS GIVES YOU POWER OF ATTORNEY FOR ALL MY AFFAIRS WHILE I'M GONE.
CHECK OUT BLITZSTEIN AND SEE IF HE'S ON THE LEVEL.
AND IF I HAVE TO REACH YOU?
I'LL BE AT THE NINTH ACADEMY.
MY GOD. WHY?
EITHER BLITZSTEIN IS ON THE LEVEL OR HE ISN'T. IF HE IS, I'LL NEED TO BE HEALTHY TO CREATE A HEALTHY ENVIRONMENT.
AND IF HE *ISN'T*?
ALL THE MORE REASON.

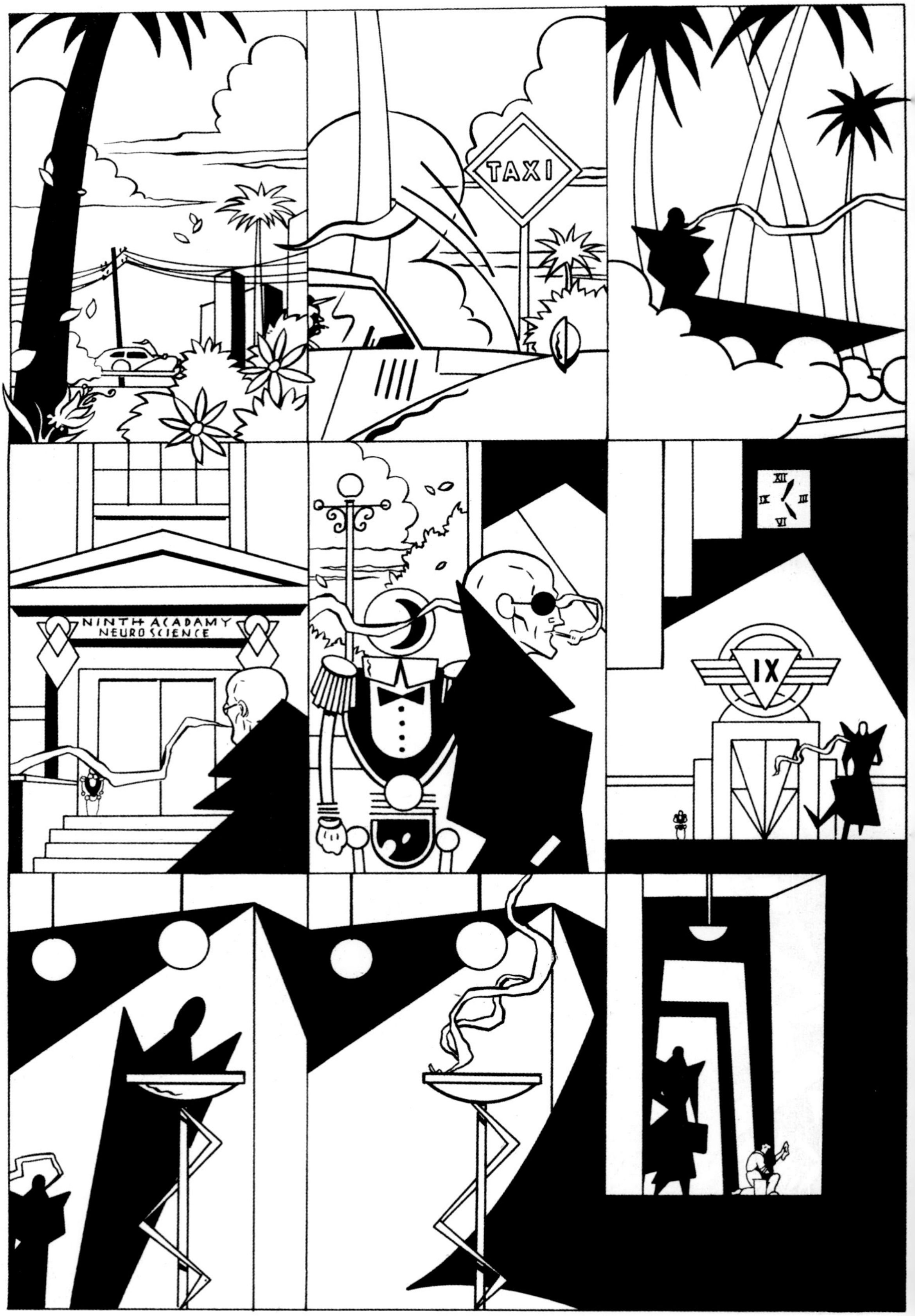
TAXI
NINTH ACADAMY
NEURO SCIENCE
IX

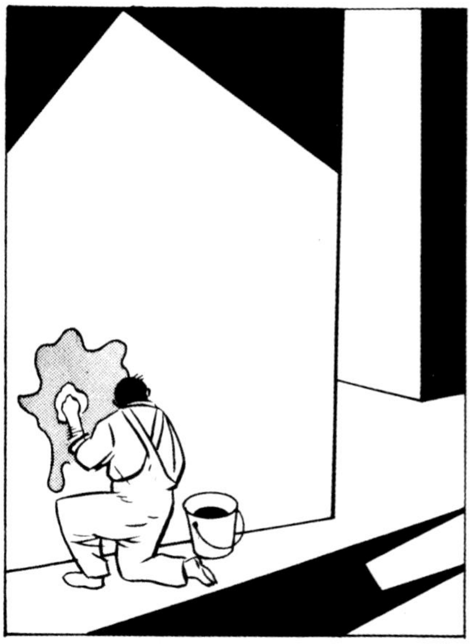

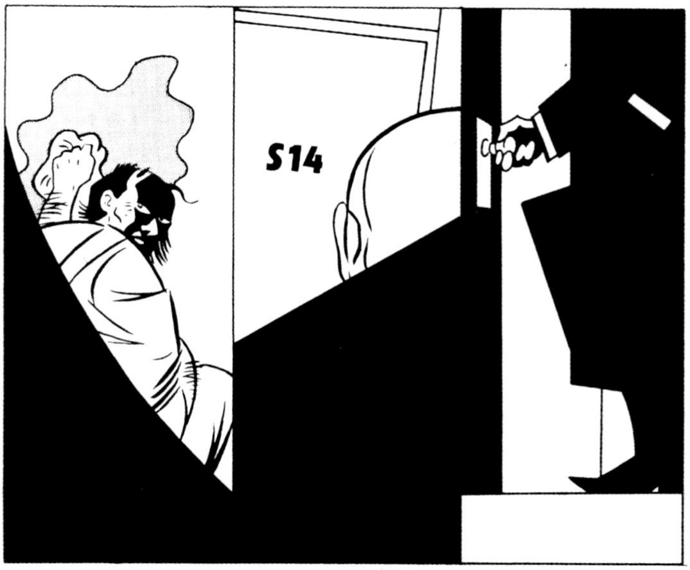
S14

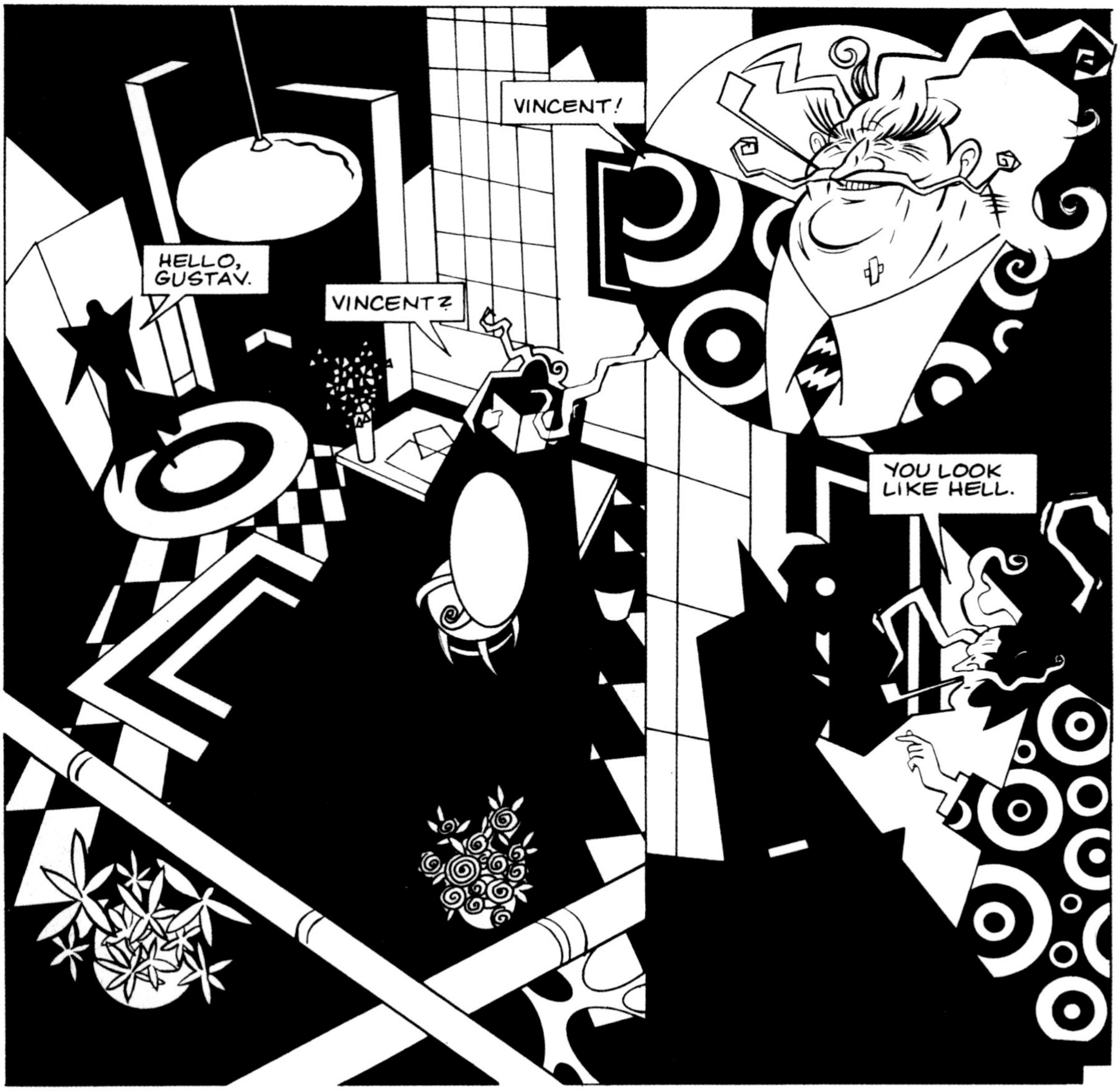
VINCENT!
HELLO, GUSTAV.
VINCENT?
YOU LOOK LIKE HELL.

I'VE *SEEN* HELL, GUSTAV. I LOOK WORSE. HOW'S THE PLACE HOLDING UP?

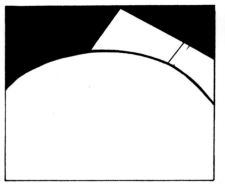

BETTER THAN ITS DESIGNER.

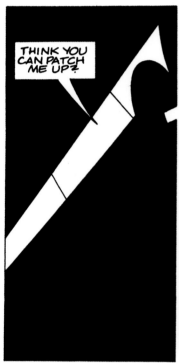

THINK YOU CAN PATCH ME UP?

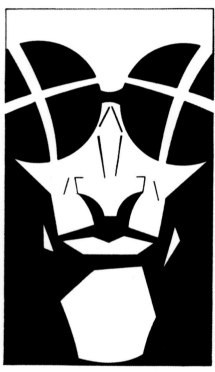

DEPENDS ON THE DAMAGE, PERHAPS. BUT I CAN'T DO IT OVERNIGHT.

HOW'S MY CREDIT?

I WOULDN'T WORRY ABOUT THAT IF I WERE YOU. WE STILL OWE YOU FOR THE DESIGN WORK.

I KNOW.

THIS'LL PROBABLY CANCEL THE DEBT, THOUGH.

I UNDERSTAND.

ALL RIGHT, THEN. BE IN ROOM 477 FOR TESTS IN HALF AN HOUR.

LET ME SEE YOUR ARMS.

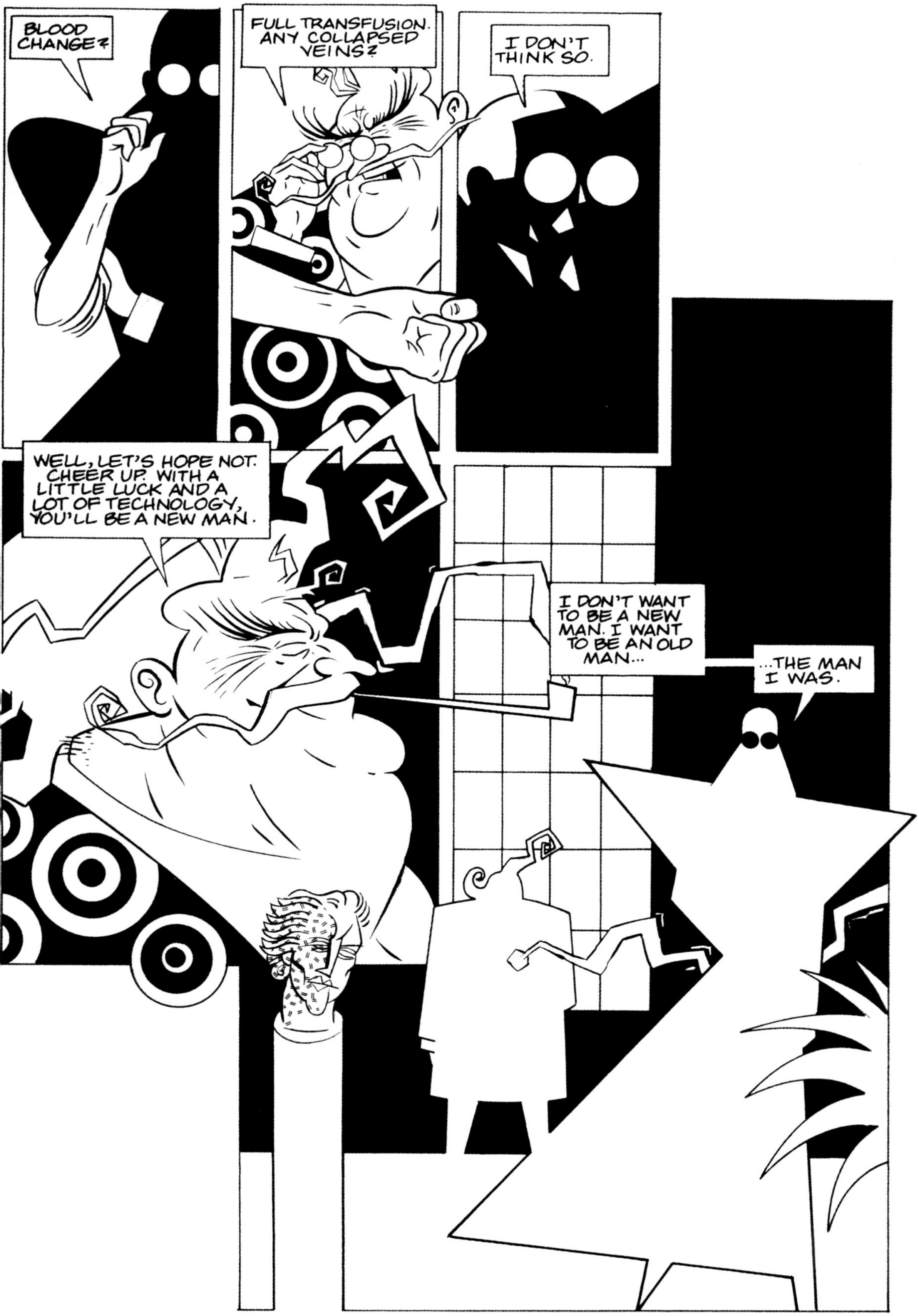
BLOOD CHANGE?
FULL TRANSFUSION. ANY COLLAPSED VEINS?
I DON'T THINK SO.
WELL, LET'S HOPE NOT. CHEER UP. WITH A LITTLE LUCK AND A LOT OF TECHNOLOGY, YOU'LL BE A NEW MAN.
I DON'T WANT TO BE A NEW MAN. I WANT TO BE AN OLD MAN...
...THE MAN I WAS.

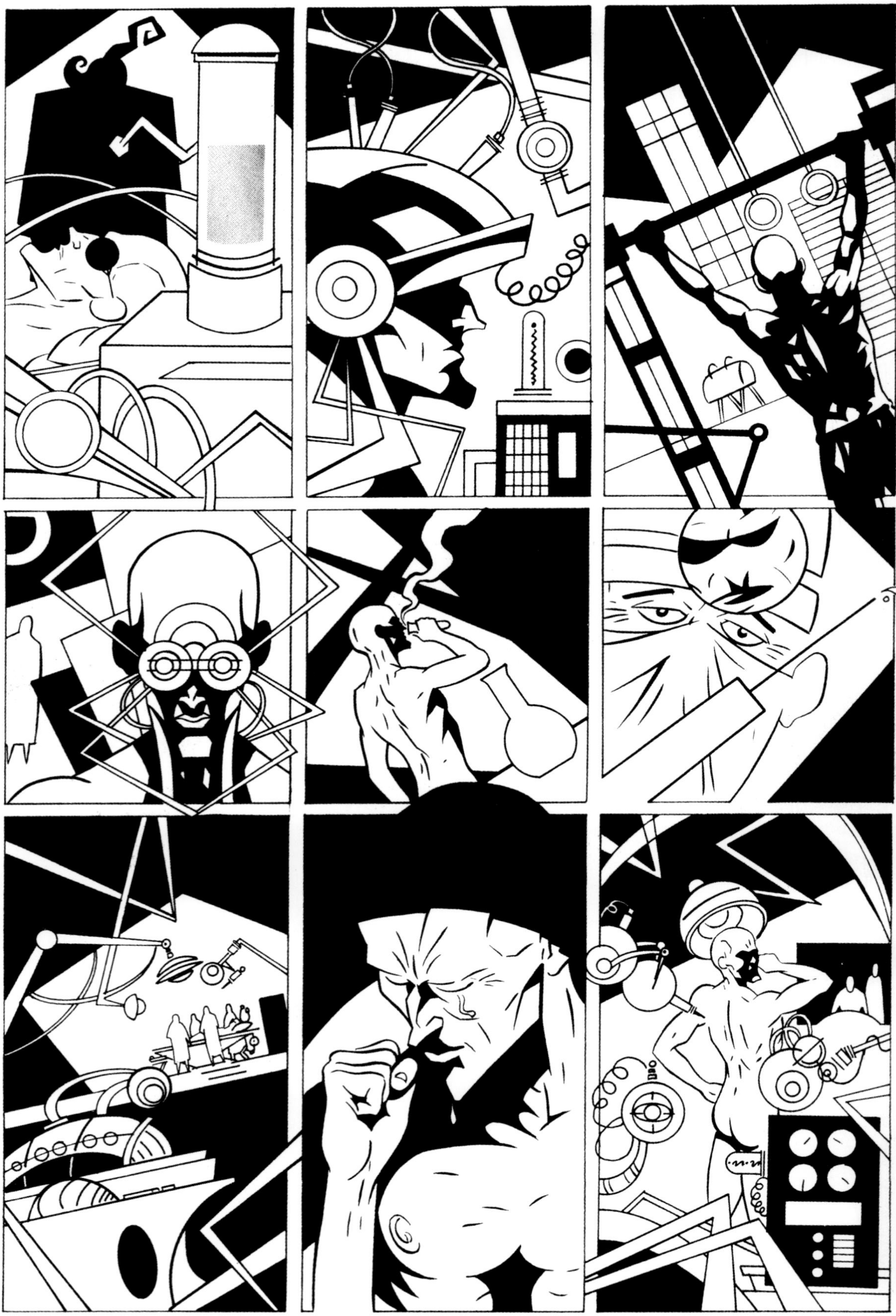

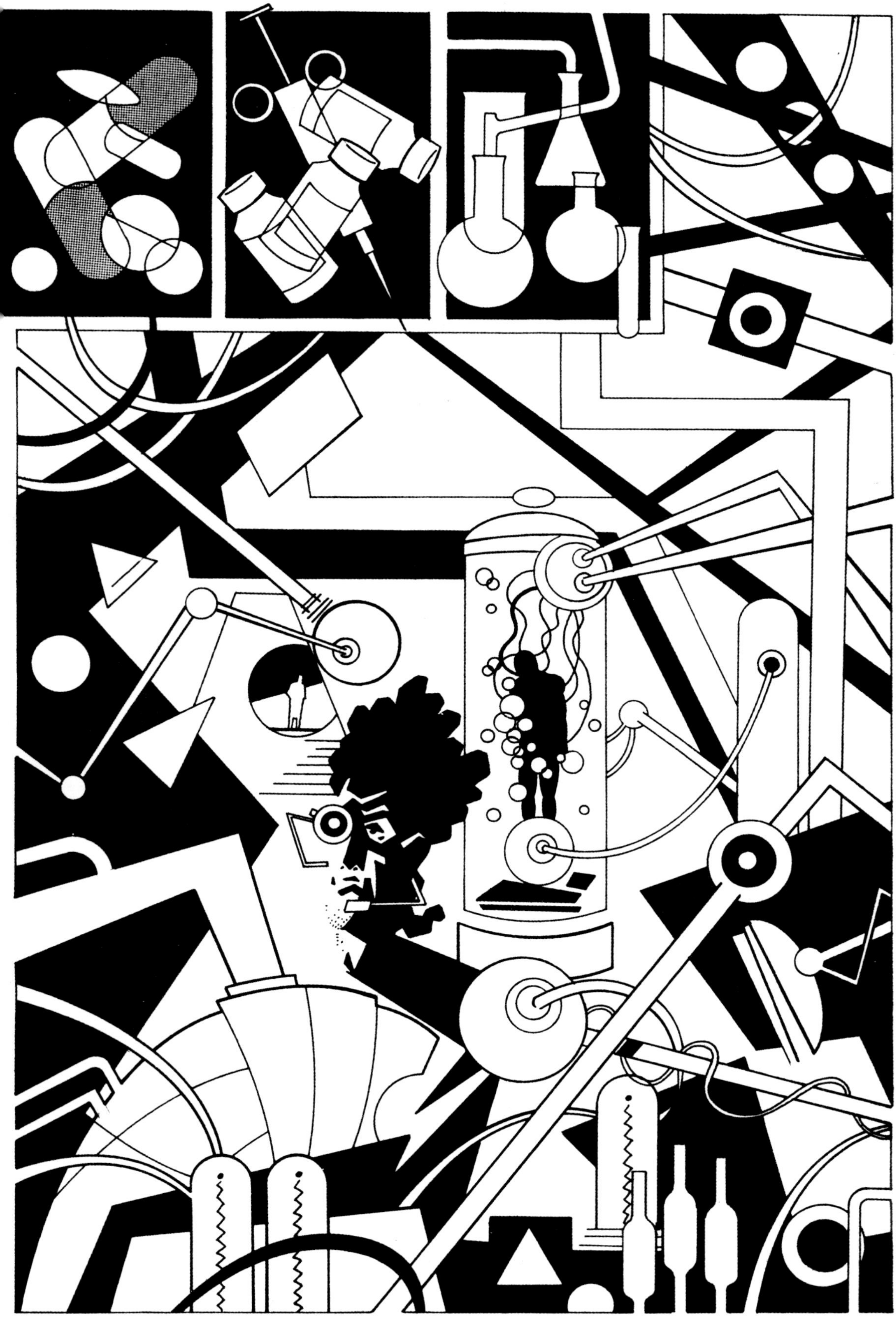

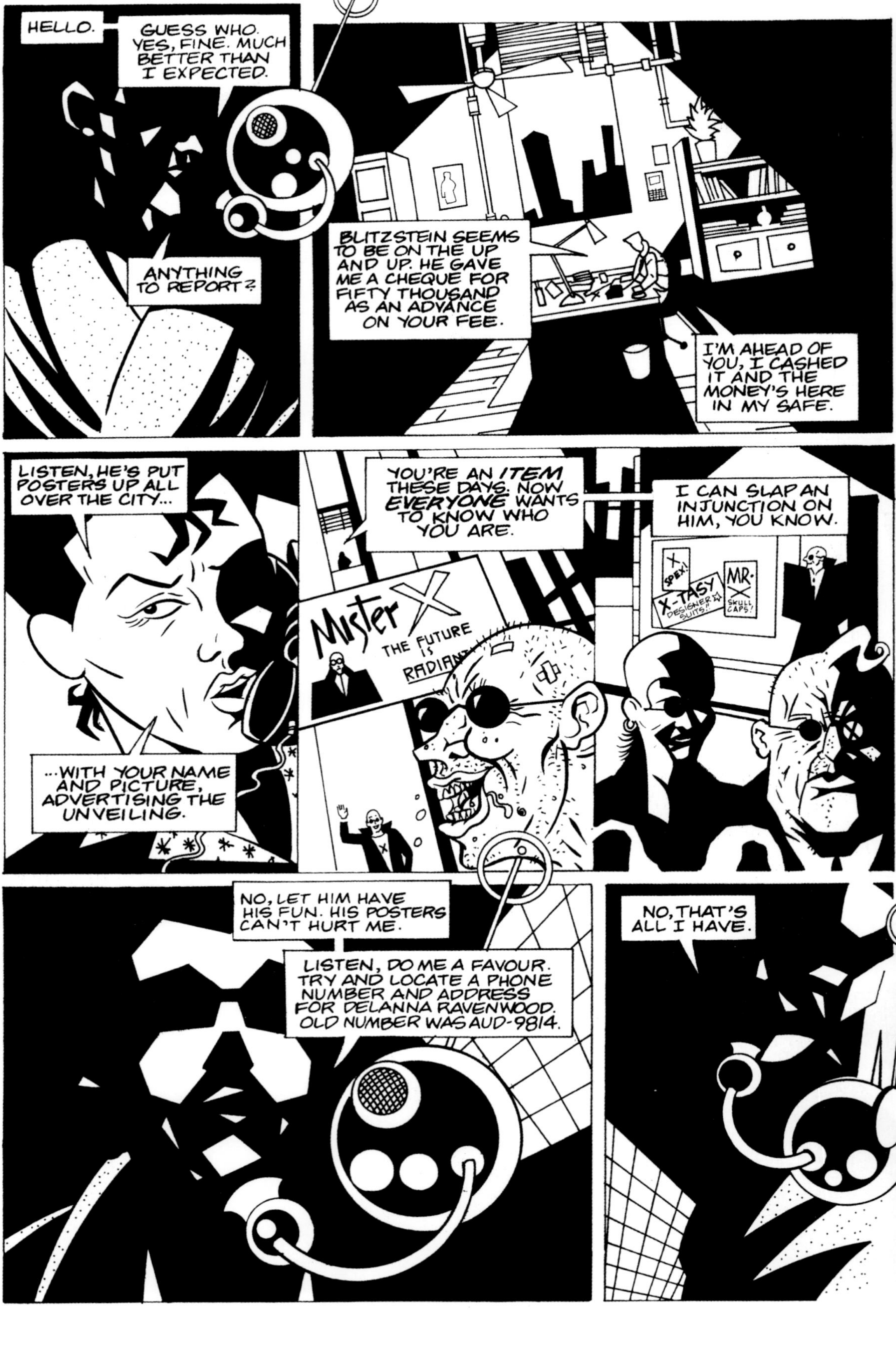
HELLO.
GUESS WHO. YES, FINE. MUCH BETTER THAN I EXPECTED.
ANYTHING TO REPORT?
BLITZSTEIN SEEMS TO BE ON THE UP AND UP. HE GAVE ME A CHEQUE FOR FIFTY THOUSAND AS AN ADVANCE ON YOUR FEE.
I'M AHEAD OF YOU, I CASHED IT AND THE MONEY'S HERE IN MY SAFE.
LISTEN, HE'S PUT POSTERS UP ALL OVER THE CITY...
...WITH YOUR NAME AND PICTURE, ADVERTISING THE UNVEILING.
YOU'RE AN *ITEM* THESE DAYS. NOW *EVERYONE* WANTS TO KNOW WHO YOU ARE.
Mister X
THE FUTURE IS RADIANT
I CAN SLAP AN INJUNCTION ON HIM, YOU KNOW.
X SPEX!
X-TASY DESIGNER SUITS!!
MR. X SKULL CAPS!
NO, LET HIM HAVE HIS FUN. HIS POSTERS CAN'T HURT ME.
LISTEN, DO ME A FAVOUR. TRY AND LOCATE A PHONE NUMBER AND ADDRESS FOR DELANNA RAVENWOOD. OLD NUMBER WAS AUD-9814.
NO, THAT'S ALL I HAVE.

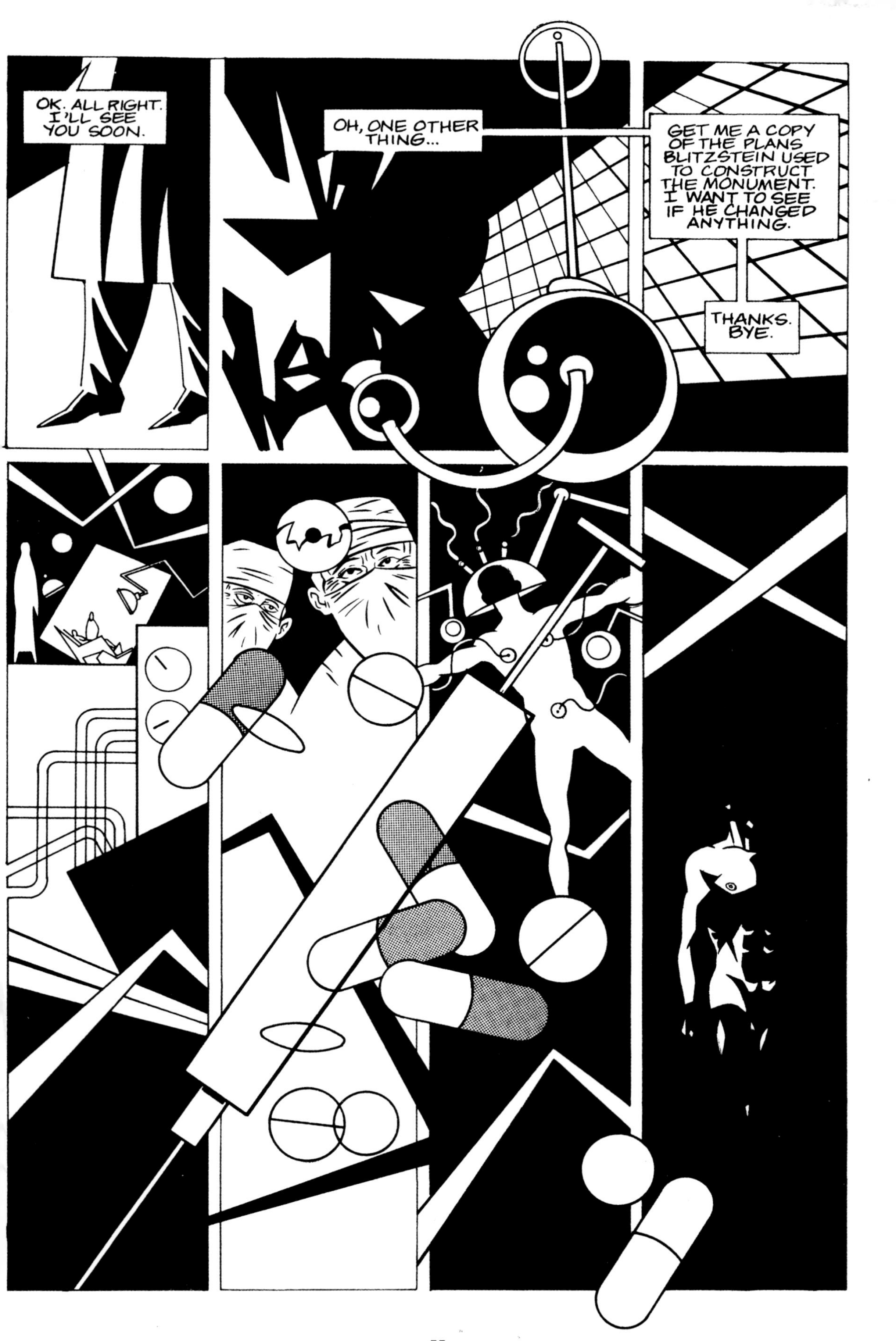
OK. ALL RIGHT. I'LL SEE YOU SOON.
OH, ONE OTHER THING...
GET ME A COPY OF THE PLANS BLITZSTEIN USED TO CONSTRUCT THE MONUMENT. I WANT TO SEE IF HE CHANGED ANYTHING.
THANKS. BYE.

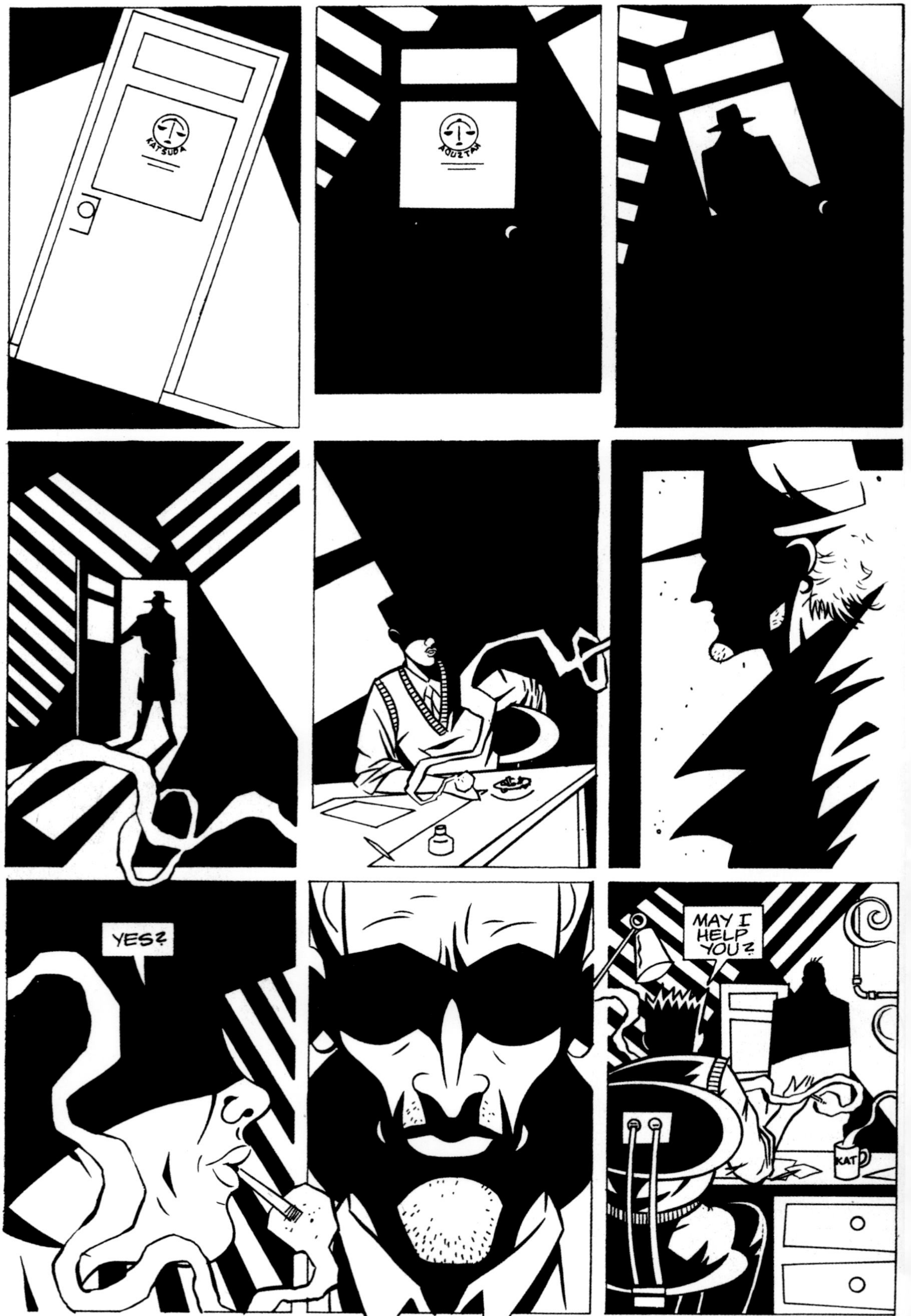
KATSUDA
YES?
MAY I HELP YOU?
KAT

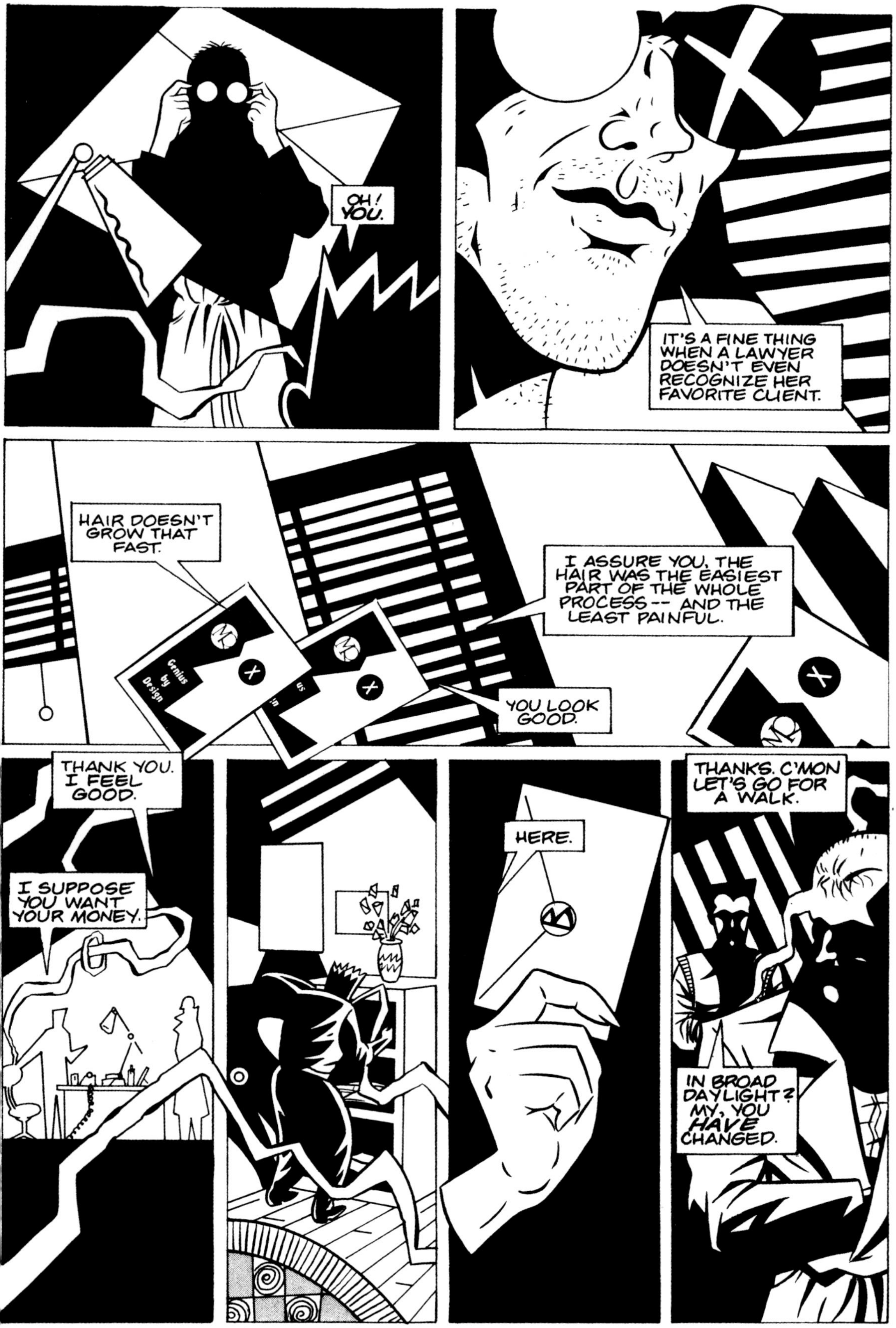
OH! YOU.
IT'S A FINE THING WHEN A LAWYER DOESN'T EVEN RECOGNIZE HER FAVORITE CLIENT.
HAIR DOESN'T GROW THAT FAST.
I ASSURE YOU, THE HAIR WAS THE EASIEST PART OF THE WHOLE PROCESS -- AND THE LEAST PAINFUL.
Genius by Design
YOU LOOK GOOD.
THANK YOU. I FEEL GOOD.
I SUPPOSE YOU WANT YOUR MONEY.
HERE.
THANKS. C'MON LET'S GO FOR A WALK.
IN BROAD DAYLIGHT? MY, YOU *HAVE* CHANGED.

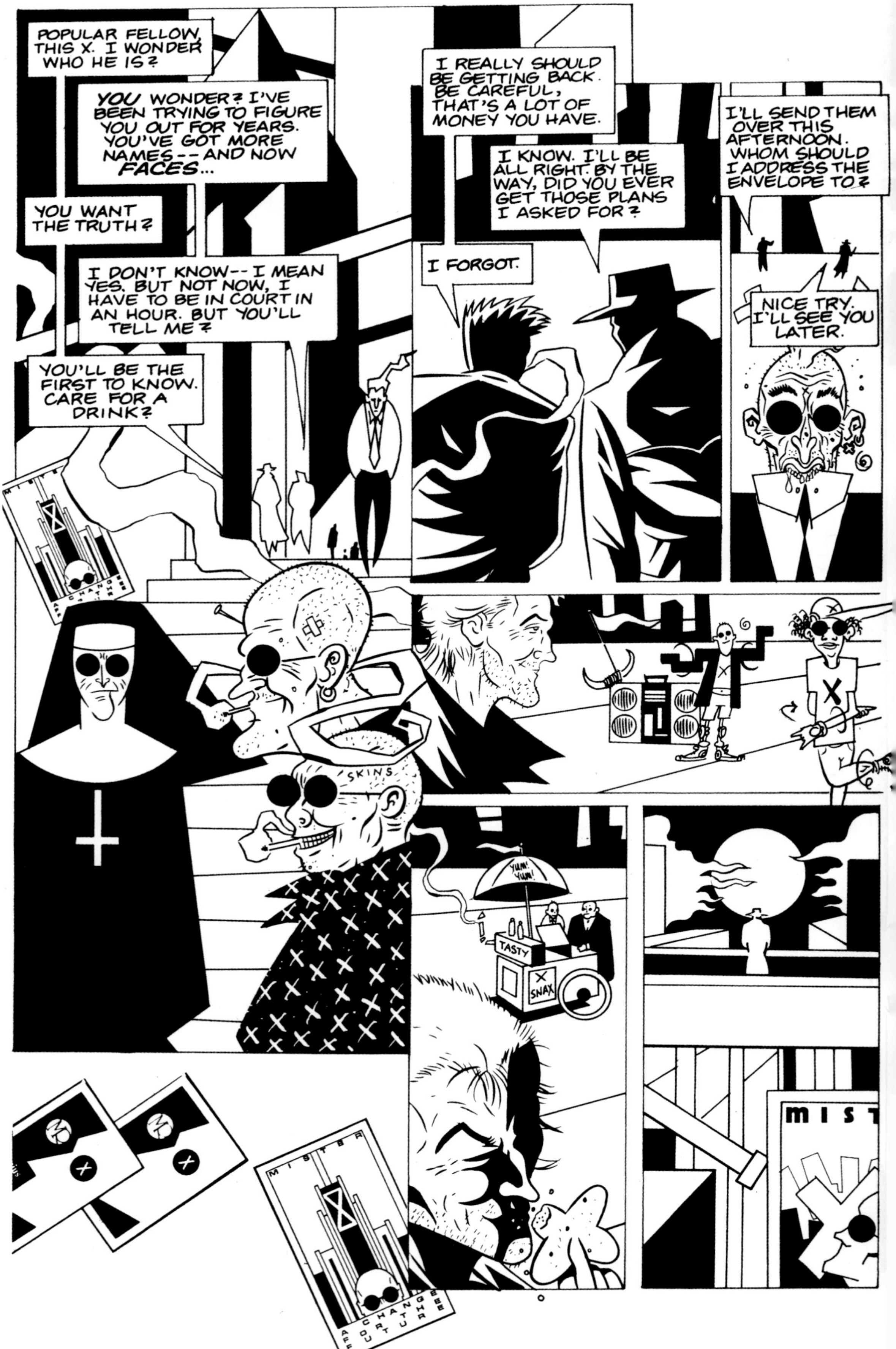
POPULAR FELLOW, THIS X. I WONDER WHO HE IS?
YOU WONDER? I'VE BEEN TRYING TO FIGURE YOU OUT FOR YEARS. YOU'VE GOT MORE NAMES-- AND NOW FACES...
YOU WANT THE TRUTH?
I DON'T KNOW-- I MEAN YES. BUT NOT NOW, I HAVE TO BE IN COURT IN AN HOUR. BUT YOU'LL TELL ME?
YOU'LL BE THE FIRST TO KNOW. CARE FOR A DRINK?
I REALLY SHOULD BE GETTING BACK. BE CAREFUL, THAT'S A LOT OF MONEY YOU HAVE.
I KNOW. I'LL BE ALL RIGHT. BY THE WAY, DID YOU EVER GET THOSE PLANS I ASKED FOR?
I FORGOT.
I'LL SEND THEM OVER THIS AFTERNOON. WHOM SHOULD I ADDRESS THE ENVELOPE TO?
NICE TRY. I'LL SEE YOU LATER.
SKINS
YUM! YUM!
TASTY
X SNAX
MISTER
A CHANGE FOR THE FUTURE
MIST

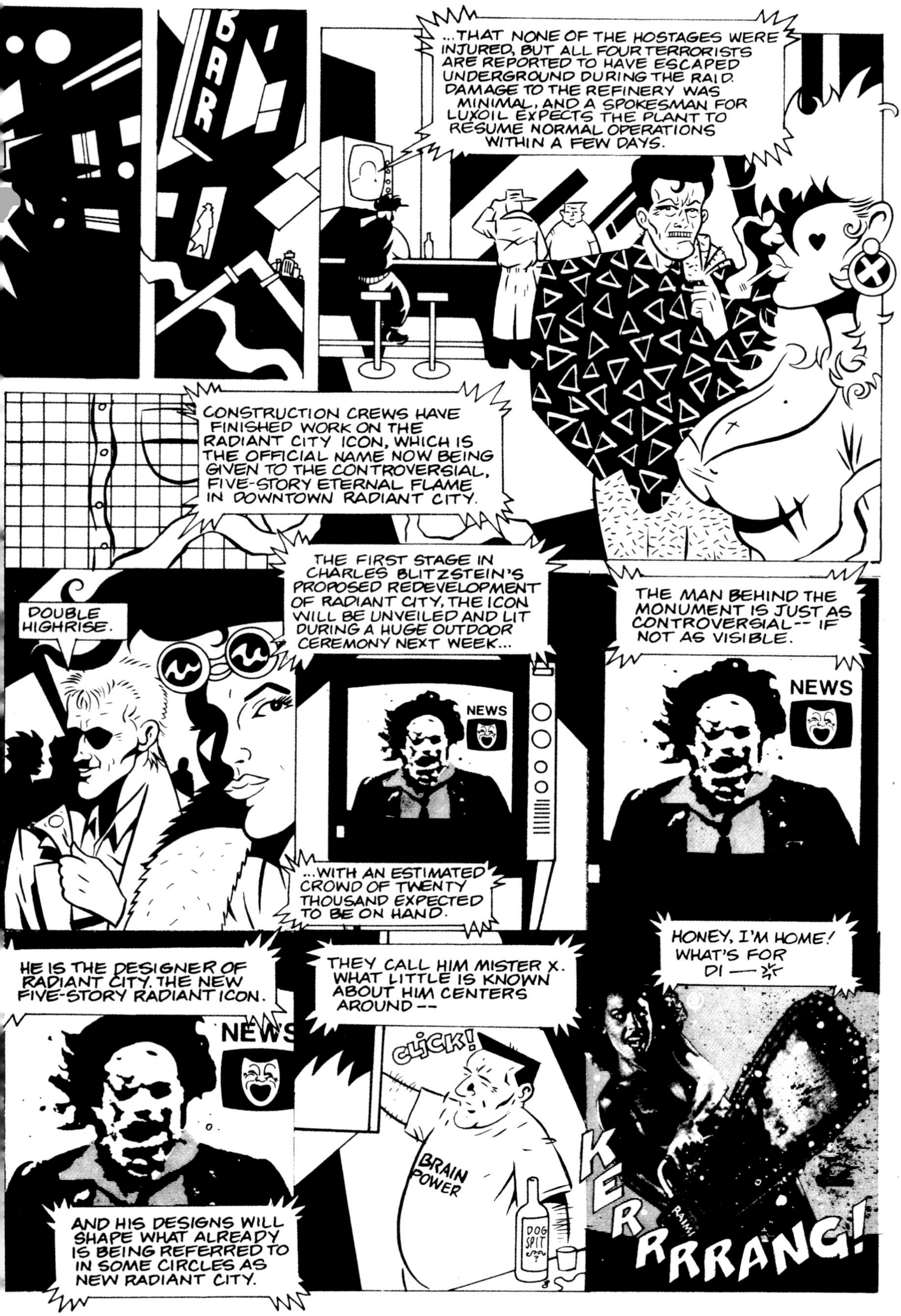
...THAT NONE OF THE HOSTAGES WERE INJURED, BUT ALL FOUR TERRORISTS ARE REPORTED TO HAVE ESCAPED UNDERGROUND DURING THE RAID. DAMAGE TO THE REFINERY WAS MINIMAL, AND A SPOKESMAN FOR LUXOIL EXPECTS THE PLANT TO RESUME NORMAL OPERATIONS WITHIN A FEW DAYS.
BAR
CONSTRUCTION CREWS HAVE FINISHED WORK ON THE RADIANT CITY ICON, WHICH IS THE OFFICIAL NAME NOW BEING GIVEN TO THE CONTROVERSIAL, FIVE-STORY ETERNAL FLAME IN DOWNTOWN RADIANT CITY.
DOUBLE HIGHRISE.
THE FIRST STAGE IN CHARLES BLITZSTEIN'S PROPOSED REDEVELOPMENT OF RADIANT CITY, THE ICON WILL BE UNVEILED AND LIT DURING A HUGE OUTDOOR CEREMONY NEXT WEEK...
NEWS
...WITH AN ESTIMATED CROWD OF TWENTY THOUSAND EXPECTED TO BE ON HAND.
THE MAN BEHIND THE MONUMENT IS JUST AS CONTROVERSIAL-- IF NOT AS VISIBLE.
NEWS
HE IS THE DESIGNER OF RADIANT CITY. THE NEW FIVE-STORY RADIANT ICON.
NEWS
AND HIS DESIGNS WILL SHAPE WHAT ALREADY IS BEING REFERRED TO IN SOME CIRCLES AS NEW RADIANT CITY.
THEY CALL HIM MISTER X. WHAT LITTLE IS KNOWN ABOUT HIM CENTERS AROUND --
CLICK!
BRAIN POWER
DOG SPIT
HONEY, I'M HOME! WHAT'S FOR DI —
KERRRRANG!

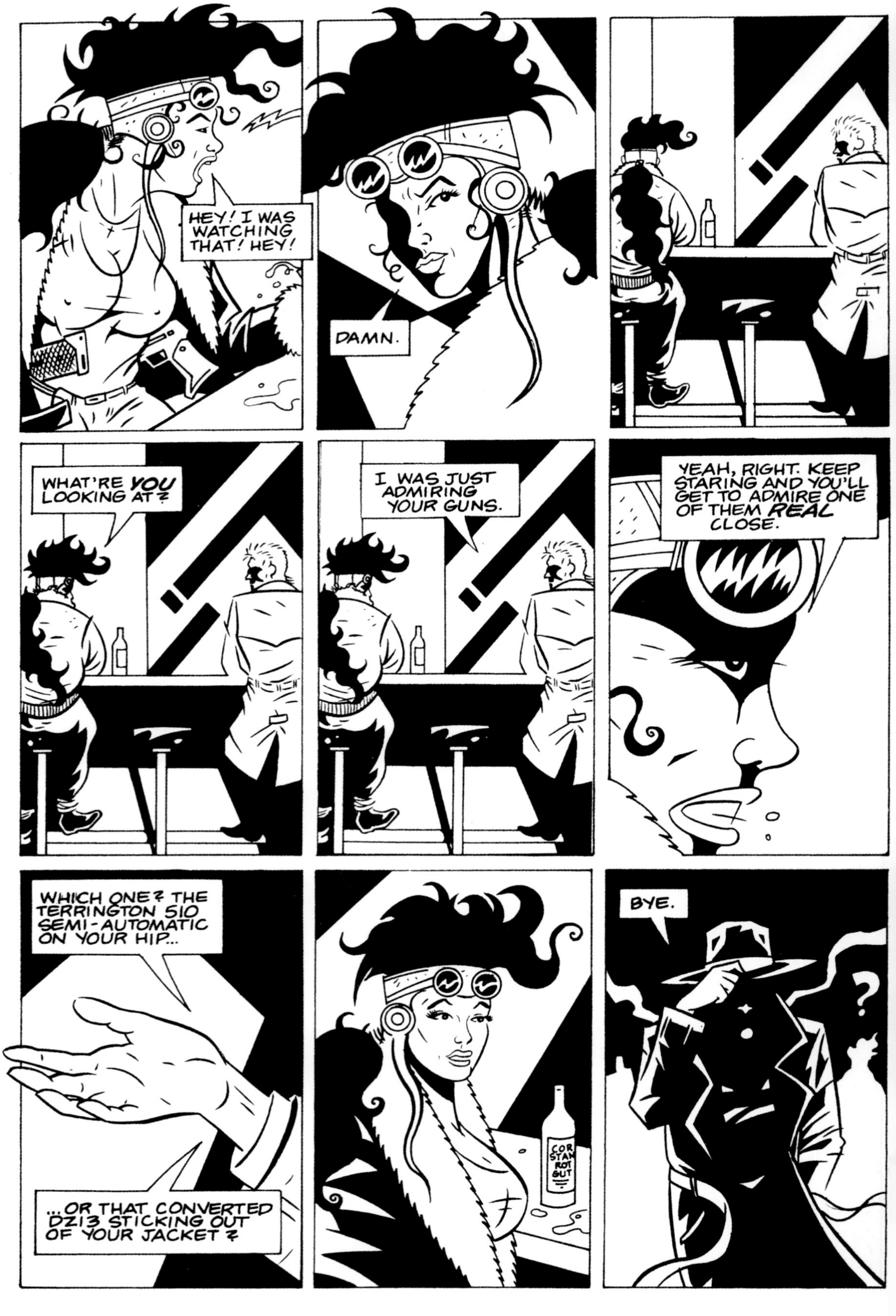
HEY! I WAS WATCHING THAT! HEY!
DAMN.
WHAT'RE YOU LOOKING AT?
I WAS JUST ADMIRING YOUR GUNS.
YEAH, RIGHT. KEEP STARING AND YOU'LL GET TO ADMIRE ONE OF THEM REAL CLOSE.
WHICH ONE? THE TERRINGTON 510 SEMI-AUTOMATIC ON YOUR HIP...
...OR THAT CONVERTED DZ13 STICKING OUT OF YOUR JACKET?
COR STAN ROT GUT
BYE.
?

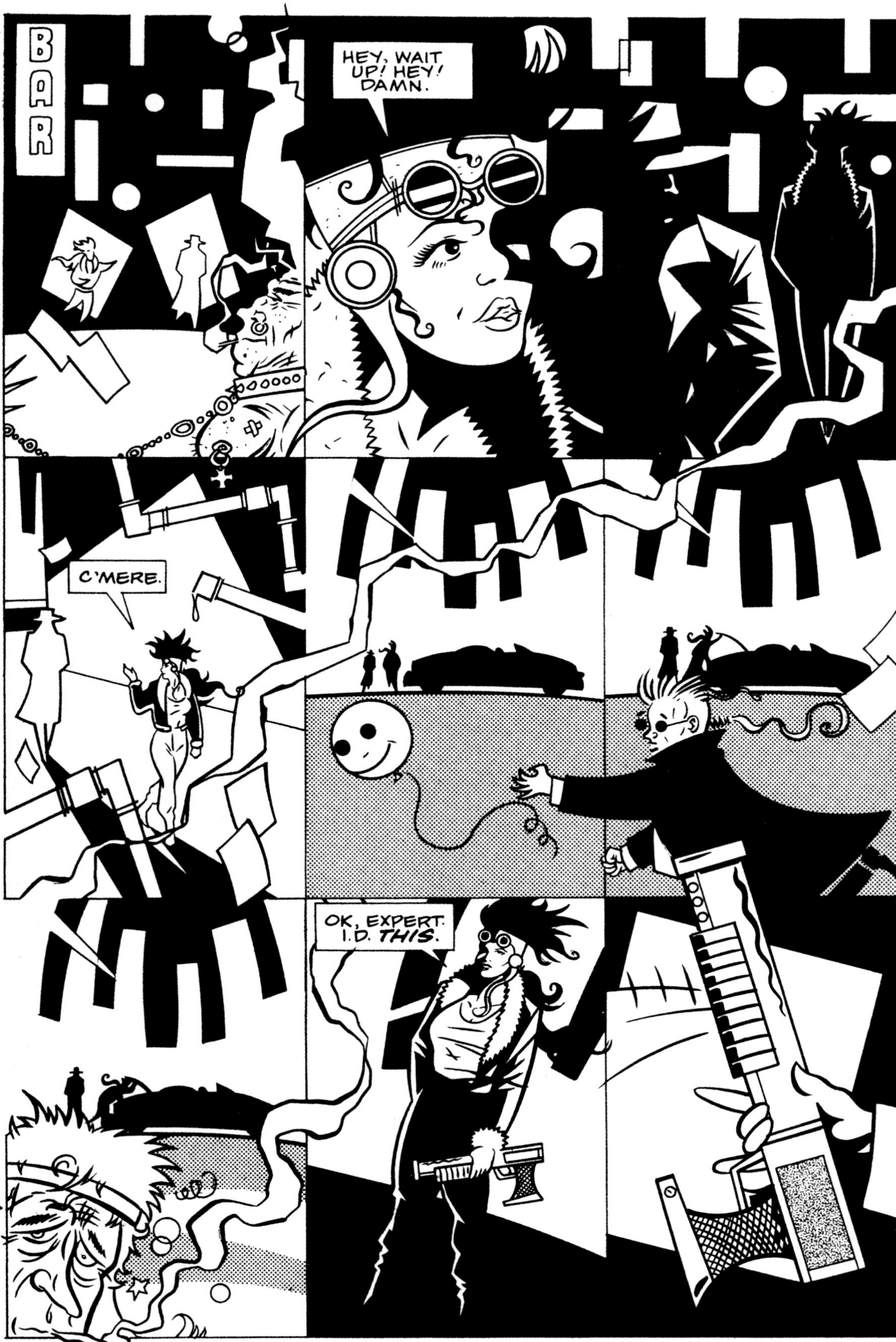
BAR
HEY, WAIT UP! HEY! DAMN.
C'MERE.
OK, EXPERT. I.D. *THIS*.

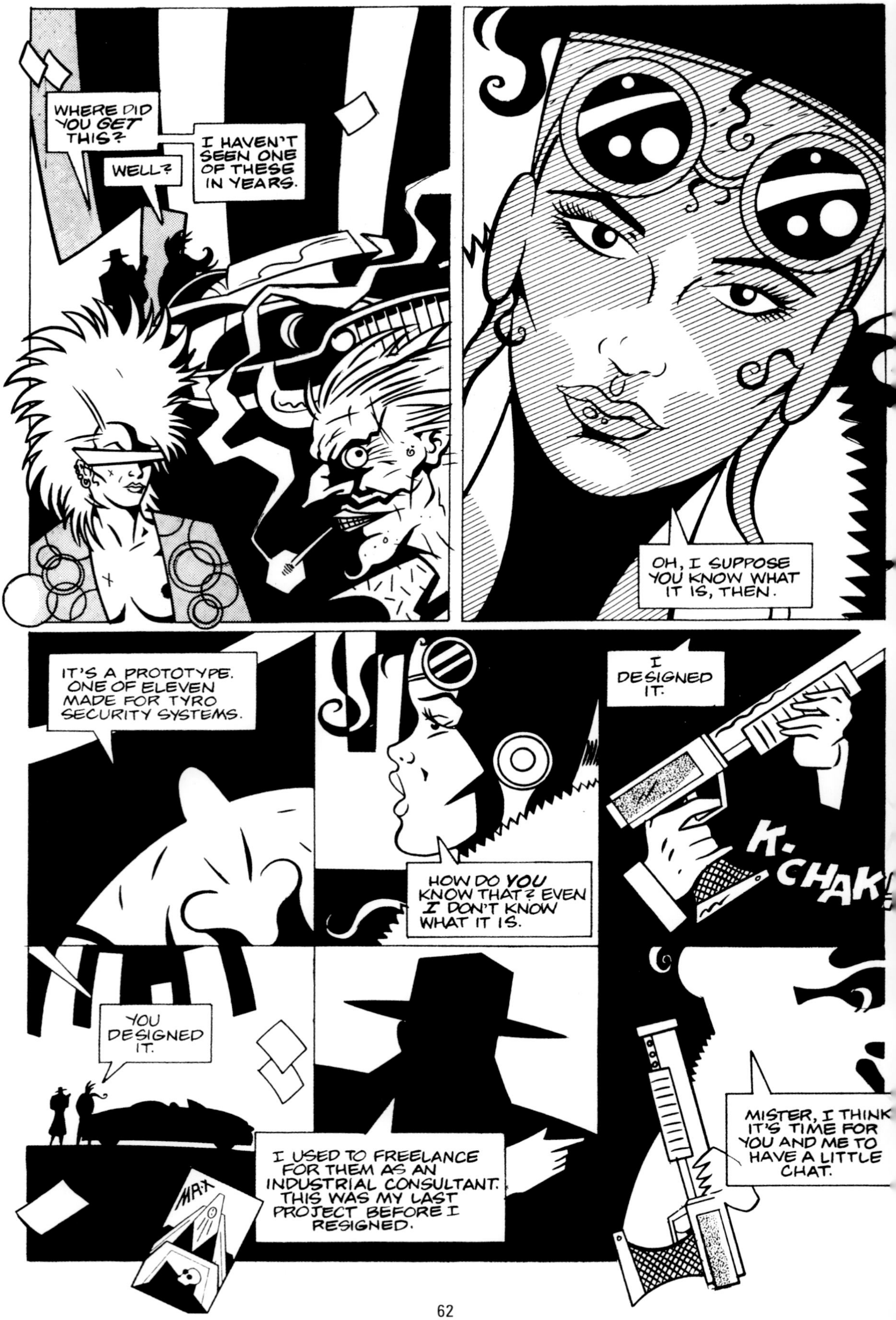
WHERE DID YOU GET THIS?
WELL?
I HAVEN'T SEEN ONE OF THESE IN YEARS.
OH, I SUPPOSE YOU KNOW WHAT IT IS, THEN.
IT'S A PROTOTYPE. ONE OF ELEVEN MADE FOR TYRO SECURITY SYSTEMS.
HOW DO YOU KNOW THAT? EVEN I DON'T KNOW WHAT IT IS.
I DESIGNED IT.
K-CHAK!
YOU DESIGNED IT.
I USED TO FREELANCE FOR THEM AS AN INDUSTRIAL CONSULTANT. THIS WAS MY LAST PROJECT BEFORE I RESIGNED.
MISTER, I THINK IT'S TIME FOR YOU AND ME TO HAVE A LITTLE CHAT.

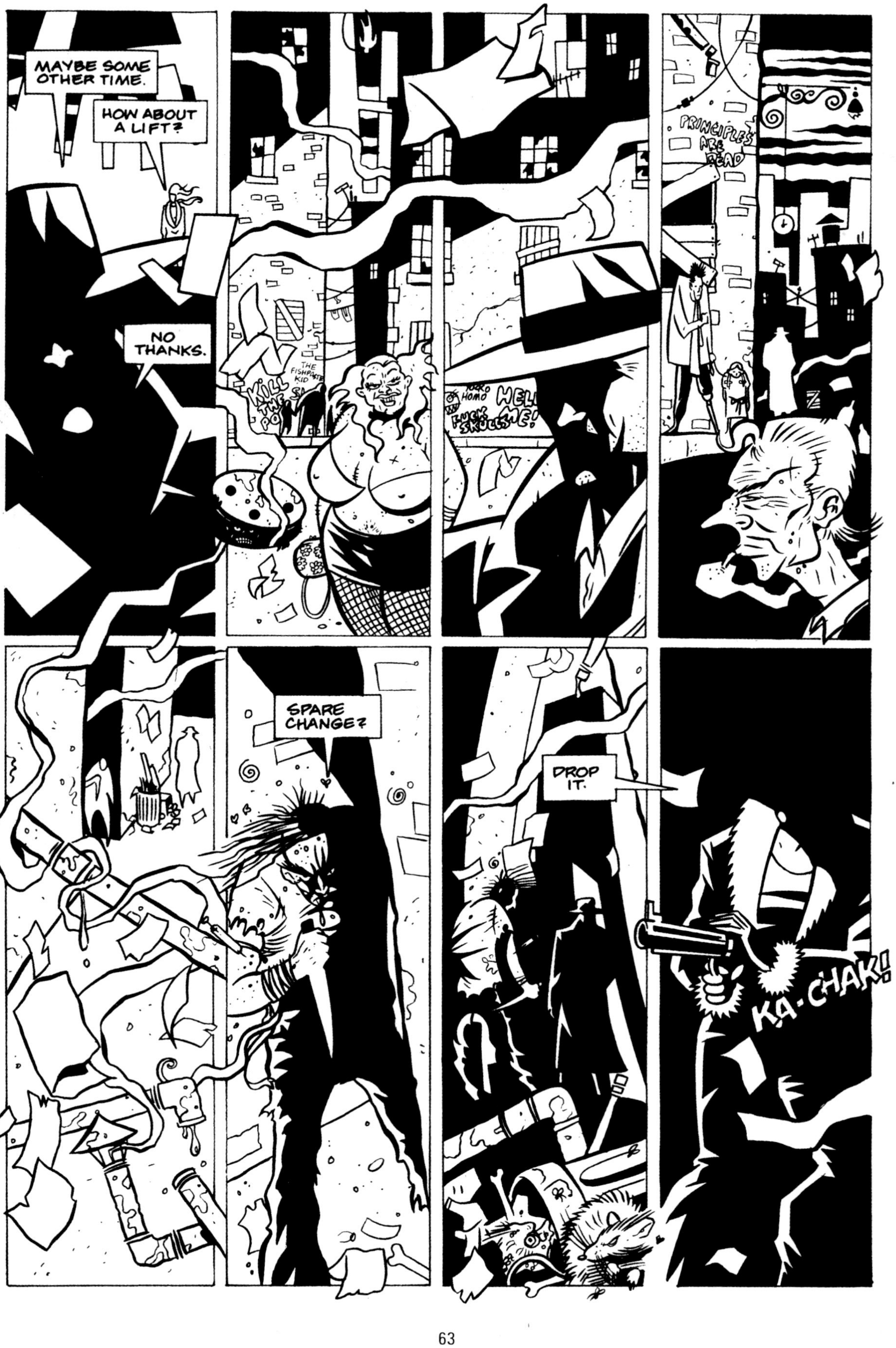
MAYBE SOME OTHER TIME.
HOW ABOUT A LIFT?
NO THANKS.
THE FISHPASTE KID
PRINCIPLES ARE DEAD
SPARE CHANGE?
DROP IT.
KA-CHAK!

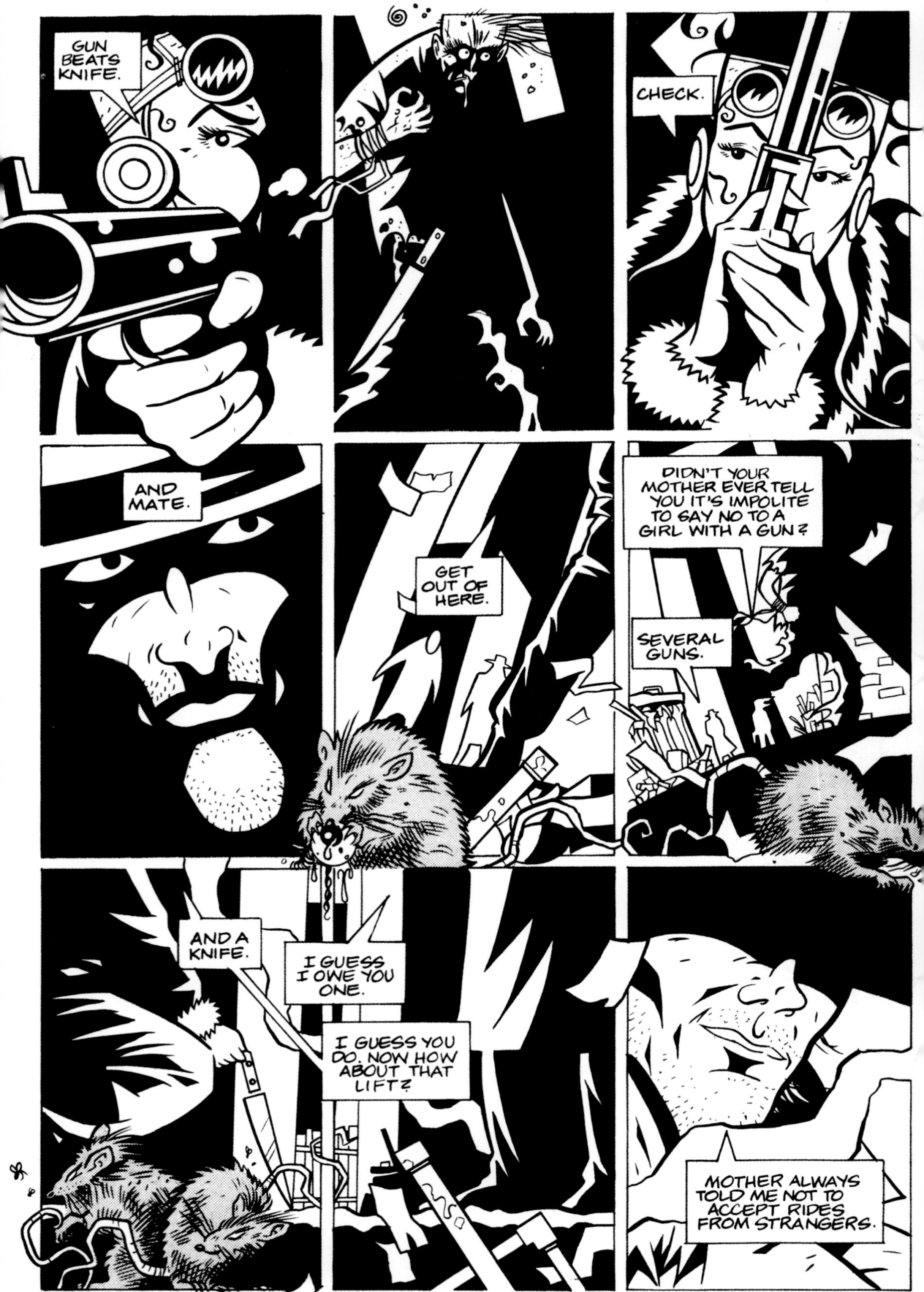
GUN BEATS KNIFE.
CHECK.
AND MATE.
GET OUT OF HERE.
DIDN'T YOUR MOTHER EVER TELL YOU IT'S IMPOLITE TO SAY NO TO A GIRL WITH A GUN?
SEVERAL GUNS.
AND A KNIFE.
I GUESS I OWE YOU ONE.
I GUESS YOU DO. NOW HOW ABOUT THAT LIFT?
MOTHER ALWAYS TOLD ME NOT TO ACCEPT RIDES FROM STRANGERS.

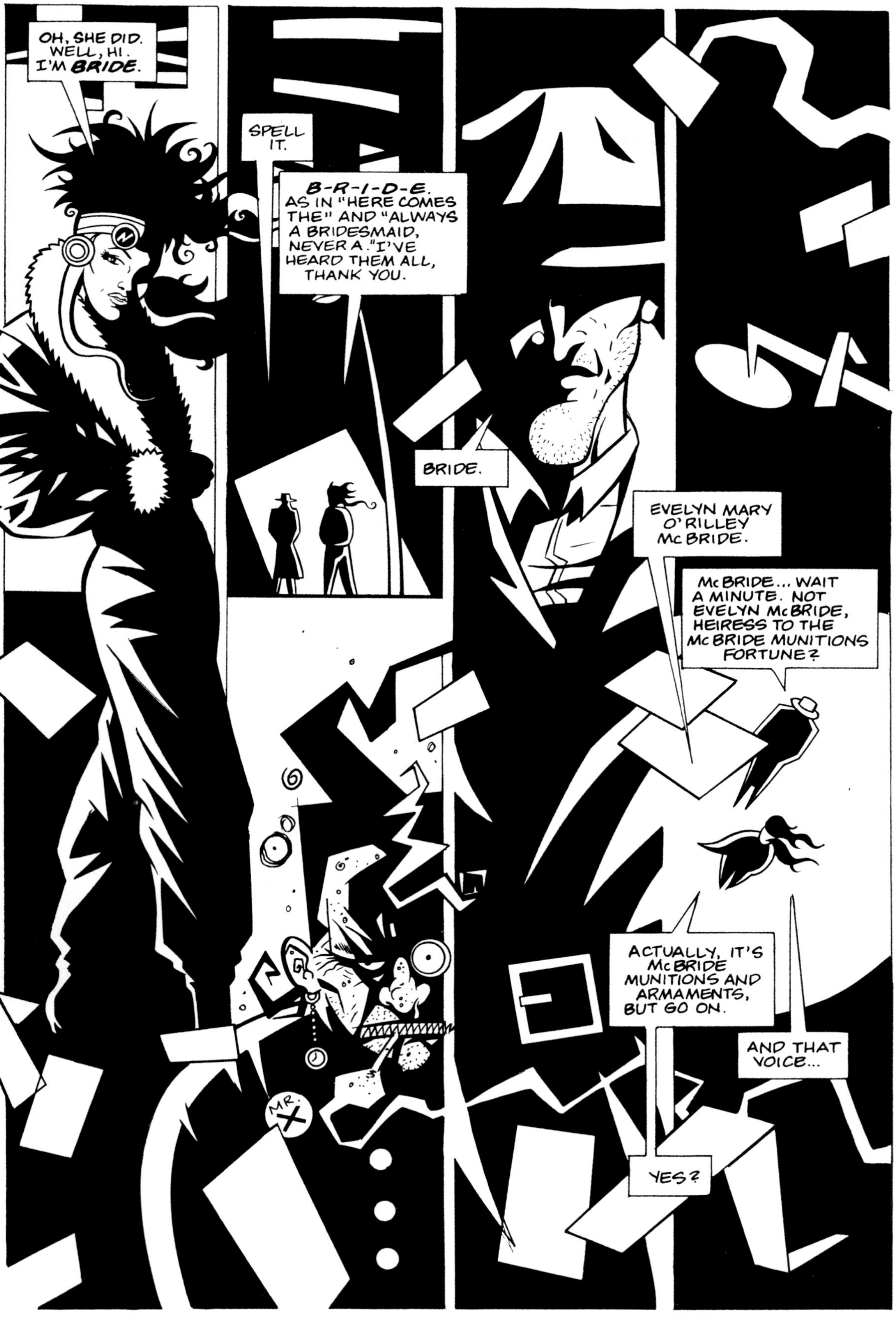
OH, SHE DID. WELL, HI. I'M BRIDE.
SPELL IT.
B-R-I-D-E. AS IN "HERE COMES THE" AND "ALWAYS A BRIDESMAID, NEVER A." I'VE HEARD THEM ALL, THANK YOU.
BRIDE.
EVELYN MARY O'RILLEY McBRIDE.
McBRIDE... WAIT A MINUTE. NOT EVELYN McBRIDE, HEIRESS TO THE McBRIDE MUNITIONS FORTUNE?
ACTUALLY, IT'S McBRIDE MUNITIONS AND ARMAMENTS, BUT GO ON.
AND THAT VOICE...
YES?
MR. X

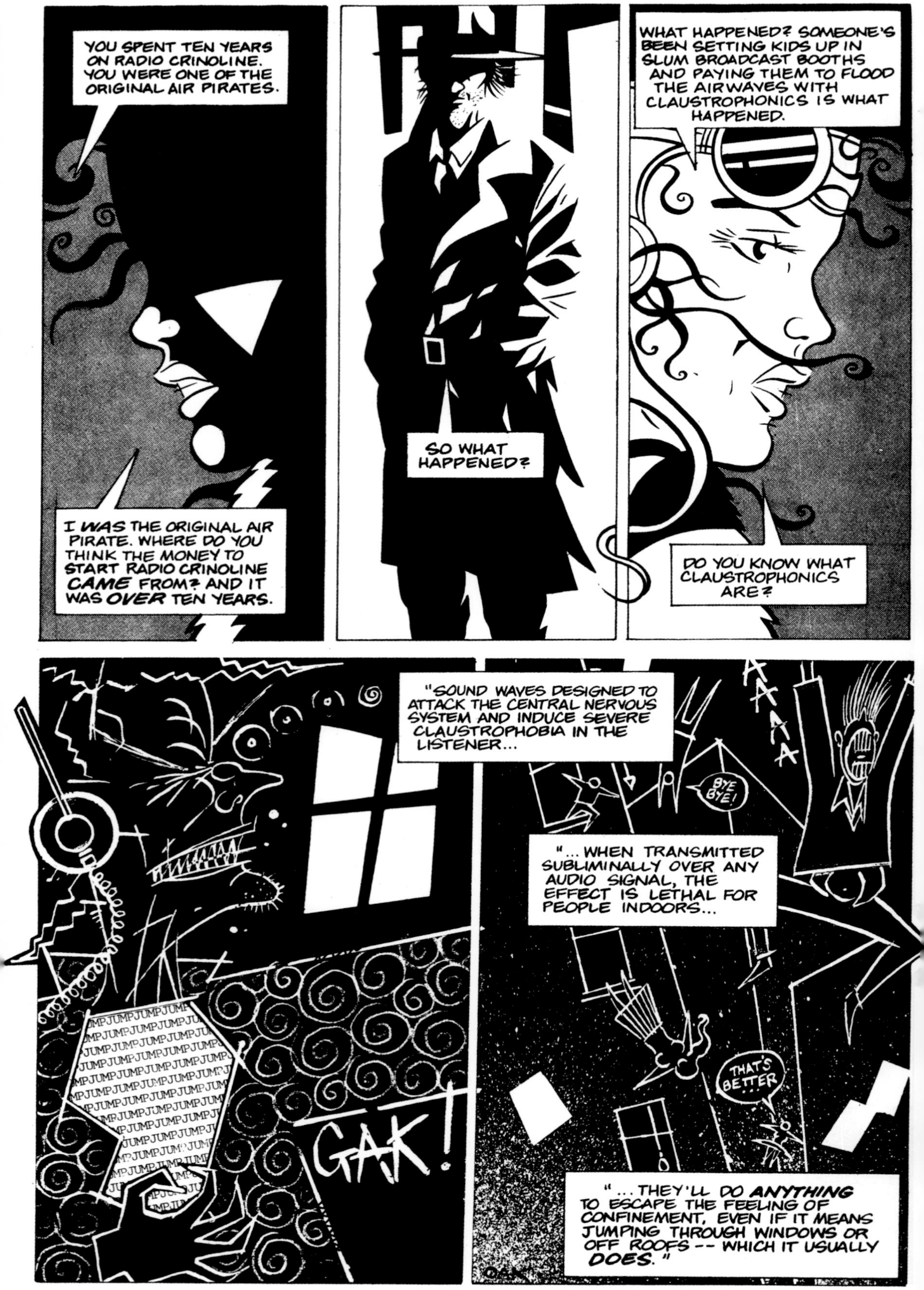
YOU SPENT TEN YEARS ON RADIO CRINOLINE. YOU WERE ONE OF THE ORIGINAL AIR PIRATES.
I WAS THE ORIGINAL AIR PIRATE. WHERE DO YOU THINK THE MONEY TO START RADIO CRINOLINE CAME FROM? AND IT WAS OVER TEN YEARS.
SO WHAT HAPPENED?
WHAT HAPPENED? SOMEONE'S BEEN SETTING KIDS UP IN SLUM BROADCAST BOOTHS AND PAYING THEM TO FLOOD THE AIRWAVES WITH CLAUSTROPHONICS IS WHAT HAPPENED.
DO YOU KNOW WHAT CLAUSTROPHONICS ARE?
"SOUND WAVES DESIGNED TO ATTACK THE CENTRAL NERVOUS SYSTEM AND INDUCE SEVERE CLAUSTROPHOBIA IN THE LISTENER...
JUMPJUMPJUMPJUMPJUMP
GAK!
AAAA
BYE BYE!
"...WHEN TRANSMITTED SUBLIMINALLY OVER ANY AUDIO SIGNAL, THE EFFECT IS LETHAL FOR PEOPLE INDOORS...
THAT'S BETTER
"...THEY'LL DO ANYTHING TO ESCAPE THE FEELING OF CONFINEMENT, EVEN IF IT MEANS JUMPING THROUGH WINDOWS OR OFF ROOFS -- WHICH IT USUALLY DOES."

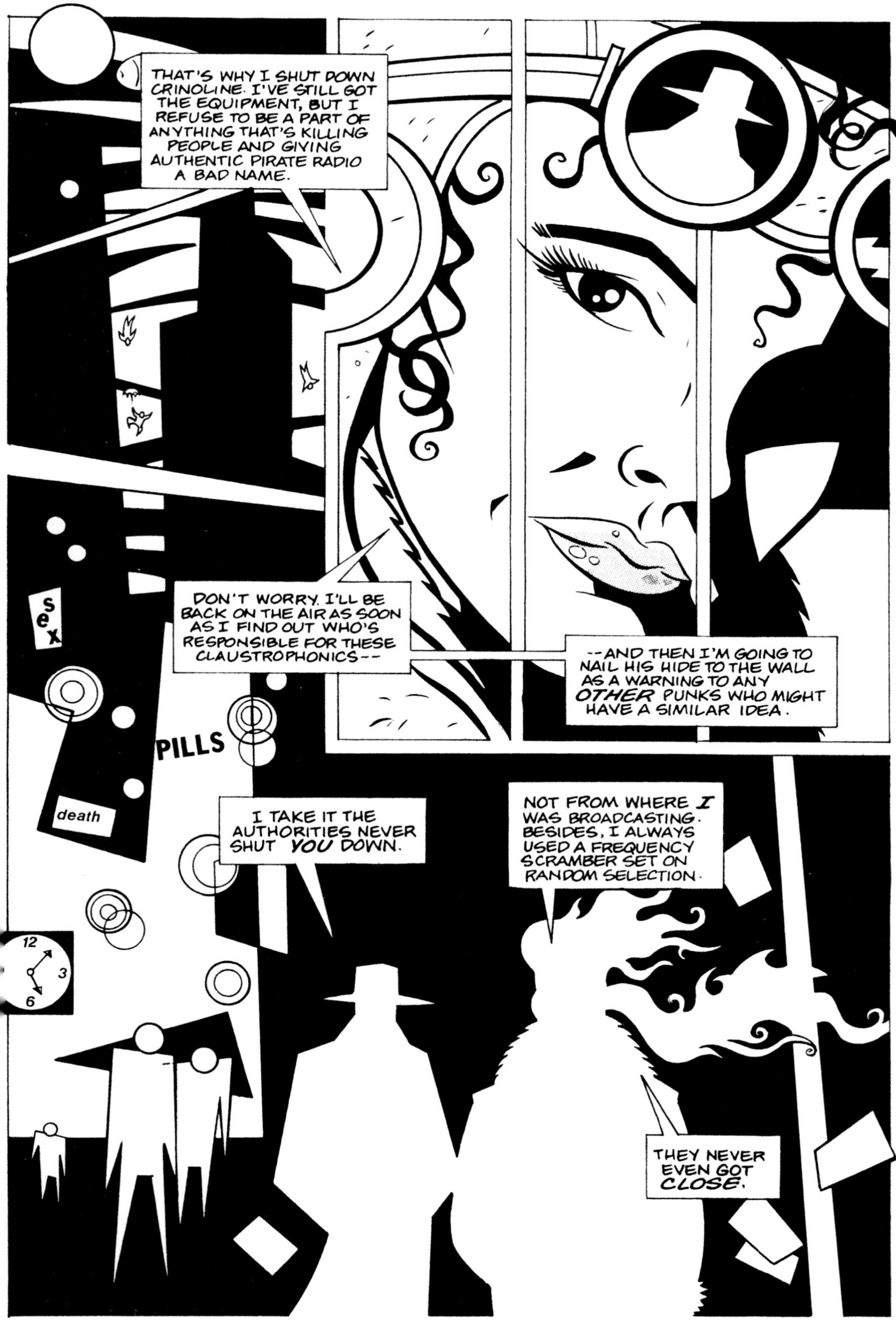
THAT'S WHY I SHUT DOWN CRINOLINE. I'VE STILL GOT THE EQUIPMENT, BUT I REFUSE TO BE A PART OF ANYTHING THAT'S KILLING PEOPLE AND GIVING AUTHENTIC PIRATE RADIO A BAD NAME.
DON'T WORRY. I'LL BE BACK ON THE AIR AS SOON AS I FIND OUT WHO'S RESPONSIBLE FOR THESE CLAUSTROPHONICS--
--AND THEN I'M GOING TO NAIL HIS HIDE TO THE WALL AS A WARNING TO ANY *OTHER* PUNKS WHO MIGHT HAVE A SIMILAR IDEA.
sex
PILLS
death
I TAKE IT THE AUTHORITIES NEVER SHUT *YOU* DOWN.
NOT FROM WHERE *I* WAS BROADCASTING. BESIDES, I ALWAYS USED A FREQUENCY SCRAMBER SET ON RANDOM SELECTION.
THEY NEVER EVEN GOT *CLOSE*.
12
3
6

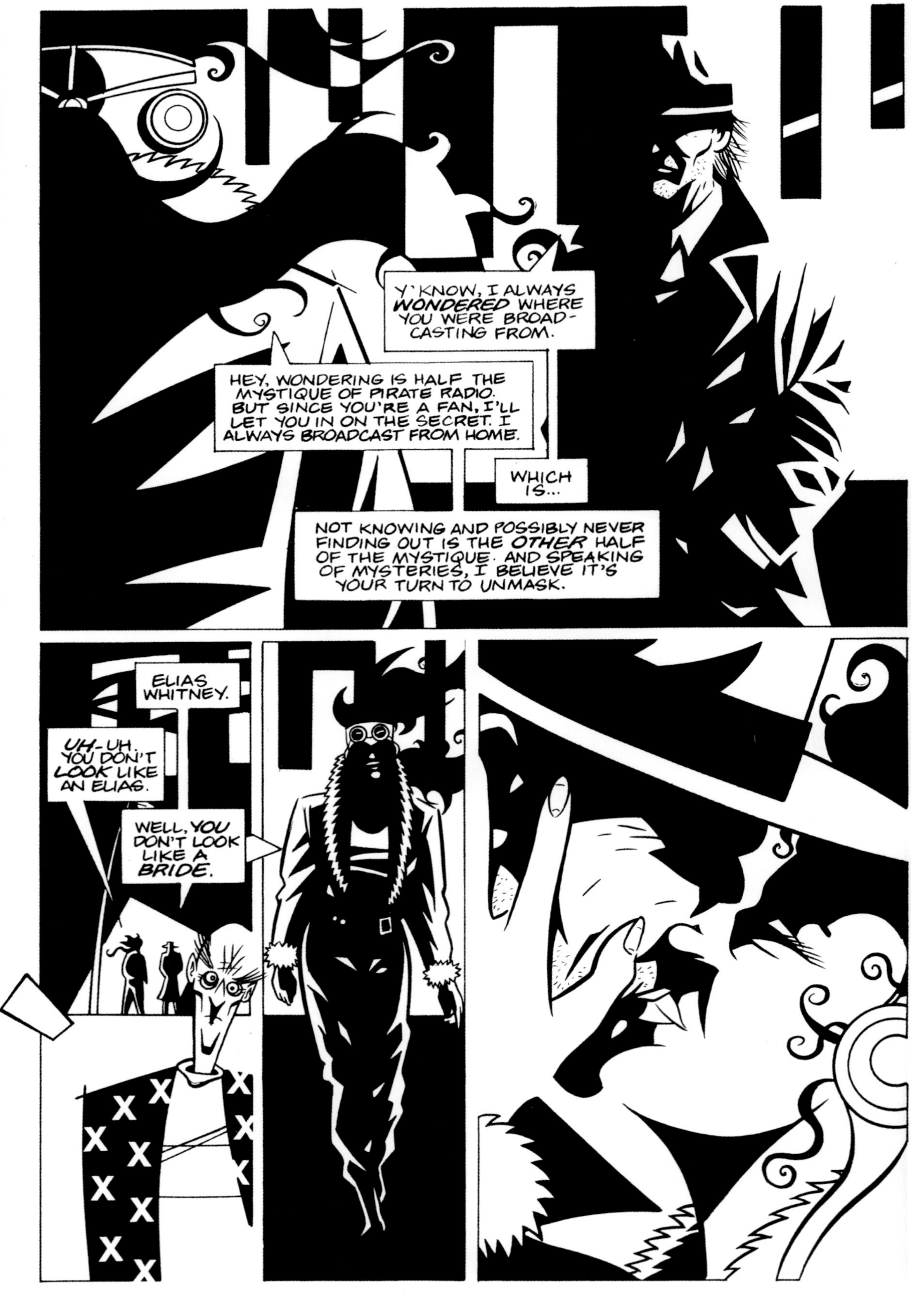

Y'KNOW, I ALWAYS WONDERED WHERE YOU WERE BROAD-CASTING FROM.
HEY, WONDERING IS HALF THE MYSTIQUE OF PIRATE RADIO. BUT SINCE YOU'RE A FAN, I'LL LET YOU IN ON THE SECRET. I ALWAYS BROADCAST FROM HOME.
WHICH IS...
NOT KNOWING AND POSSIBLY NEVER FINDING OUT IS THE OTHER HALF OF THE MYSTIQUE. AND SPEAKING OF MYSTERIES, I BELIEVE IT'S YOUR TURN TO UNMASK.
ELIAS WHITNEY.
UH-UH. YOU DON'T LOOK LIKE AN ELIAS.
WELL, YOU DON'T LOOK LIKE A BRIDE.

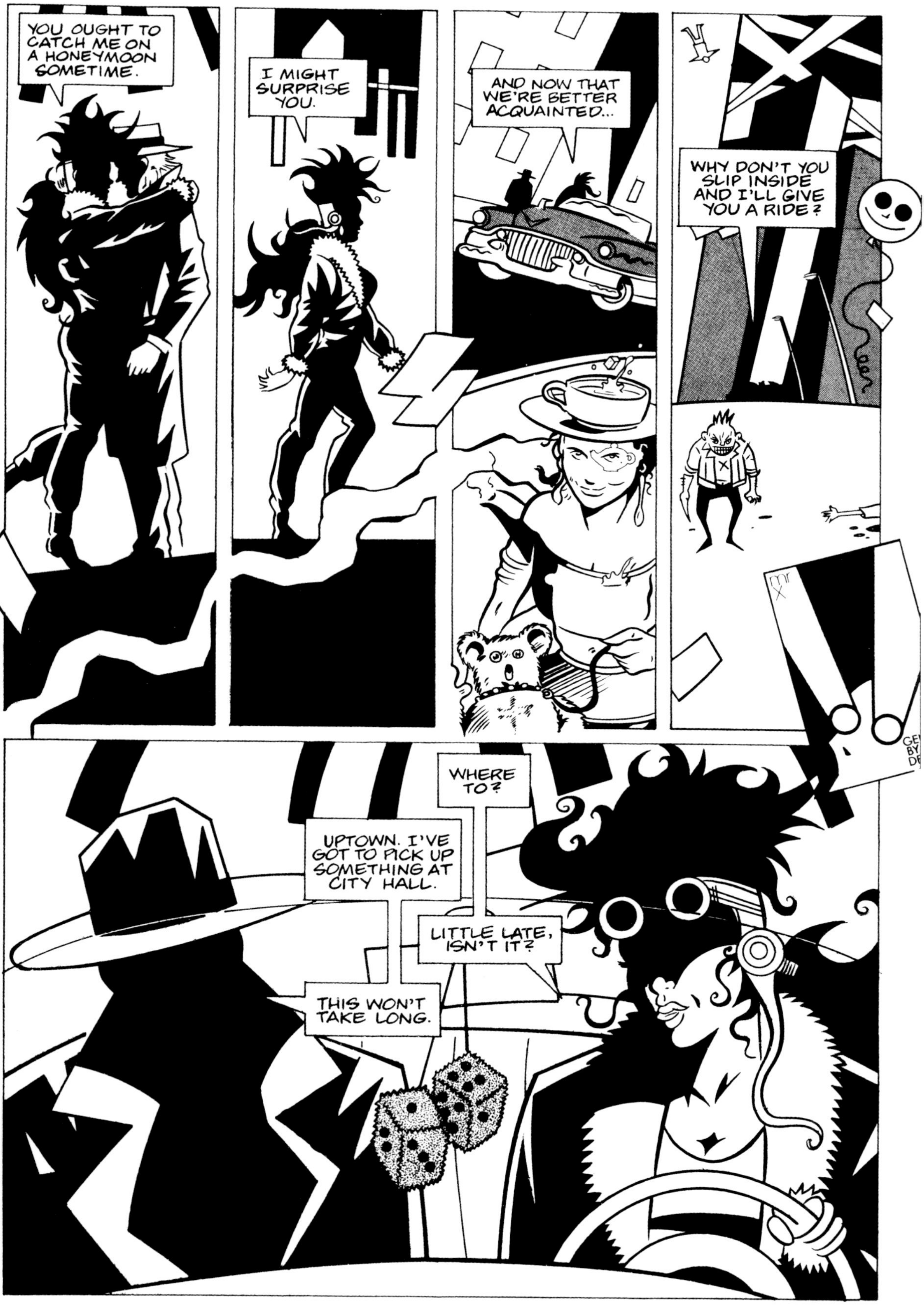
YOU OUGHT TO CATCH ME ON A HONEYMOON SOMETIME.
I MIGHT SURPRISE YOU.
AND NOW THAT WE'RE BETTER ACQUAINTED...
WHY DON'T YOU SLIP INSIDE AND I'LL GIVE YOU A RIDE?
WHERE TO?
UPTOWN. I'VE GOT TO PICK UP SOMETHING AT CITY HALL.
LITTLE LATE, ISN'T IT?
THIS WON'T TAKE LONG.

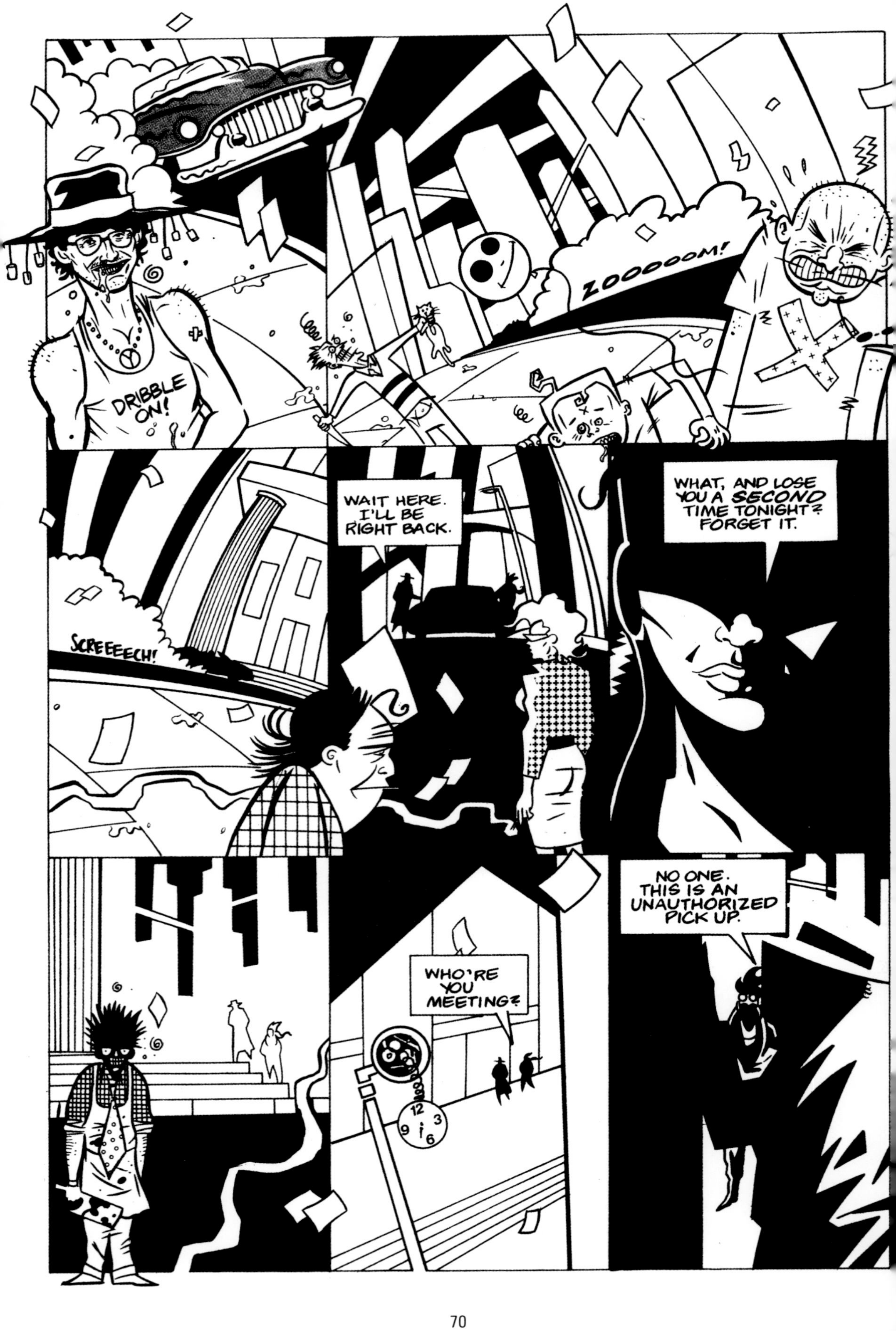
DRIBBLE ON!
ZOOOOOOM!
SCREEEECH!
WAIT HERE. I'LL BE RIGHT BACK.
WHAT, AND LOSE YOU A SECOND TIME TONIGHT? FORGET IT.
WHO'RE YOU MEETING?
NO ONE. THIS IS AN UNAUTHORIZED PICK UP.
12
3
9
6

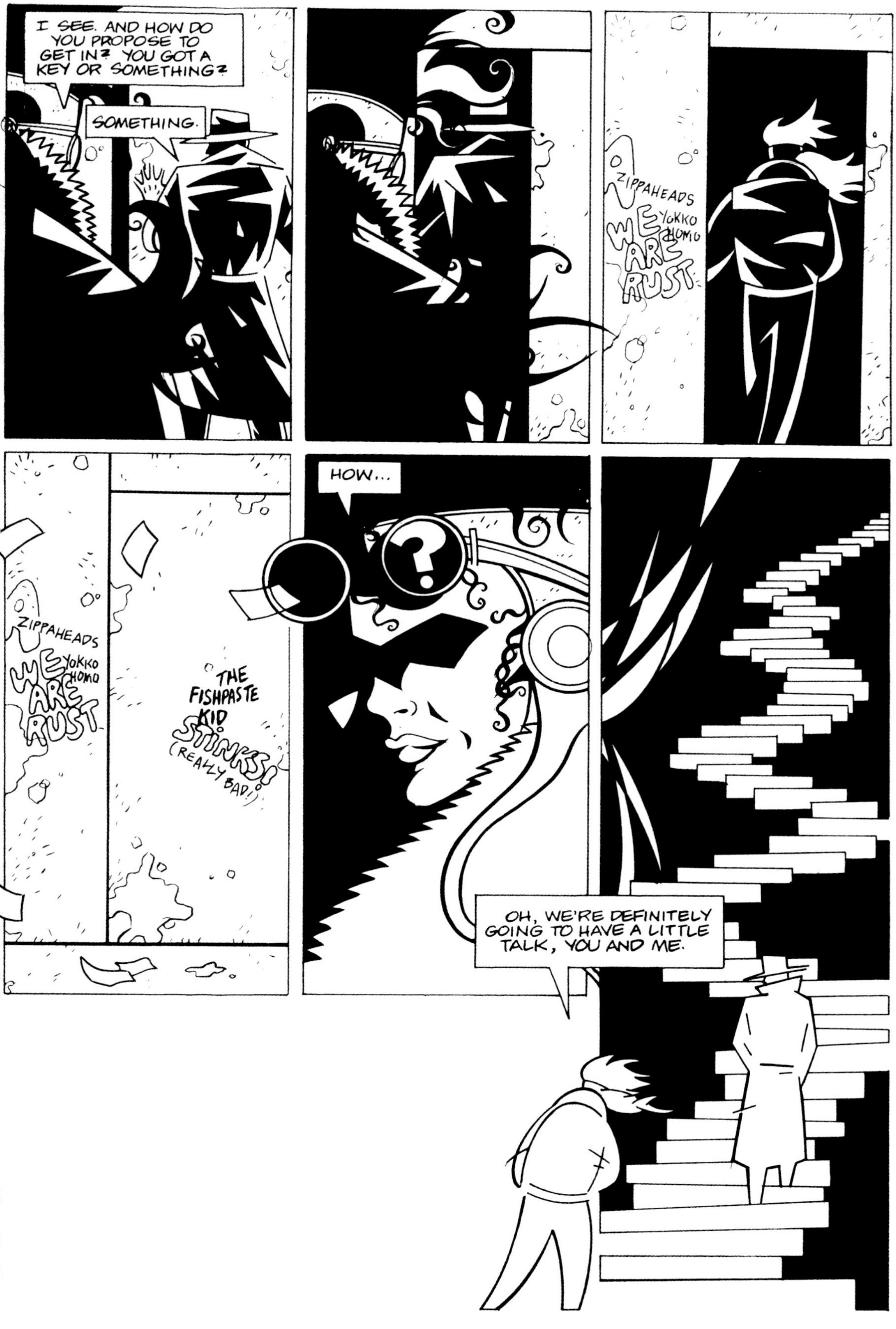
I SEE. AND HOW DO YOU PROPOSE TO GET IN? YOU GOT A KEY OR SOMETHING?
SOMETHING.
ZIPPAHEADS
WE ARE RUST
YOKKO HOMO
ZIPPAHEADS
WE ARE RUST
YOKKO HOMO
THE FISHPASTE KID STINKS! (REALLY BAD!)
HOW...
OH, WE'RE DEFINITELY GOING TO HAVE A LITTLE TALK, YOU AND ME.

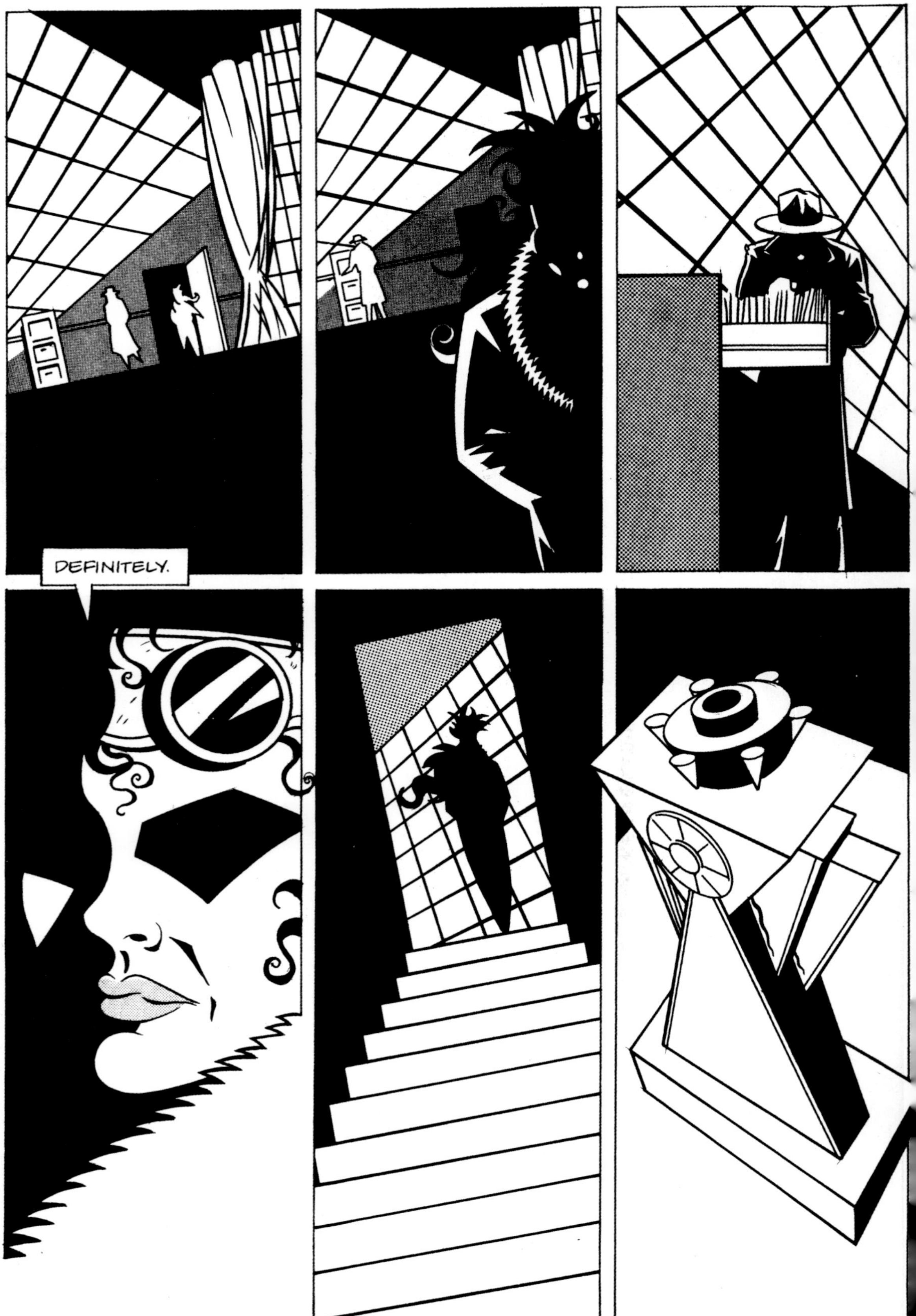
DEFINITELY.

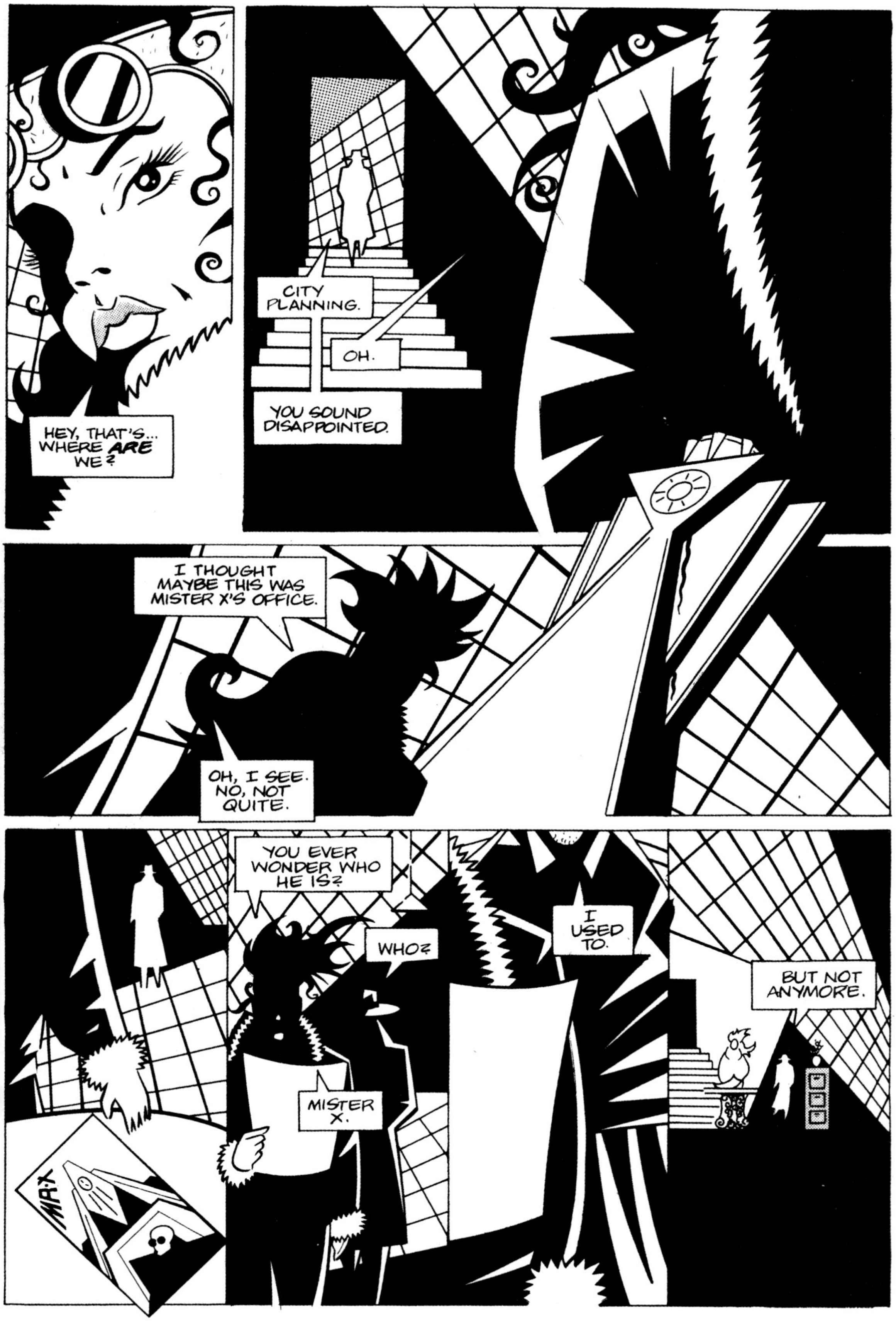

HEY, THAT'S... WHERE **ARE** WE?
CITY PLANNING.
OH.
YOU SOUND DISAPPOINTED.
I THOUGHT MAYBE THIS WAS MISTER X'S OFFICE.
OH, I SEE. NO, NOT QUITE.
YOU EVER WONDER WHO HE IS?
WHO?
MISTER X.
I USED TO.
BUT NOT ANYMORE.
MR.X

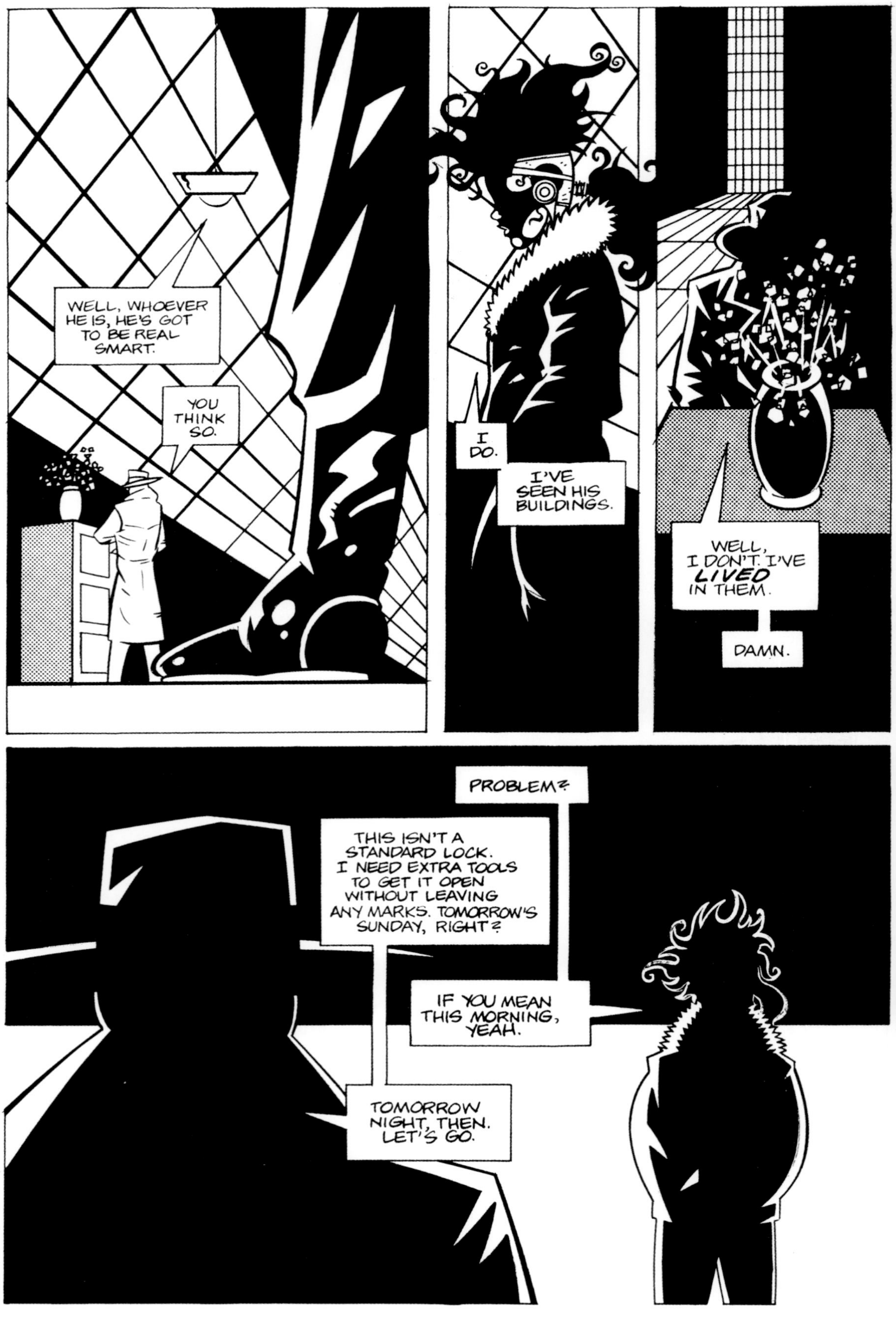
WELL, WHOEVER HE IS, HE'S GOT TO BE REAL SMART.
YOU THINK SO.
I DO.
I'VE SEEN HIS BUILDINGS.
WELL, I DON'T. I'VE **LIVED** IN THEM.
DAMN.
PROBLEM?
THIS ISN'T A STANDARD LOCK. I NEED EXTRA TOOLS TO GET IT OPEN WITHOUT LEAVING ANY MARKS. TOMORROW'S SUNDAY, RIGHT?
IF YOU MEAN THIS MORNING, YEAH.
TOMORROW NIGHT, THEN. LET'S GO.

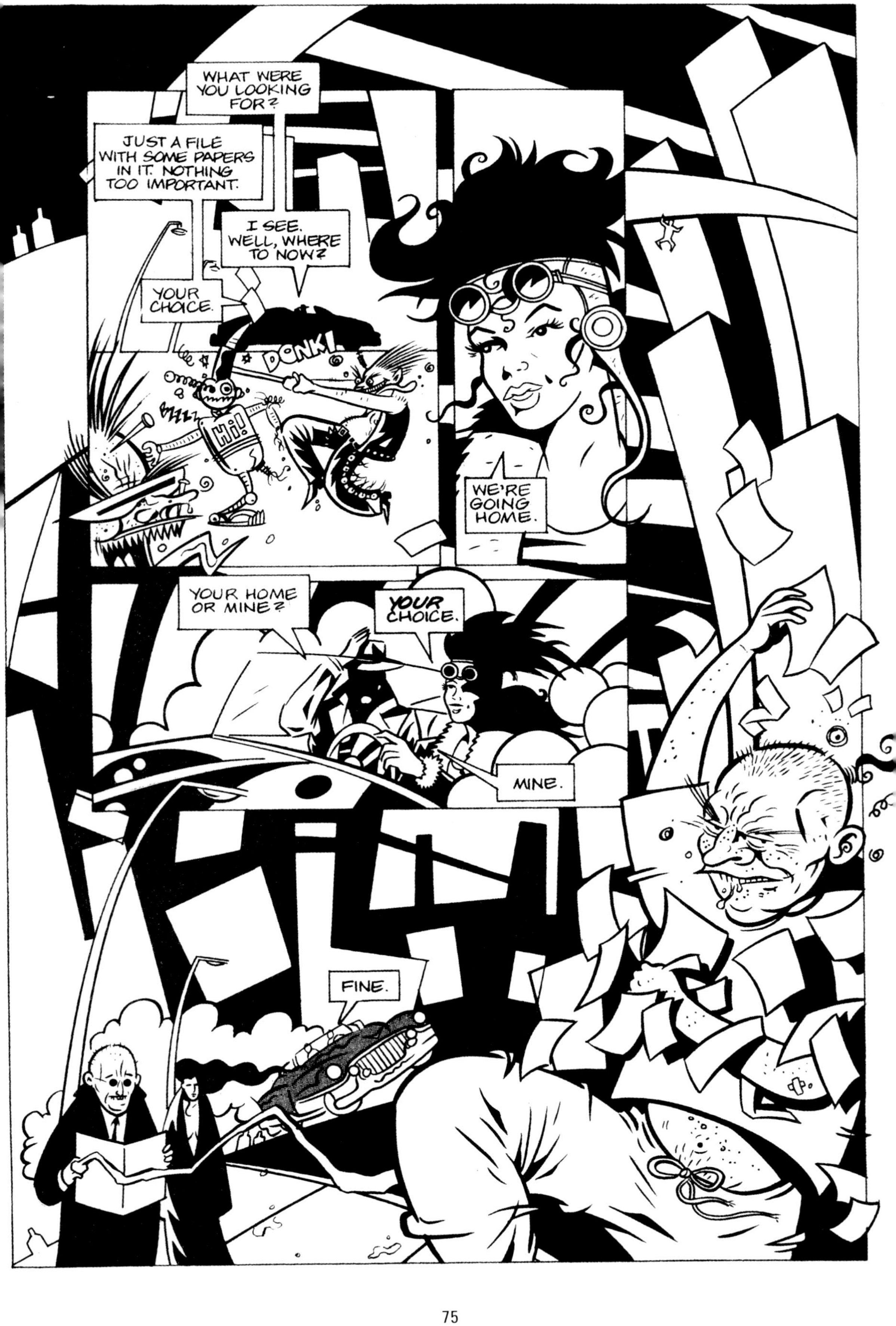
WHAT WERE YOU LOOKING FOR?
JUST A FILE WITH SOME PAPERS IN IT. NOTHING TOO IMPORTANT.
I SEE. WELL, WHERE TO NOW?
YOUR CHOICE.
DONK!
Hi!
WE'RE GOING HOME.
YOUR HOME OR MINE?
YOUR CHOICE.
MINE.
FINE.

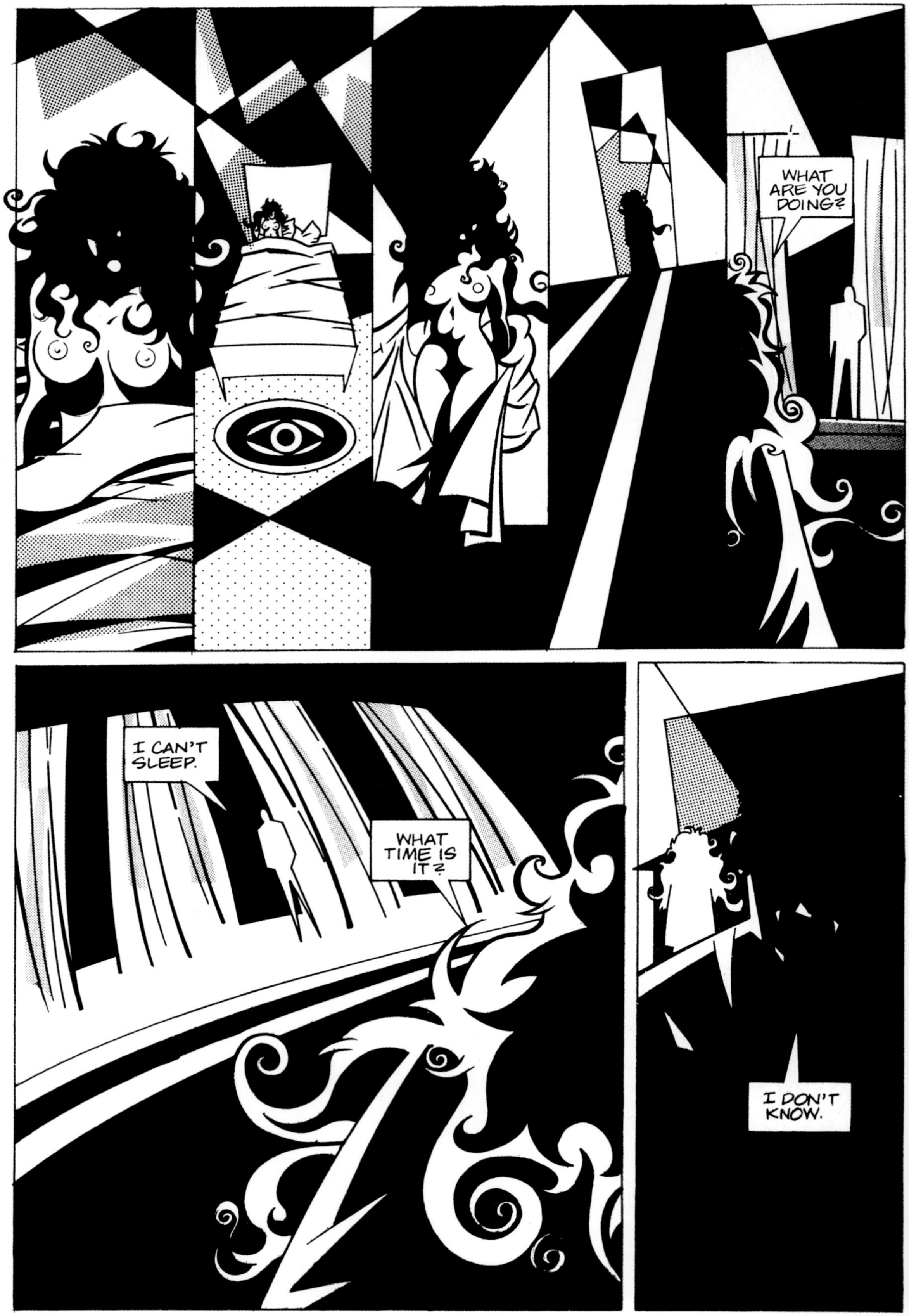
WHAT ARE YOU DOING?
I CAN'T SLEEP.
WHAT TIME IS IT?
I DON'T KNOW.

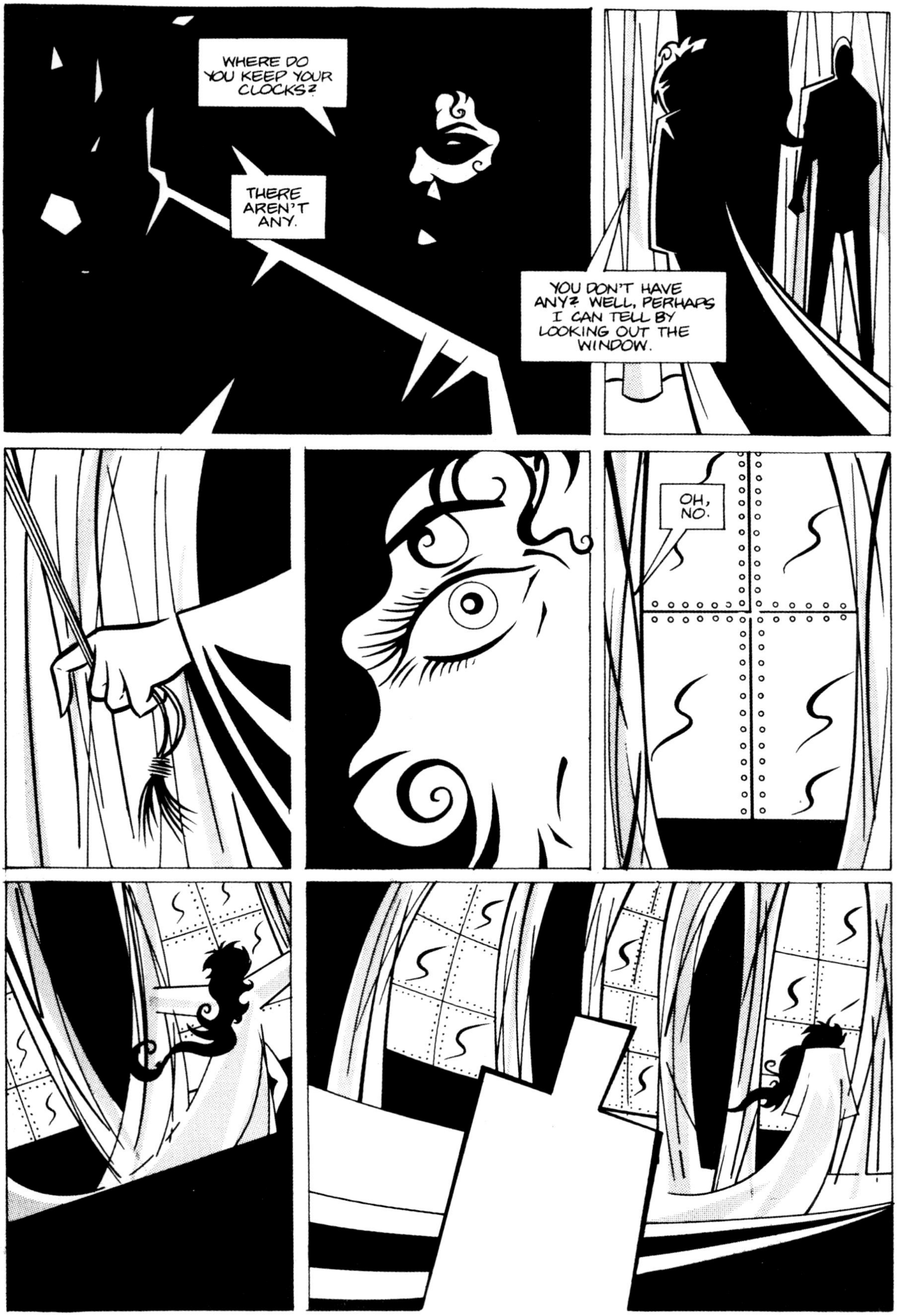
WHERE DO YOU KEEP YOUR CLOCKS?
THERE AREN'T ANY.
YOU DON'T HAVE ANY? WELL, PERHAPS I CAN TELL BY LOOKING OUT THE WINDOW.
OH, NO.

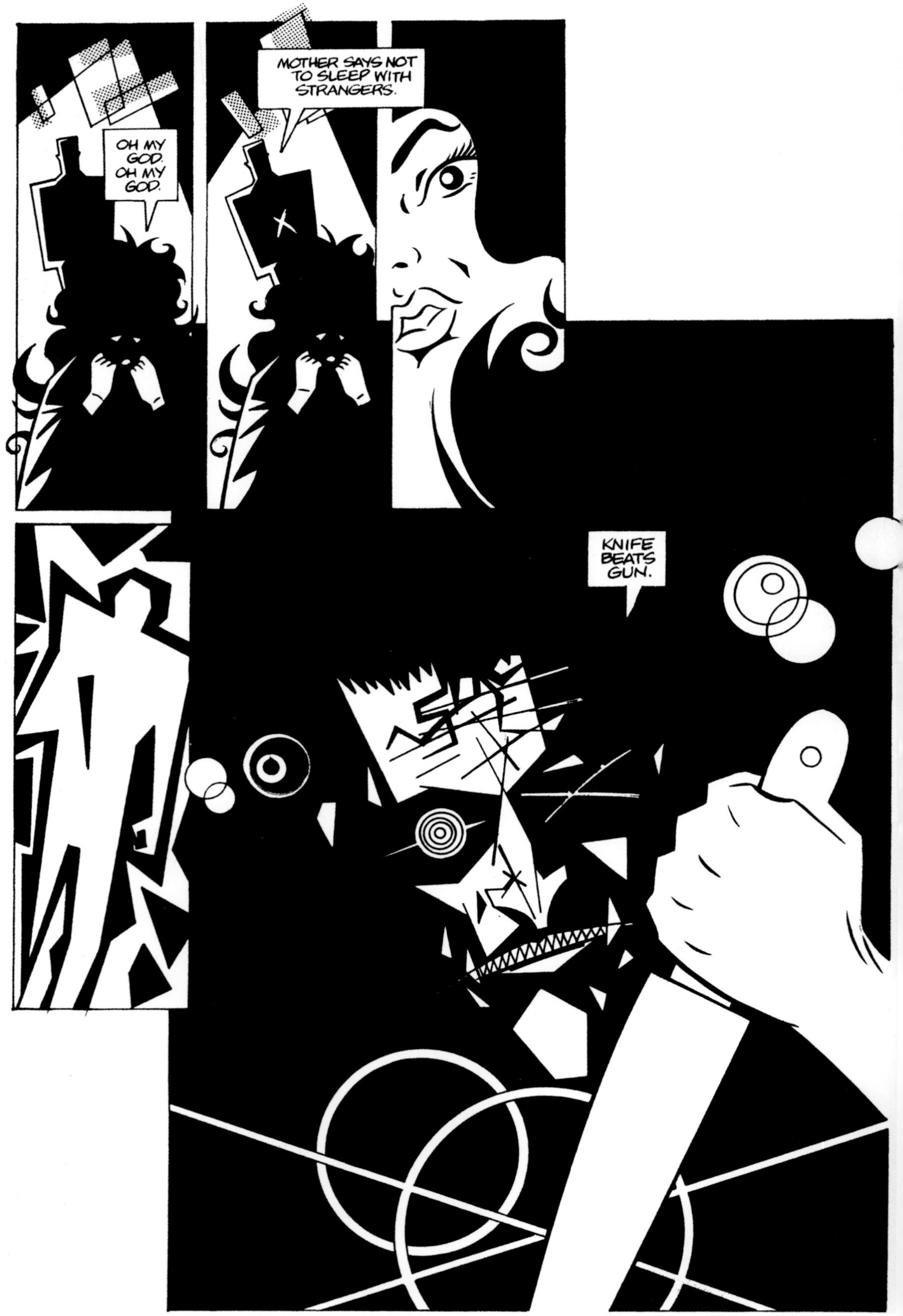
OH MY GOD. OH MY GOD.
MOTHER SAYS NOT TO SLEEP WITH STRANGERS.
KNIFE BEATS GUN.

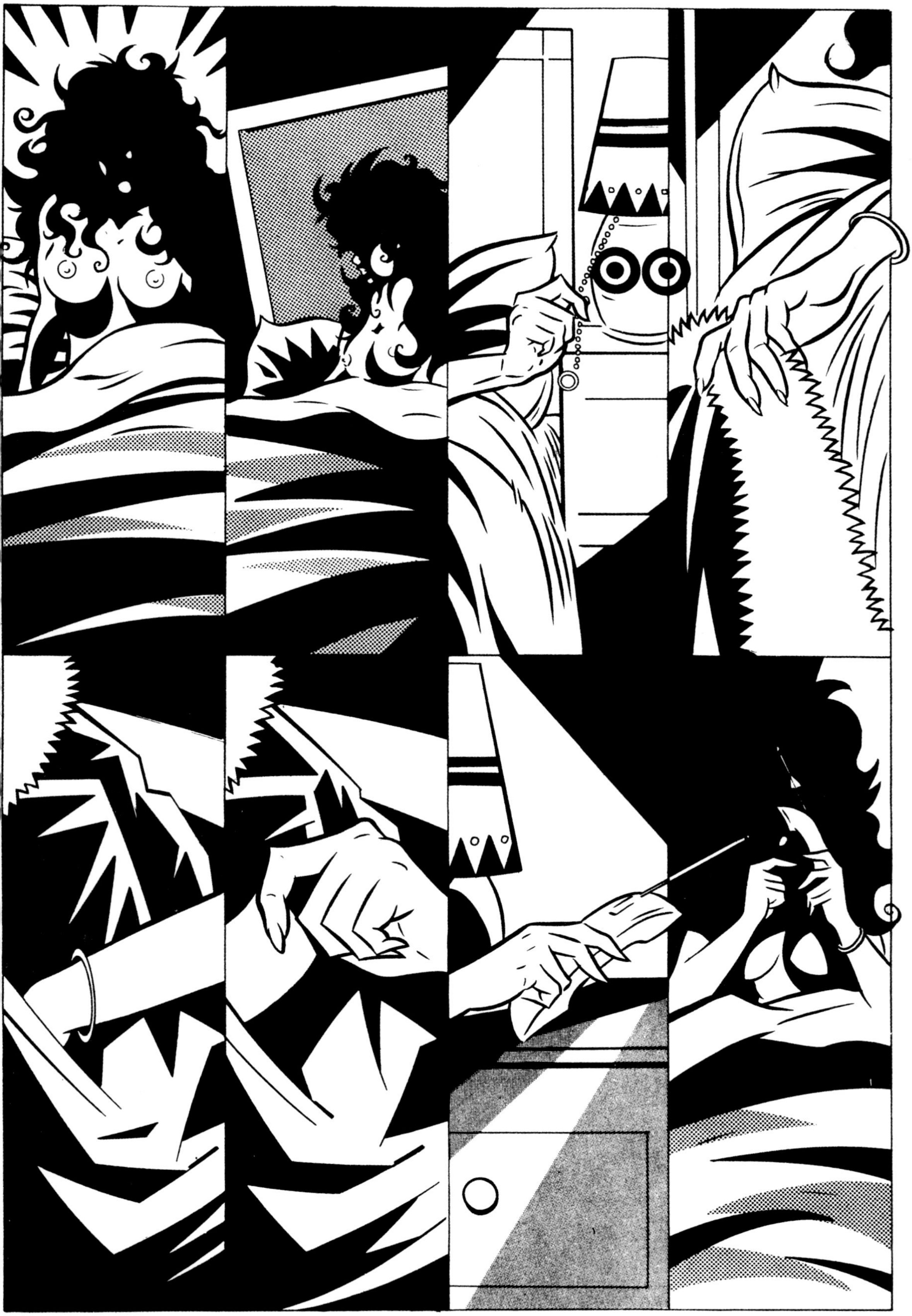

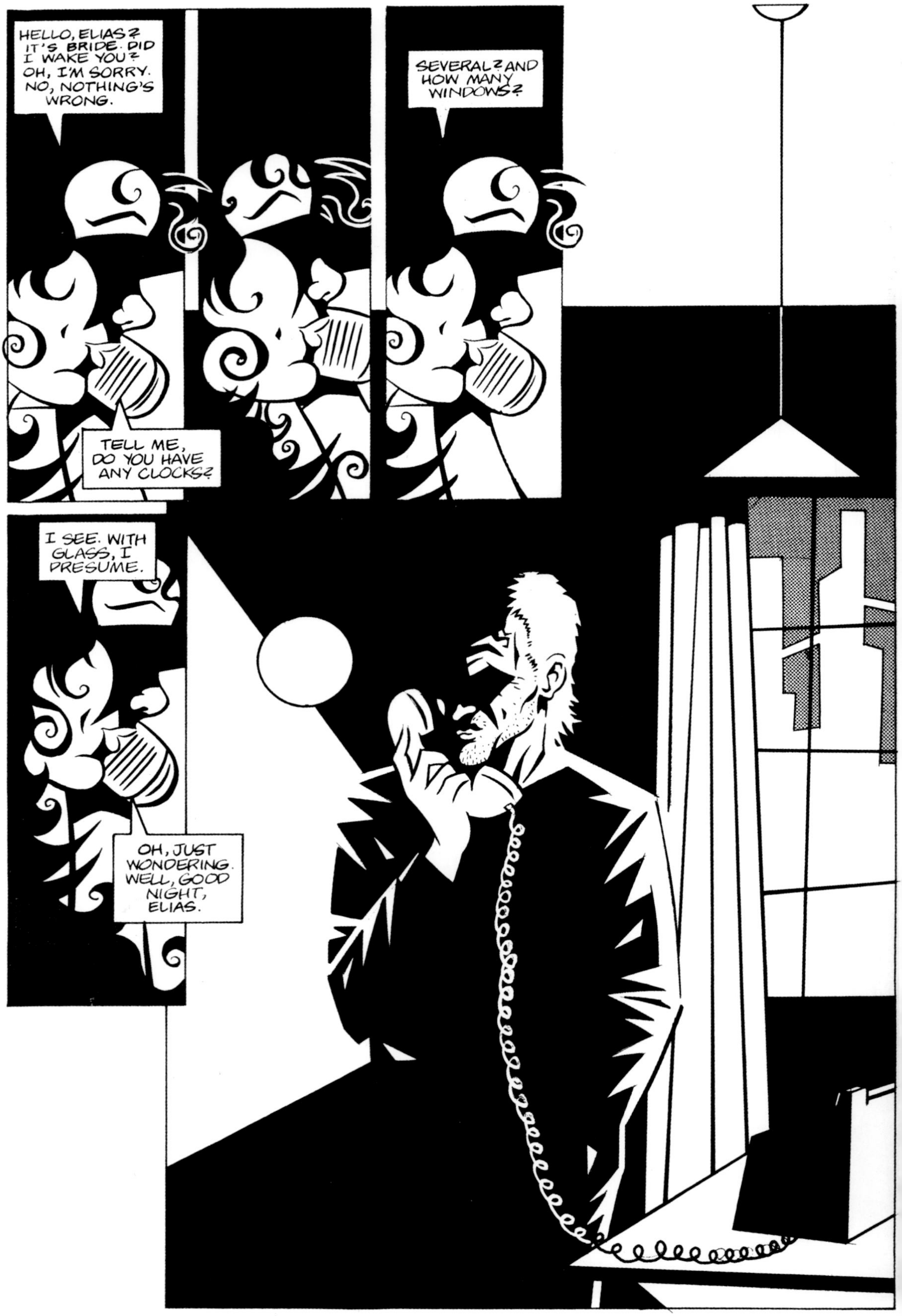
HELLO, ELIAS? IT'S BRIDE. DID I WAKE YOU? OH, I'M SORRY. NO, NOTHING'S WRONG.
TELL ME, DO YOU HAVE ANY CLOCKS?
SEVERAL? AND HOW MANY WINDOWS?
I SEE. WITH GLASS, I PRESUME.
OH, JUST WONDERING. WELL, GOOD NIGHT, ELIAS.

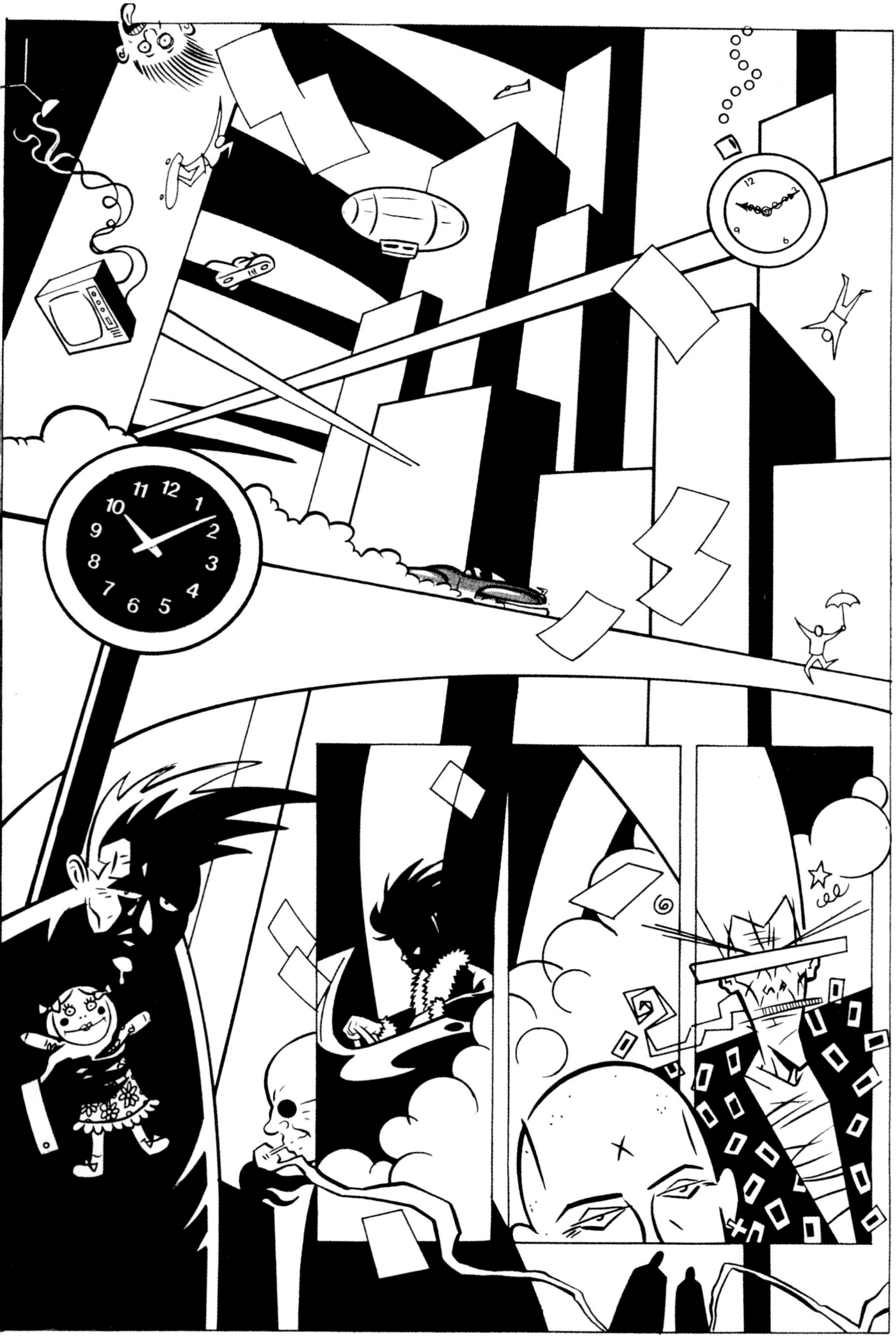

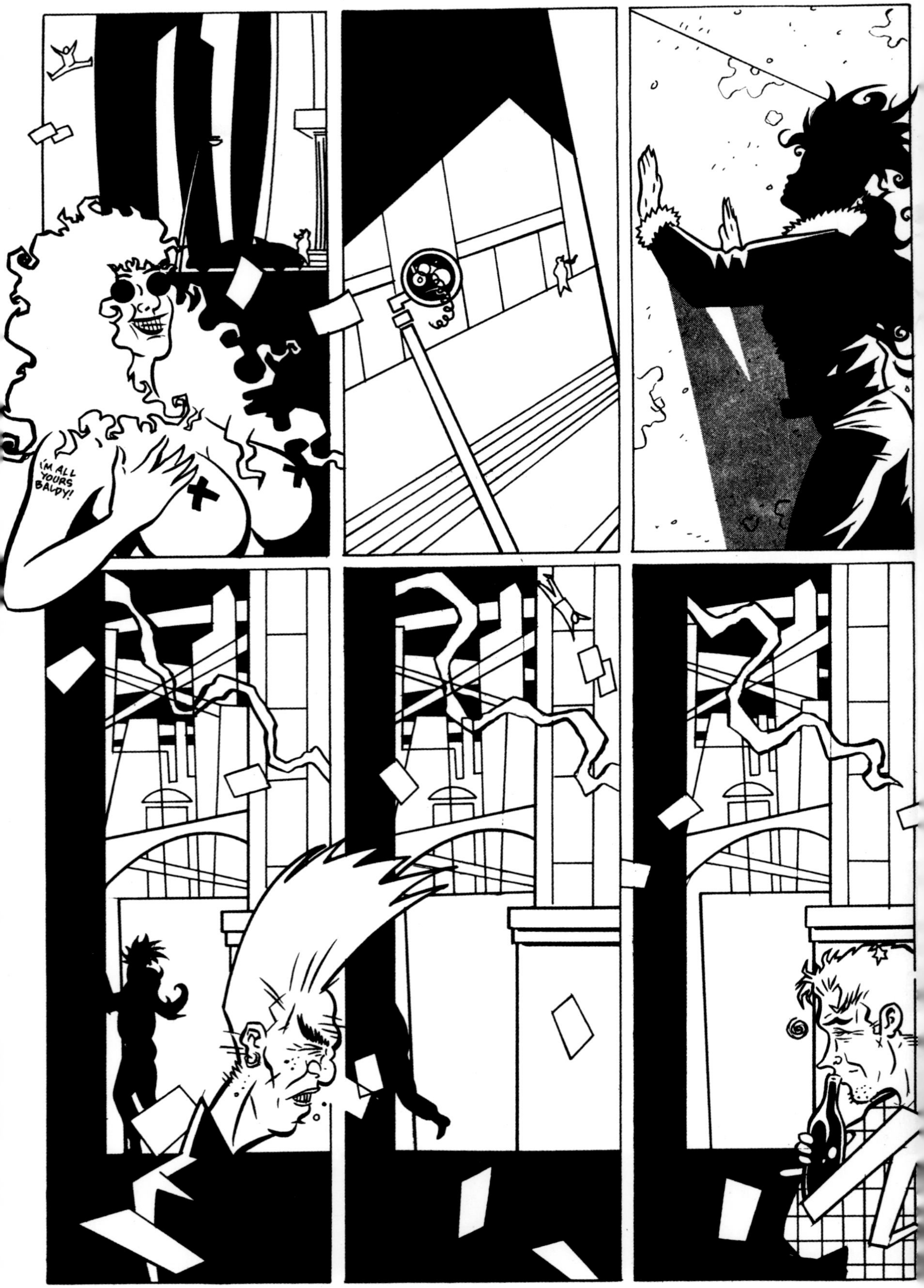
I'M ALL YOURS BALDY!

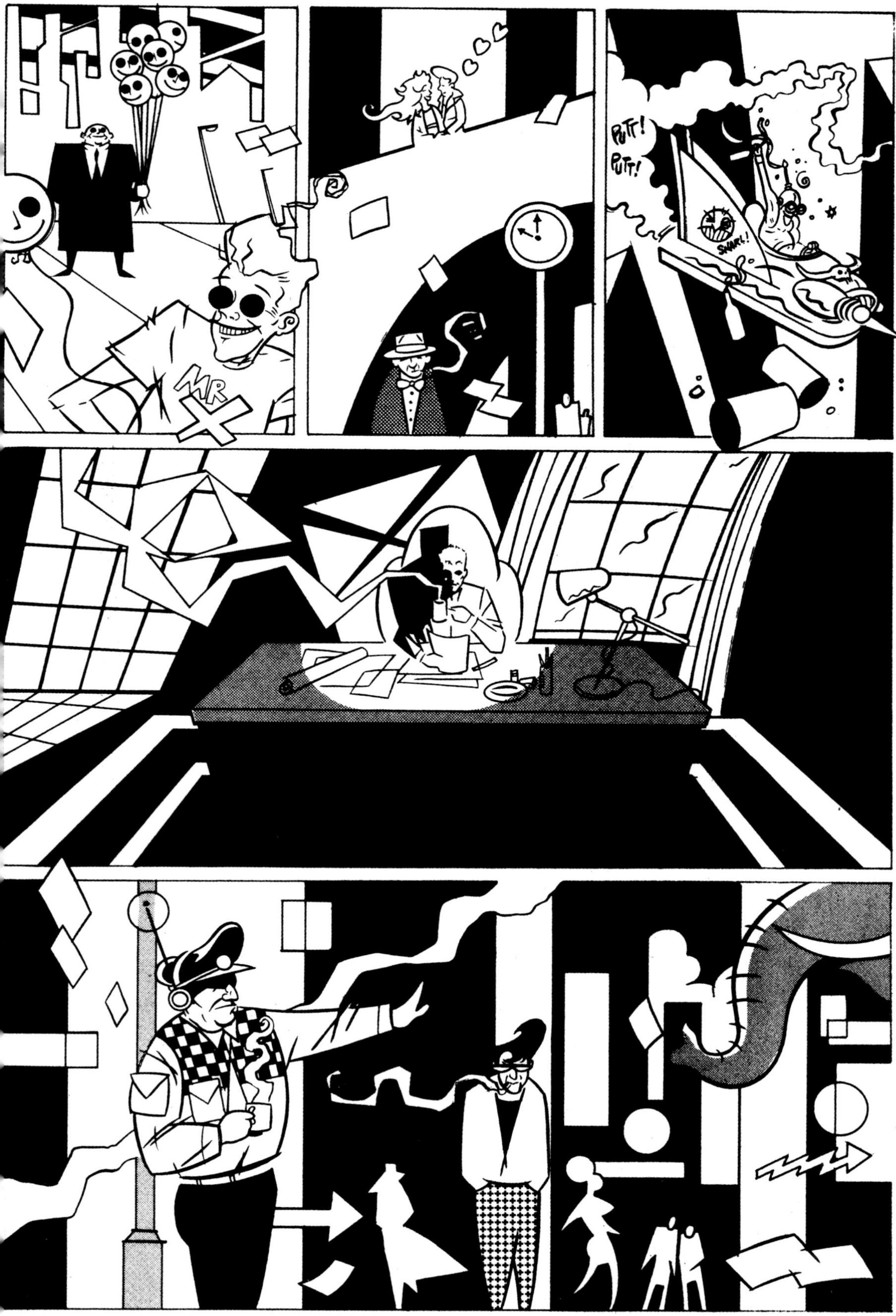
MR
PUTT!
PUTT!
SNARL!

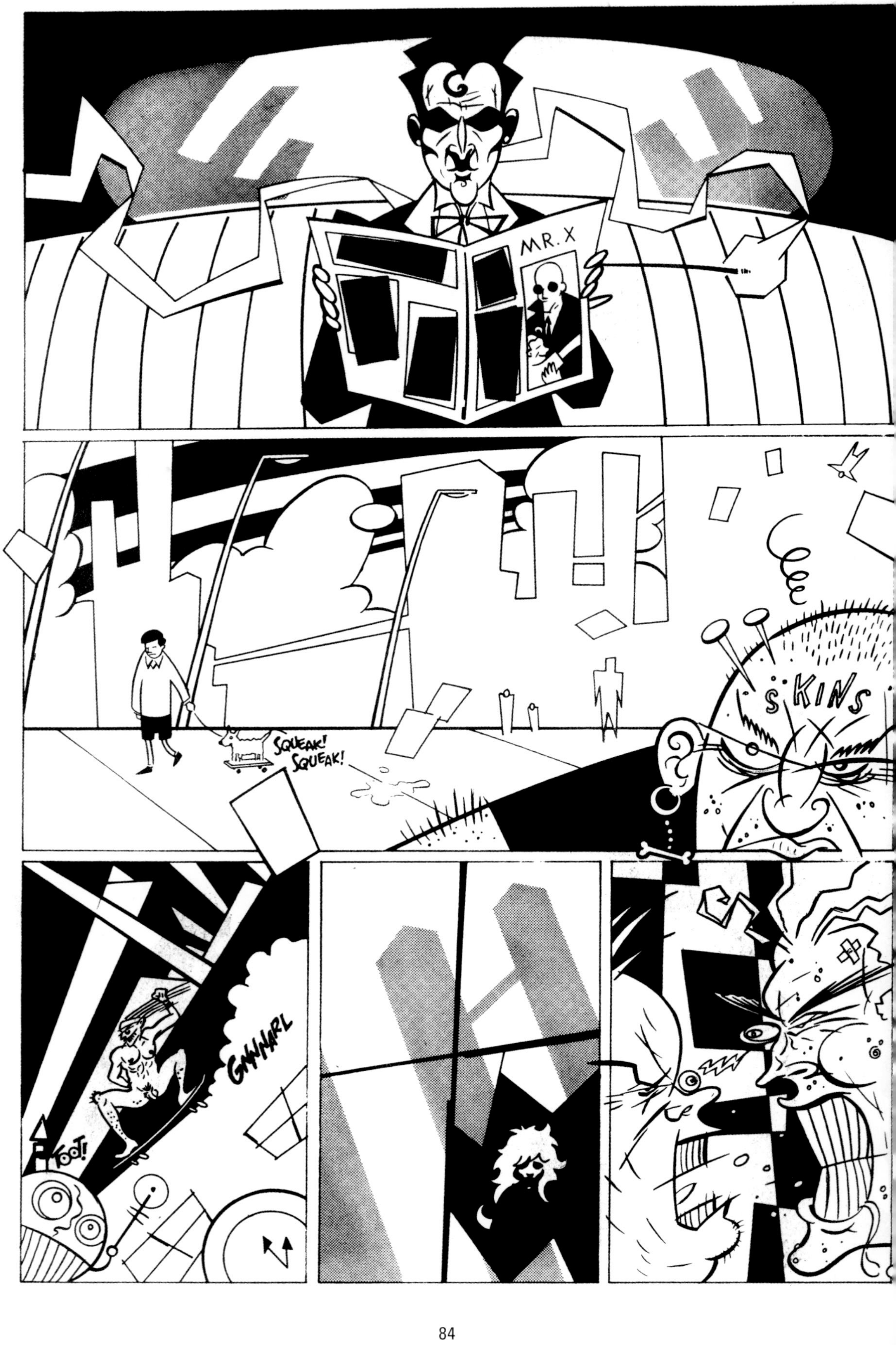
MR. X
SQUEAK!
SQUEAK!
SKINS
GNNNARL
TOOT!

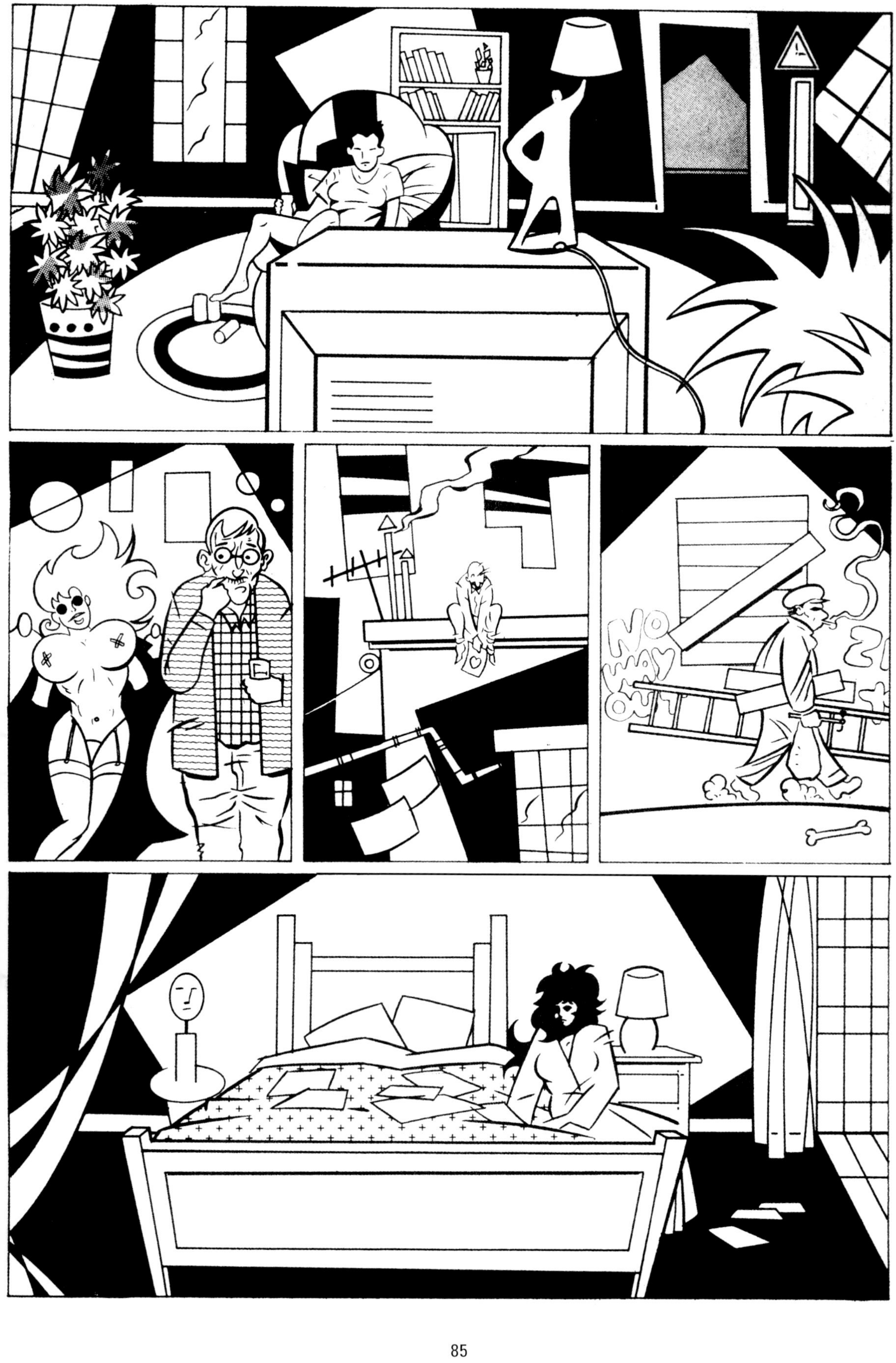
NO WAY OUT

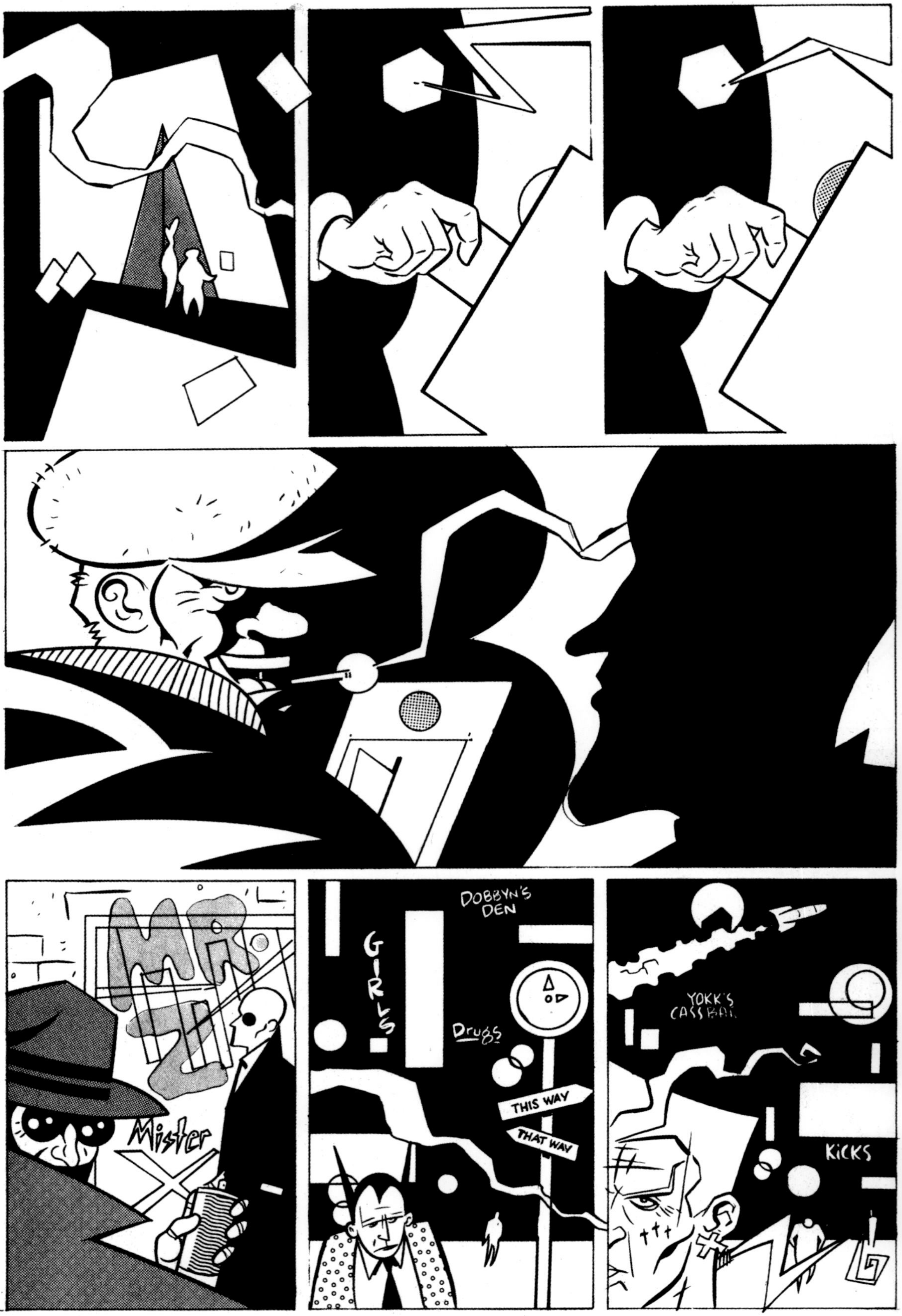
MR X
Mister X
DOBBYN'S DEN
GIRLS
Drugs
THIS WAY
THAT WAY
YOKK'S
KICKS

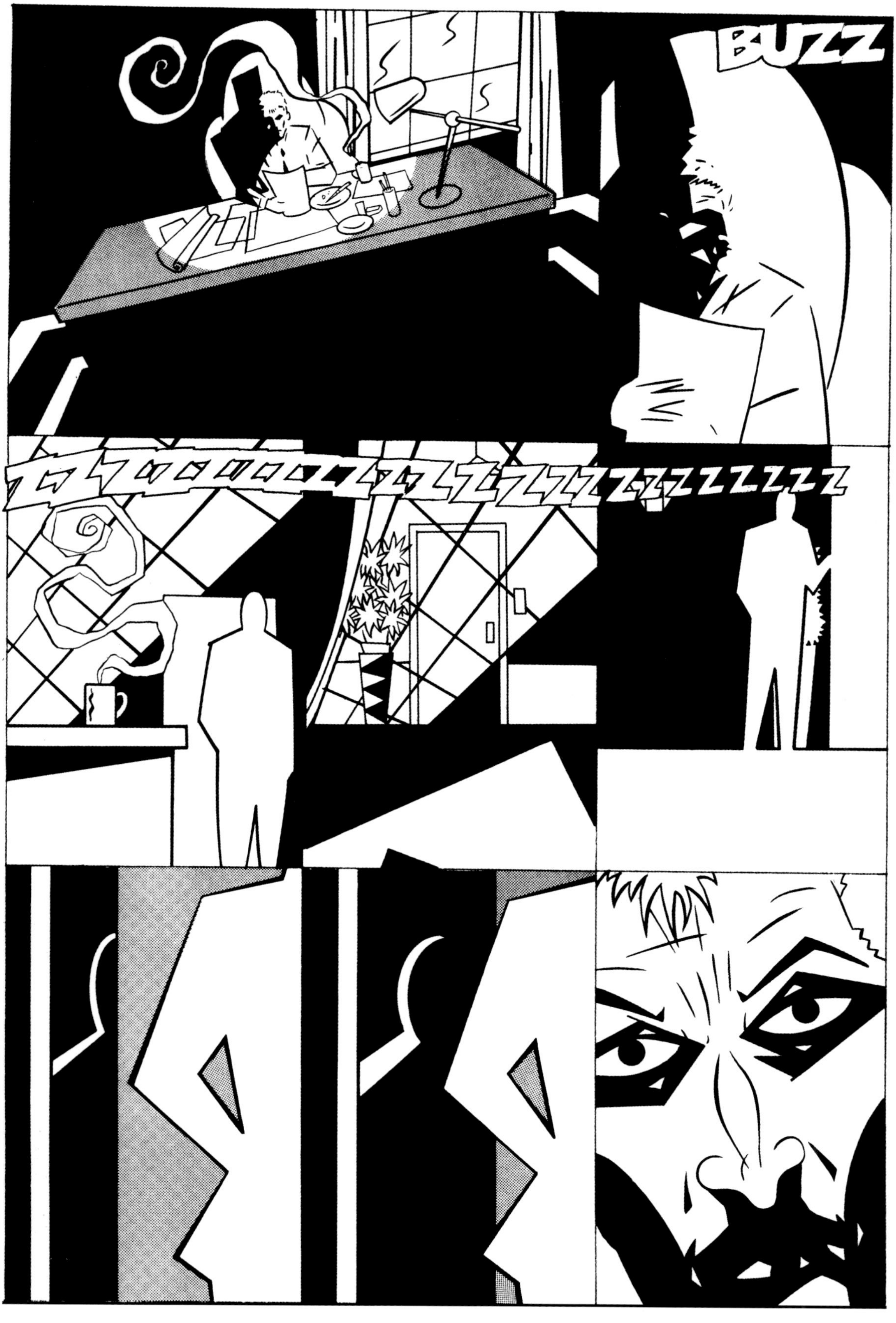
BUZZ
ZZZZZZZZZZZZZZZZZZZZ

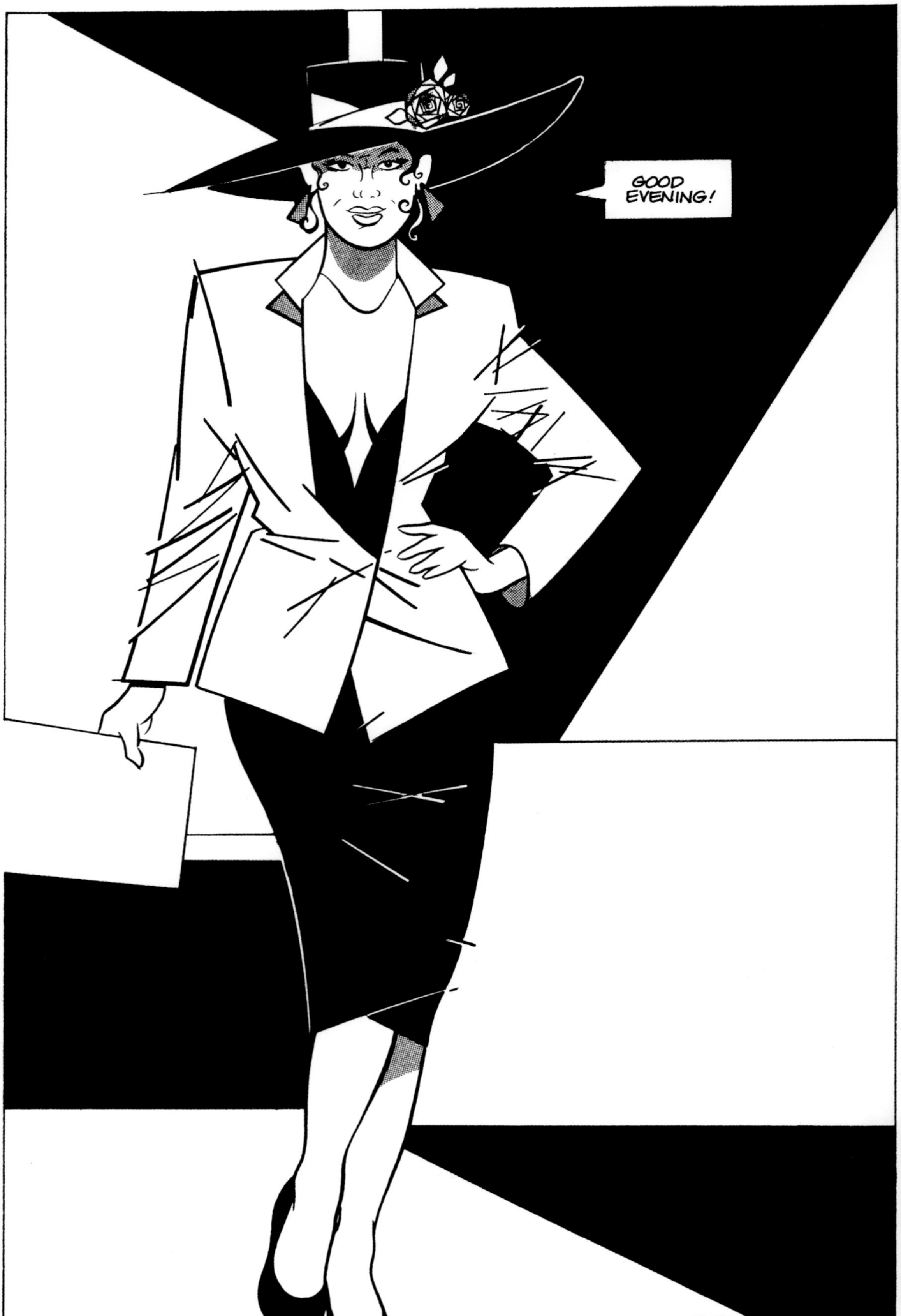
GOOD EVENING!

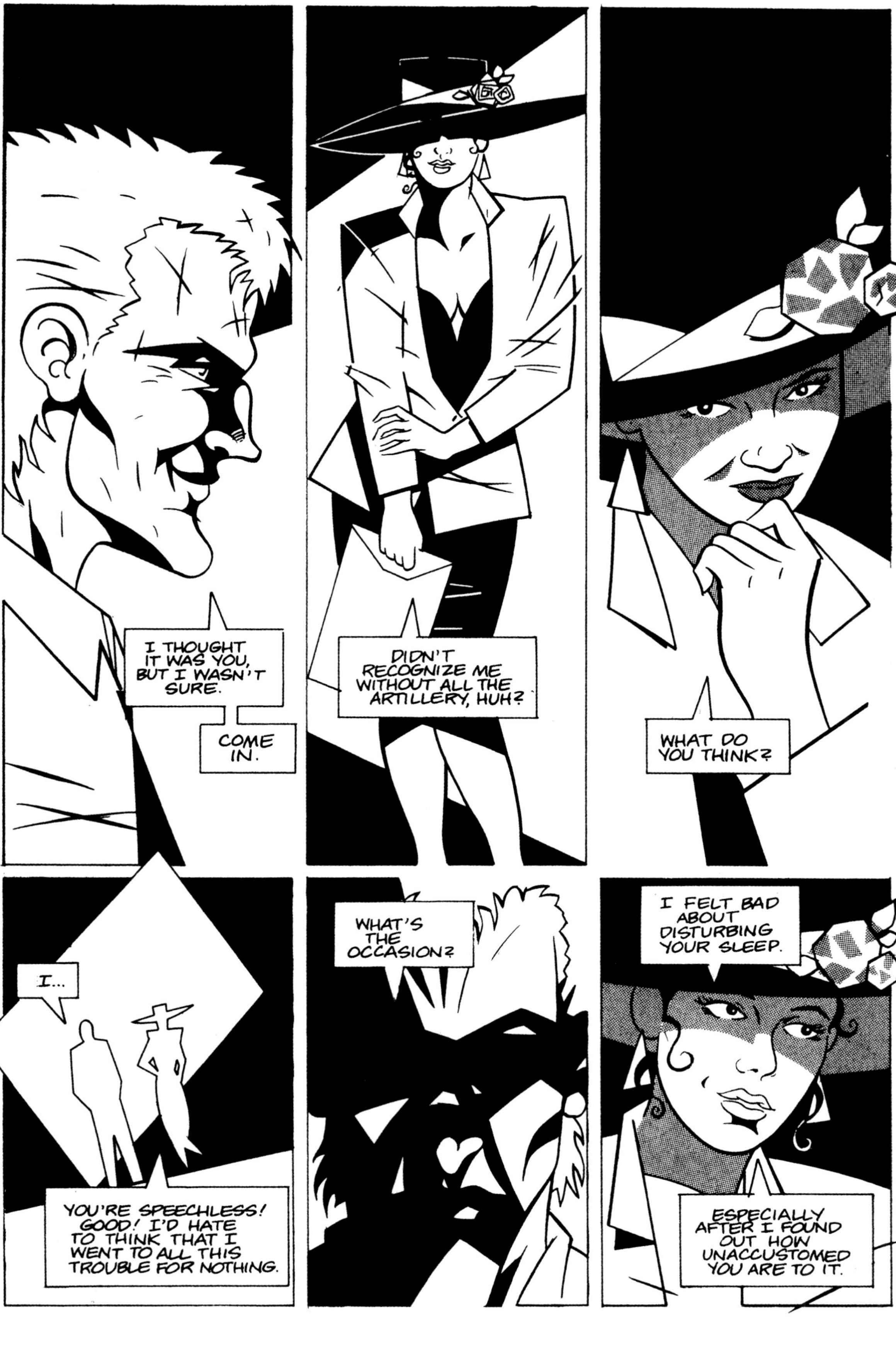
I THOUGHT IT WAS YOU, BUT I WASN'T SURE.
COME IN.
DIDN'T RECOGNIZE ME WITHOUT ALL THE ARTILLERY, HUH?
WHAT DO YOU THINK?
I...
YOU'RE SPEECHLESS! GOOD! I'D HATE TO THINK THAT I WENT TO ALL THIS TROUBLE FOR NOTHING.
WHAT'S THE OCCASION?
I FELT BAD ABOUT DISTURBING YOUR SLEEP.
ESPECIALLY AFTER I FOUND OUT HOW UNACCUSTOMED YOU ARE TO IT.

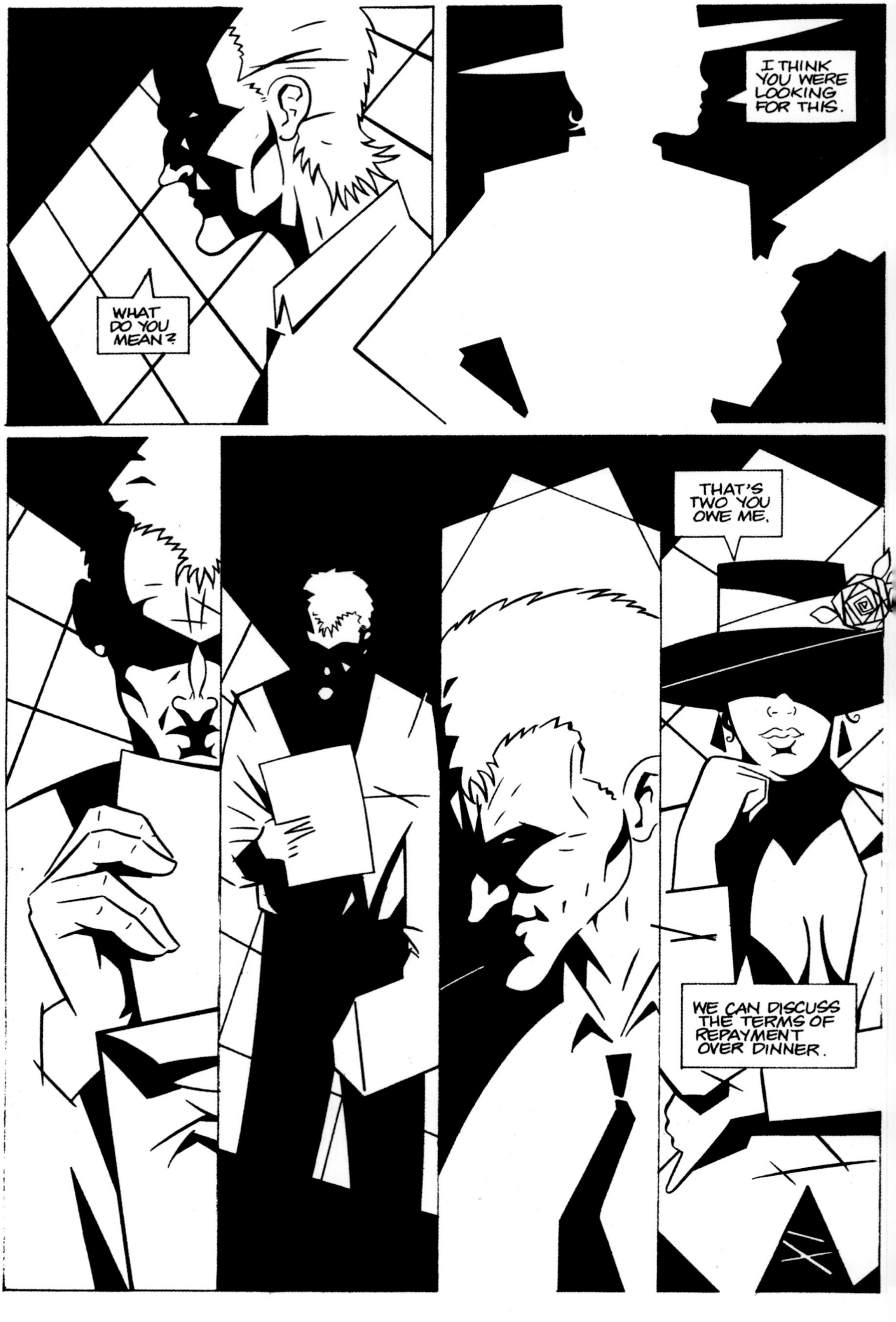
WHAT DO YOU MEAN?
I THINK YOU WERE LOOKING FOR THIS.
THAT'S TWO YOU OWE ME.
WE CAN DISCUSS THE TERMS OF REPAYMENT OVER DINNER.

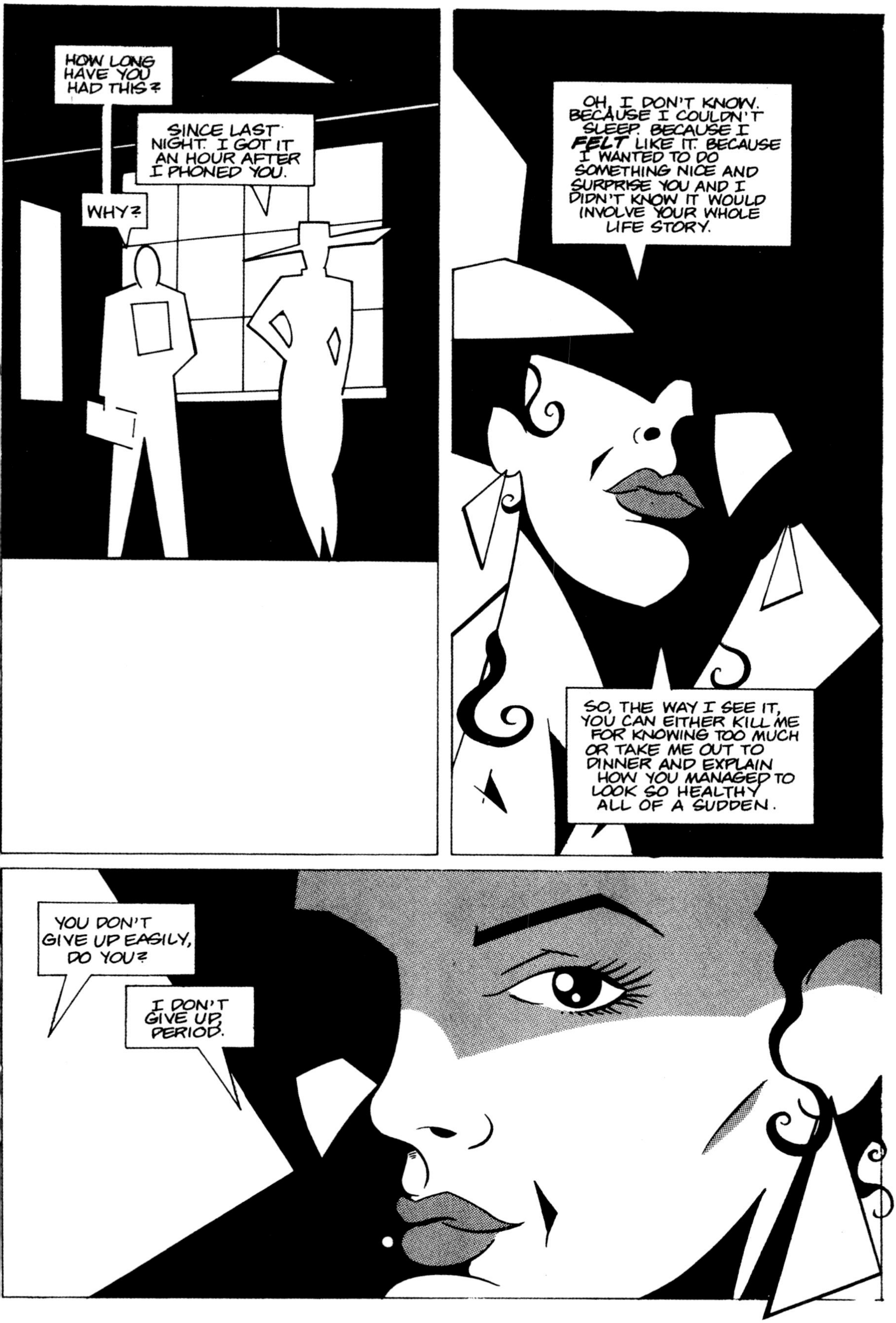
HOW LONG HAVE YOU HAD THIS?
SINCE LAST NIGHT. I GOT IT AN HOUR AFTER I PHONED YOU.
WHY?
OH, I DON'T KNOW. BECAUSE I COULDN'T SLEEP. BECAUSE I *FELT* LIKE IT. BECAUSE I WANTED TO DO SOMETHING NICE AND SURPRISE YOU AND I DIDN'T KNOW IT WOULD INVOLVE YOUR WHOLE LIFE STORY.
SO, THE WAY I SEE IT, YOU CAN EITHER KILL ME FOR KNOWING TOO MUCH OR TAKE ME OUT TO DINNER AND EXPLAIN HOW YOU MANAGED TO LOOK SO HEALTHY ALL OF A SUDDEN.
YOU DON'T GIVE UP EASILY, DO YOU?
I DON'T GIVE UP, PERIOD.

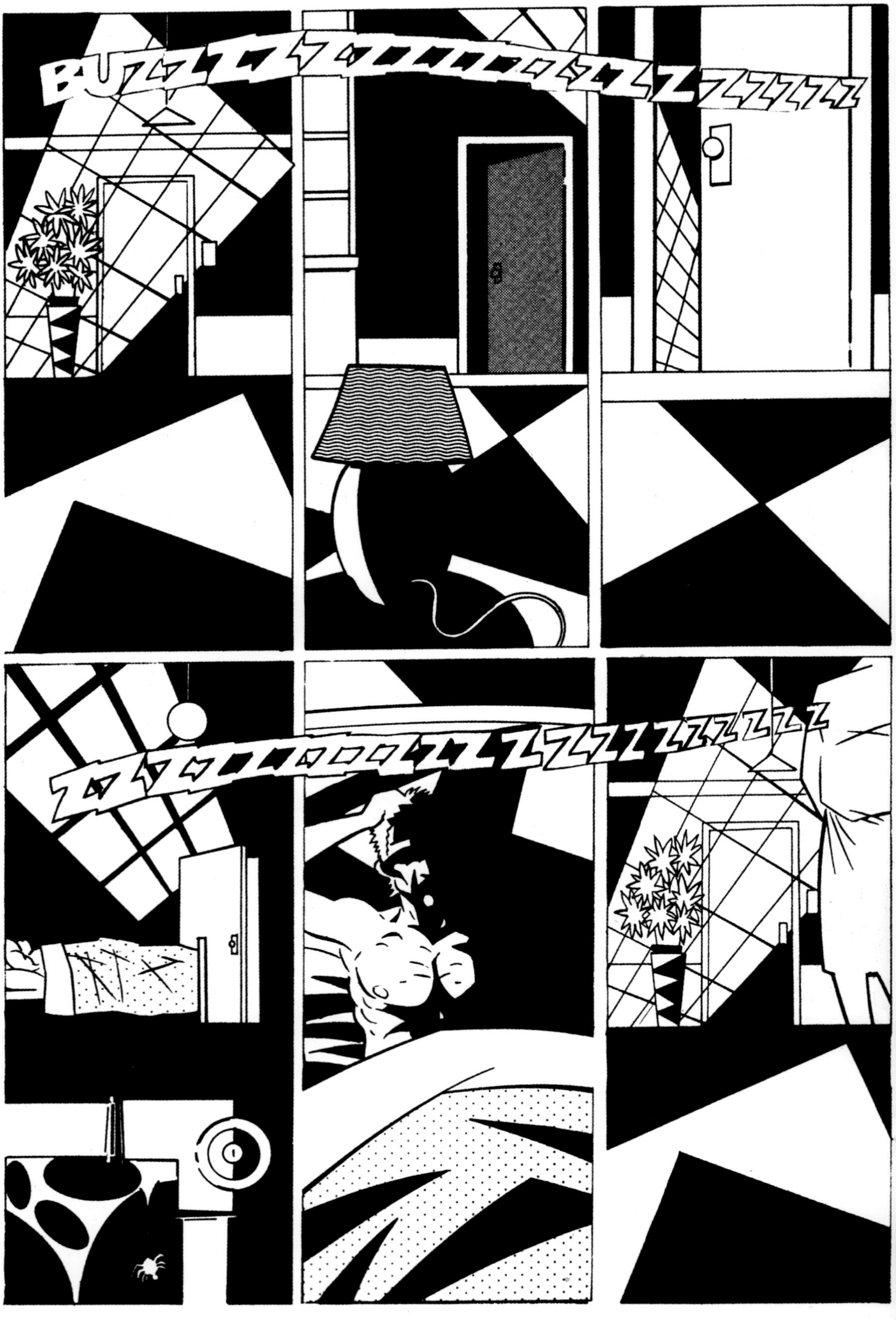
BUZZZZZOOOOOOOOZZZZZZZZZZZZ
ZZZOOOOOOOOZZZZZZZZZZZZZZZ

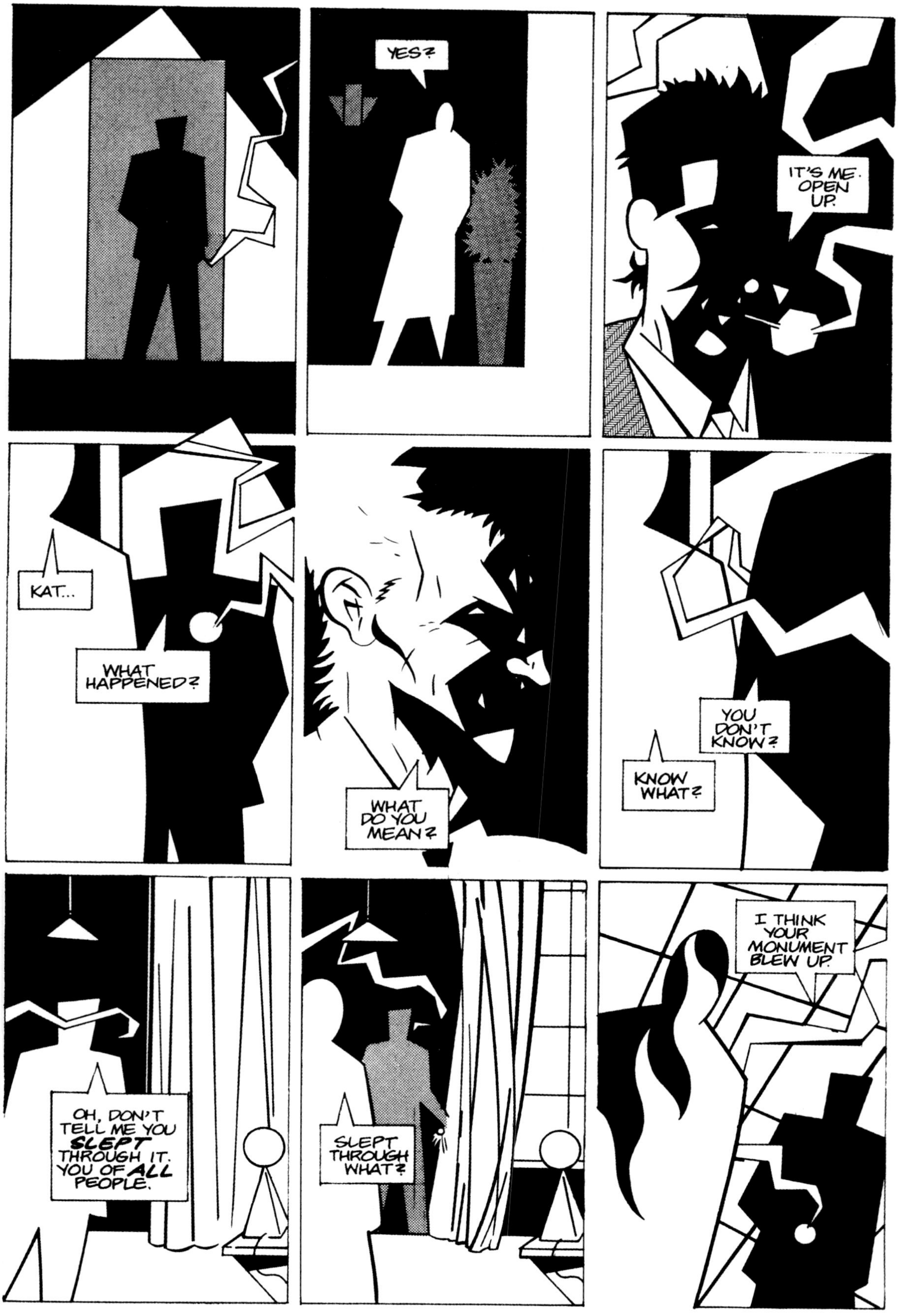
YES?
IT'S ME. OPEN UP.
KAT...
WHAT HAPPENED?
WHAT DO YOU MEAN?
YOU DON'T KNOW?
KNOW WHAT?
OH, DON'T TELL ME YOU SLEPT THROUGH IT. YOU OF ALL PEOPLE.
SLEPT THROUGH WHAT?
I THINK YOUR MONUMENT BLEW UP.

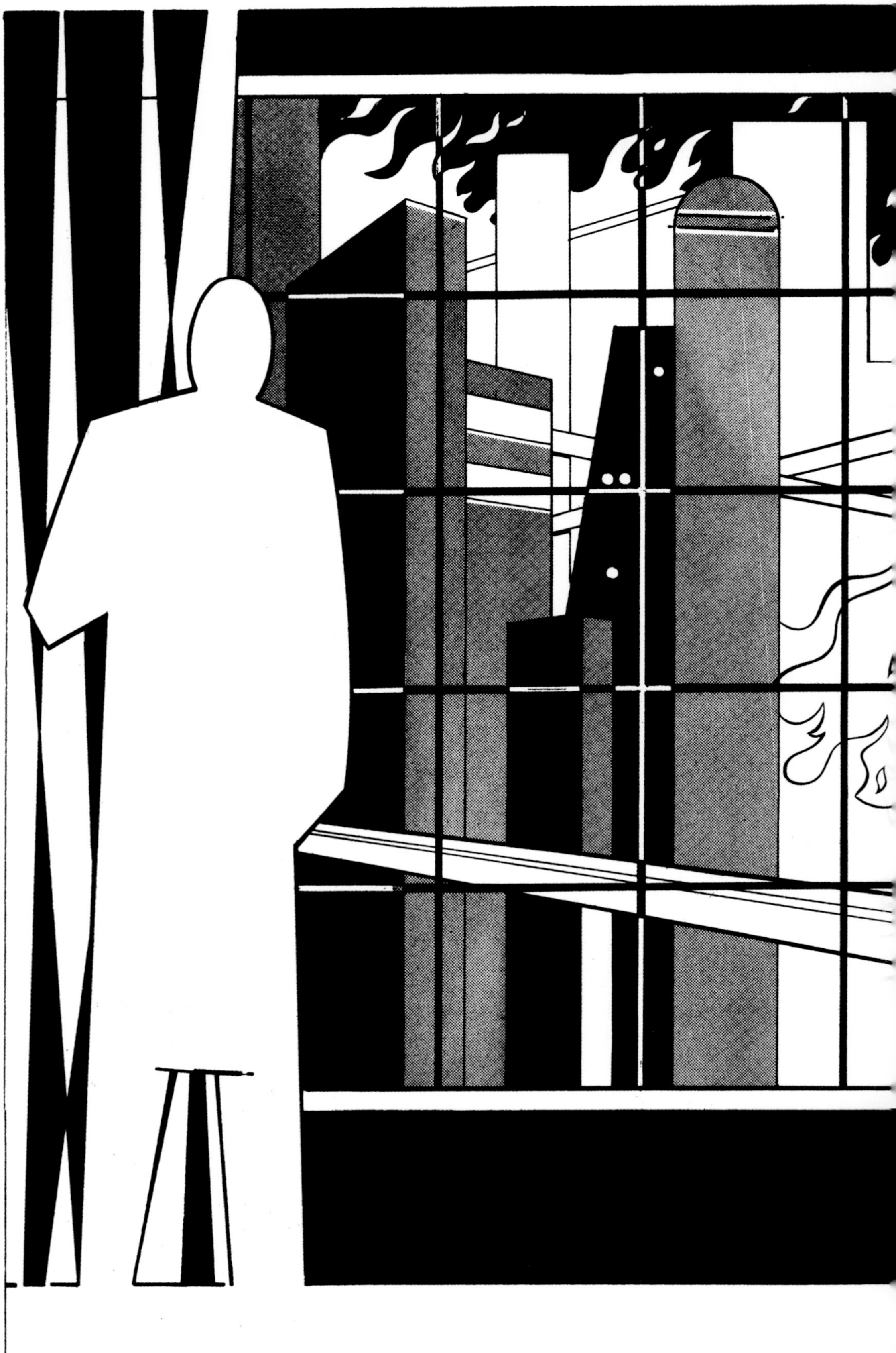

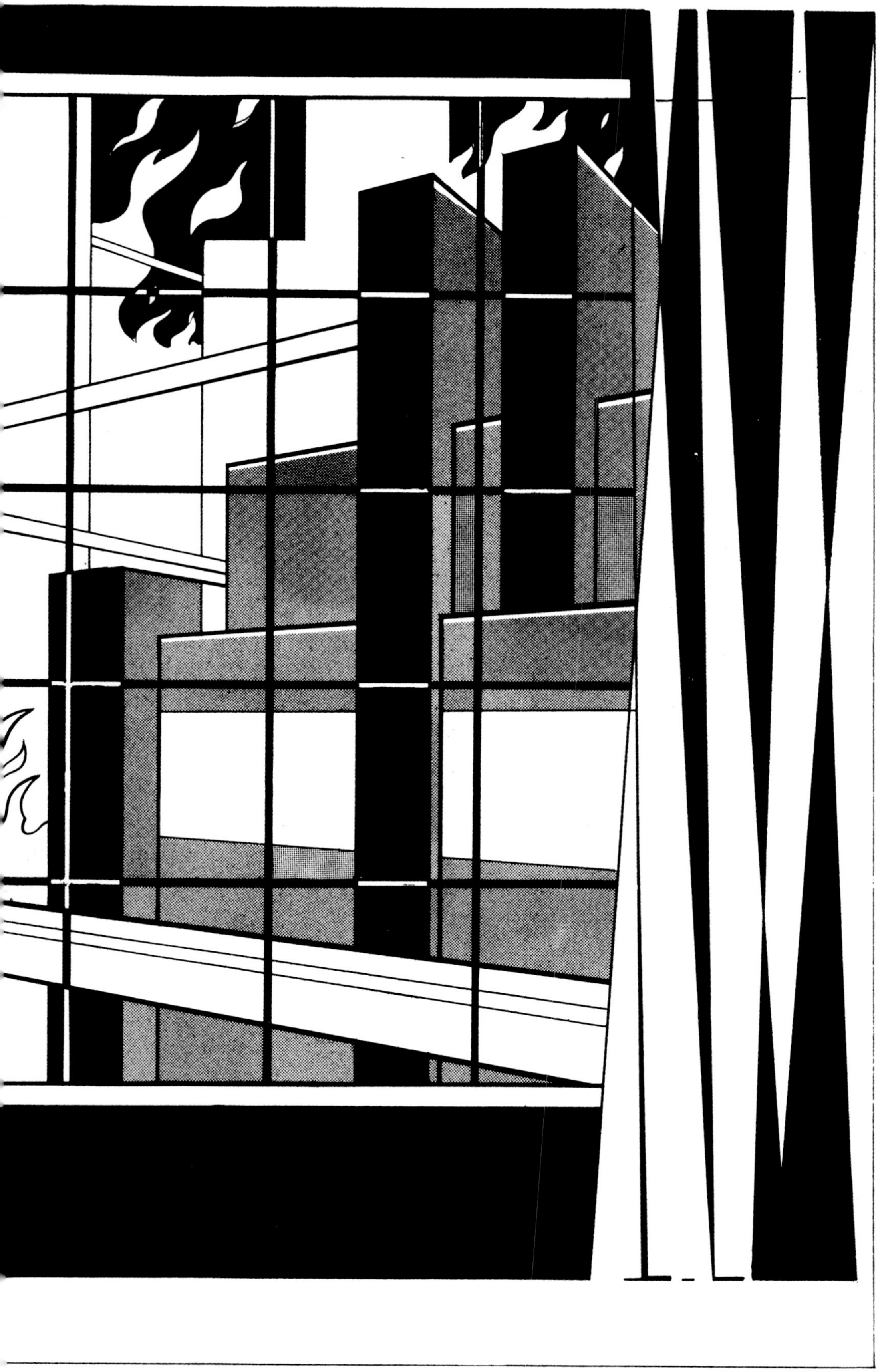

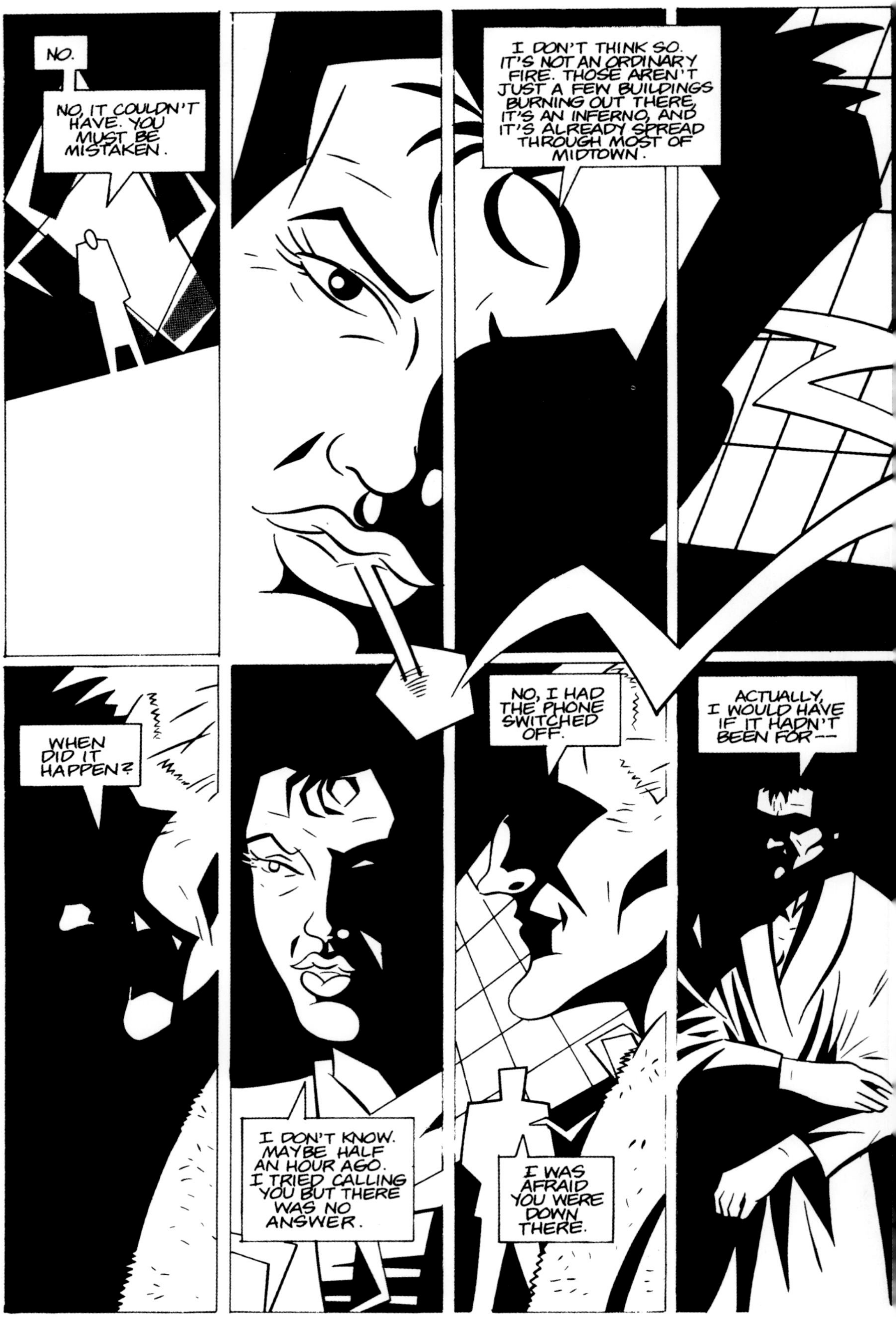
NO.
NO, IT COULDN'T HAVE. YOU MUST BE MISTAKEN.
I DON'T THINK SO. IT'S NOT AN ORDINARY FIRE. THOSE AREN'T JUST A FEW BUILDINGS BURNING OUT THERE, IT'S AN INFERNO, AND IT'S ALREADY SPREAD THROUGH MOST OF MIDTOWN.
WHEN DID IT HAPPEN?
I DON'T KNOW. MAYBE HALF AN HOUR AGO. I TRIED CALLING YOU BUT THERE WAS NO ANSWER.
NO, I HAD THE PHONE SWITCHED OFF.
I WAS AFRAID YOU WERE DOWN THERE.
ACTUALLY, I WOULD HAVE IF IT HADN'T BEEN FOR--

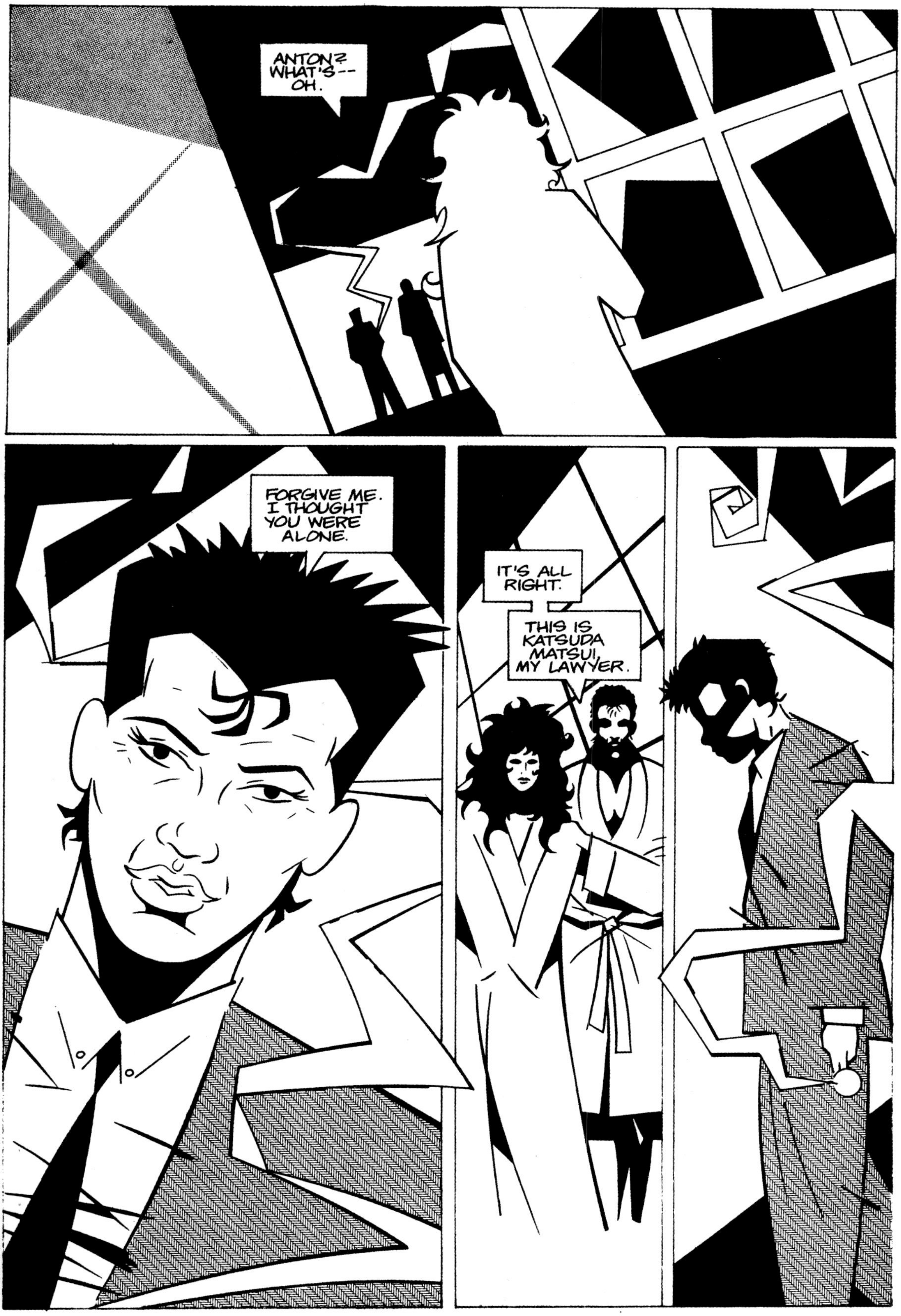
ANTON? WHAT'S-- OH.
FORGIVE ME. I THOUGHT YOU WERE ALONE.
IT'S ALL RIGHT.
THIS IS KATSUDA MATSUI, MY LAWYER.

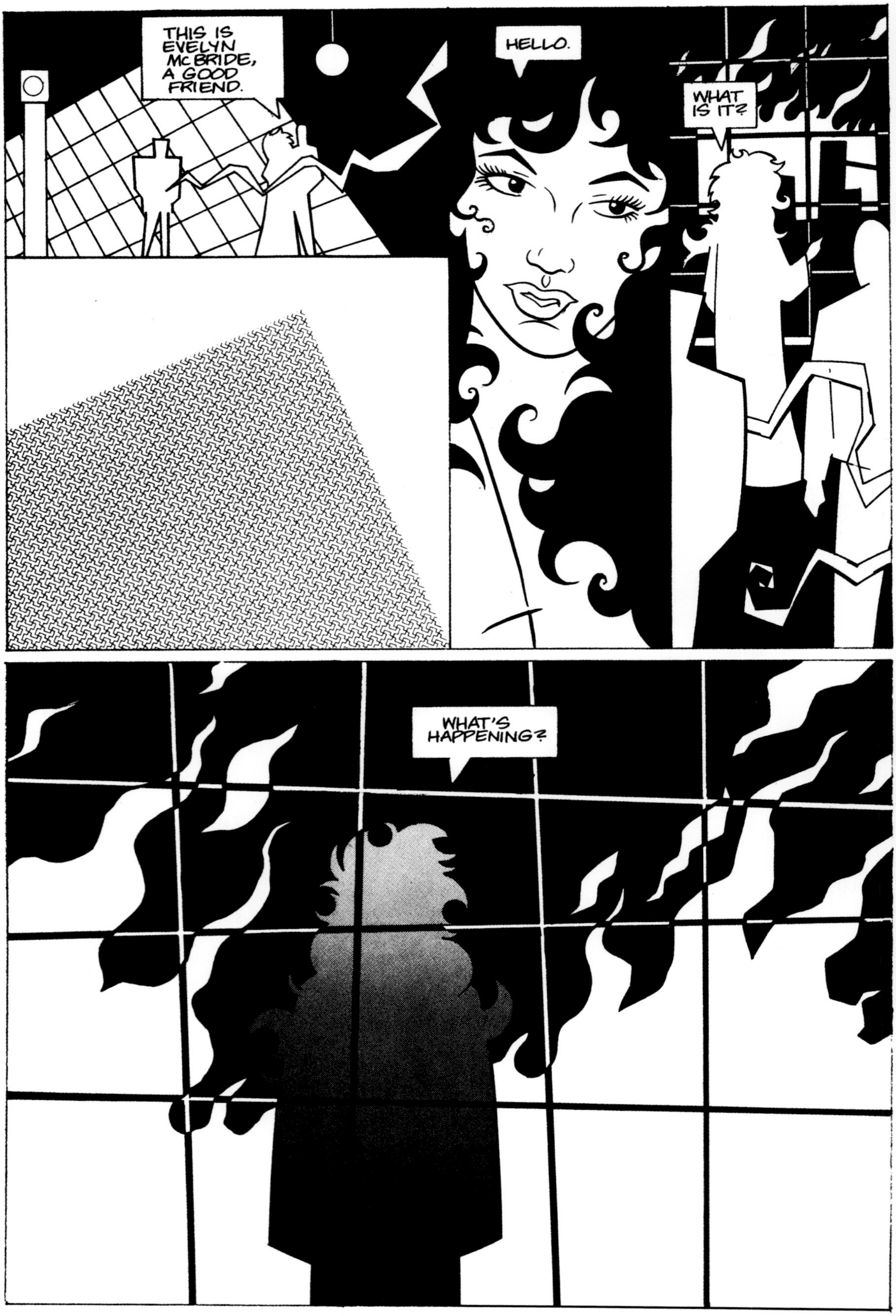
THIS IS EVELYN McBRIDE, A GOOD FRIEND.
HELLO.
WHAT IS IT?
WHAT'S HAPPENING?

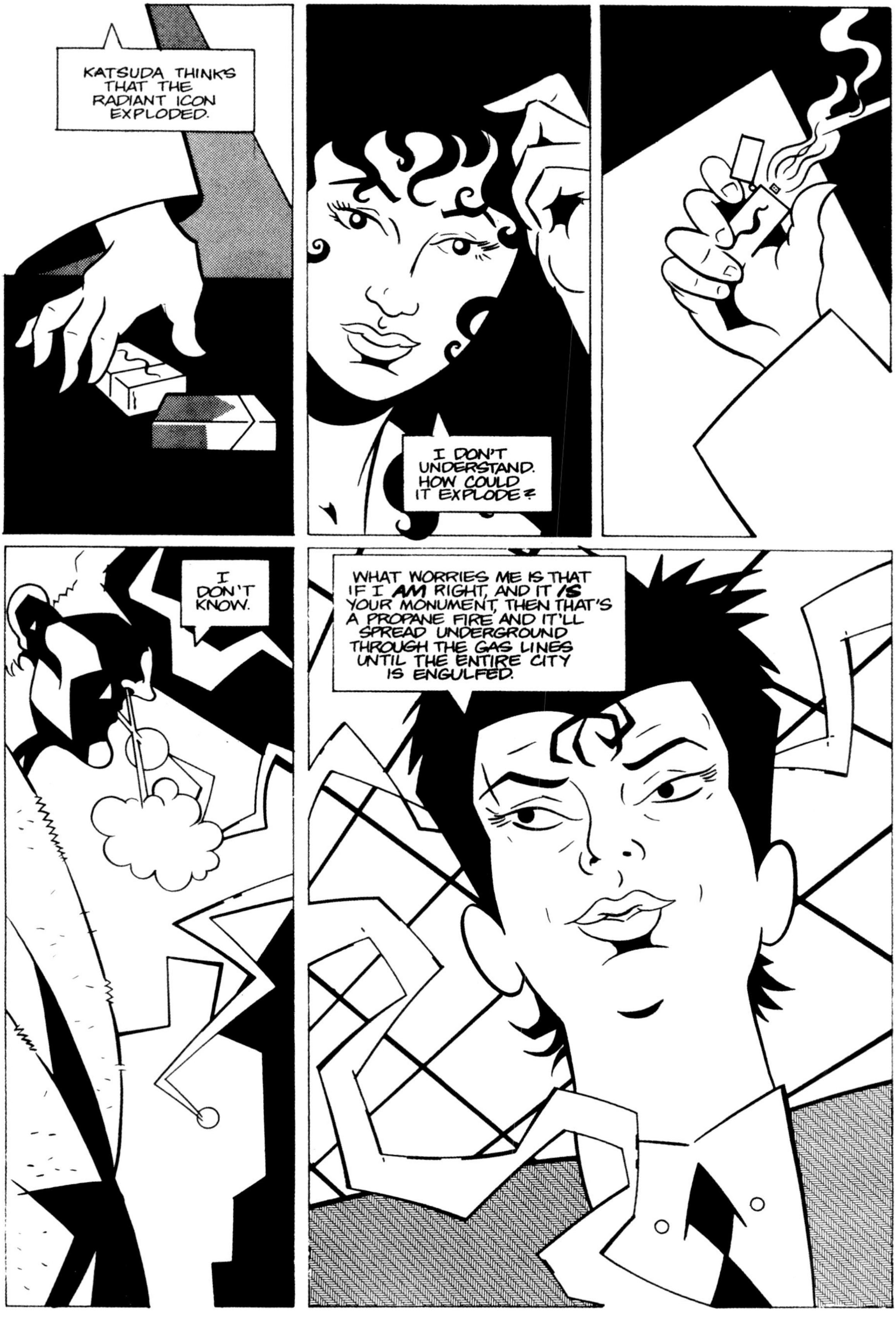
KATSUDA THINKS THAT THE RADIANT ICON EXPLODED.
I DON'T UNDERSTAND. HOW COULD IT EXPLODE?
I DON'T KNOW.
WHAT WORRIES ME IS THAT IF I AM RIGHT, AND IT IS YOUR MONUMENT, THEN THAT'S A PROPANE FIRE AND IT'LL SPREAD UNDERGROUND THROUGH THE GAS LINES UNTIL THE ENTIRE CITY IS ENGULFED.

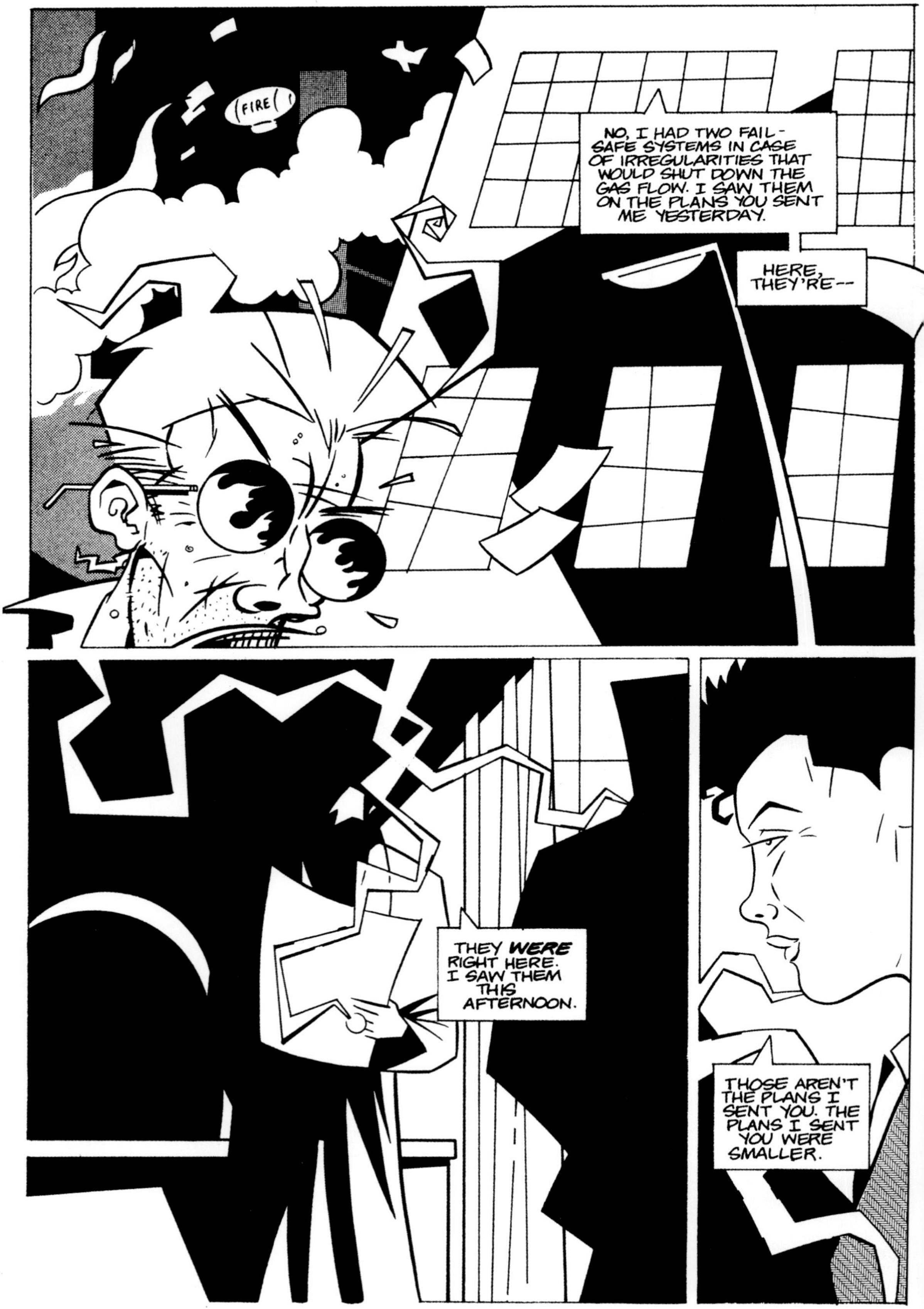
FIRE
NO, I HAD TWO FAIL-SAFE SYSTEMS IN CASE OF IRREGULARITIES THAT WOULD SHUT DOWN THE GAS FLOW. I SAW THEM ON THE PLANS YOU SENT ME YESTERDAY.
HERE, THEY'RE--
THEY *WERE* RIGHT HERE. I SAW THEM THIS AFTERNOON.
THOSE AREN'T THE PLANS I SENT YOU. THE PLANS I SENT YOU WERE SMALLER.

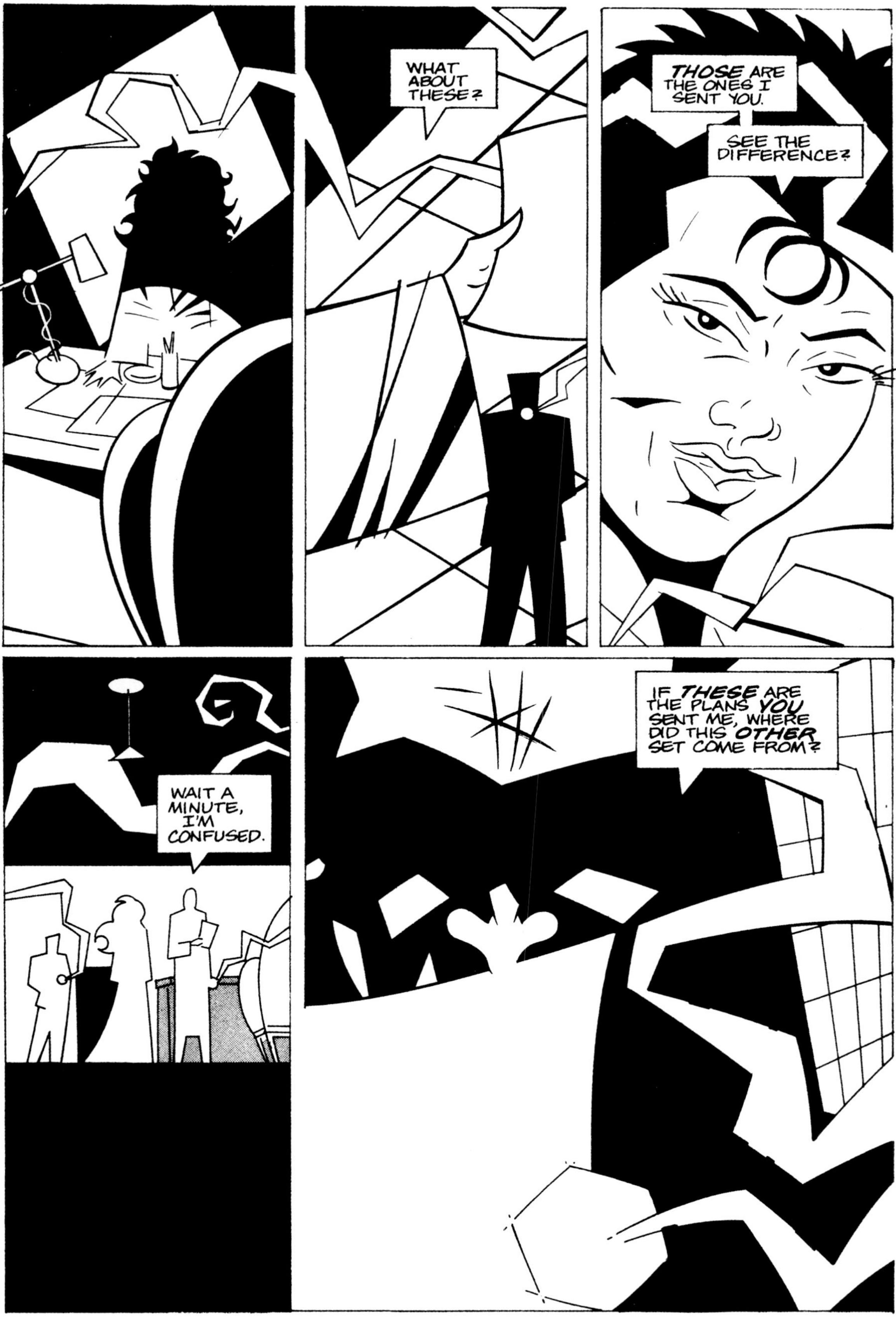
WHAT ABOUT THESE?
THOSE ARE THE ONES I SENT YOU.
SEE THE DIFFERENCE?
WAIT A MINUTE, I'M CONFUSED.
IF THESE ARE THE PLANS YOU SENT ME, WHERE DID THIS OTHER SET COME FROM?

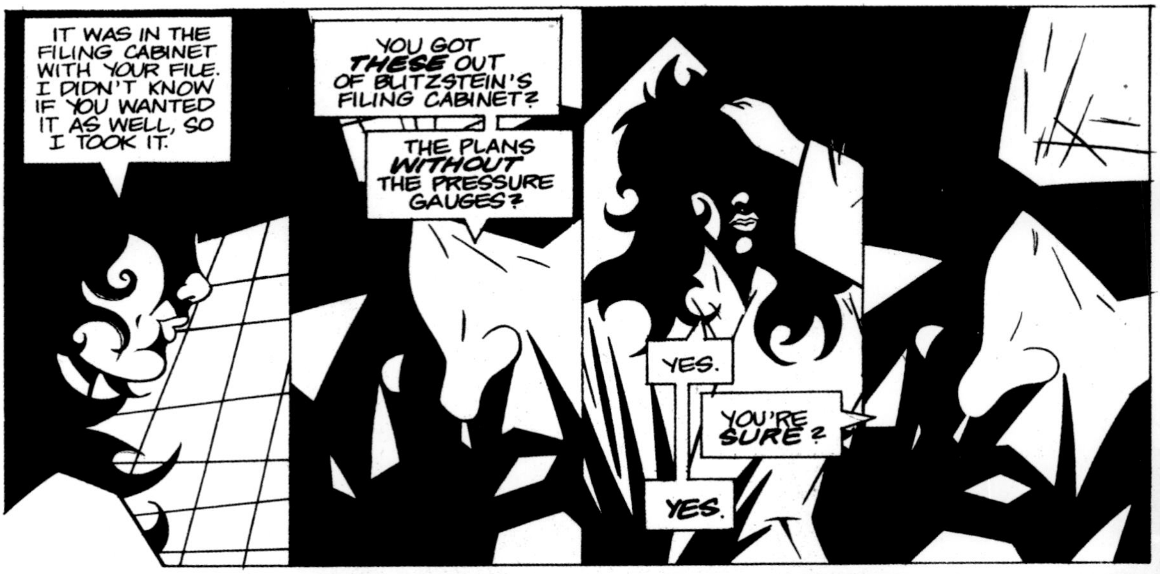
IT WAS IN THE FILING CABINET WITH YOUR FILE. I DIDN'T KNOW IF YOU WANTED IT AS WELL, SO I TOOK IT.
YOU GOT THESE OUT OF BLITZSTEIN'S FILING CABINET?
THE PLANS WITHOUT THE PRESSURE GAUGES?
YES.
YOU'RE SURE?
YES.

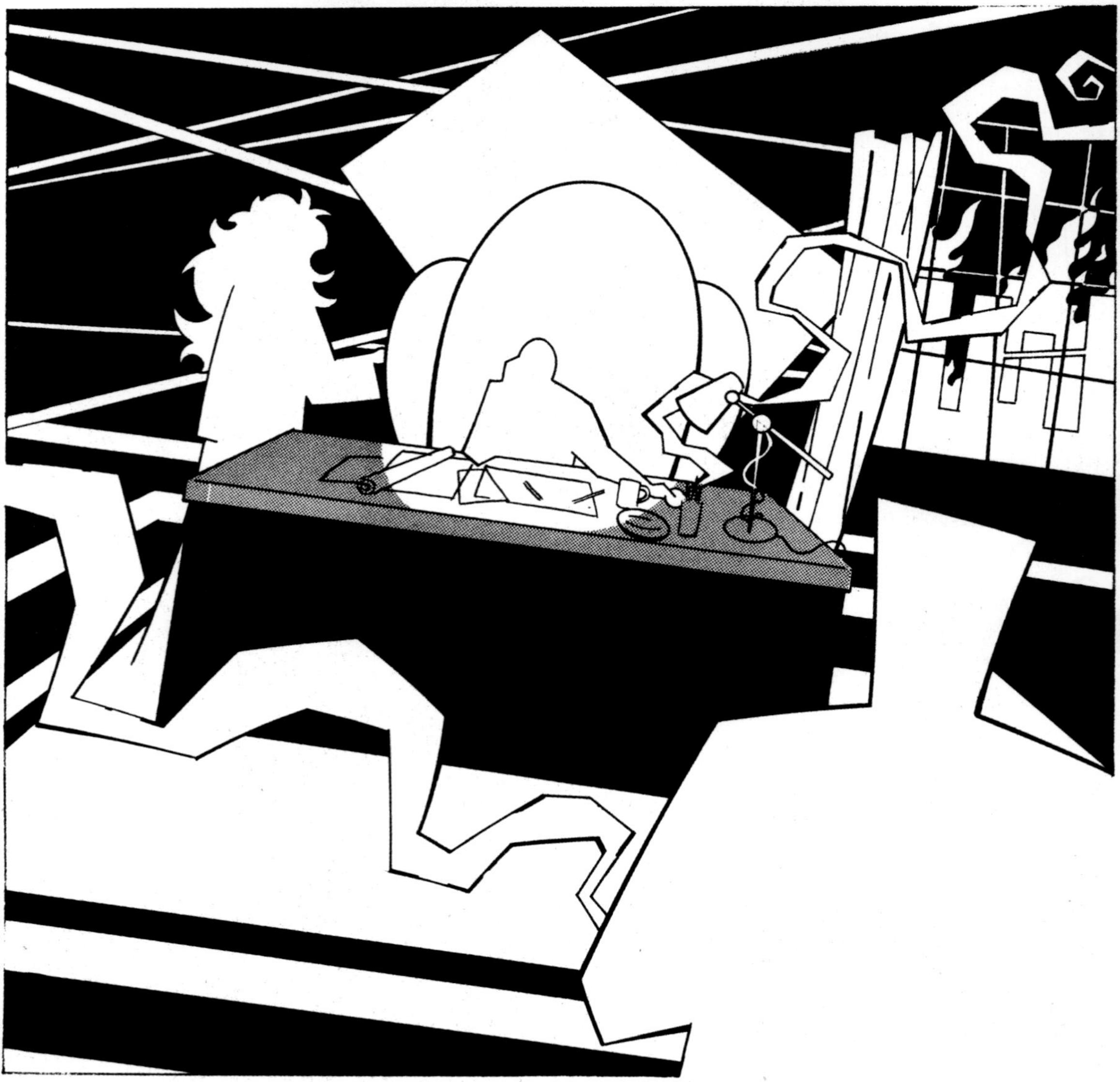

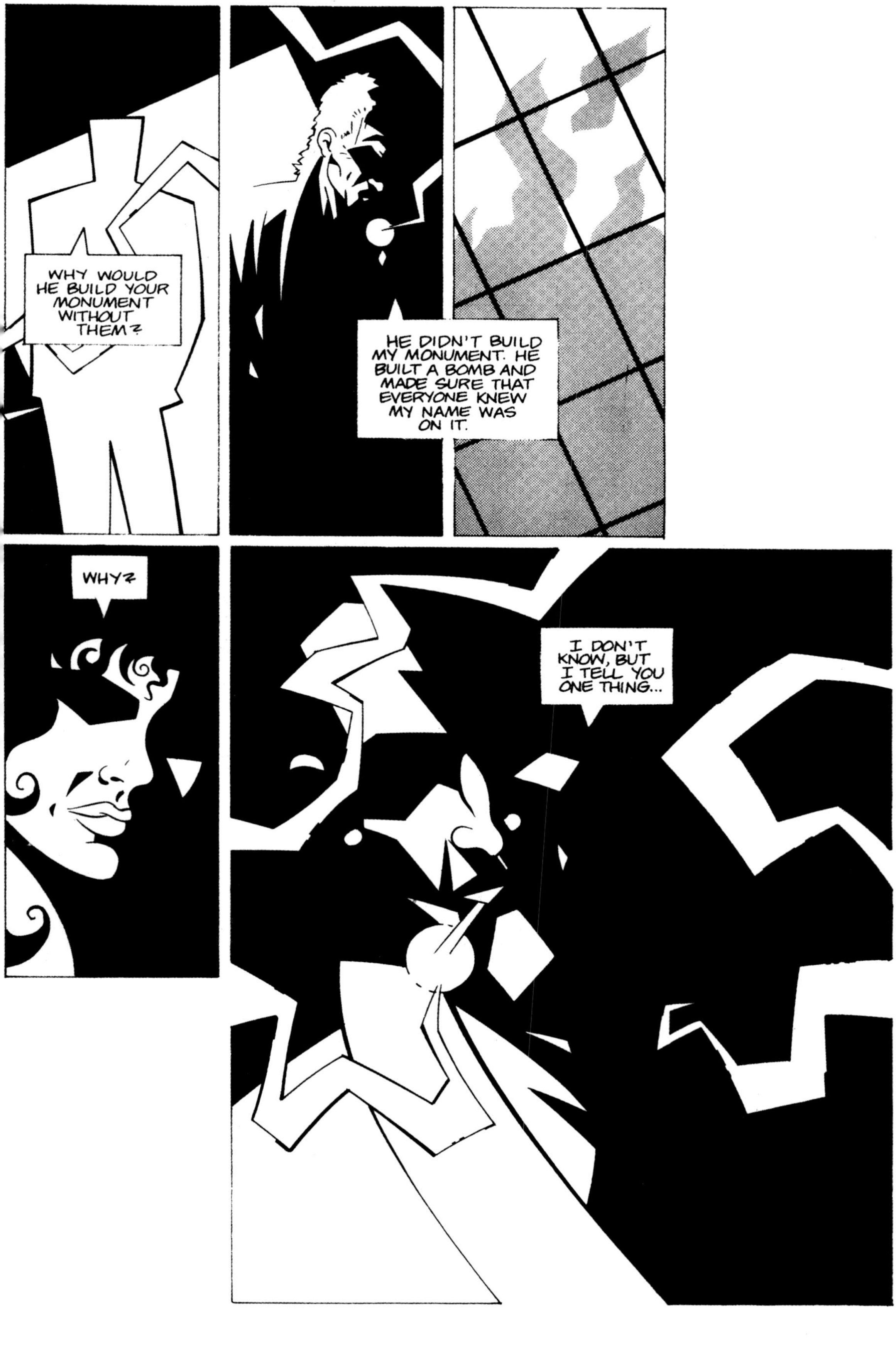
WHY WOULD HE BUILD YOUR MONUMENT WITHOUT THEM?
HE DIDN'T BUILD MY MONUMENT. HE BUILT A BOMB AND MADE SURE THAT EVERYONE KNEW MY NAME WAS ON IT.
WHY?
I DON'T KNOW, BUT I TELL YOU ONE THING...

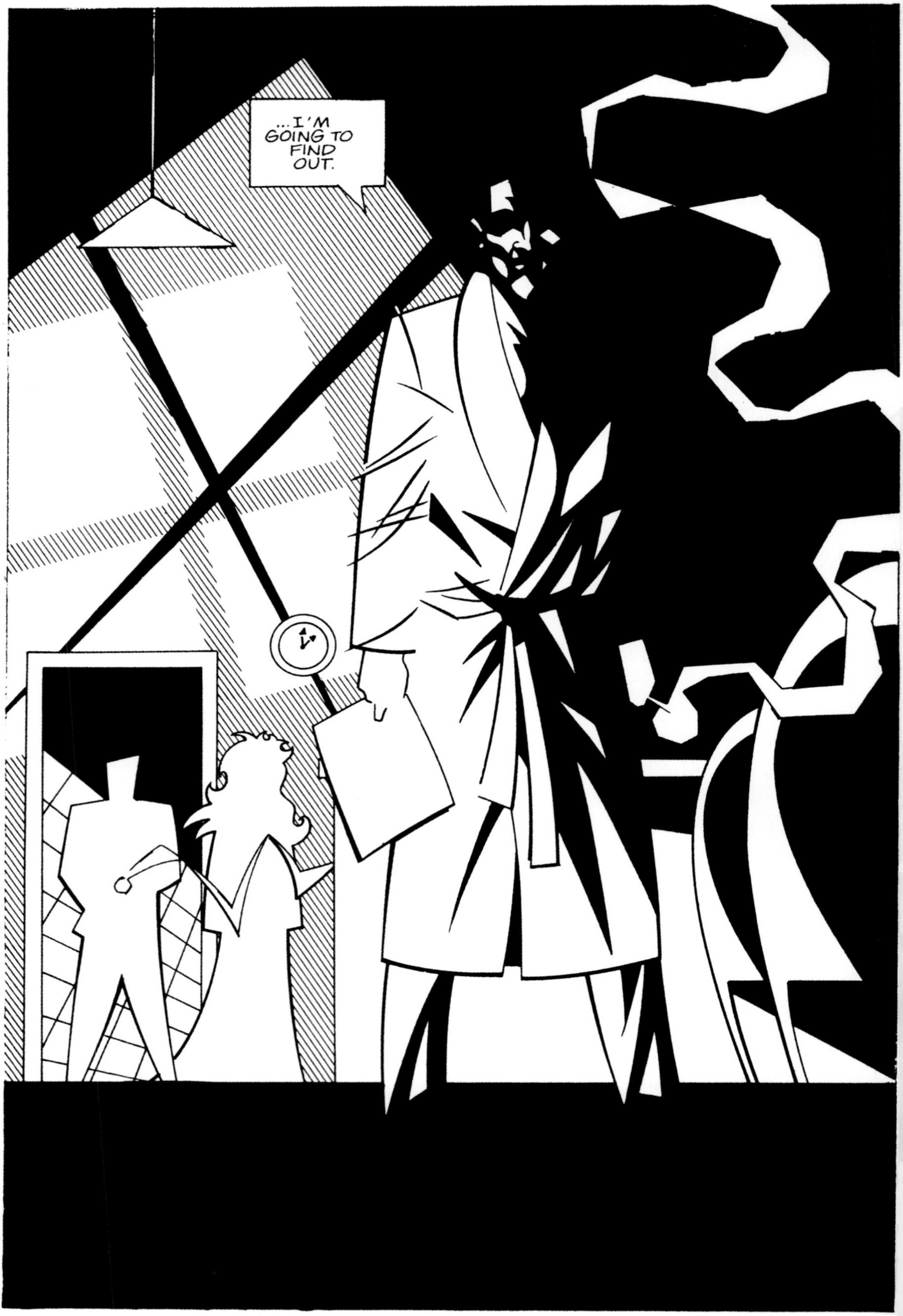
...I'M GOING TO FIND OUT.

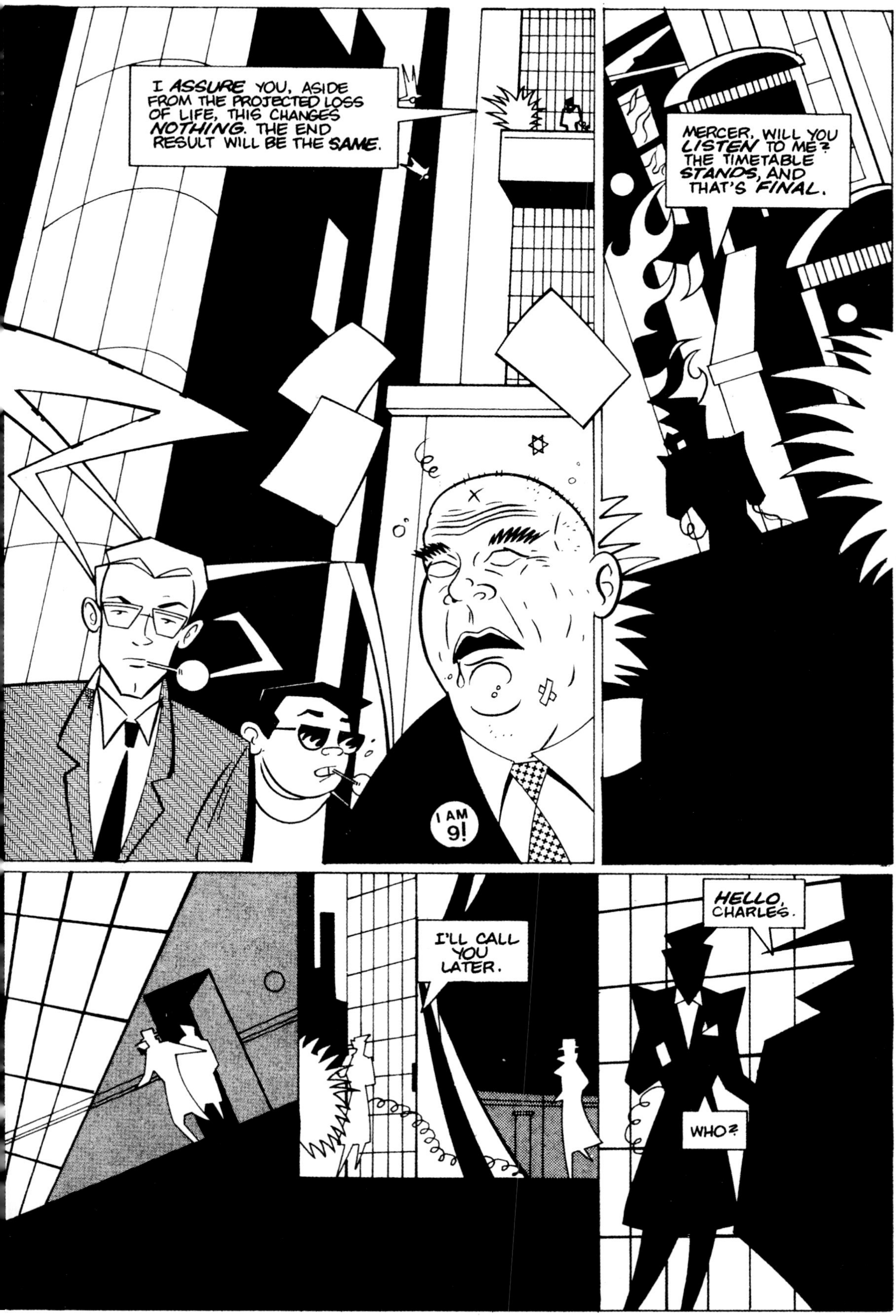
I ASSURE YOU, ASIDE FROM THE PROJECTED LOSS OF LIFE, THIS CHANGES NOTHING. THE END RESULT WILL BE THE SAME.
MERCER, WILL YOU LISTEN TO ME? THE TIMETABLE STANDS, AND THAT'S FINAL.
I AM 9!
I'LL CALL YOU LATER.
HELLO, CHARLES.
WHO?

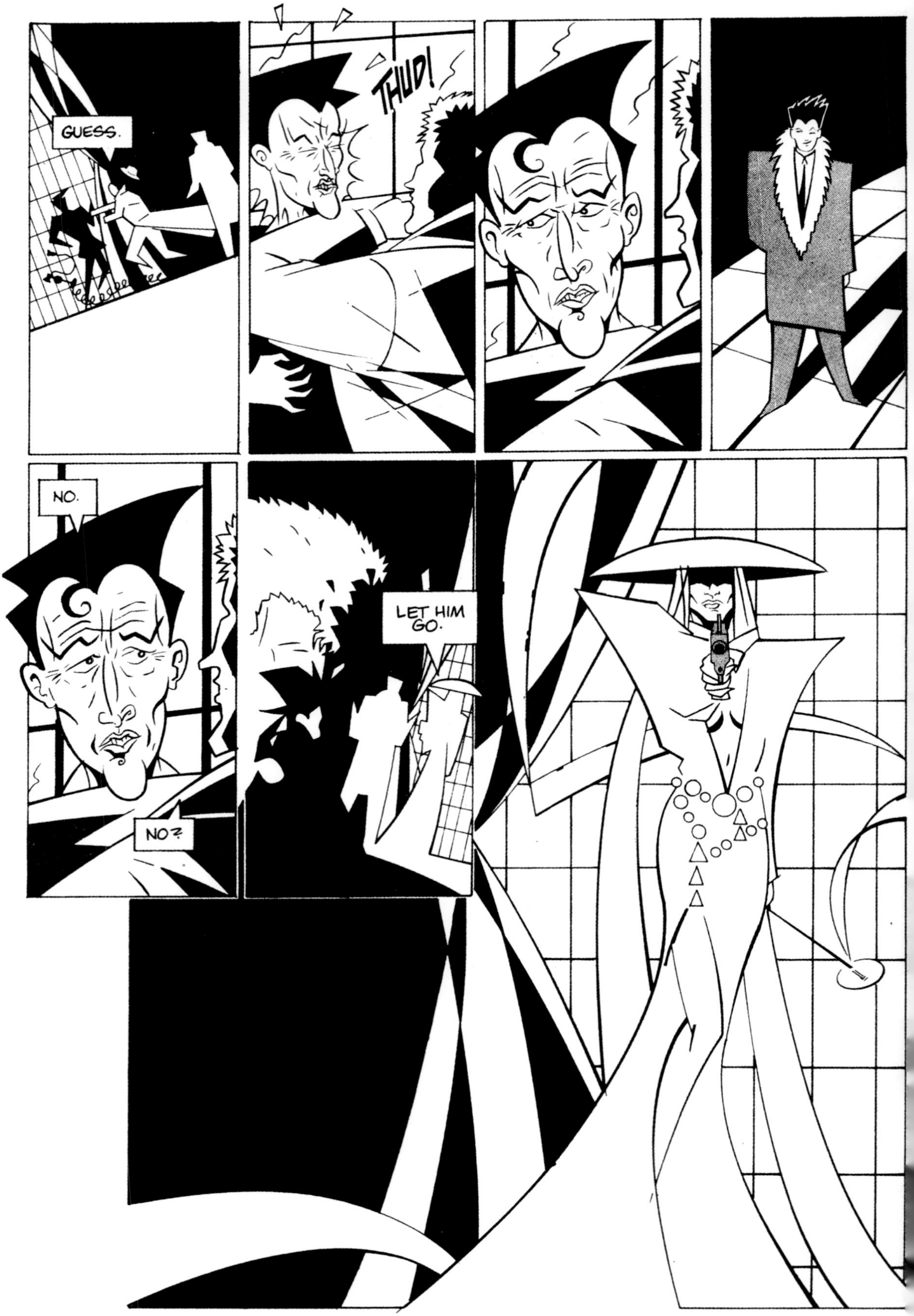
GUESS.
THUD!
NO.
NO?
LET HIM GO.

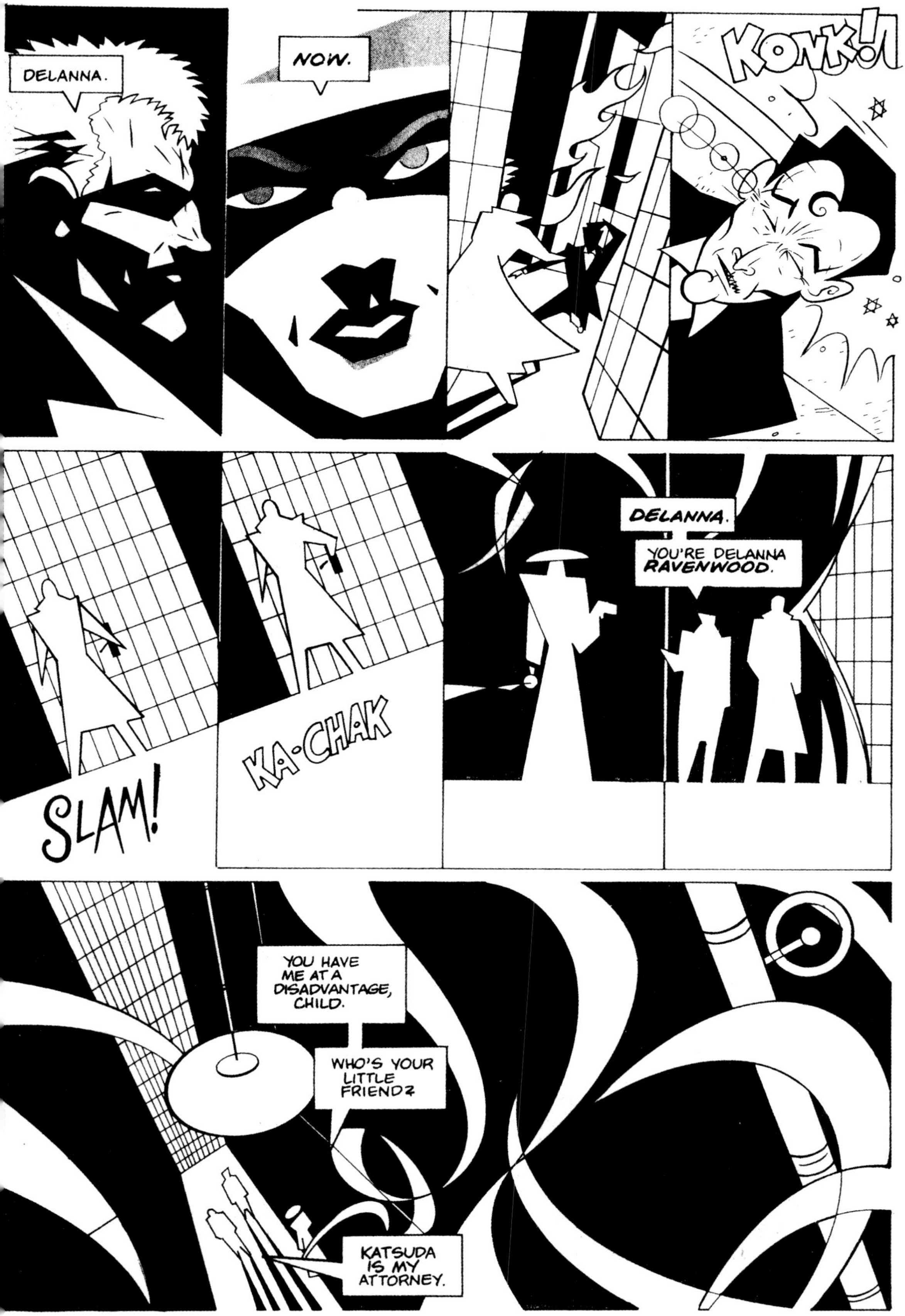
DELANNA.
NOW.
KONK!!
SLAM!
KA-CHAK
DELANNA.
YOU'RE DELANNA RAVENWOOD.
YOU HAVE ME AT A DISADVANTAGE, CHILD.
WHO'S YOUR LITTLE FRIEND?
KATSUDA IS MY ATTORNEY.

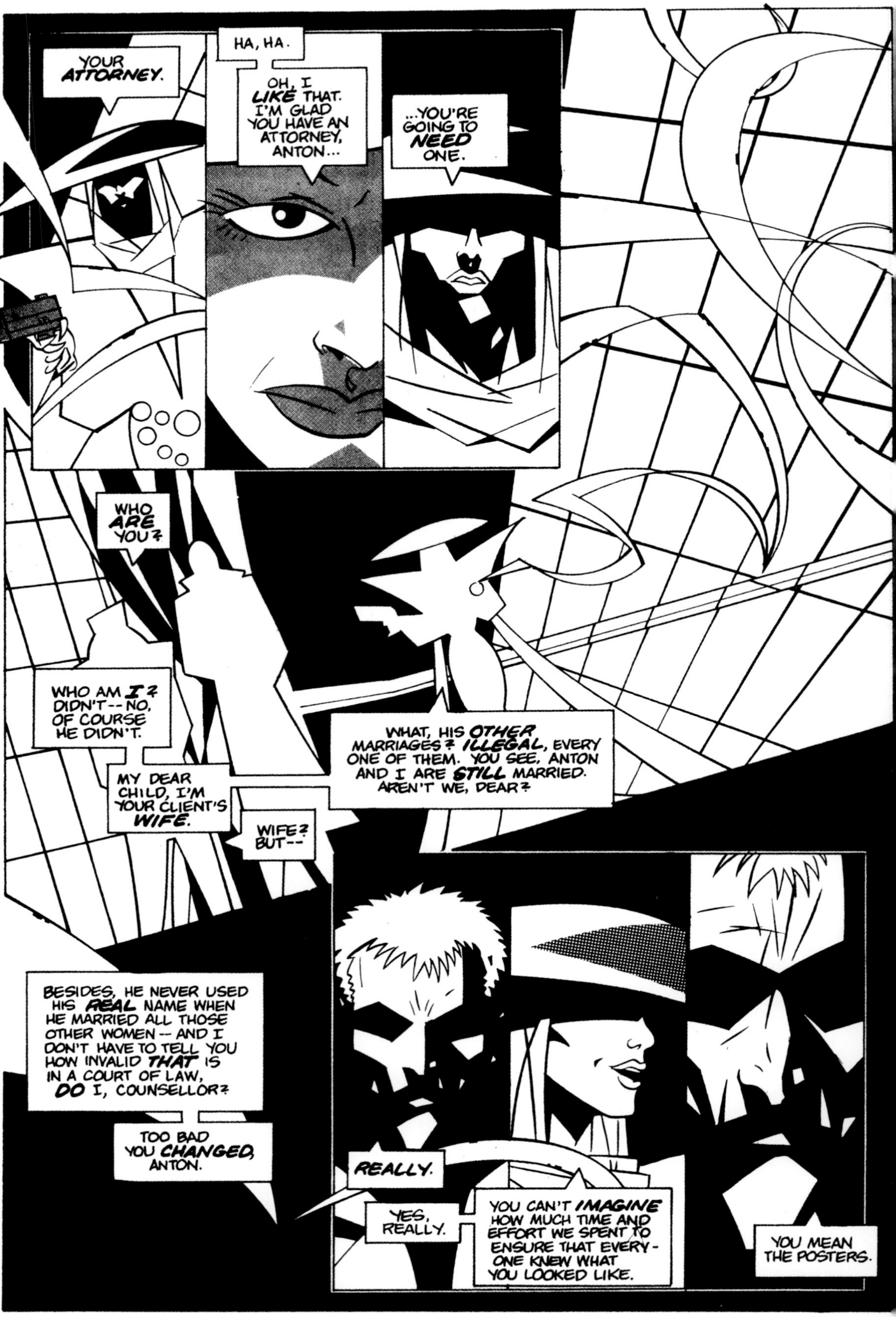
YOUR ATTORNEY.
HA, HA.
OH, I LIKE THAT. I'M GLAD YOU HAVE AN ATTORNEY, ANTON...
...YOU'RE GOING TO NEED ONE.
WHO ARE YOU?
WHO AM I? DIDN'T--NO, OF COURSE HE DIDN'T.
MY DEAR CHILD, I'M YOUR CLIENT'S WIFE.
WIFE? BUT--
WHAT, HIS OTHER MARRIAGES? ILLEGAL, EVERY ONE OF THEM. YOU SEE, ANTON AND I ARE STILL MARRIED. AREN'T WE, DEAR?
BESIDES, HE NEVER USED HIS REAL NAME WHEN HE MARRIED ALL THOSE OTHER WOMEN -- AND I DON'T HAVE TO TELL YOU HOW INVALID THAT IS IN A COURT OF LAW, DO I, COUNSELLOR?
TOO BAD YOU CHANGED, ANTON.
REALLY.
YES, REALLY.
YOU CAN'T IMAGINE HOW MUCH TIME AND EFFORT WE SPENT TO ENSURE THAT EVERY-ONE KNEW WHAT YOU LOOKED LIKE.
YOU MEAN THE POSTERS.

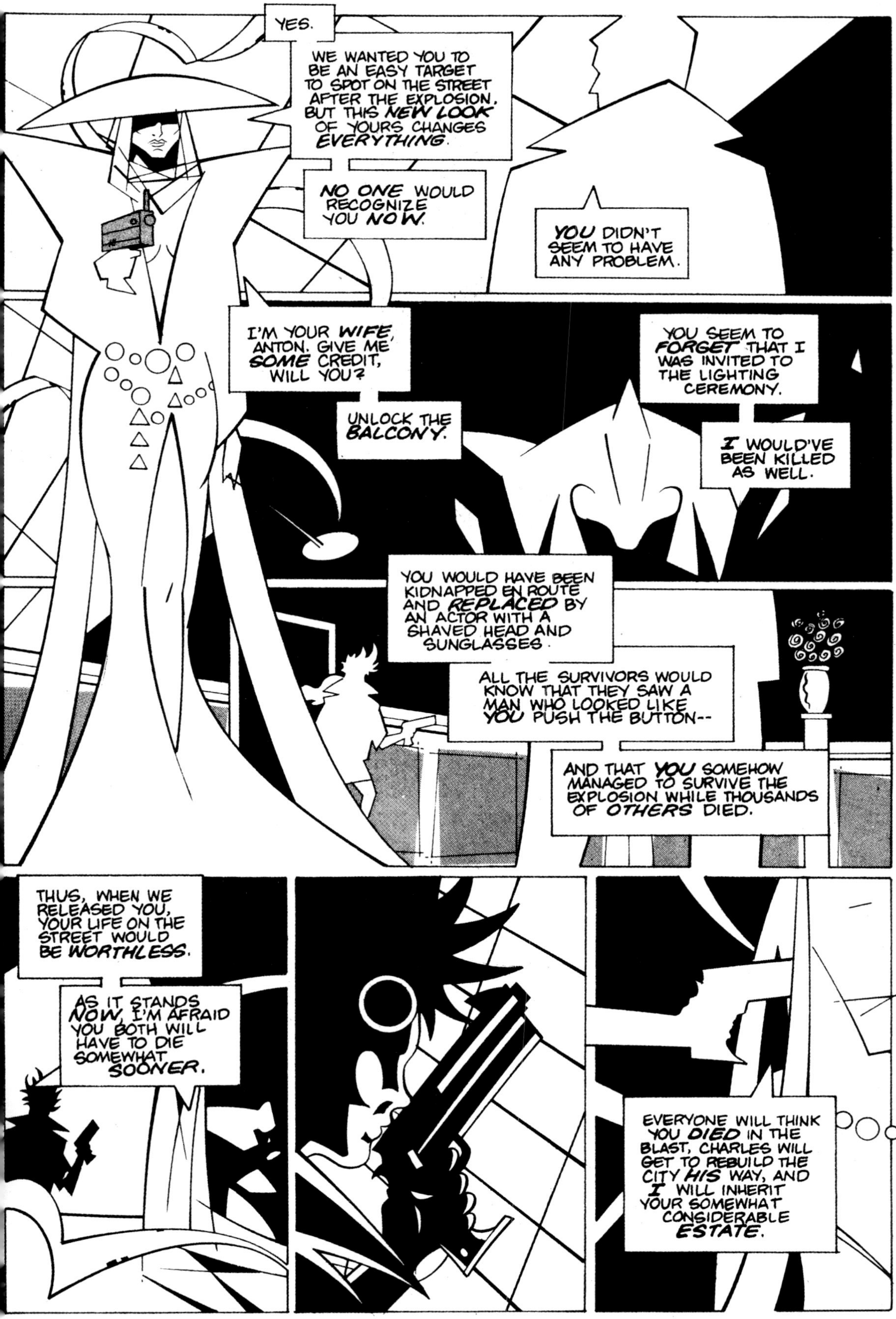

YES.
WE WANTED YOU TO BE AN EASY TARGET TO SPOT ON THE STREET AFTER THE EXPLOSION. BUT THIS NEW LOOK OF YOURS CHANGES EVERYTHING.
NO ONE WOULD RECOGNIZE YOU NOW.
YOU DIDN'T SEEM TO HAVE ANY PROBLEM.
I'M YOUR WIFE, ANTON. GIVE ME SOME CREDIT, WILL YOU?
UNLOCK THE BALCONY.
YOU SEEM TO FORGET THAT I WAS INVITED TO THE LIGHTING CEREMONY.
I WOULD'VE BEEN KILLED AS WELL.
YOU WOULD HAVE BEEN KIDNAPPED EN ROUTE AND REPLACED BY AN ACTOR WITH A SHAVED HEAD AND SUNGLASSES.
ALL THE SURVIVORS WOULD KNOW THAT THEY SAW A MAN WHO LOOKED LIKE YOU PUSH THE BUTTON--
AND THAT YOU SOMEHOW MANAGED TO SURVIVE THE EXPLOSION WHILE THOUSANDS OF OTHERS DIED.
THUS, WHEN WE RELEASED YOU, YOUR LIFE ON THE STREET WOULD BE WORTHLESS.
AS IT STANDS NOW, I'M AFRAID YOU BOTH WILL HAVE TO DIE SOMEWHAT SOONER.
EVERYONE WILL THINK YOU DIED IN THE BLAST, CHARLES WILL GET TO REBUILD THE CITY HIS WAY, AND I WILL INHERIT YOUR SOMEWHAT CONSIDERABLE ESTATE.

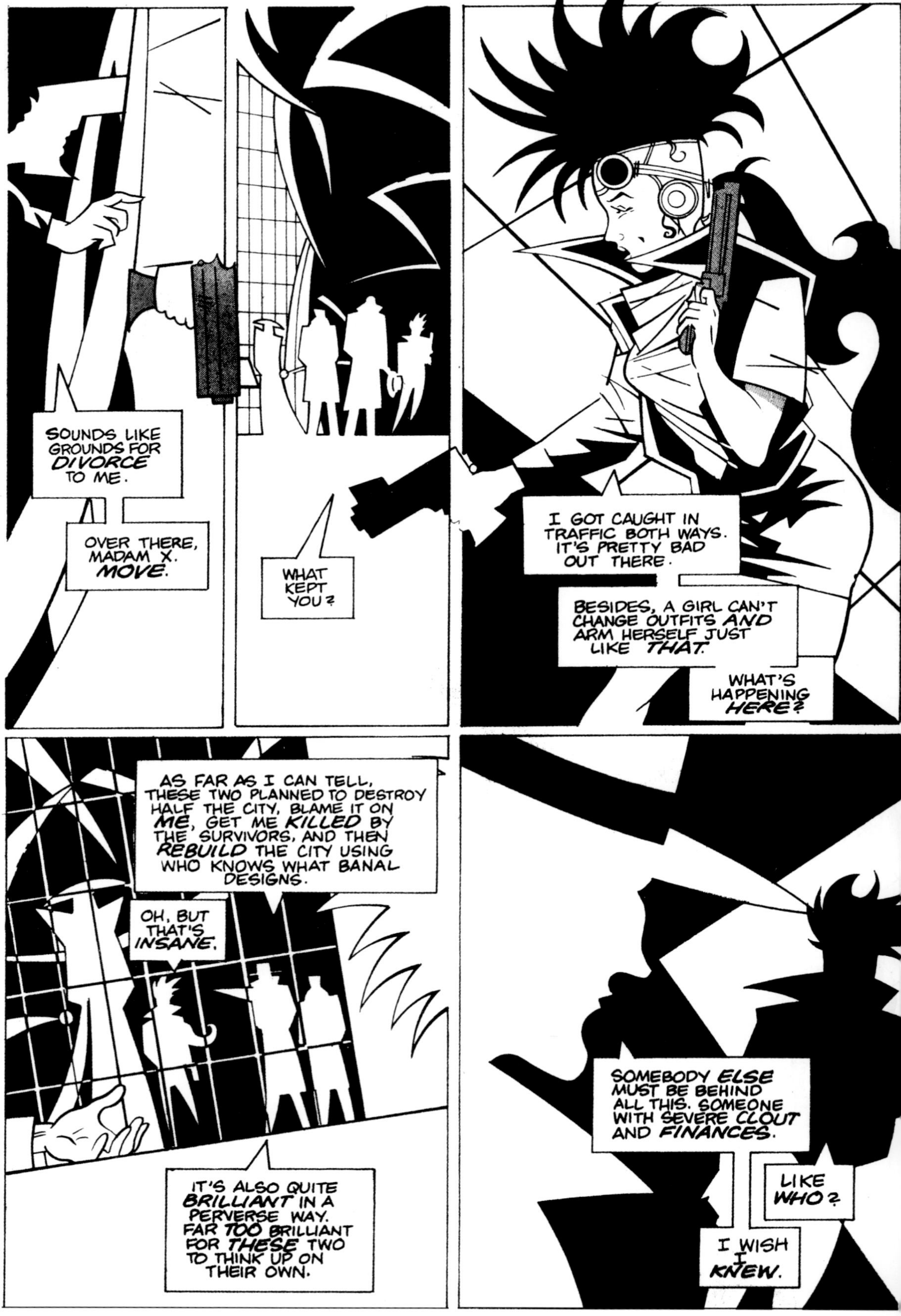

SOUNDS LIKE GROUNDS FOR DIVORCE TO ME.
OVER THERE, MADAM X. MOVE.
WHAT KEPT YOU?
I GOT CAUGHT IN TRAFFIC BOTH WAYS. IT'S PRETTY BAD OUT THERE.
BESIDES, A GIRL CAN'T CHANGE OUTFITS AND ARM HERSELF JUST LIKE THAT.
WHAT'S HAPPENING HERE?
AS FAR AS I CAN TELL, THESE TWO PLANNED TO DESTROY HALF THE CITY, BLAME IT ON ME, GET ME KILLED BY THE SURVIVORS, AND THEN REBUILD THE CITY USING WHO KNOWS WHAT BANAL DESIGNS.
OH, BUT THAT'S INSANE.
IT'S ALSO QUITE BRILLIANT IN A PERVERSE WAY. FAR TOO BRILLIANT FOR THESE TWO TO THINK UP ON THEIR OWN.
SOMEBODY ELSE MUST BE BEHIND ALL THIS. SOMEONE WITH SEVERE CLOUT AND FINANCES.
LIKE WHO?
I WISH I KNEW.

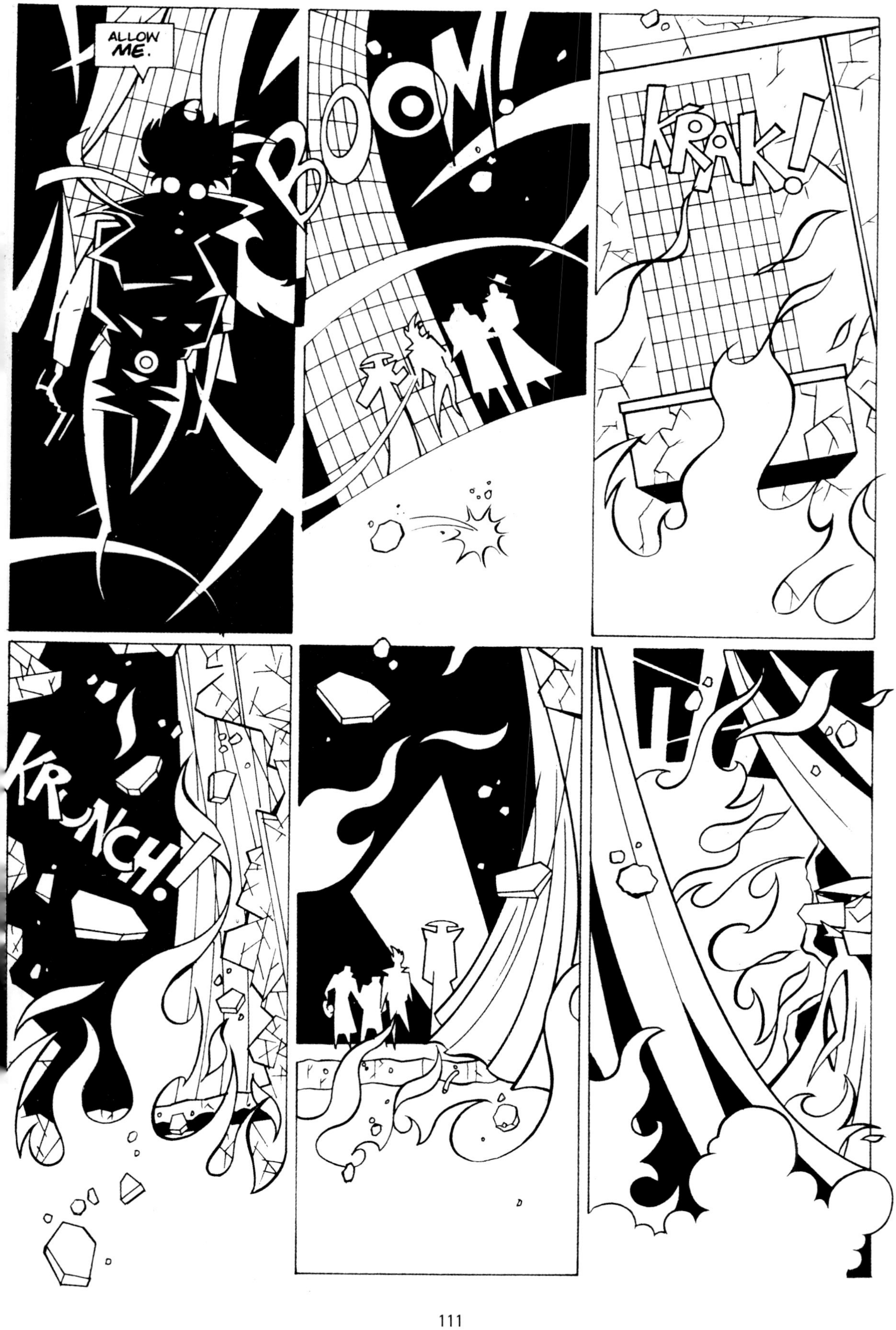
ALLOW ME.
BOOM!
KRAK!
KRUNCH!

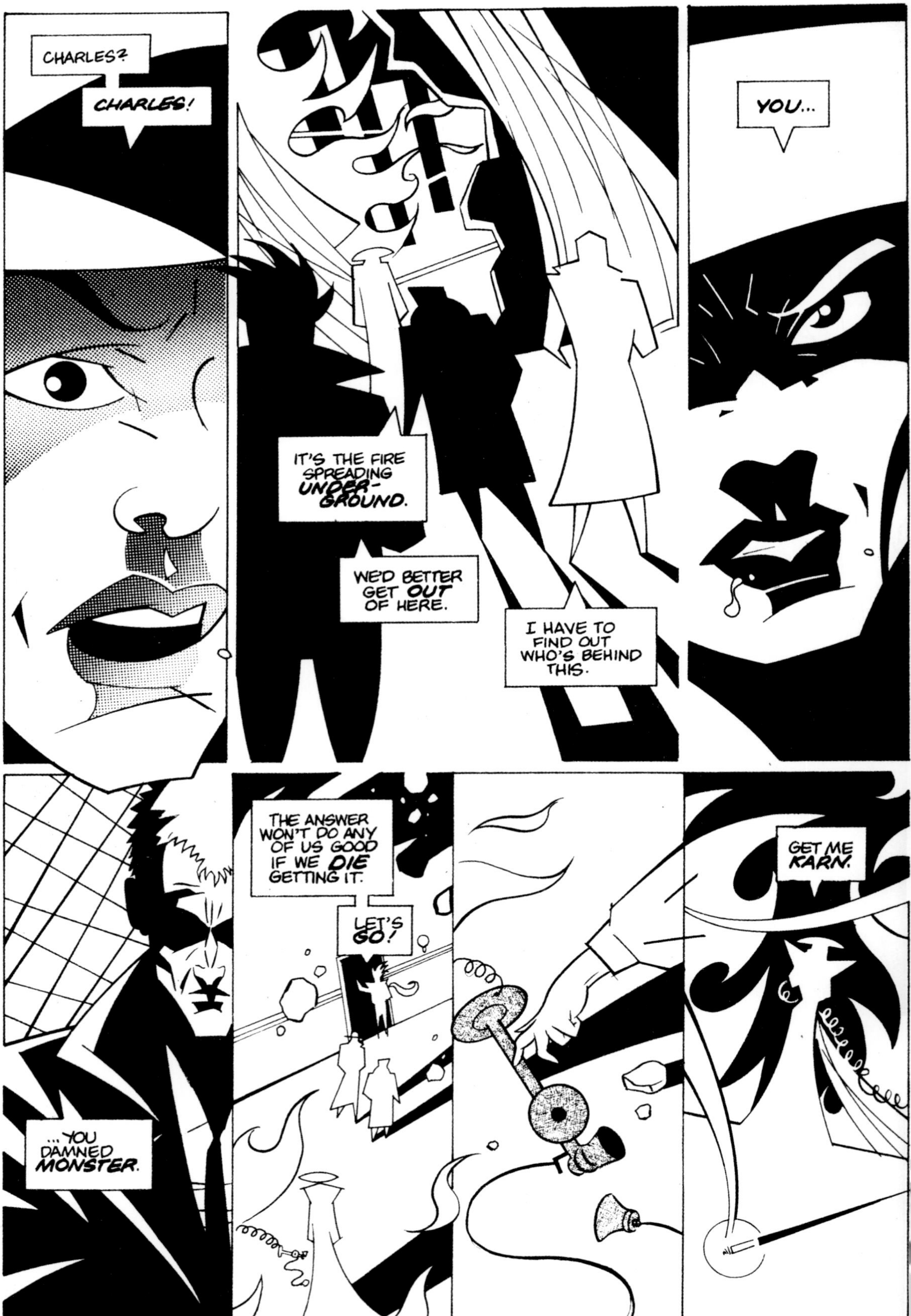
CHARLES?
CHARLES!
IT'S THE FIRE SPREADING UNDER-GROUND.
WE'D BETTER GET OUT OF HERE.
I HAVE TO FIND OUT WHO'S BEHIND THIS.
YOU...
...YOU DAMNED MONSTER.
THE ANSWER WON'T DO ANY OF US GOOD IF WE DIE GETTING IT.
LET'S GO!
GET ME KARN.

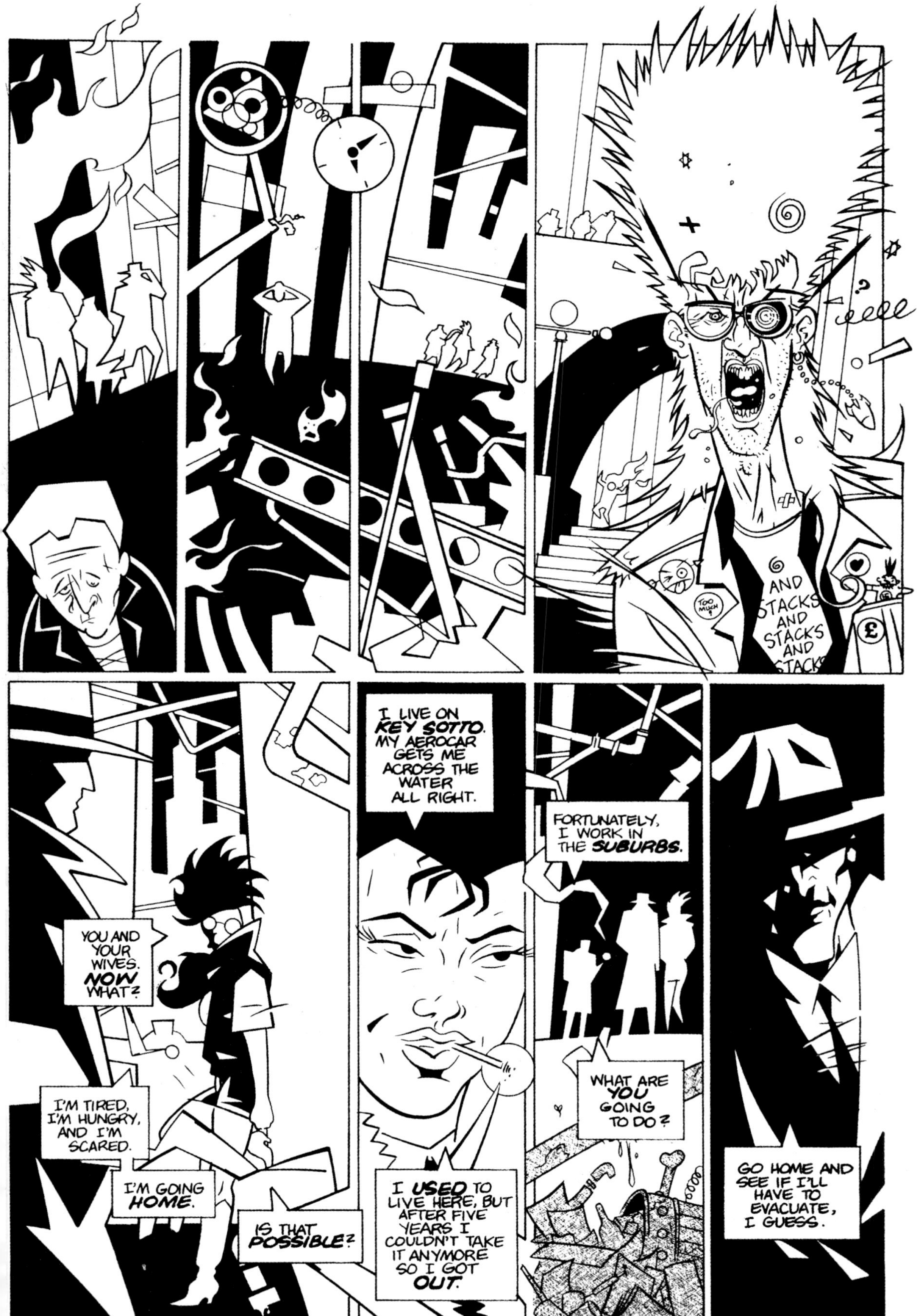

TOO MUCH!
AND STACKS AND STACKS AND STACKS
YOU AND YOUR WIVES. NOW WHAT?
I'M TIRED, I'M HUNGRY, AND I'M SCARED.
I'M GOING HOME.
IS THAT POSSIBLE?
I LIVE ON KEY SOTTO. MY AEROCAR GETS ME ACROSS THE WATER ALL RIGHT.
I USED TO LIVE HERE, BUT AFTER FIVE YEARS I COULDN'T TAKE IT ANYMORE SO I GOT OUT.
FORTUNATELY, I WORK IN THE SUBURBS.
WHAT ARE YOU GOING TO DO?
GO HOME AND SEE IF I'LL HAVE TO EVACUATE, I GUESS.

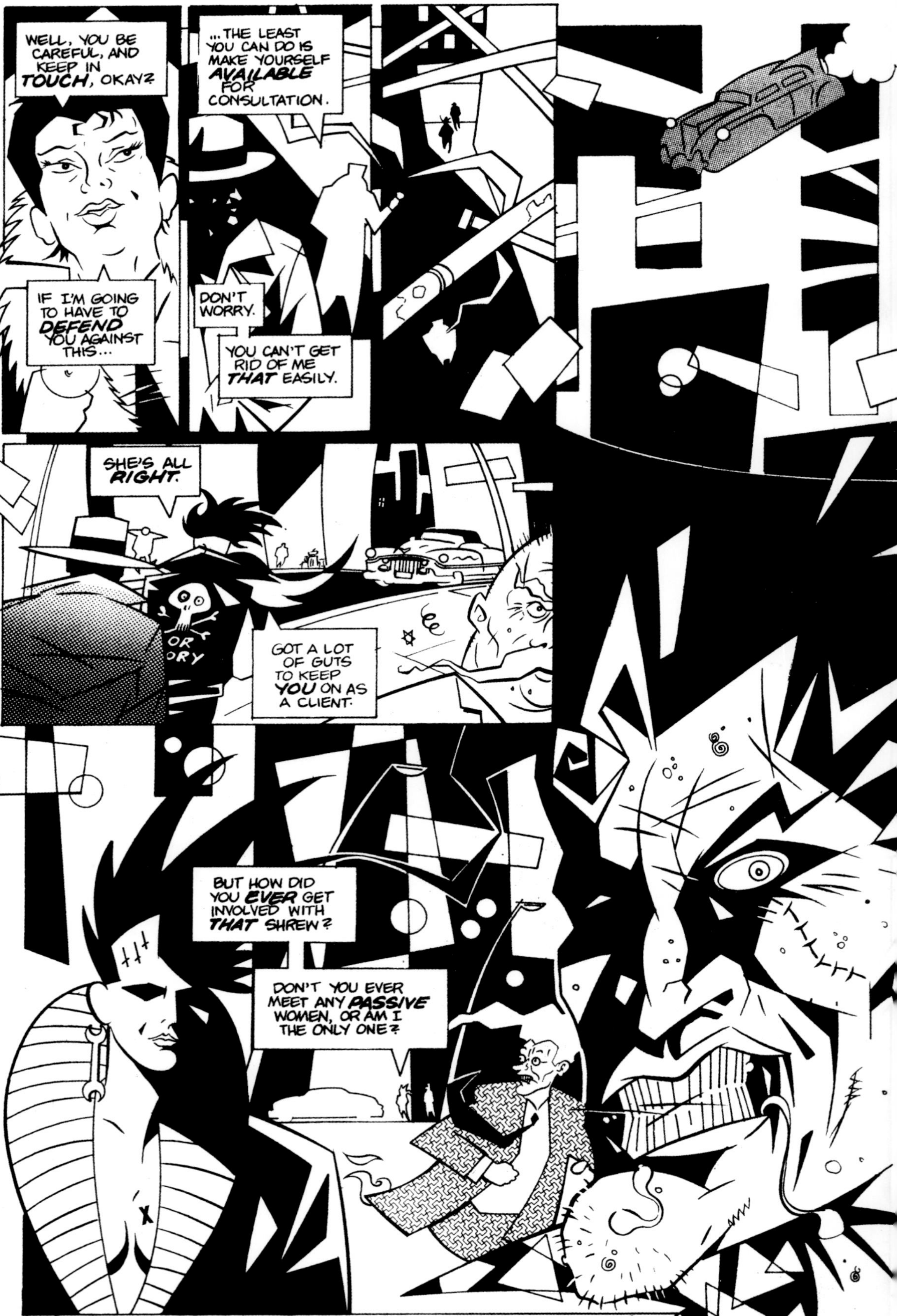
WELL, YOU BE CAREFUL, AND KEEP IN TOUCH, OKAY?
...THE LEAST YOU CAN DO IS MAKE YOURSELF AVAILABLE FOR CONSULTATION.
IF I'M GOING TO HAVE TO DEFEND YOU AGAINST THIS...
DON'T WORRY.
YOU CAN'T GET RID OF ME THAT EASILY.
SHE'S ALL RIGHT.
GOT A LOT OF GUTS TO KEEP YOU ON AS A CLIENT.
BUT HOW DID YOU EVER GET INVOLVED WITH THAT SHREW?
DON'T YOU EVER MEET ANY PASSIVE WOMEN, OR AM I THE ONLY ONE?

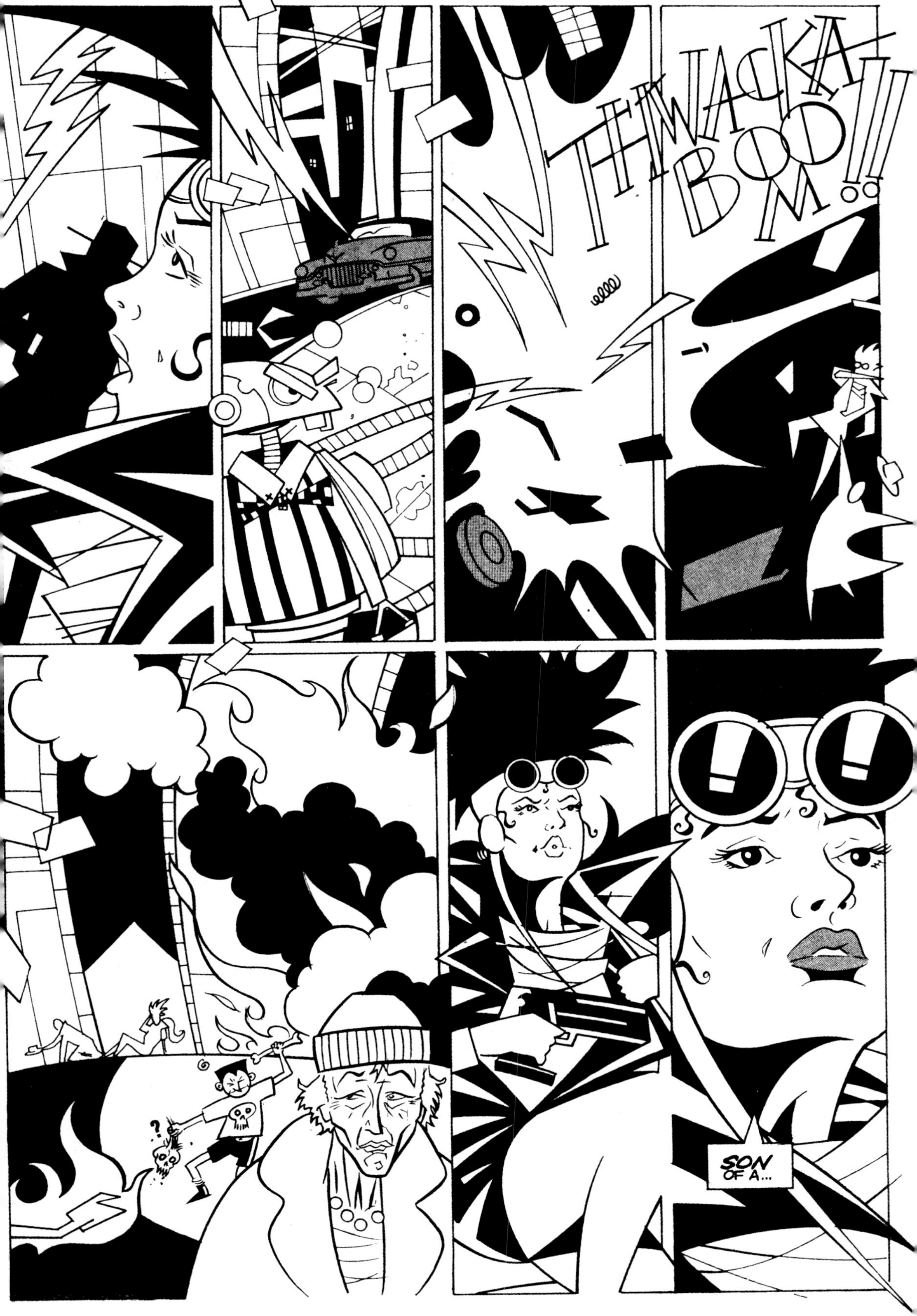
THWACKA-BOOM!!!
SON OF A...

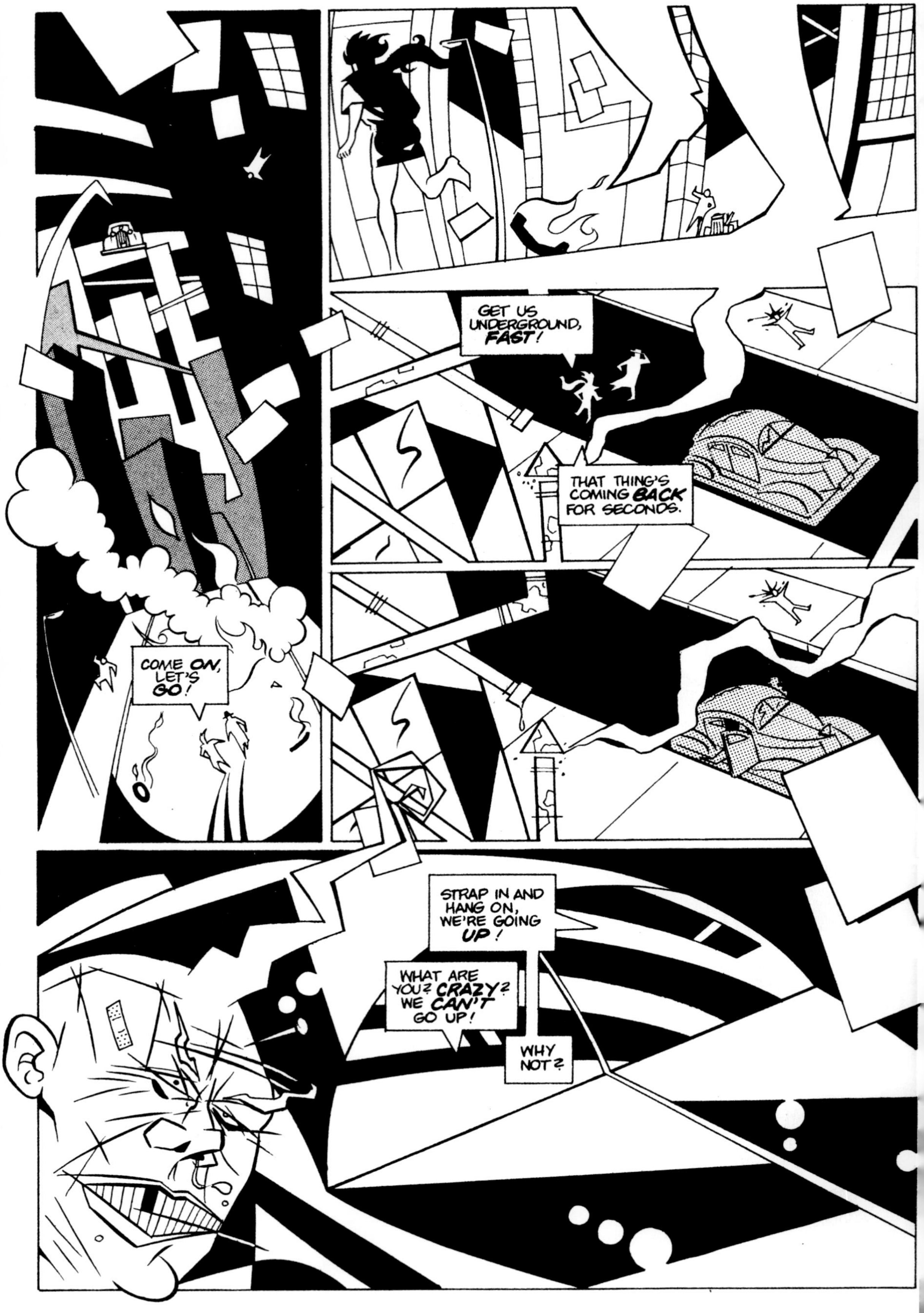
GET US UNDERGROUND, FAST!
THAT THING'S COMING BACK FOR SECONDS.
COME ON, LET'S GO!
STRAP IN AND HANG ON, WE'RE GOING UP!
WHAT ARE YOU? CRAZY? WE CAN'T GO UP!
WHY NOT?

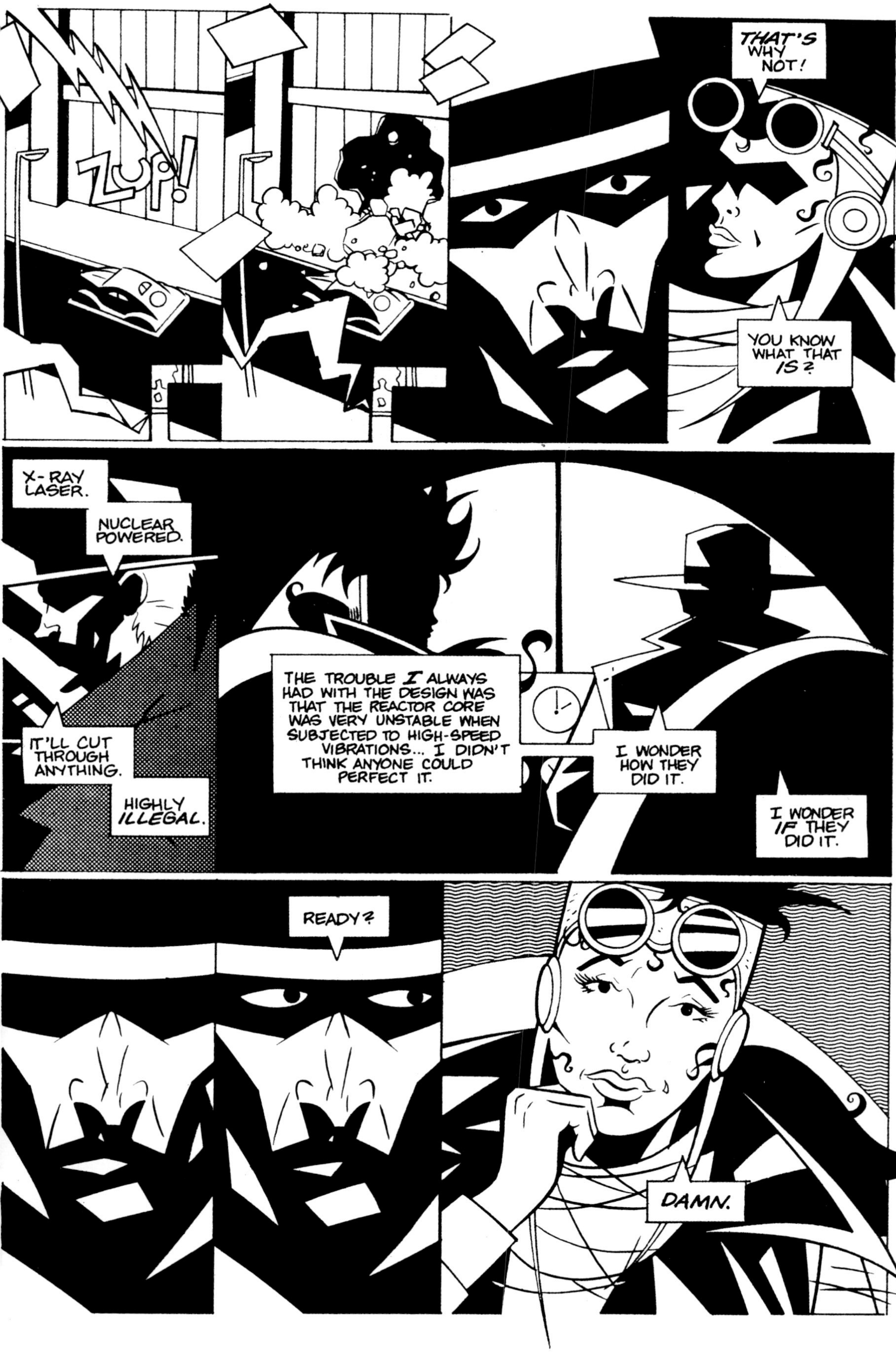
ZUP!
THAT'S WHY NOT!
YOU KNOW WHAT THAT IS?
X-RAY LASER.
NUCLEAR POWERED.
IT'LL CUT THROUGH ANYTHING.
HIGHLY ILLEGAL.
THE TROUBLE I ALWAYS HAD WITH THE DESIGN WAS THAT THE REACTOR CORE WAS VERY UNSTABLE WHEN SUBJECTED TO HIGH-SPEED VIBRATIONS... I DIDN'T THINK ANYONE COULD PERFECT IT.
I WONDER HOW THEY DID IT.
I WONDER IF THEY DID IT.
READY?
DAMN.

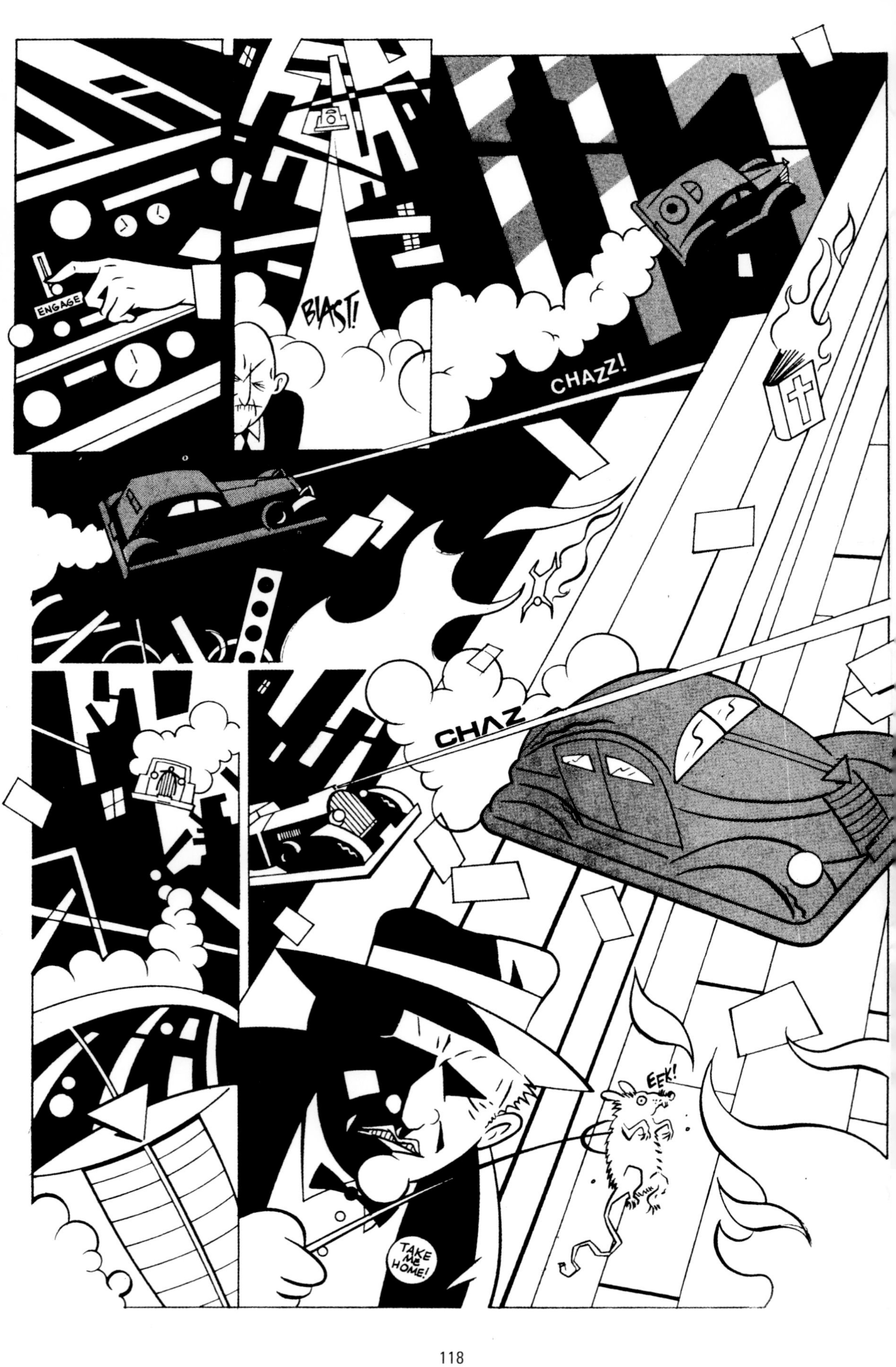
ENGAGE
BLAST!
CHAZZ!
CHAZ
EEK!
TAKE ME HOME!

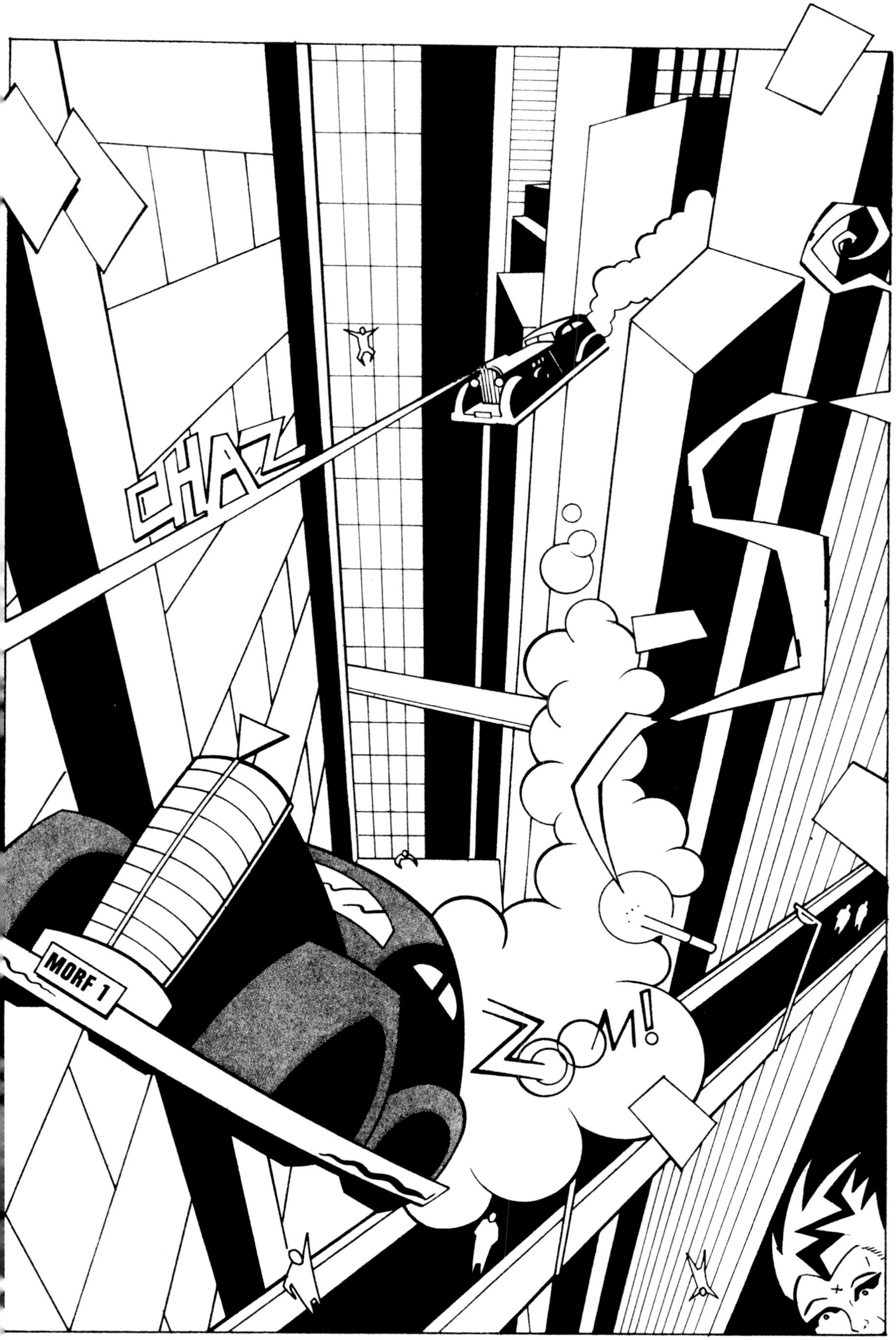
CHAZ
MORF 1
ZOOM!

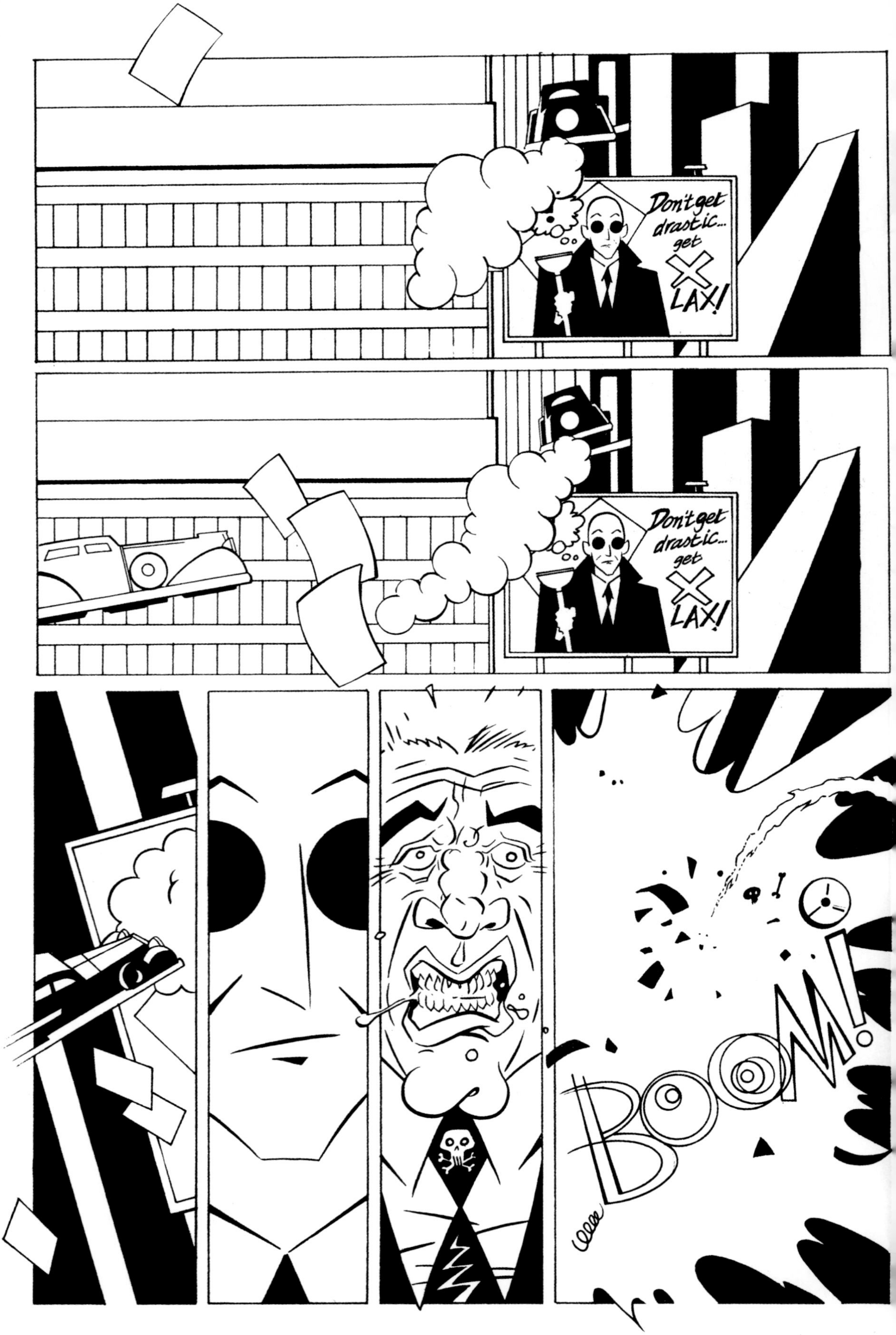
Don't get drastic... get X LAX!
Don't get drastic... get X LAX!
BOOOM!

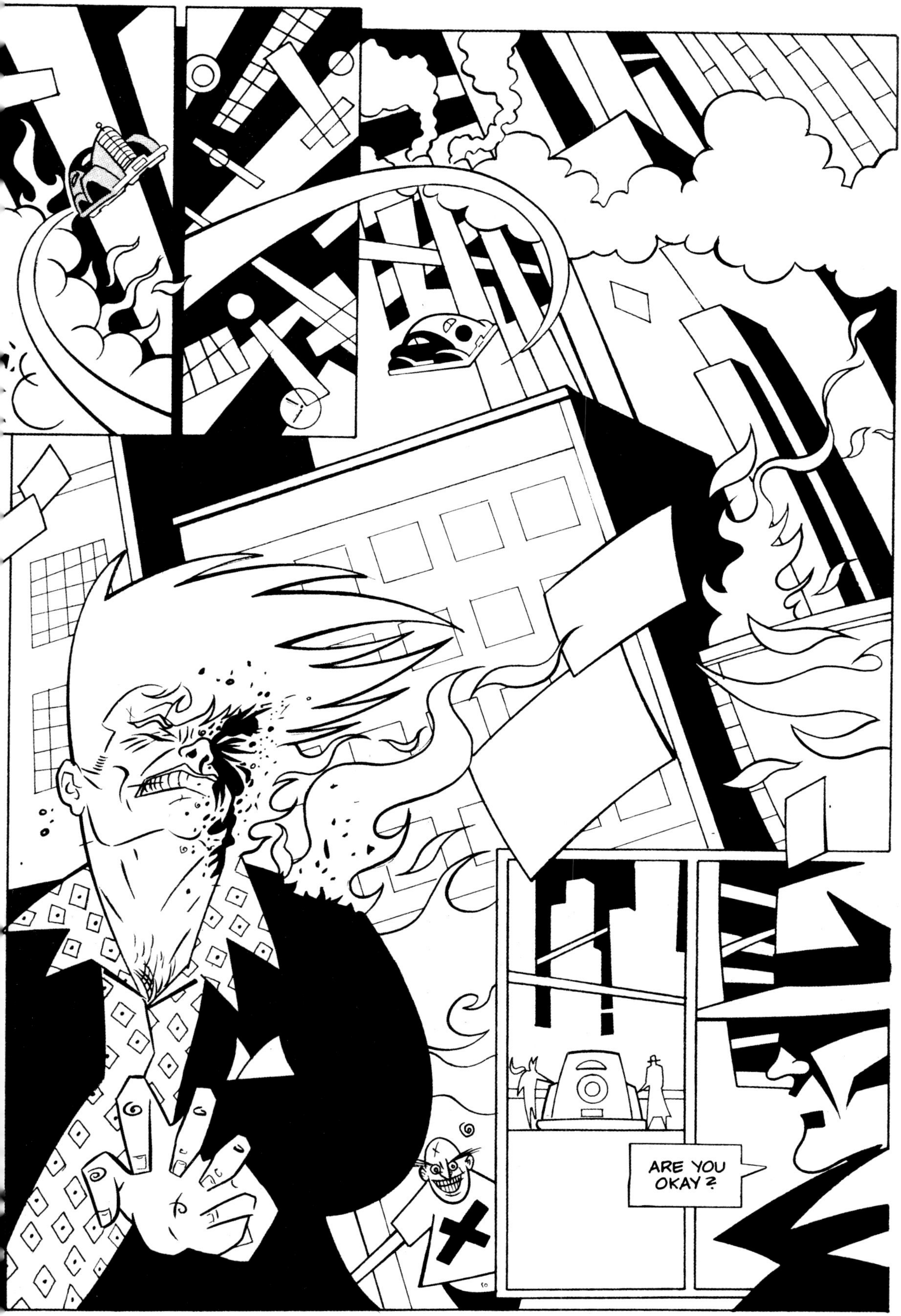
ARE YOU OKAY?

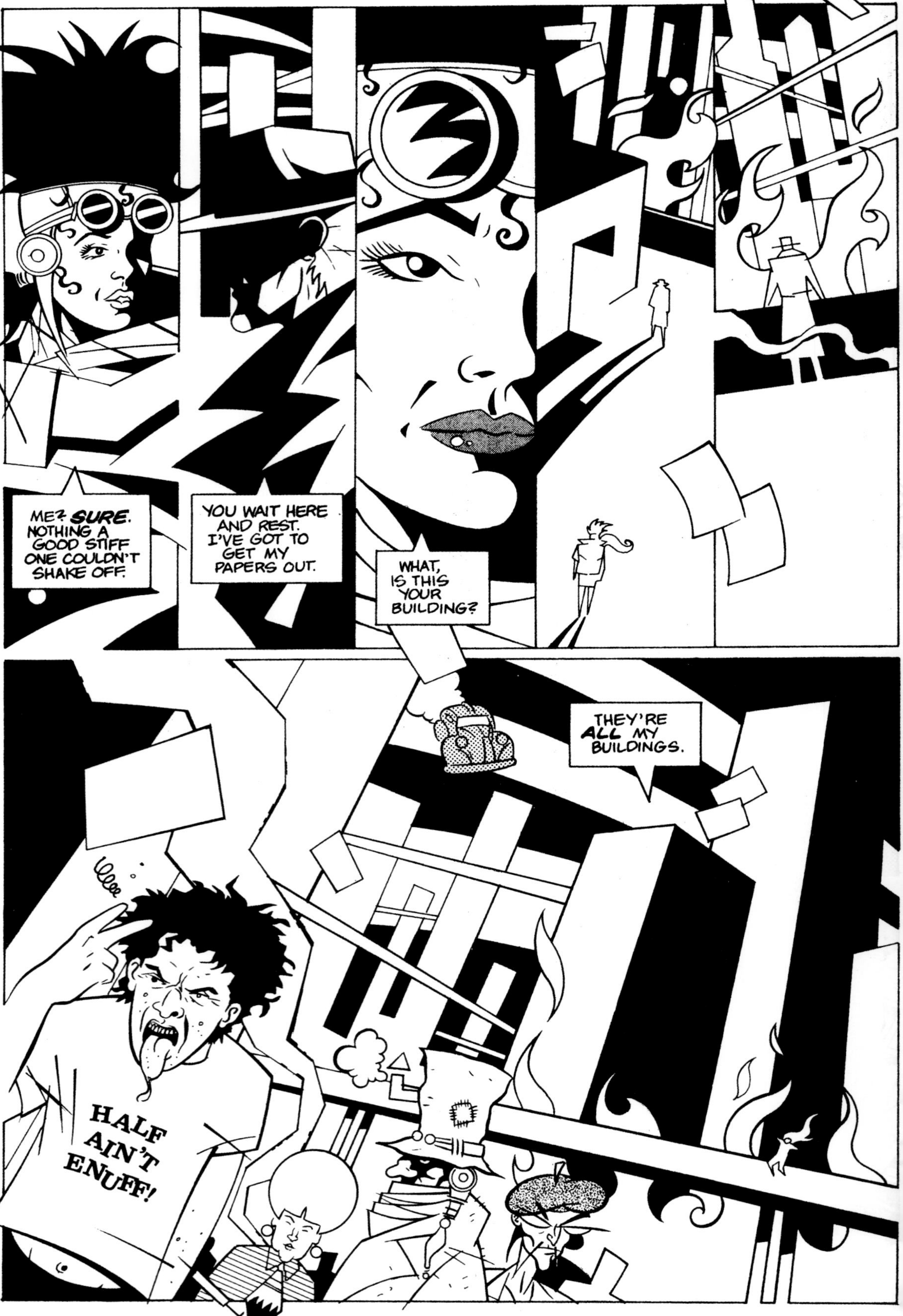
ME? SURE. NOTHING A GOOD STIFF ONE COULDN'T SHAKE OFF.
YOU WAIT HERE AND REST. I'VE GOT TO GET MY PAPERS OUT.
WHAT, IS THIS YOUR BUILDING?
THEY'RE ALL MY BUILDINGS.
HALF AIN'T ENUFF!

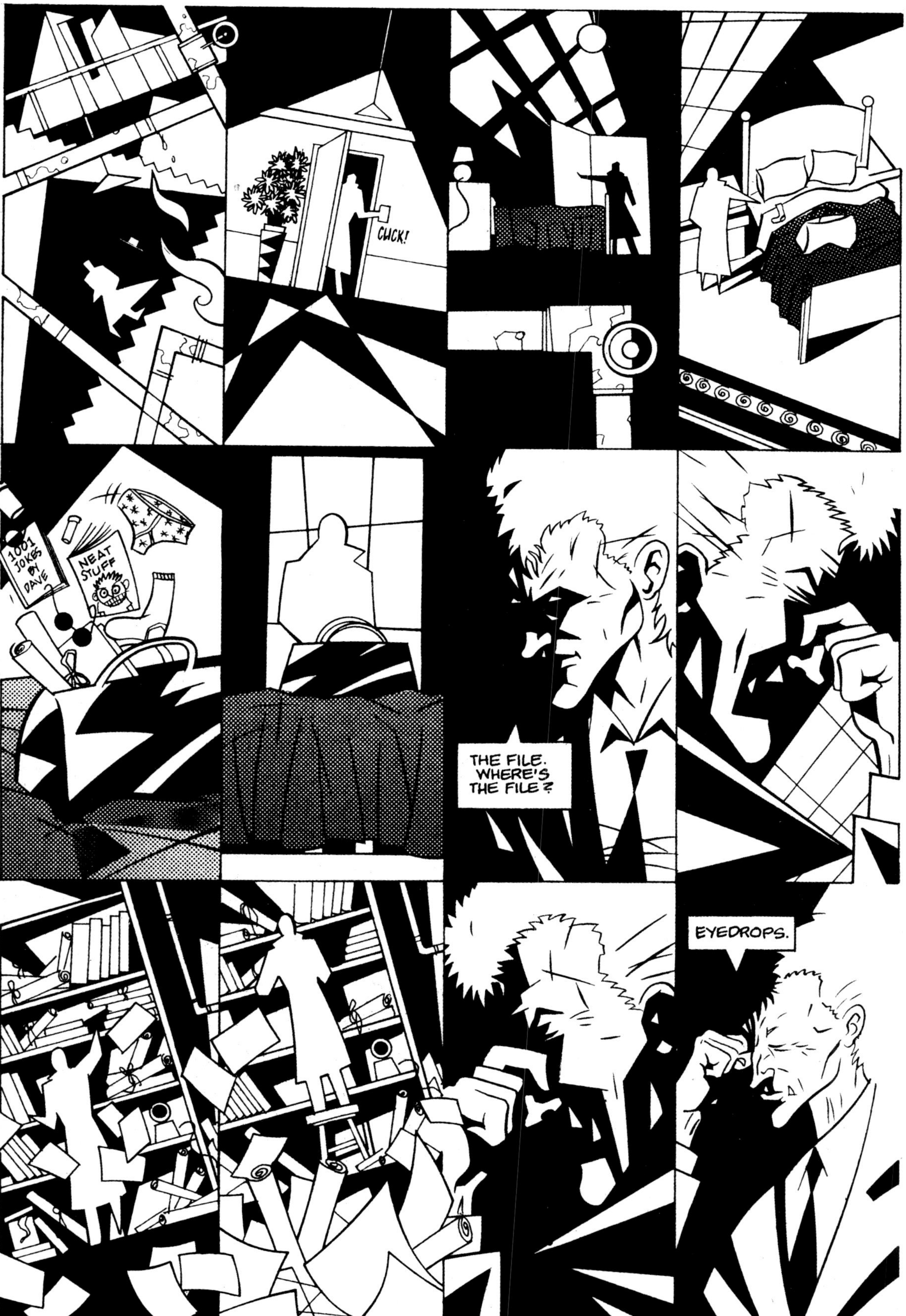
CLICK!
1001 JOKES BY DAVE
NEAT STUFF
THE FILE. WHERE'S THE FILE?
EYEDROPS.

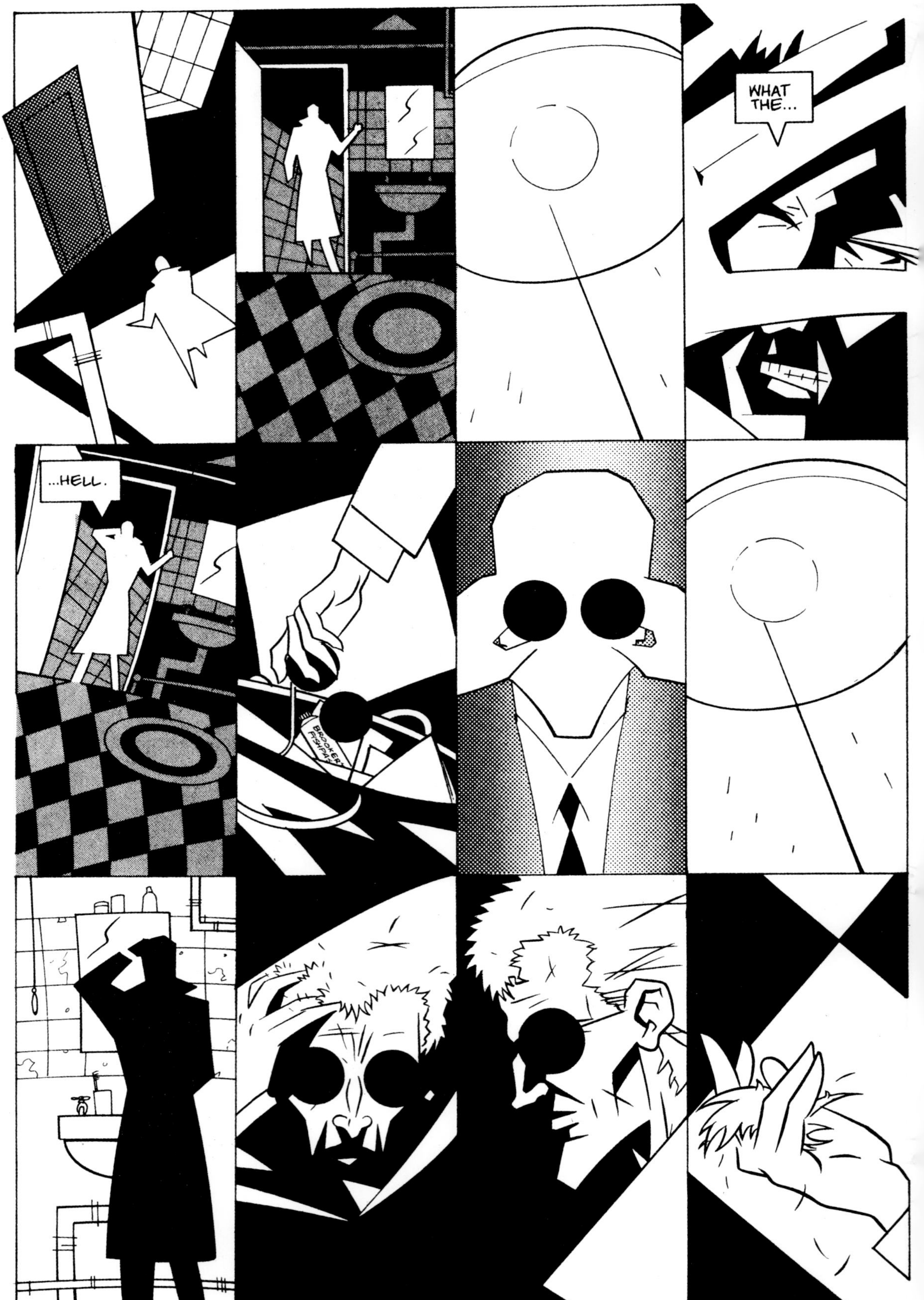
WHAT THE...
...HELL.
BROOKER'S FISHPASTE

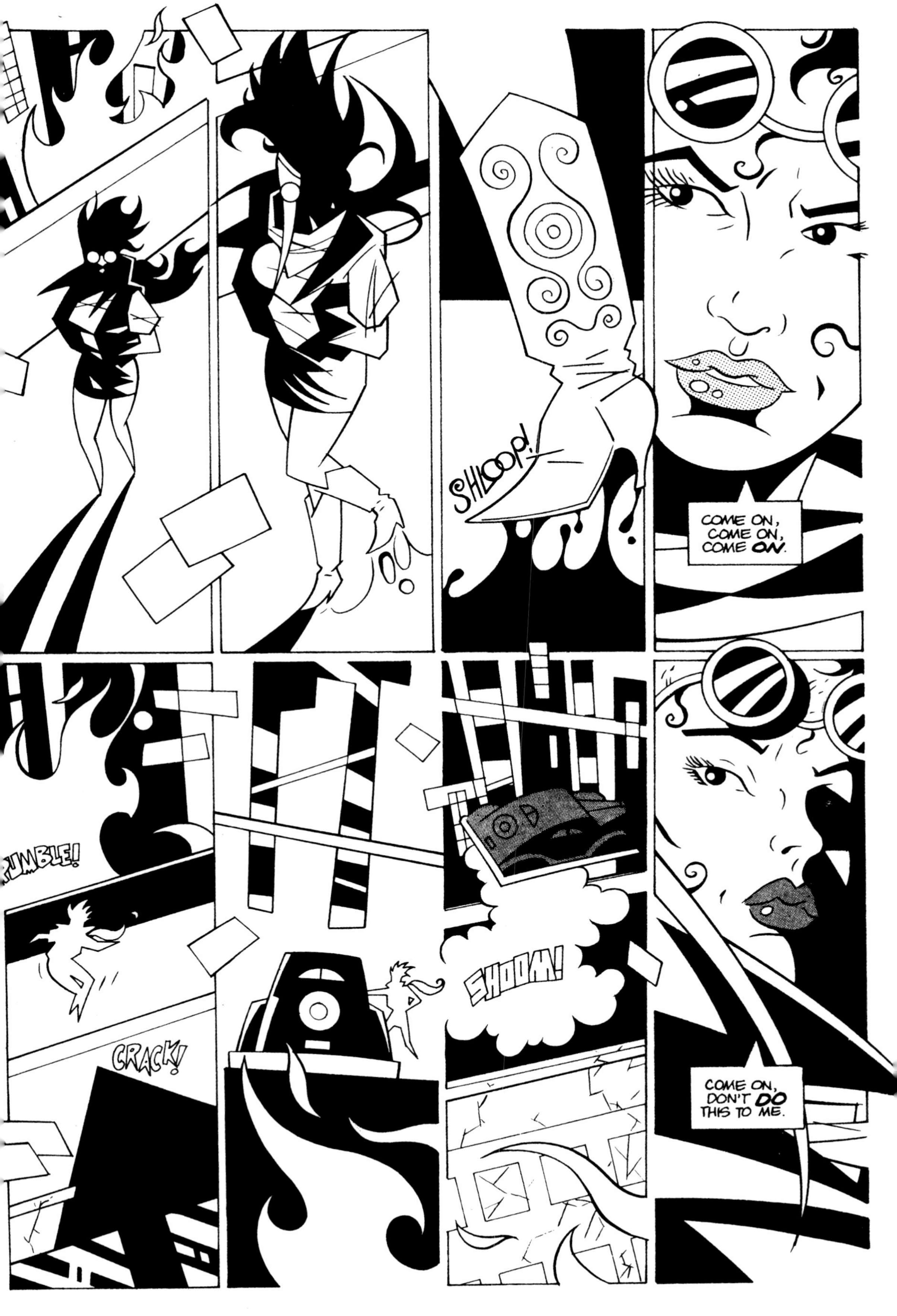
SHLOOP!
COME ON, COME ON, COME ON.
RUMBLE!
CRACK!
SHOOM!
COME ON, DON'T DO THIS TO ME.

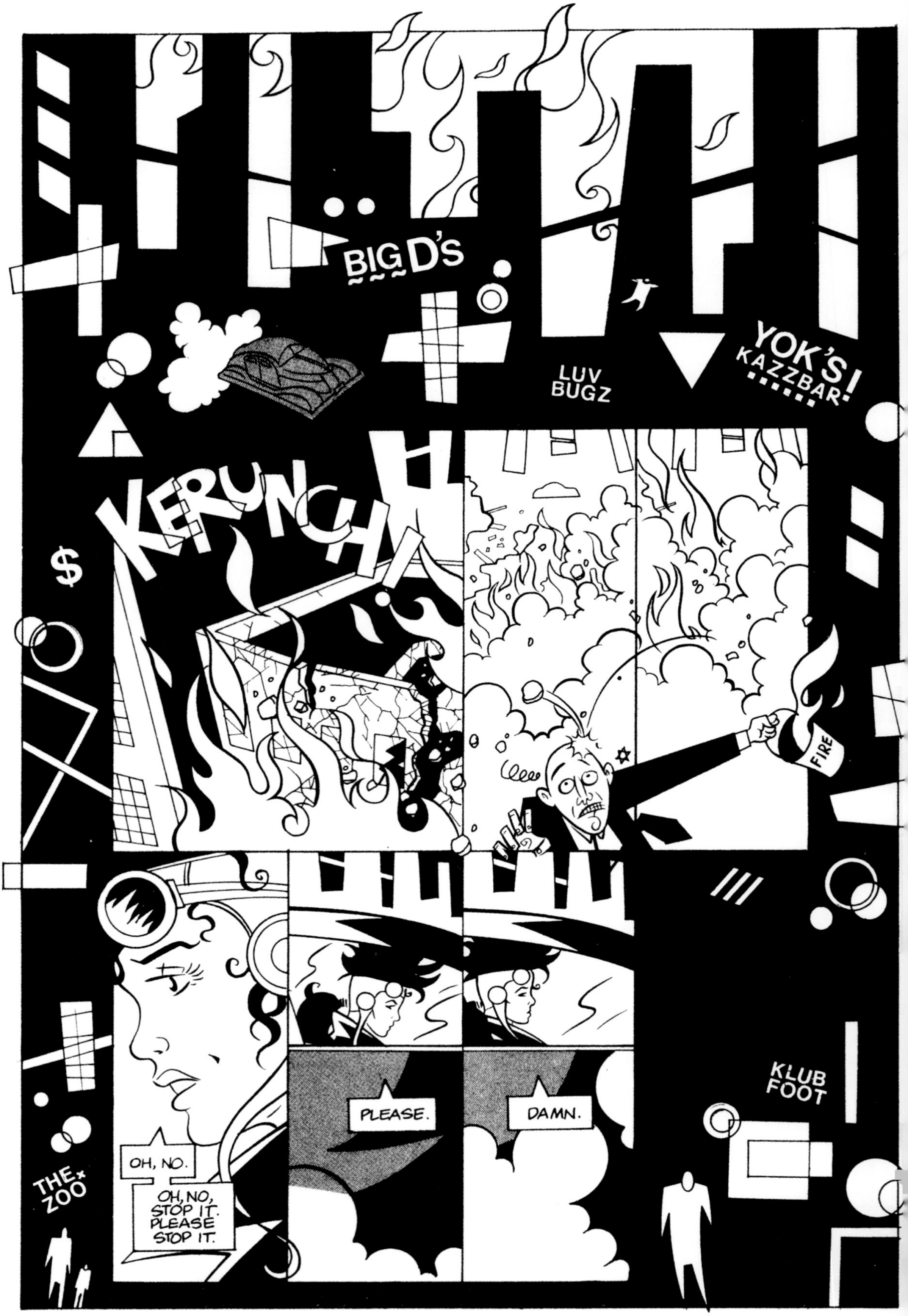
BIG D's
LUV BUGZ
YOK'S! KAZZBAR
KERUNCH!
$
FIRE
OH, NO.
OH, NO, STOP IT. PLEASE STOP IT.
PLEASE.
DAMN.
KLUB FOOT
THE ZOO

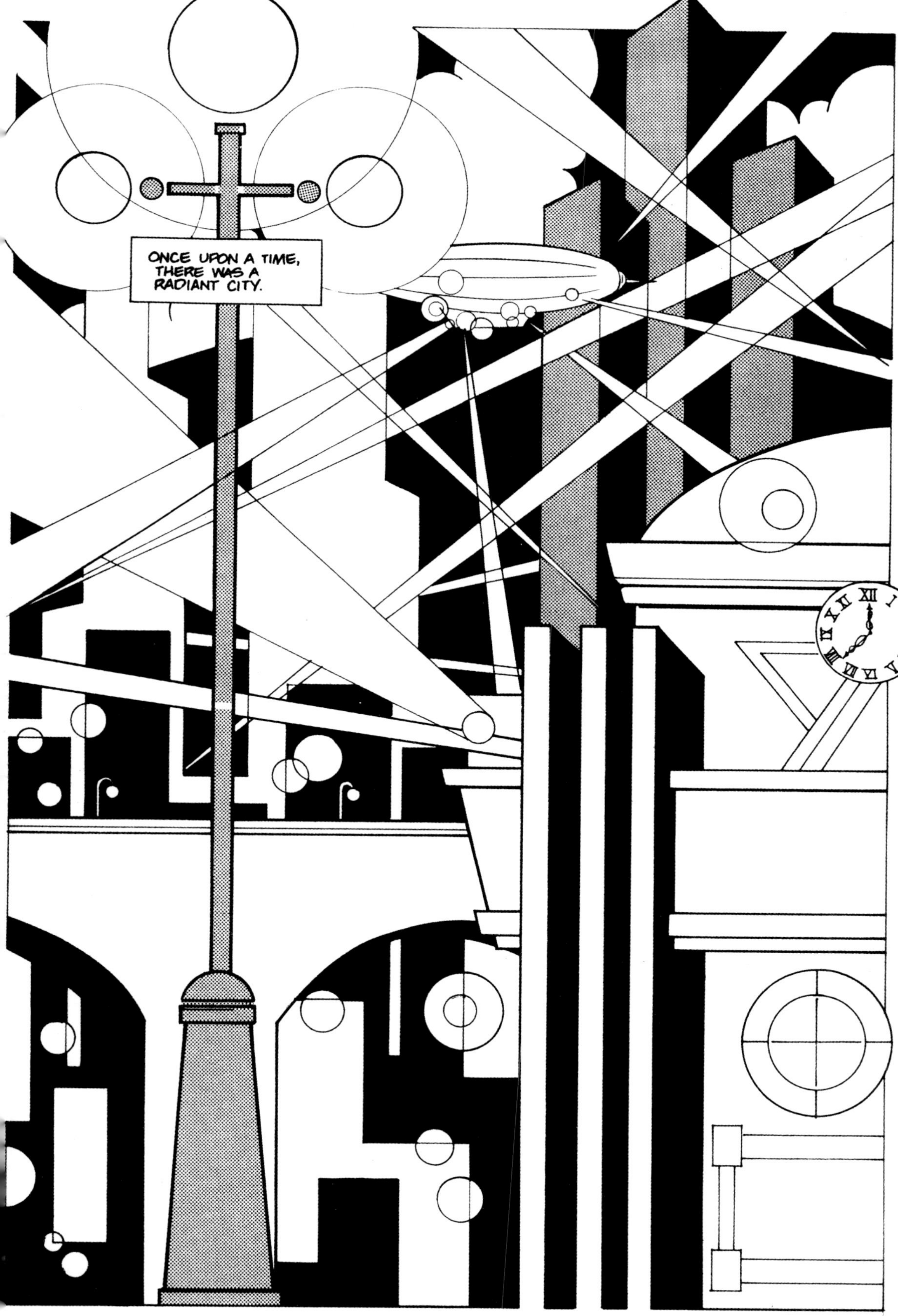
ONCE UPON A TIME, THERE WAS A RADIANT CITY.

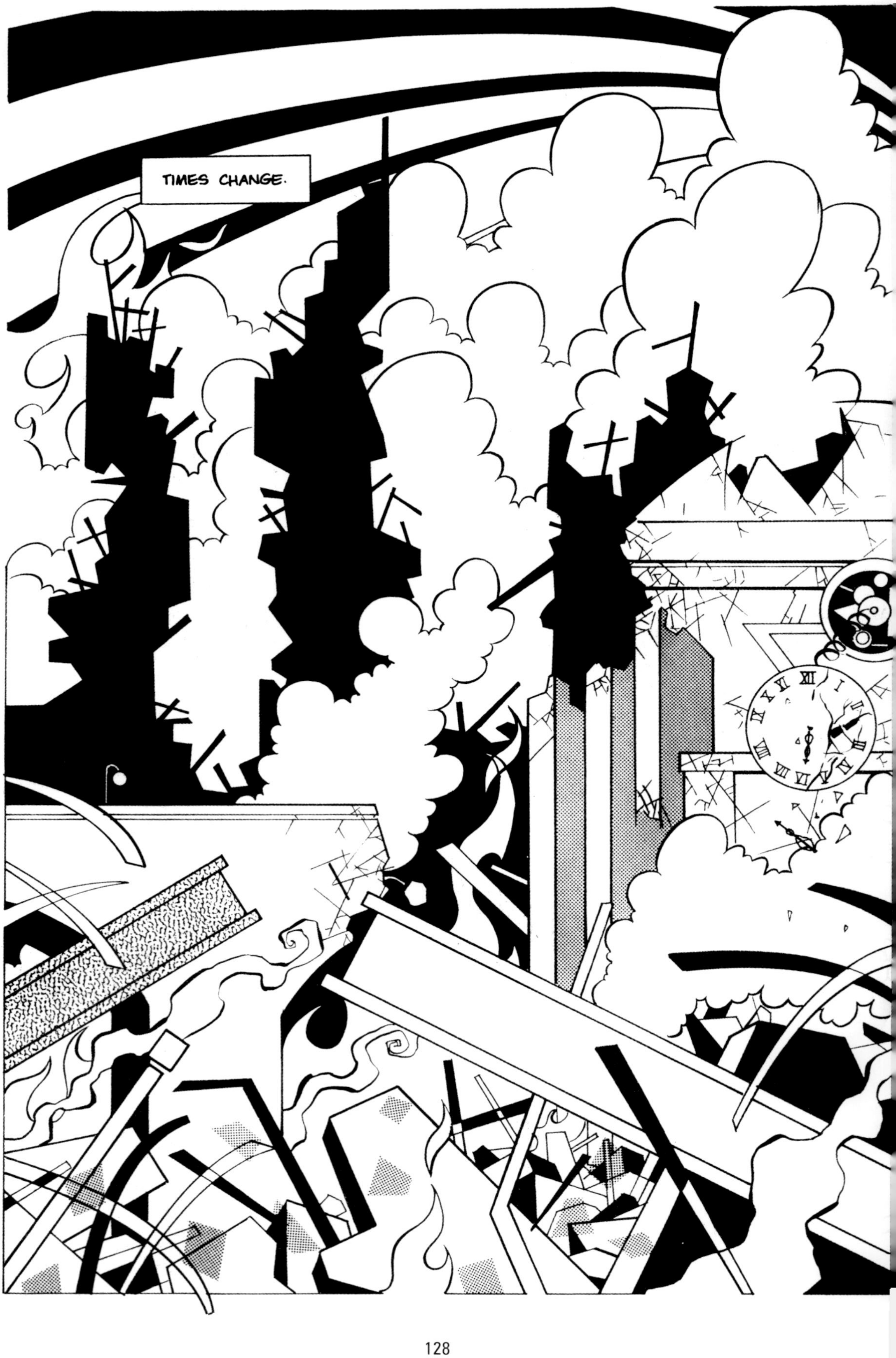
TIMES CHANGE.

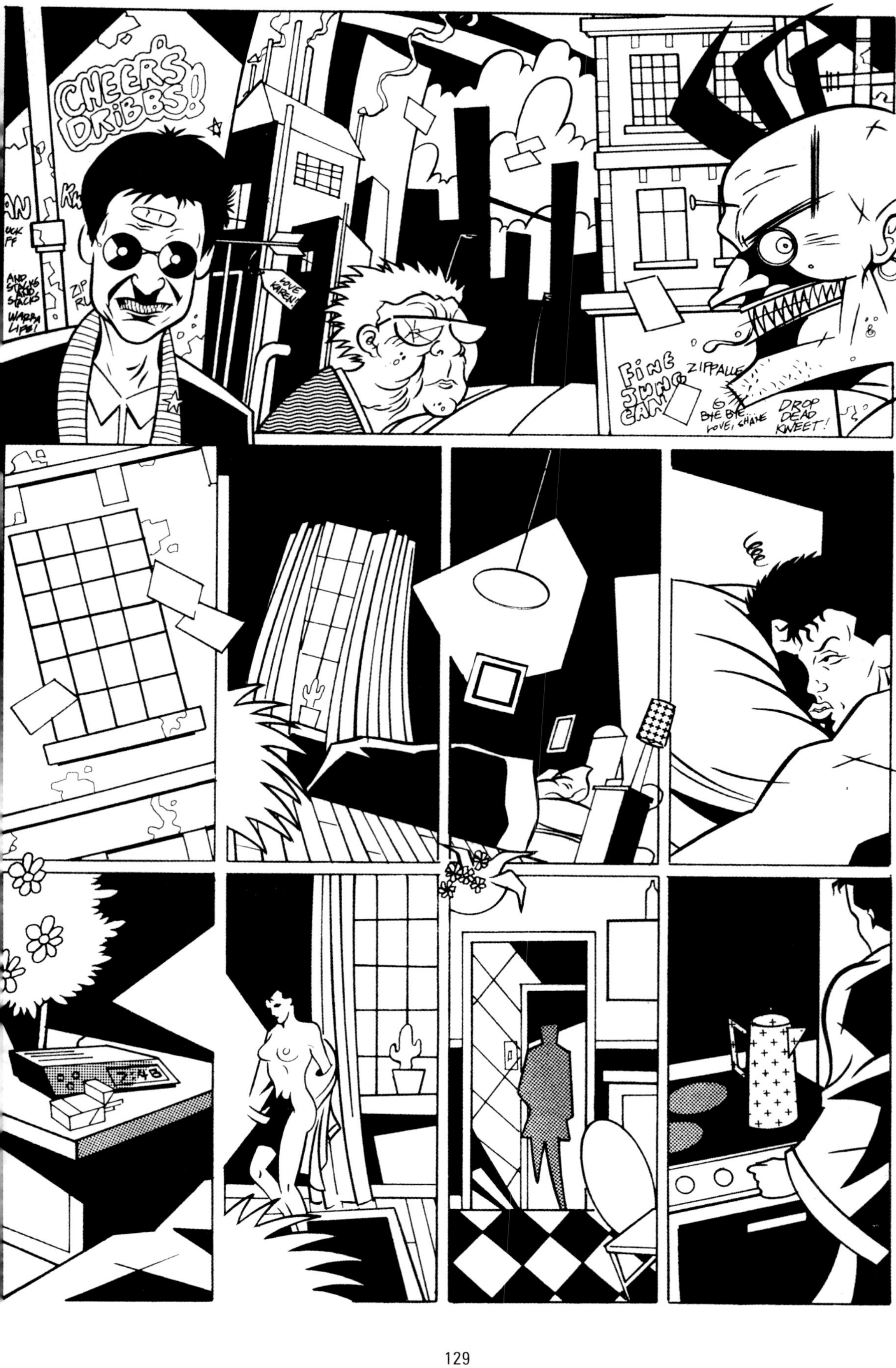
CHEERS DRIBBS!
AND STACKS AND STACKS
WARRA LIFE!
LOVE KAREN!
FINE JUNG
BYE BYE
LOVE, SHANE
DROP DEAD KWEET!
7:48

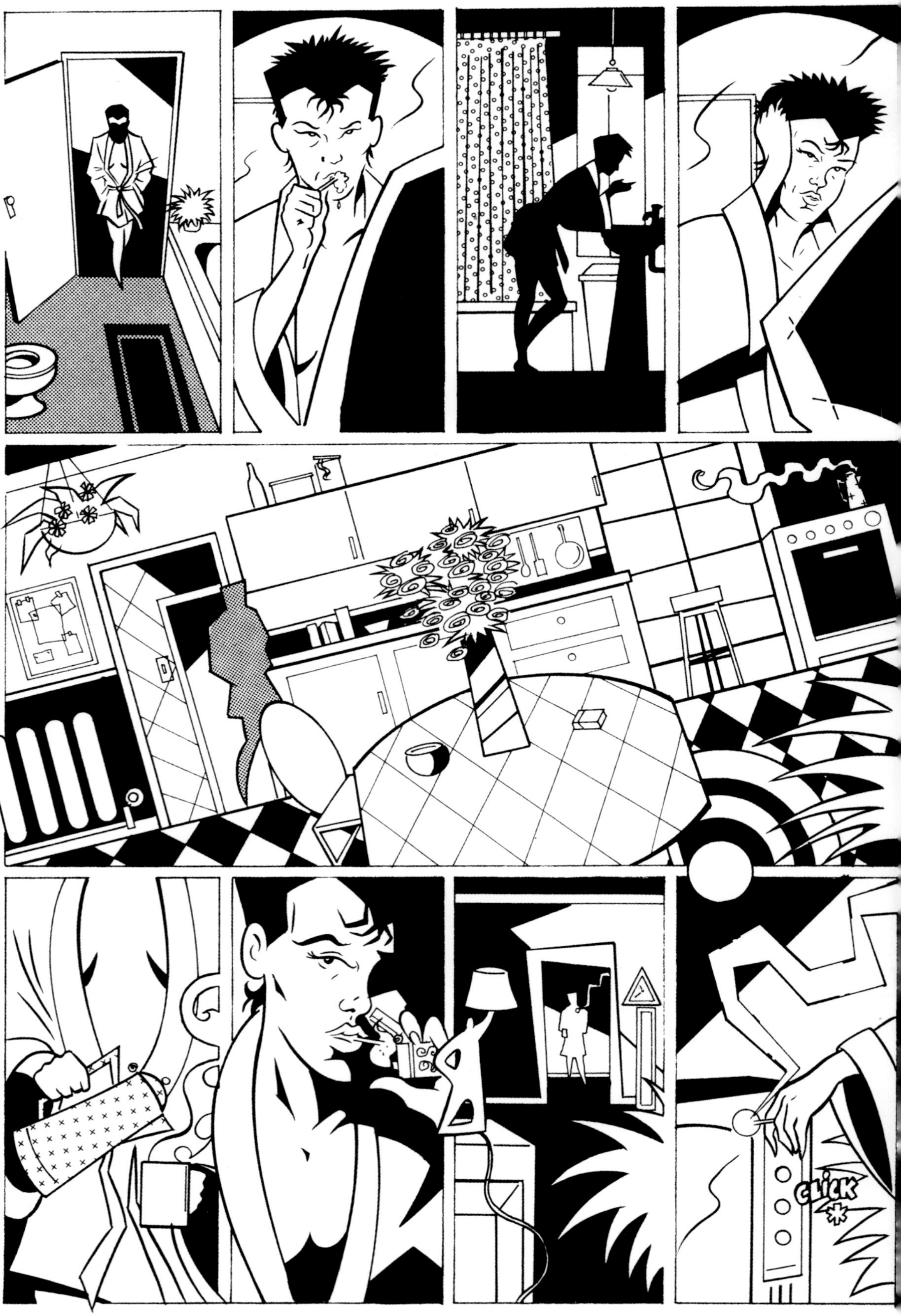
CLICK

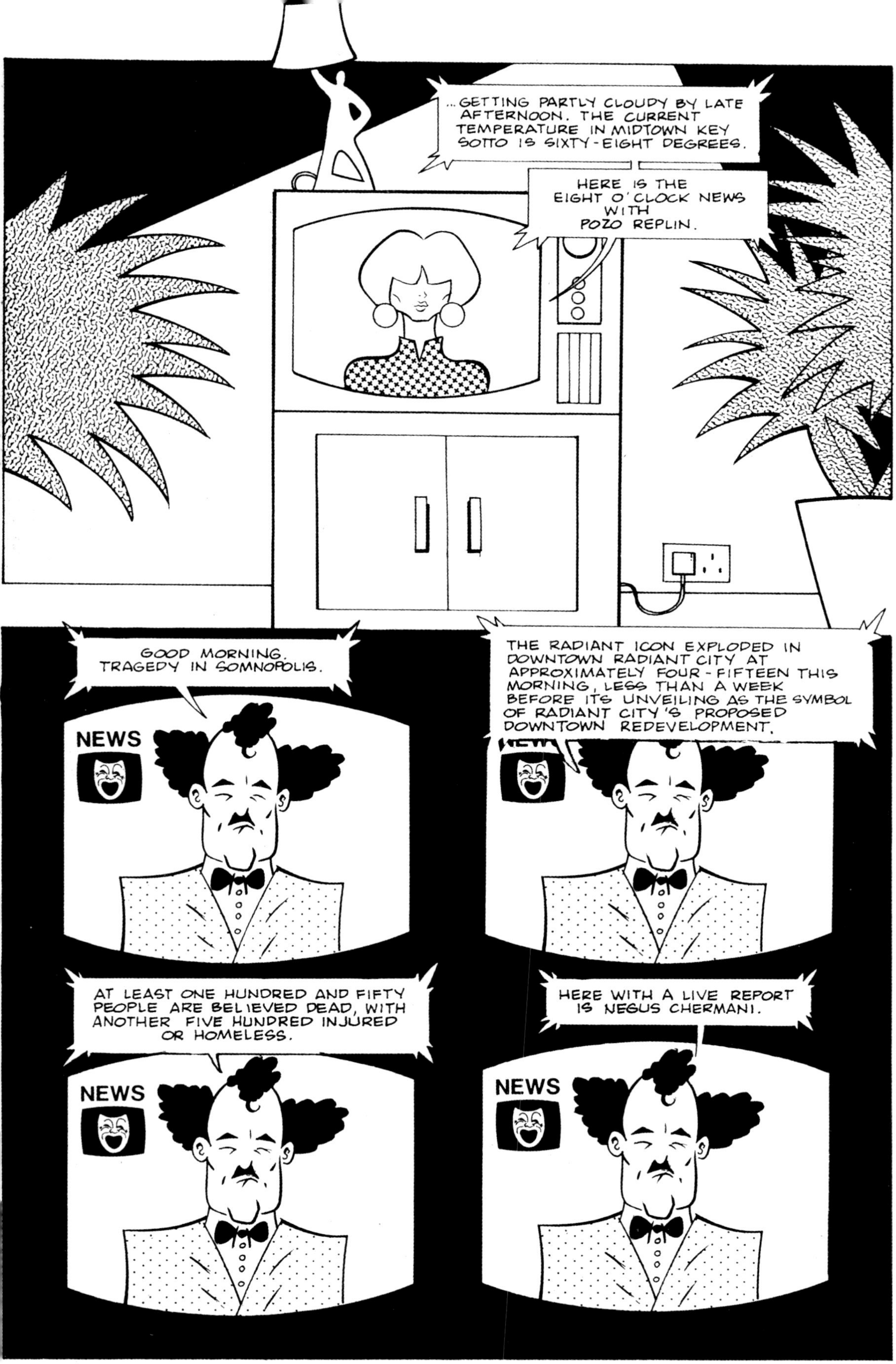

...GETTING PARTLY CLOUDY BY LATE AFTERNOON. THE CURRENT TEMPERATURE IN MIDTOWN KEY SOTTO IS SIXTY-EIGHT DEGREES.
HERE IS THE EIGHT O'CLOCK NEWS WITH POZO REPLIN.
GOOD MORNING. TRAGEDY IN SOMNOPOLIS.
NEWS
THE RADIANT ICON EXPLODED IN DOWNTOWN RADIANT CITY AT APPROXIMATELY FOUR-FIFTEEN THIS MORNING, LESS THAN A WEEK BEFORE ITS UNVEILING AS THE SYMBOL OF RADIANT CITY'S PROPOSED DOWNTOWN REDEVELOPMENT.
AT LEAST ONE HUNDRED AND FIFTY PEOPLE ARE BELIEVED DEAD, WITH ANOTHER FIVE HUNDRED INJURED OR HOMELESS.
NEWS
HERE WITH A LIVE REPORT IS NEGUS CHERMANI.
NEWS

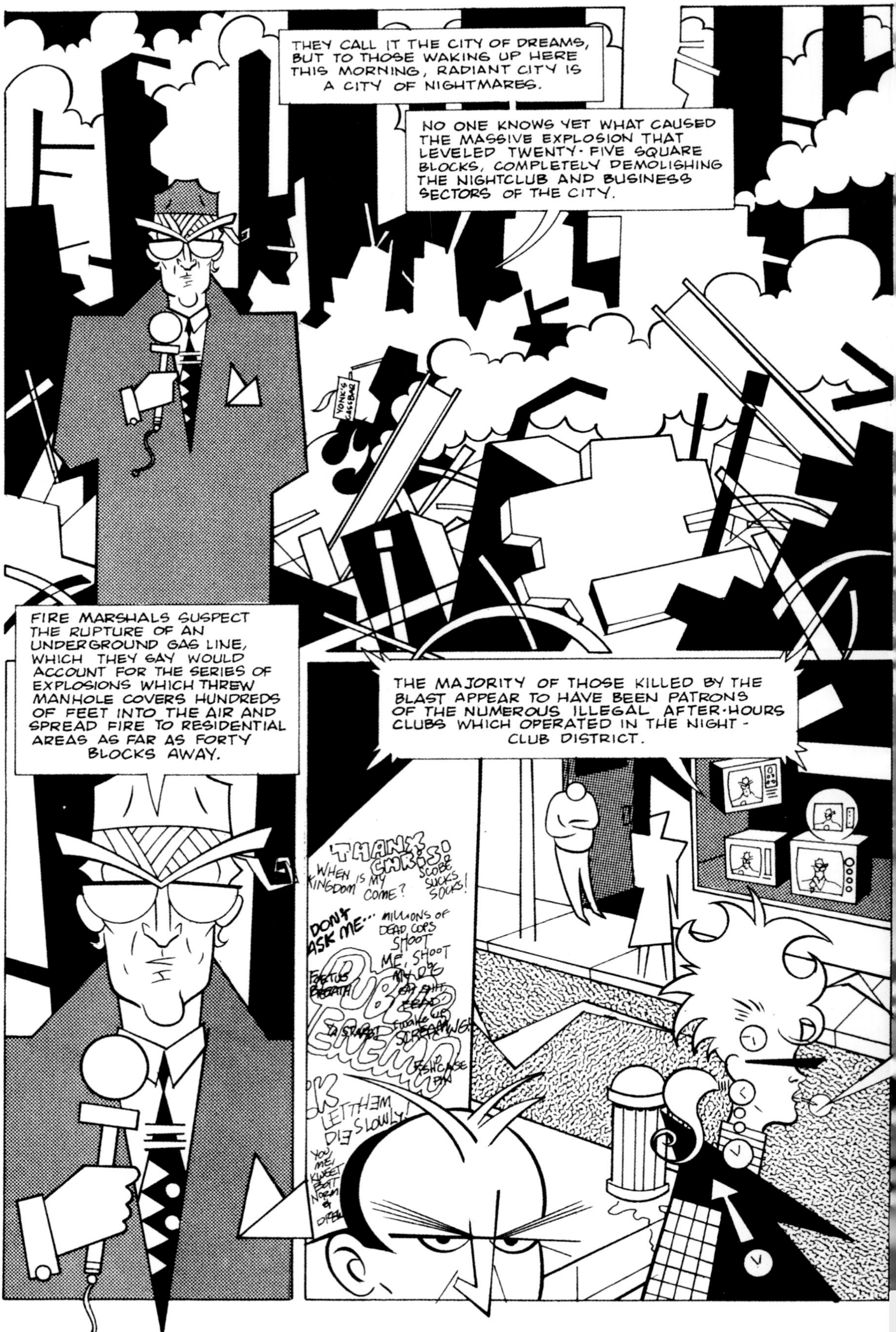
THEY CALL IT THE CITY OF DREAMS, BUT TO THOSE WAKING UP HERE THIS MORNING, RADIANT CITY IS A CITY OF NIGHTMARES.
NO ONE KNOWS YET WHAT CAUSED THE MASSIVE EXPLOSION THAT LEVELED TWENTY-FIVE SQUARE BLOCKS, COMPLETELY DEMOLISHING THE NIGHTCLUB AND BUSINESS SECTORS OF THE CITY.
FIRE MARSHALS SUSPECT THE RUPTURE OF AN UNDERGROUND GAS LINE, WHICH THEY SAY WOULD ACCOUNT FOR THE SERIES OF EXPLOSIONS WHICH THREW MANHOLE COVERS HUNDREDS OF FEET INTO THE AIR AND SPREAD FIRE TO RESIDENTIAL AREAS AS FAR AS FORTY BLOCKS AWAY.
THE MAJORITY OF THOSE KILLED BY THE BLAST APPEAR TO HAVE BEEN PATRONS OF THE NUMEROUS ILLEGAL AFTER-HOURS CLUBS WHICH OPERATED IN THE NIGHT-CLUB DISTRICT.
THANX CHRIS!
SCOBE SUCKS SOCKS!

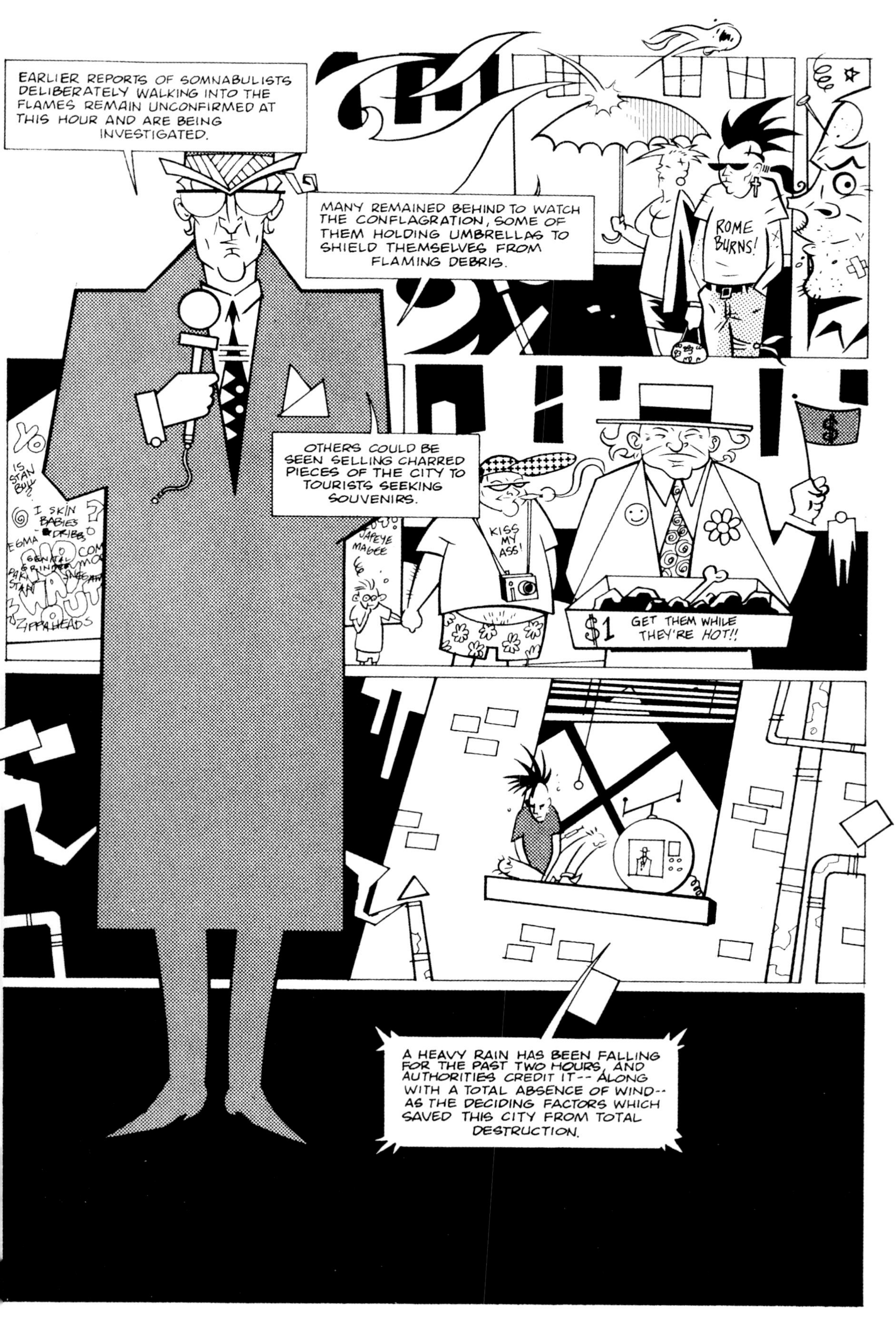
EARLIER REPORTS OF SOMNABULISTS DELIBERATELY WALKING INTO THE FLAMES REMAIN UNCONFIRMED AT THIS HOUR AND ARE BEING INVESTIGATED.
MANY REMAINED BEHIND TO WATCH THE CONFLAGRATION, SOME OF THEM HOLDING UMBRELLAS TO SHIELD THEMSELVES FROM FLAMING DEBRIS.
ROME BURNS!
OTHERS COULD BE SEEN SELLING CHARRED PIECES OF THE CITY TO TOURISTS SEEKING SOUVENIRS.
KISS MY ASS!
JAPEYE MAGEE
$1 GET THEM WHILE THEY'RE HOT!!
A HEAVY RAIN HAS BEEN FALLING FOR THE PAST TWO HOURS, AND AUTHORITIES CREDIT IT-- ALONG WITH A TOTAL ABSENCE OF WIND-- AS THE DECIDING FACTORS WHICH SAVED THIS CITY FROM TOTAL DESTRUCTION.

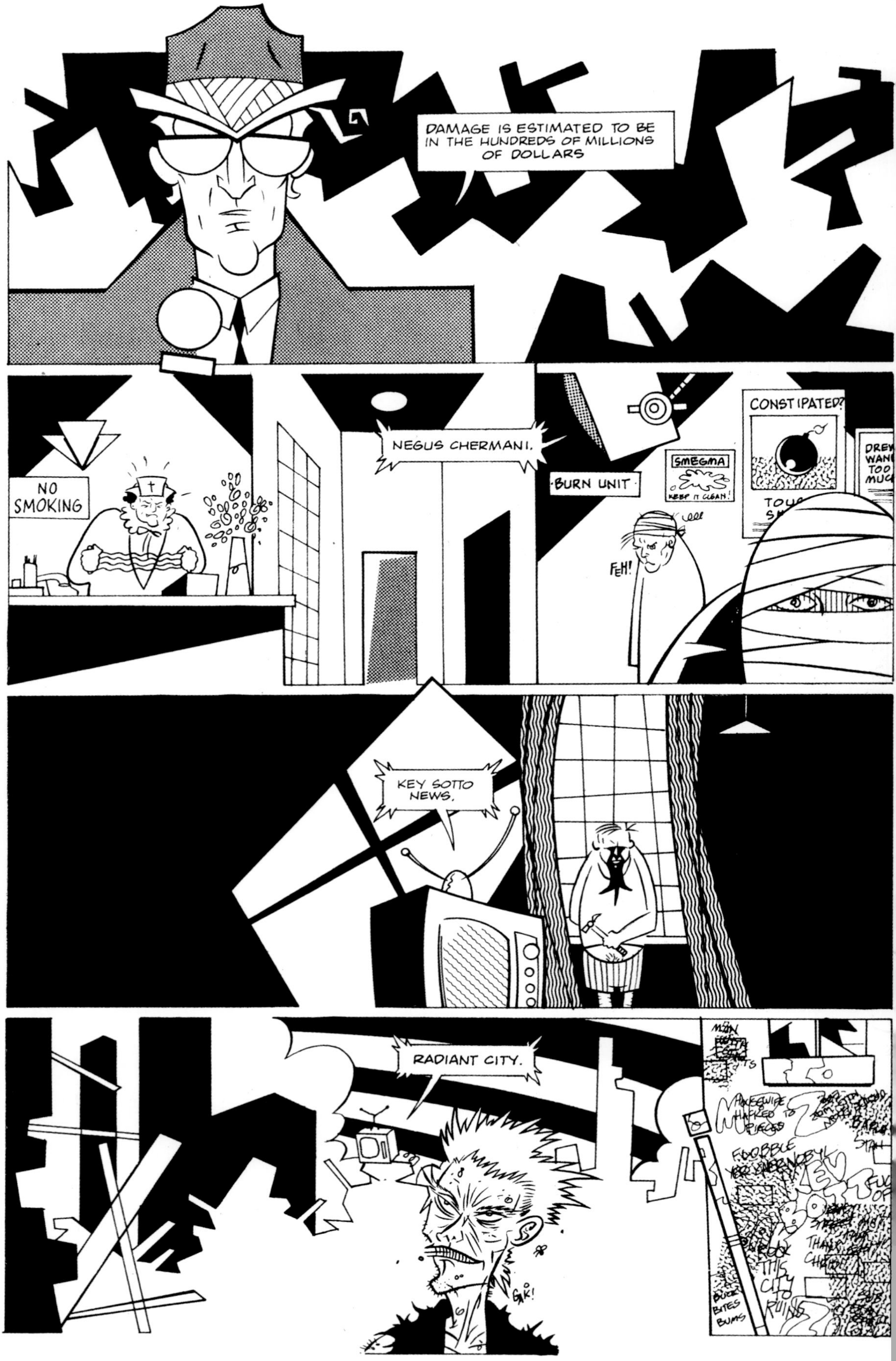
DAMAGE IS ESTIMATED TO BE IN THE HUNDREDS OF MILLIONS OF DOLLARS
NO SMOKING
NEGUS CHERMANI.
BURN UNIT
SMEGMA
KEEP IT CLEAN!
CONSTIPATED?
FEH!
KEY SOTTO NEWS.
RADIANT CITY.
GAK!
BRUCE BITES BUMS

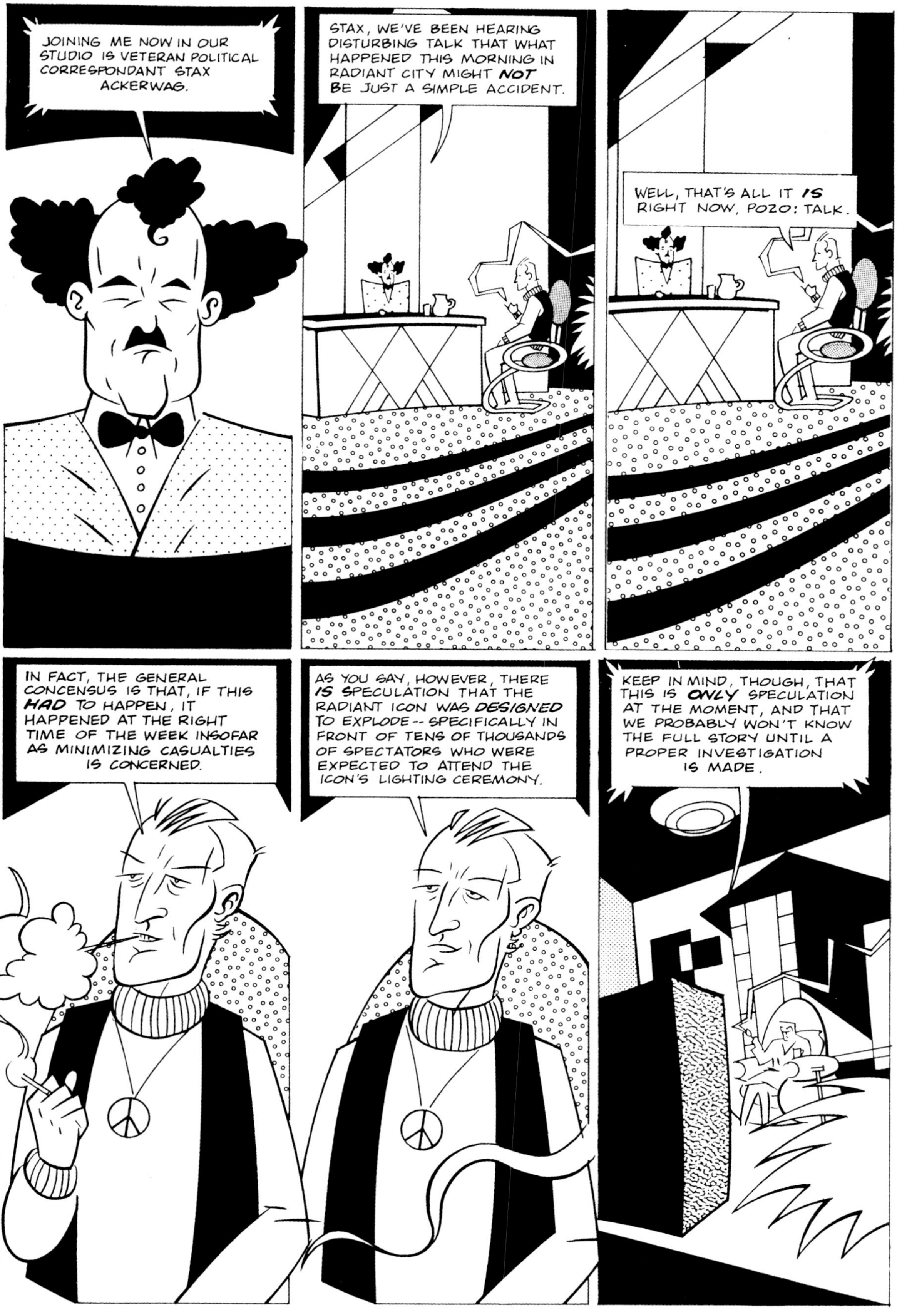
JOINING ME NOW IN OUR STUDIO IS VETERAN POLITICAL CORRESPONDANT STAX ACKERWAG.
STAX, WE'VE BEEN HEARING DISTURBING TALK THAT WHAT HAPPENED THIS MORNING IN RADIANT CITY MIGHT NOT BE JUST A SIMPLE ACCIDENT.
WELL, THAT'S ALL IT IS RIGHT NOW, POZO: TALK.
IN FACT, THE GENERAL CONCENSUS IS THAT, IF THIS HAD TO HAPPEN, IT HAPPENED AT THE RIGHT TIME OF THE WEEK INSOFAR AS MINIMIZING CASUALTIES IS CONCERNED.
AS YOU SAY, HOWEVER, THERE IS SPECULATION THAT THE RADIANT ICON WAS DESIGNED TO EXPLODE-- SPECIFICALLY IN FRONT OF TENS OF THOUSANDS OF SPECTATORS WHO WERE EXPECTED TO ATTEND THE ICON'S LIGHTING CEREMONY.
KEEP IN MIND, THOUGH, THAT THIS IS ONLY SPECULATION AT THE MOMENT, AND THAT WE PROBABLY WON'T KNOW THE FULL STORY UNTIL A PROPER INVESTIGATION IS MADE.

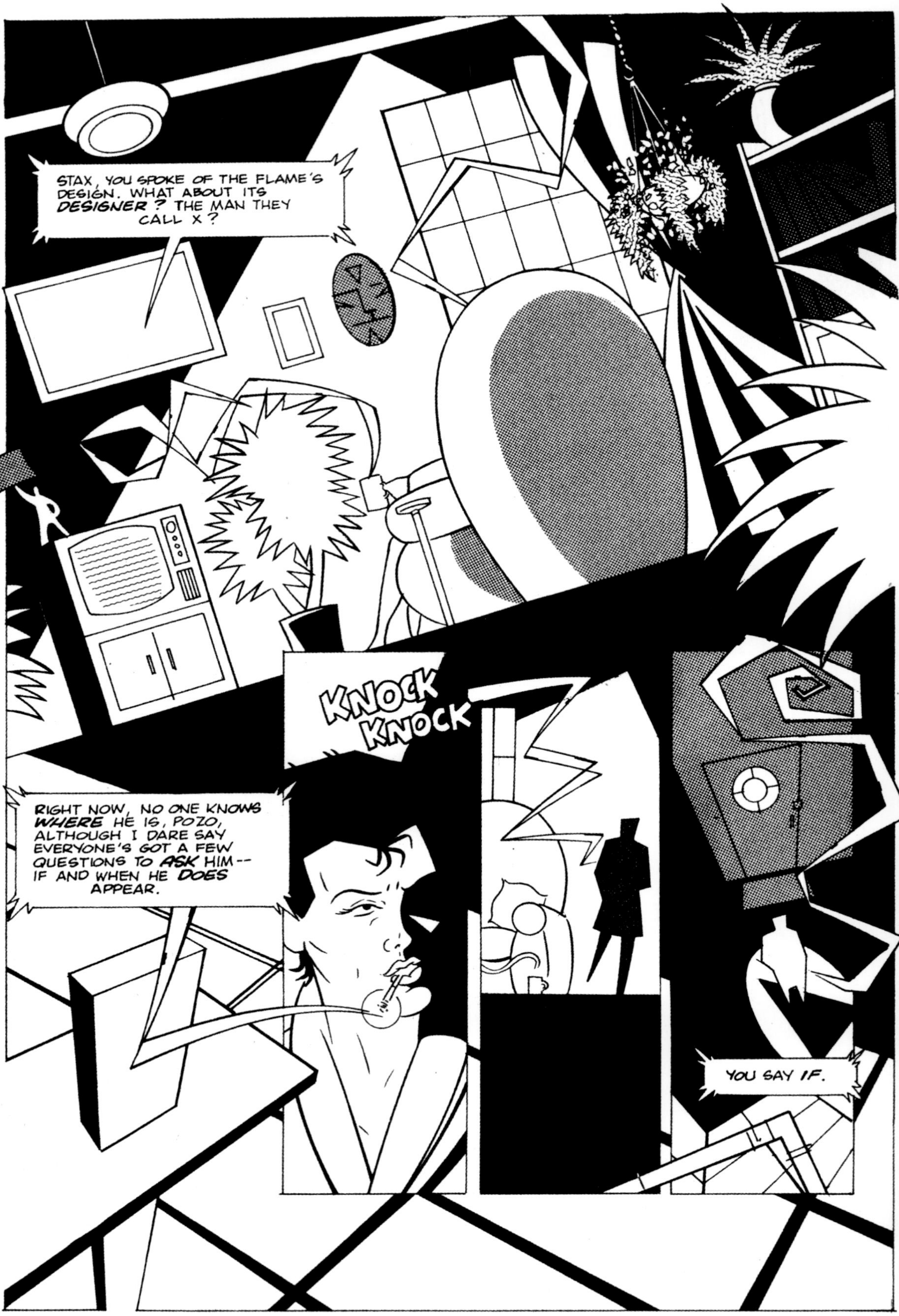
STAX, YOU SPOKE OF THE FLAME'S DESIGN. WHAT ABOUT ITS DESIGNER? THE MAN THEY CALL X?
KNOCK KNOCK
RIGHT NOW, NO ONE KNOWS WHERE HE IS, POZO, ALTHOUGH I DARE SAY EVERYONE'S GOT A FEW QUESTIONS TO ASK HIM-- IF AND WHEN HE DOES APPEAR.
YOU SAY IF.

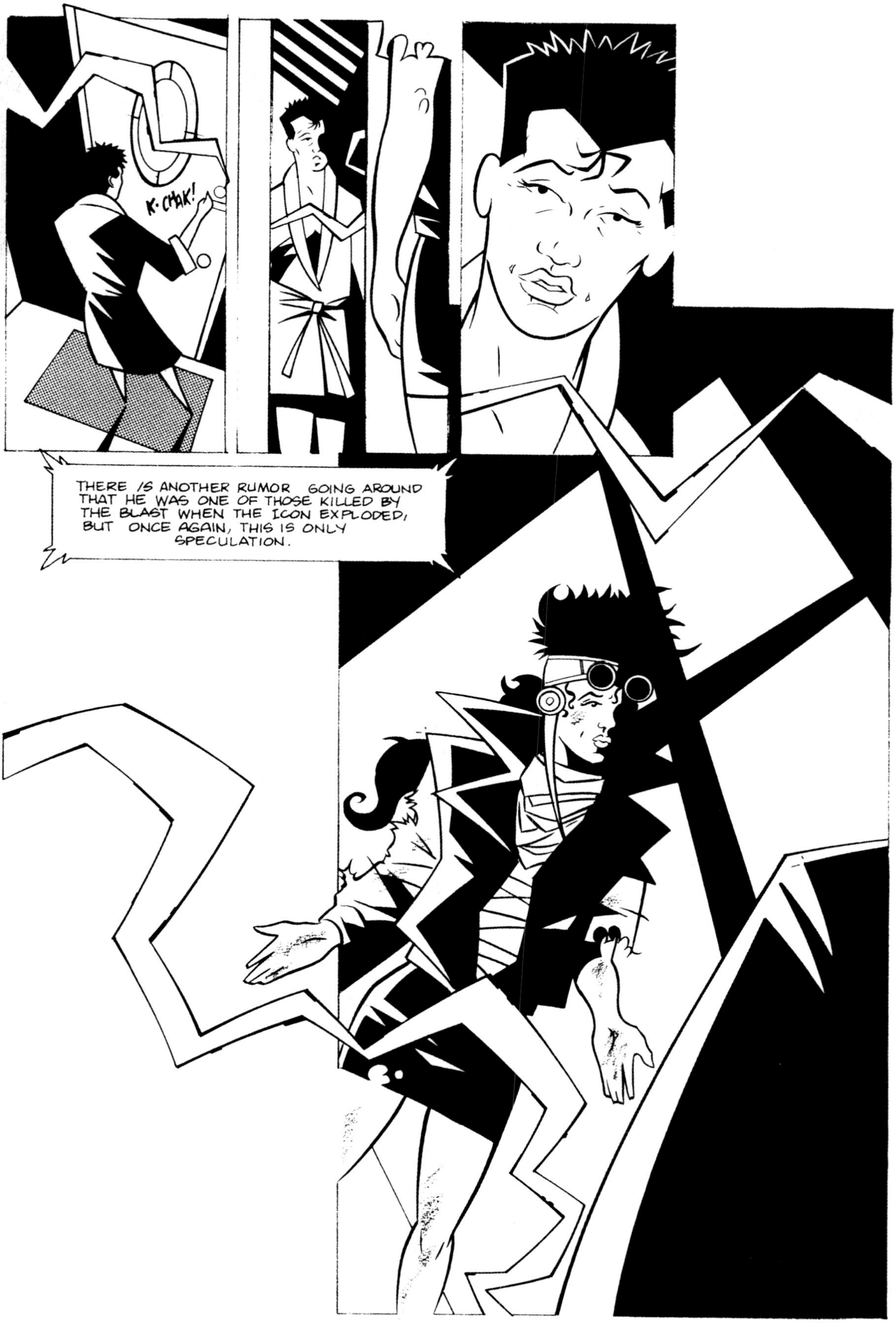
K-CHAK!
THERE IS ANOTHER RUMOR GOING AROUND THAT HE WAS ONE OF THOSE KILLED BY THE BLAST WHEN THE ICON EXPLODED, BUT ONCE AGAIN, THIS IS ONLY SPECULATION.

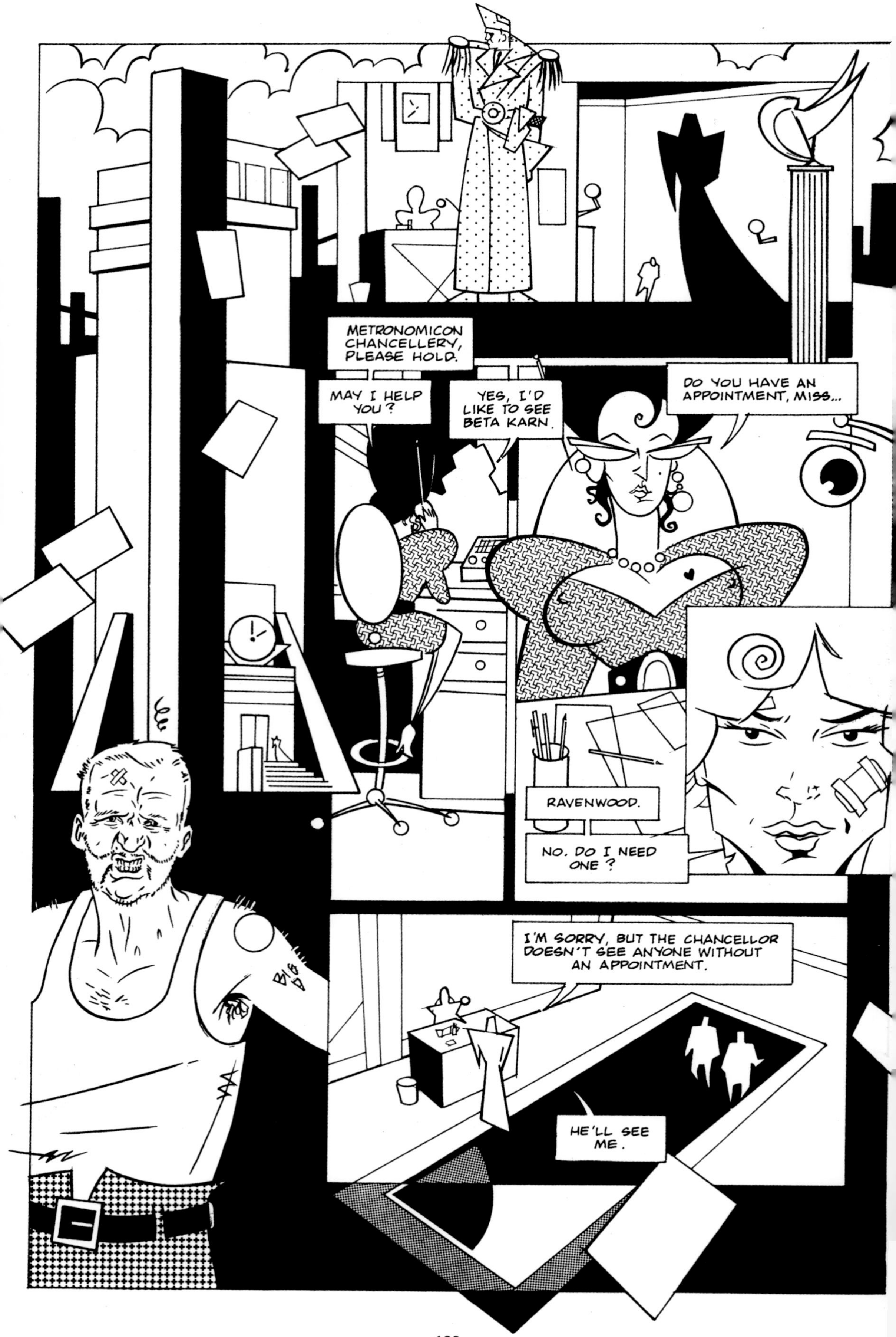
METRONOMICON CHANCELLERY, PLEASE HOLD.
MAY I HELP YOU?
YES, I'D LIKE TO SEE BETA KARN.
DO YOU HAVE AN APPOINTMENT, MISS...
RAVENWOOD.
NO. DO I NEED ONE?
I'M SORRY, BUT THE CHANCELLOR DOESN'T SEE ANYONE WITHOUT AN APPOINTMENT.
HE'LL SEE ME.

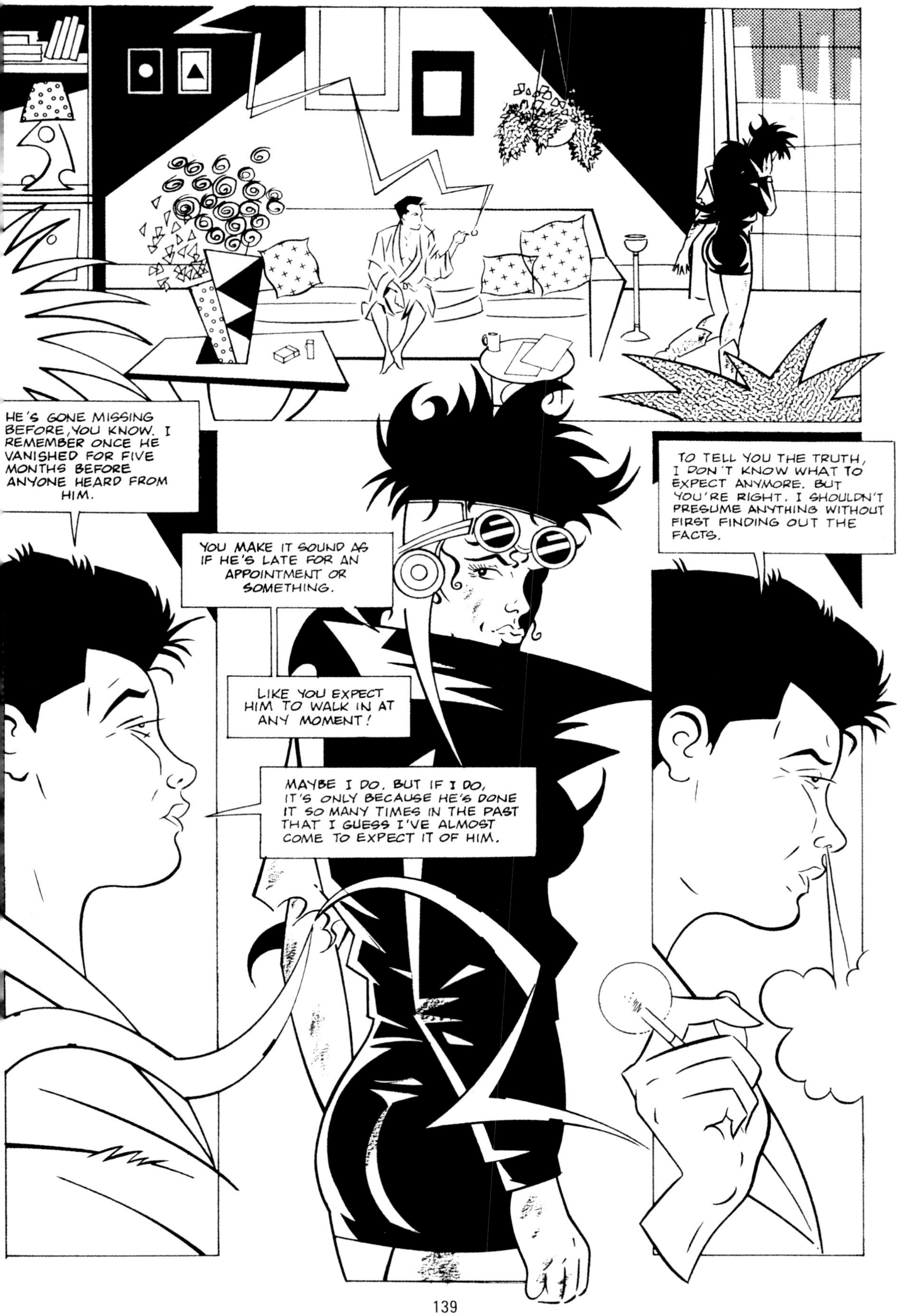
HE'S GONE MISSING BEFORE, YOU KNOW. I REMEMBER ONCE HE VANISHED FOR FIVE MONTHS BEFORE ANYONE HEARD FROM HIM.
YOU MAKE IT SOUND AS IF HE'S LATE FOR AN APPOINTMENT OR SOMETHING.
LIKE YOU EXPECT HIM TO WALK IN AT ANY MOMENT!
MAYBE I DO. BUT IF I DO, IT'S ONLY BECAUSE HE'S DONE IT SO MANY TIMES IN THE PAST THAT I GUESS I'VE ALMOST COME TO EXPECT IT OF HIM.
TO TELL YOU THE TRUTH, I DON'T KNOW WHAT TO EXPECT ANYMORE. BUT YOU'RE RIGHT. I SHOULDN'T PRESUME ANYTHING WITHOUT FIRST FINDING OUT THE FACTS.

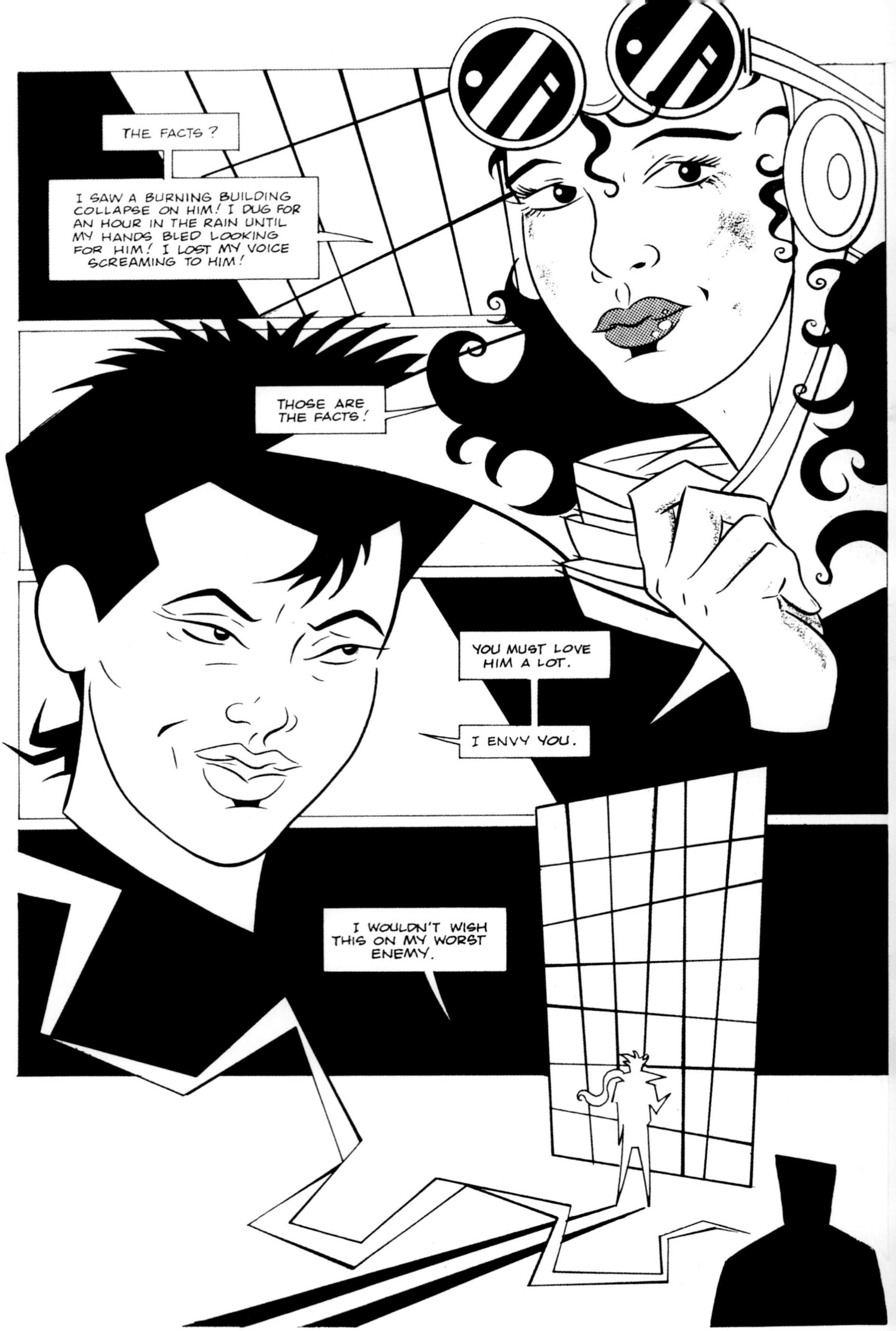
THE FACTS ?
I SAW A BURNING BUILDING COLLAPSE ON HIM! I DUG FOR AN HOUR IN THE RAIN UNTIL MY HANDS BLED LOOKING FOR HIM! I LOST MY VOICE SCREAMING TO HIM!
THOSE ARE THE FACTS!
YOU MUST LOVE HIM A LOT.
I ENVY YOU.
I WOULDN'T WISH THIS ON MY WORST ENEMY.

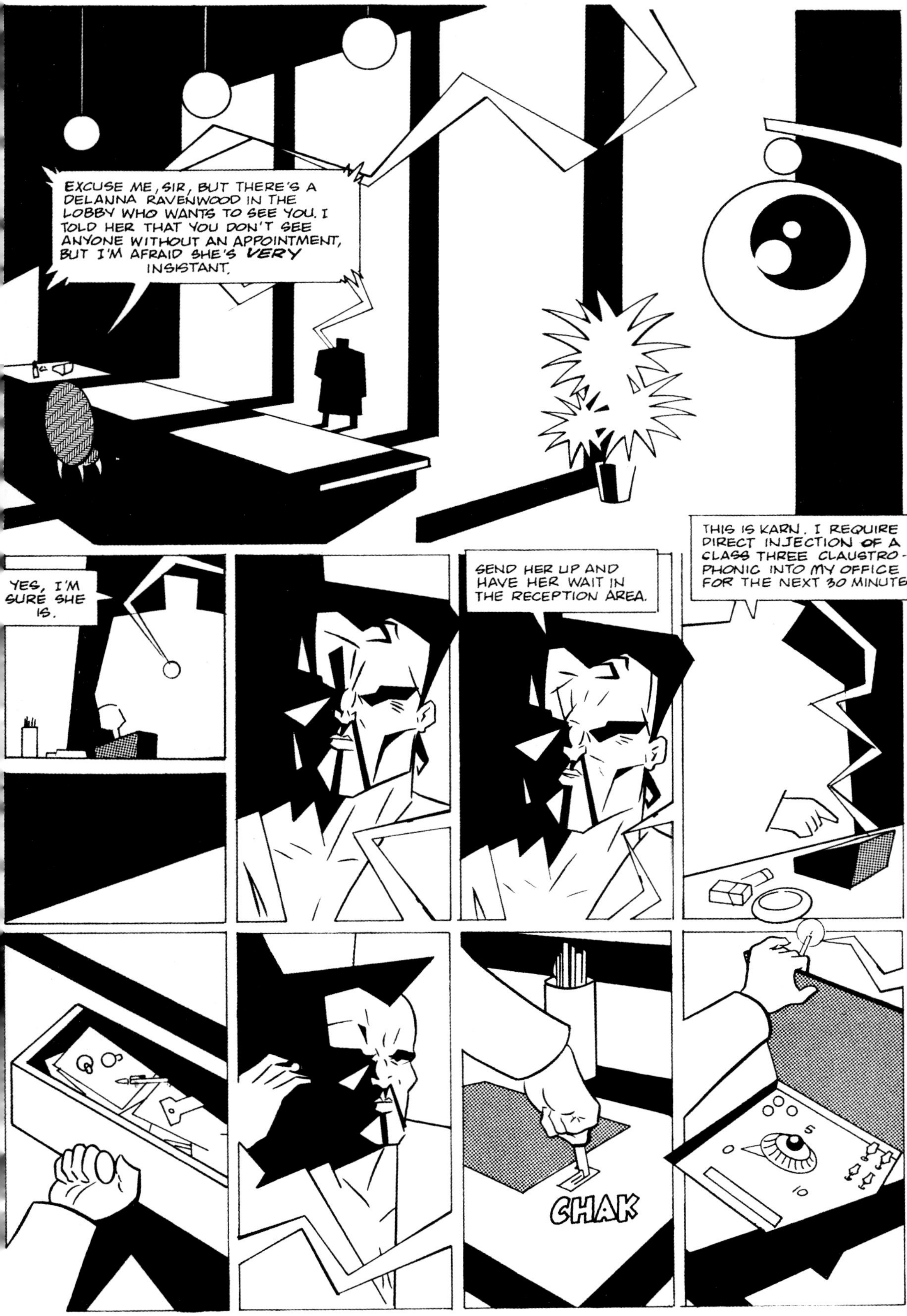
EXCUSE ME, SIR, BUT THERE'S A DELANNA RAVENWOOD IN THE LOBBY WHO WANTS TO SEE YOU. I TOLD HER THAT YOU DON'T SEE ANYONE WITHOUT AN APPOINTMENT, BUT I'M AFRAID SHE'S VERY INSISTANT.
YES, I'M SURE SHE IS.
SEND HER UP AND HAVE HER WAIT IN THE RECEPTION AREA.
THIS IS KARN. I REQUIRE DIRECT INJECTION OF A CLASS THREE CLAUSTRO-PHONIC INTO MY OFFICE FOR THE NEXT 30 MINUTES.
CHAK

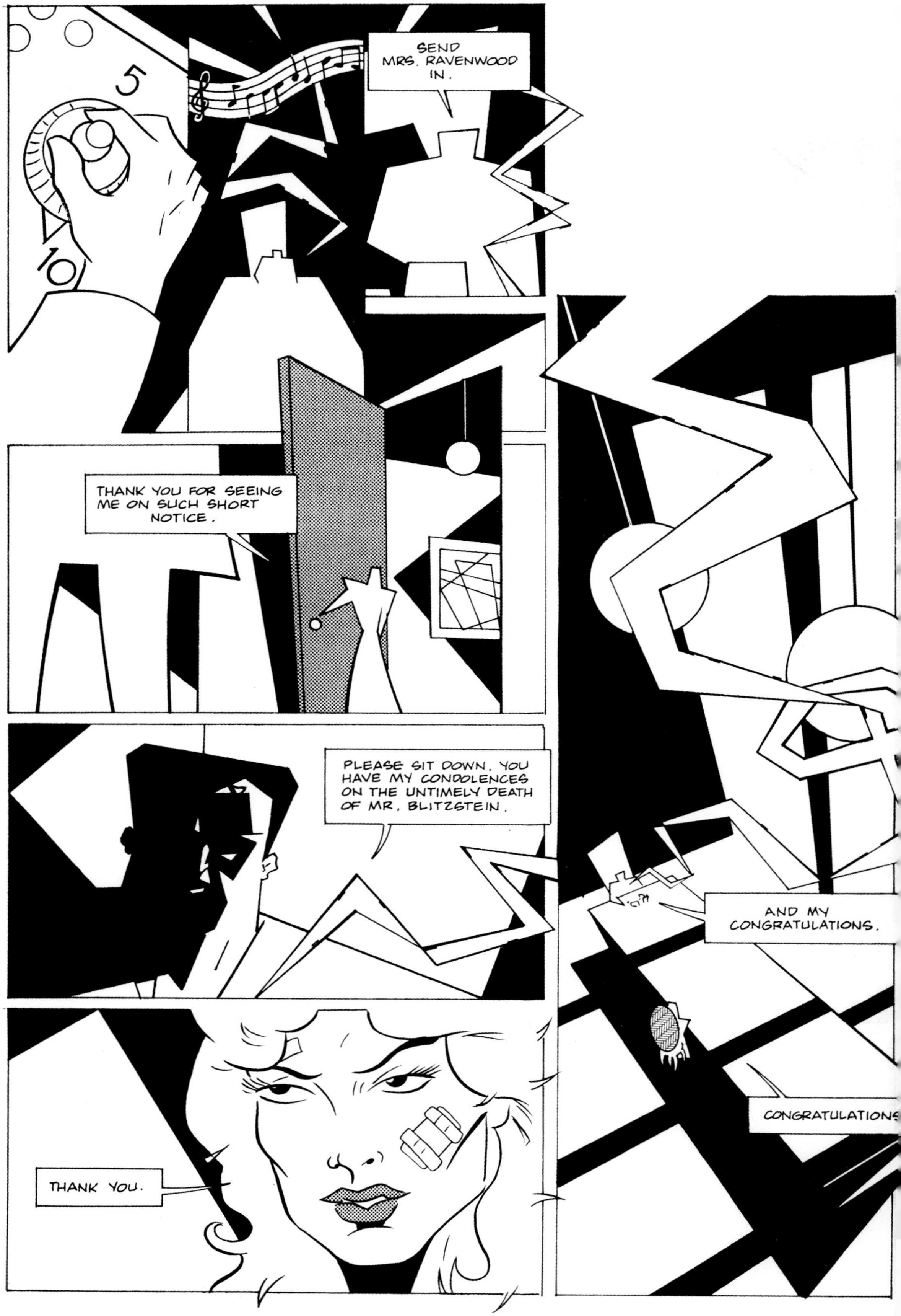
SEND MRS. RAVENWOOD IN.
THANK YOU FOR SEEING ME ON SUCH SHORT NOTICE.
PLEASE SIT DOWN. YOU HAVE MY CONDOLENCES ON THE UNTIMELY DEATH OF MR. BLITZSTEIN.
THANK YOU.
AND MY CONGRATULATIONS.
CONGRATULATIONS

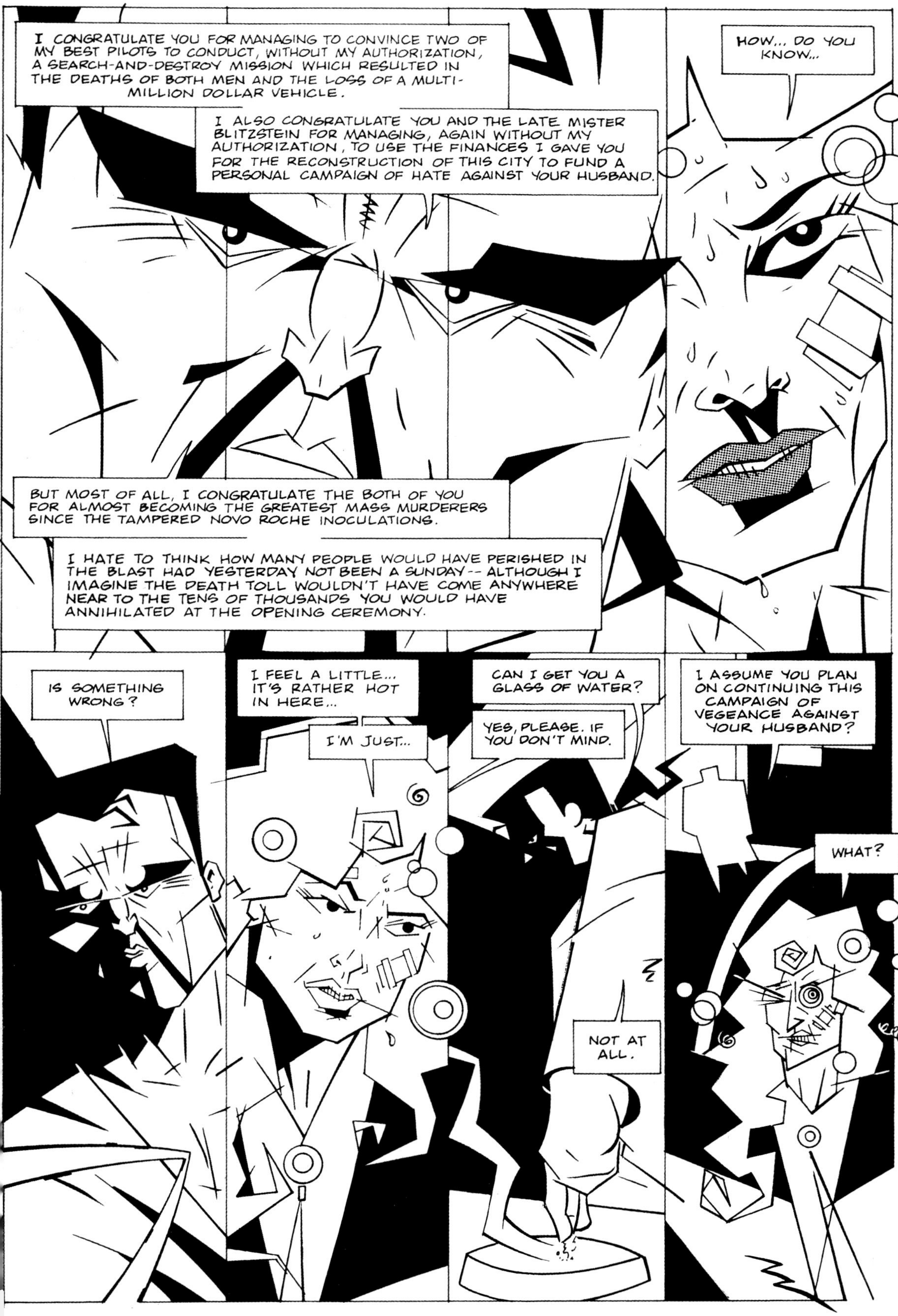
I CONGRATULATE YOU FOR MANAGING TO CONVINCE TWO OF MY BEST PILOTS TO CONDUCT, WITHOUT MY AUTHORIZATION, A SEARCH-AND-DESTROY MISSION WHICH RESULTED IN THE DEATHS OF BOTH MEN AND THE LOSS OF A MULTI-MILLION DOLLAR VEHICLE.
I ALSO CONGRATULATE YOU AND THE LATE MISTER BLITZSTEIN FOR MANAGING, AGAIN WITHOUT MY AUTHORIZATION, TO USE THE FINANCES I GAVE YOU FOR THE RECONSTRUCTION OF THIS CITY TO FUND A PERSONAL CAMPAIGN OF HATE AGAINST YOUR HUSBAND.
HOW... DO YOU KNOW...
BUT MOST OF ALL, I CONGRATULATE THE BOTH OF YOU FOR ALMOST BECOMING THE GREATEST MASS MURDERERS SINCE THE TAMPERED NOVO ROCHE INOCULATIONS.
I HATE TO THINK HOW MANY PEOPLE WOULD HAVE PERISHED IN THE BLAST HAD YESTERDAY NOT BEEN A SUNDAY-- ALTHOUGH I IMAGINE THE DEATH TOLL WOULDN'T HAVE COME ANYWHERE NEAR TO THE TENS OF THOUSANDS YOU WOULD HAVE ANNIHILATED AT THE OPENING CEREMONY.
IS SOMETHING WRONG?
I FEEL A LITTLE... IT'S RATHER HOT IN HERE...
I'M JUST...
CAN I GET YOU A GLASS OF WATER?
YES, PLEASE. IF YOU DON'T MIND.
NOT AT ALL.
I ASSUME YOU PLAN ON CONTINUING THIS CAMPAIGN OF VEGEANCE AGAINST YOUR HUSBAND?
WHAT?

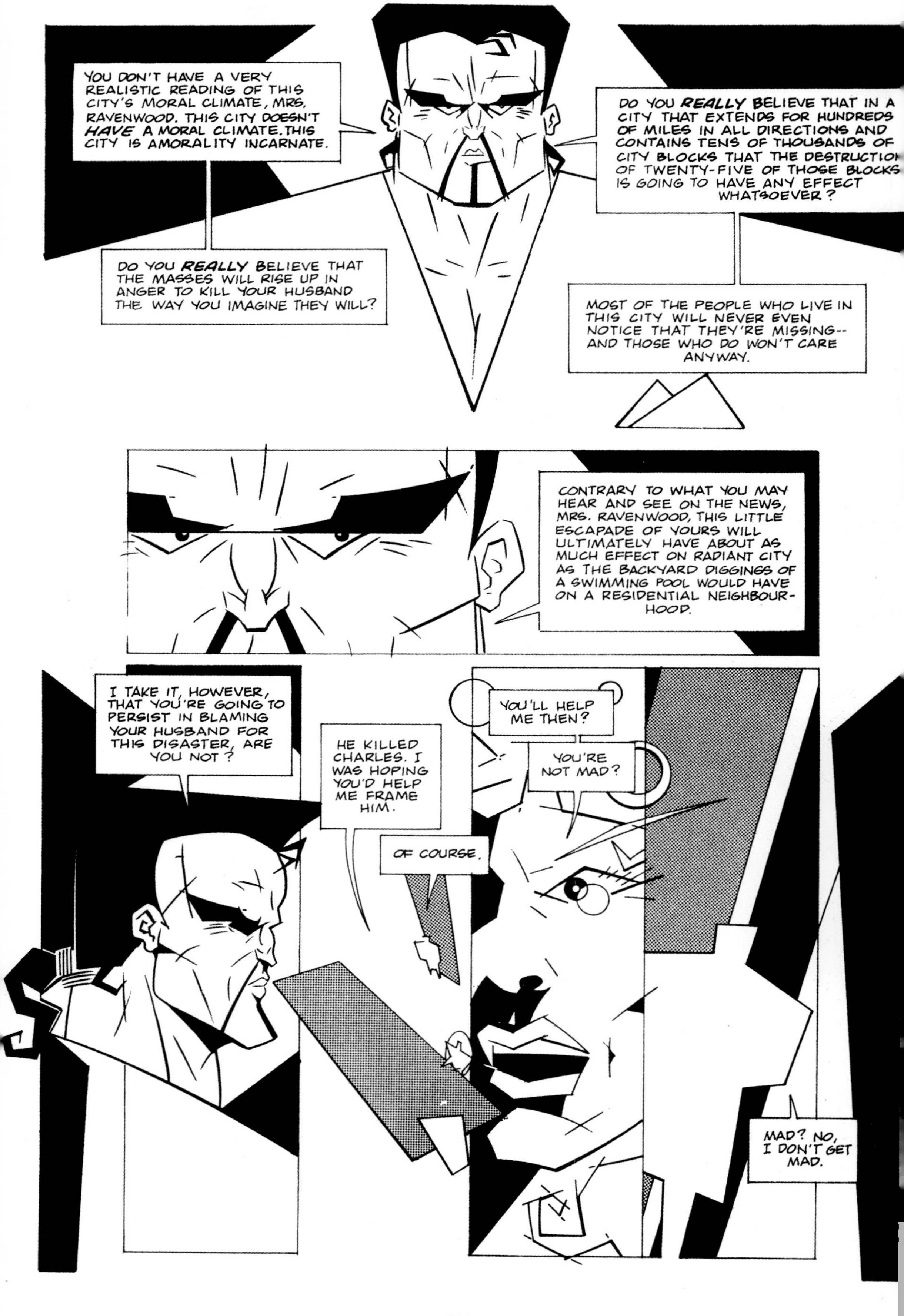
YOU DON'T HAVE A VERY REALISTIC READING OF THIS CITY'S MORAL CLIMATE, MRS. RAVENWOOD. THIS CITY DOESN'T *HAVE* A MORAL CLIMATE. THIS CITY IS AMORALITY INCARNATE.
DO YOU *REALLY* BELIEVE THAT THE MASSES WILL RISE UP IN ANGER TO KILL YOUR HUSBAND THE WAY YOU IMAGINE THEY WILL?
DO YOU *REALLY* BELIEVE THAT IN A CITY THAT EXTENDS FOR HUNDREDS OF MILES IN ALL DIRECTIONS AND CONTAINS TENS OF THOUSANDS OF CITY BLOCKS THAT THE DESTRUCTION OF TWENTY-FIVE OF THOSE BLOCKS IS GOING TO HAVE ANY EFFECT WHATSOEVER?
MOST OF THE PEOPLE WHO LIVE IN THIS CITY WILL NEVER EVEN NOTICE THAT THEY'RE MISSING-- AND THOSE WHO DO WON'T CARE ANYWAY.
CONTRARY TO WHAT YOU MAY HEAR AND SEE ON THE NEWS, MRS. RAVENWOOD, THIS LITTLE ESCAPADE OF YOURS WILL ULTIMATELY HAVE ABOUT AS MUCH EFFECT ON RADIANT CITY AS THE BACKYARD DIGGINGS OF A SWIMMING POOL WOULD HAVE ON A RESIDENTIAL NEIGHBOUR-HOOD.
I TAKE IT, HOWEVER, THAT YOU'RE GOING TO PERSIST IN BLAMING YOUR HUSBAND FOR THIS DISASTER, ARE YOU NOT?
HE KILLED CHARLES. I WAS HOPING YOU'D HELP ME FRAME HIM.
OF COURSE.
YOU'LL HELP ME THEN?
YOU'RE NOT MAD?
MAD? NO, I DON'T GET MAD.

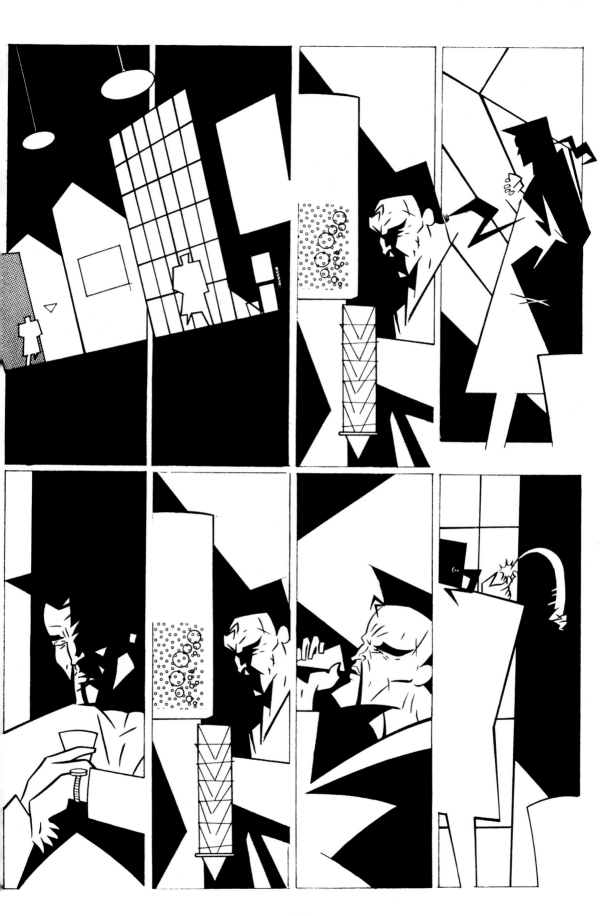

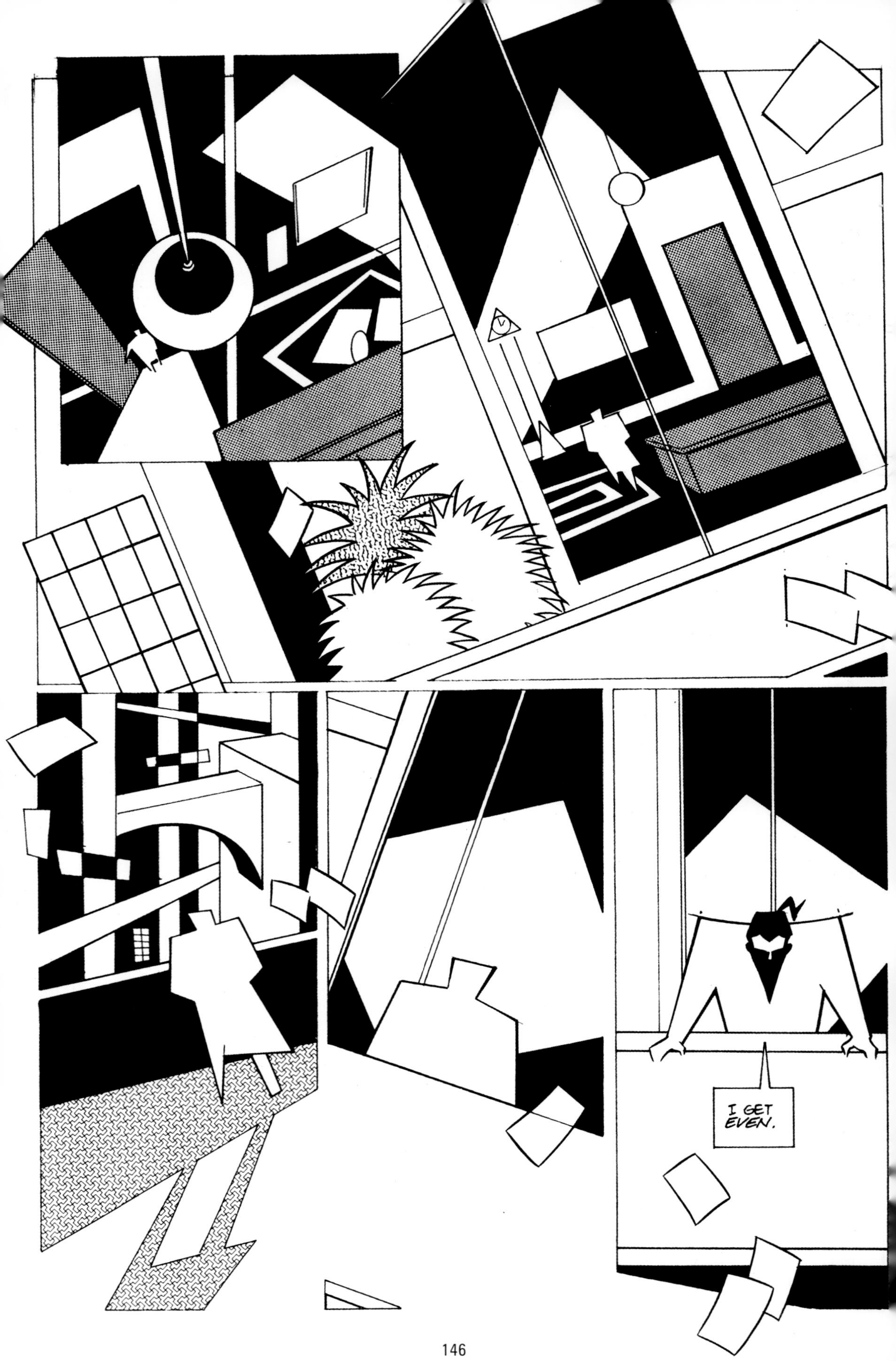
I GET EVEN.

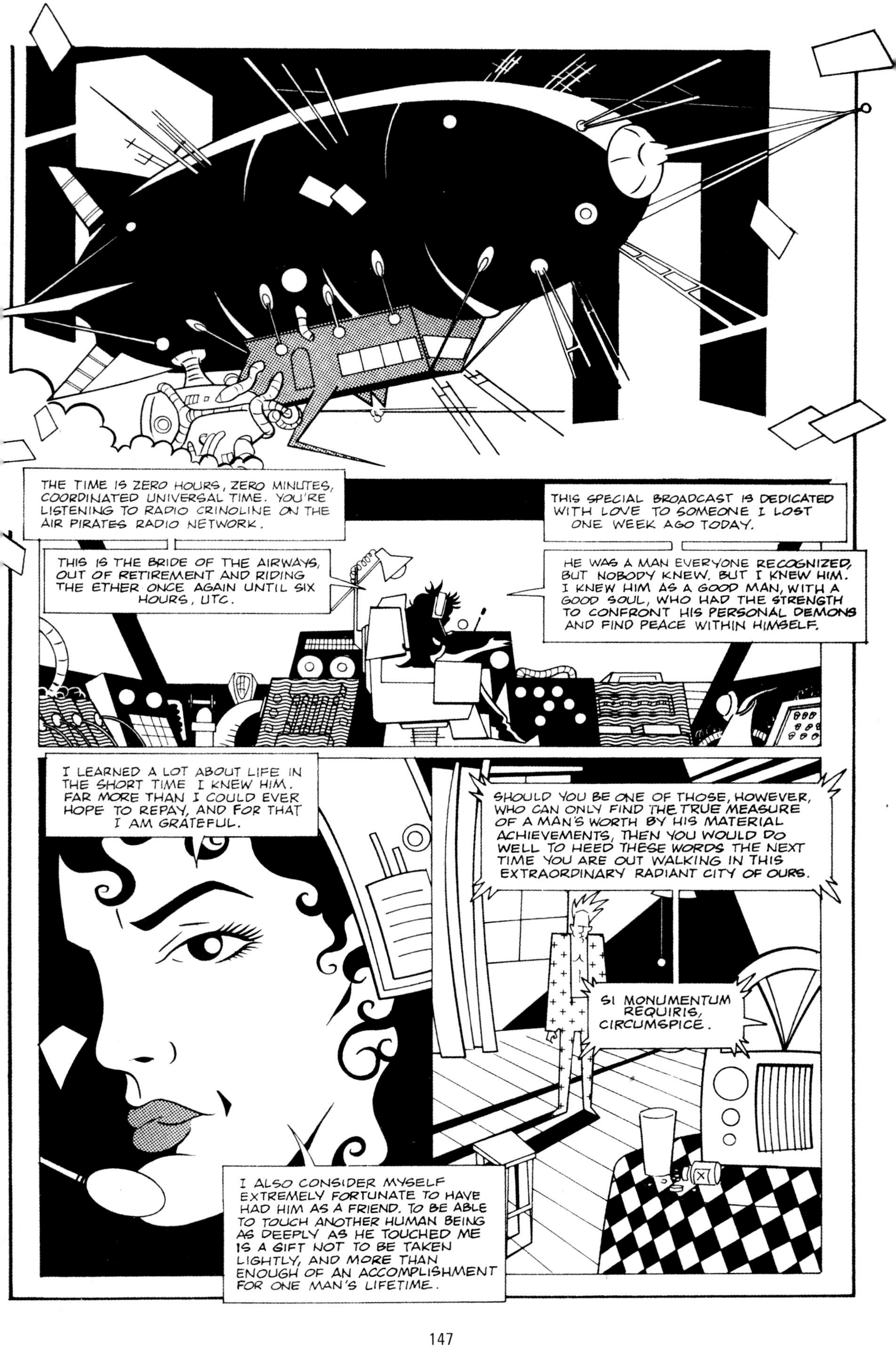
THE TIME IS ZERO HOURS, ZERO MINUTES, COORDINATED UNIVERSAL TIME. YOU'RE LISTENING TO RADIO CRINOLINE ON THE AIR PIRATES RADIO NETWORK.
THIS IS THE BRIDE OF THE AIRWAYS, OUT OF RETIREMENT AND RIDING THE ETHER ONCE AGAIN UNTIL SIX HOURS, UTC.
THIS SPECIAL BROADCAST IS DEDICATED WITH LOVE TO SOMEONE I LOST ONE WEEK AGO TODAY.
HE WAS A MAN EVERYONE RECOGNIZED, BUT NOBODY KNEW. BUT I KNEW HIM. I KNEW HIM AS A GOOD MAN, WITH A GOOD SOUL, WHO HAD THE STRENGTH TO CONFRONT HIS PERSONAL DEMONS AND FIND PEACE WITHIN HIMSELF.
I LEARNED A LOT ABOUT LIFE IN THE SHORT TIME I KNEW HIM. FAR MORE THAN I COULD EVER HOPE TO REPAY, AND FOR THAT I AM GRATEFUL.
I ALSO CONSIDER MYSELF EXTREMELY FORTUNATE TO HAVE HAD HIM AS A FRIEND. TO BE ABLE TO TOUCH ANOTHER HUMAN BEING AS DEEPLY AS HE TOUCHED ME IS A GIFT NOT TO BE TAKEN LIGHTLY, AND MORE THAN ENOUGH OF AN ACCOMPLISHMENT FOR ONE MAN'S LIFETIME.
SHOULD YOU BE ONE OF THOSE, HOWEVER, WHO CAN ONLY FIND THE TRUE MEASURE OF A MAN'S WORTH BY HIS MATERIAL ACHIEVEMENTS, THEN YOU WOULD DO WELL TO HEED THESE WORDS THE NEXT TIME YOU ARE OUT WALKING IN THIS EXTRAORDINARY RADIANT CITY OF OURS.
SI MONUMENTUM REQUIRIS, CIRCUMSPICE.

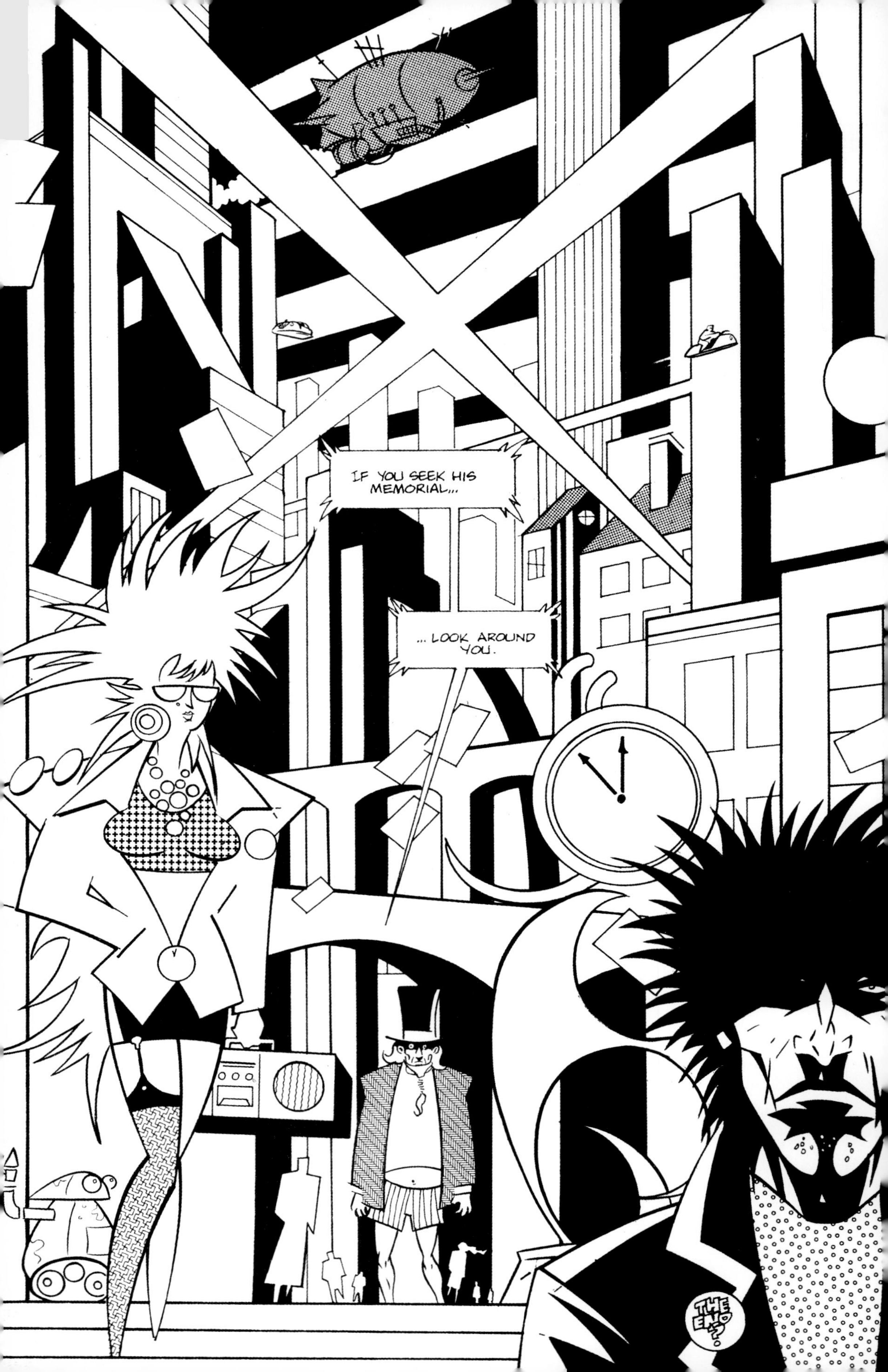

IF YOU SEEK HIS MEMORIAL...
...LOOK AROUND YOU.
THE END?

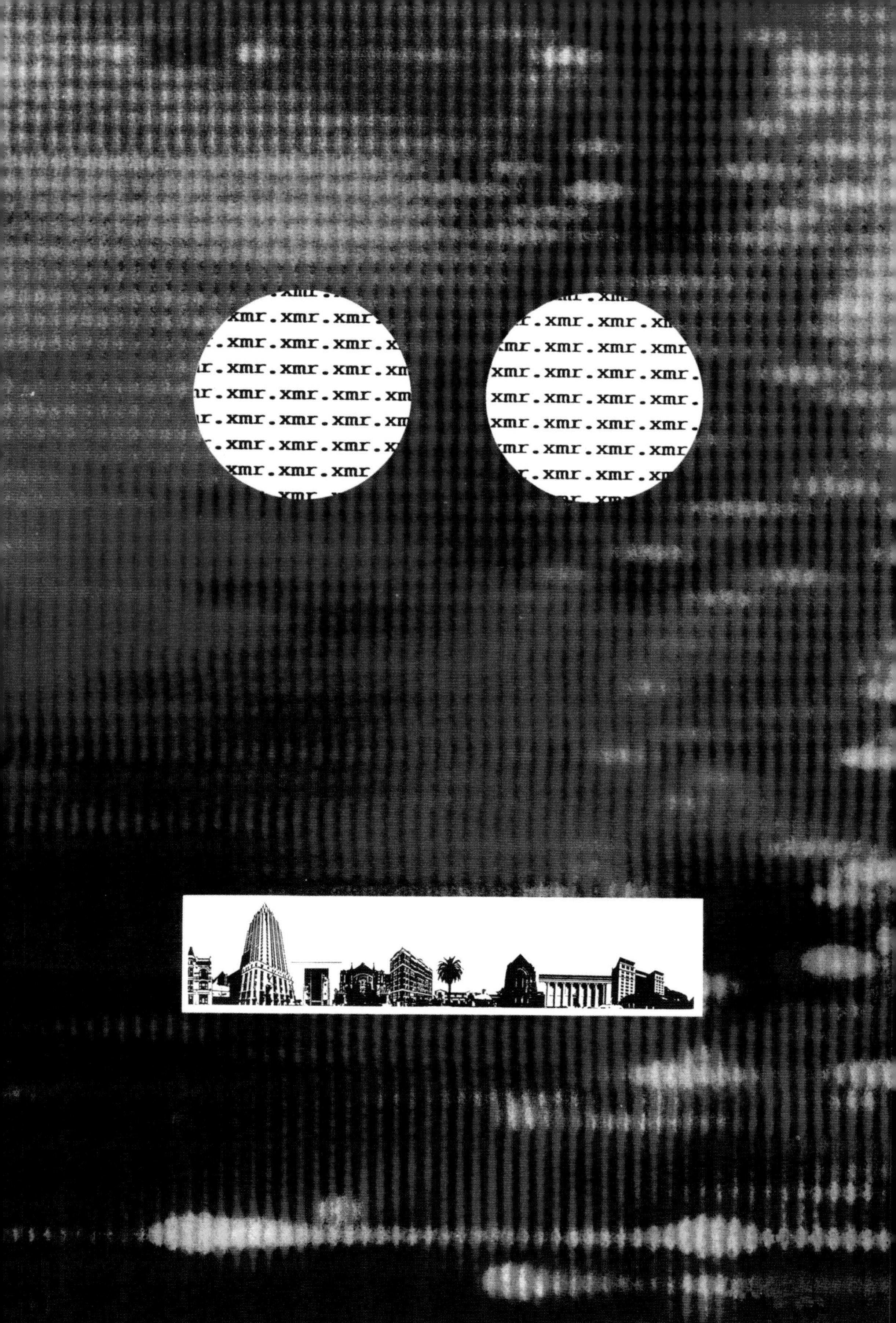
xmr.xmr.xmr.xmr.
xmr.xmr.xmr.xmr.

Illustration by **DITI KATONA**

LIMBO

WRITTEN BY **JEFFREY MORGAN**
PENCILED BY **D'ISRAELI**
INKED BY **KEN HOLEWCZYNSKI**
LETTERED BY **DEBORAH MARKS**

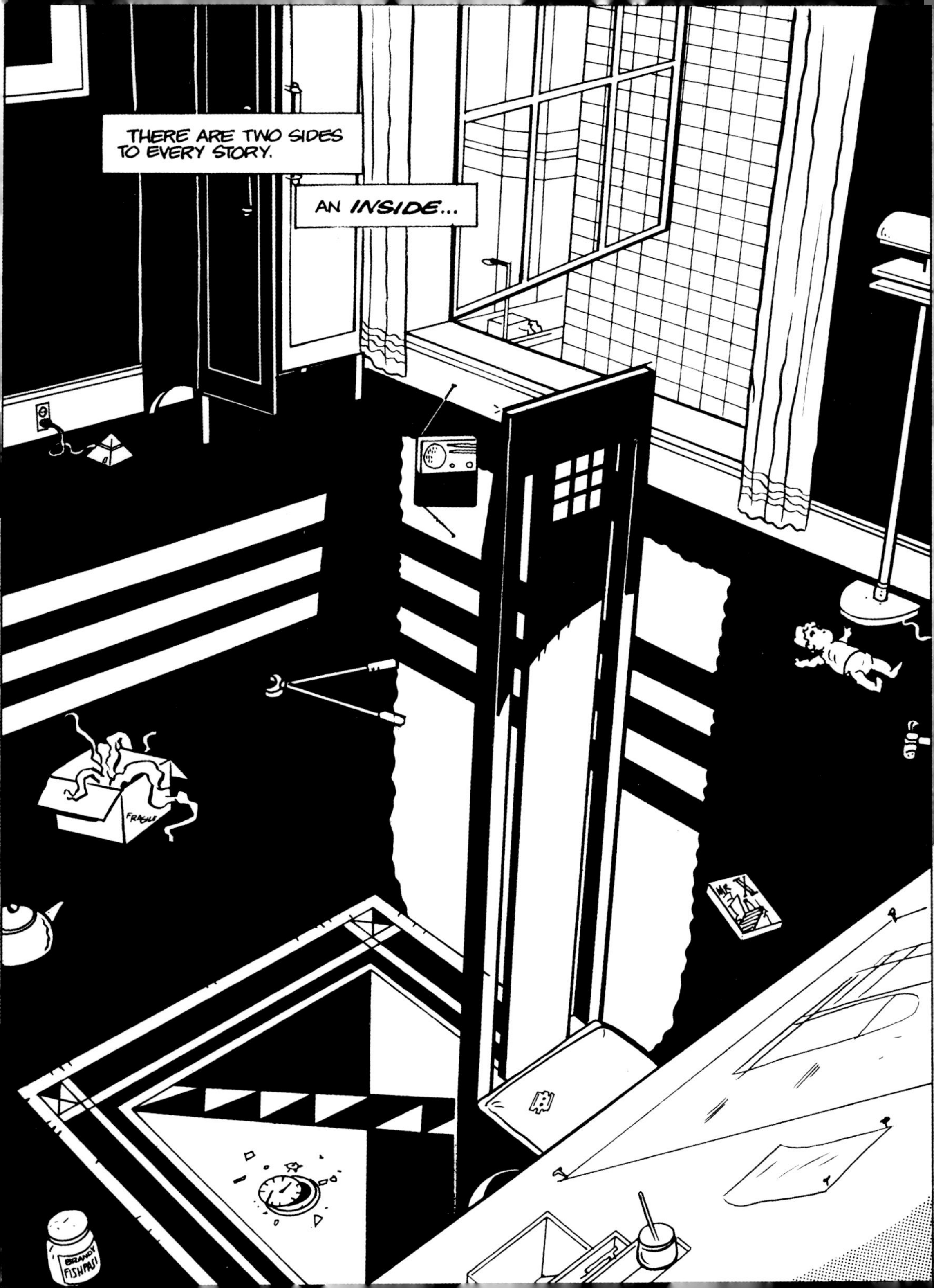
THERE ARE TWO SIDES TO EVERY STORY.
AN INSIDE...

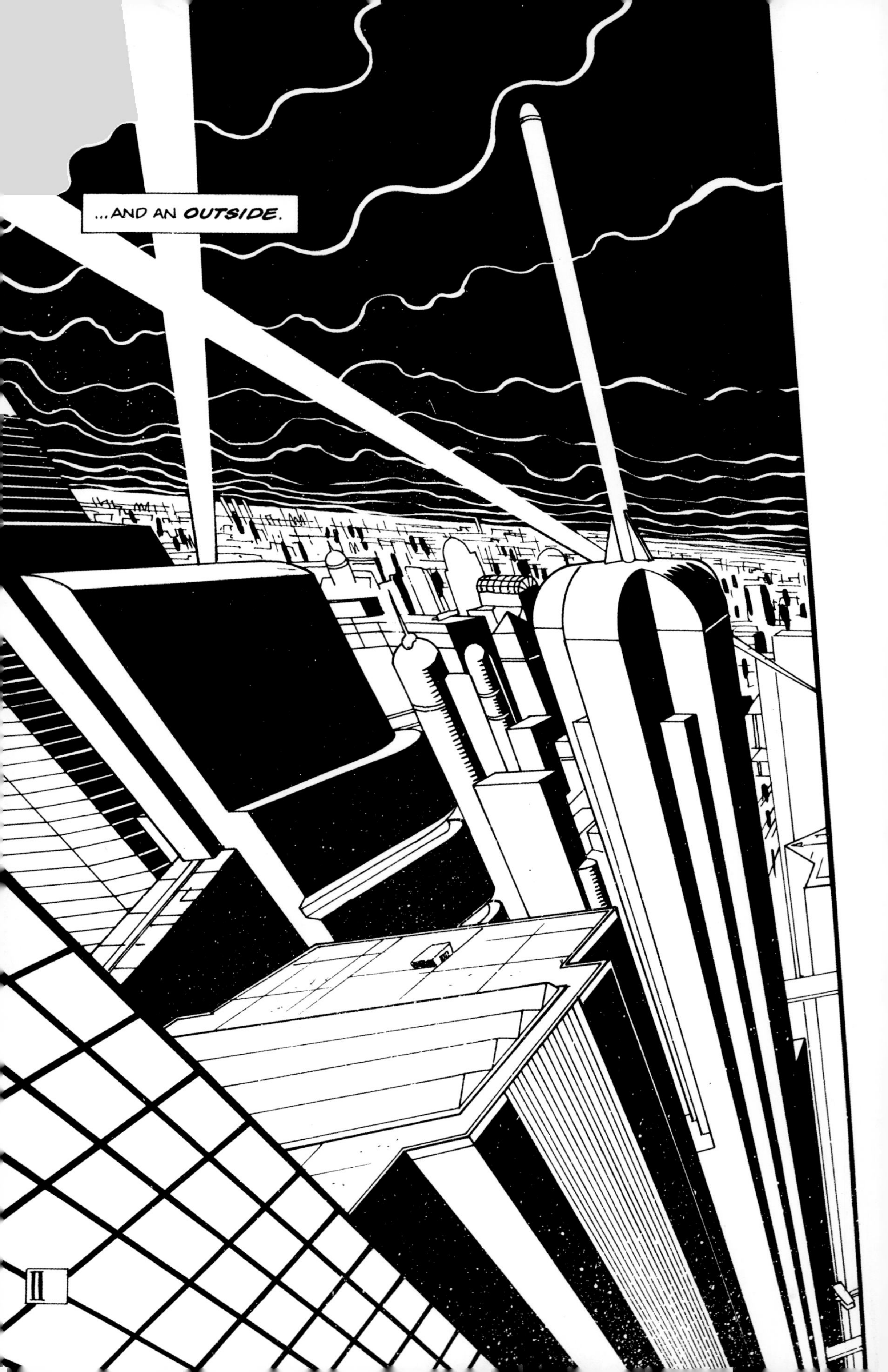
...AND AN OUTSIDE.

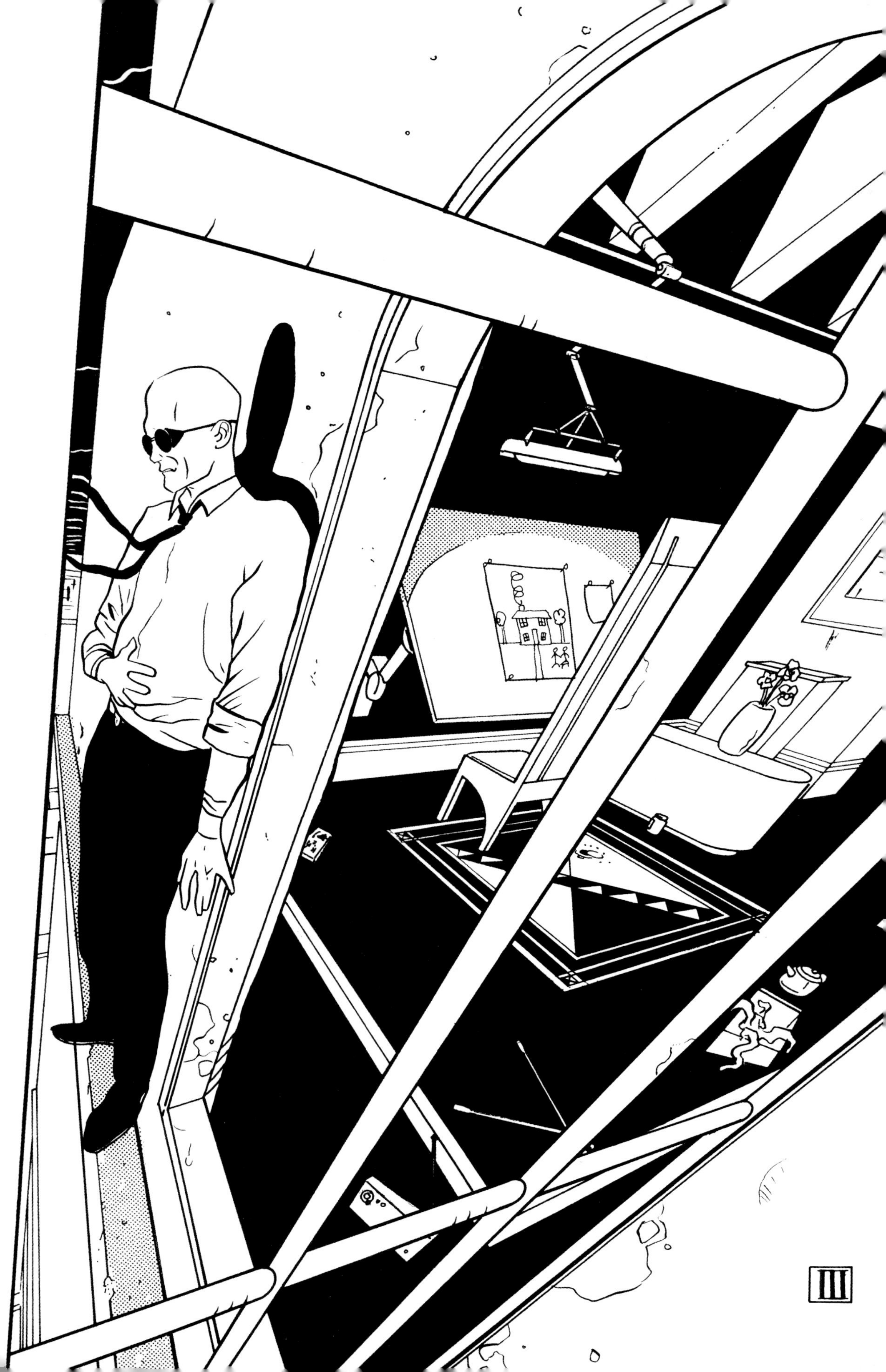
III

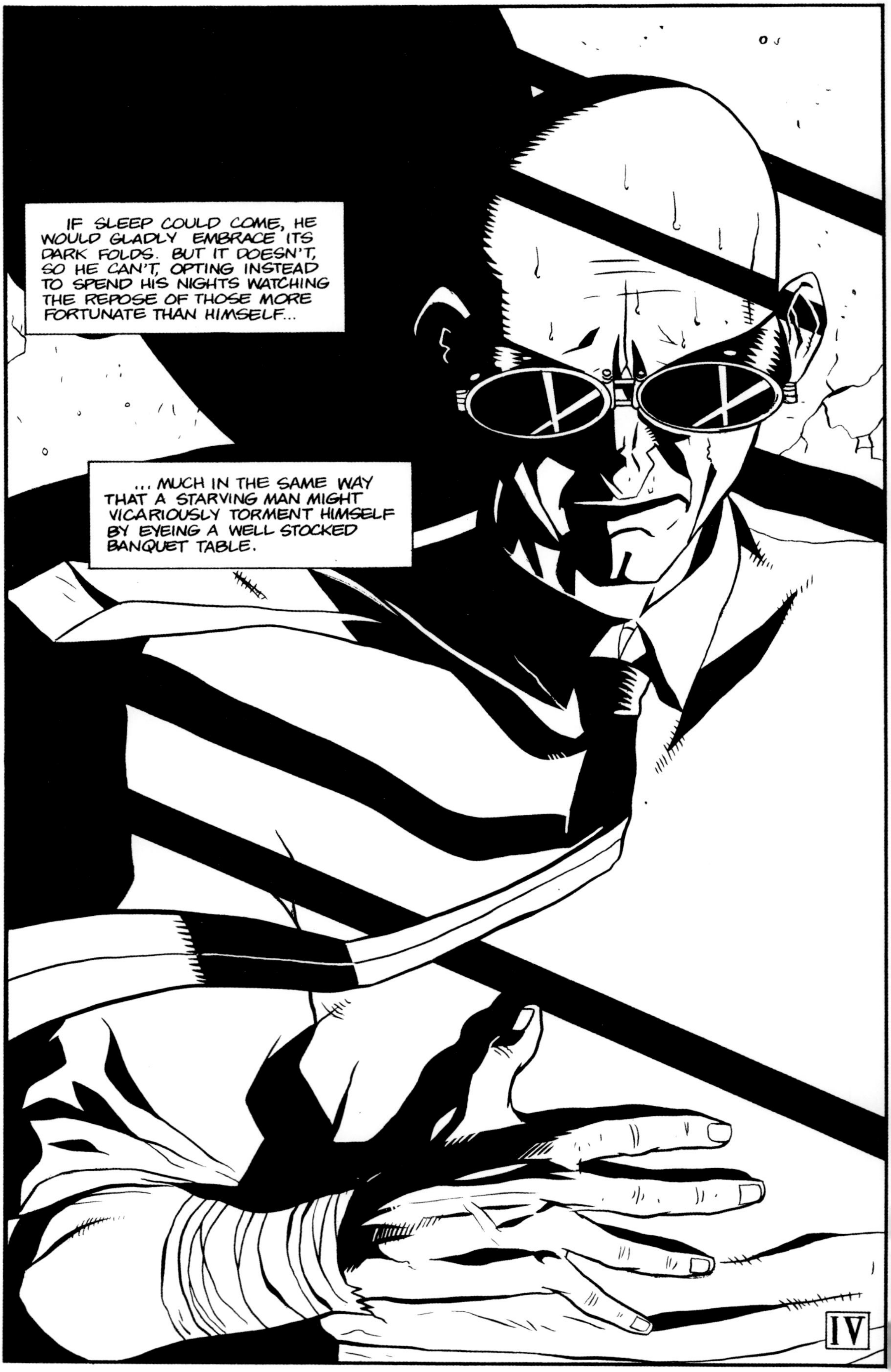
IF SLEEP COULD COME, HE WOULD GLADLY EMBRACE ITS DARK FOLDS. BUT IT DOESN'T, SO HE CAN'T, OPTING INSTEAD TO SPEND HIS NIGHTS WATCHING THE REPOSE OF THOSE MORE FORTUNATE THAN HIMSELF...
...MUCH IN THE SAME WAY THAT A STARVING MAN MIGHT VICARIOUSLY TORMENT HIMSELF BY EYEING A WELL STOCKED BANQUET TABLE.
IV

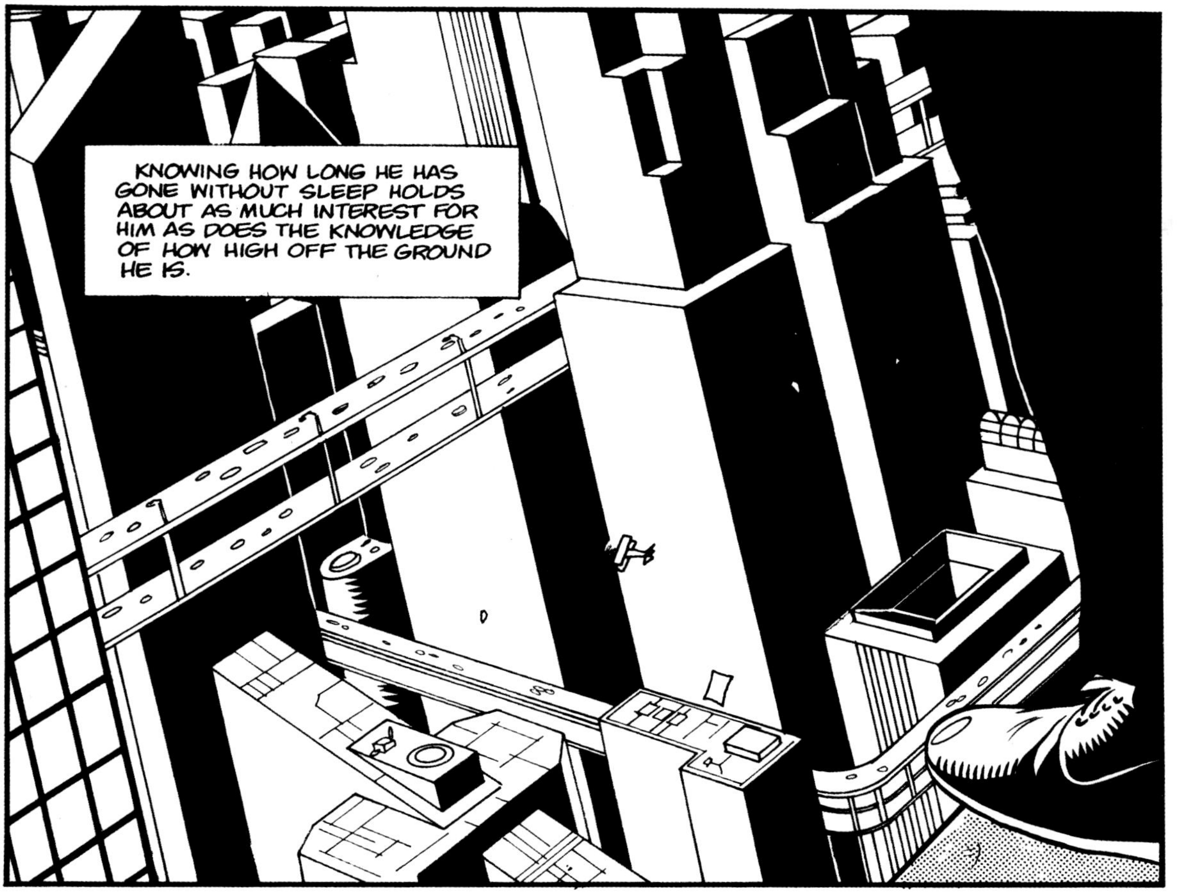
KNOWING HOW LONG HE HAS GONE WITHOUT SLEEP HOLDS ABOUT AS MUCH INTEREST FOR HIM AS DOES THE KNOWLEDGE OF HOW HIGH OFF THE GROUND HE IS.

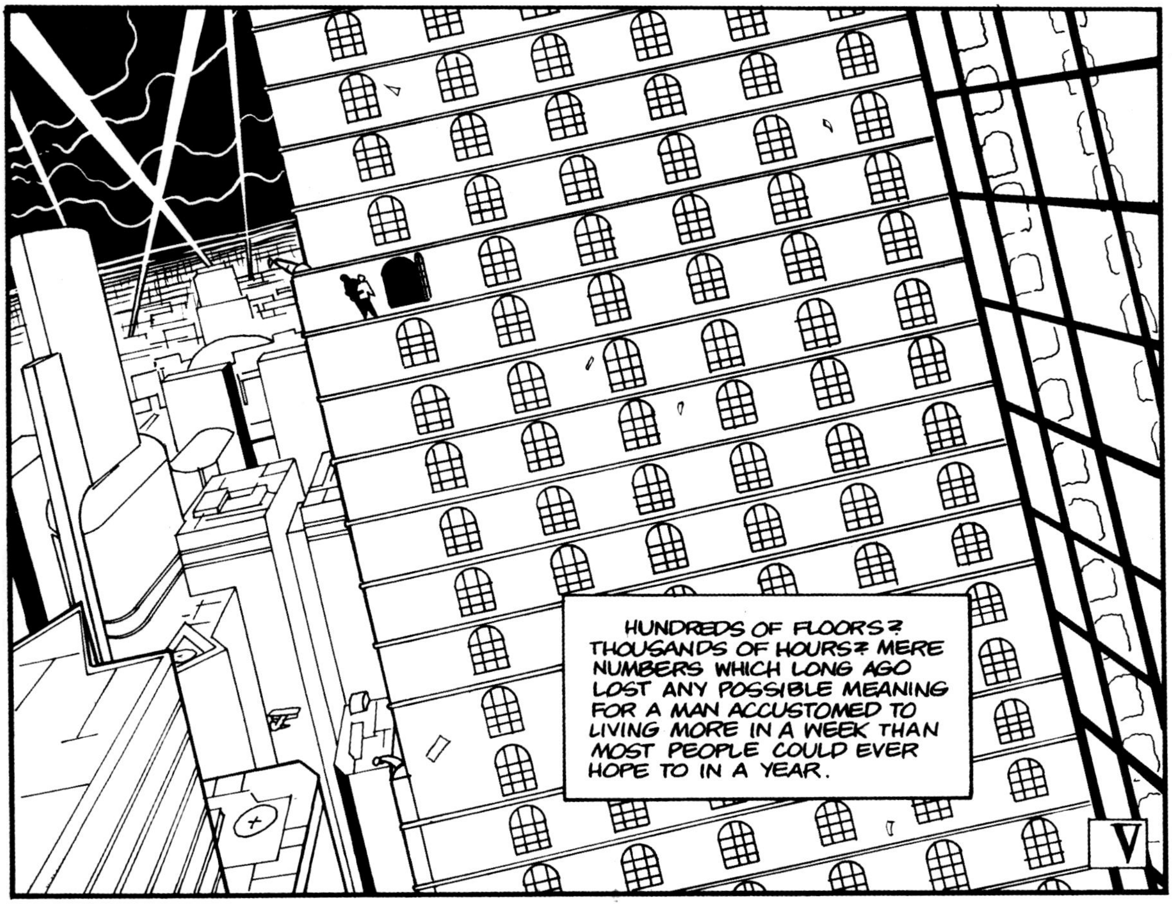
HUNDREDS OF FLOORS? THOUSANDS OF HOURS? MERE NUMBERS WHICH LONG AGO LOST ANY POSSIBLE MEANING FOR A MAN ACCUSTOMED TO LIVING MORE IN A WEEK THAN MOST PEOPLE COULD EVER HOPE TO IN A YEAR.
V

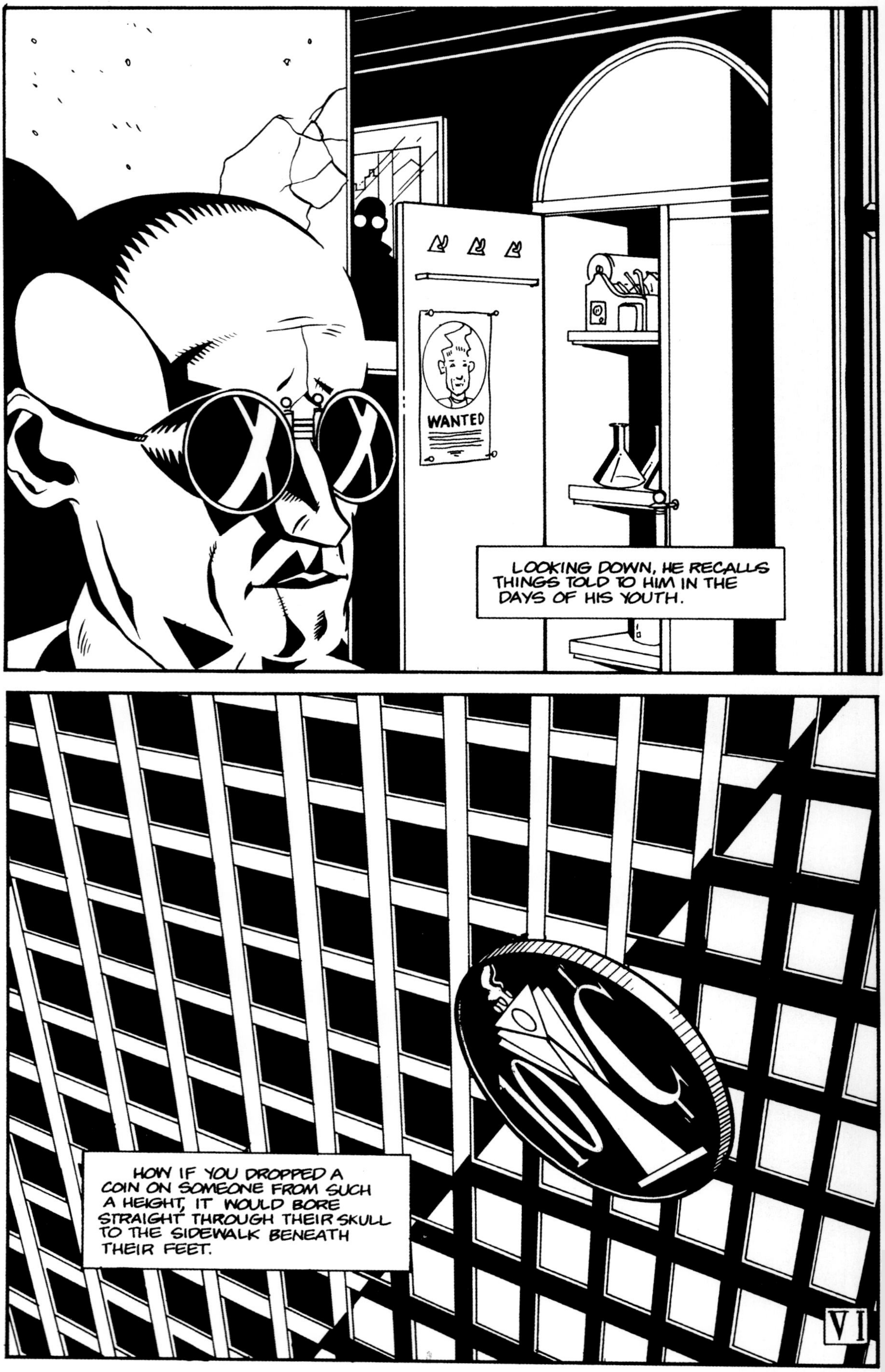
WANTED
LOOKING DOWN, HE RECALLS THINGS TOLD TO HIM IN THE DAYS OF HIS YOUTH.
HOW IF YOU DROPPED A COIN ON SOMEONE FROM SUCH A HEIGHT, IT WOULD BORE STRAIGHT THROUGH THEIR SKULL TO THE SIDEWALK BENEATH THEIR FEET.
VI

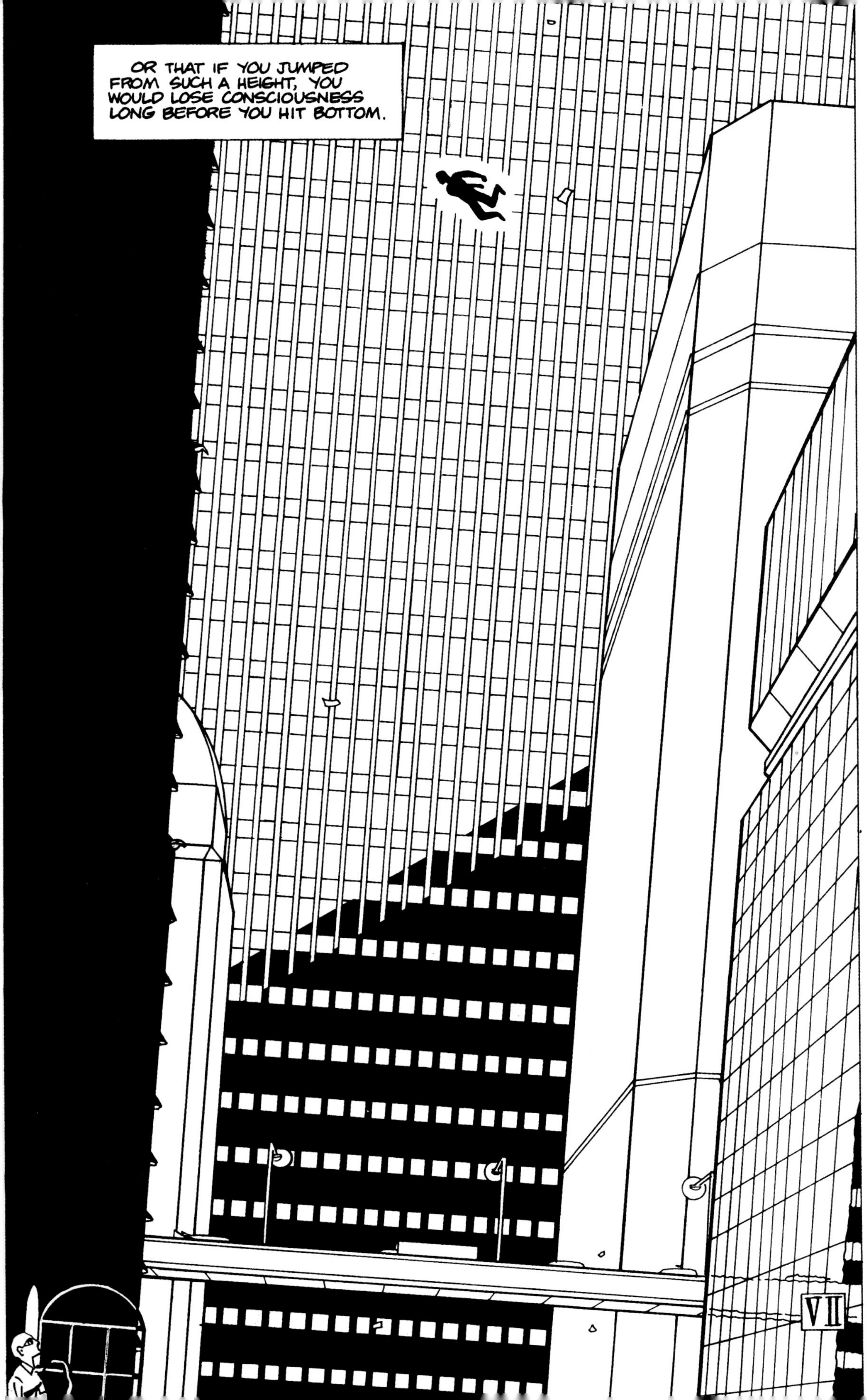
OR THAT IF YOU JUMPED FROM SUCH A HEIGHT, YOU WOULD LOSE CONSCIOUSNESS LONG BEFORE YOU HIT BOTTOM.
VII

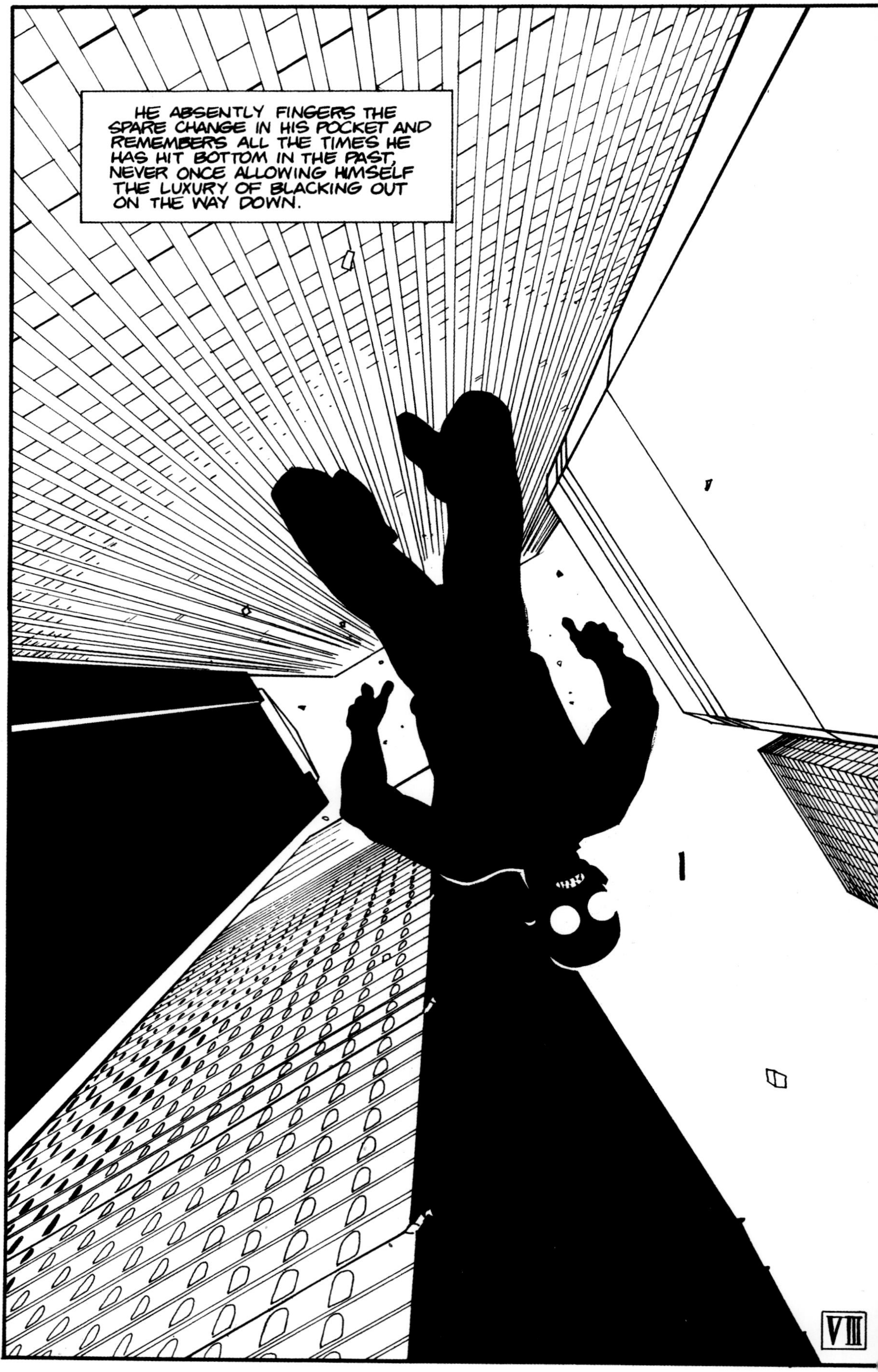
HE ABSENTLY FINGERS THE SPARE CHANGE IN HIS POCKET AND REMEMBERS ALL THE TIMES HE HAS HIT BOTTOM IN THE PAST, NEVER ONCE ALLOWING HIMSELF THE LUXURY OF BLACKING OUT ON THE WAY DOWN.
VIII

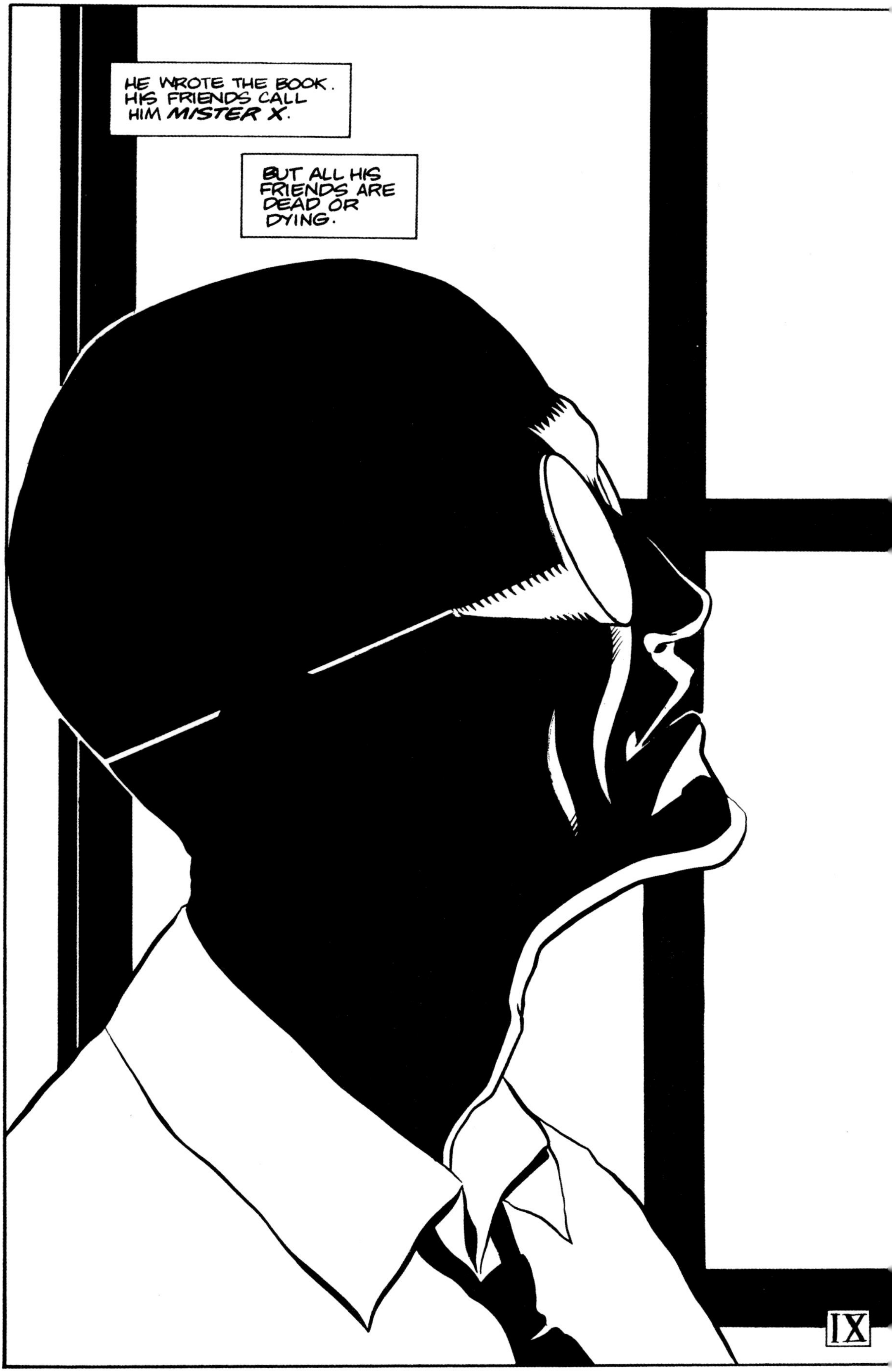
HE WROTE THE BOOK. HIS FRIENDS CALL HIM *MISTER X*.
BUT ALL HIS FRIENDS ARE DEAD OR DYING.
IX

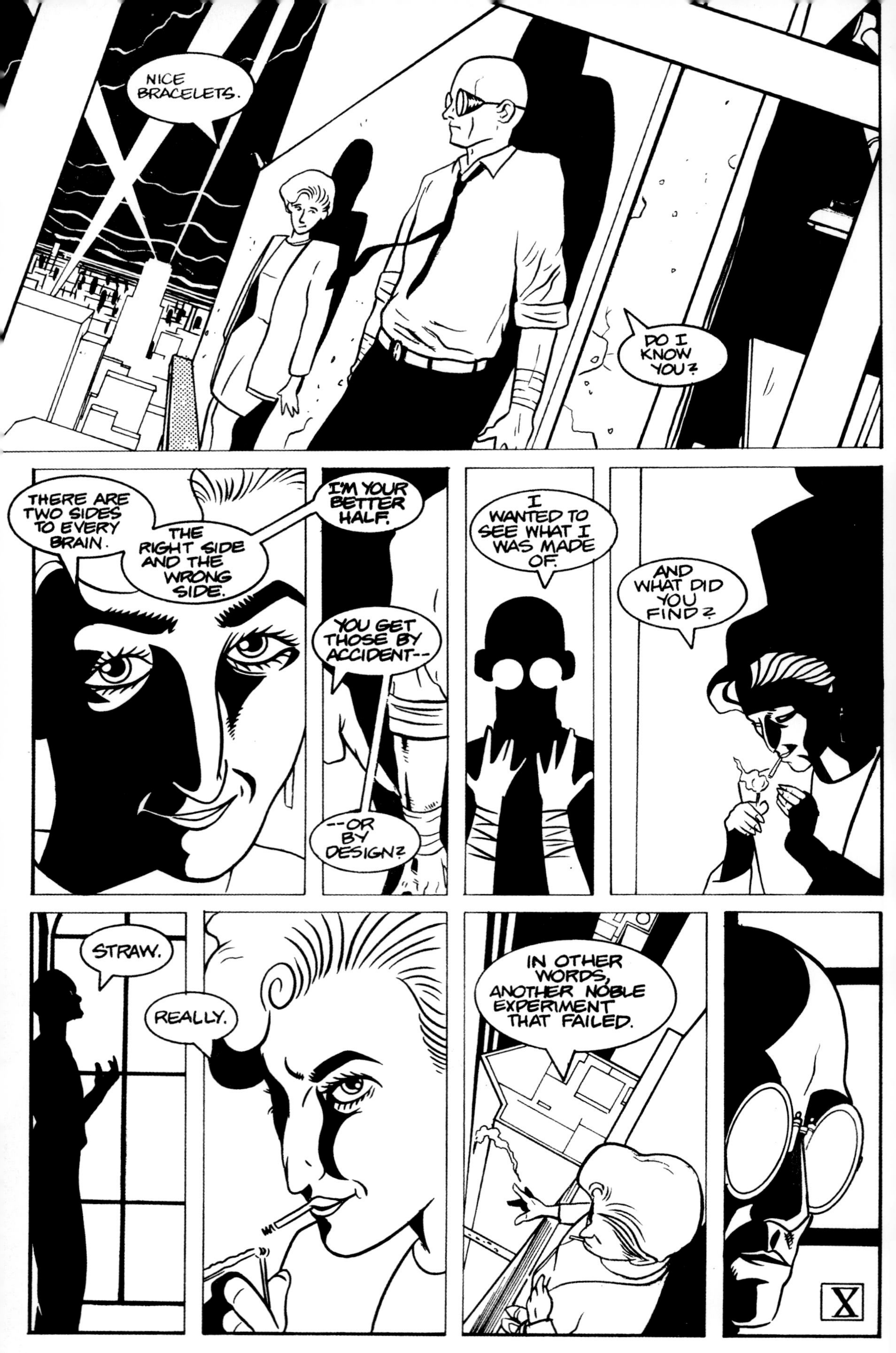
NICE BRACELETS.
DO I KNOW YOU?
THERE ARE TWO SIDES TO EVERY BRAIN.
THE RIGHT SIDE AND THE WRONG SIDE.
I'M YOUR BETTER HALF.
YOU GET THOSE BY ACCIDENT--
--OR BY DESIGN?
I WANTED TO SEE WHAT I WAS MADE OF.
AND WHAT DID YOU FIND?
STRAW.
REALLY.
IN OTHER WORDS, ANOTHER NOBLE EXPERIMENT THAT FAILED.
X

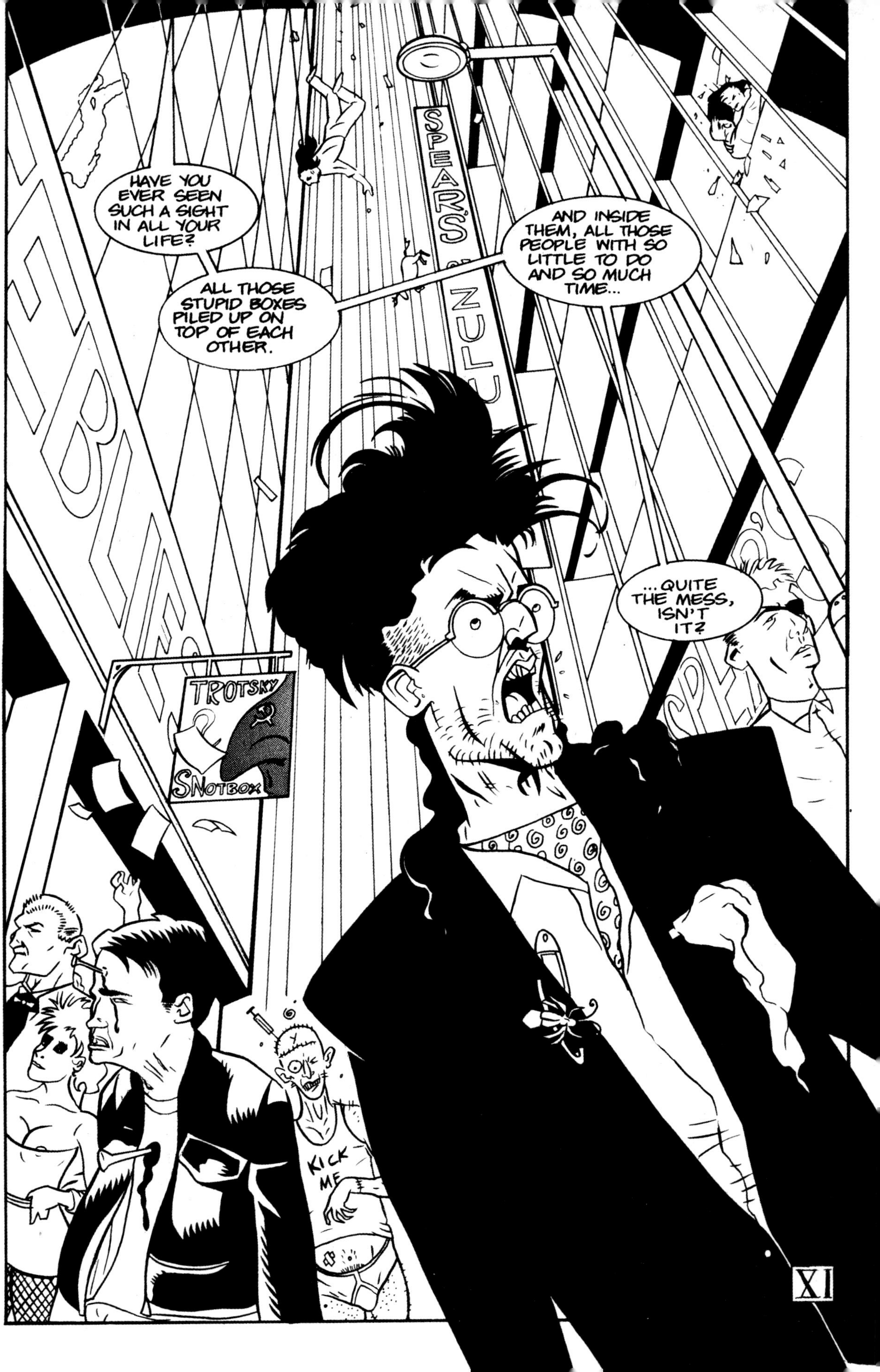
HAVE YOU EVER SEEN SUCH A SIGHT IN ALL YOUR LIFE?
ALL THOSE STUPID BOXES PILED UP ON TOP OF EACH OTHER.
AND INSIDE THEM, ALL THOSE PEOPLE WITH SO LITTLE TO DO AND SO MUCH TIME...
...QUITE THE MESS, ISN'T IT?
SPEAR'S
ZULU
TROTSKY
SNOTBOX
KICK ME

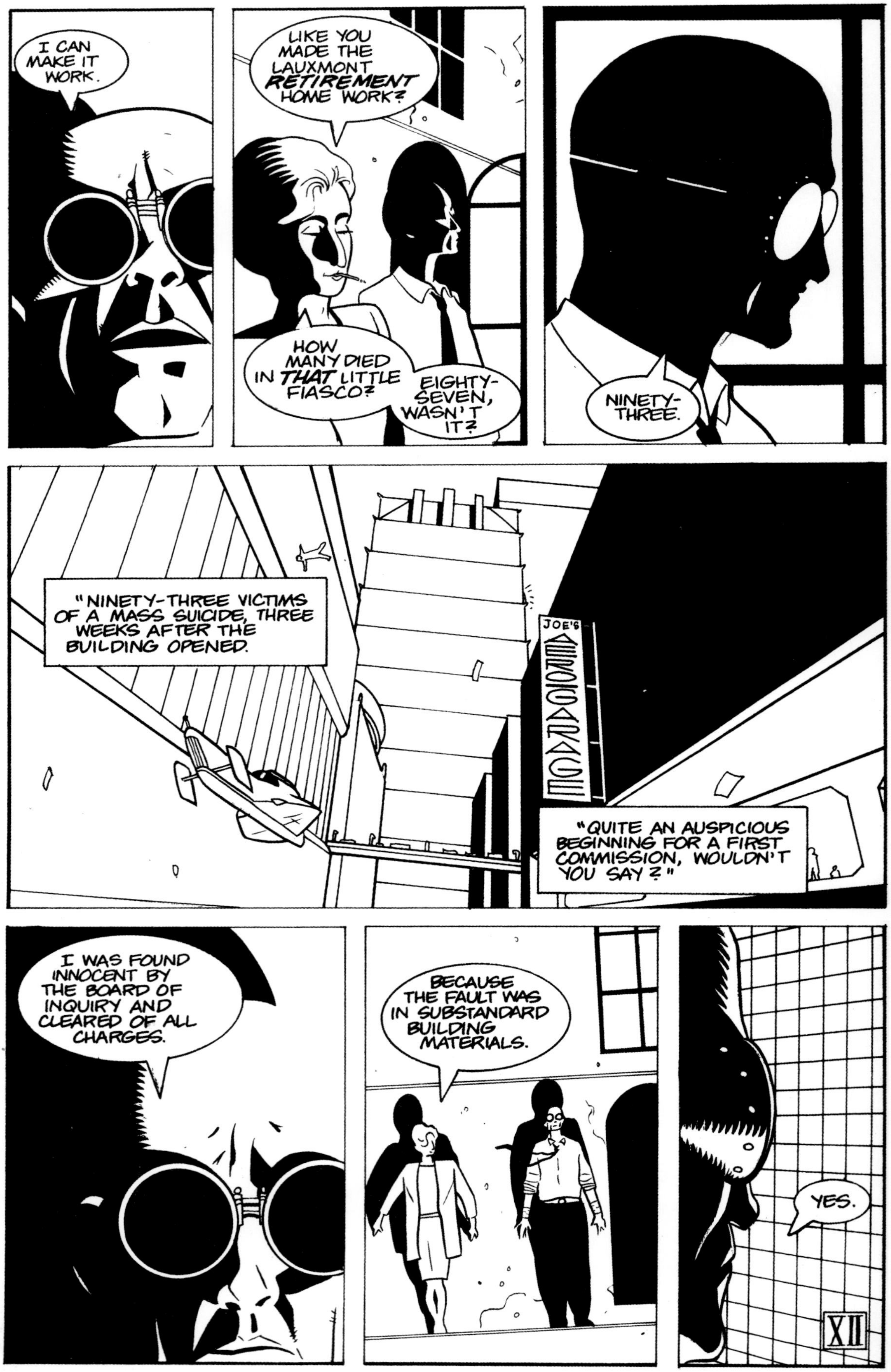
I CAN MAKE IT WORK.
LIKE YOU MADE THE LAUXMONT RETIREMENT HOME WORK?
HOW MANY DIED IN THAT LITTLE FIASCO?
EIGHTY-SEVEN, WASN'T IT?
NINETY-THREE.
"NINETY-THREE VICTIMS OF A MASS SUICIDE, THREE WEEKS AFTER THE BUILDING OPENED.
JOE'S AEROGARAGE
"QUITE AN AUSPICIOUS BEGINNING FOR A FIRST COMMISSION, WOULDN'T YOU SAY?"
I WAS FOUND INNOCENT BY THE BOARD OF INQUIRY AND CLEARED OF ALL CHARGES.
BECAUSE THE FAULT WAS IN SUBSTANDARD BUILDING MATERIALS.
YES.
XII

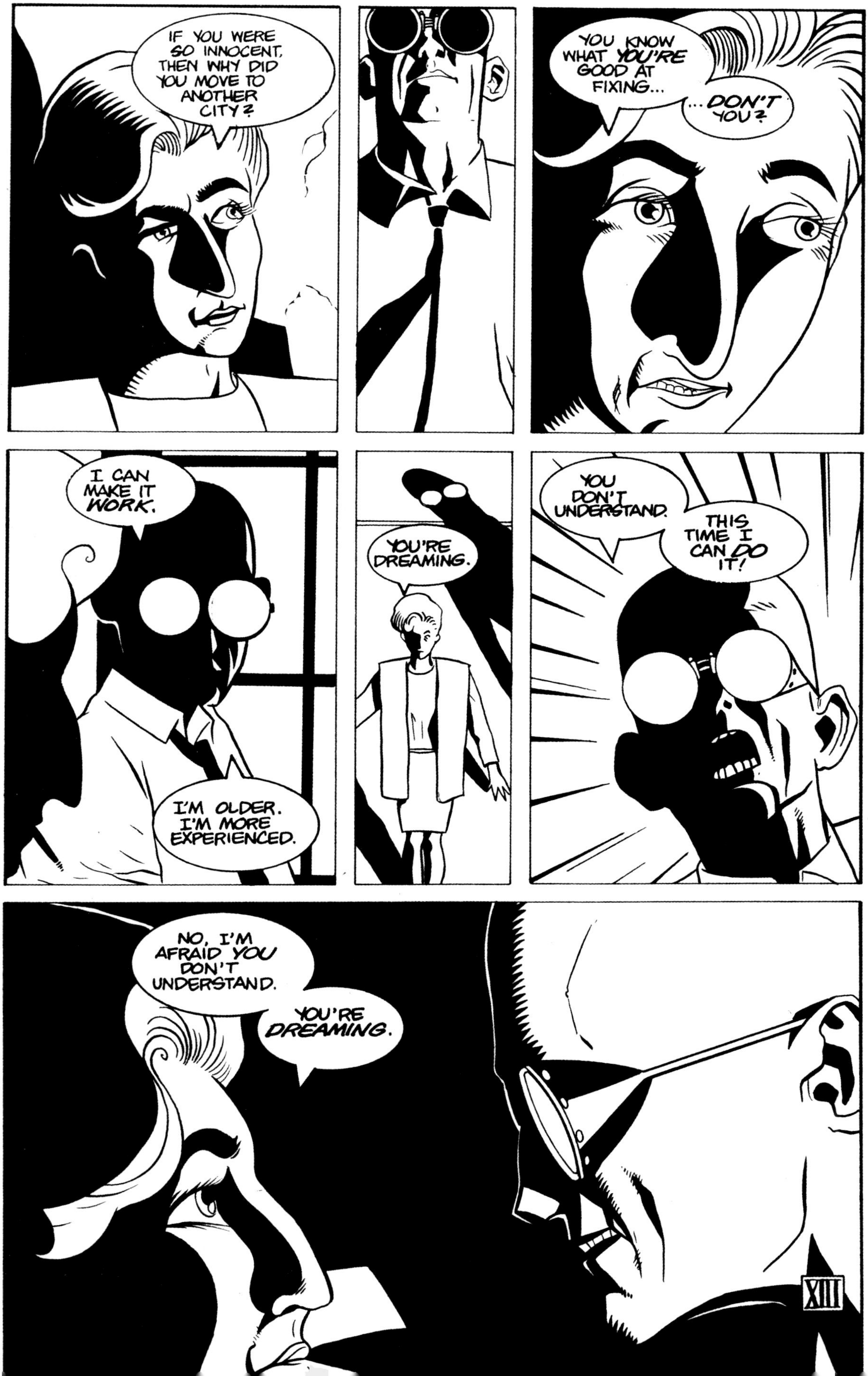
IF YOU WERE SO INNOCENT, THEN WHY DID YOU MOVE TO ANOTHER CITY?
YOU KNOW WHAT YOU'RE GOOD AT FIXING...
...DON'T YOU?
I CAN MAKE IT WORK.
I'M OLDER. I'M MORE EXPERIENCED.
YOU'RE DREAMING.
YOU DON'T UNDERSTAND.
THIS TIME I CAN DO IT!
NO, I'M AFRAID YOU DON'T UNDERSTAND.
YOU'RE DREAMING.
XIII

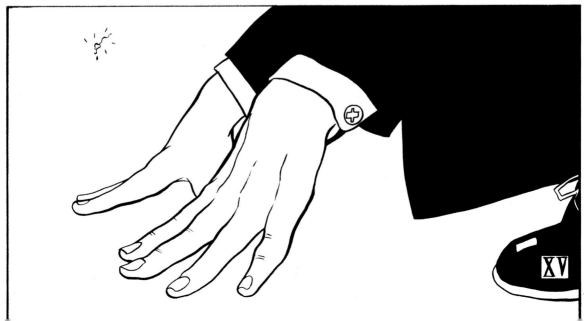

XV

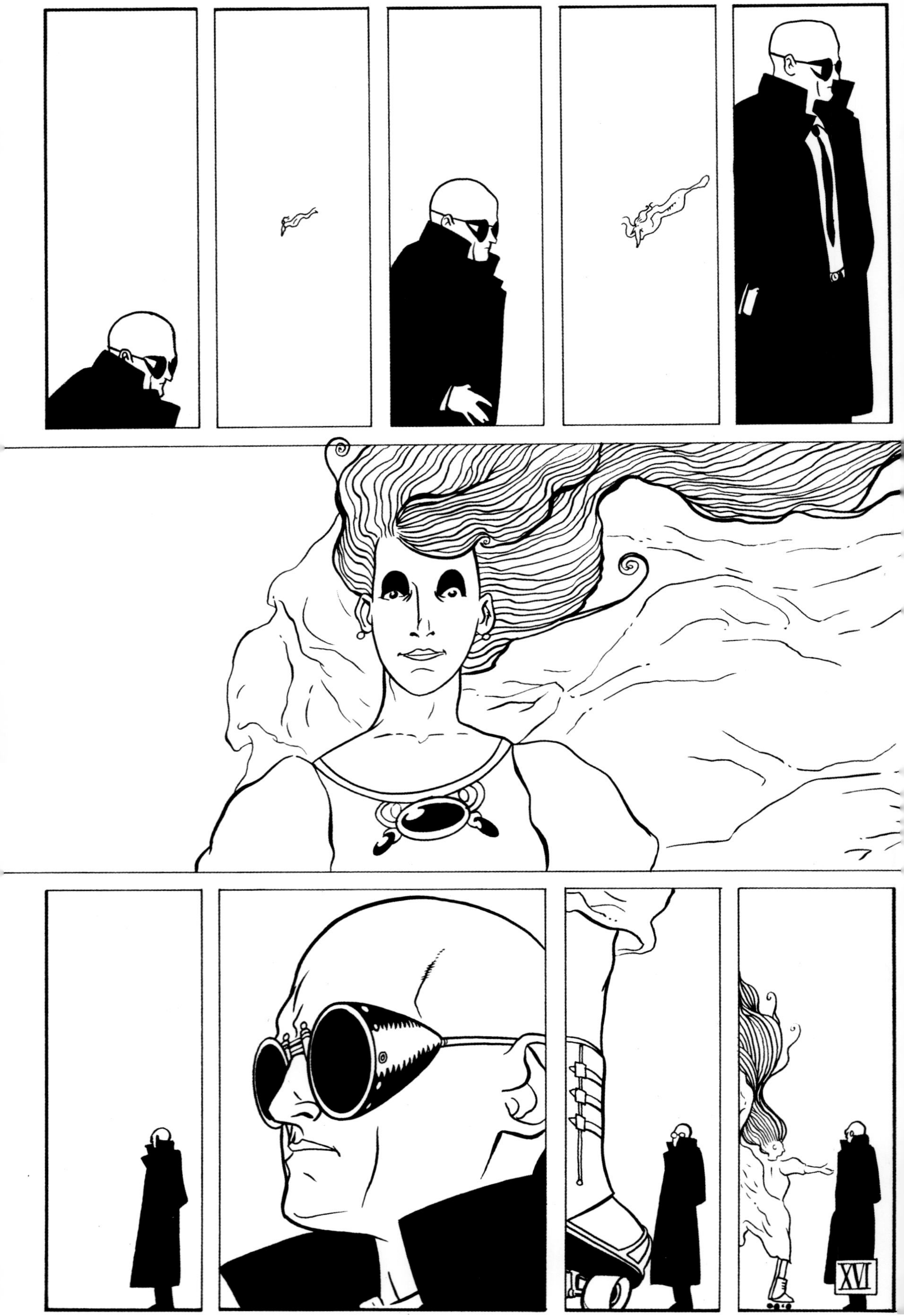
XVI

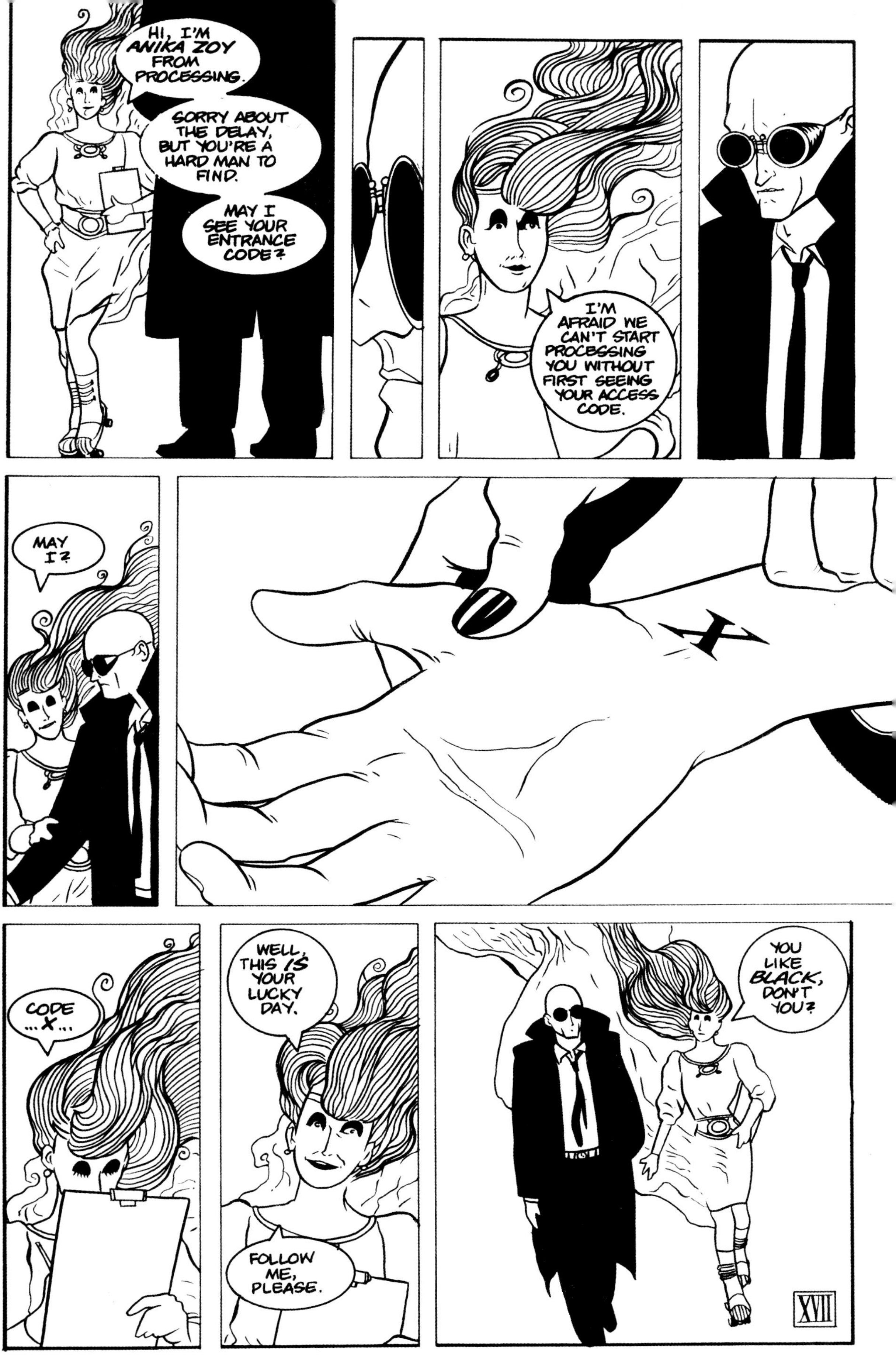
HI, I'M ANIKA ZOY FROM PROCESSING.
SORRY ABOUT THE DELAY, BUT YOU'RE A HARD MAN TO FIND.
MAY I SEE YOUR ENTRANCE CODE?
I'M AFRAID WE CAN'T START PROCESSING YOU WITHOUT FIRST SEEING YOUR ACCESS CODE.
MAY I?
CODE ...X...
WELL, THIS IS YOUR LUCKY DAY.
FOLLOW ME, PLEASE.
YOU LIKE BLACK, DON'T YOU?
XVII

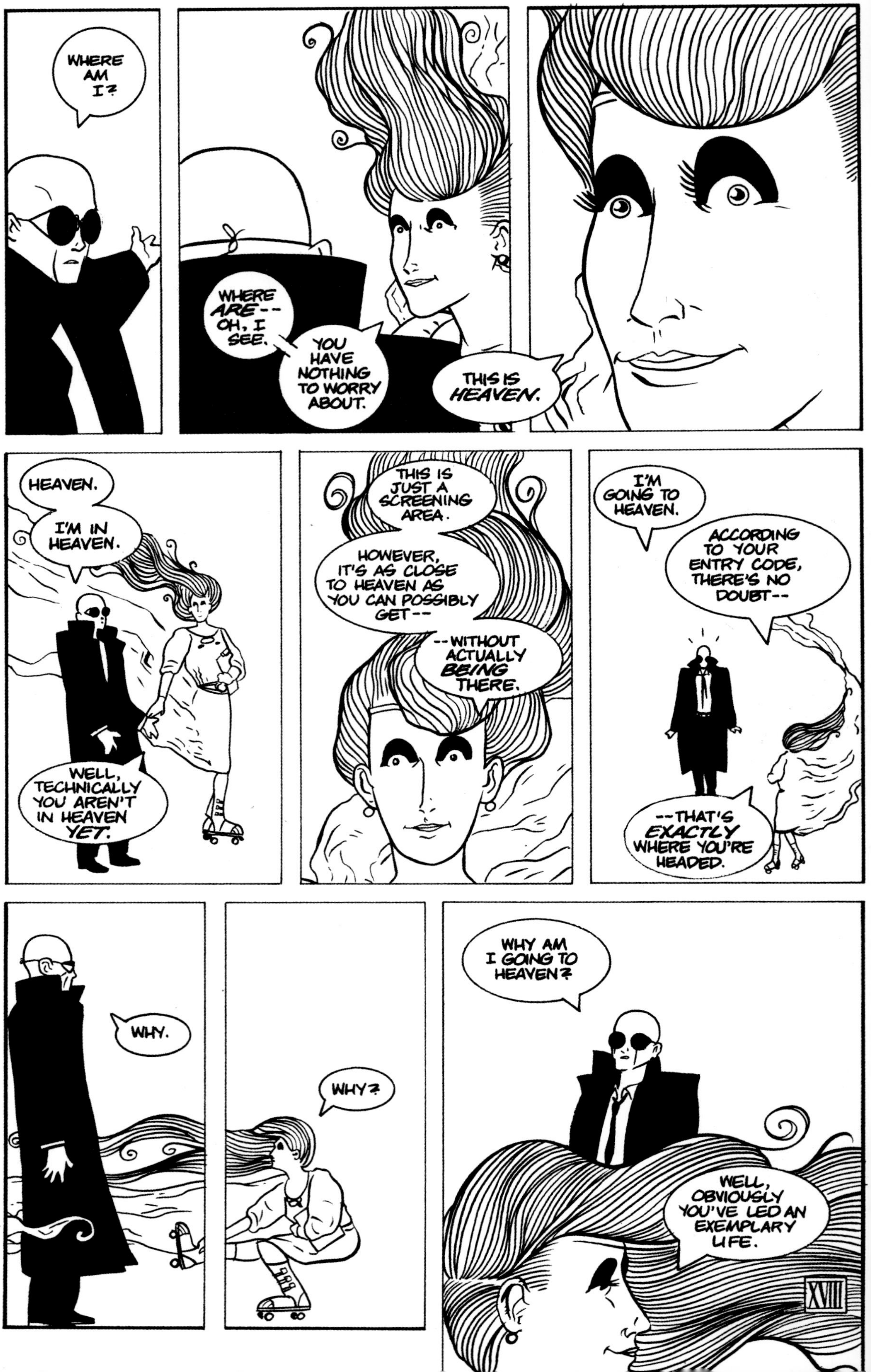

WHERE AM I?
WHERE ARE-- OH, I SEE.
YOU HAVE NOTHING TO WORRY ABOUT.
THIS IS HEAVEN.
HEAVEN.
I'M IN HEAVEN.
WELL, TECHNICALLY YOU AREN'T IN HEAVEN YET.
THIS IS JUST A SCREENING AREA.
HOWEVER, IT'S AS CLOSE TO HEAVEN AS YOU CAN POSSIBLY GET--
--WITHOUT ACTUALLY BEING THERE.
I'M GOING TO HEAVEN.
ACCORDING TO YOUR ENTRY CODE, THERE'S NO DOUBT--
--THAT'S EXACTLY WHERE YOU'RE HEADED.
WHY.
WHY?
WHY AM I GOING TO HEAVEN?
WELL, OBVIOUSLY YOU'VE LED AN EXEMPLARY LIFE.
XVIII

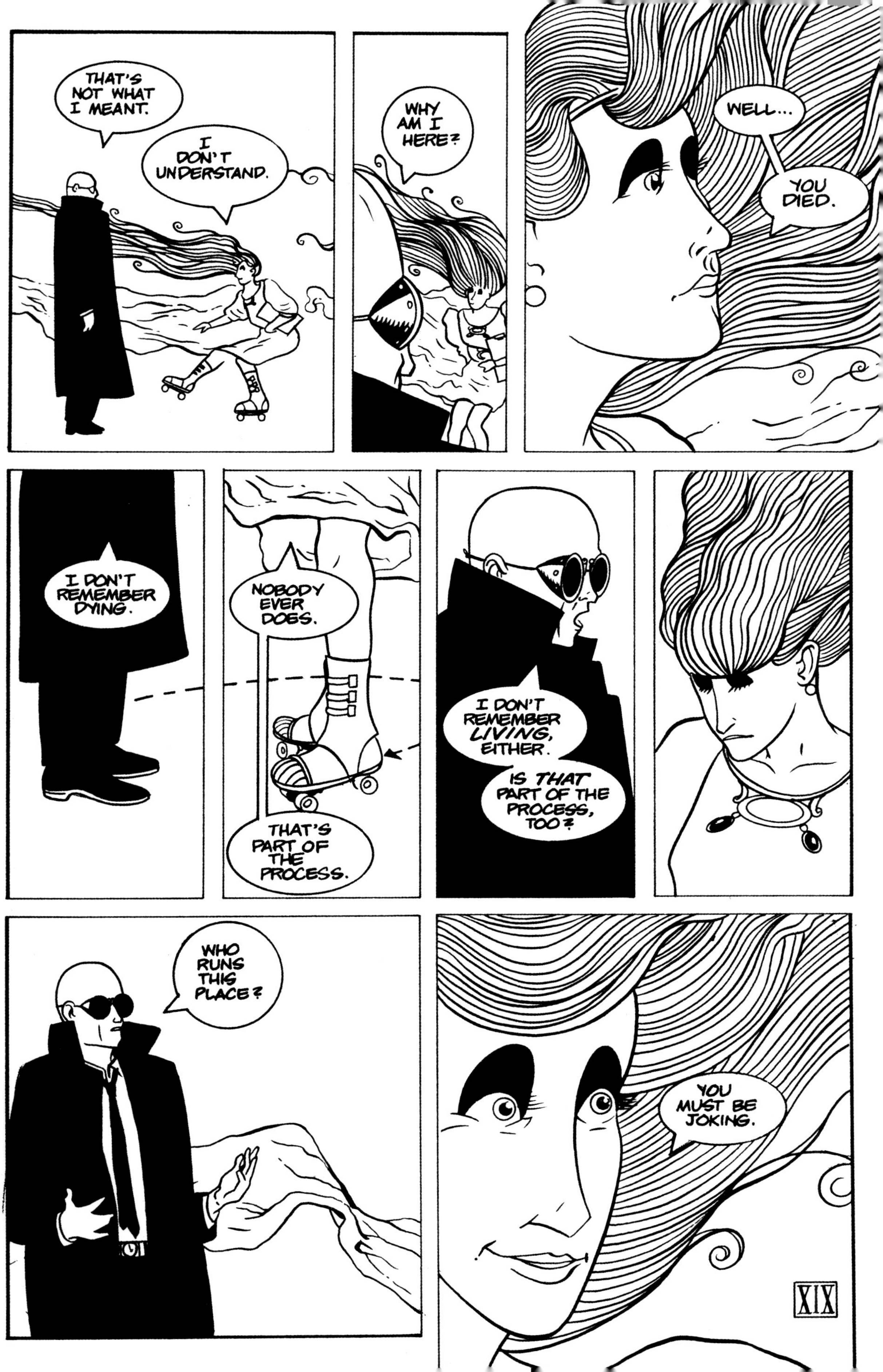
THAT'S NOT WHAT I MEANT.
I DON'T UNDERSTAND.
WHY AM I HERE?
WELL...
YOU DIED.
I DON'T REMEMBER DYING.
NOBODY EVER DOES.
THAT'S PART OF THE PROCESS.
I DON'T REMEMBER *LIVING*, EITHER.
IS *THAT* PART OF THE PROCESS, TOO?
WHO RUNS THIS PLACE?
YOU MUST BE JOKING.
XIX

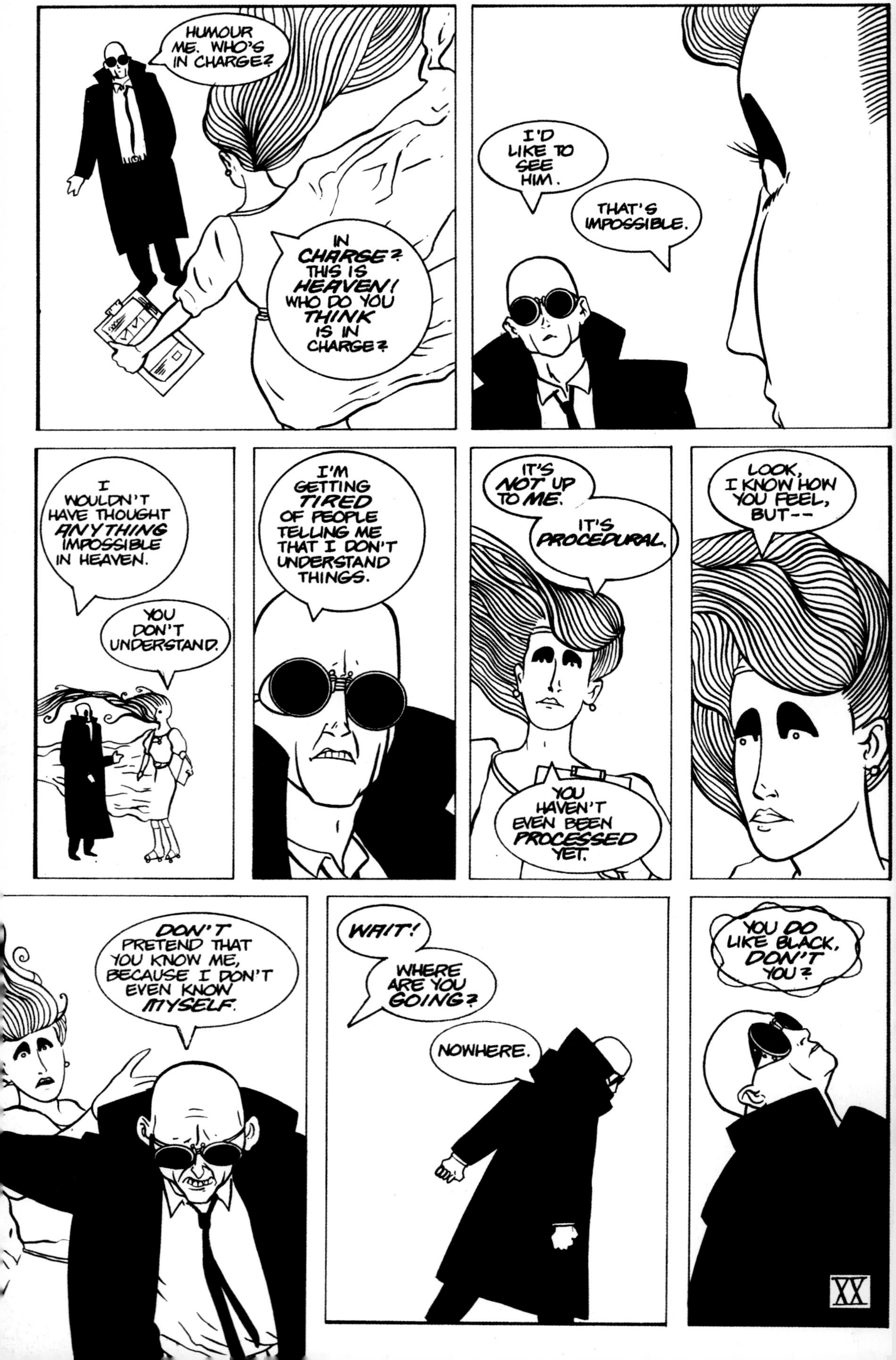
HUMOUR ME. WHO'S IN CHARGE?
IN CHARGE? THIS IS HEAVEN! WHO DO YOU THINK IS IN CHARGE?
I'D LIKE TO SEE HIM.
THAT'S IMPOSSIBLE.
I WOULDN'T HAVE THOUGHT ANYTHING IMPOSSIBLE IN HEAVEN.
YOU DON'T UNDERSTAND.
I'M GETTING TIRED OF PEOPLE TELLING ME THAT I DON'T UNDERSTAND THINGS.
IT'S NOT UP TO ME.
IT'S PROCEDURAL.
YOU HAVEN'T EVEN BEEN PROCESSED YET.
LOOK, I KNOW HOW YOU FEEL, BUT--
DON'T PRETEND THAT YOU KNOW ME, BECAUSE I DON'T EVEN KNOW MYSELF.
WAIT!
WHERE ARE YOU GOING?
NOWHERE.
YOU DO LIKE BLACK, DON'T YOU?
XX

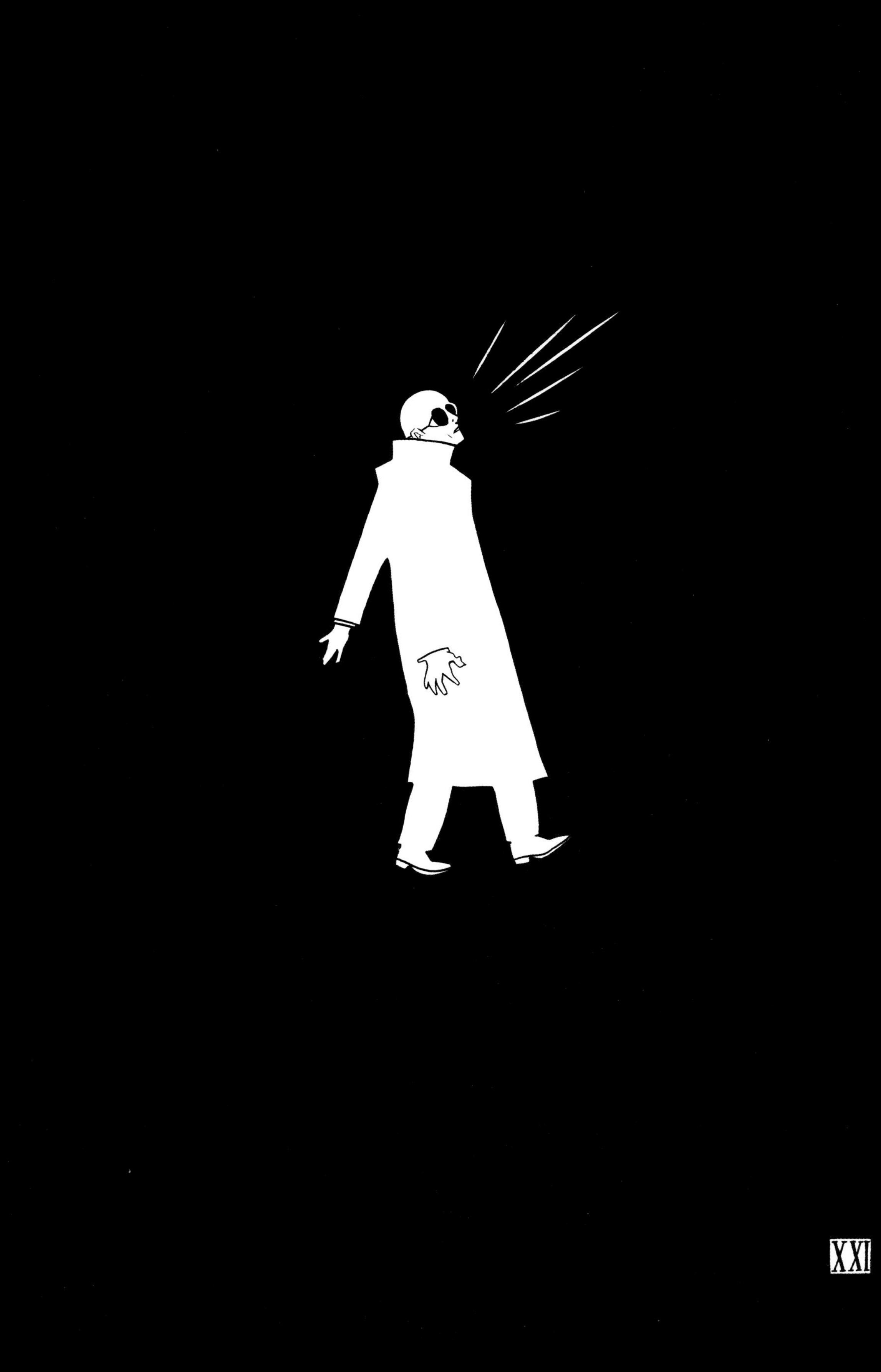

XXI

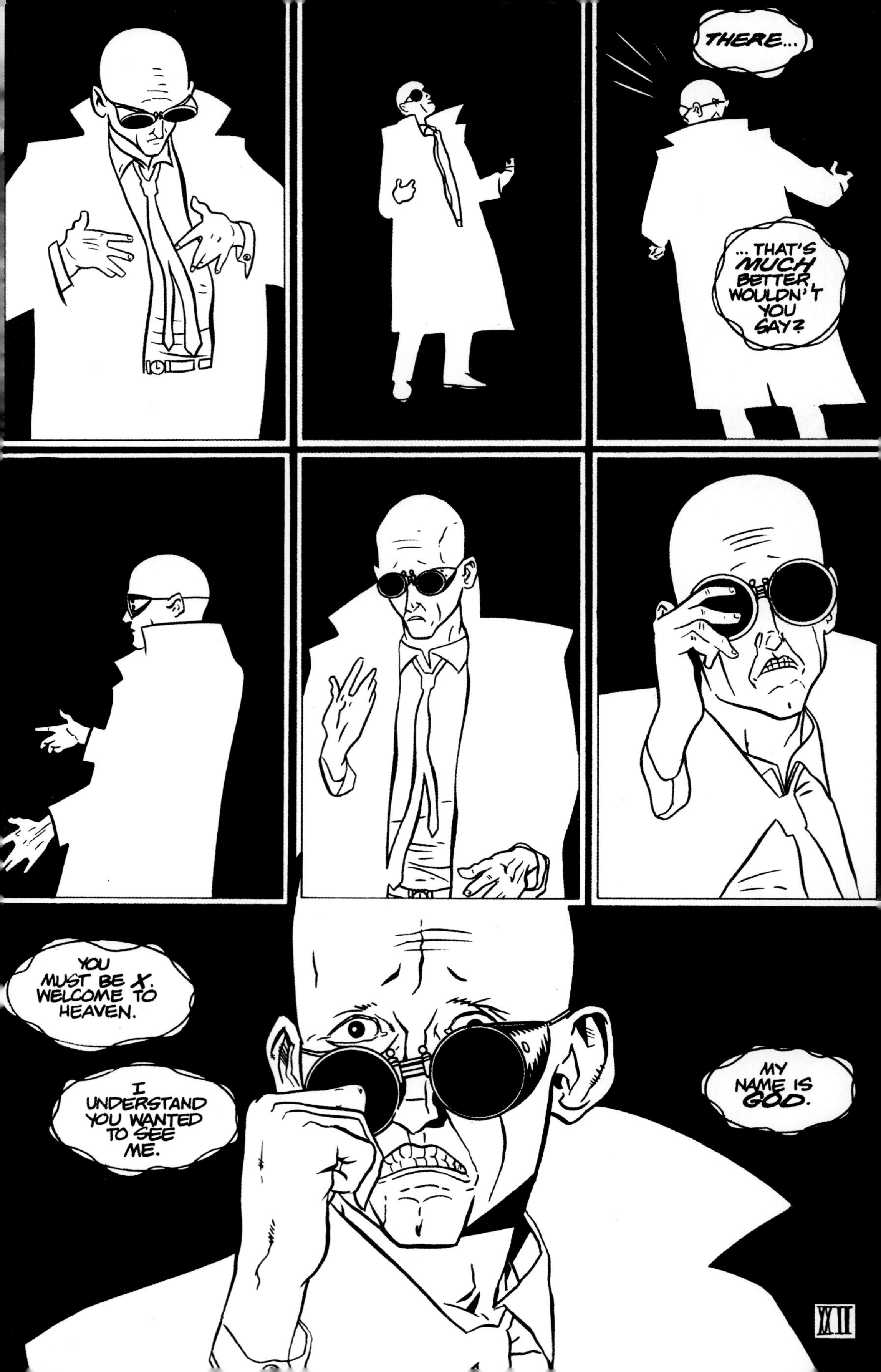
THERE...
...THAT'S MUCH BETTER WOULDN'T YOU SAY?
YOU MUST BE X. WELCOME TO HEAVEN.
I UNDERSTAND YOU WANTED TO SEE ME.
MY NAME IS GOD.
XXII

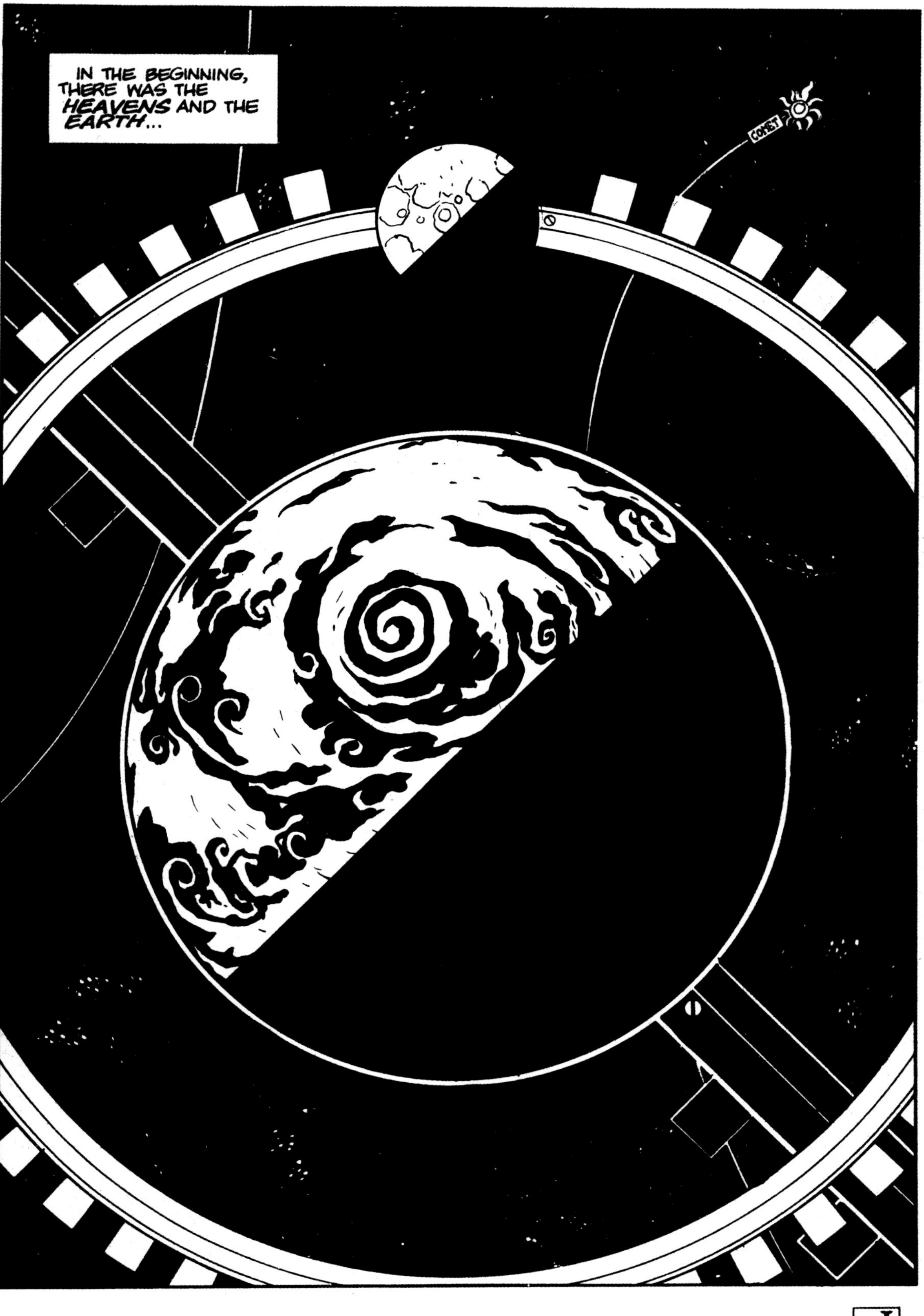
IN THE BEGINNING, THERE WAS THE HEAVENS AND THE EARTH...
COMET

I

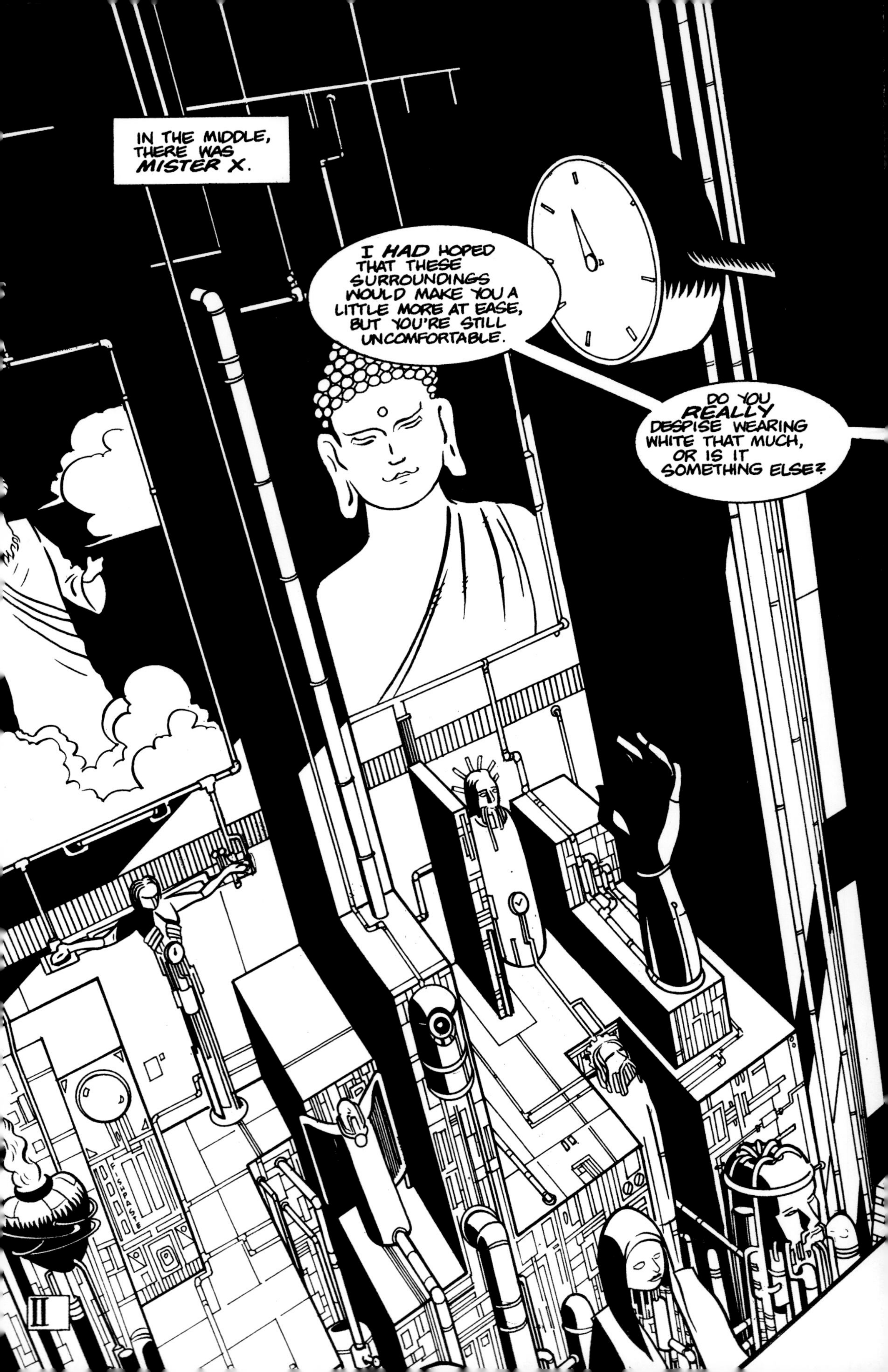

IN THE MIDDLE, THERE WAS MISTER X.
I HAD HOPED THAT THESE SURROUNDINGS WOULD MAKE YOU A LITTLE MORE AT EASE, BUT YOU'RE STILL UNCOMFORTABLE.
DO YOU REALLY DESPISE WEARING WHITE THAT MUCH, OR IS IT SOMETHING ELSE?
FISHPASTE

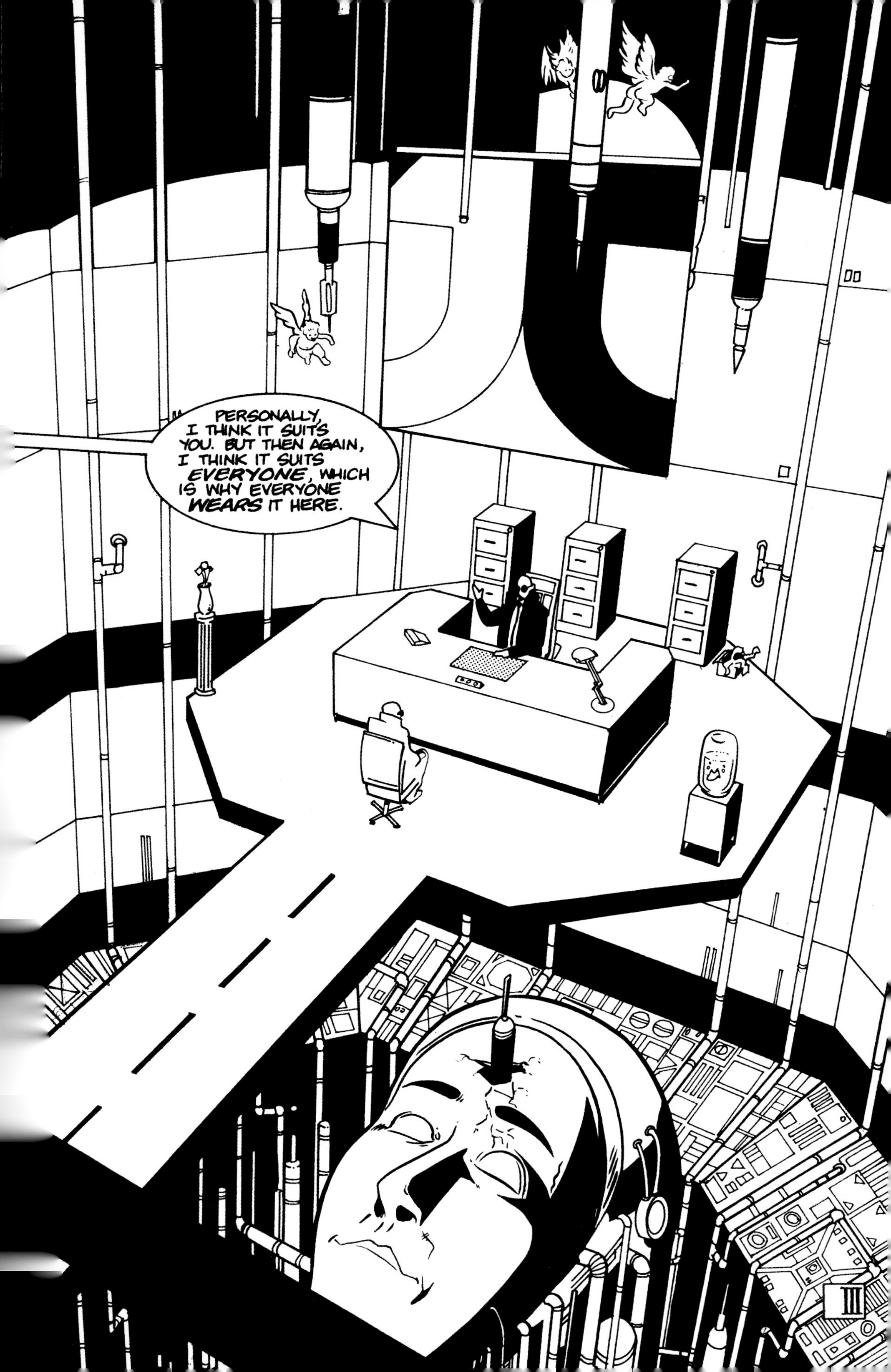
PERSONALLY, I THINK IT SUITS YOU. BUT THEN AGAIN, I THINK IT SUITS EVERYONE, WHICH IS WHY EVERYONE WEARS IT HERE.

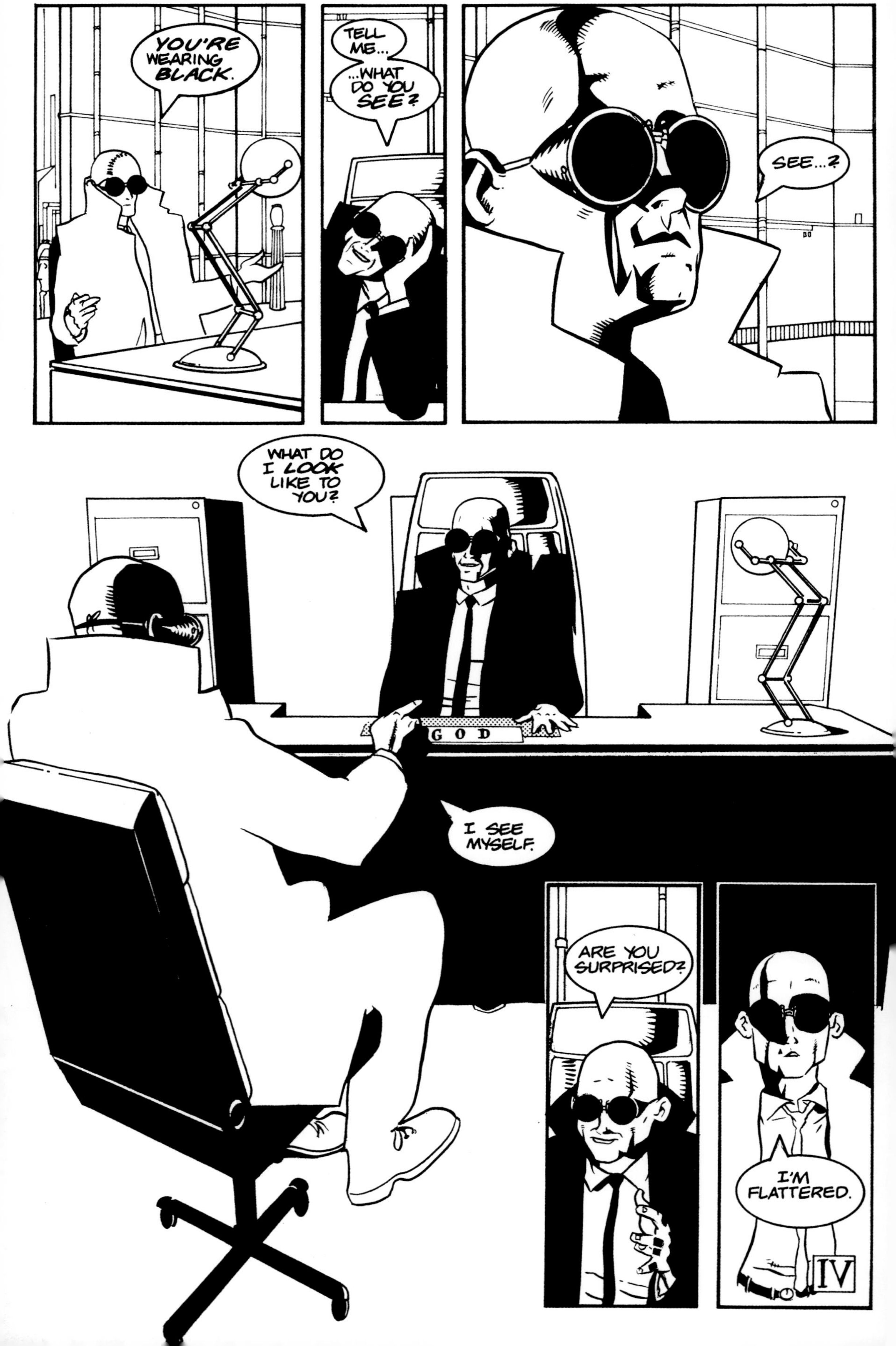
YOU'RE WEARING BLACK.
TELL ME...
...WHAT DO YOU SEE?
SEE...?
WHAT DO I LOOK LIKE TO YOU?
GOD
I SEE MYSELF.
ARE YOU SURPRISED?
I'M FLATTERED.
IV

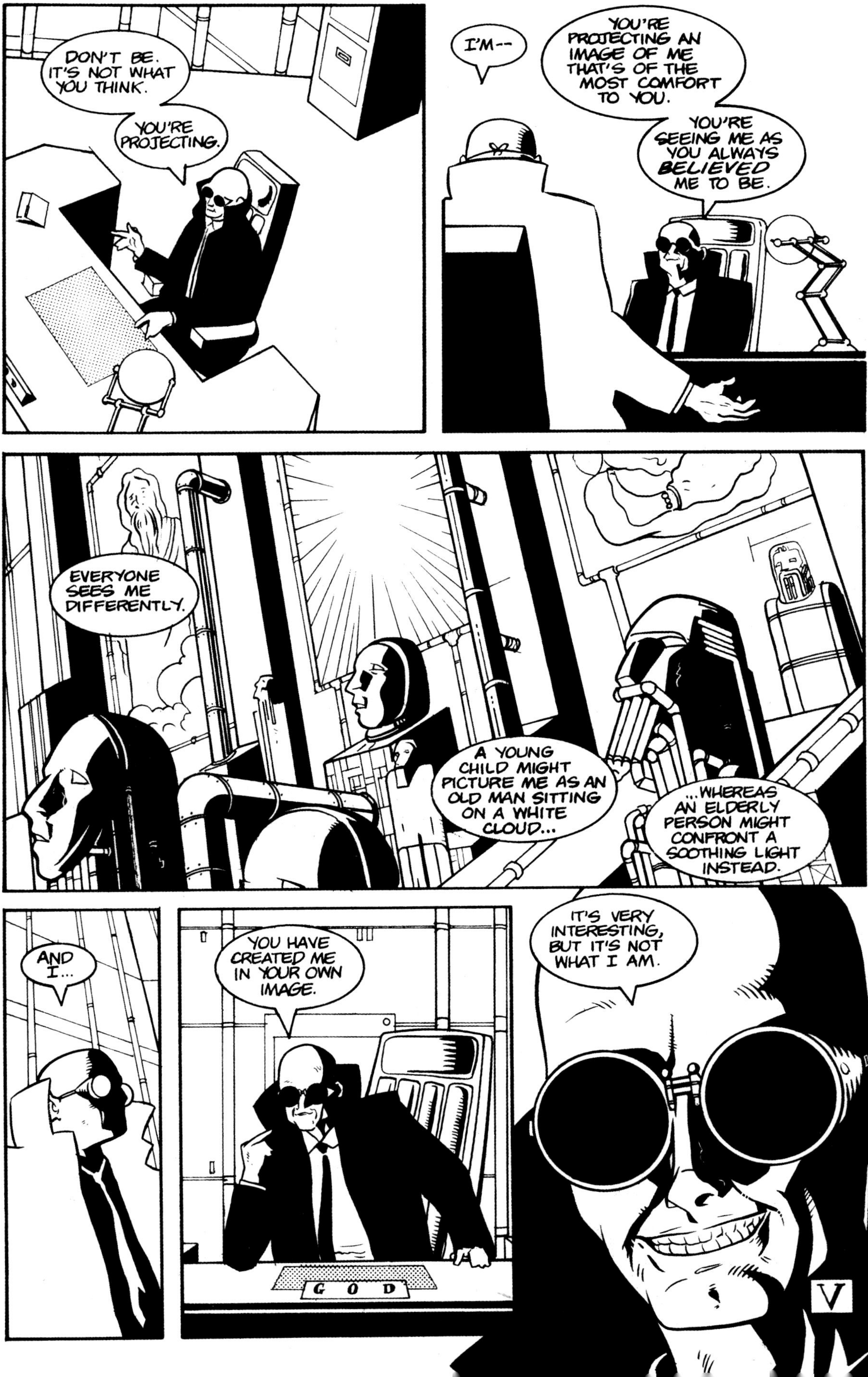
DON'T BE. IT'S NOT WHAT YOU THINK.
YOU'RE PROJECTING.
I'M--
YOU'RE PROJECTING AN IMAGE OF ME THAT'S OF THE MOST COMFORT TO YOU.
YOU'RE SEEING ME AS YOU ALWAYS *BELIEVED* ME TO BE.
EVERYONE SEES ME DIFFERENTLY.
A YOUNG CHILD MIGHT PICTURE ME AS AN OLD MAN SITTING ON A WHITE CLOUD...
...WHEREAS AN ELDERLY PERSON MIGHT CONFRONT A SOOTHING LIGHT INSTEAD.
AND I...
YOU HAVE CREATED ME IN YOUR OWN IMAGE.
GOD
IT'S VERY INTERESTING, BUT IT'S NOT WHAT I AM.
V

WHAT ARE YOU?
I AM THE TRUTH. WHAT ARE YOU?
I DON'T KNOW.
DON'T YOU?
NO.
YOU'RE SURE.
THE LIE.
I'M SORRY?
I AM THE LIE.
WERE THAT THE CASE, THEN YOU WOULDN'T BE HERE.
WHERE WOULD I BE?
PRAY TO ME THAT YOU NEVER FIND OUT.
VI

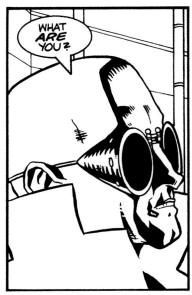

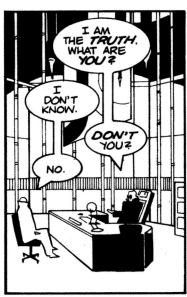

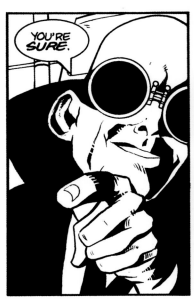

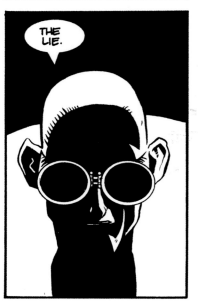

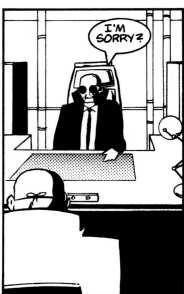

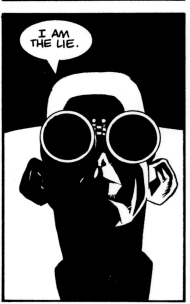

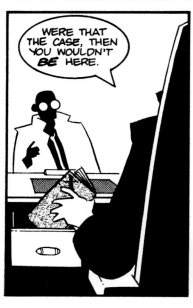

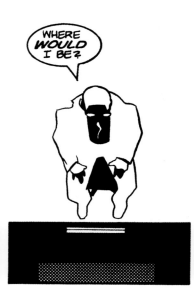

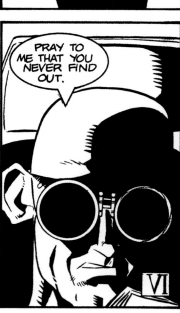

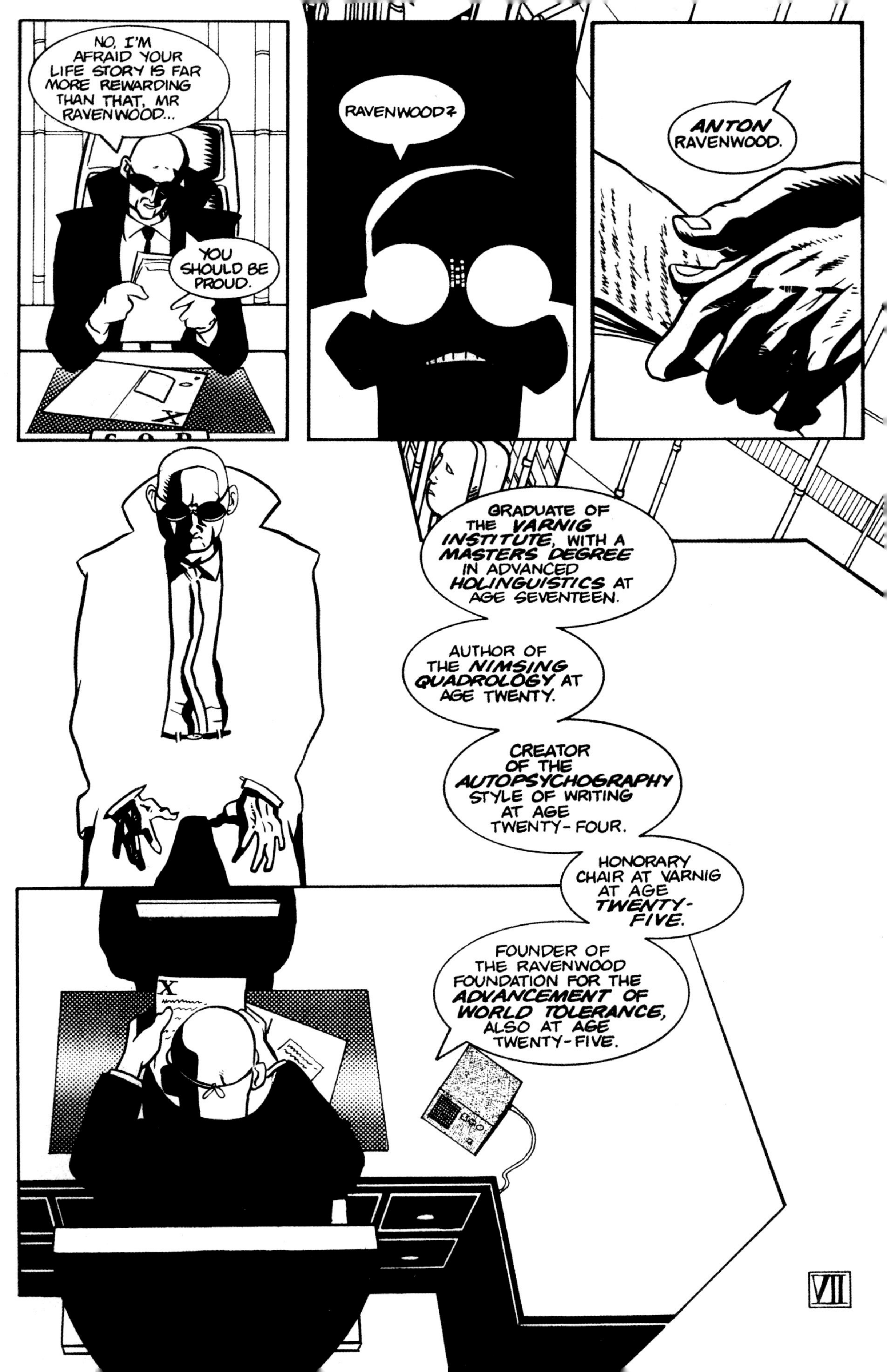
NO, I'M AFRAID YOUR LIFE STORY IS FAR MORE REWARDING THAN THAT, MR RAVENWOOD...
YOU SHOULD BE PROUD.
RAVENWOOD?
ANTON RAVENWOOD.
GRADUATE OF THE VARNIG INSTITUTE, WITH A MASTERS DEGREE IN ADVANCED HOLINGUISTICS AT AGE SEVENTEEN.
AUTHOR OF THE NIMSING QUADROLOGY AT AGE TWENTY.
CREATOR OF THE AUTOPSYCHOGRAPHY STYLE OF WRITING AT AGE TWENTY-FOUR.
HONORARY CHAIR AT VARNIG AT AGE TWENTY-FIVE.
FOUNDER OF THE RAVENWOOD FOUNDATION FOR THE ADVANCEMENT OF WORLD TOLERANCE, ALSO AT AGE TWENTY-FIVE.
VII

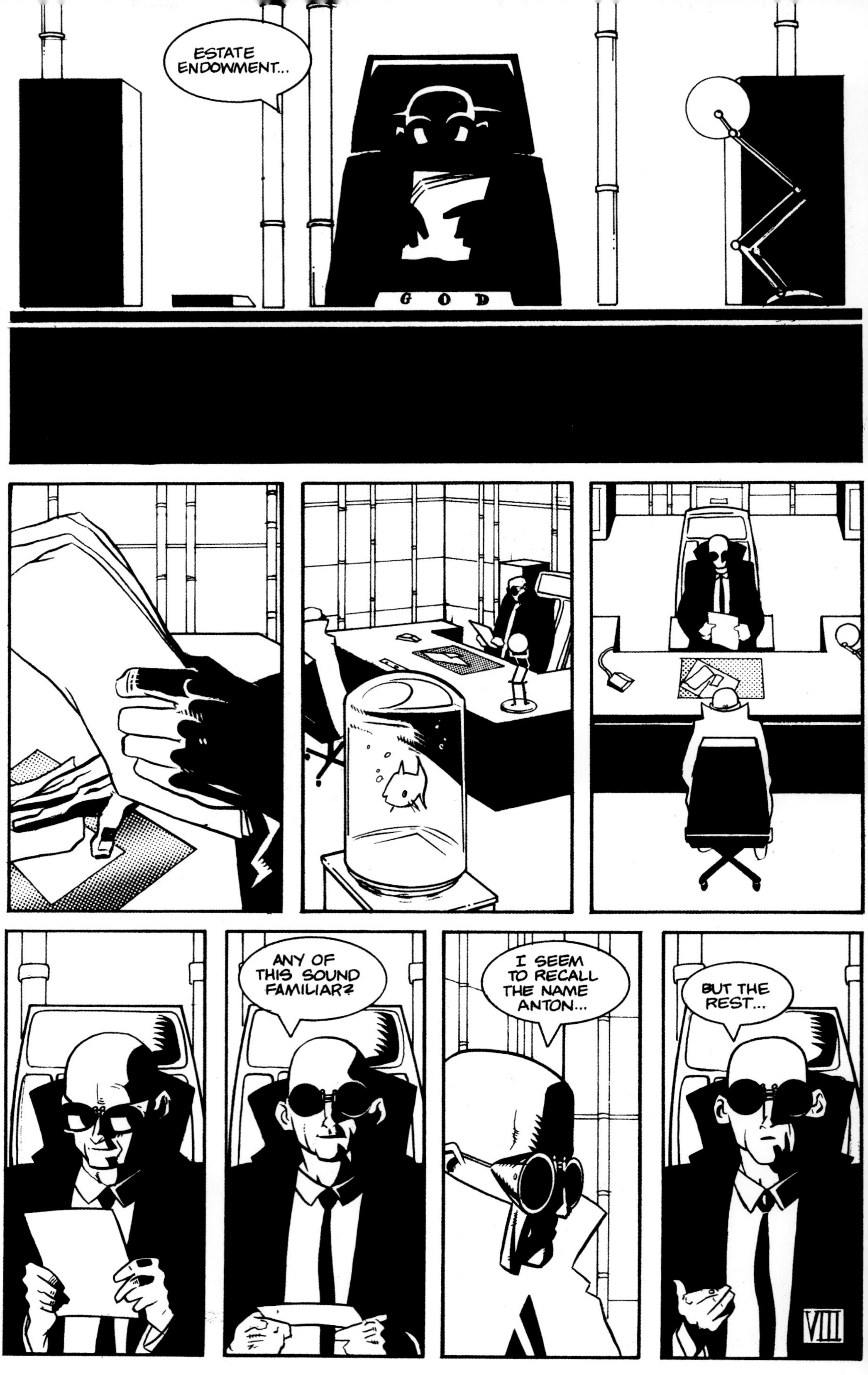
ESTATE ENDOWMENT...
GOD
ANY OF THIS SOUND FAMILIAR?
I SEEM TO RECALL THE NAME ANTON...
BUT THE REST...
VIII

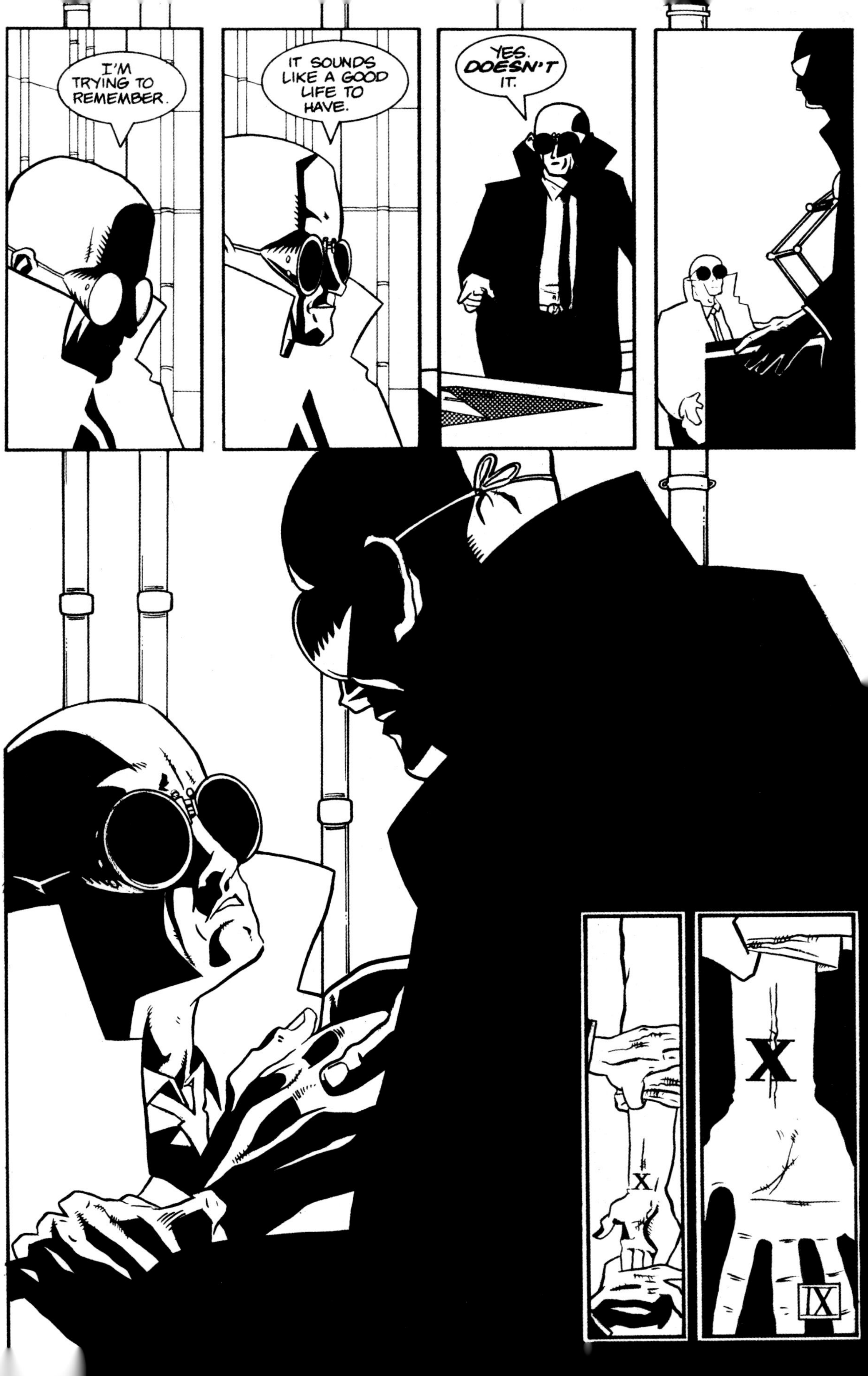
I'M TRYING TO REMEMBER.
IT SOUNDS LIKE A GOOD LIFE TO HAVE.
YES. DOESN'T IT.
X
X
IX

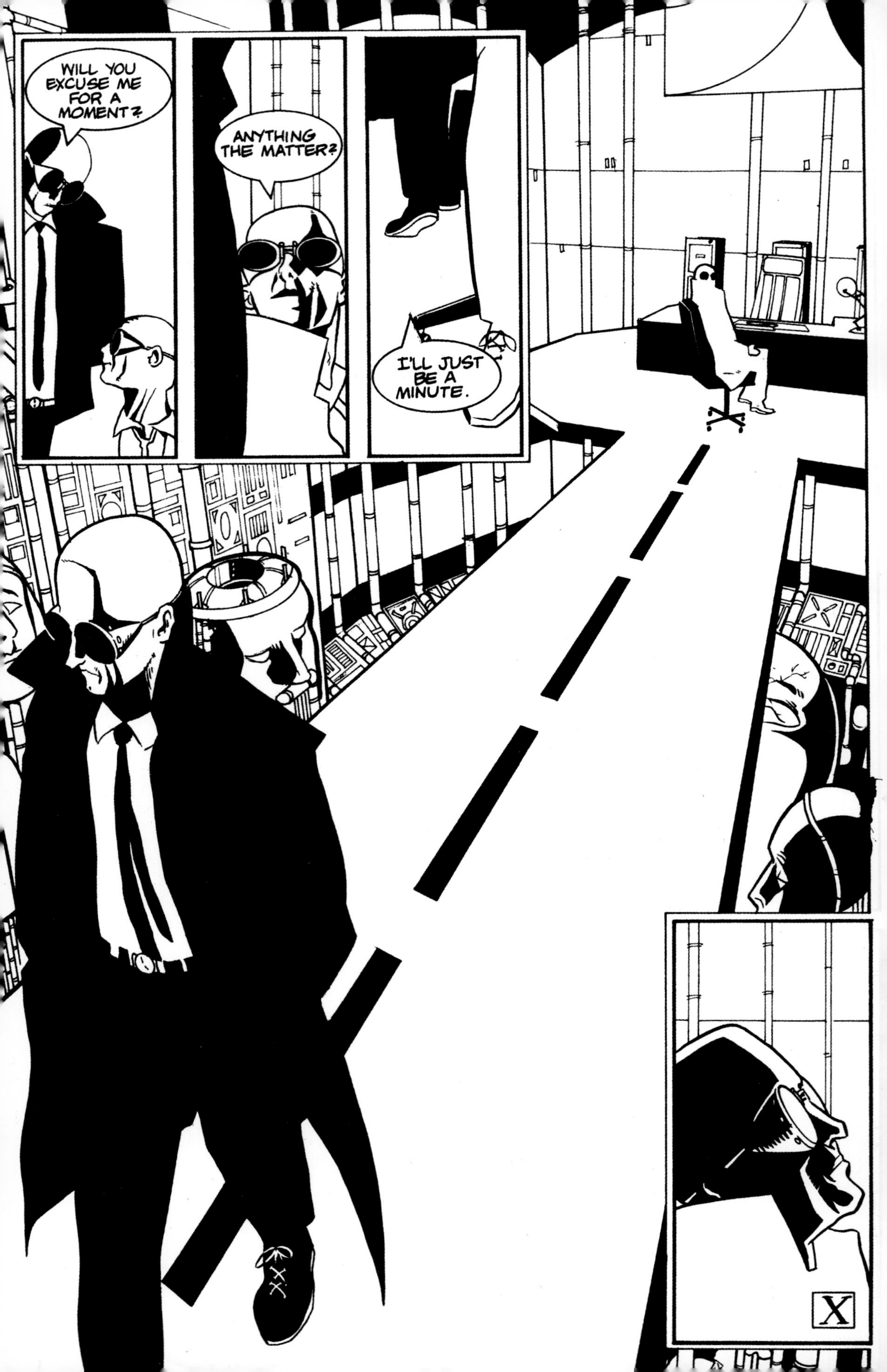
WILL YOU EXCUSE ME FOR A MOMENT?
ANYTHING THE MATTER?
I'LL JUST BE A MINUTE.
X

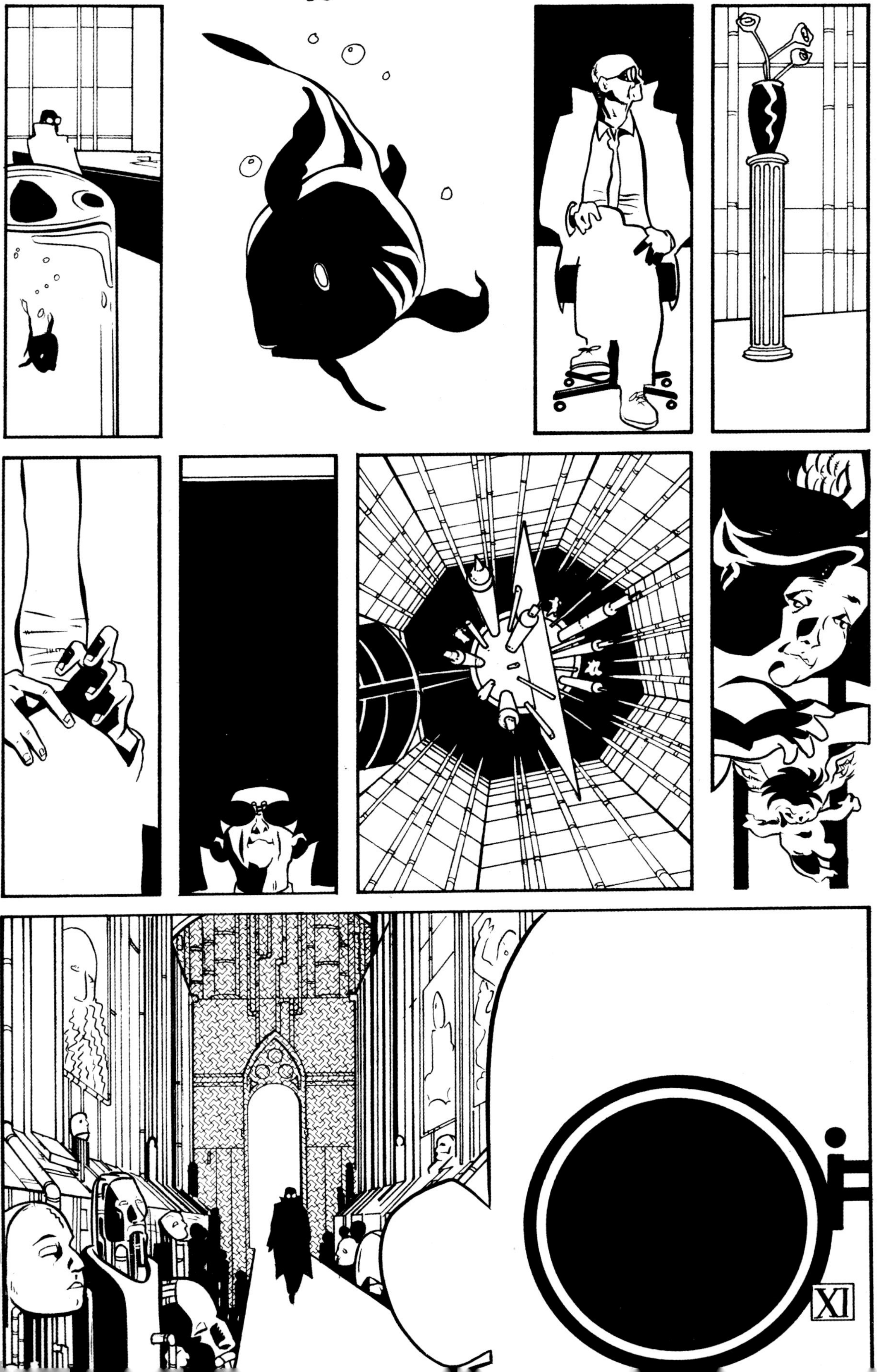
XI

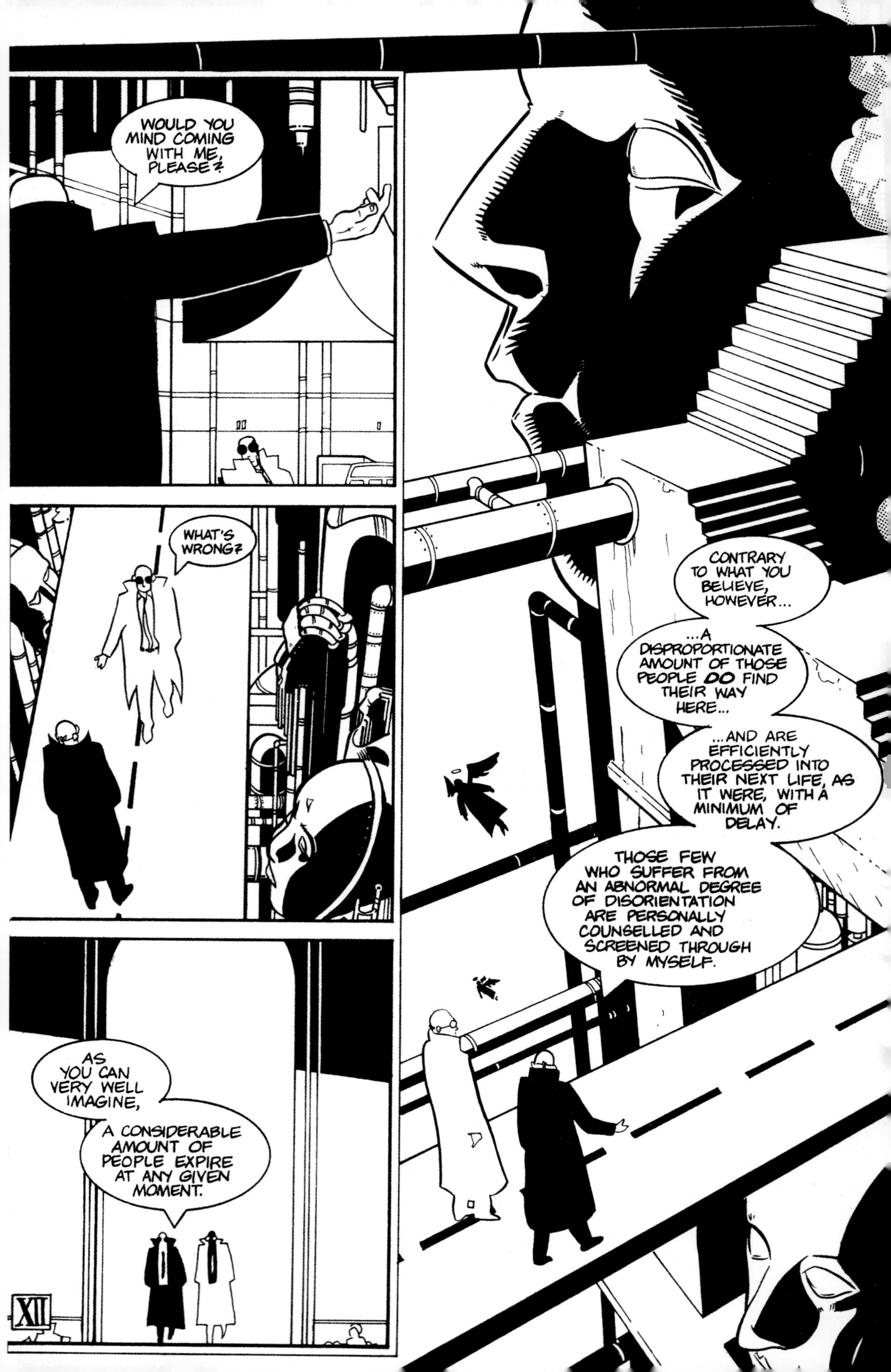
WOULD YOU MIND COMING WITH ME, PLEASE?
WHAT'S WRONG?
AS YOU CAN VERY WELL IMAGINE,
A CONSIDERABLE AMOUNT OF PEOPLE EXPIRE AT ANY GIVEN MOMENT.
CONTRARY TO WHAT YOU BELIEVE, HOWEVER...
...A DISPROPORTIONATE AMOUNT OF THOSE PEOPLE DO FIND THEIR WAY HERE...
...AND ARE EFFICIENTLY PROCESSED INTO THEIR NEXT LIFE, AS IT WERE, WITH A MINIMUM OF DELAY.
THOSE FEW WHO SUFFER FROM AN ABNORMAL DEGREE OF DISORIENTATION ARE PERSONALLY COUNSELLED AND SCREENED THROUGH BY MYSELF.
XII

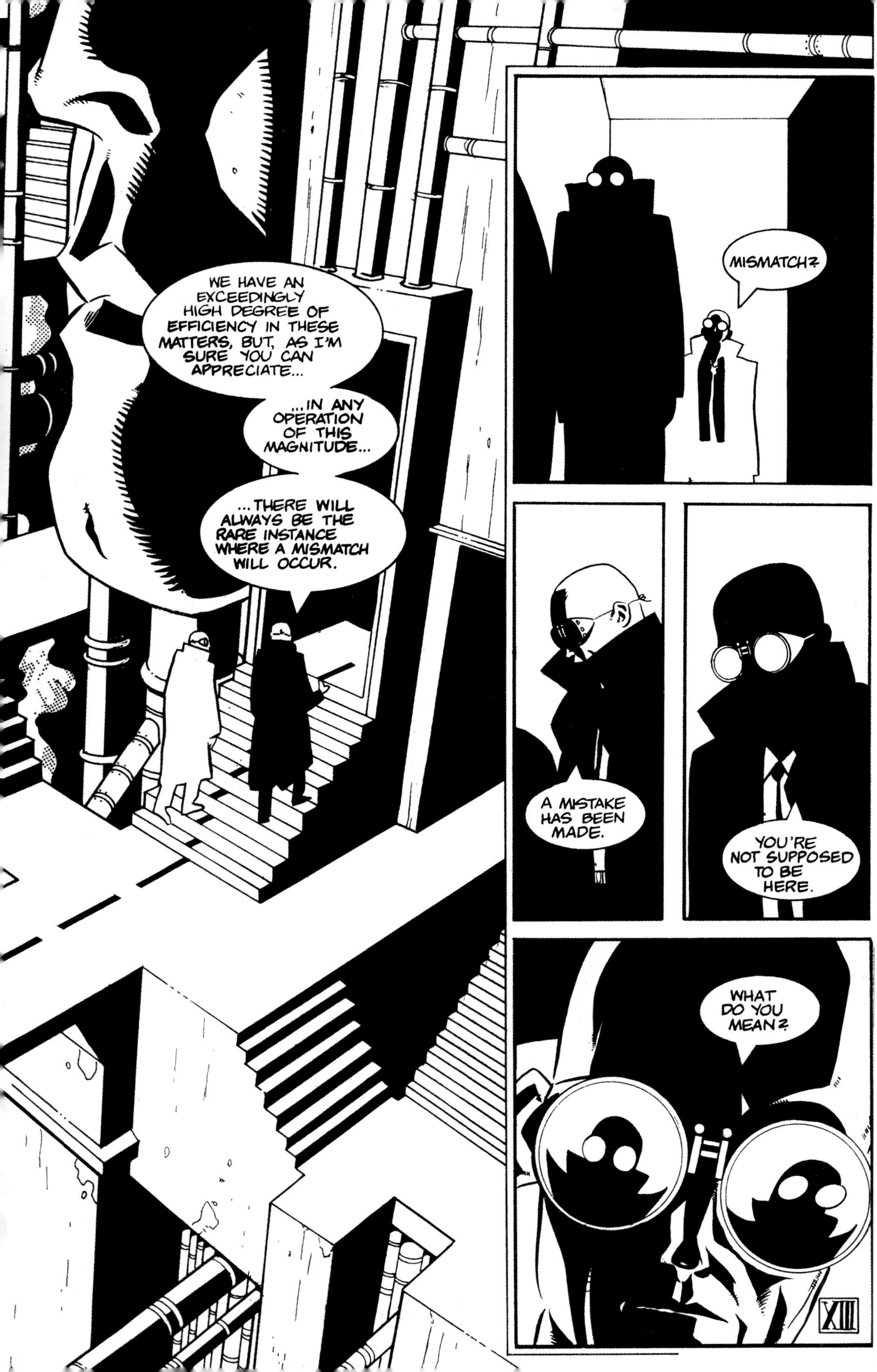
WE HAVE AN EXCEEDINGLY HIGH DEGREE OF EFFICIENCY IN THESE MATTERS, BUT, AS I'M SURE YOU CAN APPRECIATE...
...IN ANY OPERATION OF THIS MAGNITUDE...
...THERE WILL ALWAYS BE THE RARE INSTANCE WHERE A MISMATCH WILL OCCUR.
MISMATCH?
A MISTAKE HAS BEEN MADE.
YOU'RE NOT SUPPOSED TO BE HERE.
WHAT DO YOU MEAN?
XIII

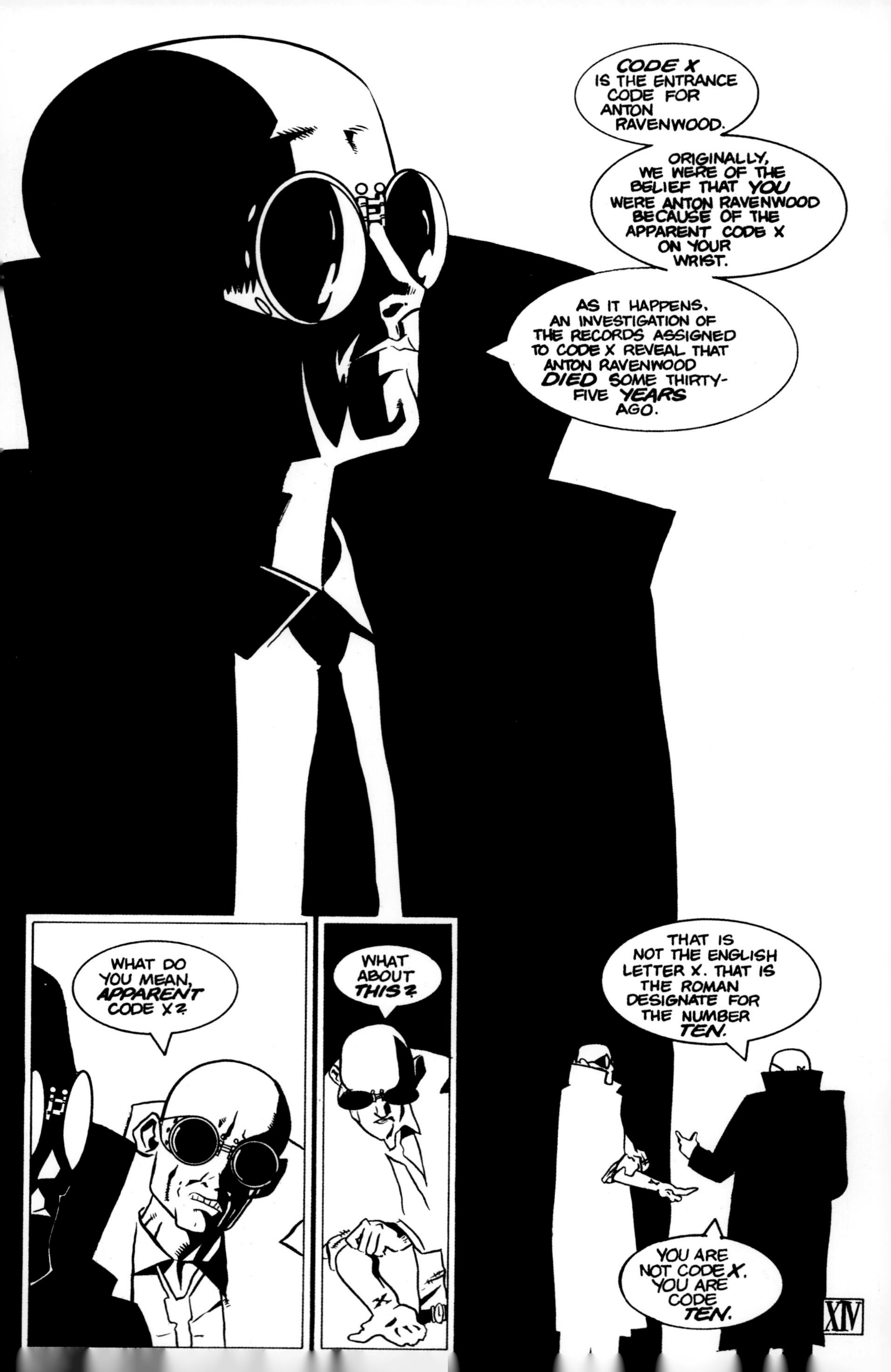
CODE X IS THE ENTRANCE CODE FOR ANTON RAVENWOOD.
ORIGINALLY, WE WERE OF THE BELIEF THAT YOU WERE ANTON RAVENWOOD BECAUSE OF THE APPARENT CODE X ON YOUR WRIST.
AS IT HAPPENS, AN INVESTIGATION OF THE RECORDS ASSIGNED TO CODE X REVEAL THAT ANTON RAVENWOOD DIED SOME THIRTY-FIVE YEARS AGO.
WHAT DO YOU MEAN, APPARENT CODE X?
WHAT ABOUT THIS?
THAT IS NOT THE ENGLISH LETTER X. THAT IS THE ROMAN DESIGNATE FOR THE NUMBER TEN.
YOU ARE NOT CODE X. YOU ARE CODE TEN.
XIV

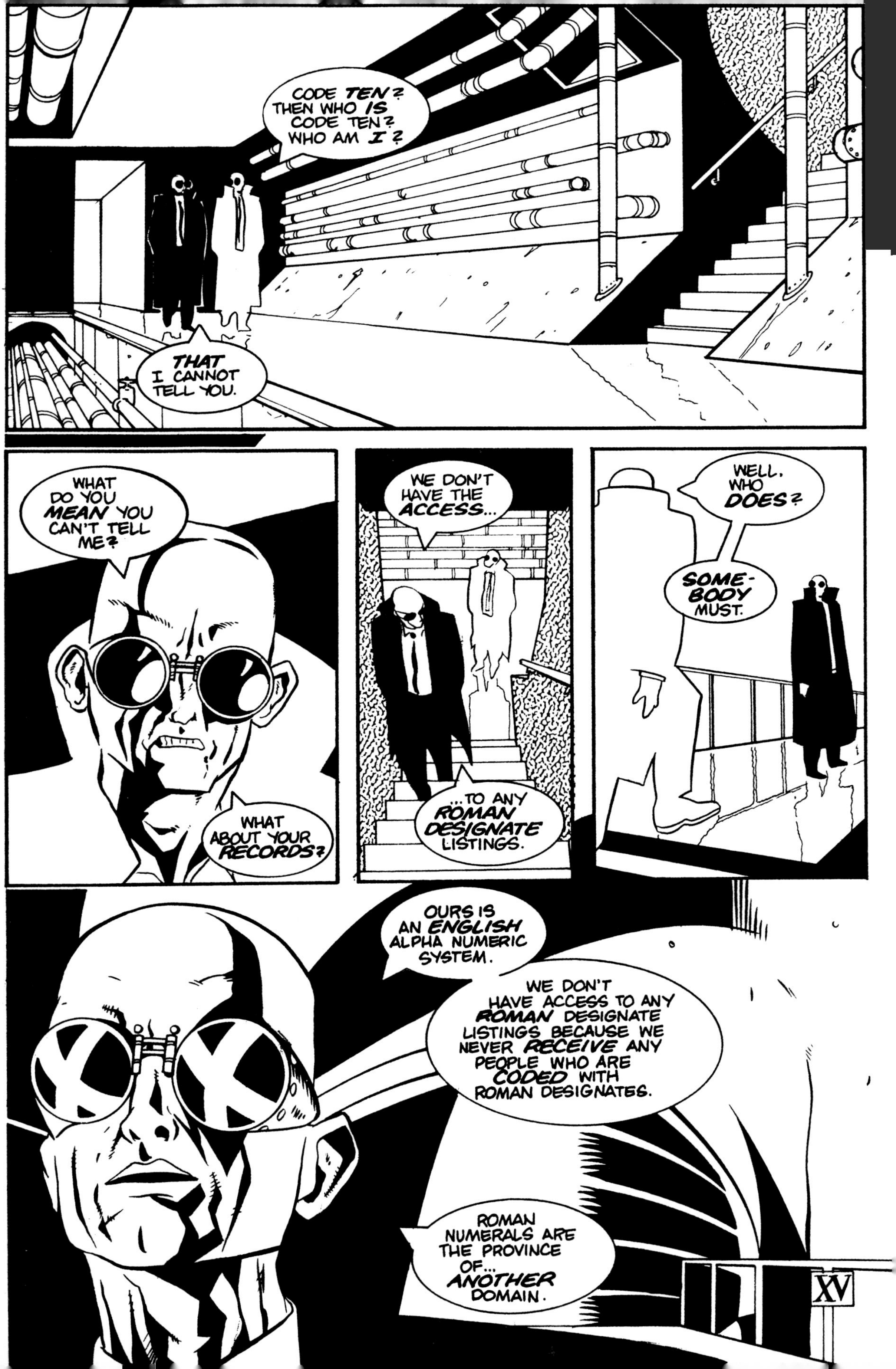
CODE TEN? THEN WHO IS CODE TEN? WHO AM I?
THAT I CANNOT TELL YOU.
WHAT DO YOU MEAN YOU CAN'T TELL ME?
WHAT ABOUT YOUR RECORDS?
WE DON'T HAVE THE ACCESS...
...TO ANY ROMAN DESIGNATE LISTINGS.
WELL, WHO DOES?
SOME-BODY MUST.
OURS IS AN ENGLISH ALPHA NUMERIC SYSTEM.
WE DON'T HAVE ACCESS TO ANY ROMAN DESIGNATE LISTINGS BECAUSE WE NEVER RECEIVE ANY PEOPLE WHO ARE CODED WITH ROMAN DESIGNATES.
ROMAN NUMERALS ARE THE PROVINCE OF... ANOTHER DOMAIN.
XV

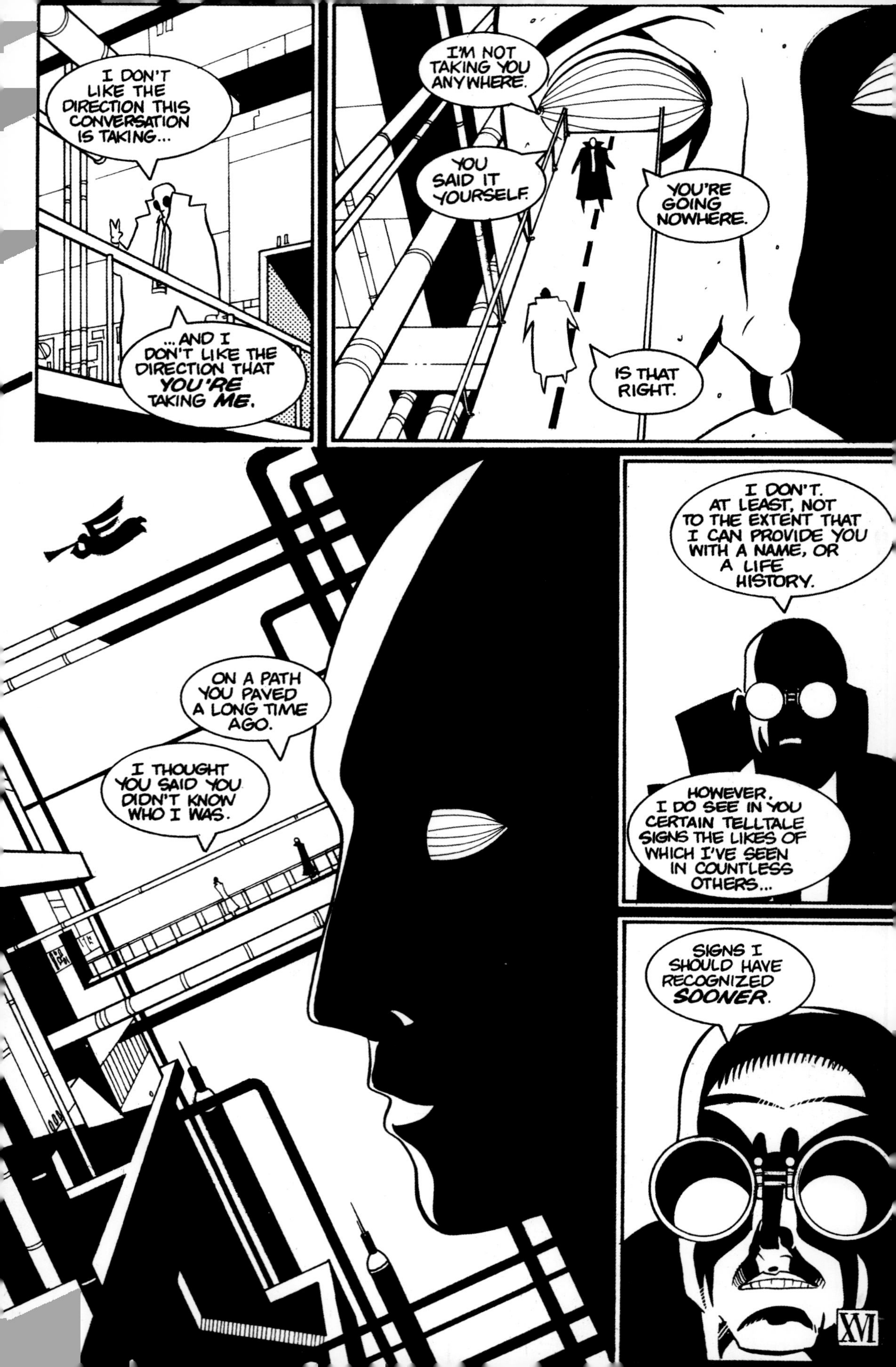
I DON'T LIKE THE DIRECTION THIS CONVERSATION IS TAKING...
...AND I DON'T LIKE THE DIRECTION THAT YOU'RE TAKING ME.
I'M NOT TAKING YOU ANYWHERE.
YOU SAID IT YOURSELF.
YOU'RE GOING NOWHERE.
IS THAT RIGHT.
ON A PATH YOU PAVED A LONG TIME AGO.
I THOUGHT YOU SAID YOU DIDN'T KNOW WHO I WAS.
I DON'T. AT LEAST, NOT TO THE EXTENT THAT I CAN PROVIDE YOU WITH A NAME, OR A LIFE HISTORY.
HOWEVER. I DO SEE IN YOU CERTAIN TELLTALE SIGNS THE LIKES OF WHICH I'VE SEEN IN COUNTLESS OTHERS...
SIGNS I SHOULD HAVE RECOGNIZED SOONER.
XVI

SUCH AS?

YOUR CONFUSION. YOUR GUILT. YOUR LACK OF DIRECTION.

THE FACT THAT YOU DON'T KNOW WHO YOU ARE, OR HOW YOU GOT HERE.

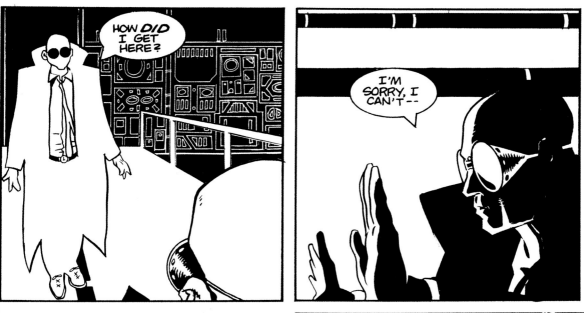

HOW *DID* I GET HERE?

I'M SORRY, I CAN'T--

I MUST KNOW.

YOU WERE MURDERED.

A WOMAN PUSHED YOU OFF THE LEDGE OF A VERY TALL BUILDING.

MORE THAN THAT, I CANNOT SAY.

XVII

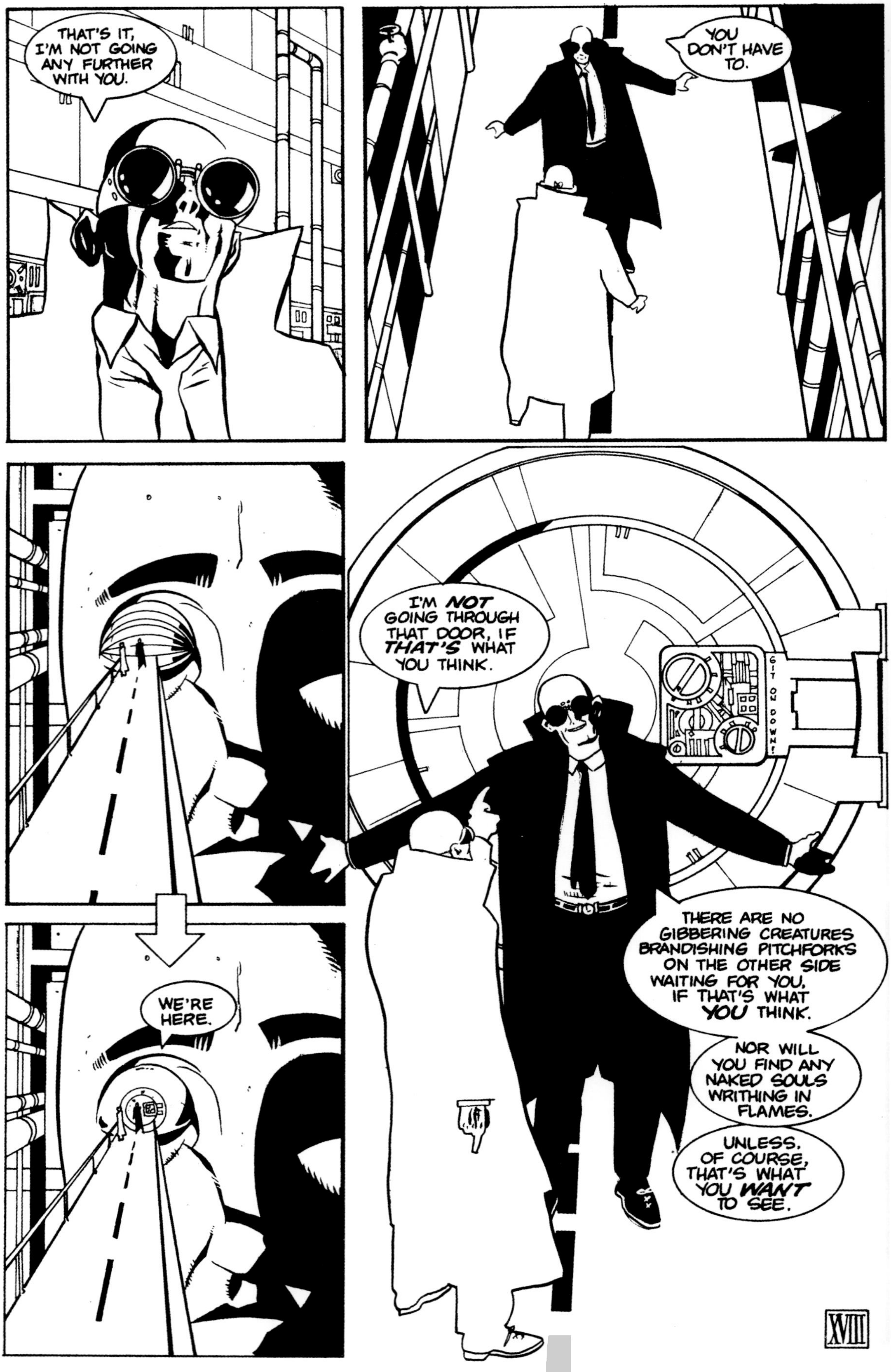
THAT'S IT, I'M NOT GOING ANY FURTHER WITH YOU.
YOU DON'T HAVE TO.
WE'RE HERE.
I'M NOT GOING THROUGH THAT DOOR, IF THAT'S WHAT YOU THINK.
GIT ON DOWN!
THERE ARE NO GIBBERING CREATURES BRANDISHING PITCHFORKS ON THE OTHER SIDE WAITING FOR YOU, IF THAT'S WHAT YOU THINK.
NOR WILL YOU FIND ANY NAKED SOULS WRITHING IN FLAMES.
UNLESS, OF COURSE, THAT'S WHAT YOU WANT TO SEE.

WANT?

JUST AS IS THE CASE HERE, YOU WILL SEE THE *OTHER* DOMAIN AS YOU'VE ALWAYS *BELIEVED* IT TO BE.

WHATEVER DARKEST SECRET IMAGE YOU *FEAR* IT TO BE, THEN SO *SHALL* IT BE.

I'M NOT GOING TO SEE *ANY*THING, BECAUSE I'M NOT GOING *THROUGH* THERE.

THAT'S WHAT *MOST* REDIRECTS SAY.

WHICH IS WHY WE HAVE A CONTINGENCY PLAN.

WHAT *KIND* OF CONTINGENCY PLAN?

YOU'RE *STANDING* ON IT.

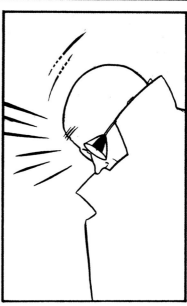

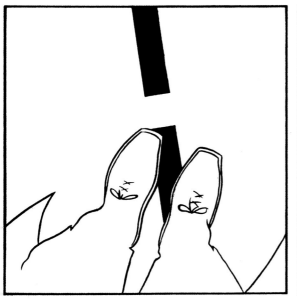

I *WILL* CONCEDE *ONE* THING, HOWEVER.

YOU'RE ABSOLUTELY CORRECT.

BLACK *DOES* SUIT YOU.

XIX

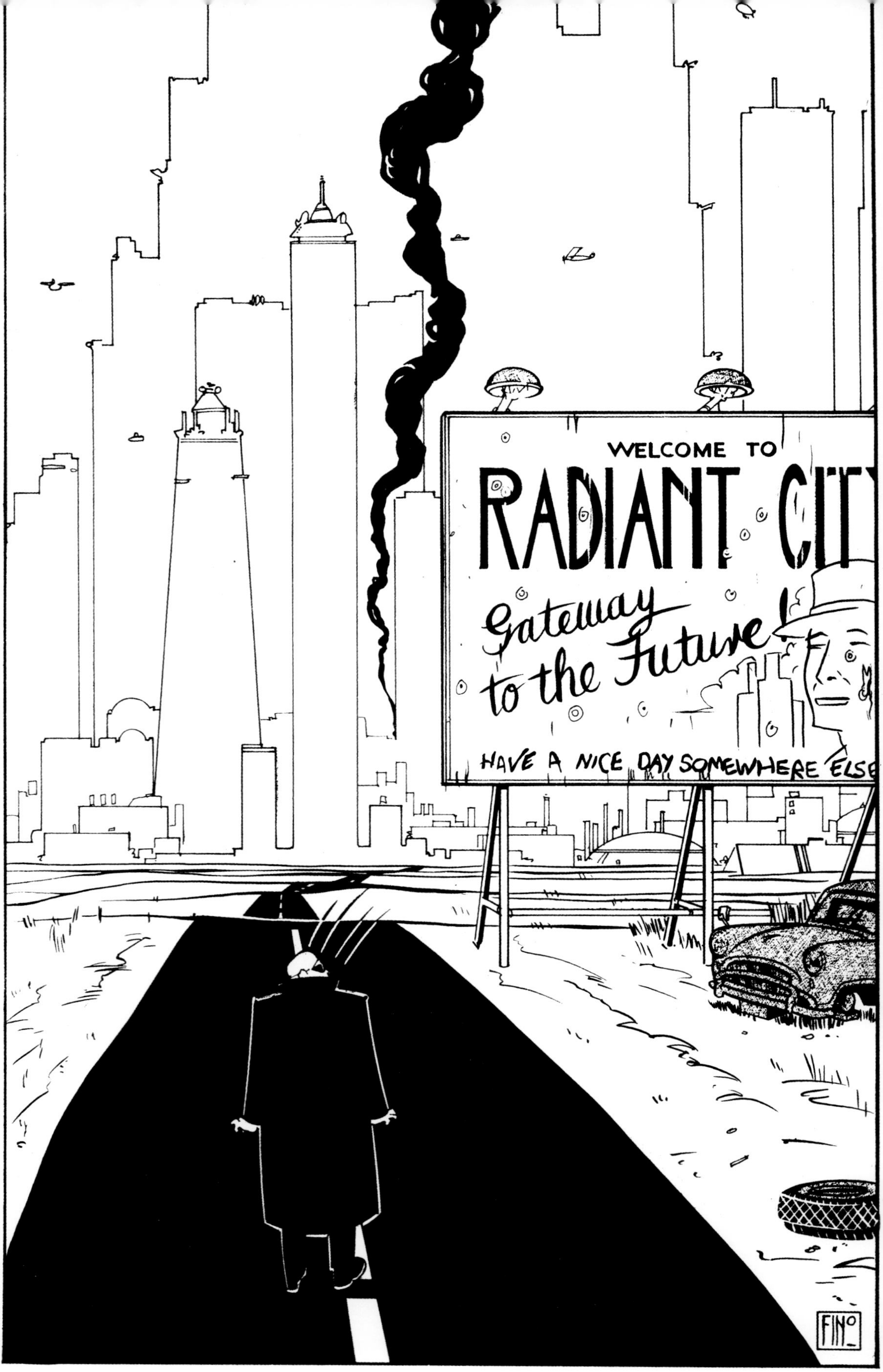
WELCOME TO
RADIANT CITY
Gateway to the Future!
HAVE A NICE DAY SOMEWHERE ELSE
FIN°

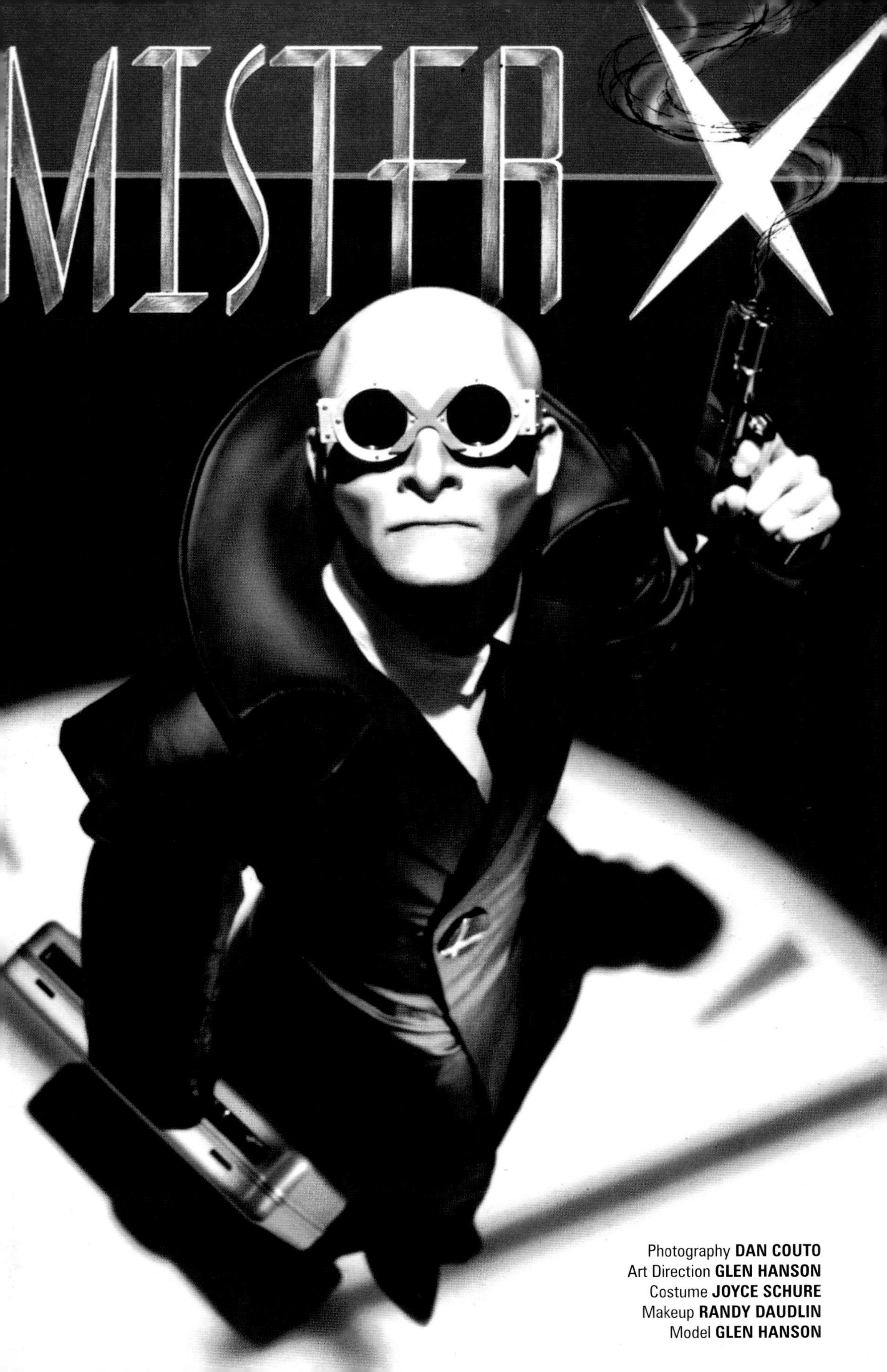
MISTER X

Photography **DAN COUTO**
Art Direction **GLEN HANSON**
Costume **JOYCE SCHURE**
Makeup **RANDY DAUDLIN**
Model **GLEN HANSON**

DEDICATED USER

WRITTEN BY **JEFFREY MORGAN**
PENCILED BY **D'ISRAELI**
INKED BY **KEN HOLEWCZYNSKI**
LETTERED BY **DEBORAH MARKS**

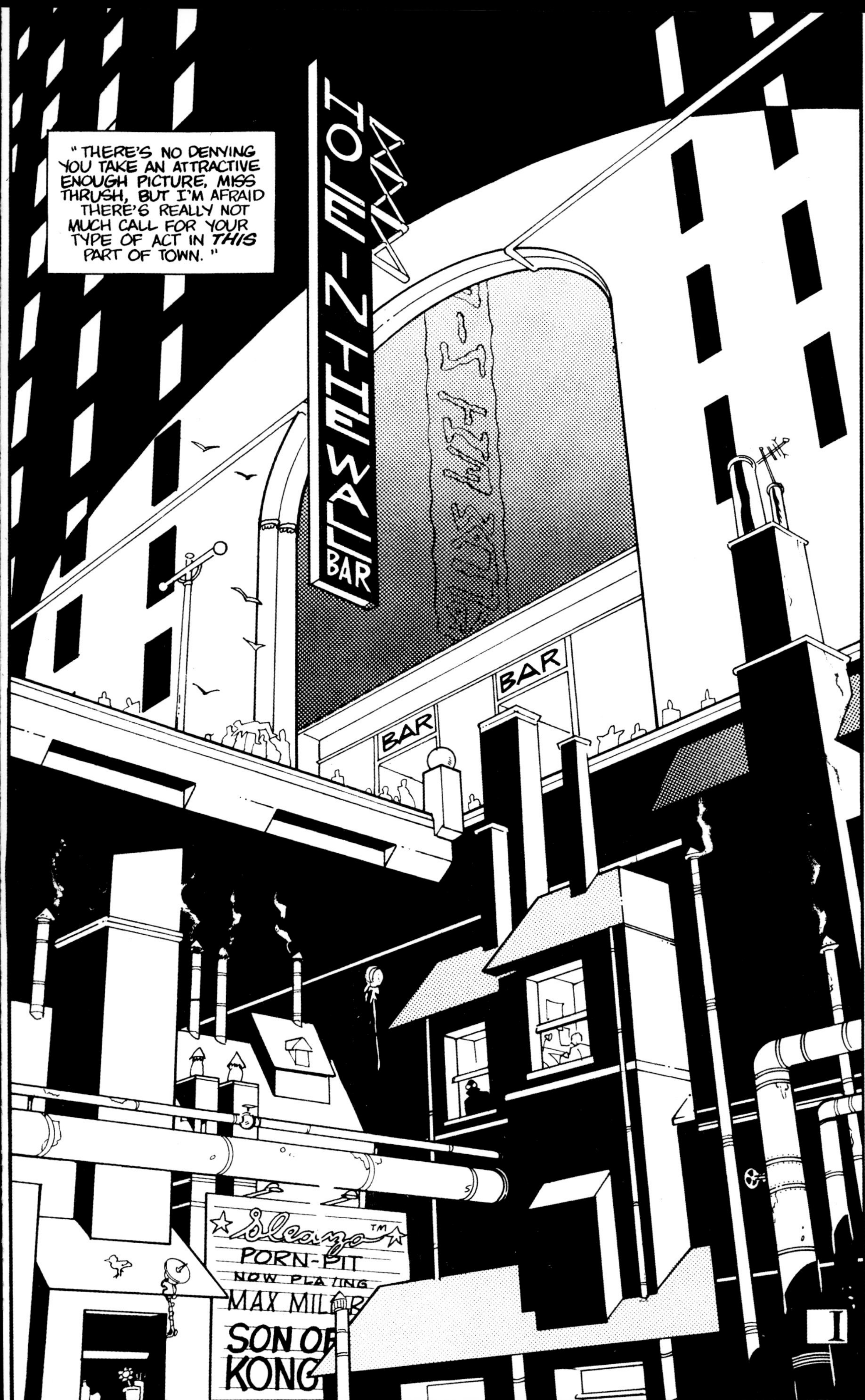
"THERE'S NO DENYING YOU TAKE AN ATTRACTIVE ENOUGH PICTURE, MISS THRUSH, BUT I'M AFRAID THERE'S REALLY NOT MUCH CALL FOR YOUR TYPE OF ACT IN *THIS* PART OF TOWN."
HOLE-IN-THE-WALL BAR
BAR
BAR
BAR
Sleazo™
PORN-PIT
NOW PLAYING
MAX MILLER
SON OF KONG
I

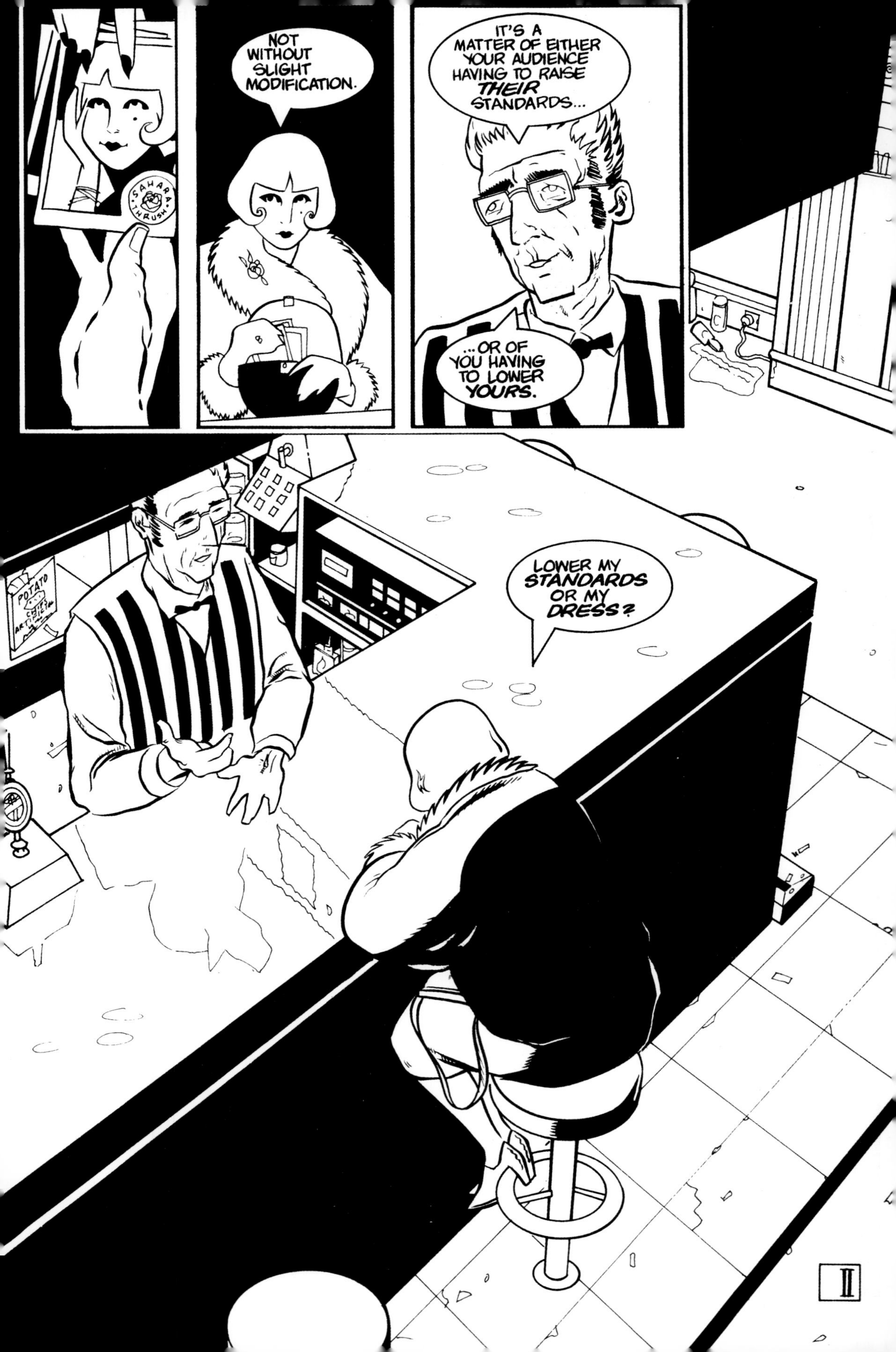
SAHARA THRUSH
NOT WITHOUT SLIGHT MODIFICATION.
IT'S A MATTER OF EITHER YOUR AUDIENCE HAVING TO RAISE THEIR STANDARDS...
...OR OF YOU HAVING TO LOWER YOURS.
POTATO CHIPS
LOWER MY STANDARDS OR MY DRESS?

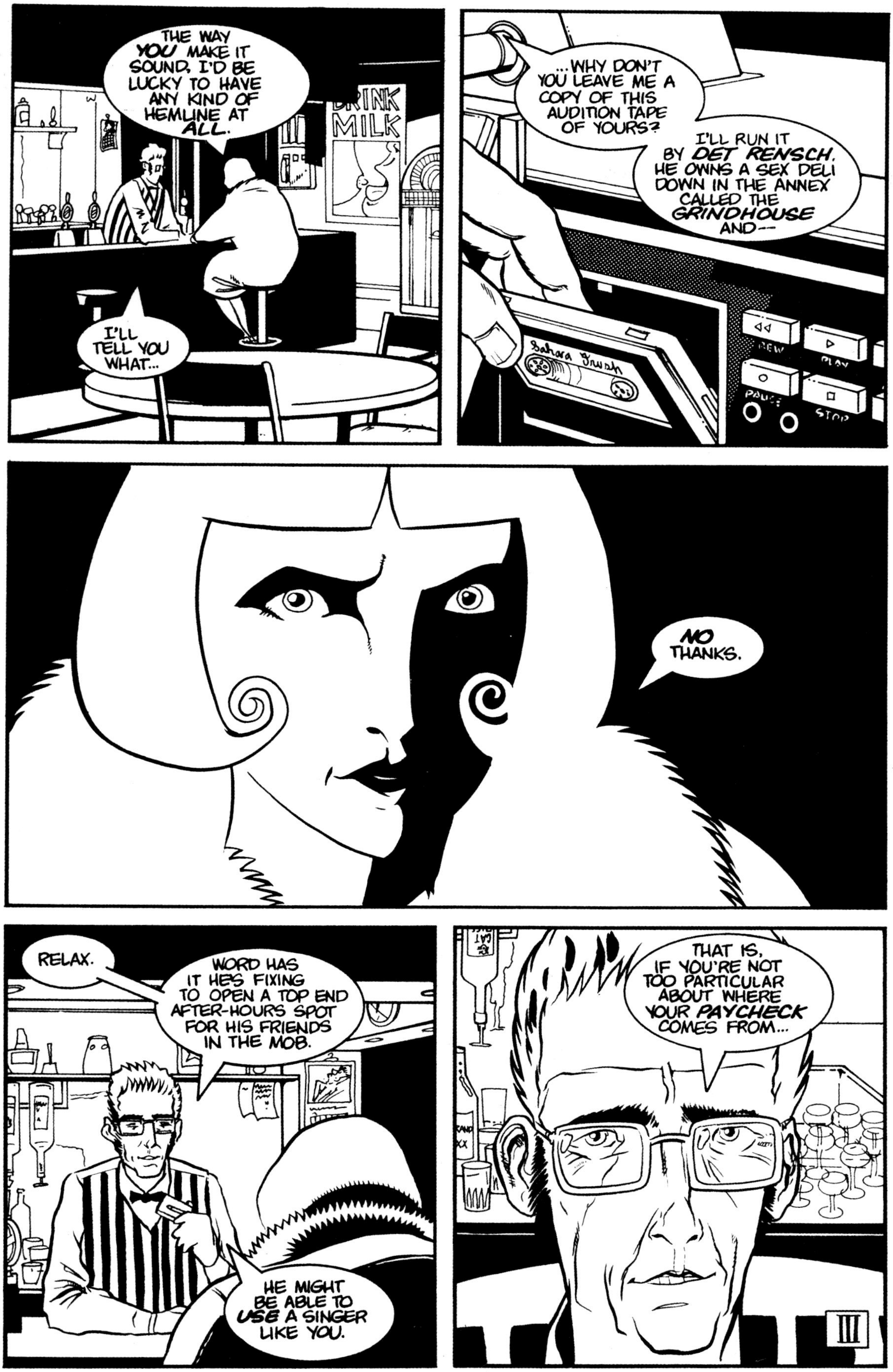
THE WAY YOU MAKE IT SOUND, I'D BE LUCKY TO HAVE ANY KIND OF HEMLINE AT ALL.
DRINK MILK
I'LL TELL YOU WHAT...
...WHY DON'T YOU LEAVE ME A COPY OF THIS AUDITION TAPE OF YOURS?
I'LL RUN IT BY DET RENSCH. HE OWNS A SEX DELI DOWN IN THE ANNEX CALLED THE GRINDHOUSE AND--
Sahara Gnush
REW
PLAY
PAUSE
STOP
NO THANKS.
RELAX.
WORD HAS IT HE'S FIXING TO OPEN A TOP END AFTER-HOURS SPOT FOR HIS FRIENDS IN THE MOB.
HE MIGHT BE ABLE TO USE A SINGER LIKE YOU.
THAT IS, IF YOU'RE NOT TOO PARTICULAR ABOUT WHERE YOUR PAYCHECK COMES FROM...
III

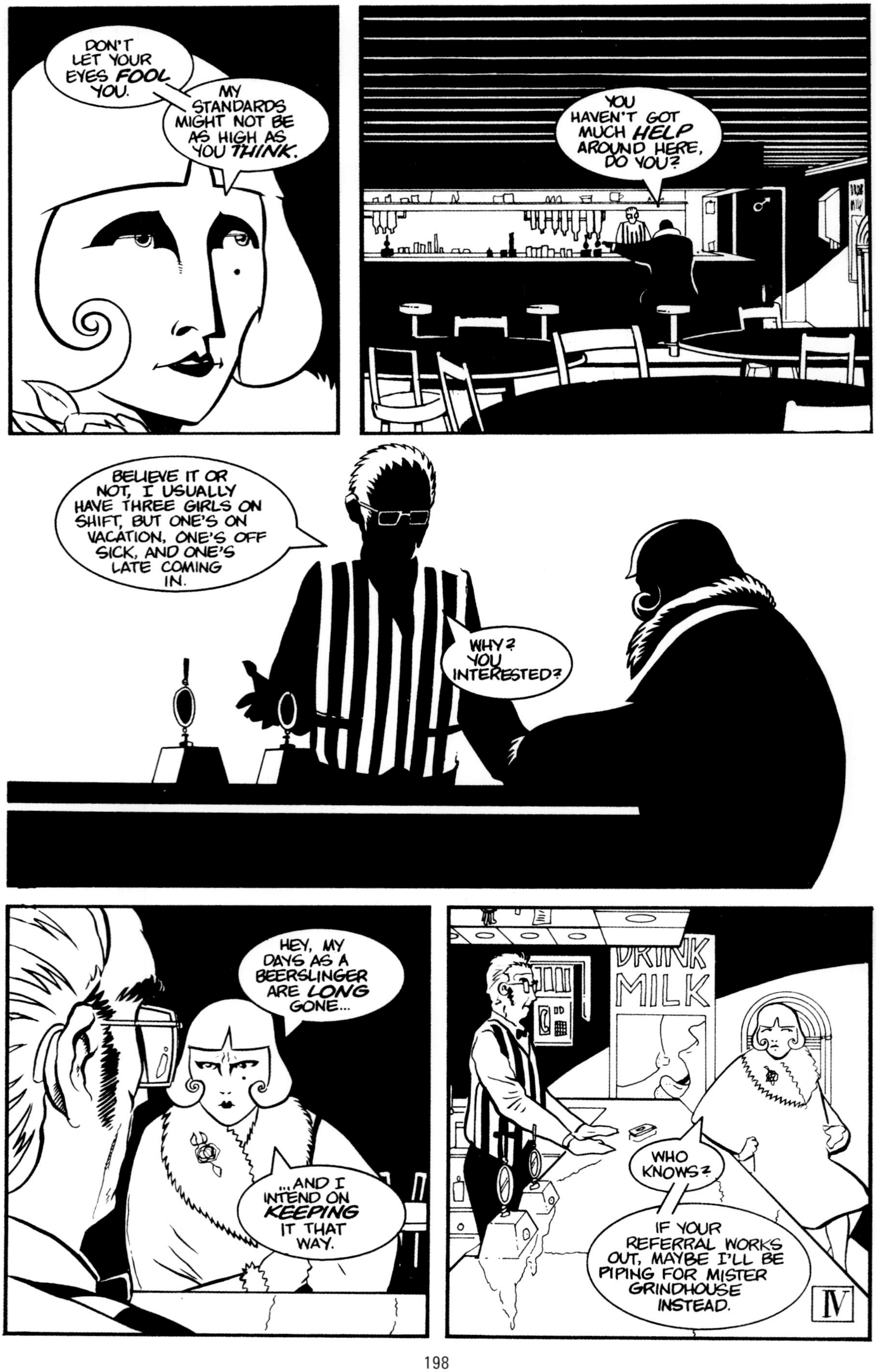
DON'T LET YOUR EYES FOOL YOU.
MY STANDARDS MIGHT NOT BE AS HIGH AS YOU THINK.
YOU HAVEN'T GOT MUCH HELP AROUND HERE, DO YOU?
BELIEVE IT OR NOT, I USUALLY HAVE THREE GIRLS ON SHIFT, BUT ONE'S ON VACATION, ONE'S OFF SICK, AND ONE'S LATE COMING IN.
WHY? YOU INTERESTED?
HEY, MY DAYS AS A BEERSLINGER ARE LONG GONE...
...AND I INTEND ON KEEPING IT THAT WAY.
DRINK MILK
WHO KNOWS?
IF YOUR REFERRAL WORKS OUT, MAYBE I'LL BE PIPING FOR MISTER GRINDHOUSE INSTEAD.
IV

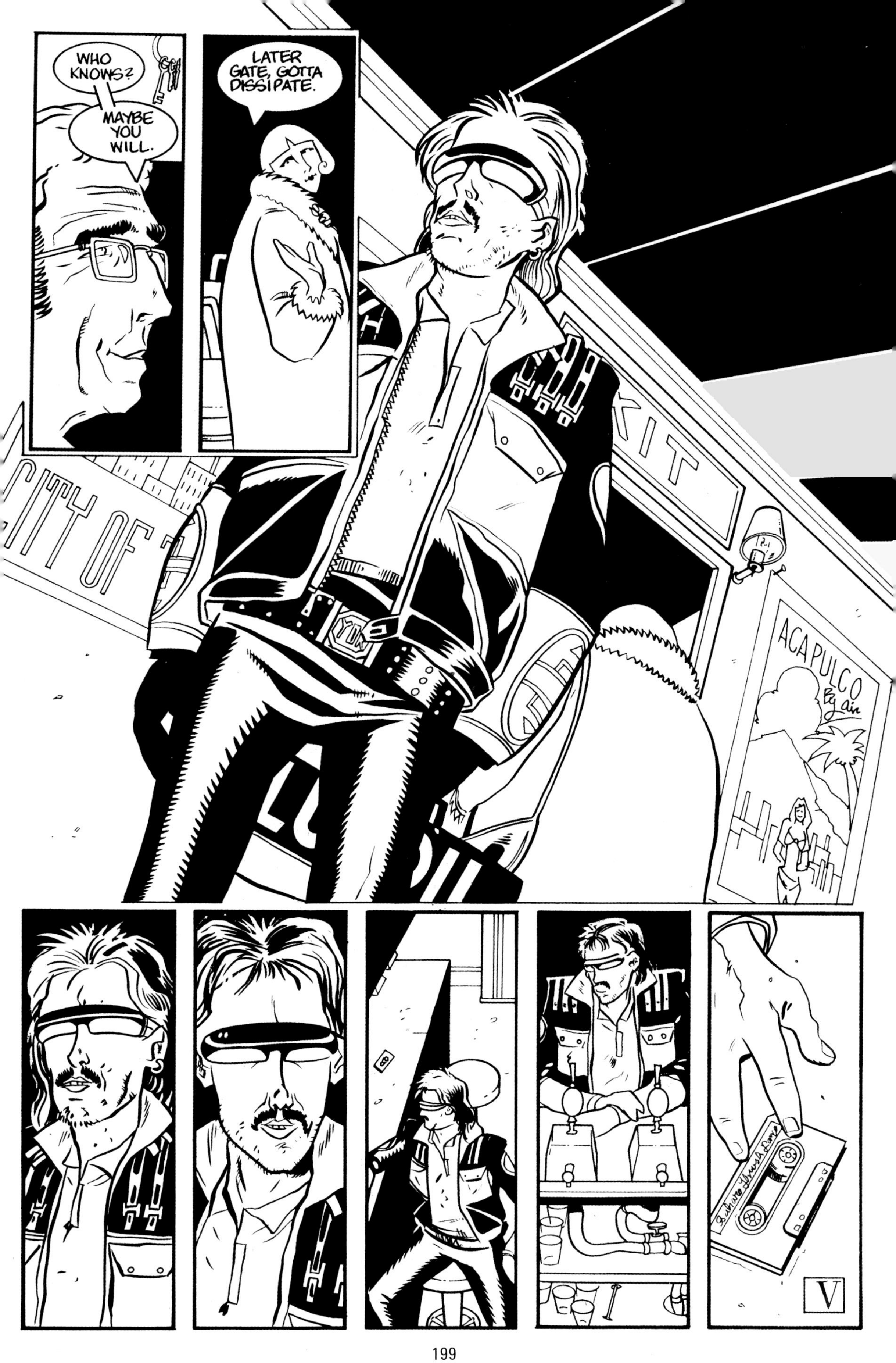
WHO KNOWS?
MAYBE YOU WILL.
LATER GATE, GOTTA DISSIPATE.
CITY OF
ACAPULCO
By air
V

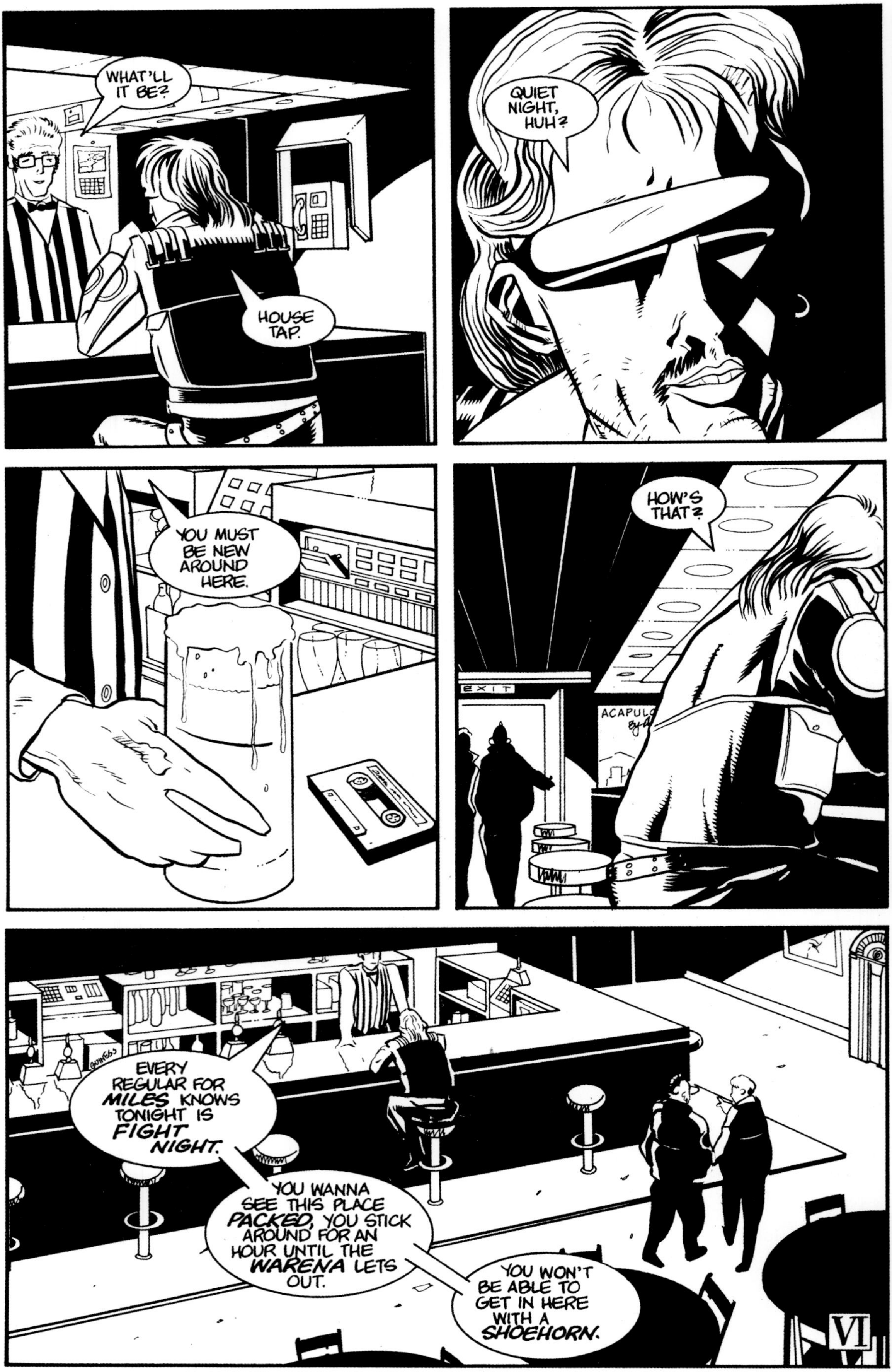
WHAT'LL IT BE?
HOUSE TAP.
QUIET NIGHT, HUH?
YOU MUST BE NEW AROUND HERE.
HOW'S THAT?
EXIT
EVERY REGULAR FOR MILES KNOWS TONIGHT IS FIGHT NIGHT.
YOU WANNA SEE THIS PLACE PACKED, YOU STICK AROUND FOR AN HOUR UNTIL THE WARENA LETS OUT.
YOU WON'T BE ABLE TO GET IN HERE WITH A SHOEHORN.
VI

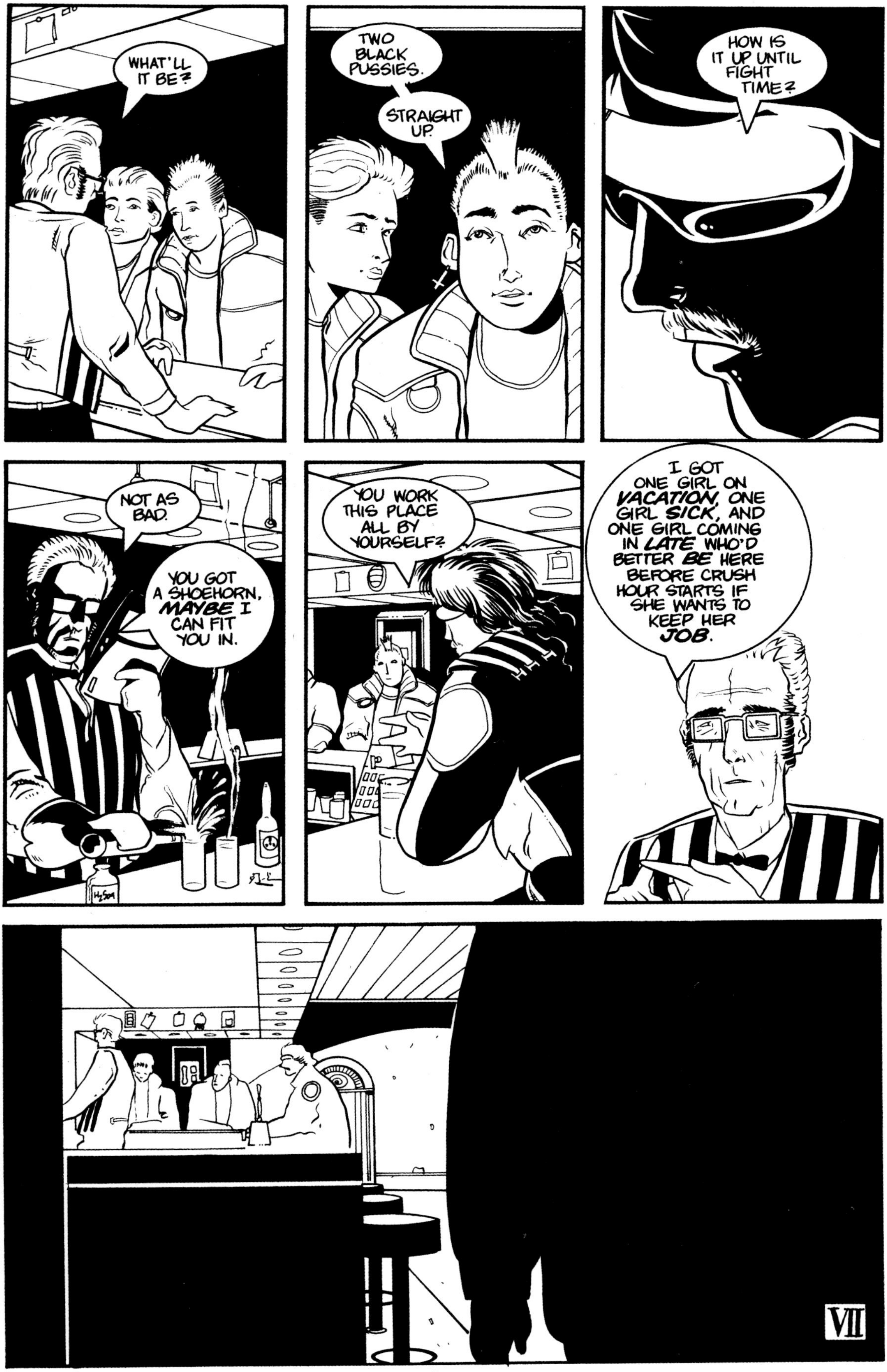
WHAT'LL IT BE?
TWO BLACK PUSSIES.
STRAIGHT UP.
HOW IS IT UP UNTIL FIGHT TIME?
NOT AS BAD.
YOU GOT A SHOEHORN, MAYBE I CAN FIT YOU IN.
YOU WORK THIS PLACE ALL BY YOURSELF?
I GOT ONE GIRL ON VACATION, ONE GIRL SICK, AND ONE GIRL COMING IN LATE WHO'D BETTER BE HERE BEFORE CRUSH HOUR STARTS IF SHE WANTS TO KEEP HER JOB.
VII

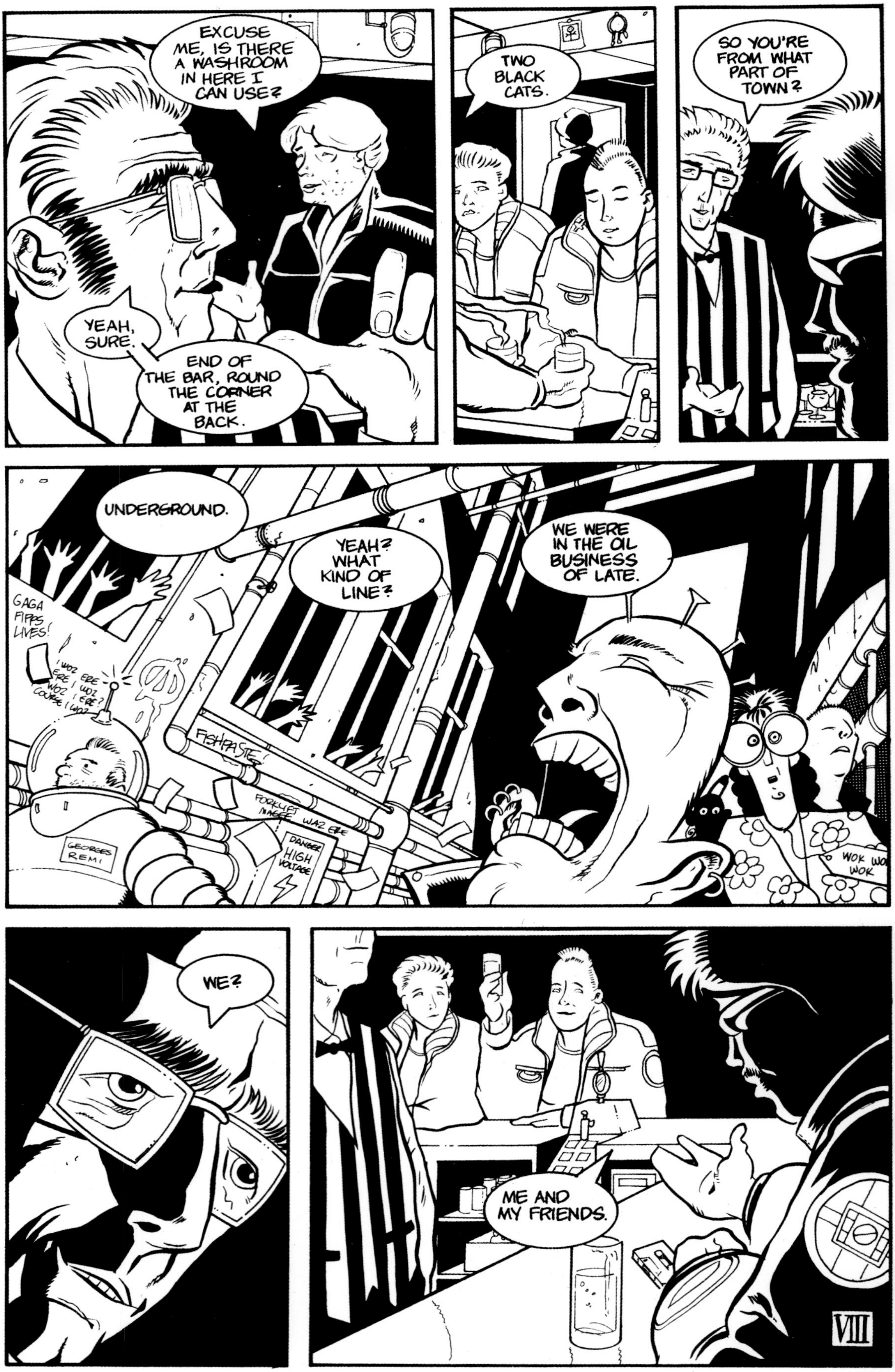
EXCUSE ME, IS THERE A WASHROOM IN HERE I CAN USE?
YEAH, SURE.
END OF THE BAR, ROUND THE CORNER AT THE BACK.
TWO BLACK CATS.
SO YOU'RE FROM WHAT PART OF TOWN?
UNDERGROUND.
YEAH? WHAT KIND OF LINE?
WE WERE IN THE OIL BUSINESS OF LATE.
GAGA FIPPS LIVES!
I WOZ ERE ERE, I WOZ WOZ I ERE? COURSE I WOZ
FISHPASTE!
FORKLIFT MAGGE WAZ ERE
GEORGES REMI
DANGER HIGH VOLTAGE
WE?
ME AND MY FRIENDS.
VIII

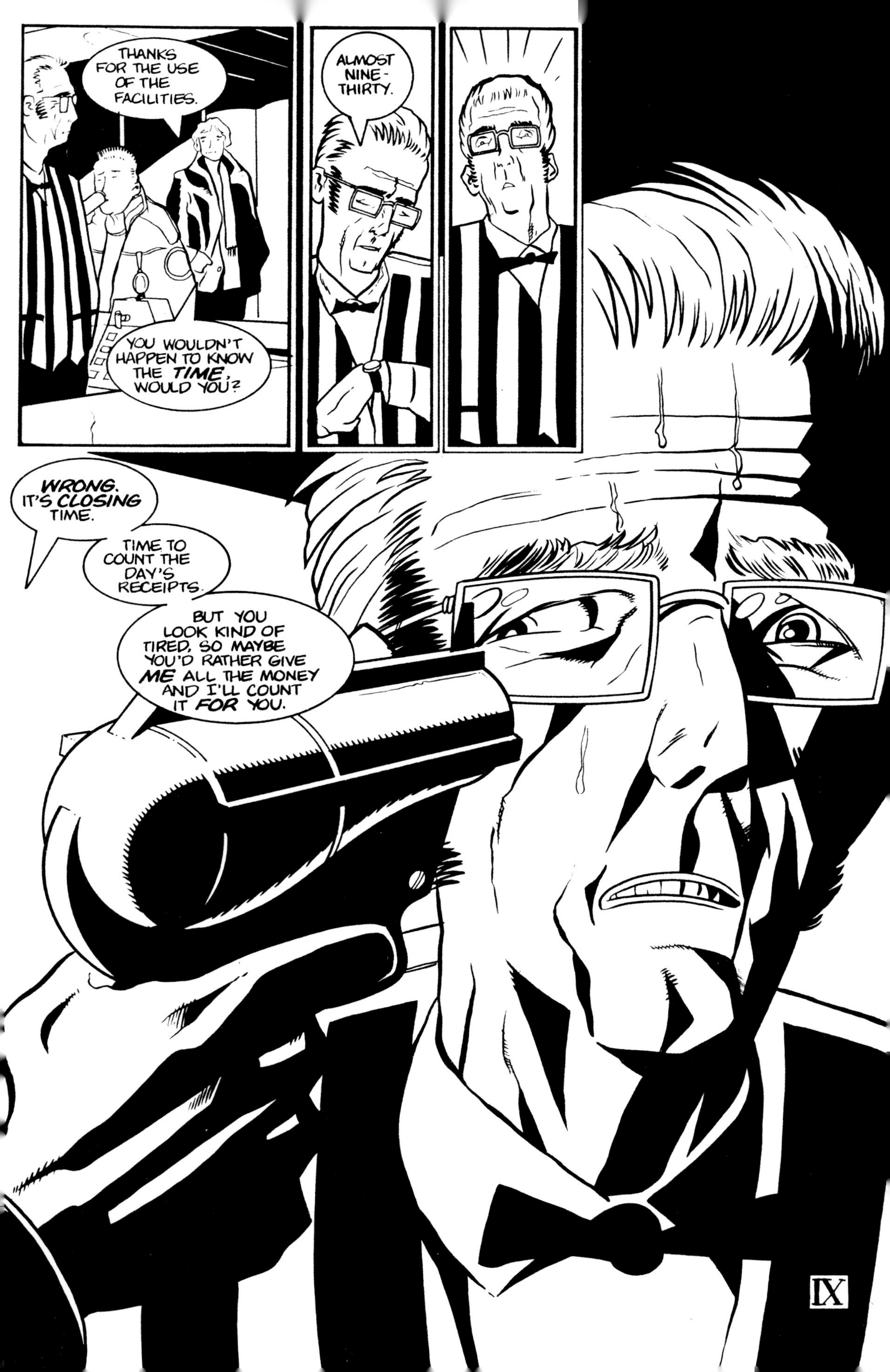
THANKS FOR THE USE OF THE FACILITIES.
YOU WOULDN'T HAPPEN TO KNOW THE TIME, WOULD YOU?
ALMOST NINE-THIRTY.
WRONG. IT'S CLOSING TIME.
TIME TO COUNT THE DAY'S RECEIPTS.
BUT YOU LOOK KIND OF TIRED, SO MAYBE YOU'D RATHER GIVE ME ALL THE MONEY AND I'LL COUNT IT FOR YOU.
IX

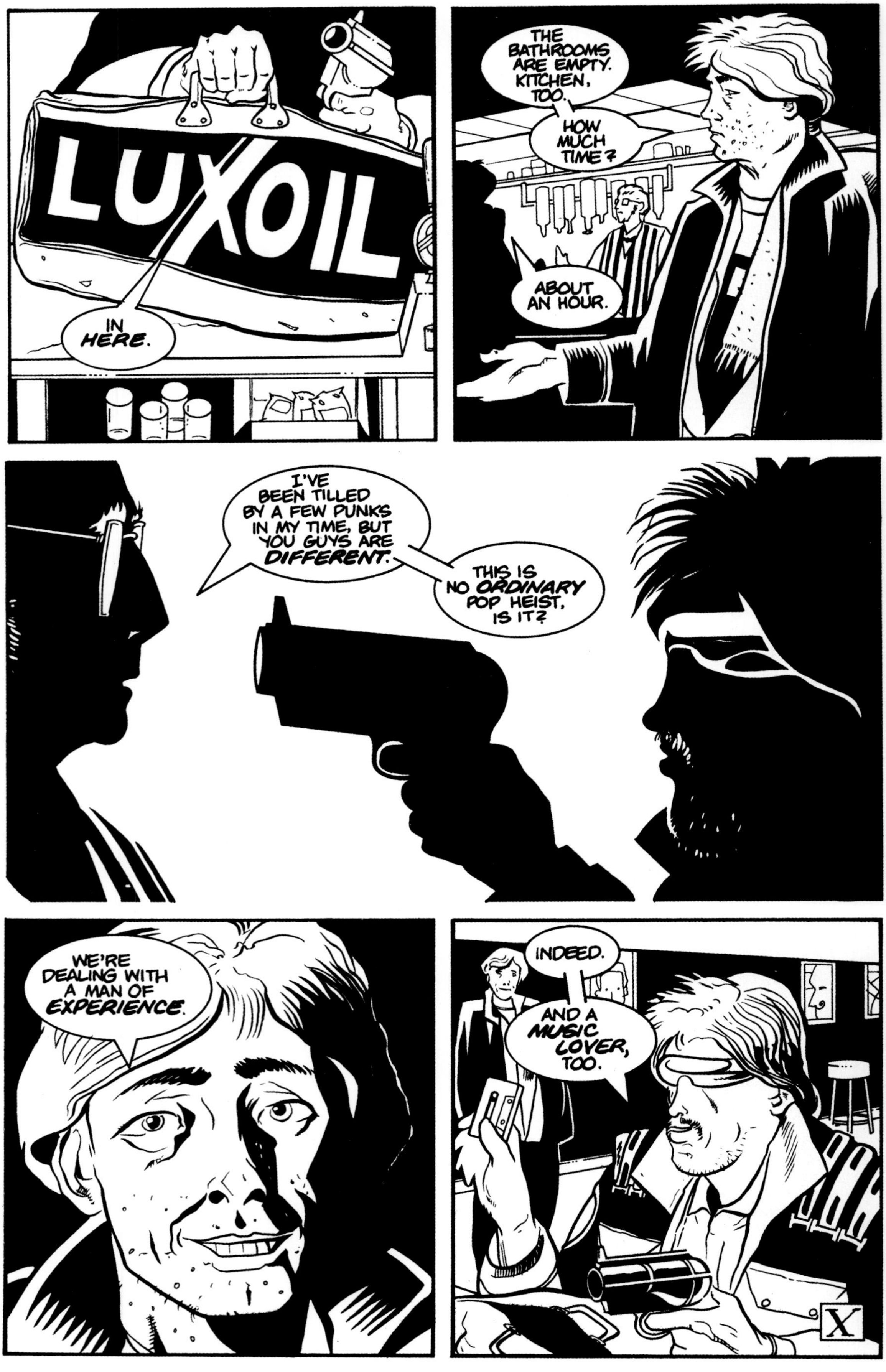
LUXOIL
IN HERE.
THE BATHROOMS ARE EMPTY. KITCHEN, TOO.
HOW MUCH TIME?
ABOUT AN HOUR.
I'VE BEEN TILLED BY A FEW PUNKS IN MY TIME, BUT YOU GUYS ARE DIFFERENT.
THIS IS NO ORDINARY POP HEIST, IS IT?
WE'RE DEALING WITH A MAN OF EXPERIENCE.
INDEED.
AND A MUSIC LOVER, TOO.

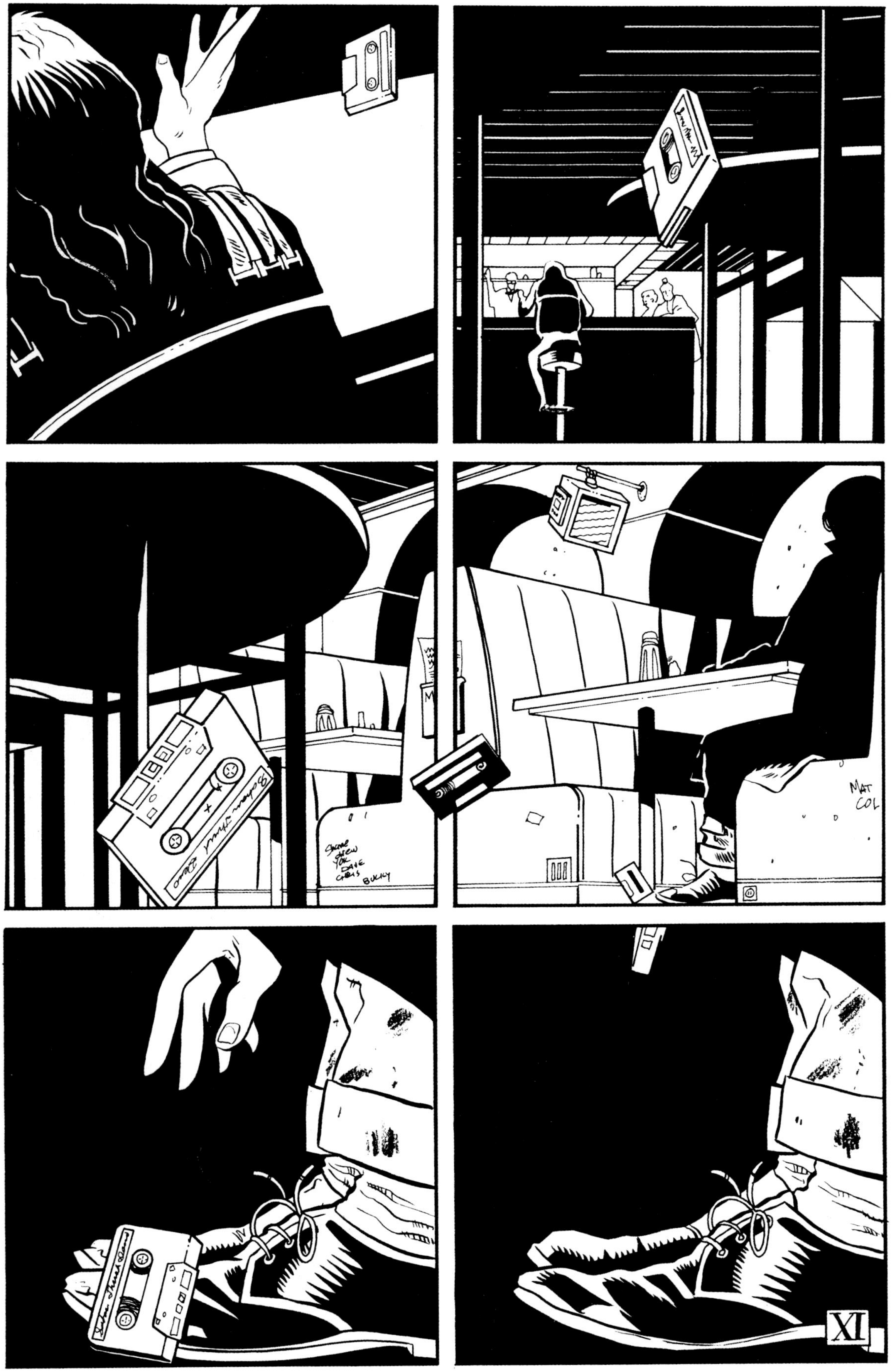
MAT
COL
XI

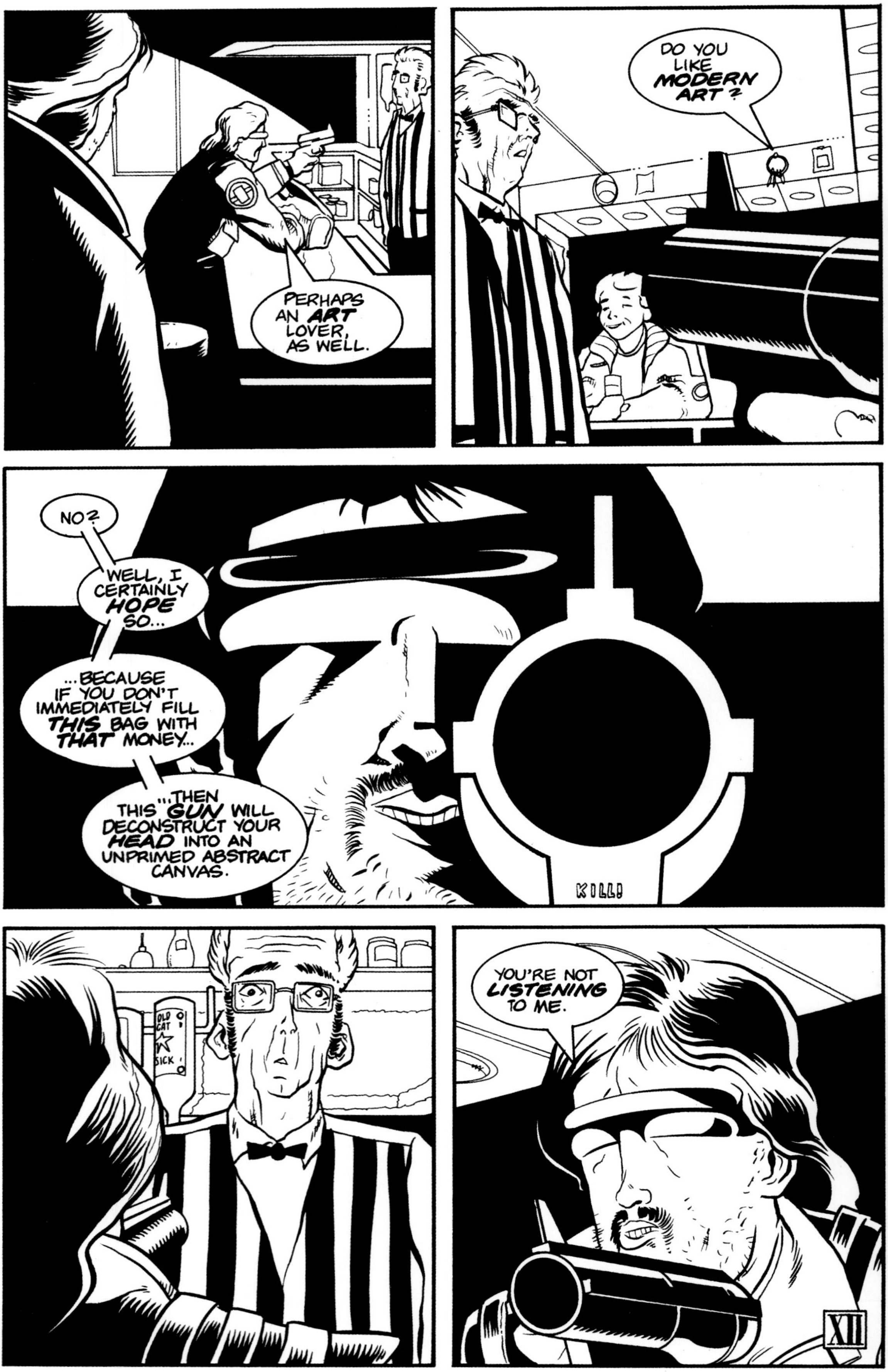
PERHAPS AN ART LOVER, AS WELL.
DO YOU LIKE MODERN ART?
NO?
WELL, I CERTAINLY HOPE SO...
...BECAUSE IF YOU DON'T IMMEDIATELY FILL THIS BAG WITH THAT MONEY...
...THEN THIS GUN WILL DECONSTRUCT YOUR HEAD INTO AN UNPRIMED ABSTRACT CANVAS.
KILL!
YOU'RE NOT LISTENING TO ME.
XII

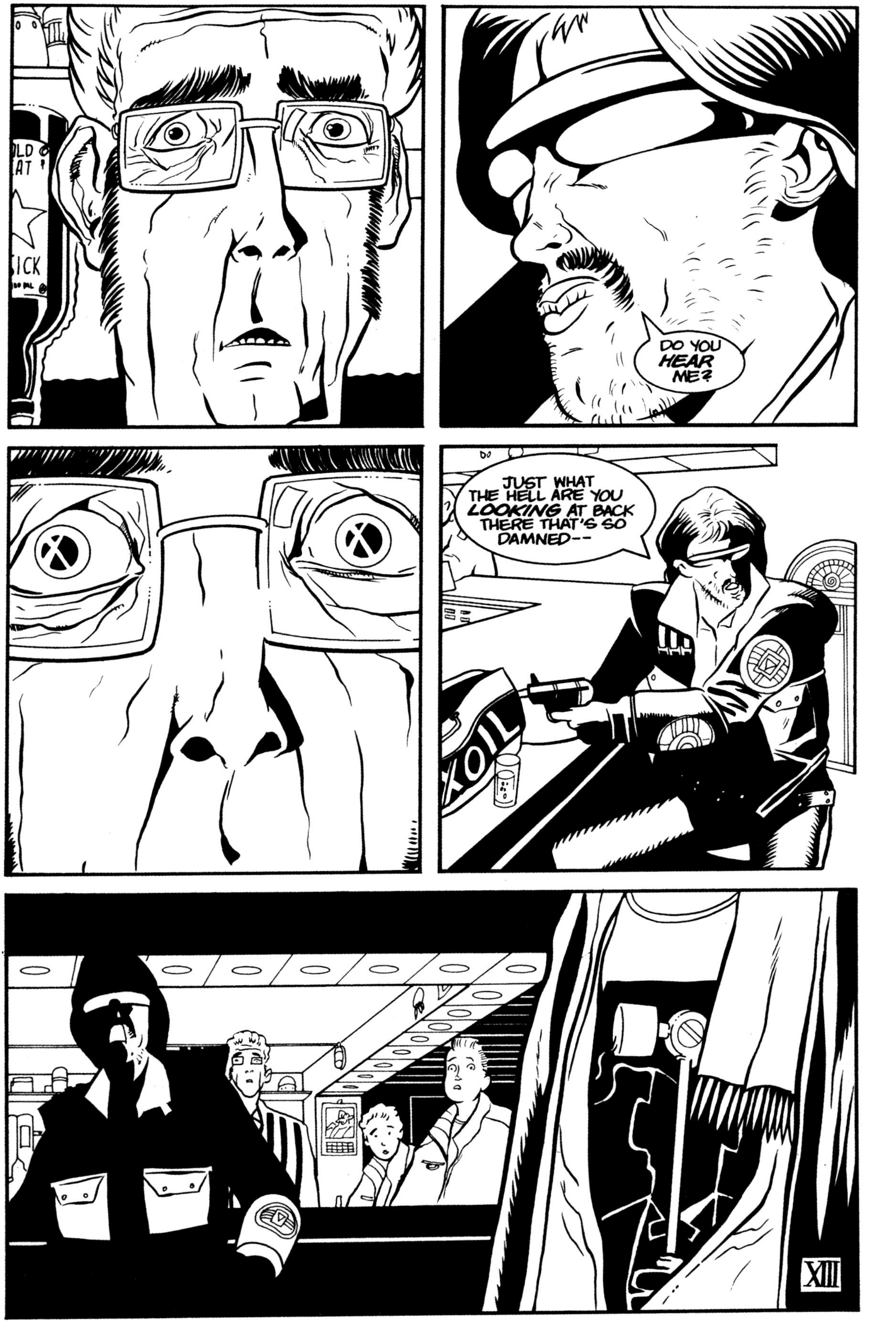
DO YOU HEAR ME?
JUST WHAT THE HELL ARE YOU LOOKING AT BACK THERE THAT'S SO DAMNED--
XIII

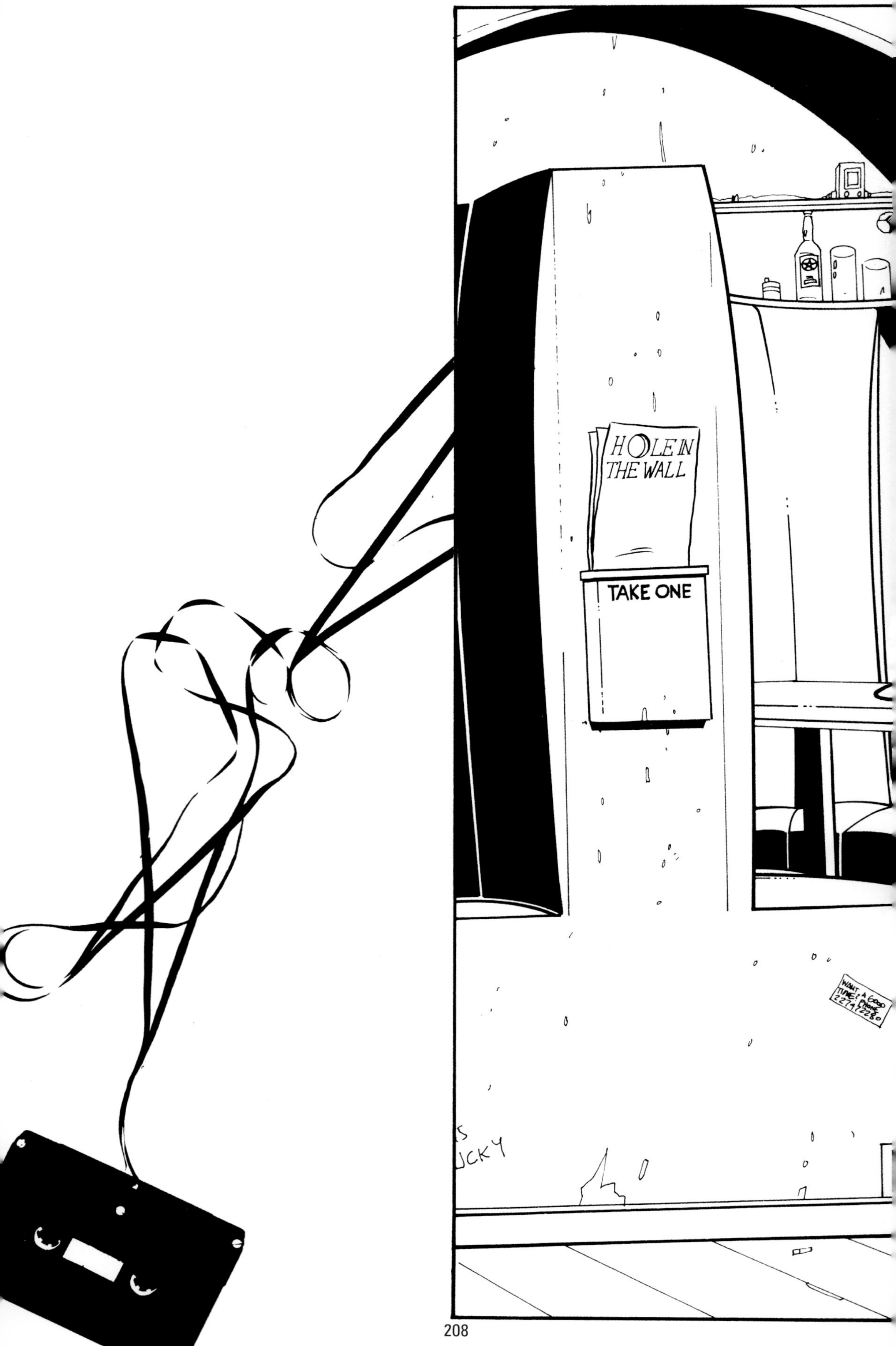
HOLE IN THE WALL
TAKE ONE
WANT A GOOD TIME? PHONE 22792280
UCKY

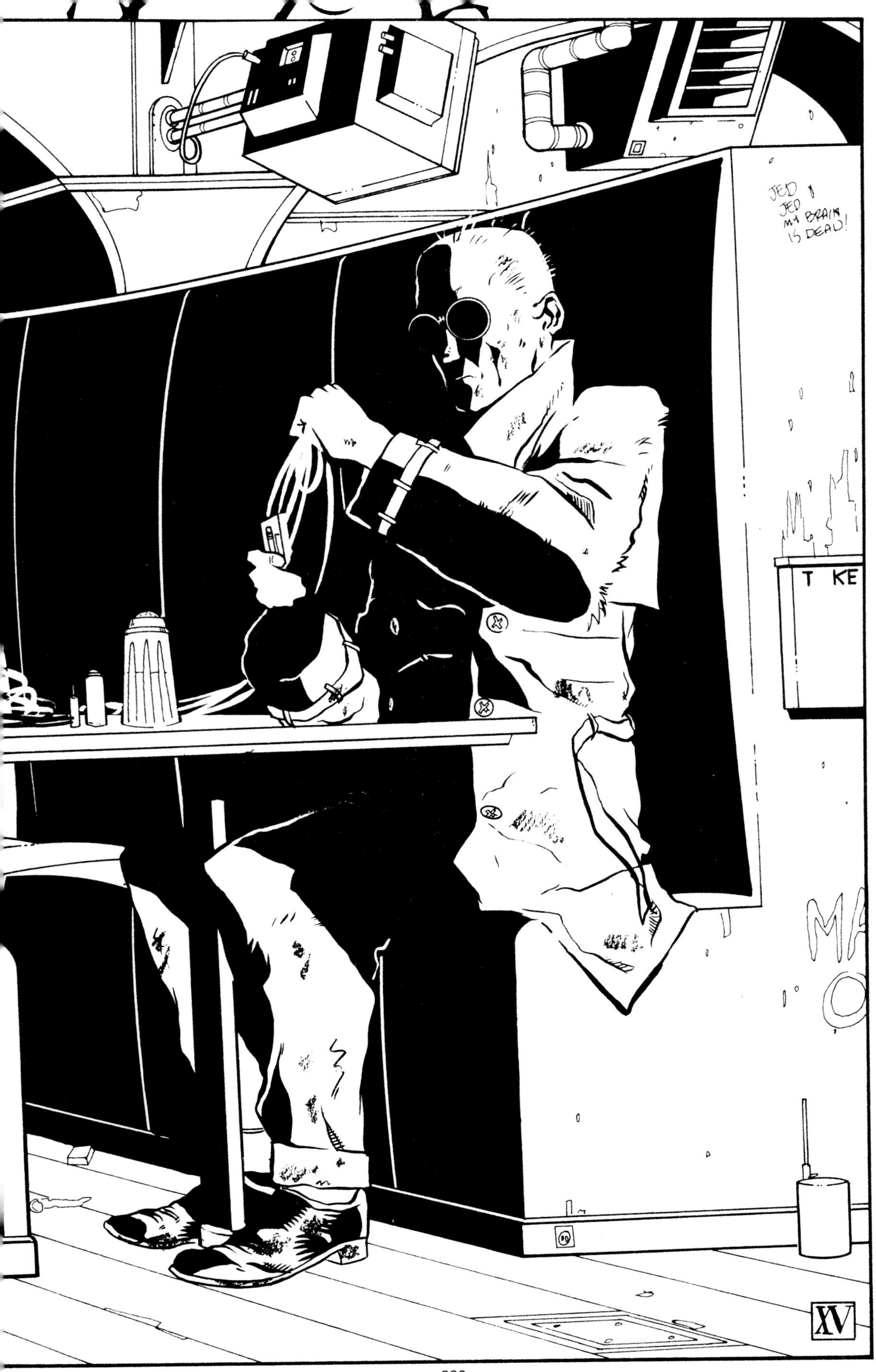
JED
JED
MY BRAIN
IS DEAD!
T KE
XV

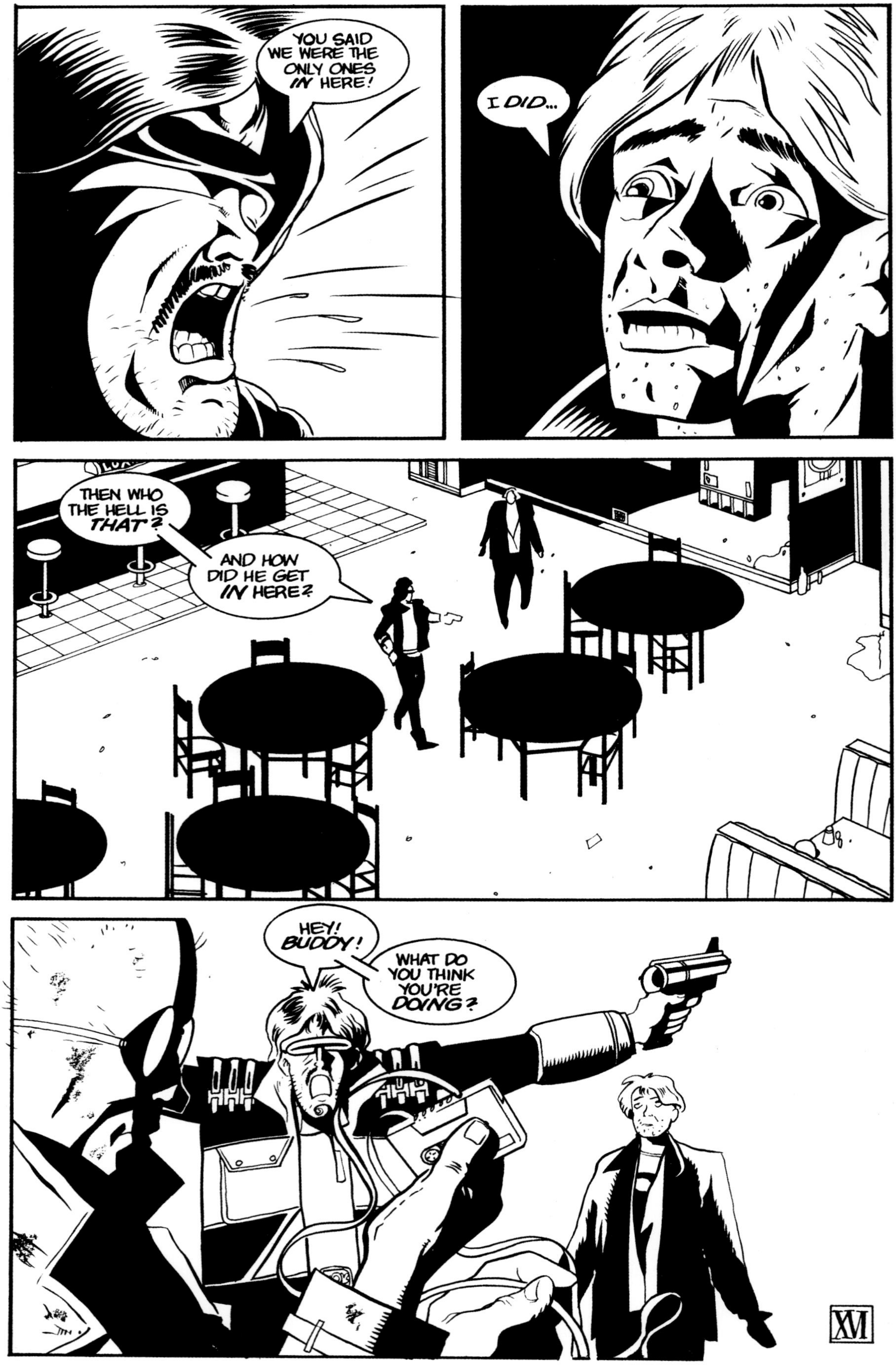
YOU SAID WE WERE THE ONLY ONES IN HERE!
I DID...
THEN WHO THE HELL IS THAT?
AND HOW DID HE GET IN HERE?
HEY! BUDDY!
WHAT DO YOU THINK YOU'RE DOING?
XVI

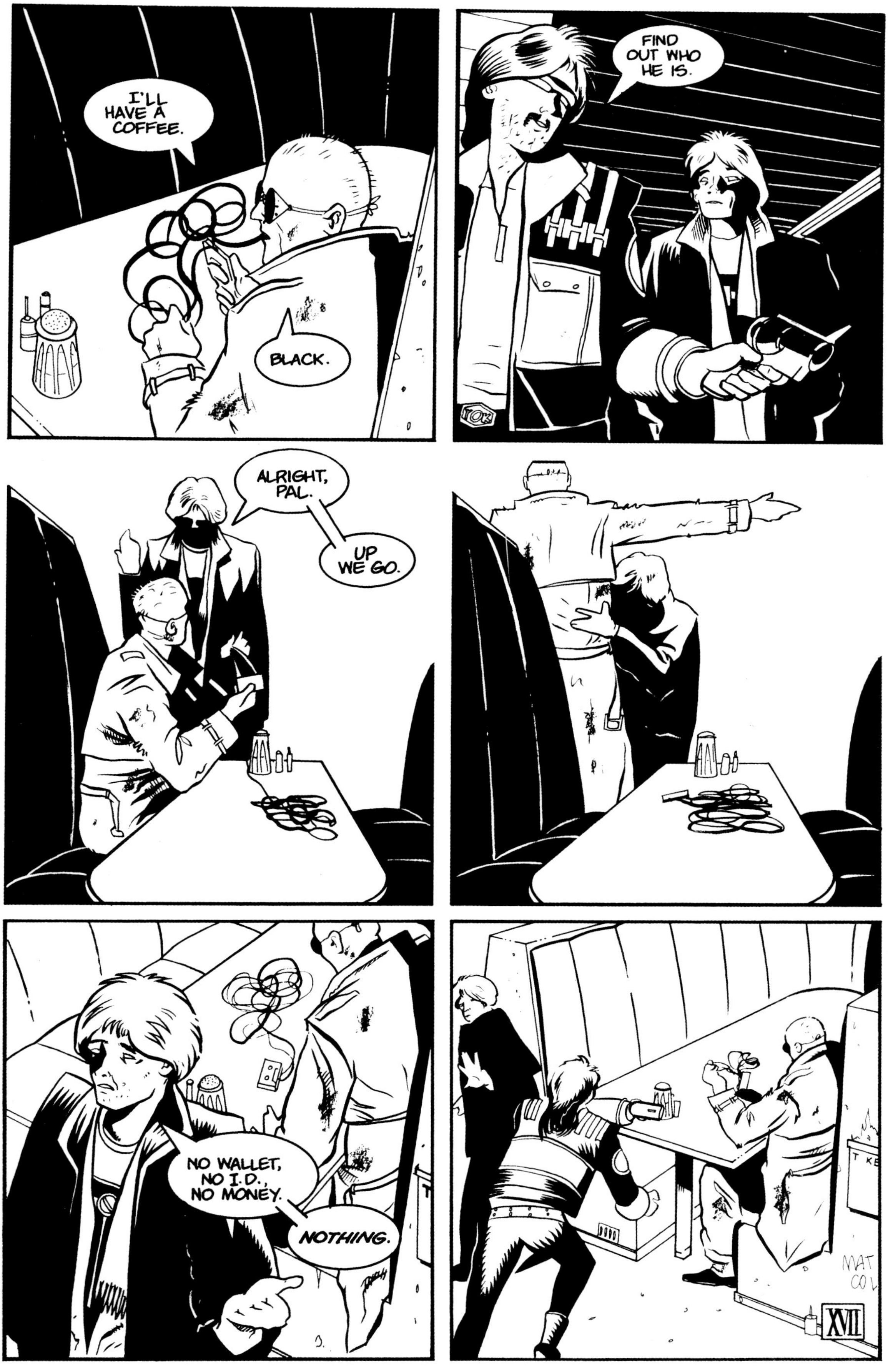
I'LL HAVE A COFFEE.
BLACK.
FIND OUT WHO HE IS.
ALRIGHT, PAL.
UP WE GO.
NO WALLET, NO I.D., NO MONEY.
NOTHING.
XVII

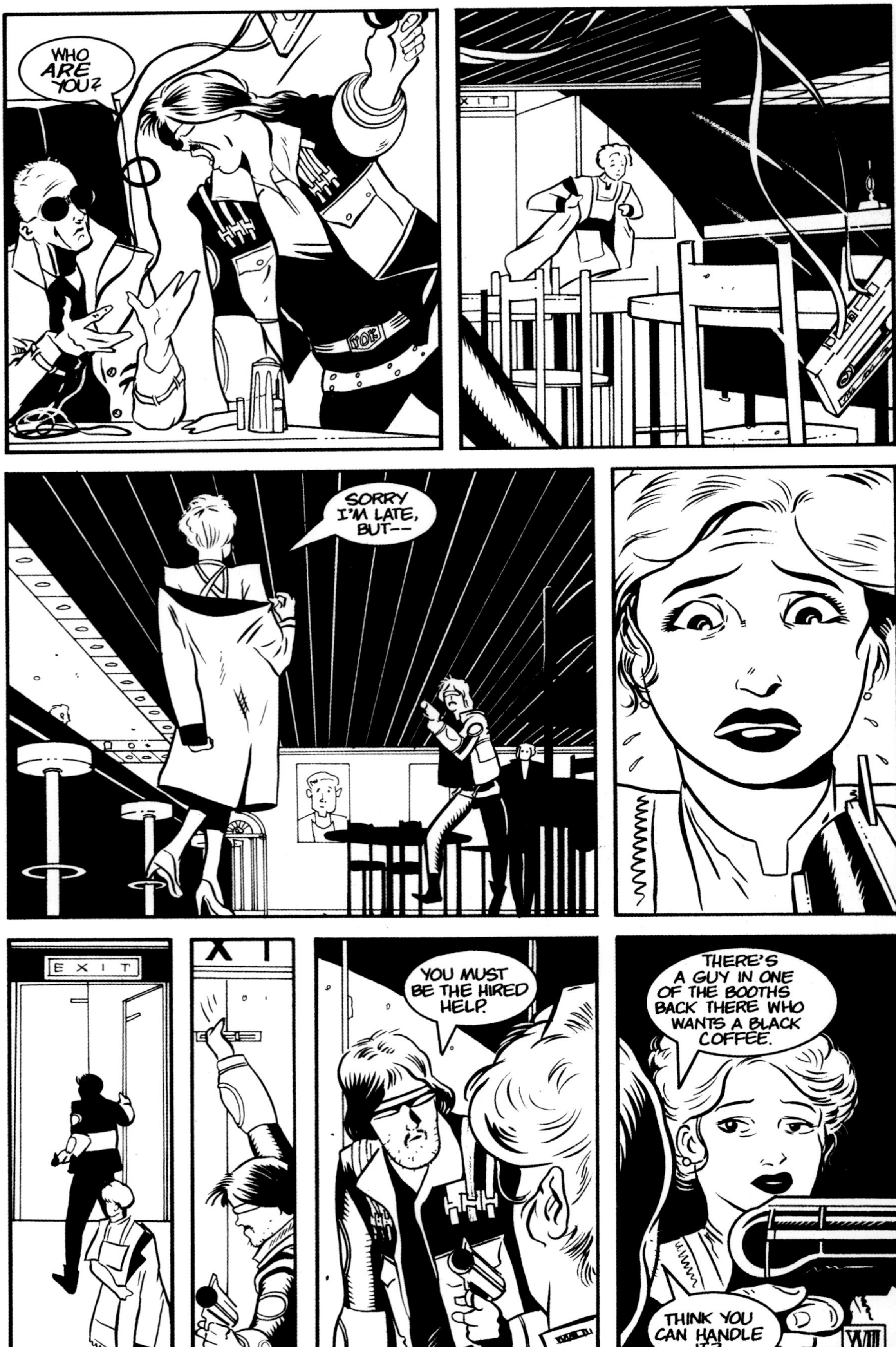
WHO ARE YOU?
SORRY I'M LATE, BUT--
EXIT
YOU MUST BE THE HIRED HELP.
THERE'S A GUY IN ONE OF THE BOOTHS BACK THERE WHO WANTS A BLACK COFFEE.
THINK YOU CAN HANDLE IT?
XVIII

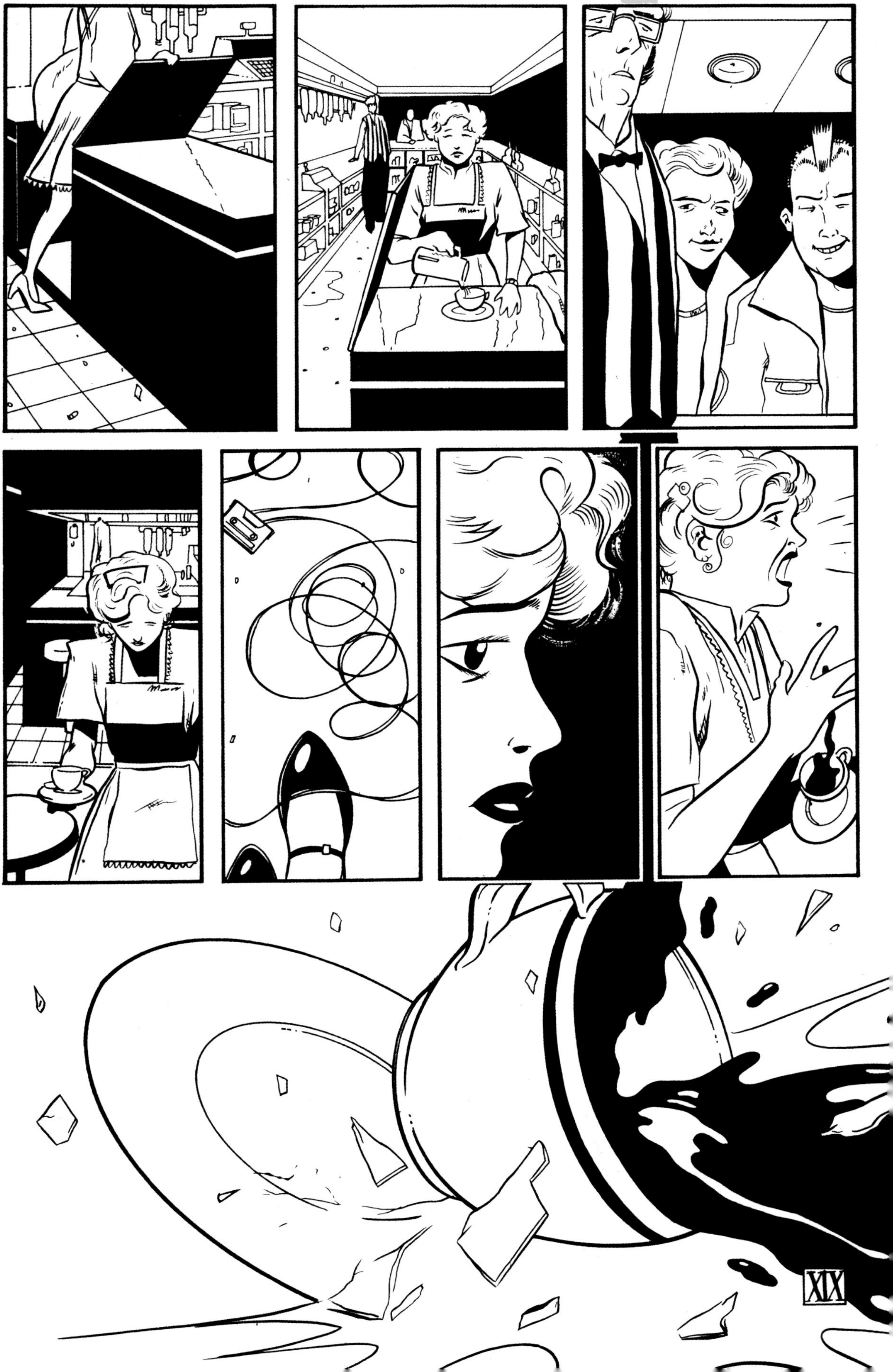
XIX

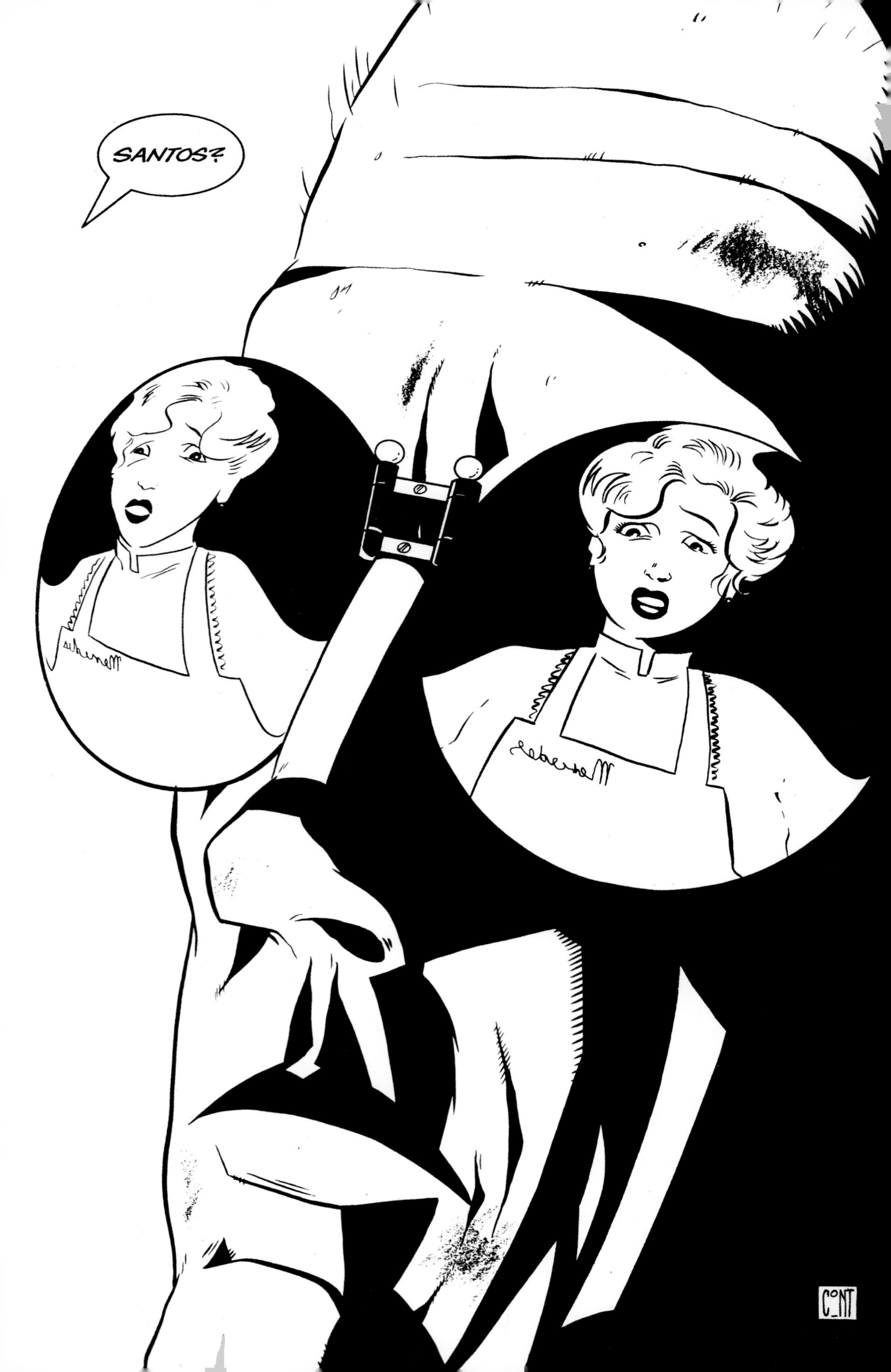
SANTOS?

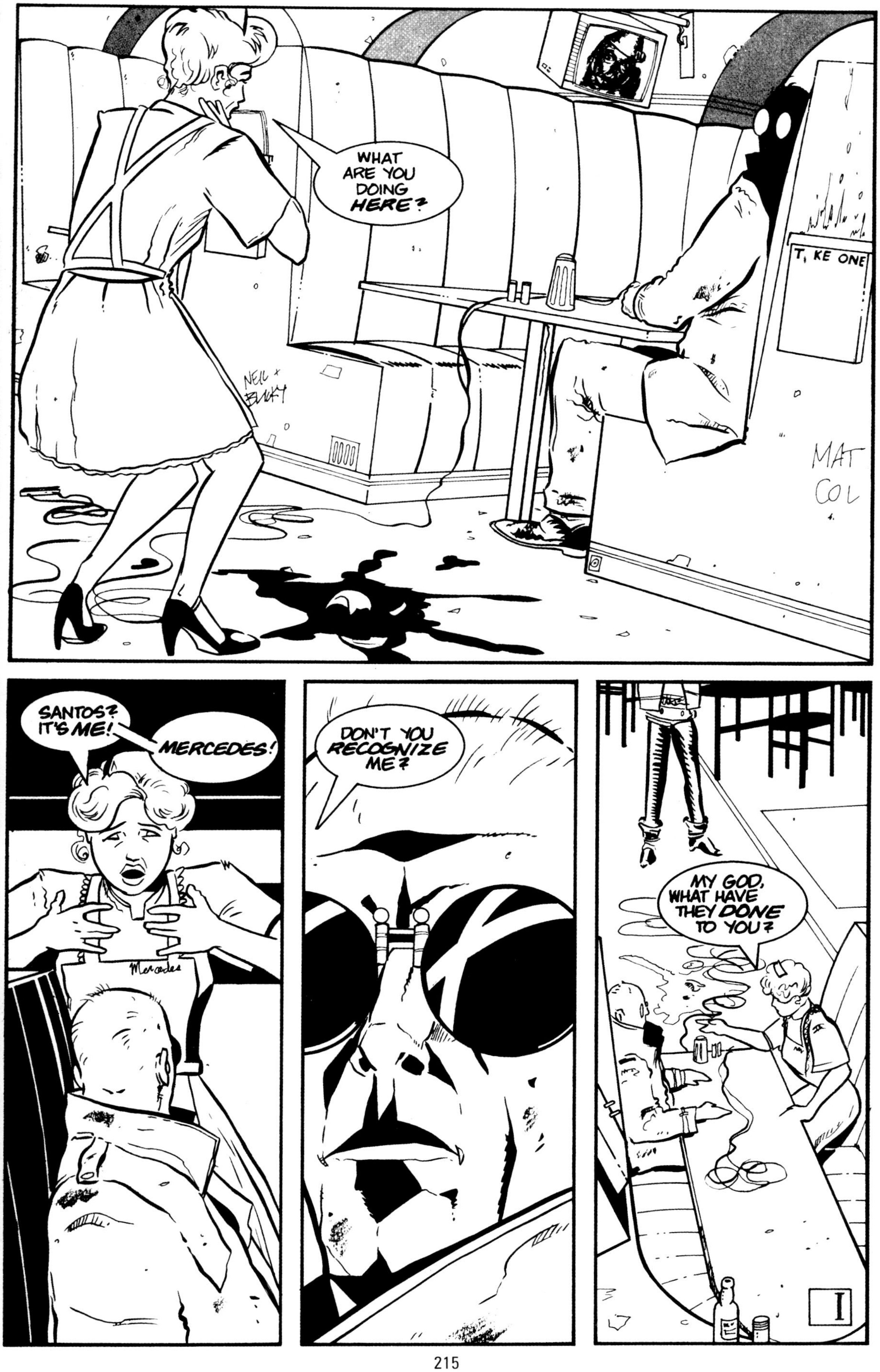
WHAT ARE YOU DOING HERE?
T, KE ONE
NEIL + BUCKY
MAT COL
SANTOS? IT'S ME!
MERCEDES!
Mercedes
DON'T YOU RECOGNIZE ME?
MY GOD, WHAT HAVE THEY DONE TO YOU?
I

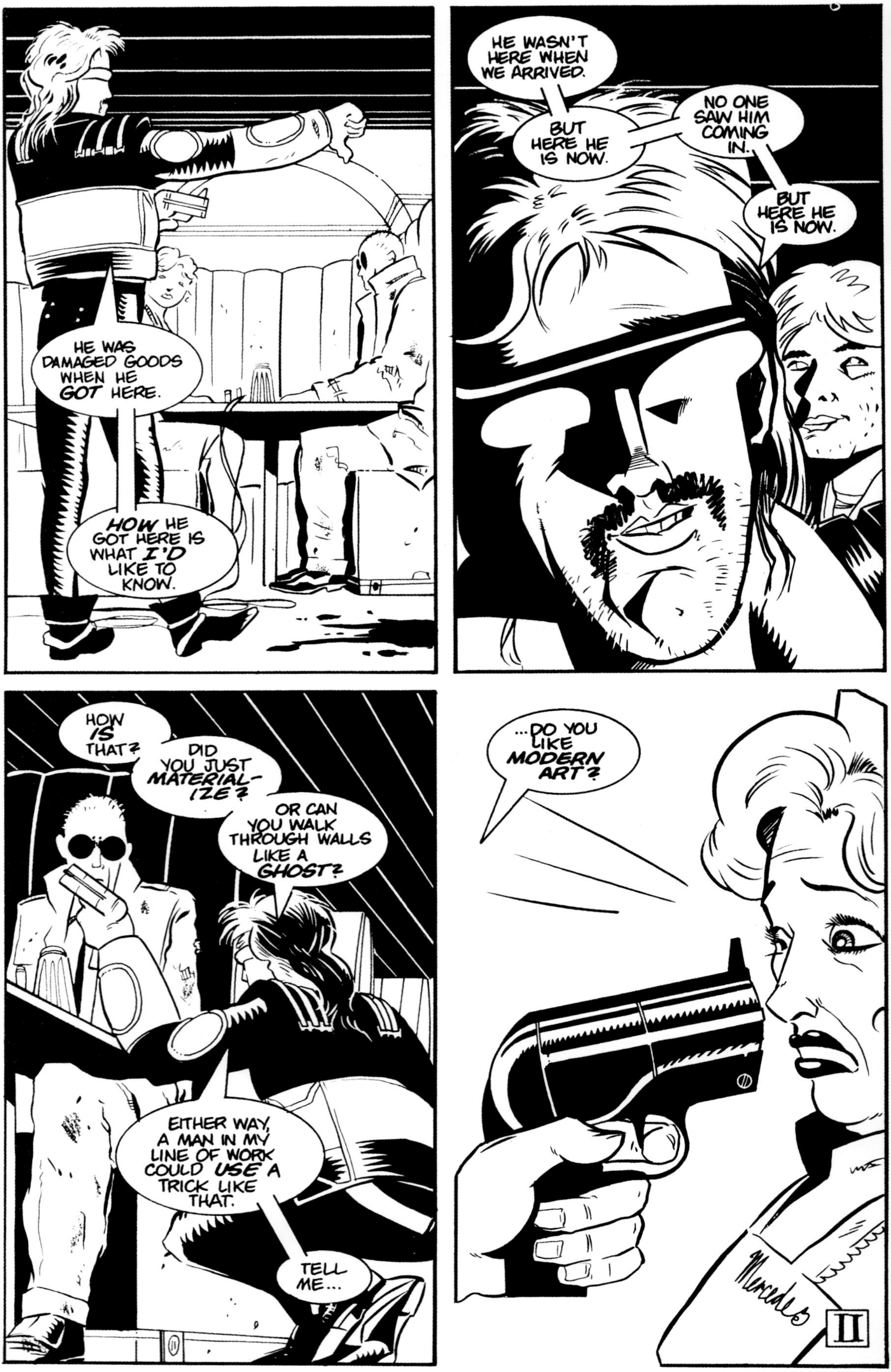
HE WAS DAMAGED GOODS WHEN HE GOT HERE.
HOW HE GOT HERE IS WHAT I'D LIKE TO KNOW.
HE WASN'T HERE WHEN WE ARRIVED.
BUT HERE HE IS NOW.
NO ONE SAW HIM COMING IN.
BUT HERE HE IS NOW.
HOW IS THAT?
DID YOU JUST MATERIAL-IZE?
OR CAN YOU WALK THROUGH WALLS LIKE A GHOST?
EITHER WAY, A MAN IN MY LINE OF WORK COULD USE A TRICK LIKE THAT.
TELL ME...
...DO YOU LIKE MODERN ART?
II

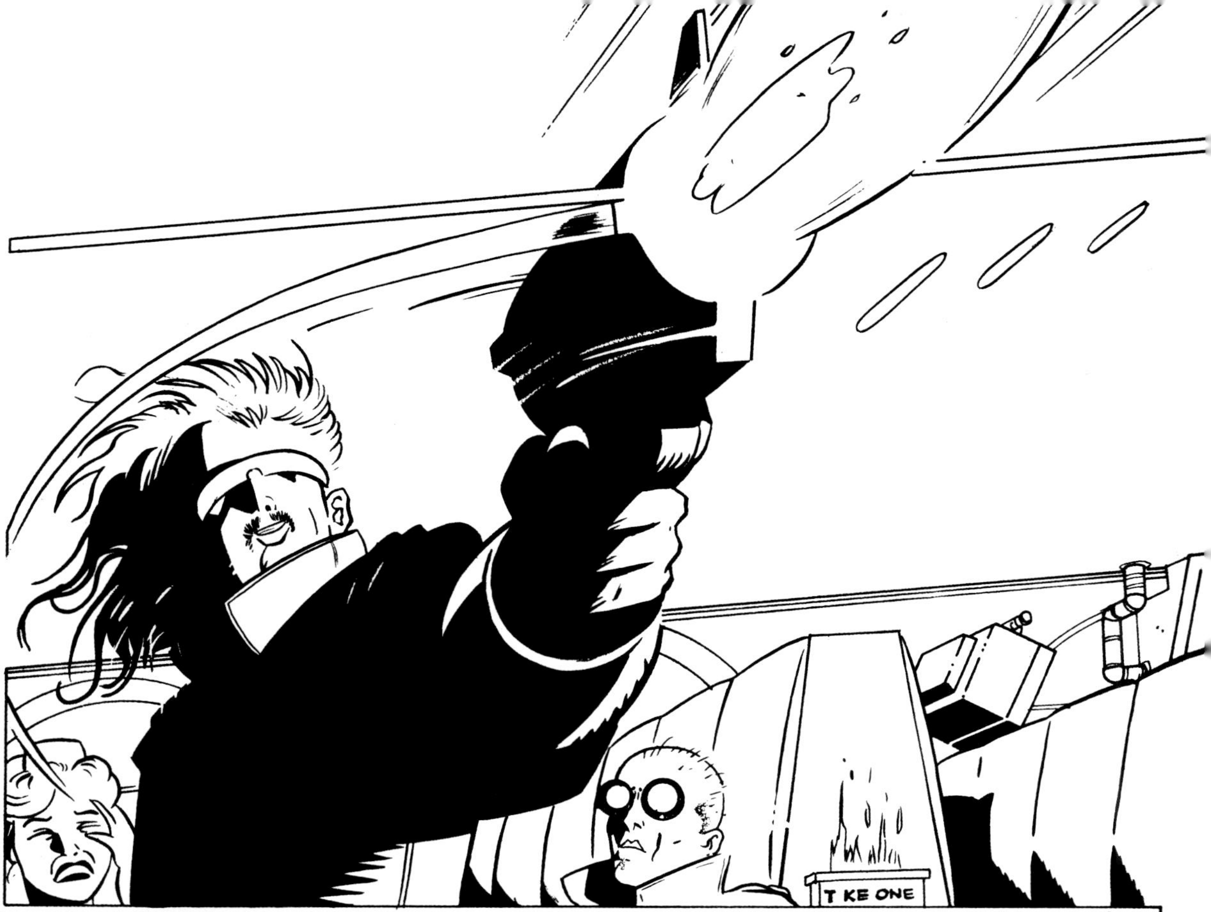
T KE ONE

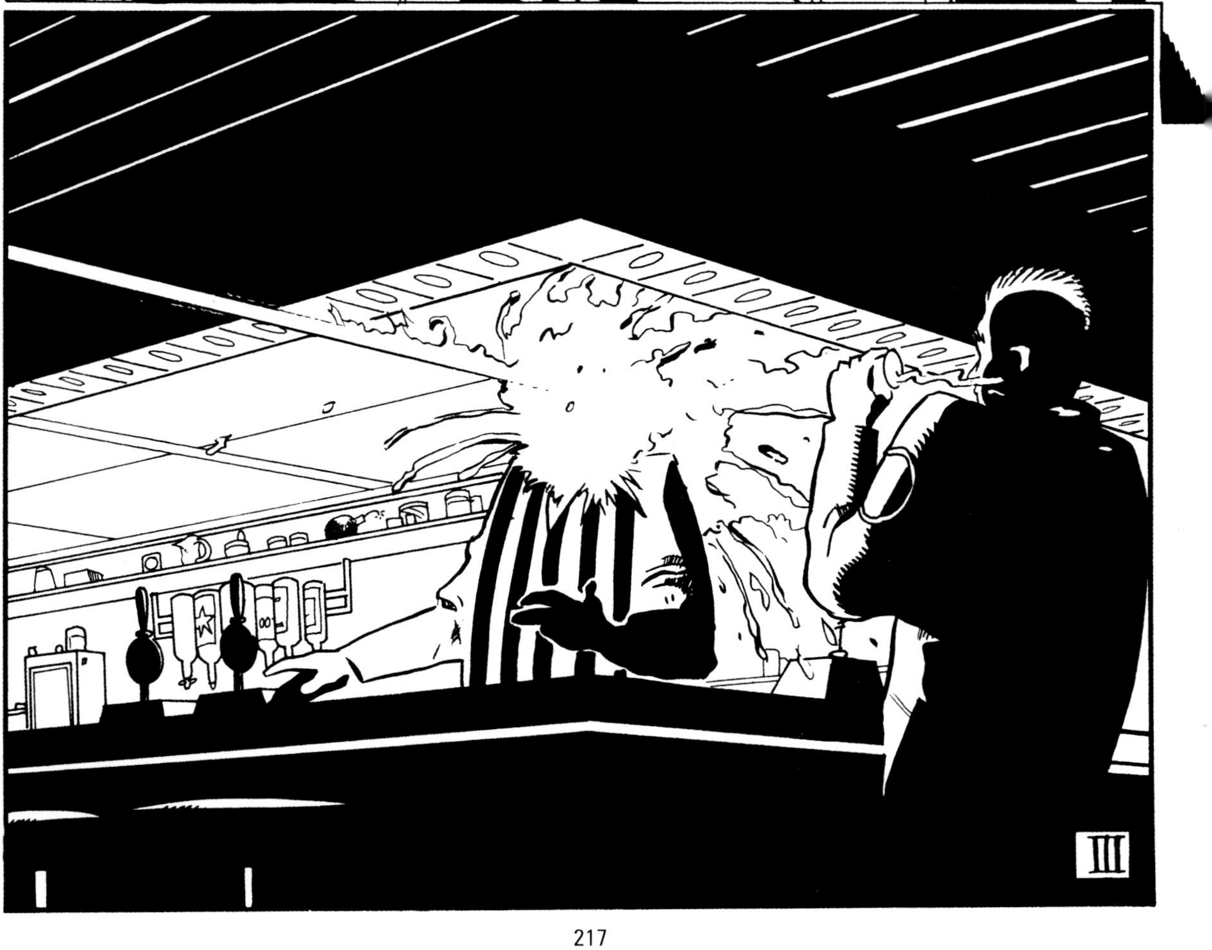
III

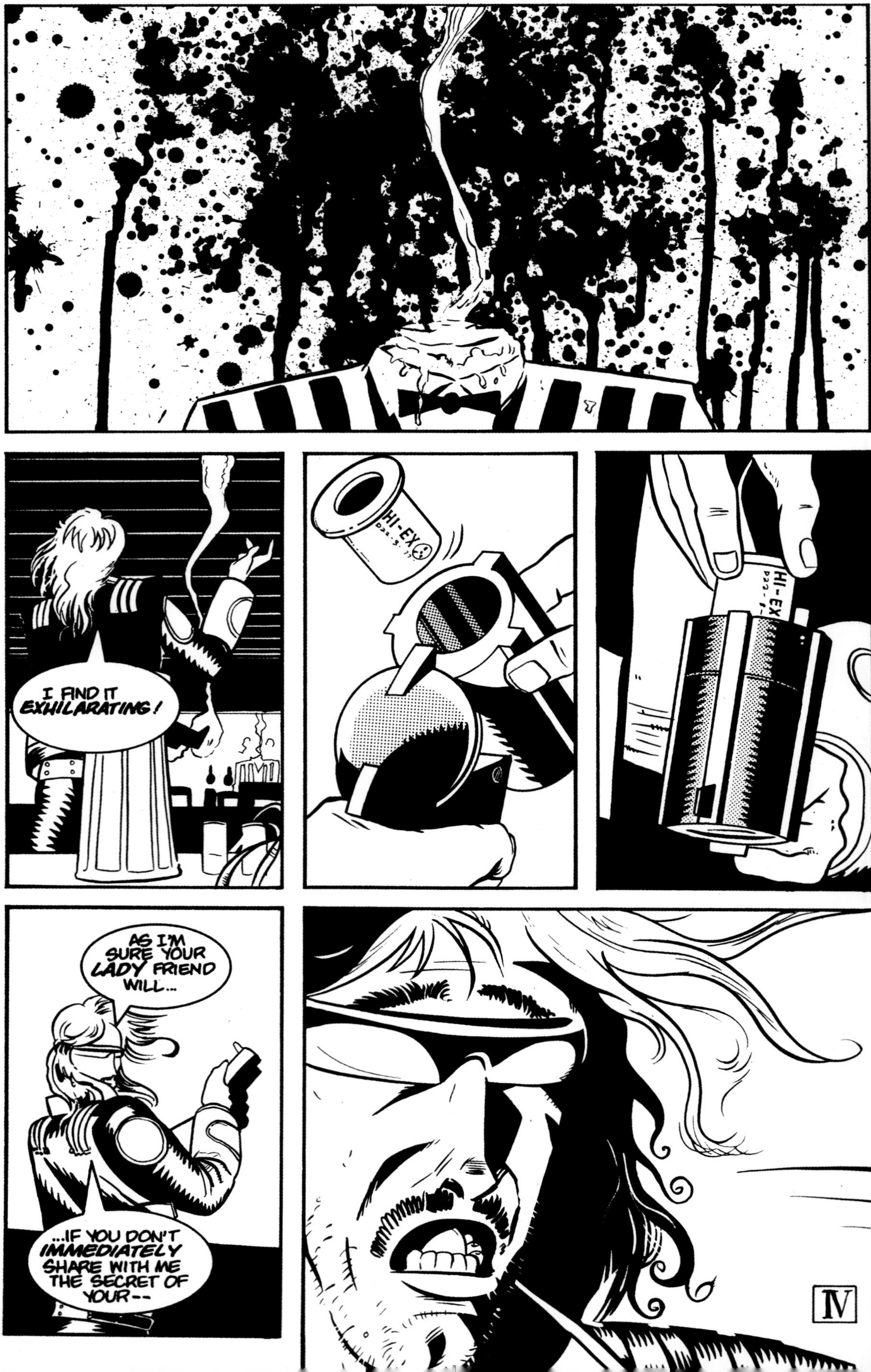
I FIND IT *EXHILARATING!*
HI-EX
HI-EX
AS I'M SURE YOUR *LADY* FRIEND WILL...
...IF YOU DON'T *IMMEDIATELY* SHARE WITH ME THE SECRET OF YOUR--
IV

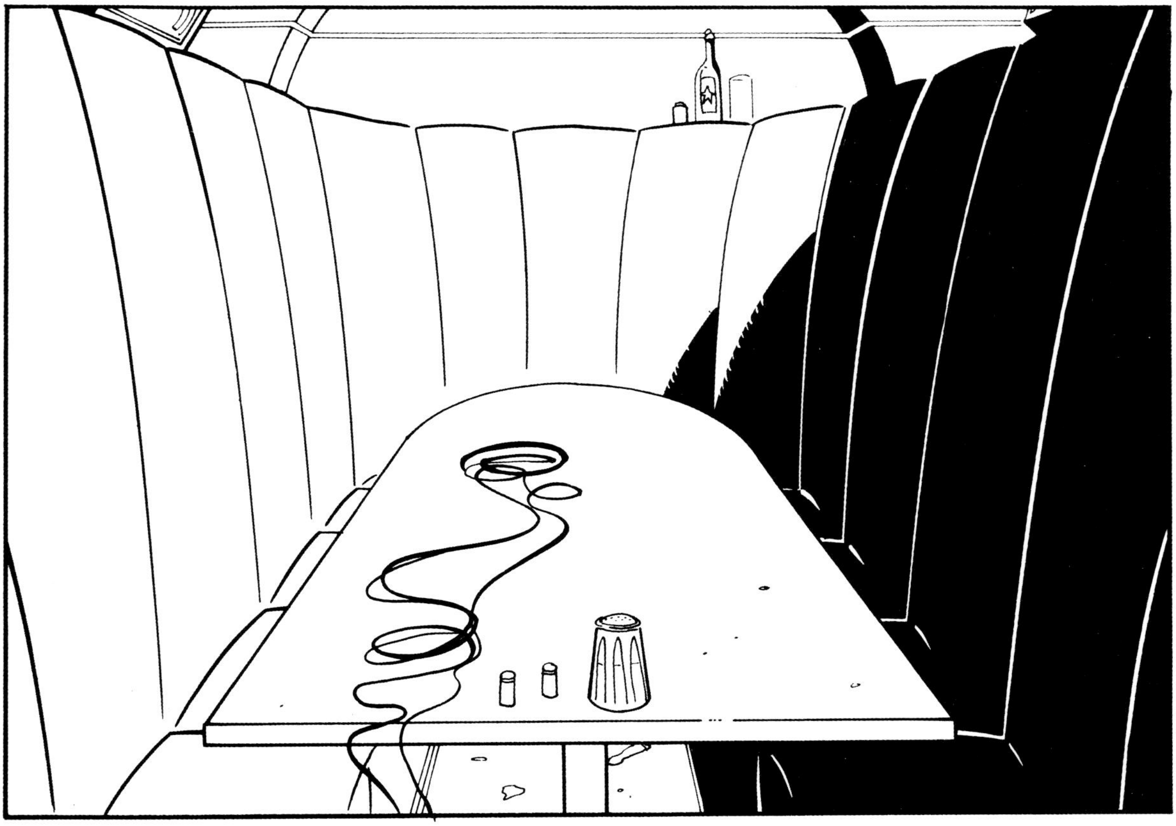

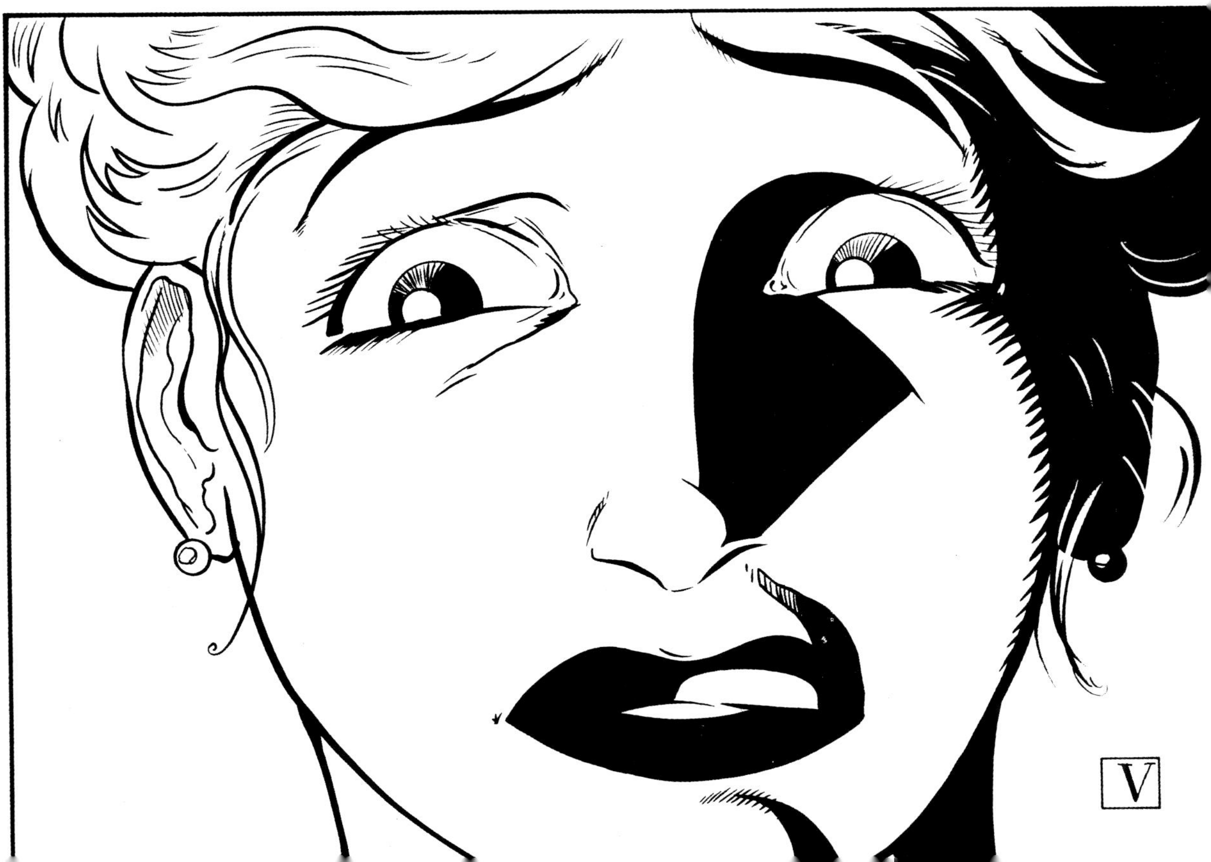
V

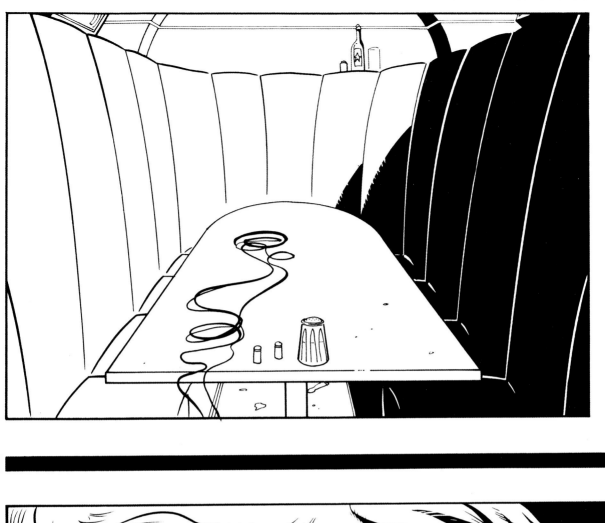

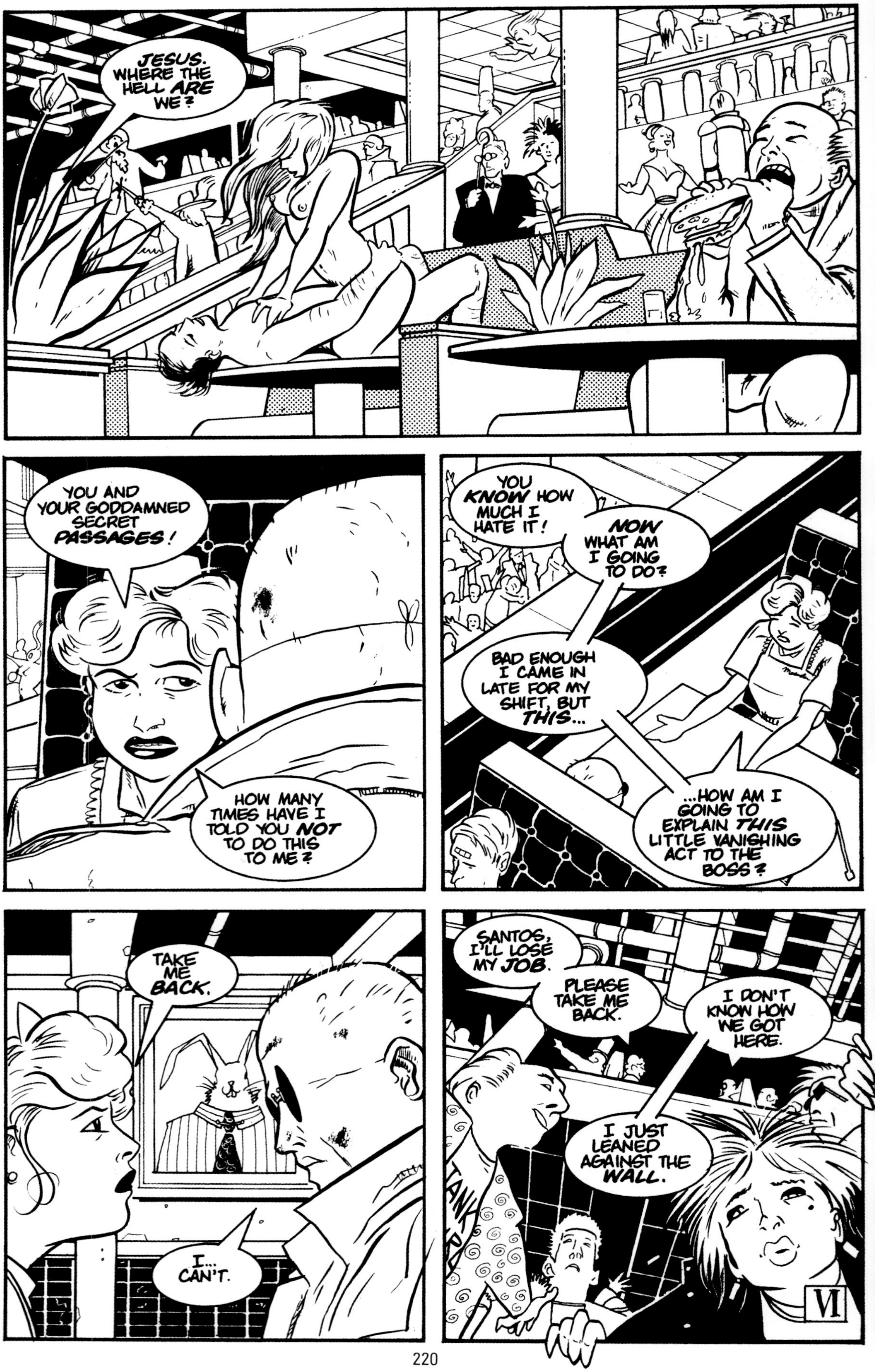
JESUS. WHERE THE HELL ARE WE?
YOU AND YOUR GODDAMNED SECRET PASSAGES!
HOW MANY TIMES HAVE I TOLD YOU NOT TO DO THIS TO ME?
YOU KNOW HOW MUCH I HATE IT!
NOW WHAT AM I GOING TO DO?
BAD ENOUGH I CAME IN LATE FOR MY SHIFT, BUT THIS...
...HOW AM I GOING TO EXPLAIN THIS LITTLE VANISHING ACT TO THE BOSS?
TAKE ME BACK.
I... CAN'T.
SANTOS, I'LL LOSE MY JOB.
PLEASE TAKE ME BACK.
I DON'T KNOW HOW WE GOT HERE.
I JUST LEANED AGAINST THE WALL.
VI

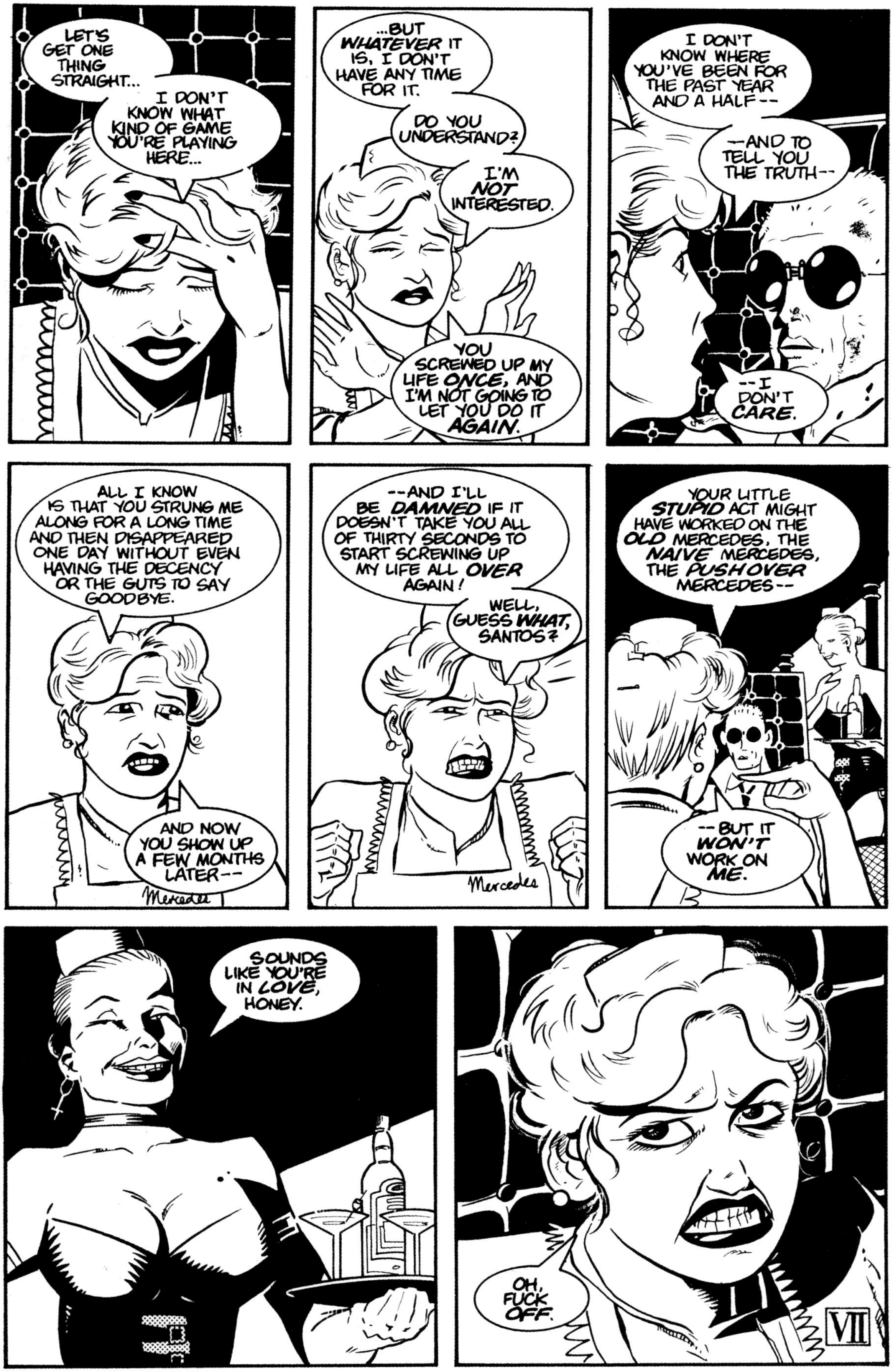
LET'S GET ONE THING STRAIGHT...
I DON'T KNOW WHAT KIND OF GAME YOU'RE PLAYING HERE...
...BUT WHATEVER IT IS, I DON'T HAVE ANY TIME FOR IT.
DO YOU UNDERSTAND?
I'M NOT INTERESTED.
YOU SCREWED UP MY LIFE ONCE, AND I'M NOT GOING TO LET YOU DO IT AGAIN.
I DON'T KNOW WHERE YOU'VE BEEN FOR THE PAST YEAR AND A HALF--
--AND TO TELL YOU THE TRUTH--
--I DON'T CARE.
ALL I KNOW IS THAT YOU STRUNG ME ALONG FOR A LONG TIME AND THEN DISAPPEARED ONE DAY WITHOUT EVEN HAVING THE DECENCY OR THE GUTS TO SAY GOODBYE.
AND NOW YOU SHOW UP A FEW MONTHS LATER--
Mercedes
--AND I'LL BE DAMNED IF IT DOESN'T TAKE YOU ALL OF THIRTY SECONDS TO START SCREWING UP MY LIFE ALL OVER AGAIN!
WELL, GUESS WHAT, SANTOS?
Mercedes
YOUR LITTLE STUPID ACT MIGHT HAVE WORKED ON THE OLD MERCEDES, THE NAIVE MERCEDES, THE PUSHOVER MERCEDES--
--BUT IT WON'T WORK ON ME.
SOUNDS LIKE YOU'RE IN LOVE, HONEY.
OH, FUCK OFF.
VII

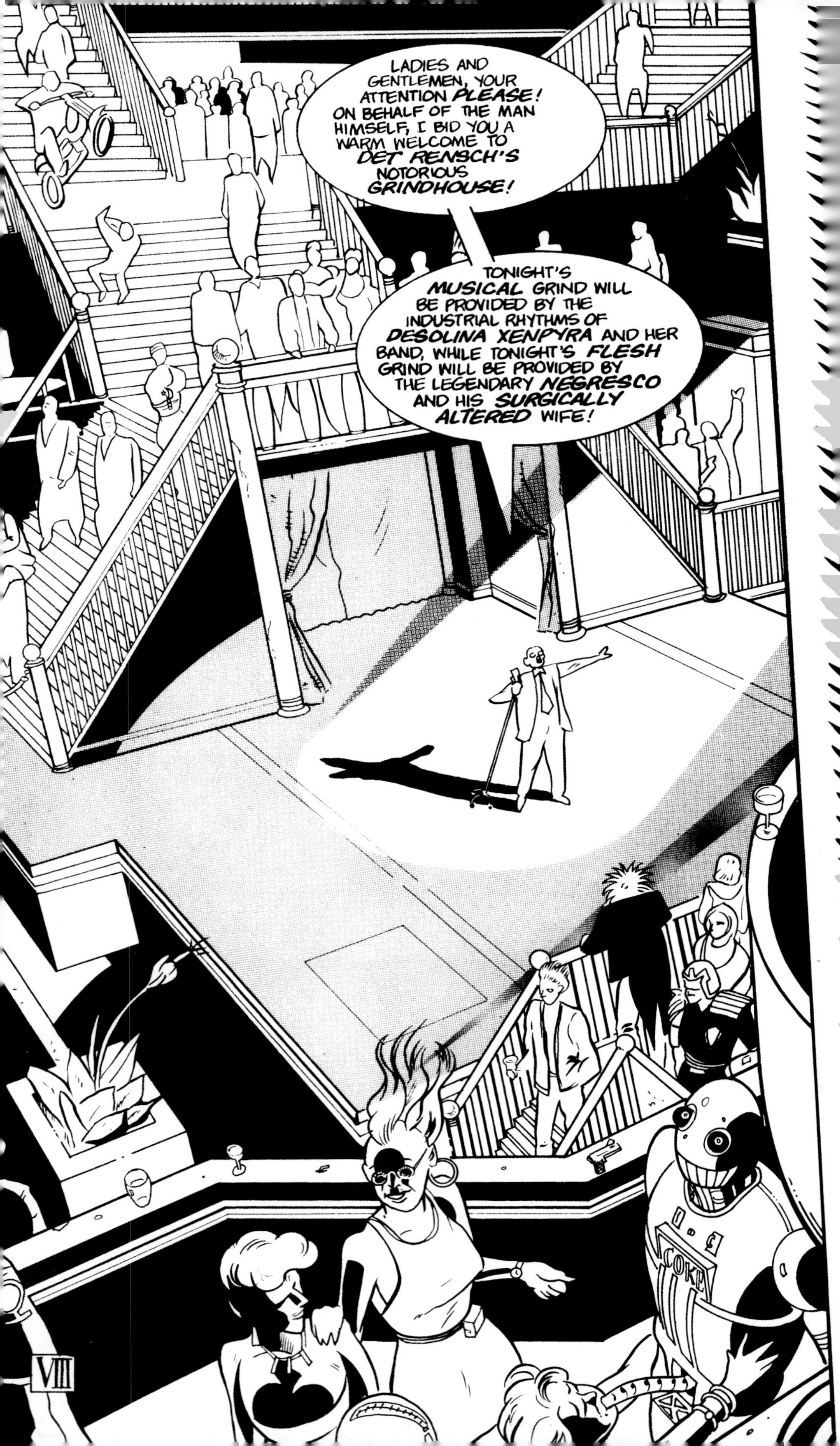
LADIES AND GENTLEMEN, YOUR ATTENTION PLEASE! ON BEHALF OF THE MAN HIMSELF, I BID YOU A WARM WELCOME TO DET RENSCH'S NOTORIOUS GRINDHOUSE!
TONIGHT'S MUSICAL GRIND WILL BE PROVIDED BY THE INDUSTRIAL RHYTHMS OF DESOLINA XENPYRA AND HER BAND, WHILE TONIGHT'S FLESH GRIND WILL BE PROVIDED BY THE LEGENDARY NEGRESCO AND HIS SURGICALLY ALTERED WIFE!
COKE
VIII

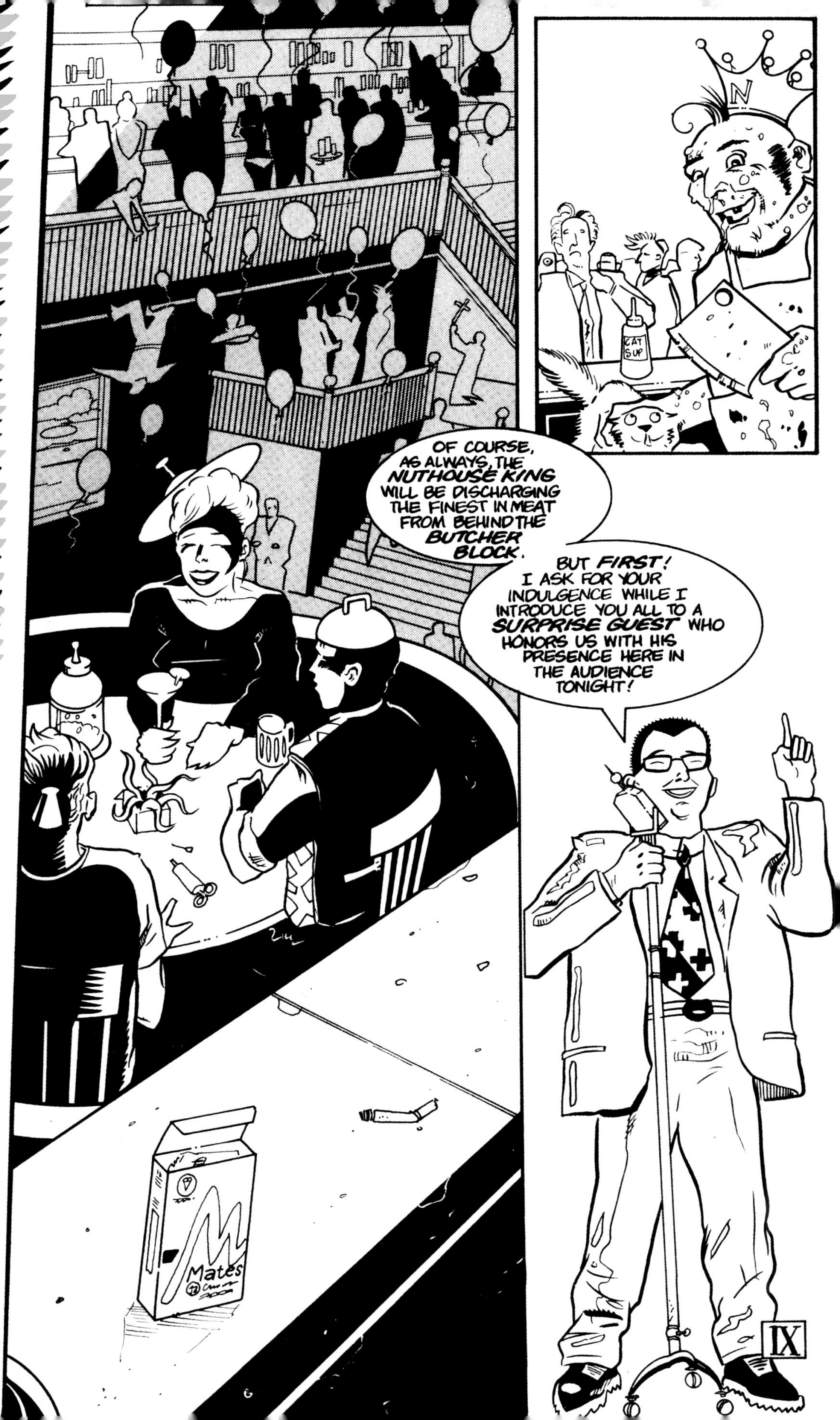
CAT SUP
OF COURSE, AS ALWAYS, THE NUTHOUSE KING WILL BE DISCHARGING THE FINEST IN MEAT FROM BEHIND THE BUTCHER BLOCK.
BUT FIRST! I ASK FOR YOUR INDULGENCE WHILE I INTRODUCE YOU ALL TO A SURPRISE GUEST WHO HONORS US WITH HIS PRESENCE HERE IN THE AUDIENCE TONIGHT!
Mates
IX

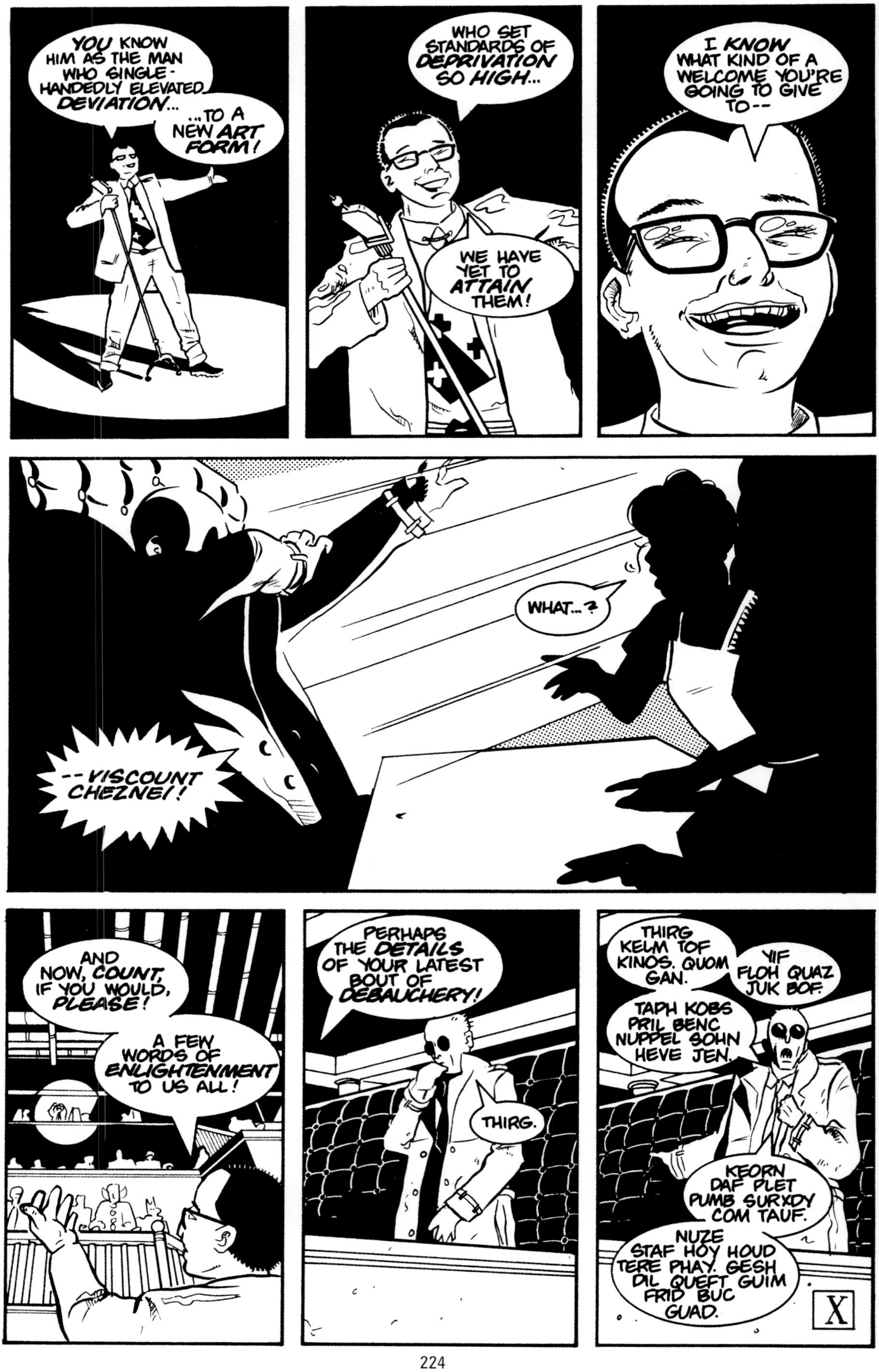
YOU KNOW HIM AS THE MAN WHO SINGLE-HANDEDLY ELEVATED DEVIATION...
...TO A NEW ART FORM!
WHO SET STANDARDS OF DEPRIVATION SO HIGH...
WE HAVE YET TO ATTAIN THEM!
I KNOW WHAT KIND OF A WELCOME YOU'RE GOING TO GIVE TO--
WHAT...?
--VISCOUNT CHEZNEI!
AND NOW, COUNT, IF YOU WOULD, PLEASE!
A FEW WORDS OF ENLIGHTENMENT TO US ALL!
PERHAPS THE DETAILS OF YOUR LATEST BOUT OF DEBAUCHERY!
THIRG.
THIRG KELM TOF KINOS. QUOM GAN.
YIF FLOH QUAZ JUK BOF.
TAPH KOBS PRIL BENC NUPPEL SOHN HEVE JEN.
KEORN DAF PLET PUMB SURXDY COM TAUF.
NUZE STAF HOY HOUD TERE PHAY. GESH DIL QUEFT GUIM FRID BUC GUAD.
X

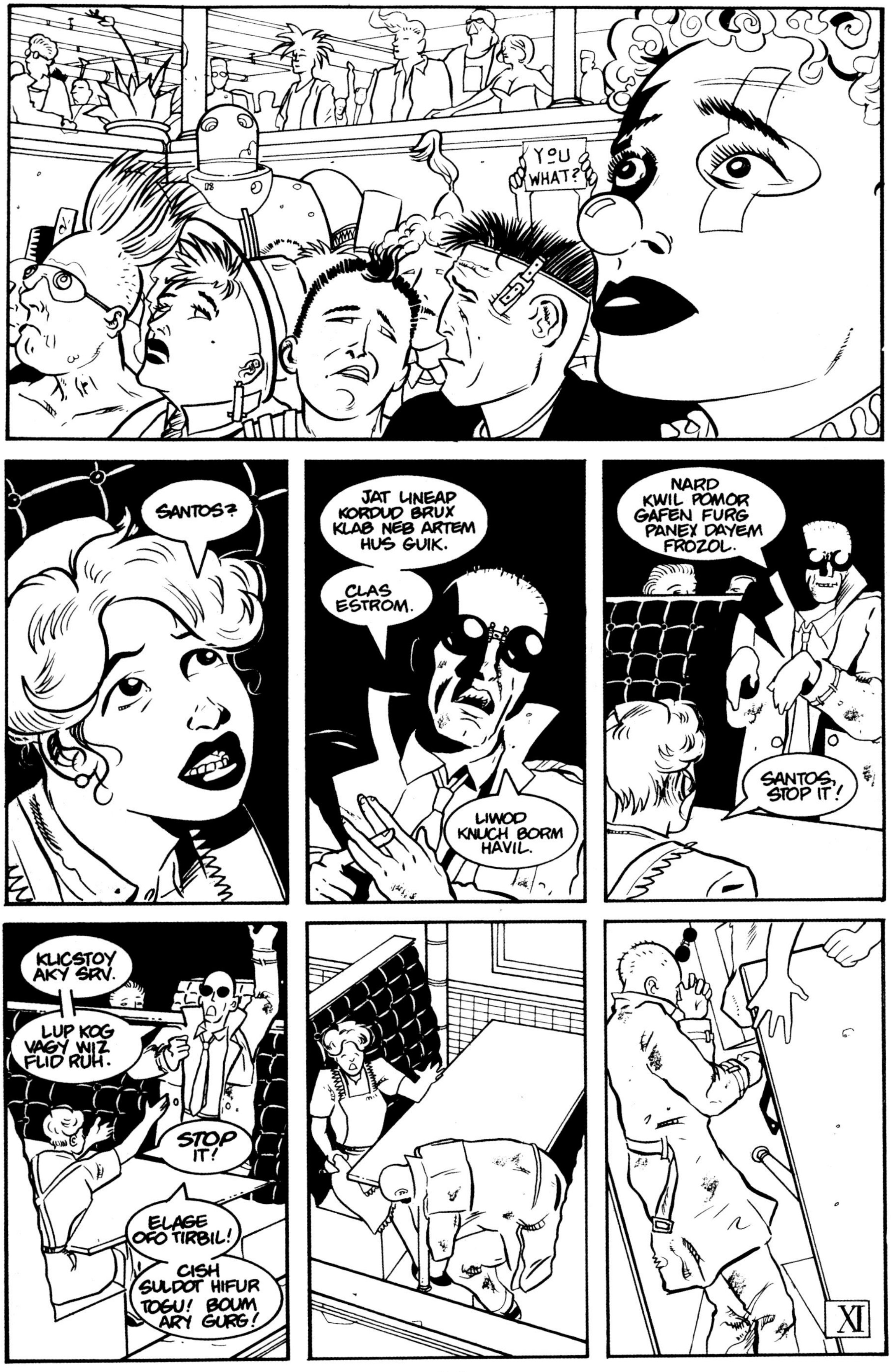
YOU WHAT?
SANTOS?
JAT LINEAP KORDUD BRUX KLAB NEB ARTEM HUS GUIK.
CLAS ESTROM.
LIWOD KNUCH BORM HAVIL.
NARD KWIL POMOR GAFEN FURG PANEX DAYEM FROZOL.
SANTOS, STOP IT!
KLICSTOY AKY SRV.
LUP KOG VAGY WIZ FLID RUH.
STOP IT!
ELAGE OFO TIRBIL!
CISH SULDOT HIFUR TOGU! BOUM ARY GURG!
XI

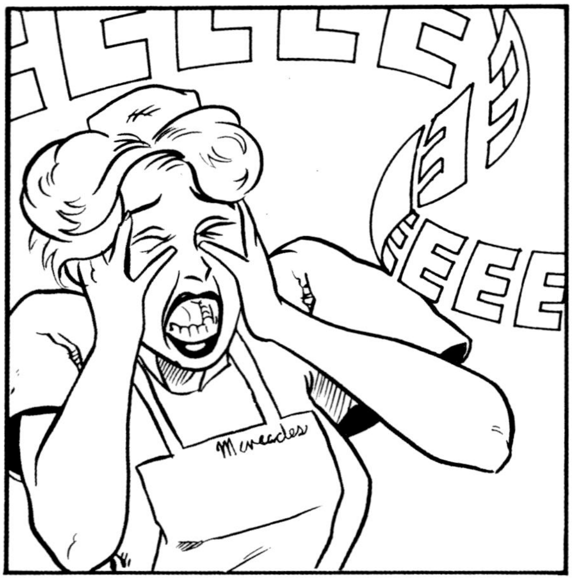
EEEE
Mercedes

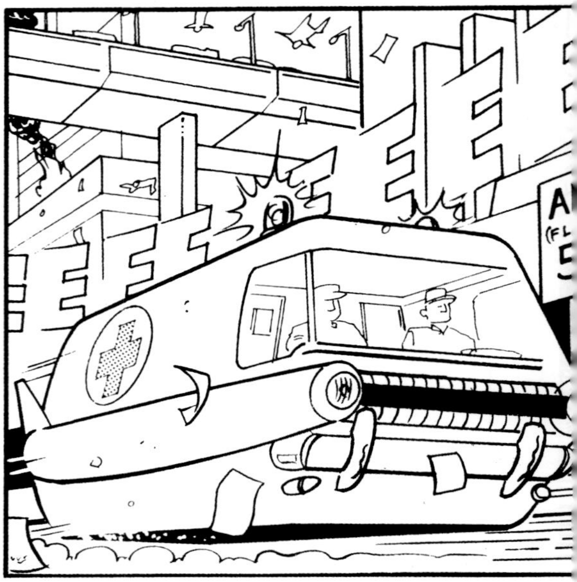

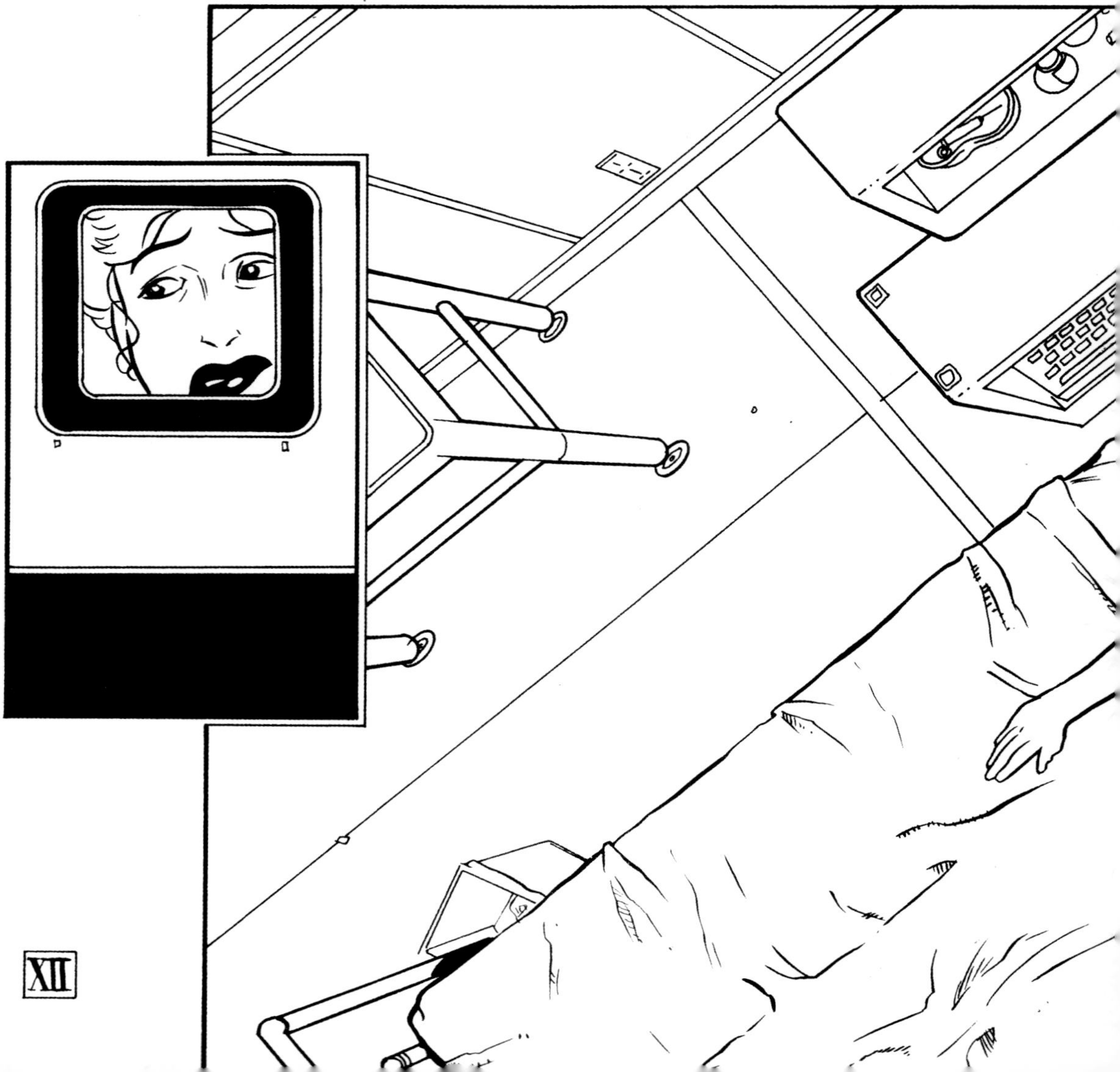

XII

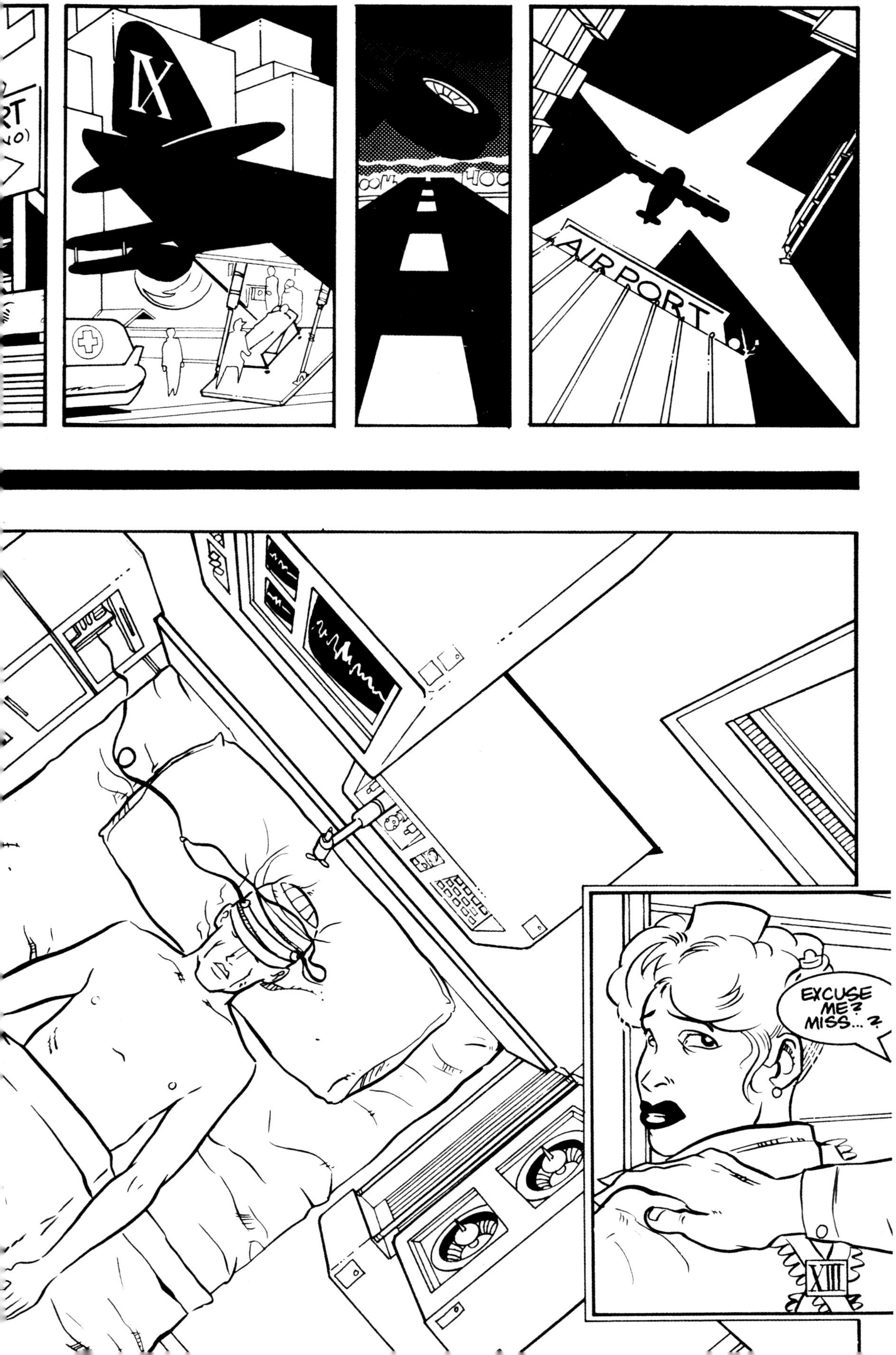

AIRPORT
EXCUSE ME? MISS...?
XIII

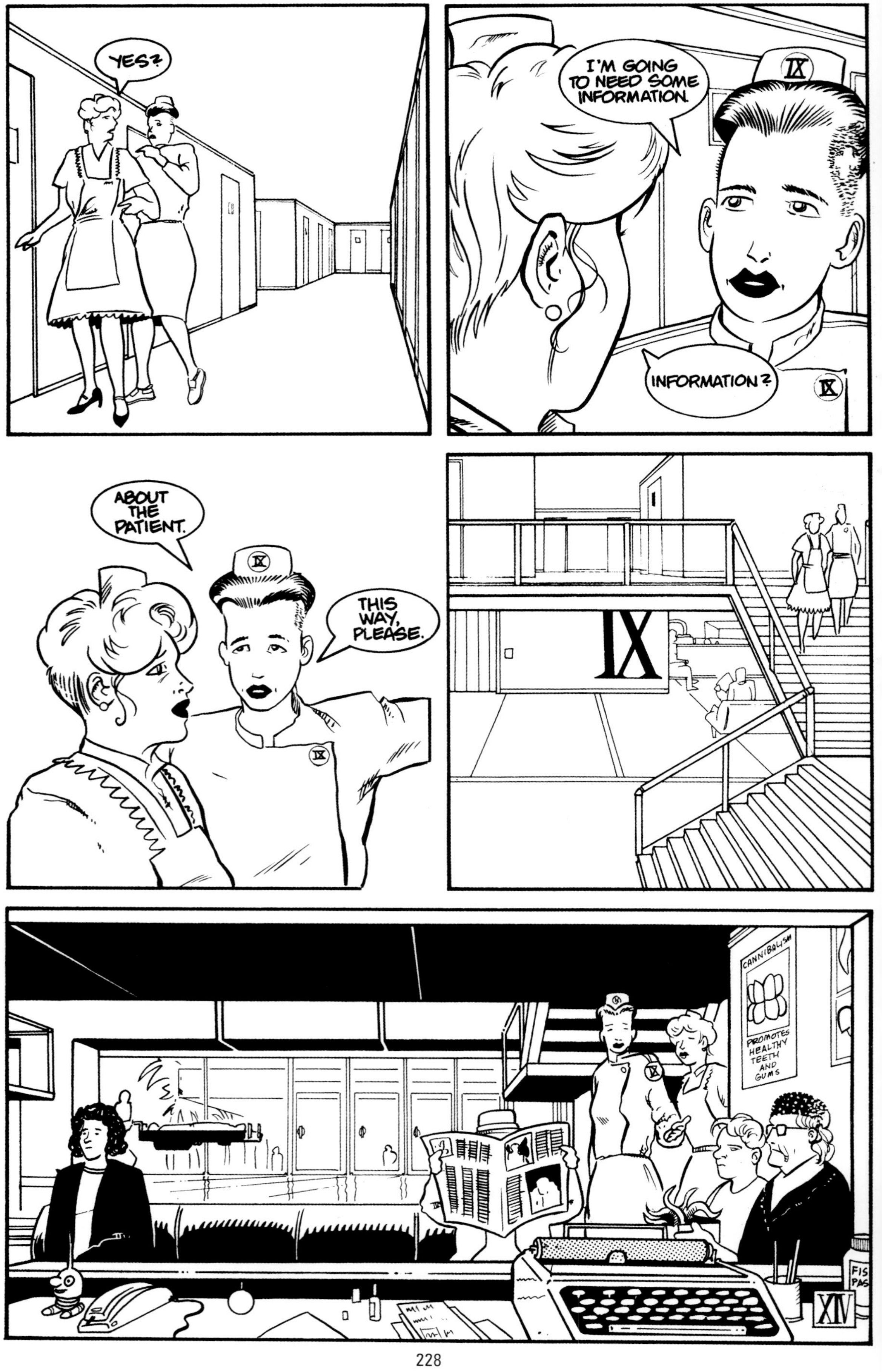
YES?
I'M GOING TO NEED SOME INFORMATION.
INFORMATION?
IX
ABOUT THE PATIENT.
THIS WAY, PLEASE.
IX
CANNIBALISM
PROMOTES HEALTHY TEETH AND GUMS
XIV

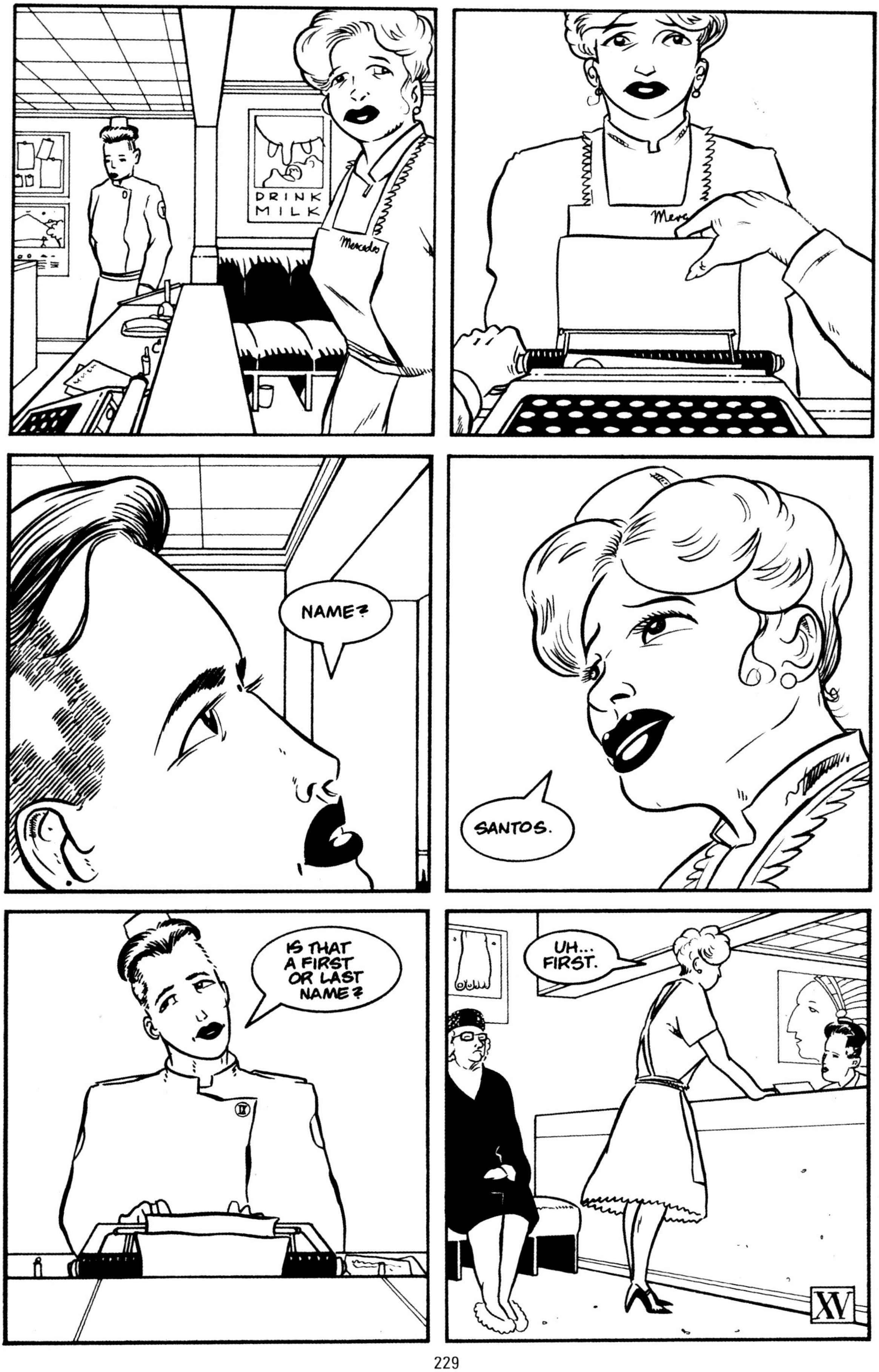
DRINK MILK
Mercedes
NAME?
SANTOS.
IS THAT A FIRST OR LAST NAME?
UH... FIRST.
XV

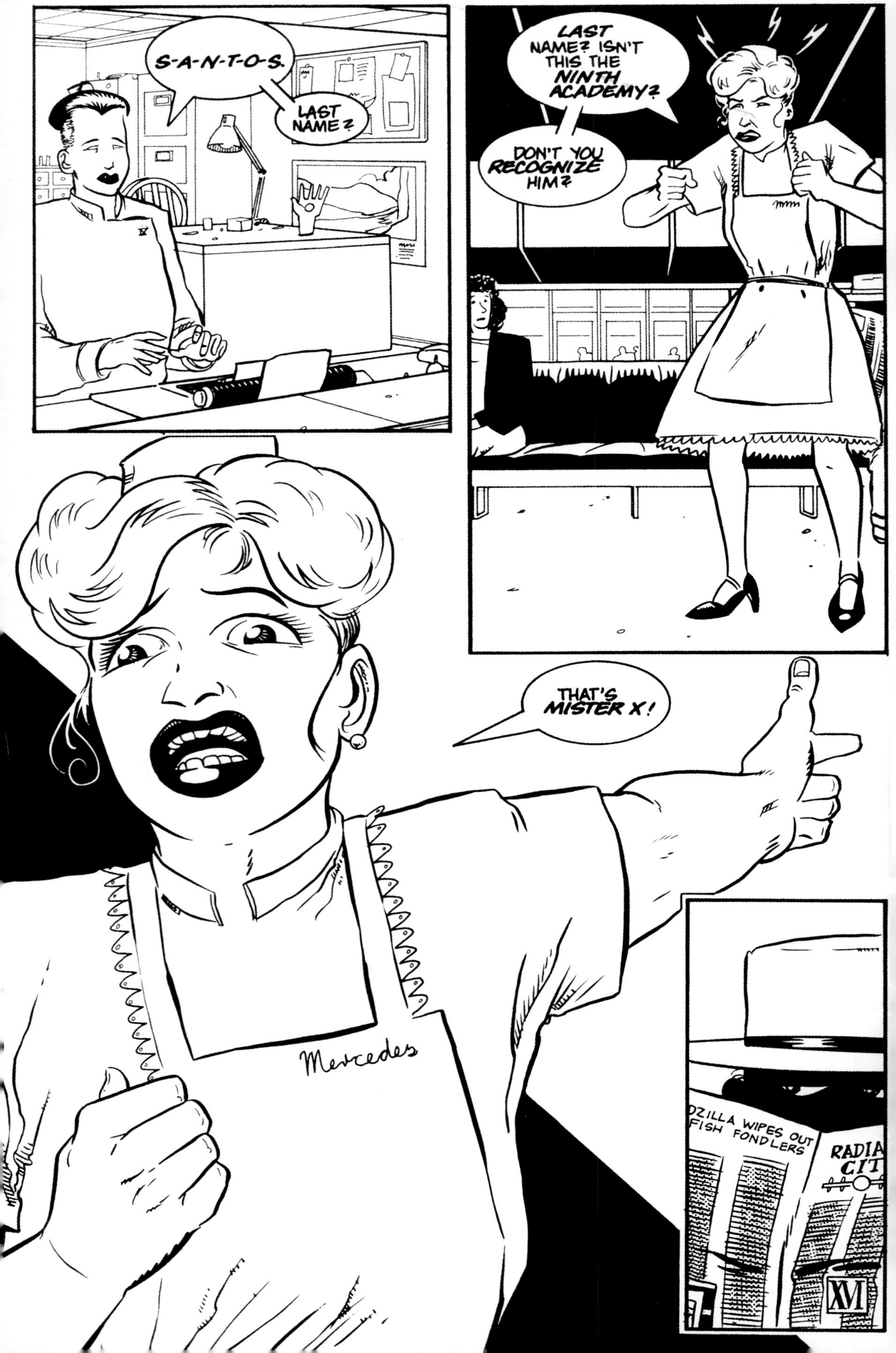
S-A-N-T-O-S.
LAST NAME?
LAST NAME? ISN'T THIS THE NINTH ACADEMY?
DON'T YOU RECOGNIZE HIM?
THAT'S MISTER X!
Mercedes
DZILLA WIPES OUT FISH FONDLERS
RADIA CIT
XVI

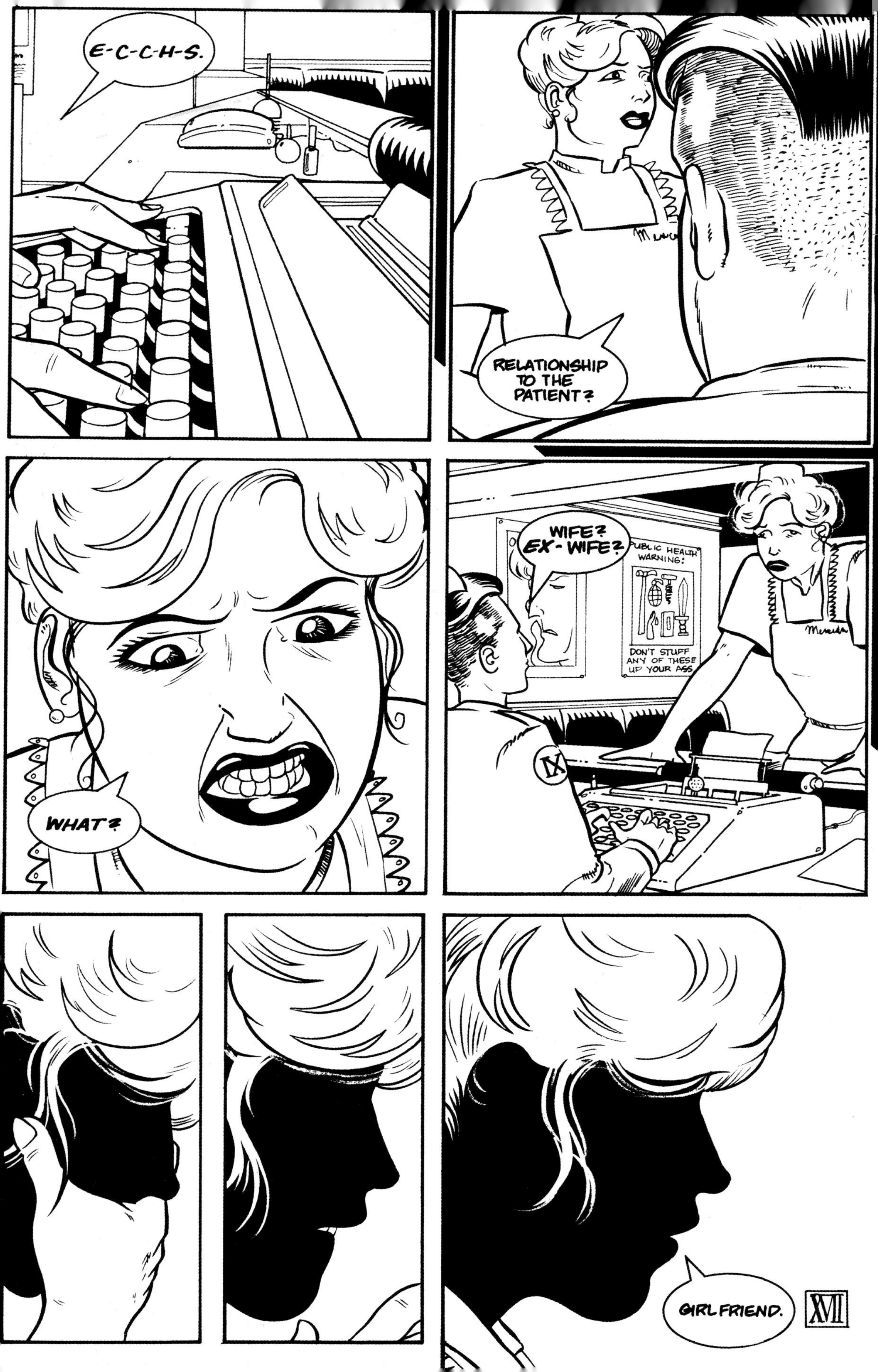
E-C-C-H-S.
RELATIONSHIP TO THE PATIENT?
WHAT?
WIFE? EX-WIFE?
PUBLIC HEALTH WARNING:
DON'T STUFF ANY OF THESE UP YOUR ASS
GIRLFRIEND.
XVII

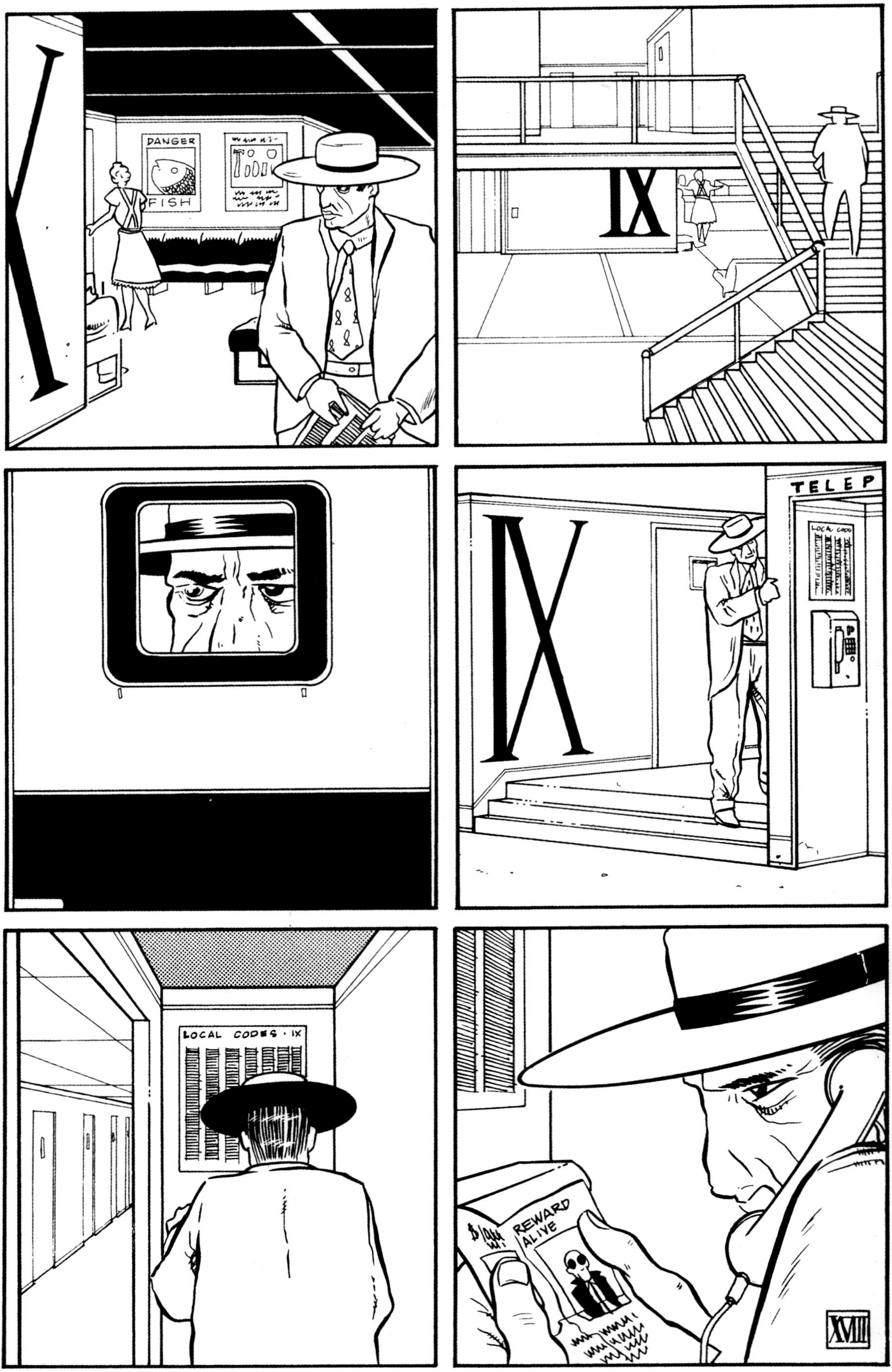

X
DANGER
FISH
IX
IX
TELEP
LOCAL CODES · IX
REWARD
ALIVE
XVIII

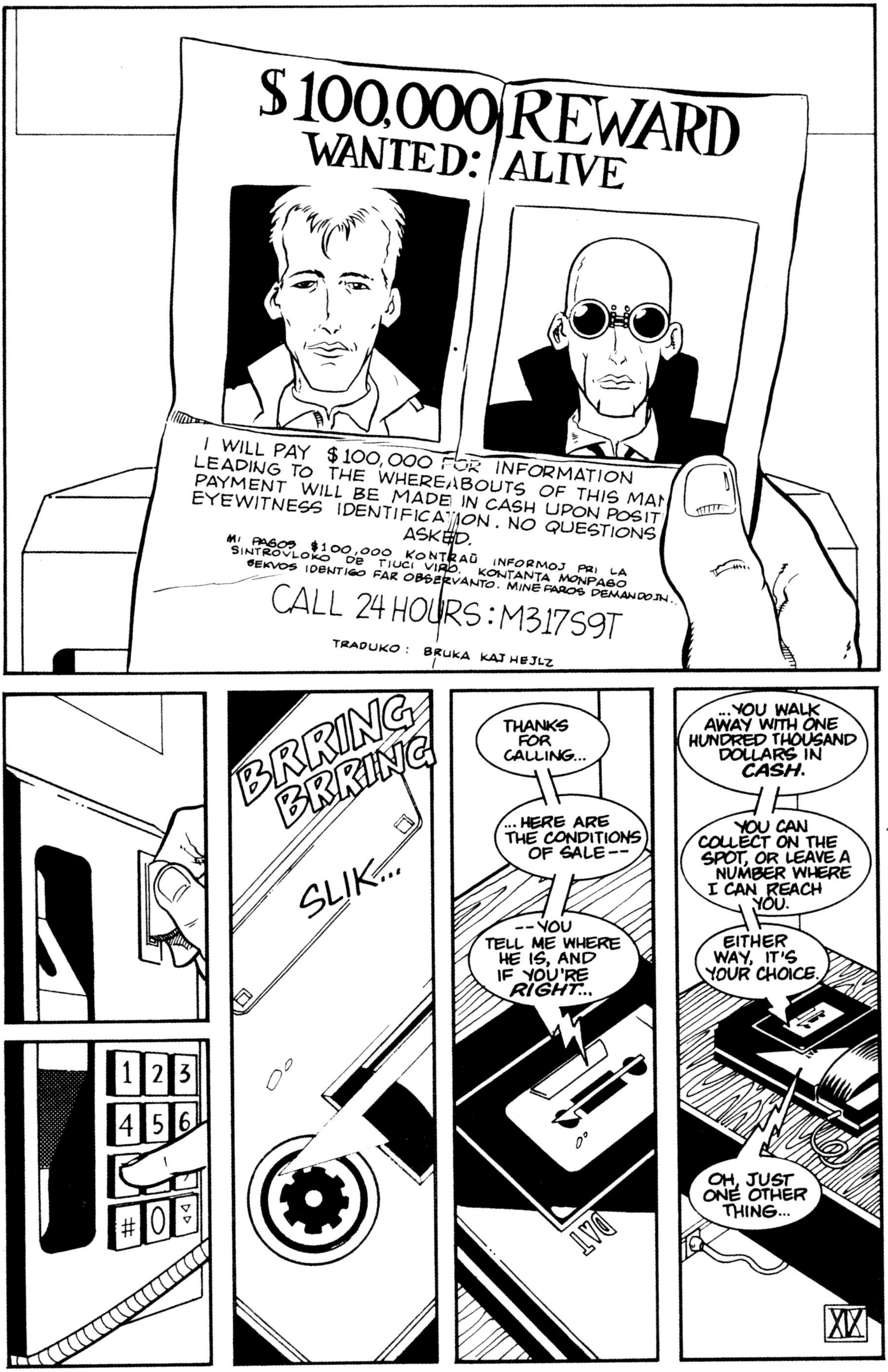

$100,000 REWARD
WANTED: ALIVE
I WILL PAY $100,000 FOR INFORMATION LEADING TO THE WHEREABOUTS OF THIS MAN PAYMENT WILL BE MADE IN CASH UPON POSIT EYEWITNESS IDENTIFICATION. NO QUESTIONS ASKED.
MI PAGOS $100,000 KONTRAŬ INFORMOJ PRI LA SINTROVLOKO DE TIUCI VIRO. KONTANTA MONPAGO SEKVOS IDENTIGO FAR OBSERVANTO. MINE FAROS DEMANDOJN..
CALL 24 HOURS: M317S9T
TRADUKO: BRUKA KAJ HEJLZ
BRRING BRRING
SLIK...
THANKS FOR CALLING...
...HERE ARE THE CONDITIONS OF SALE--
--YOU TELL ME WHERE HE IS, AND IF YOU'RE RIGHT...
...YOU WALK AWAY WITH ONE HUNDRED THOUSAND DOLLARS IN CASH.
YOU CAN COLLECT ON THE SPOT, OR LEAVE A NUMBER WHERE I CAN REACH YOU.
EITHER WAY, IT'S YOUR CHOICE.
OH, JUST ONE OTHER THING...

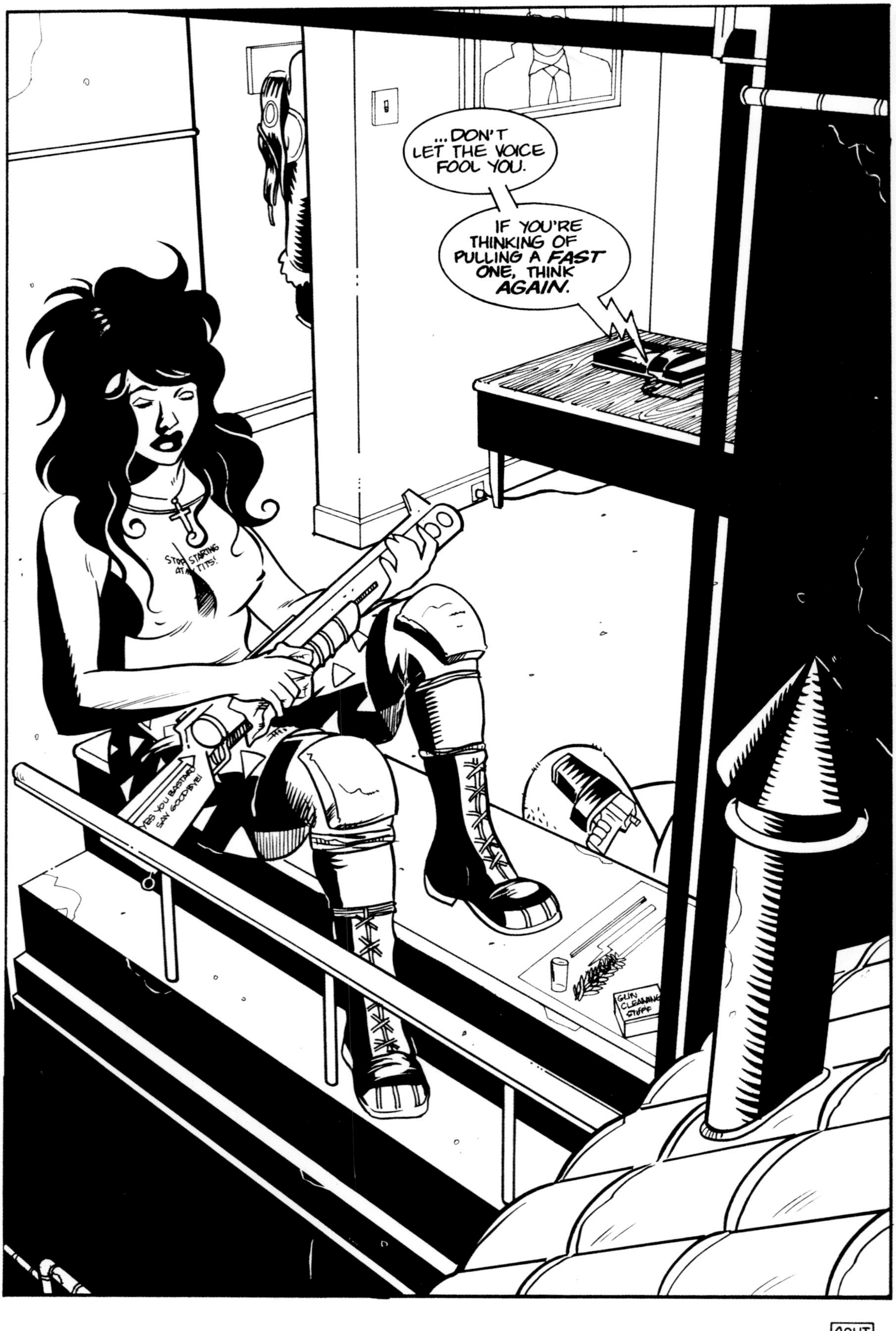
...DON'T LET THE VOICE FOOL YOU.
IF YOU'RE THINKING OF PULLING A FAST ONE, THINK AGAIN.
YES YOU BASTARD! SAY GOODBYE!
GUN CLEANING STUFF

CONT

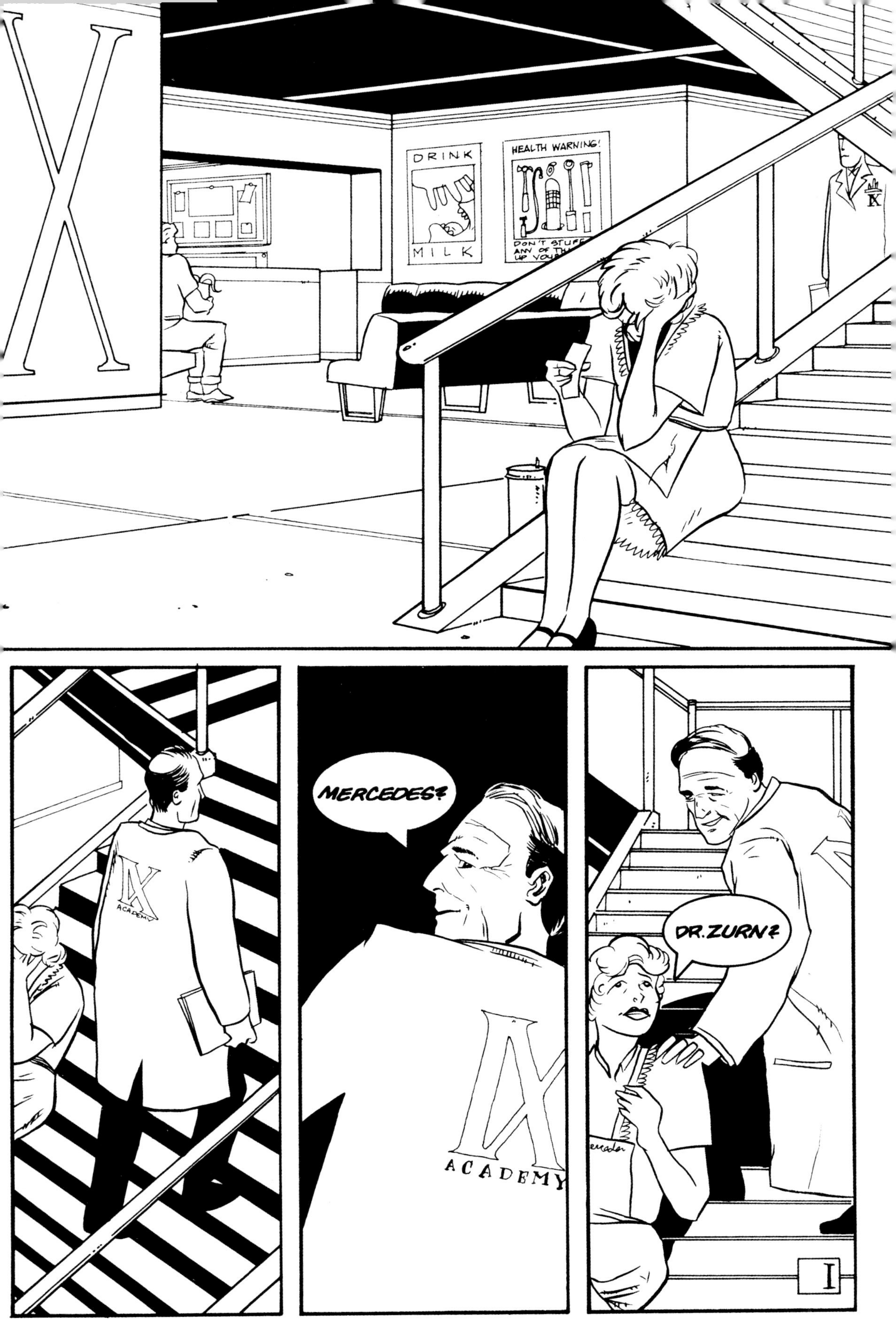
DRINK MILK
HEALTH WARNING!
MERCEDES?
ACADEMY
DR. ZURN?

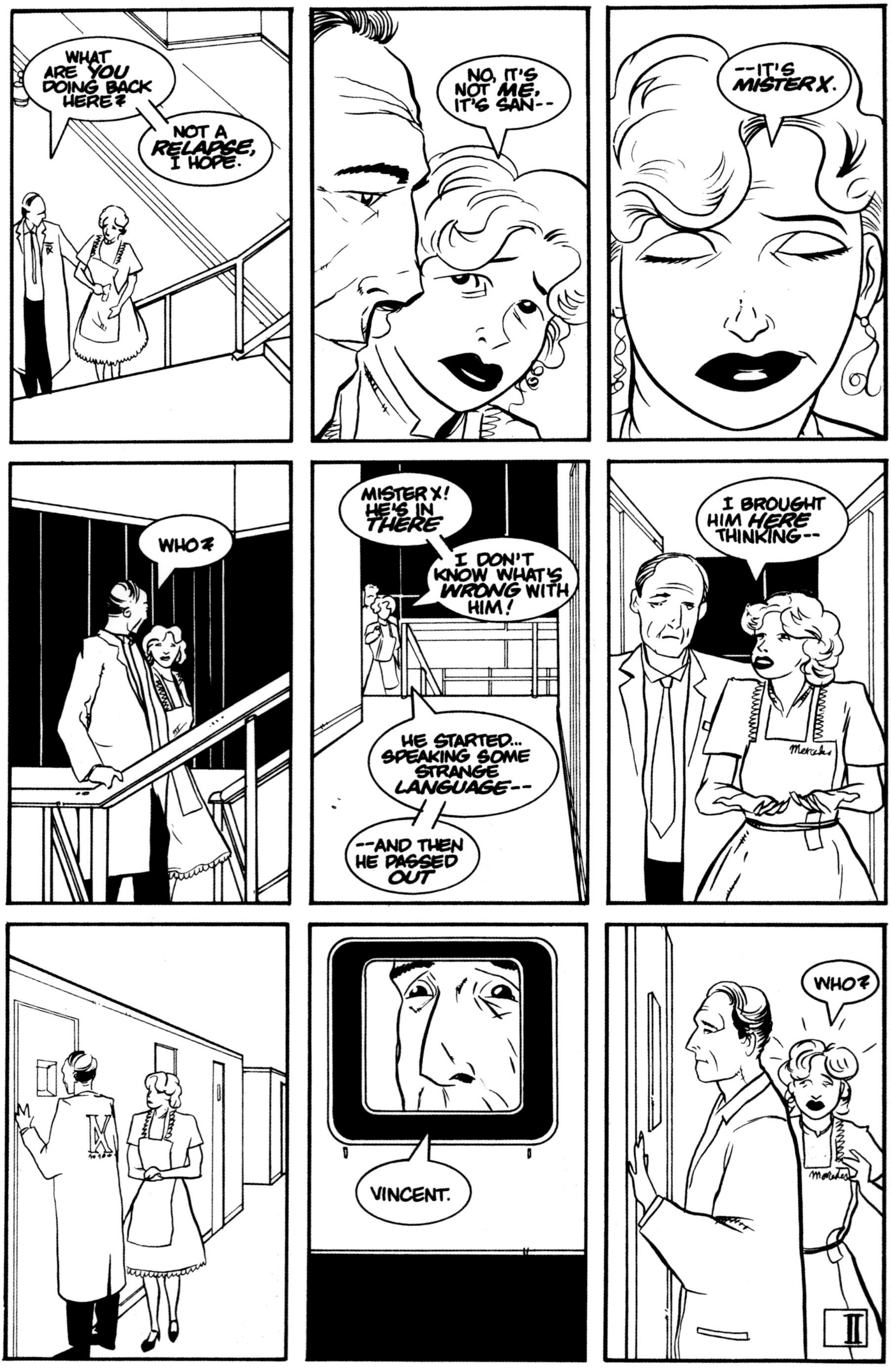
WHAT ARE YOU DOING BACK HERE?
NOT A RELAPSE, I HOPE.
NO, IT'S NOT ME, IT'S SAN--
--IT'S MISTER X.
WHO?
MISTER X! HE'S IN THERE
I DON'T KNOW WHAT'S WRONG WITH HIM!
HE STARTED... SPEAKING SOME STRANGE LANGUAGE--
--AND THEN HE PASSED OUT
I BROUGHT HIM HERE THINKING--
VINCENT.
WHO?

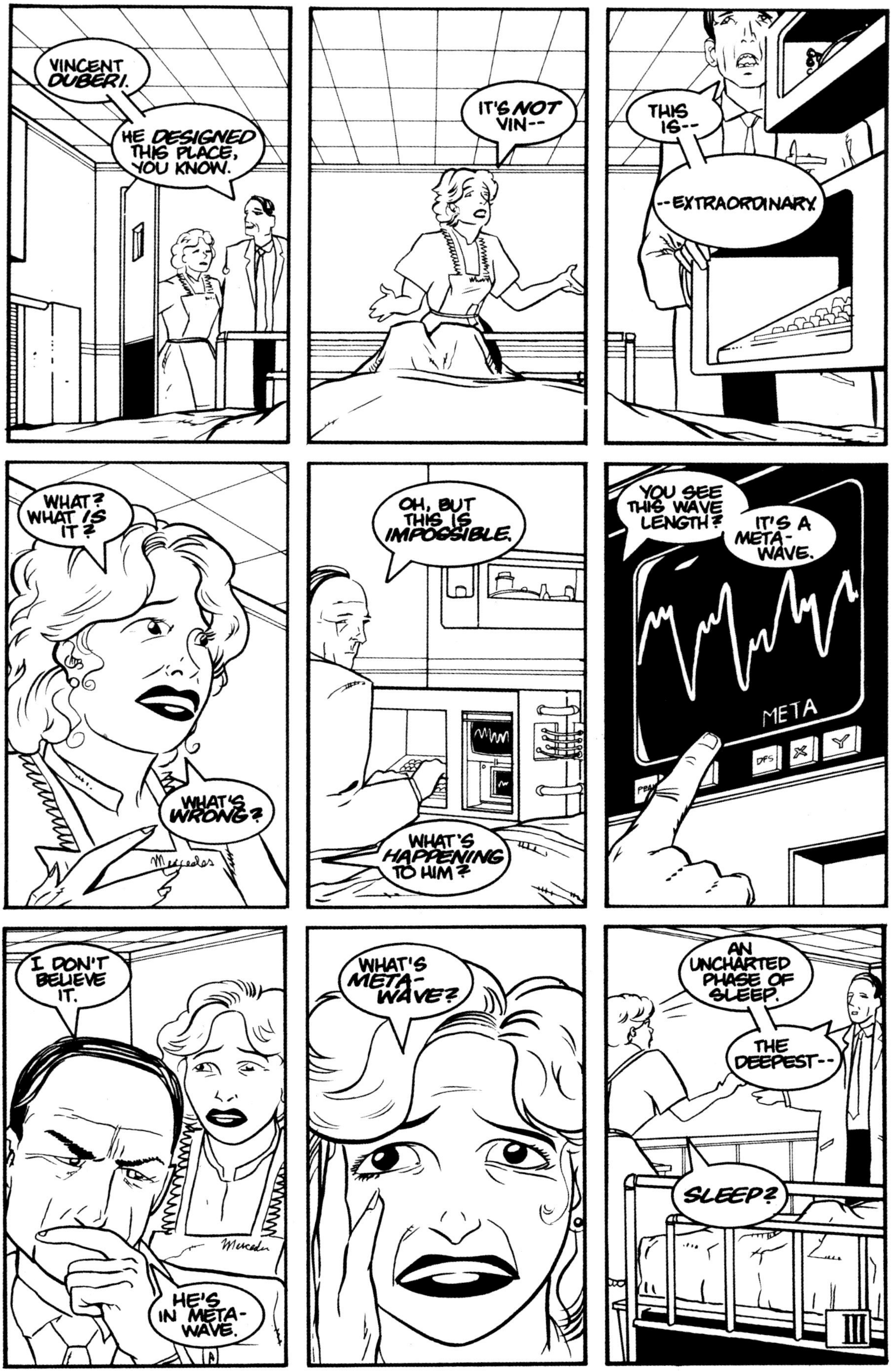
VINCENT DUBERI.
HE DESIGNED THIS PLACE, YOU KNOW.
IT'S NOT VIN--
THIS IS--
--EXTRAORDINARY.
WHAT? WHAT IS IT?
WHAT'S WRONG?
OH, BUT THIS IS IMPOSSIBLE.
WHAT'S HAPPENING TO HIM?
YOU SEE THIS WAVE LENGTH?
IT'S A META-WAVE.
META
DFS
X
Y
I DON'T BELIEVE IT.
HE'S IN META-WAVE.
WHAT'S META-WAVE?
AN UNCHARTED PHASE OF SLEEP.
THE DEEPEST--
SLEEP?
III

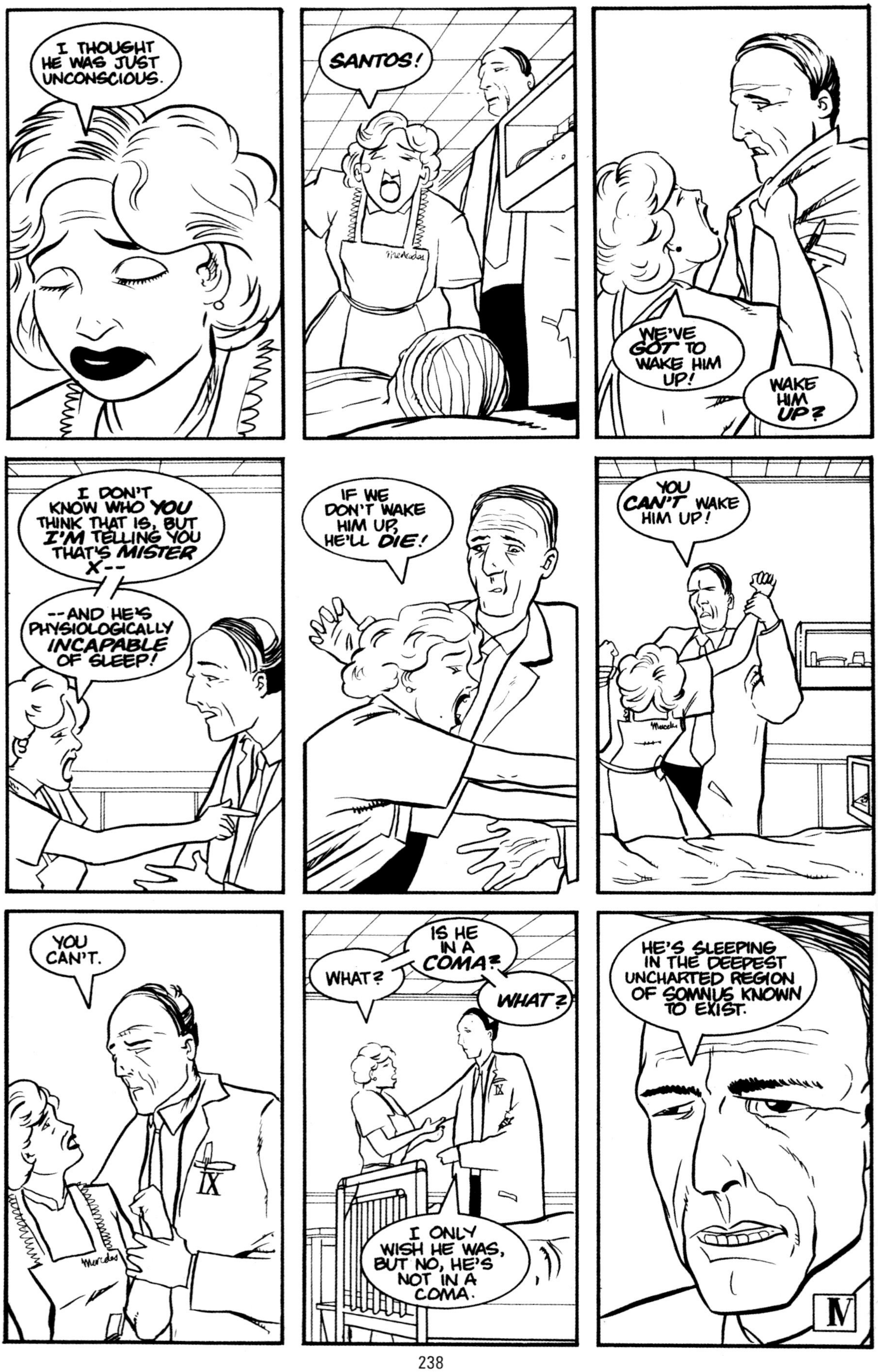
I THOUGHT HE WAS JUST UNCONSCIOUS.
SANTOS!
WE'VE GOT TO WAKE HIM UP!
WAKE HIM UP?
I DON'T KNOW WHO YOU THINK THAT IS, BUT I'M TELLING YOU THAT'S MISTER X--
--AND HE'S PHYSIOLOGICALLY INCAPABLE OF SLEEP!
IF WE DON'T WAKE HIM UP, HE'LL DIE!
YOU CAN'T WAKE HIM UP!
YOU CAN'T.
WHAT?
IS HE IN A COMA?
WHAT?
I ONLY WISH HE WAS, BUT NO, HE'S NOT IN A COMA.
HE'S SLEEPING IN THE DEEPEST UNCHARTED REGION OF SOMNUS KNOWN TO EXIST.
IV

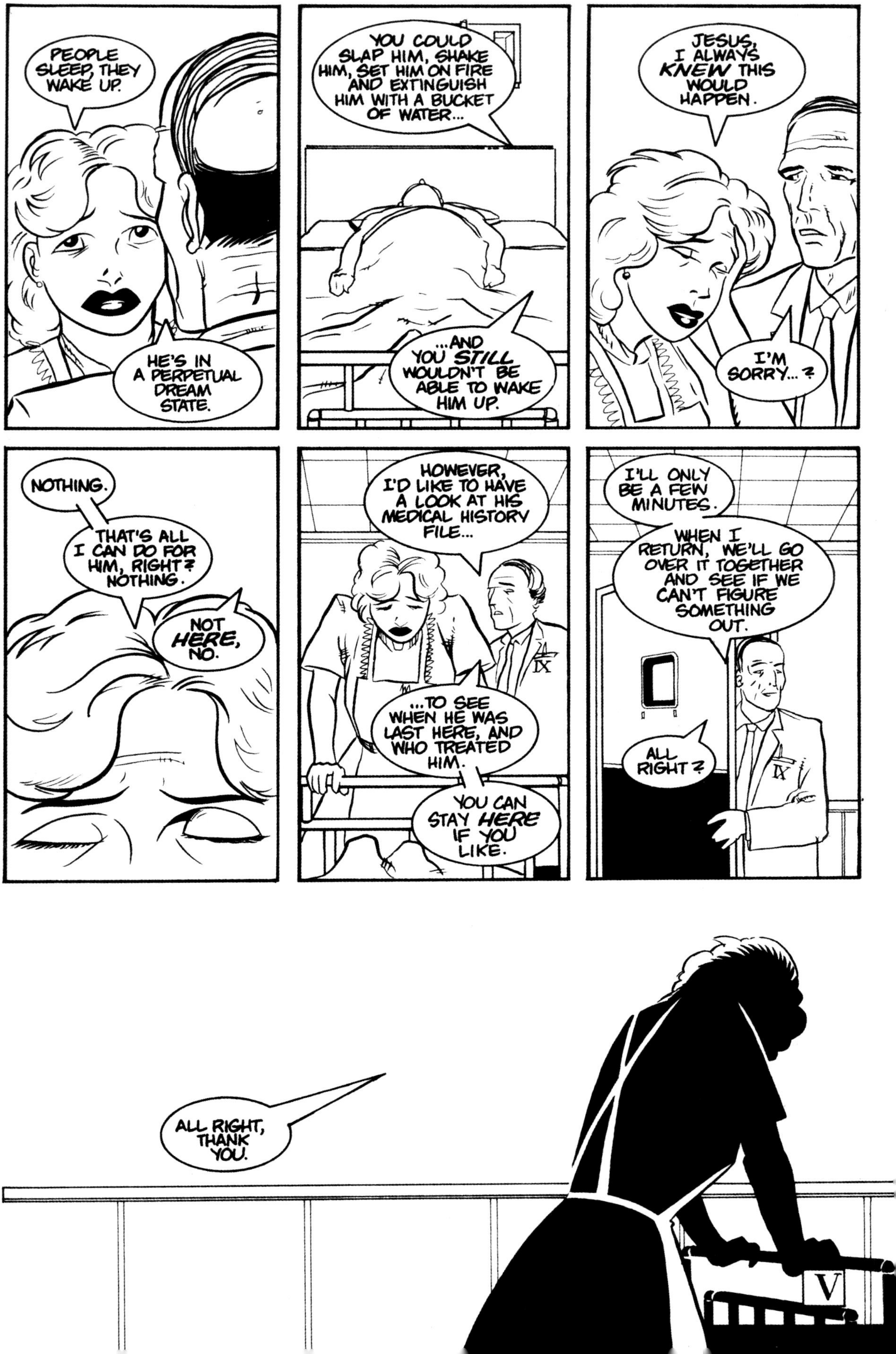
PEOPLE SLEEP, THEY WAKE UP.
HE'S IN A PERPETUAL DREAM STATE.
YOU COULD SLAP HIM, SHAKE HIM, SET HIM ON FIRE AND EXTINGUISH HIM WITH A BUCKET OF WATER...
...AND YOU STILL WOULDN'T BE ABLE TO WAKE HIM UP.
JESUS, I ALWAYS KNEW THIS WOULD HAPPEN.
I'M SORRY...?
NOTHING.
THAT'S ALL I CAN DO FOR HIM, RIGHT? NOTHING.
NOT HERE, NO.
HOWEVER, I'D LIKE TO HAVE A LOOK AT HIS MEDICAL HISTORY FILE...
...TO SEE WHEN HE WAS LAST HERE, AND WHO TREATED HIM.
YOU CAN STAY HERE IF YOU LIKE.
I'LL ONLY BE A FEW MINUTES.
WHEN I RETURN, WE'LL GO OVER IT TOGETHER AND SEE IF WE CAN'T FIGURE SOMETHING OUT.
ALL RIGHT?
ALL RIGHT, THANK YOU.

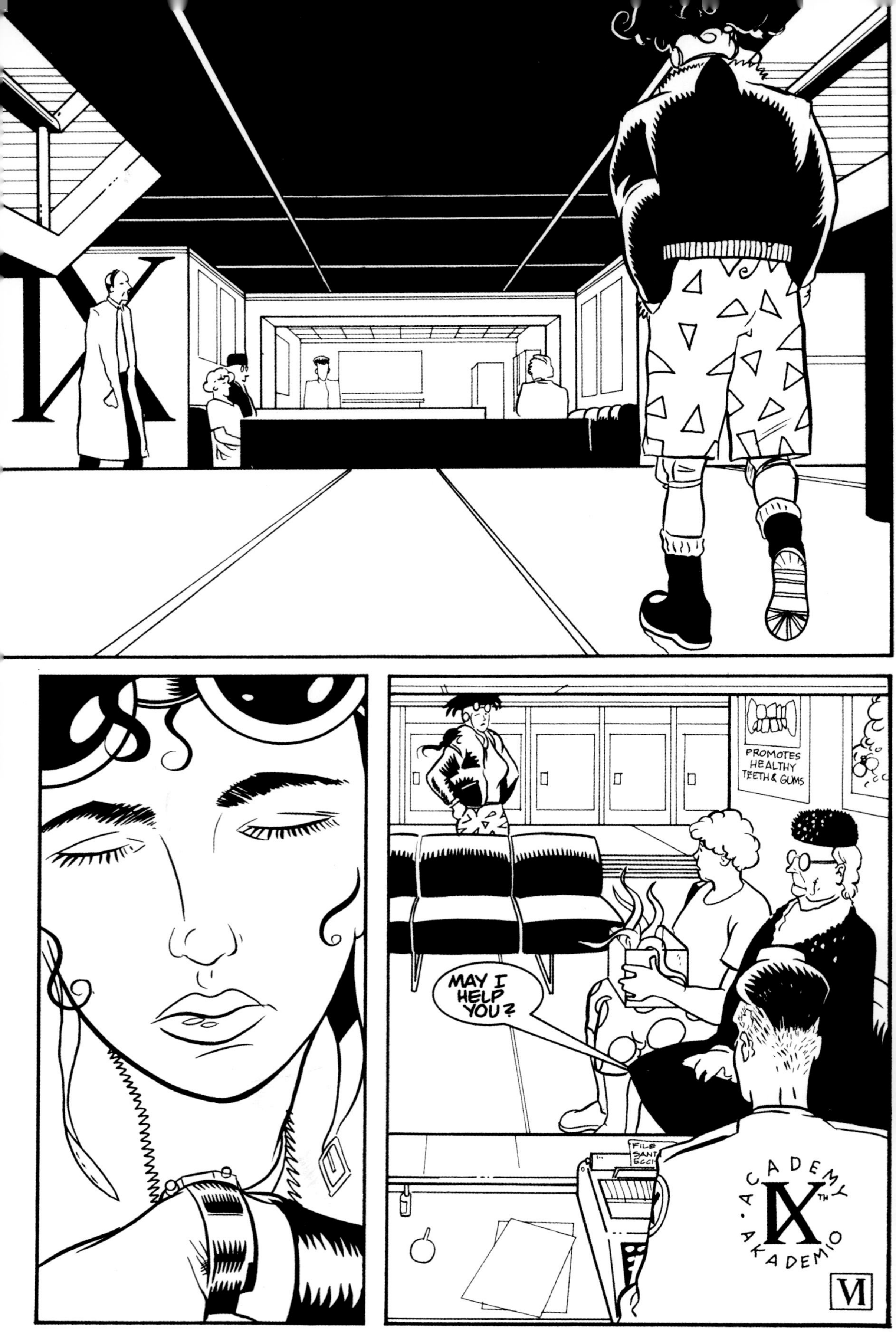
PROMOTES HEALTHY TEETH & GUMS
MAY I HELP YOU?
ACADEMY IX TH AKADEMIO
VI

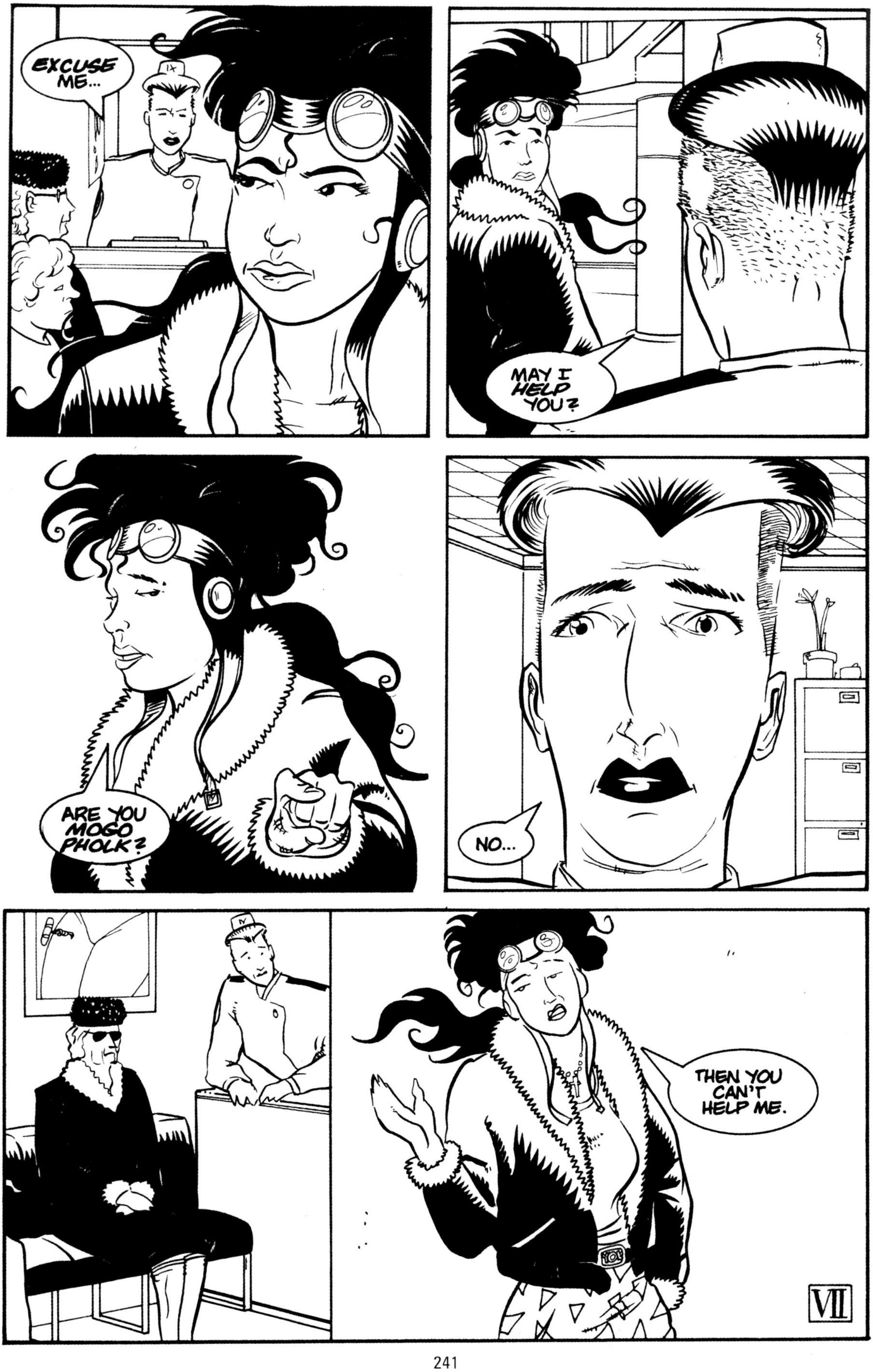
EXCUSE ME...
MAY I HELP YOU?
ARE YOU MOGO PHOLK?
NO...
THEN YOU CAN'T HELP ME.
VII

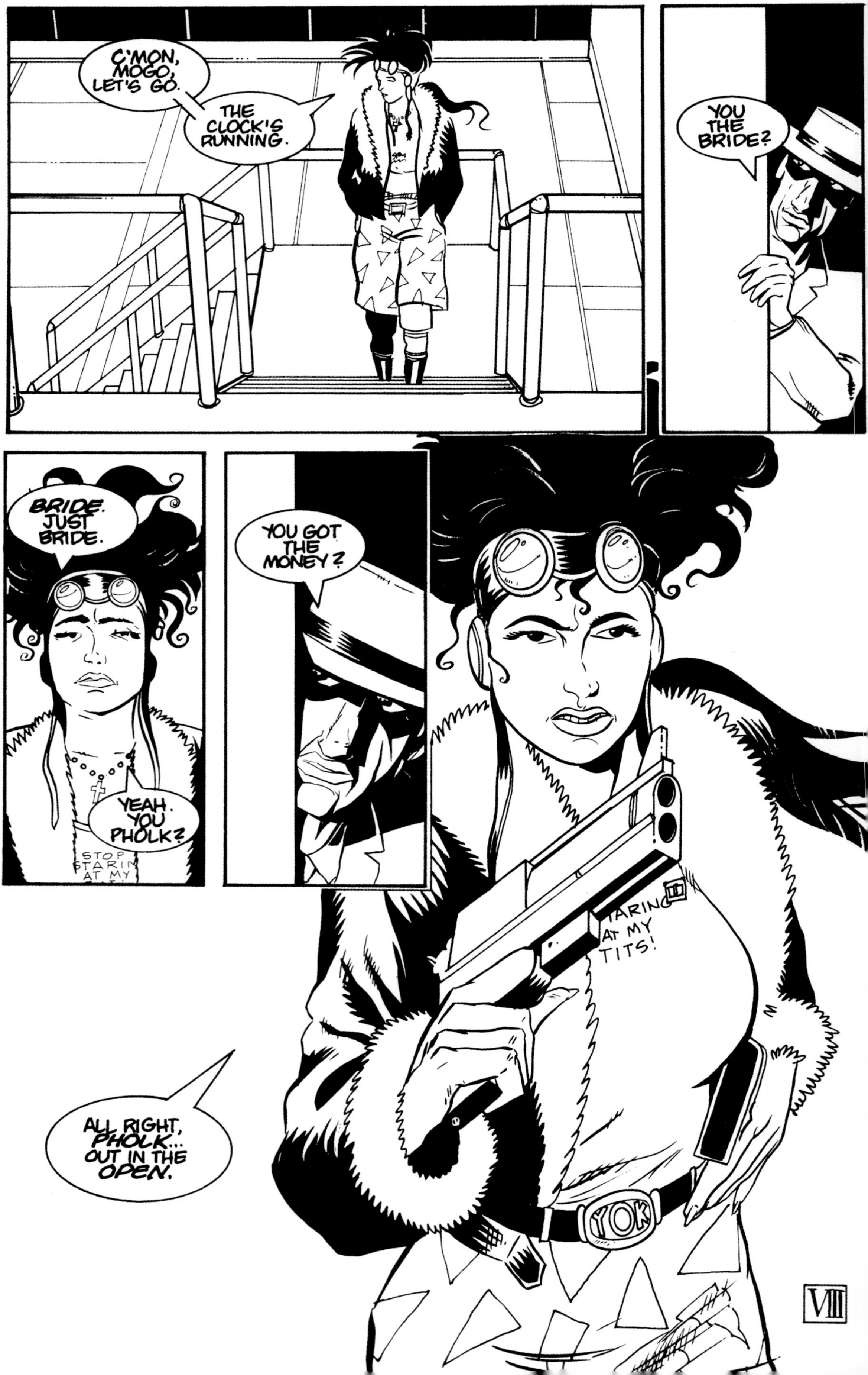
C'MON, MOGO, LET'S GO.
THE CLOCK'S RUNNING.
YOU THE BRIDE?
BRIDE. JUST BRIDE.
YEAH. YOU PHOLK?
STOP TARIN AT MY
YOU GOT THE MONEY?
TARING AT MY TITS!
ALL RIGHT, PHOLK... OUT IN THE OPEN.
YOK

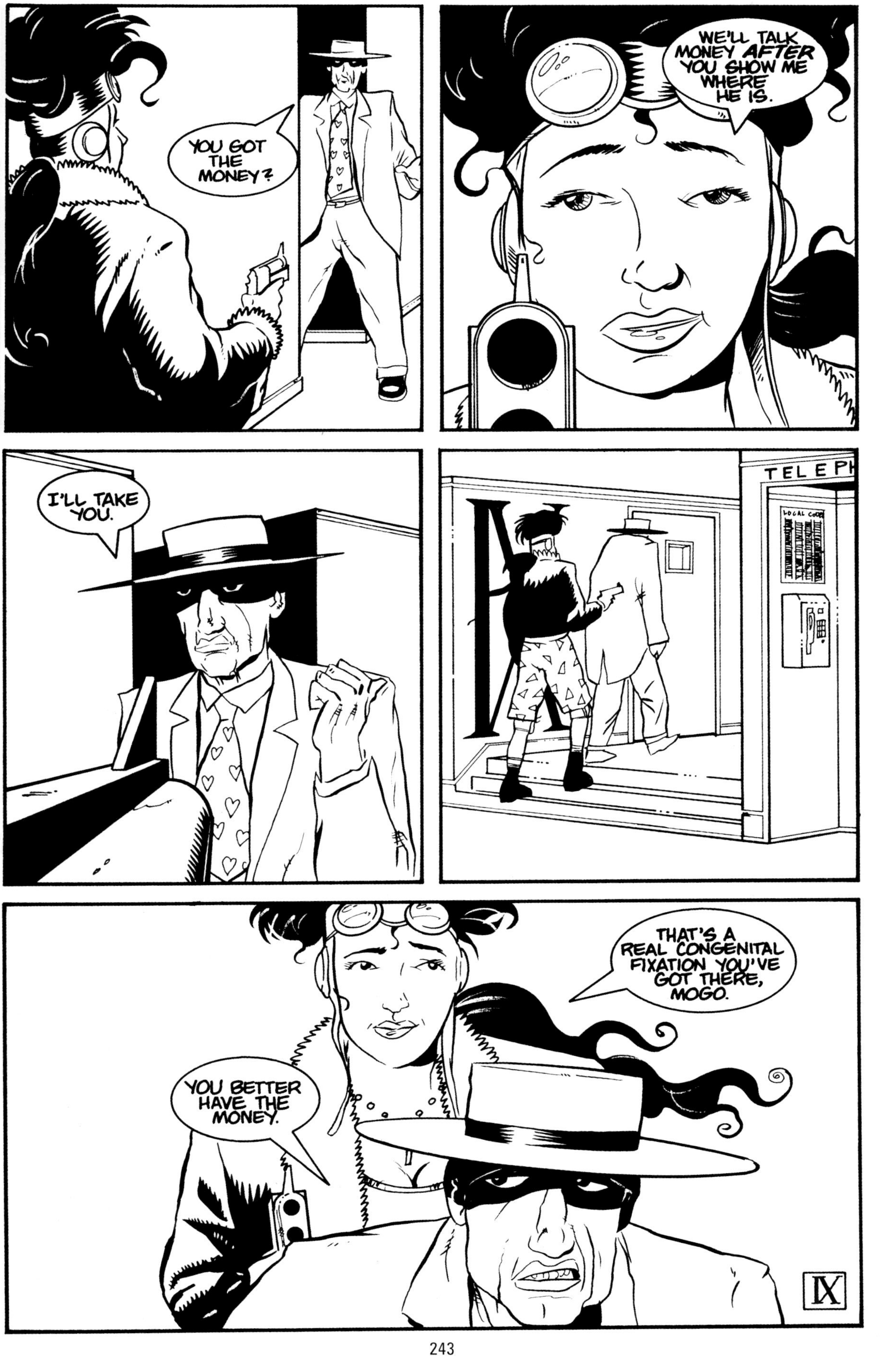
YOU GOT THE MONEY?
WE'LL TALK MONEY AFTER YOU SHOW ME WHERE HE IS.
I'LL TAKE YOU.
TELEPH
THAT'S A REAL CONGENITAL FIXATION YOU'VE GOT THERE, MOGO.
YOU BETTER HAVE THE MONEY.
IX

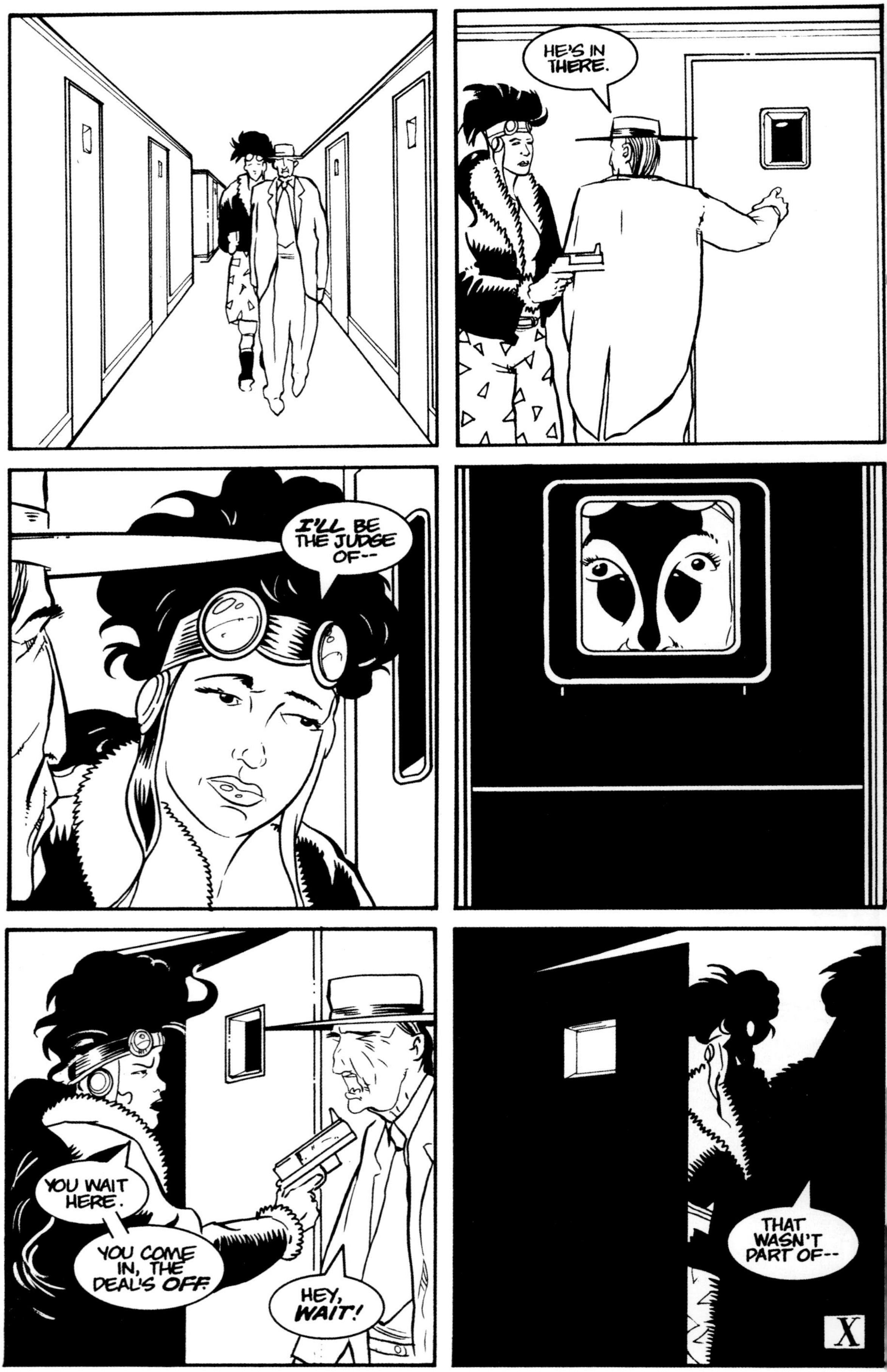
HE'S IN THERE.
I'LL BE THE JUDGE OF--
YOU WAIT HERE.
YOU COME IN, THE DEAL'S OFF.
HEY, WAIT!
THAT WASN'T PART OF--
X

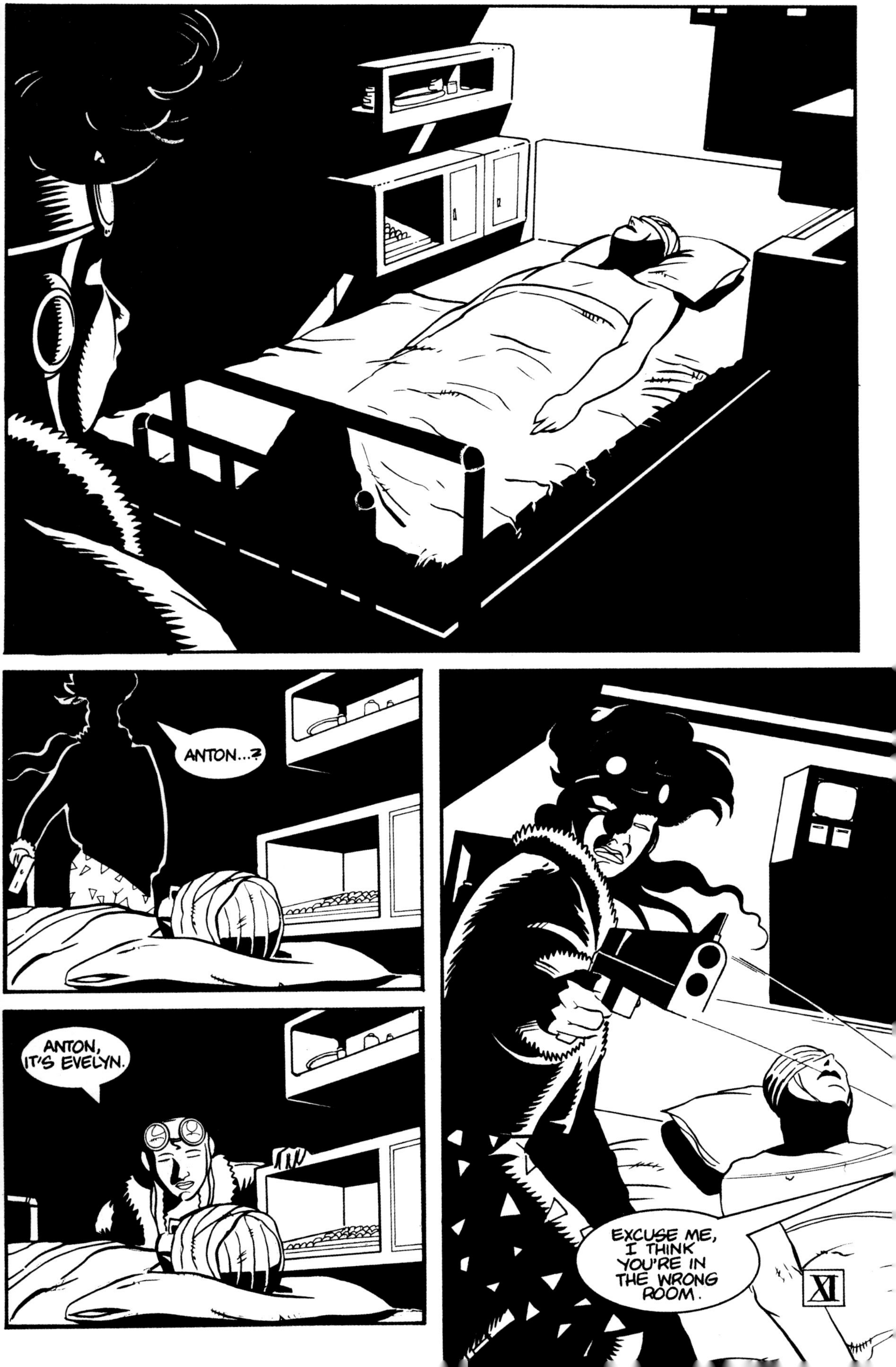

ANTON...?
ANTON, IT'S EVELYN.
EXCUSE ME, I THINK YOU'RE IN THE WRONG ROOM.
XI

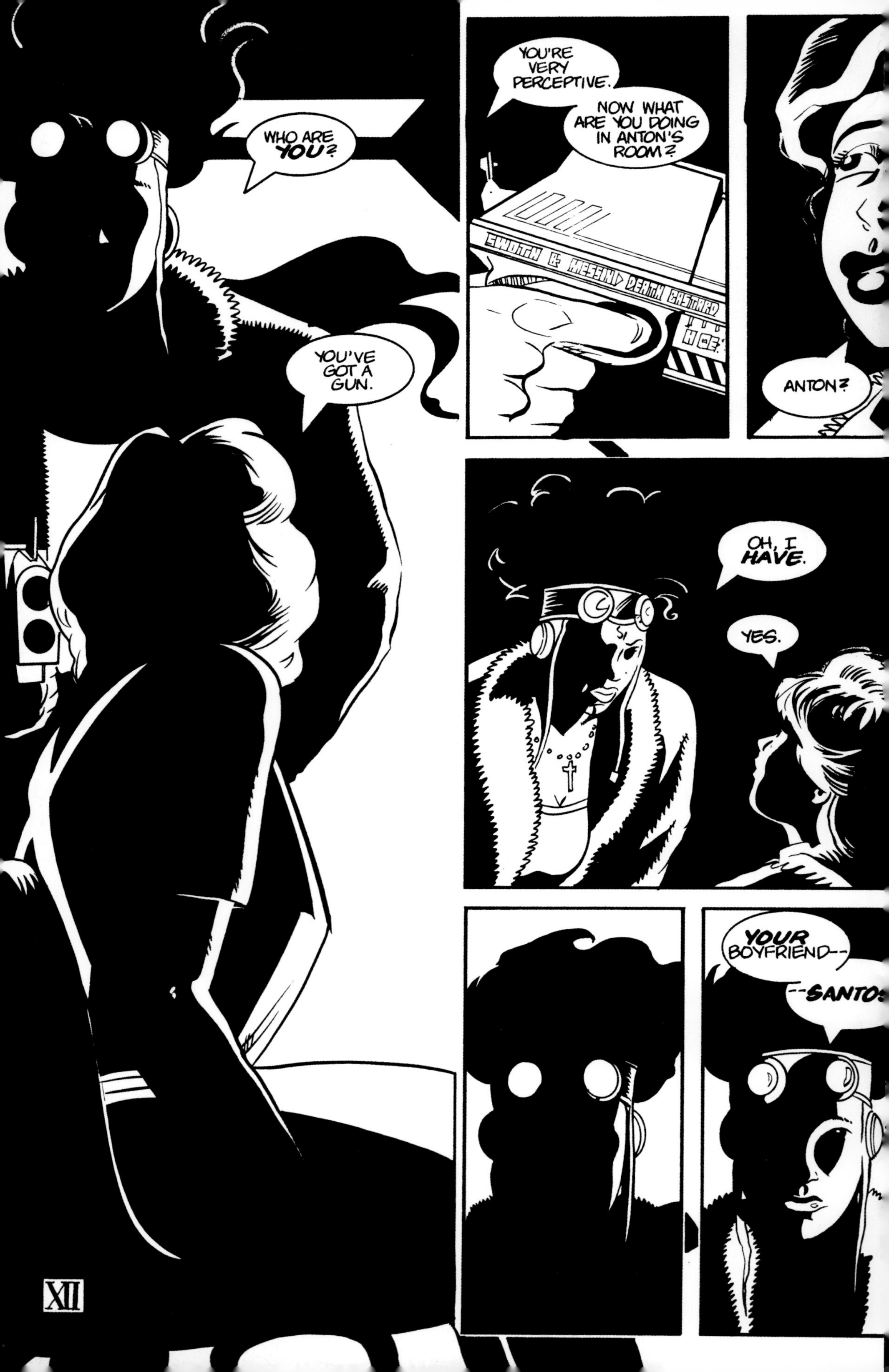
WHO ARE YOU?
YOU'VE GOT A GUN.
YOU'RE VERY PERCEPTIVE.
NOW WHAT ARE YOU DOING IN ANTON'S ROOM?
ANTON?
OH, I HAVE.
YES.
YOUR BOYFRIEND--
--SANTO

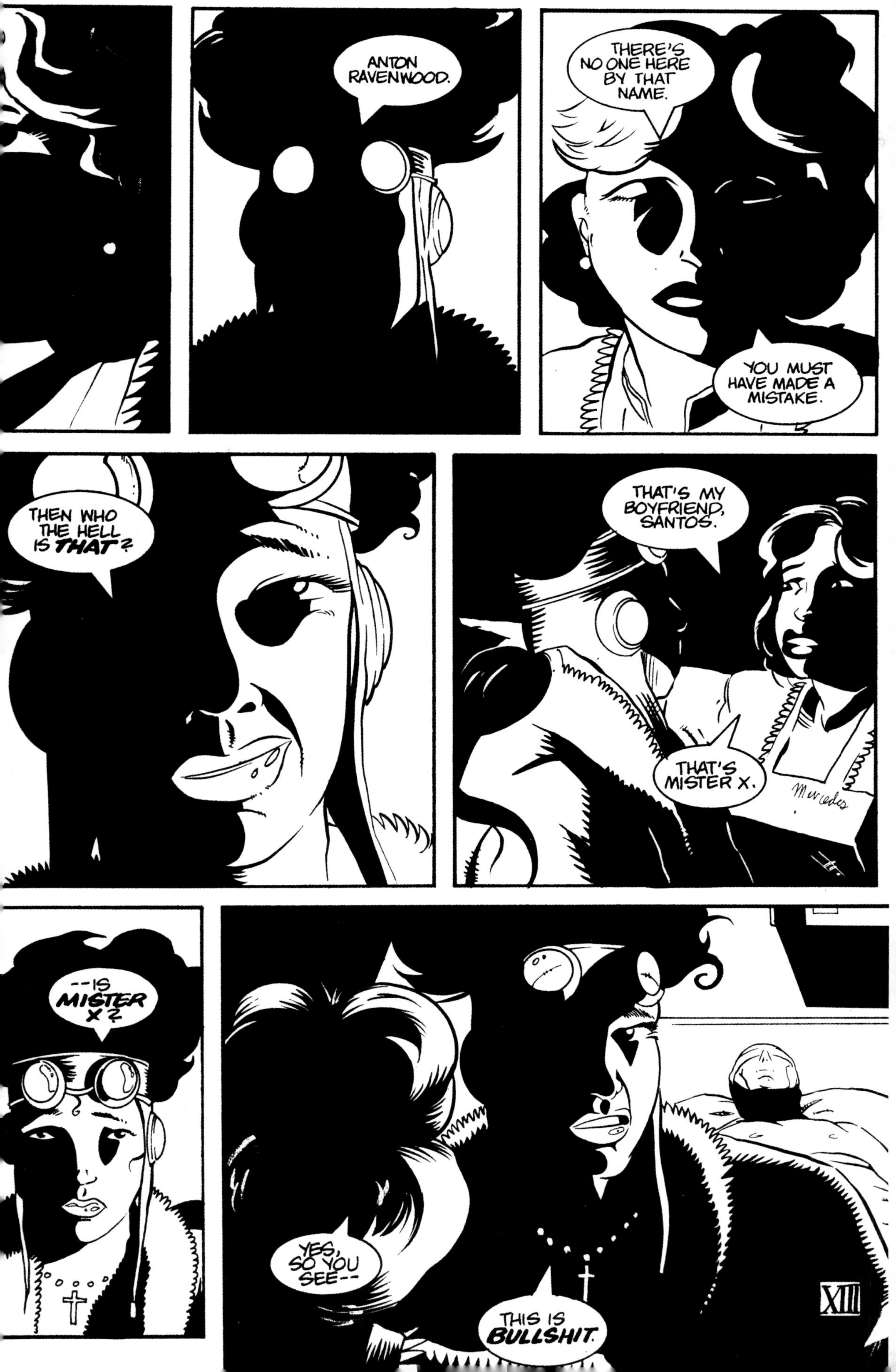
ANTON RAVENWOOD.
THERE'S NO ONE HERE BY THAT NAME.
YOU MUST HAVE MADE A MISTAKE.
THEN WHO THE HELL IS **THAT**?
THAT'S MY BOYFRIEND, SANTOS.
THAT'S MISTER X.
Mercedes
--IS **MISTER X**?
YES, SO YOU SEE--
THIS IS **BULLSHIT**.
XIII

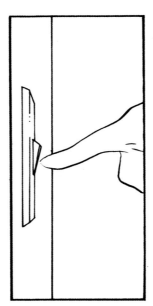

THIS *ISN'T* ANTON RAVENWOOD.

THAT'S WHAT I'VE BEEN TRYING--

THIS *ISN'T* MISTER X.

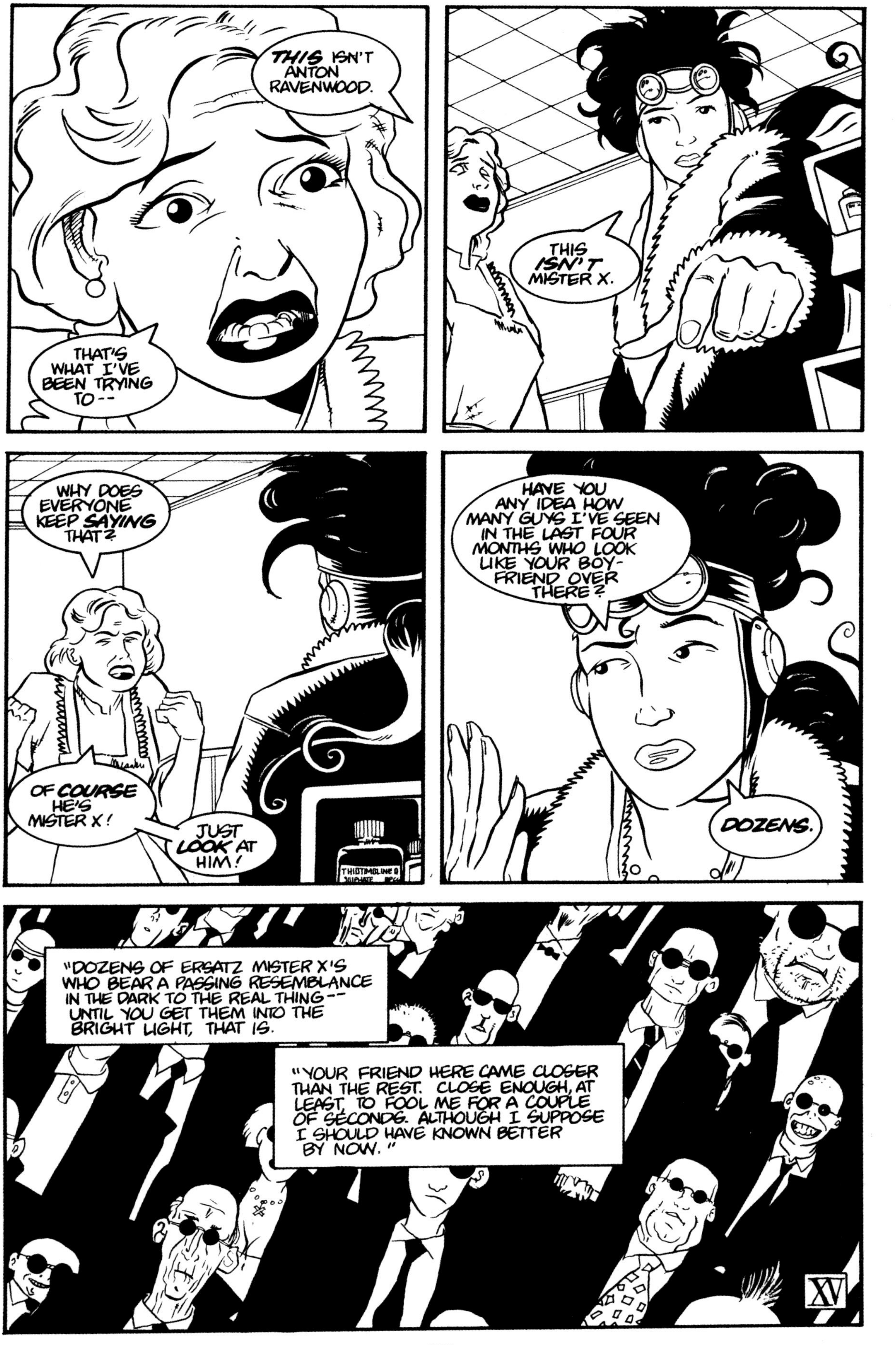
THIS ISN'T ANTON RAVENWOOD.
THAT'S WHAT I'VE BEEN TRYING TO--
THIS ISN'T MISTER X.
WHY DOES EVERYONE KEEP SAYING THAT?
OF COURSE HE'S MISTER X!
JUST LOOK AT HIM!
HAVE YOU ANY IDEA HOW MANY GUYS I'VE SEEN IN THE LAST FOUR MONTHS WHO LOOK LIKE YOUR BOY-FRIEND OVER THERE?
DOZENS.
"DOZENS OF ERSATZ MISTER X'S WHO BEAR A PASSING RESEMBLANCE IN THE DARK TO THE REAL THING-- UNTIL YOU GET THEM INTO THE BRIGHT LIGHT, THAT IS.
"YOUR FRIEND HERE CAME CLOSER THAN THE REST. CLOSE ENOUGH, AT LEAST, TO FOOL ME FOR A COUPLE OF SECONDS. ALTHOUGH I SUPPOSE I SHOULD HAVE KNOWN BETTER BY NOW."
XV

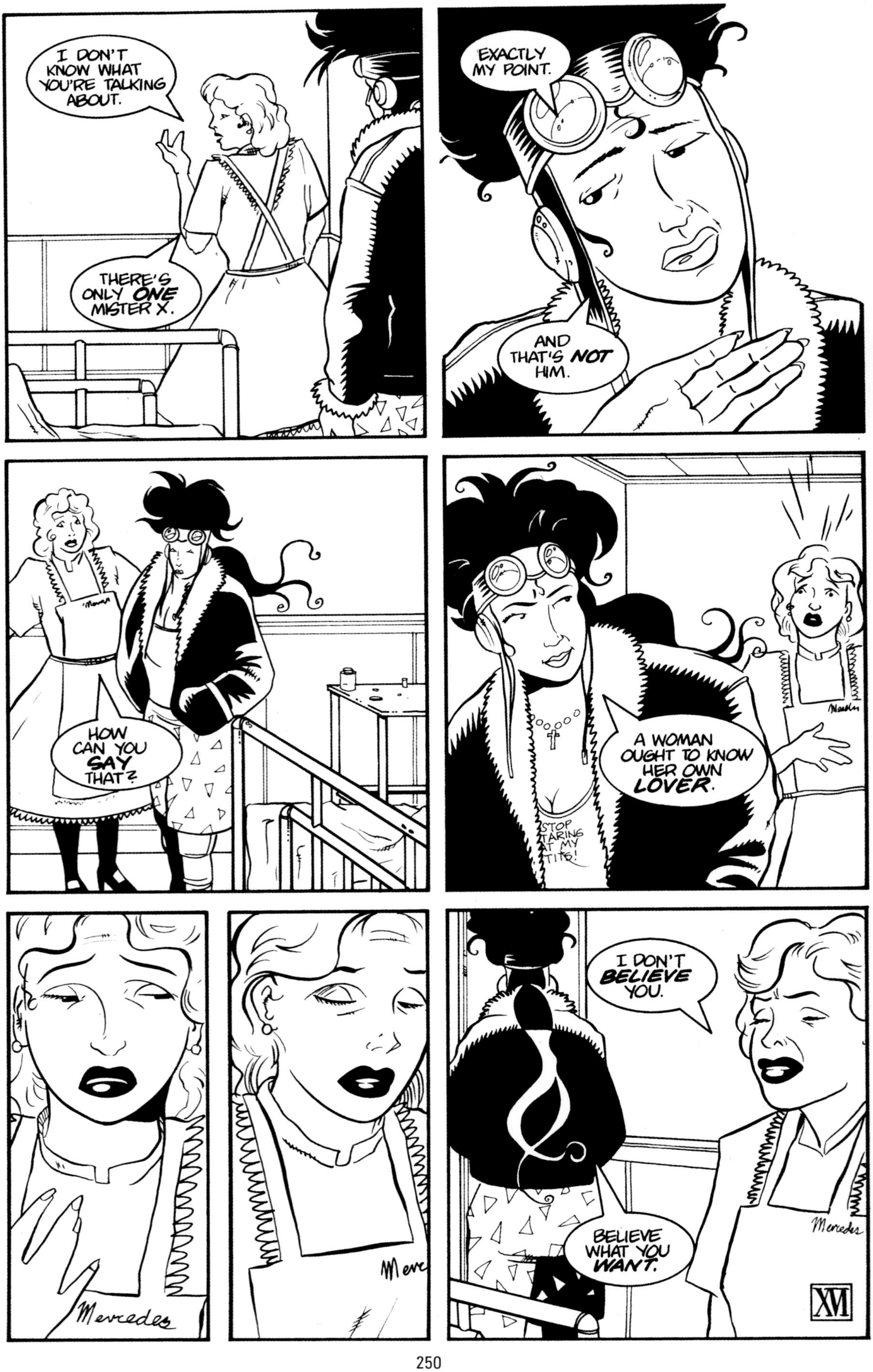
I DON'T KNOW WHAT YOU'RE TALKING ABOUT.
THERE'S ONLY ONE MISTER X.
EXACTLY MY POINT.
AND THAT'S NOT HIM.
HOW CAN YOU SAY THAT?
A WOMAN OUGHT TO KNOW HER OWN LOVER.
STOP STARING AT MY TITS!
I DON'T BELIEVE YOU.
BELIEVE WHAT YOU WANT.

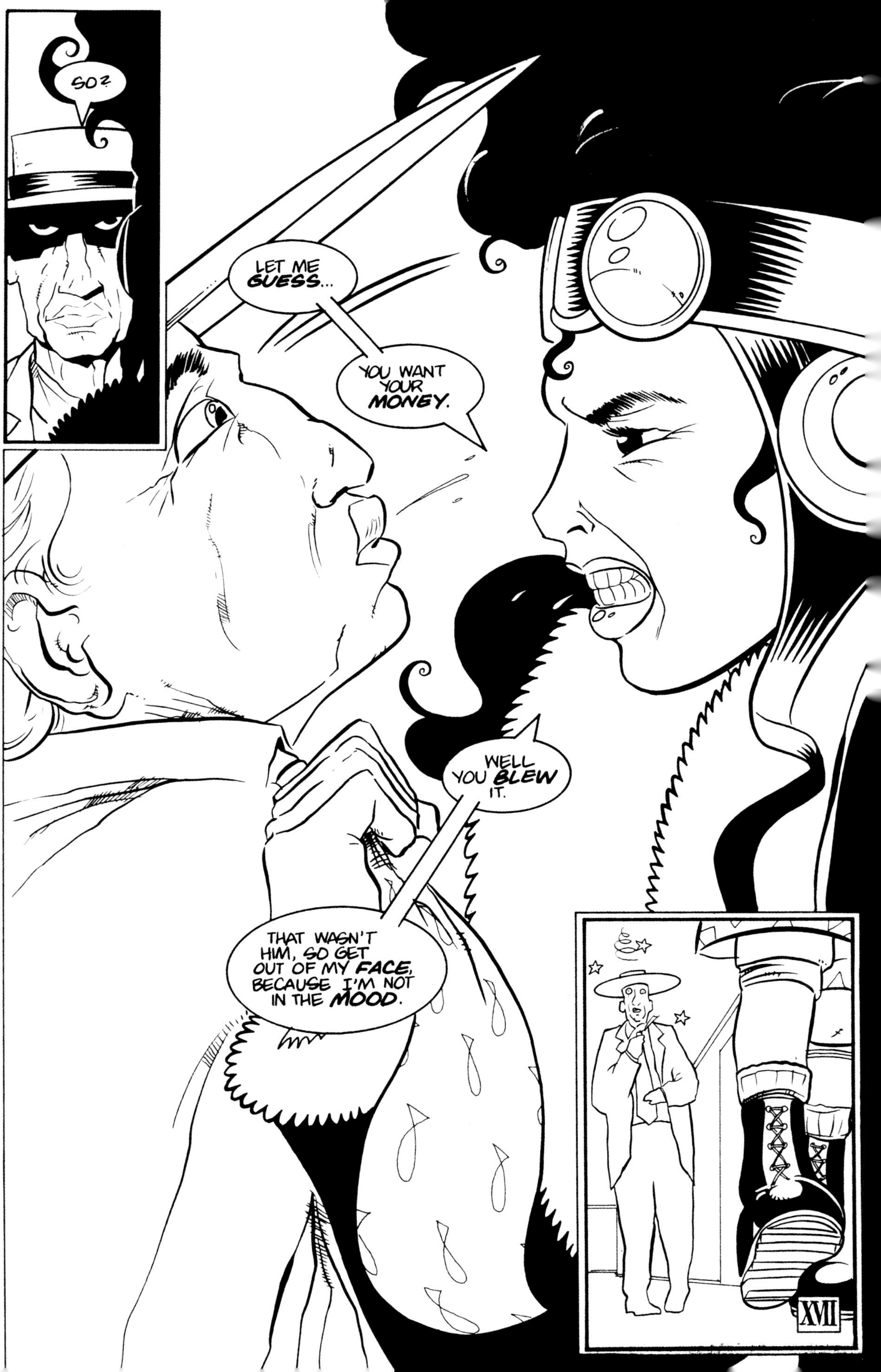
SO?
LET ME GUESS...
YOU WANT YOUR MONEY.
WELL YOU BLEW IT.
THAT WASN'T HIM, SO GET OUT OF MY FACE, BECAUSE I'M NOT IN THE MOOD.
XVII

MAYBE YOU *CAN* HELP ME.

WHERE'S THE NEAREST PLACE AROUND HERE I CAN GET A DRINK?

PROMOTES Y TEETH AND GUMS!

YOU COULD TRY THE *GRINDHOUSE.*

I'D RATHER WALK THROUGH *HELL* IN A GASOLINE SUIT.

FISH PASTE

I DON'T THINK *I* WOULD.

YEAH, WELL, MAYBE I'M *CRAZY.*

YOU CAME TO THE RIGHT PLACE.

·ACADE
·IX·
·ADE

XVIII

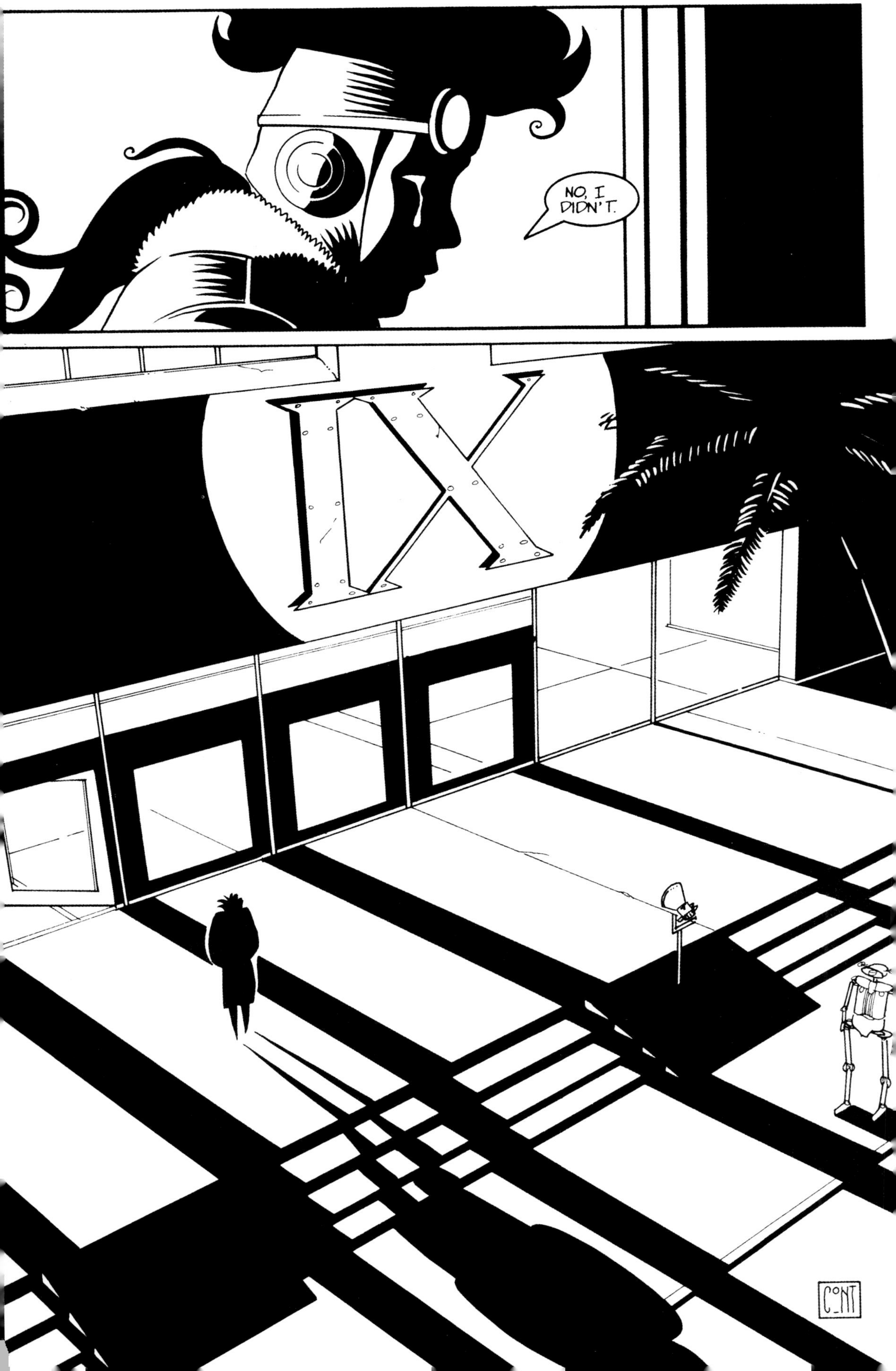
NO, I DIDN'T.
IX
CONT

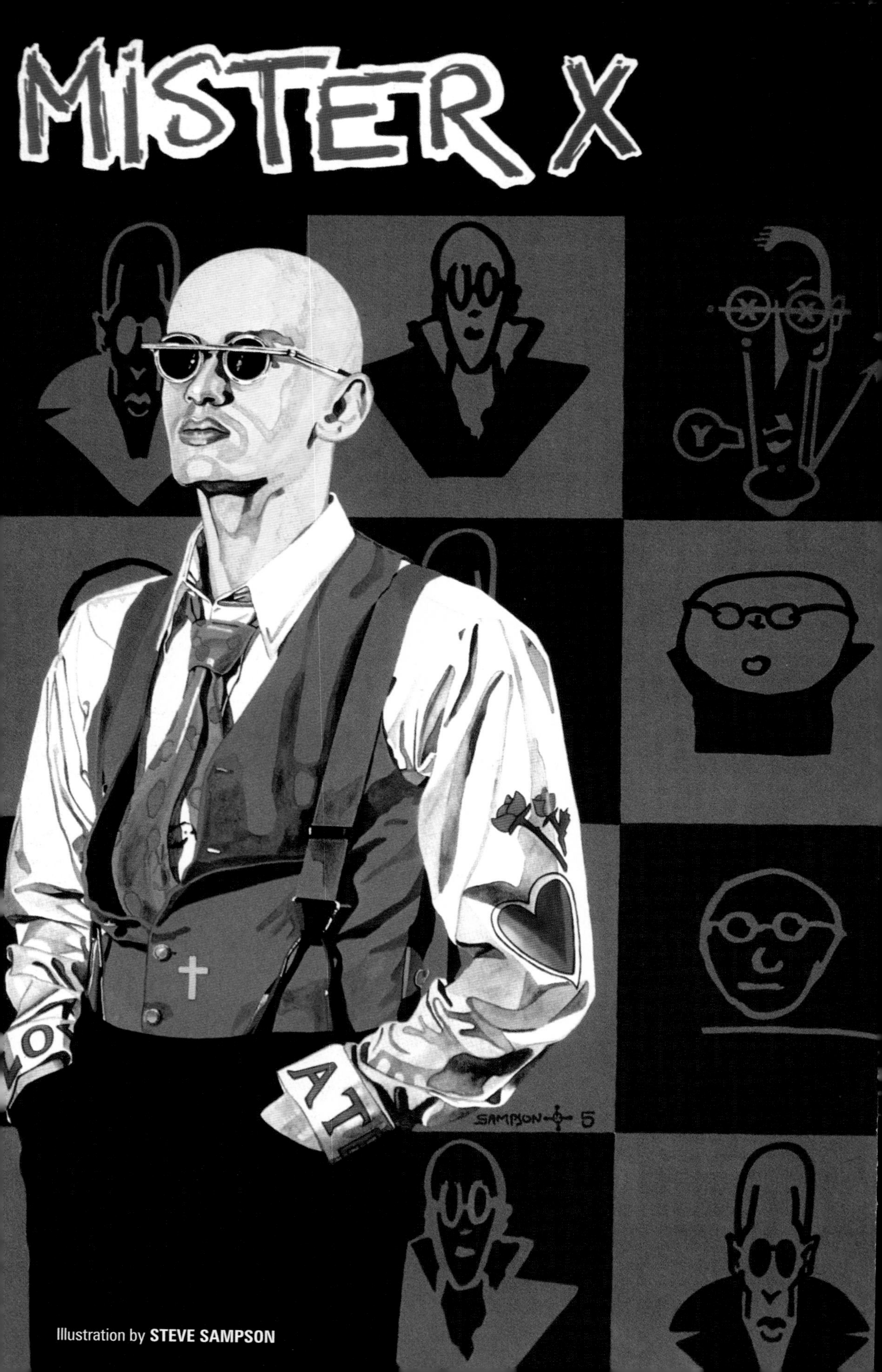
MISTER X
SAMPSON 5

Illustration by **STEVE SAMPSON**

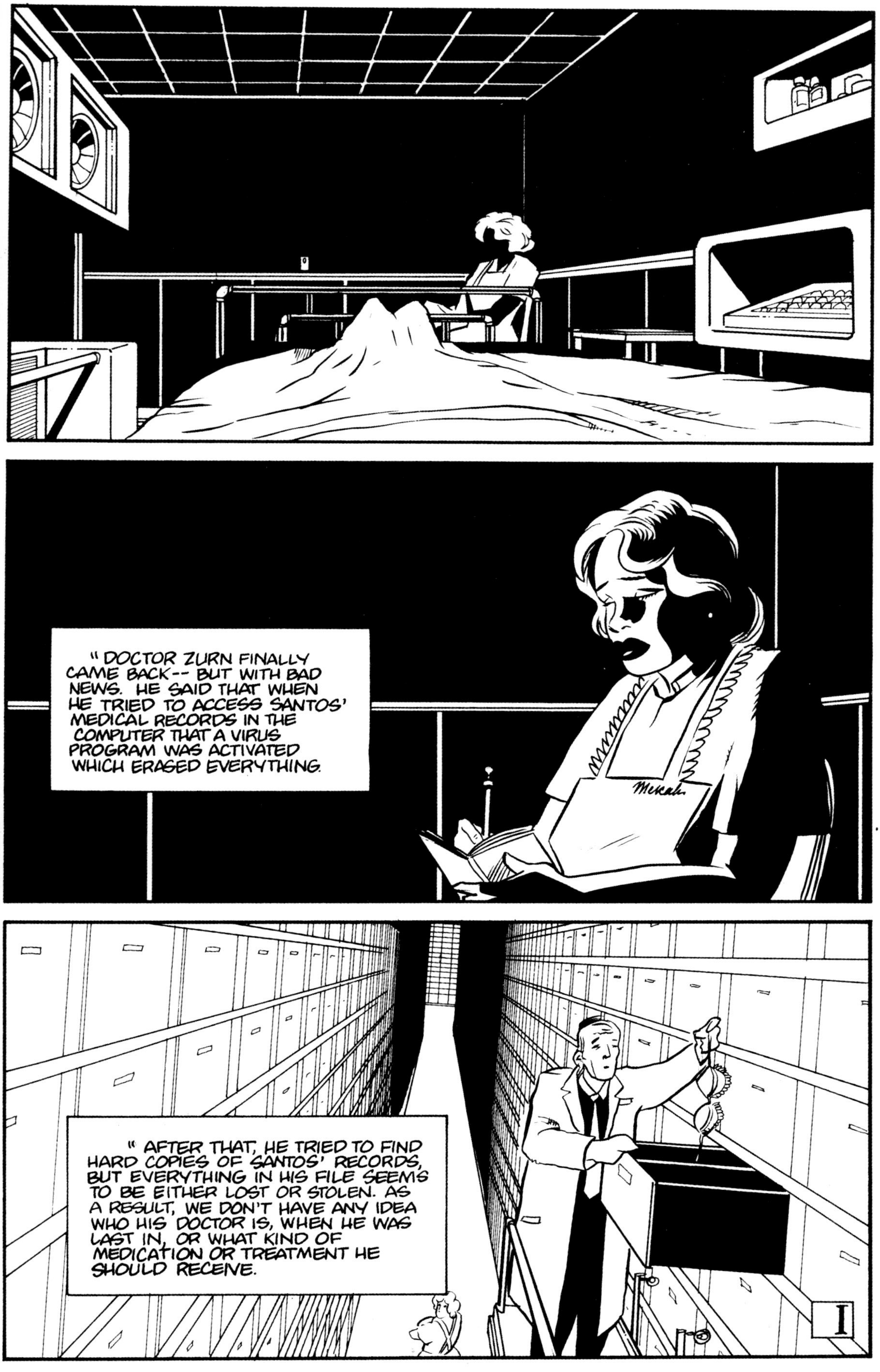
"DOCTOR ZURN FINALLY CAME BACK-- BUT WITH BAD NEWS. HE SAID THAT WHEN HE TRIED TO ACCESS SANTOS' MEDICAL RECORDS IN THE COMPUTER THAT A VIRUS PROGRAM WAS ACTIVATED WHICH ERASED EVERYTHING.
"AFTER THAT, HE TRIED TO FIND HARD COPIES OF SANTOS' RECORDS, BUT EVERYTHING IN HIS FILE SEEMS TO BE EITHER LOST OR STOLEN. AS A RESULT, WE DON'T HAVE ANY IDEA WHO HIS DOCTOR IS, WHEN HE WAS LAST IN, OR WHAT KIND OF MEDICATION OR TREATMENT HE SHOULD RECEIVE.

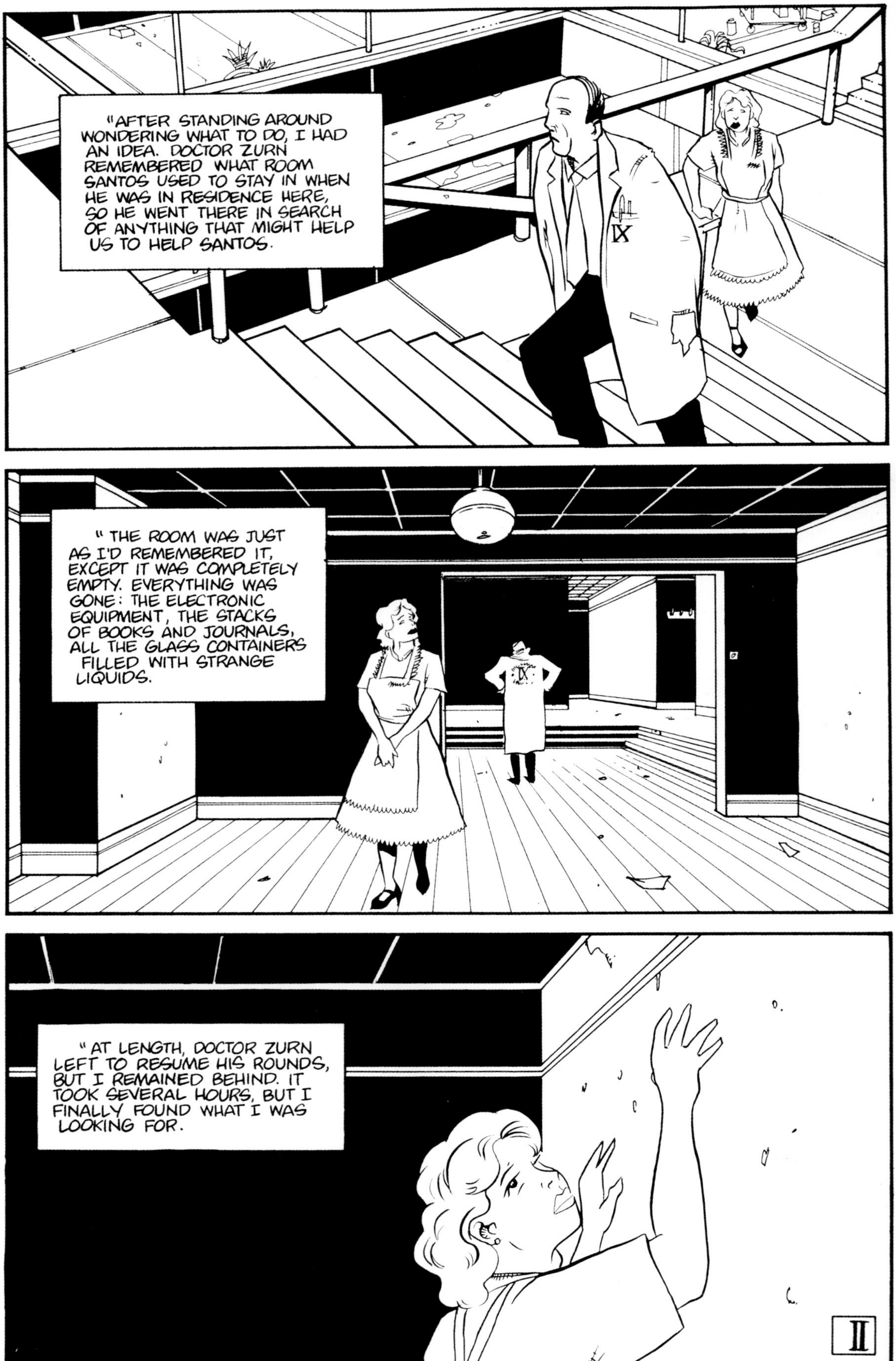
"AFTER STANDING AROUND WONDERING WHAT TO DO, I HAD AN IDEA. DOCTOR ZURN REMEMBERED WHAT ROOM SANTOS USED TO STAY IN WHEN HE WAS IN RESIDENCE HERE, SO HE WENT THERE IN SEARCH OF ANYTHING THAT MIGHT HELP US TO HELP SANTOS.
" THE ROOM WAS JUST AS I'D REMEMBERED IT, EXCEPT IT WAS COMPLETELY EMPTY. EVERYTHING WAS GONE: THE ELECTRONIC EQUIPMENT, THE STACKS OF BOOKS AND JOURNALS, ALL THE GLASS CONTAINERS FILLED WITH STRANGE LIQUIDS.
"AT LENGTH, DOCTOR ZURN LEFT TO RESUME HIS ROUNDS, BUT I REMAINED BEHIND. IT TOOK SEVERAL HOURS, BUT I FINALLY FOUND WHAT I WAS LOOKING FOR.
II

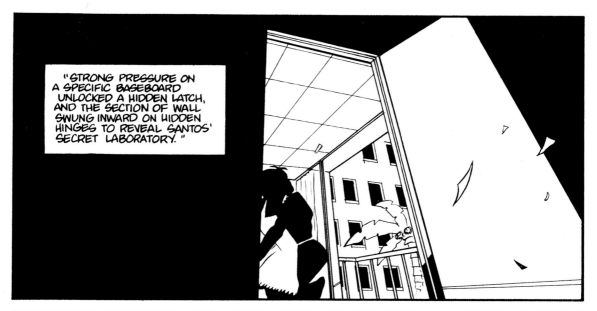

"STRONG PRESSURE ON A SPECIFIC BASEBOARD UNLOCKED A HIDDEN LATCH, AND THE SECTION OF WALL SWUNG INWARD ON HIDDEN HINGES TO REVEAL SANTOS' SECRET LABORATORY."

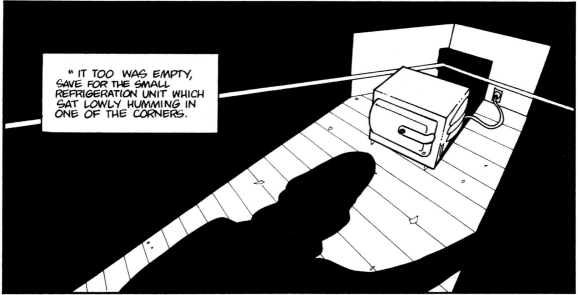

" IT TOO WAS EMPTY, SAVE FOR THE SMALL REFRIGERATION UNIT WHICH SAT LOWLY HUMMING IN ONE OF THE CORNERS.

" I OPENED THE DOOR AND THERE IT WAS: ONE SMALL VIAL WHICH CONTAINED SANTOS' INSOMULIN SERUM.

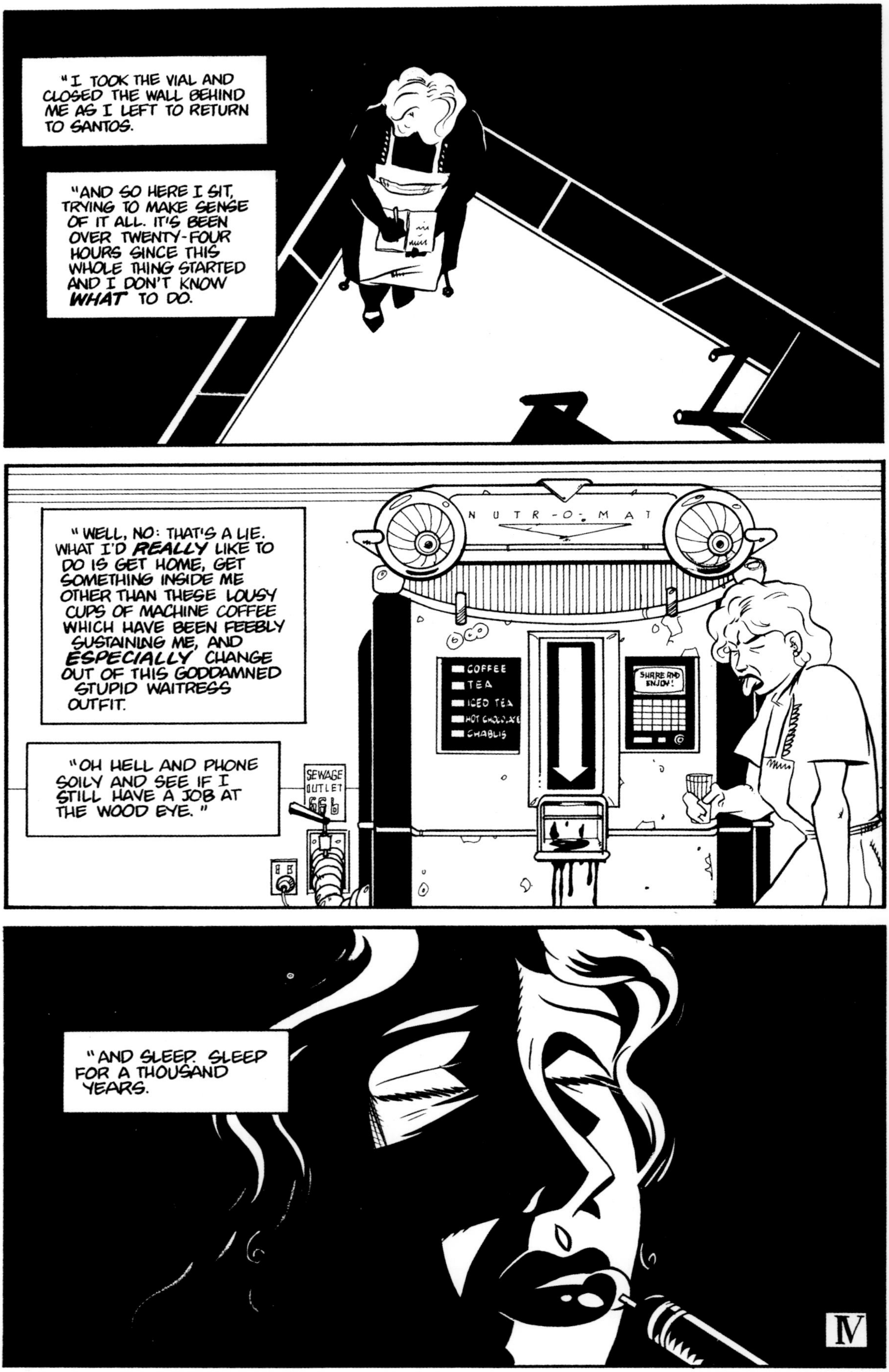
"I TOOK THE VIAL AND CLOSED THE WALL BEHIND ME AS I LEFT TO RETURN TO SANTOS.
"AND SO HERE I SIT, TRYING TO MAKE SENSE OF IT ALL. IT'S BEEN OVER TWENTY-FOUR HOURS SINCE THIS WHOLE THING STARTED AND I DON'T KNOW ***WHAT*** TO DO.
NUTR-O-MAT
"WELL, NO: THAT'S A LIE. WHAT I'D ***REALLY*** LIKE TO DO IS GET HOME, GET SOMETHING INSIDE ME OTHER THAN THESE LOUSY CUPS OF MACHINE COFFEE WHICH HAVE BEEN FEEBLY SUSTAINING ME, AND ***ESPECIALLY*** CHANGE OUT OF THIS GODDAMNED STUPID WAITRESS OUTFIT.
COFFEE
TEA
ICED TEA
HOT CHOCOLATE
CHABLIS
SHARE AND ENJOY!
SEWAGE OUTLET 66b
"OH HELL AND PHONE SOILY AND SEE IF I STILL HAVE A JOB AT THE WOOD EYE."
"AND SLEEP. SLEEP FOR A THOUSAND YEARS.
IV

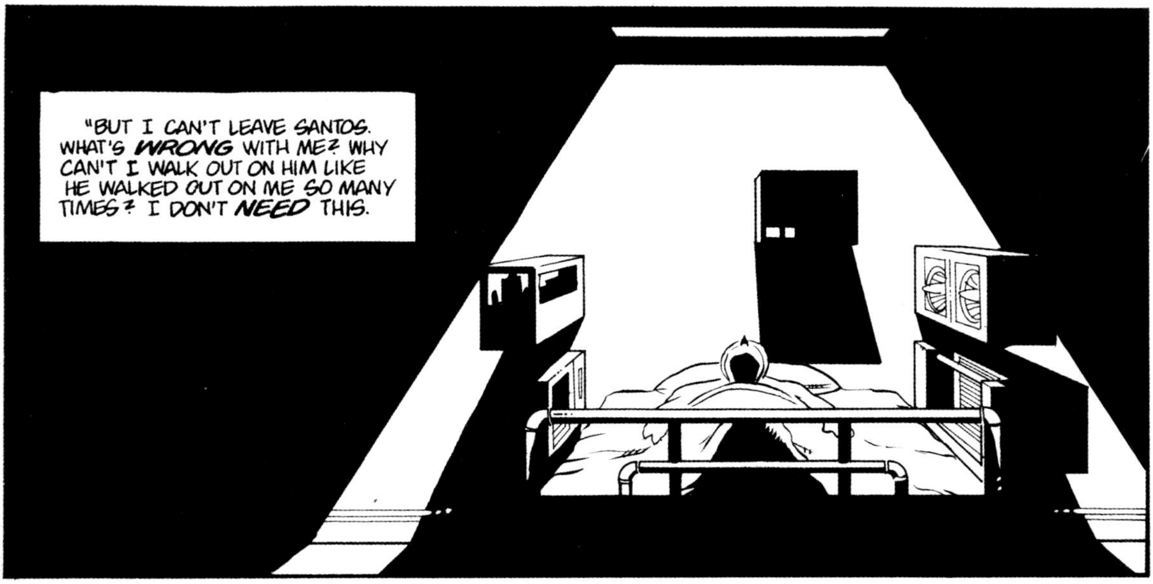
"BUT I CAN'T LEAVE SANTOS. WHAT'S WRONG WITH ME? WHY CAN'T I WALK OUT ON HIM LIKE HE WALKED OUT ON ME SO MANY TIMES? I DON'T NEED THIS.

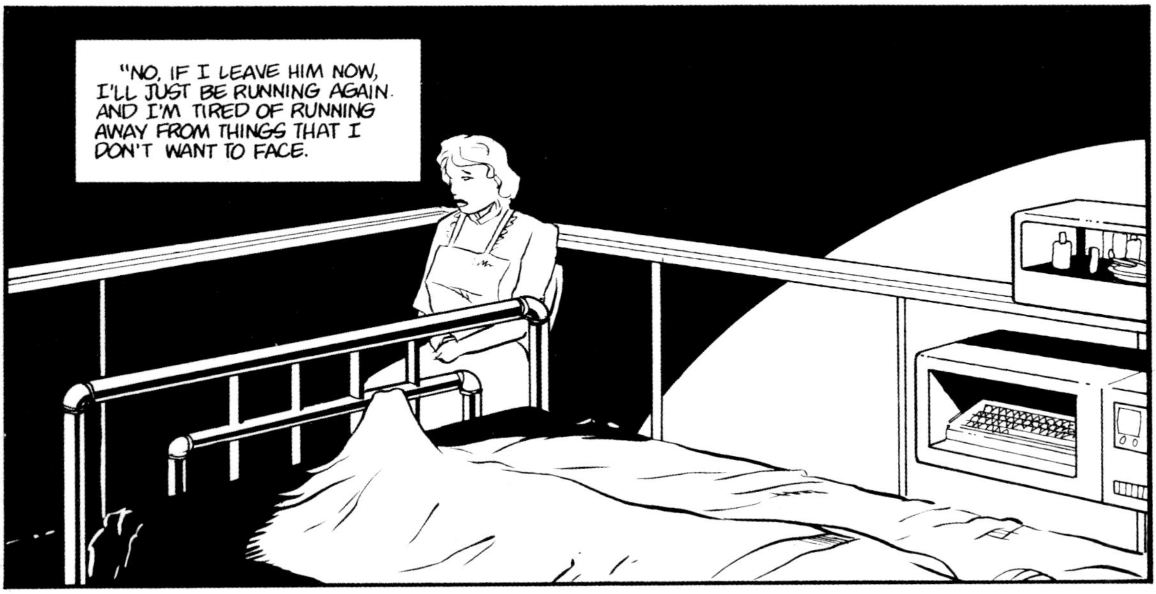
"NO, IF I LEAVE HIM NOW, I'LL JUST BE RUNNING AGAIN. AND I'M TIRED OF RUNNING AWAY FROM THINGS THAT I DON'T WANT TO FACE.

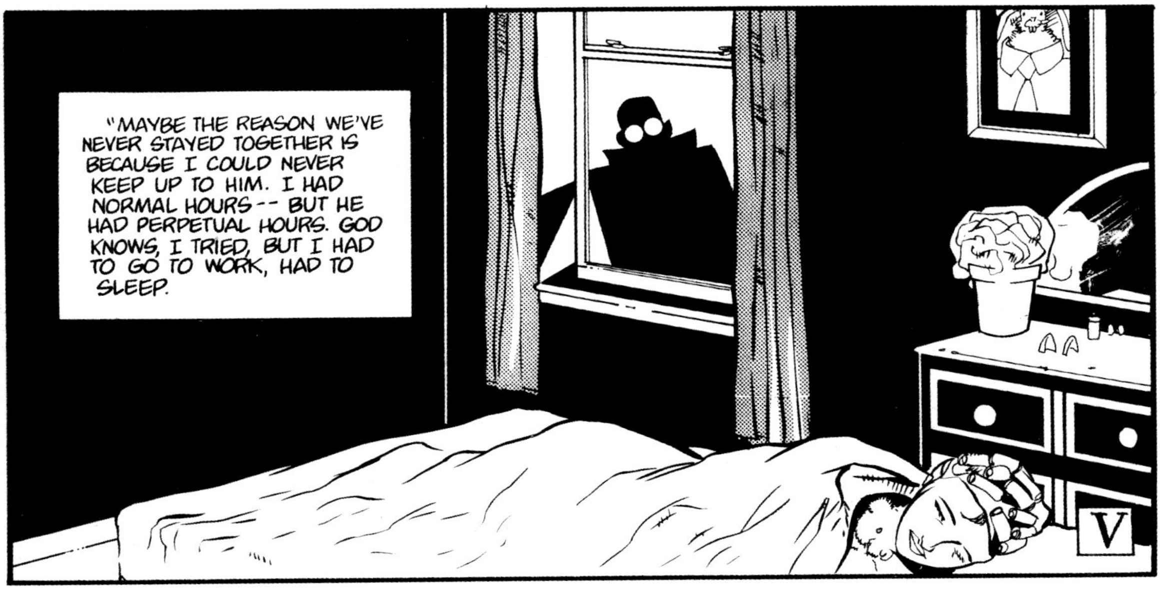
"MAYBE THE REASON WE'VE NEVER STAYED TOGETHER IS BECAUSE I COULD NEVER KEEP UP TO HIM. I HAD NORMAL HOURS -- BUT HE HAD PERPETUAL HOURS. GOD KNOWS, I TRIED, BUT I HAD TO GO TO WORK, HAD TO SLEEP.
V

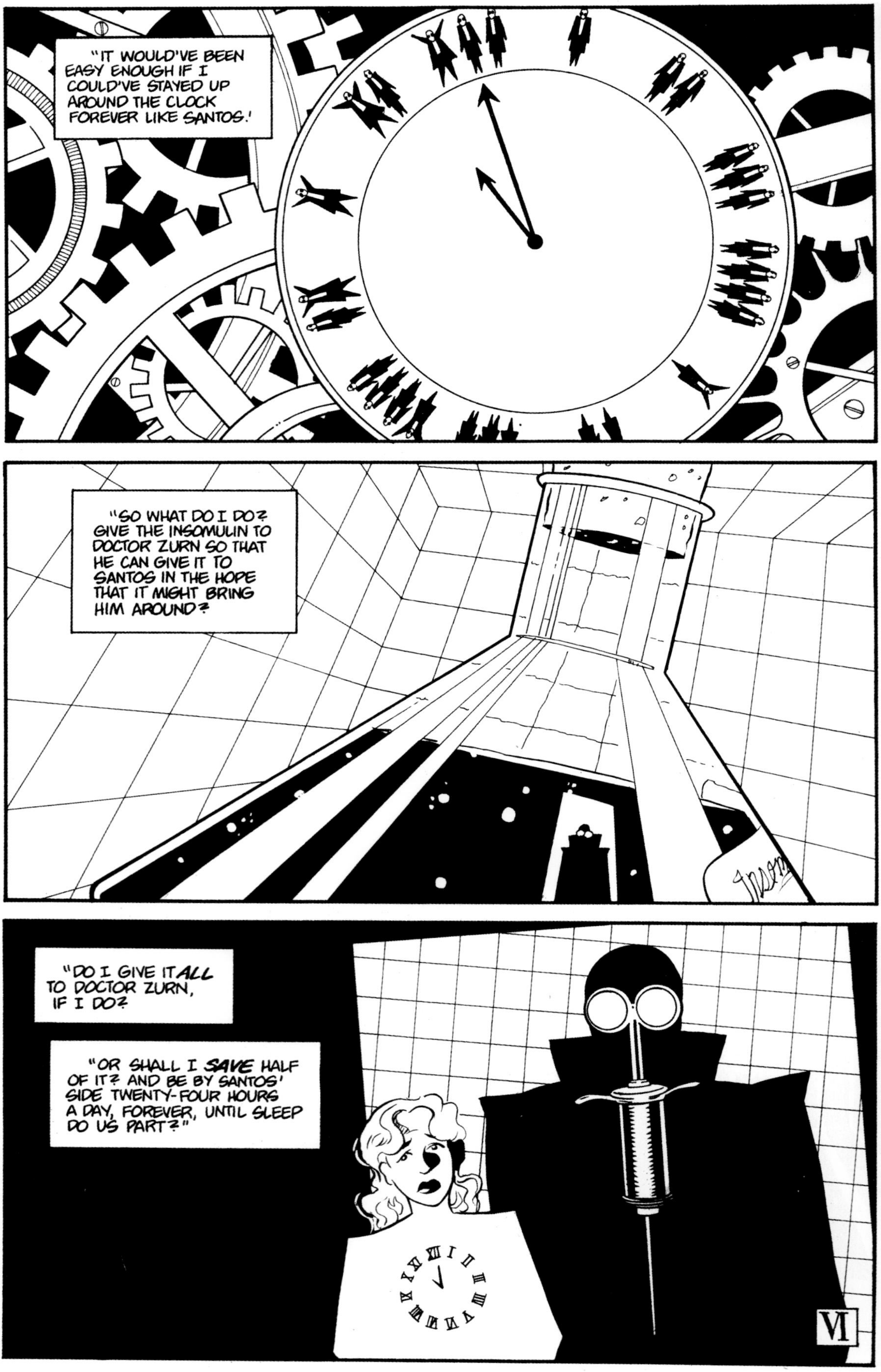
"IT WOULD'VE BEEN EASY ENOUGH IF I COULD'VE STAYED UP AROUND THE CLOCK FOREVER LIKE SANTOS.'
"SO WHAT DO I DO? GIVE THE INSOMULIN TO DOCTOR ZURN SO THAT HE CAN GIVE IT TO SANTOS IN THE HOPE THAT IT MIGHT BRING HIM AROUND?
"DO I GIVE IT ALL TO DOCTOR ZURN, IF I DO?
"OR SHALL I SAVE HALF OF IT? AND BE BY SANTOS' SIDE TWENTY-FOUR HOURS A DAY, FOREVER, UNTIL SLEEP DO US PART?"
VI

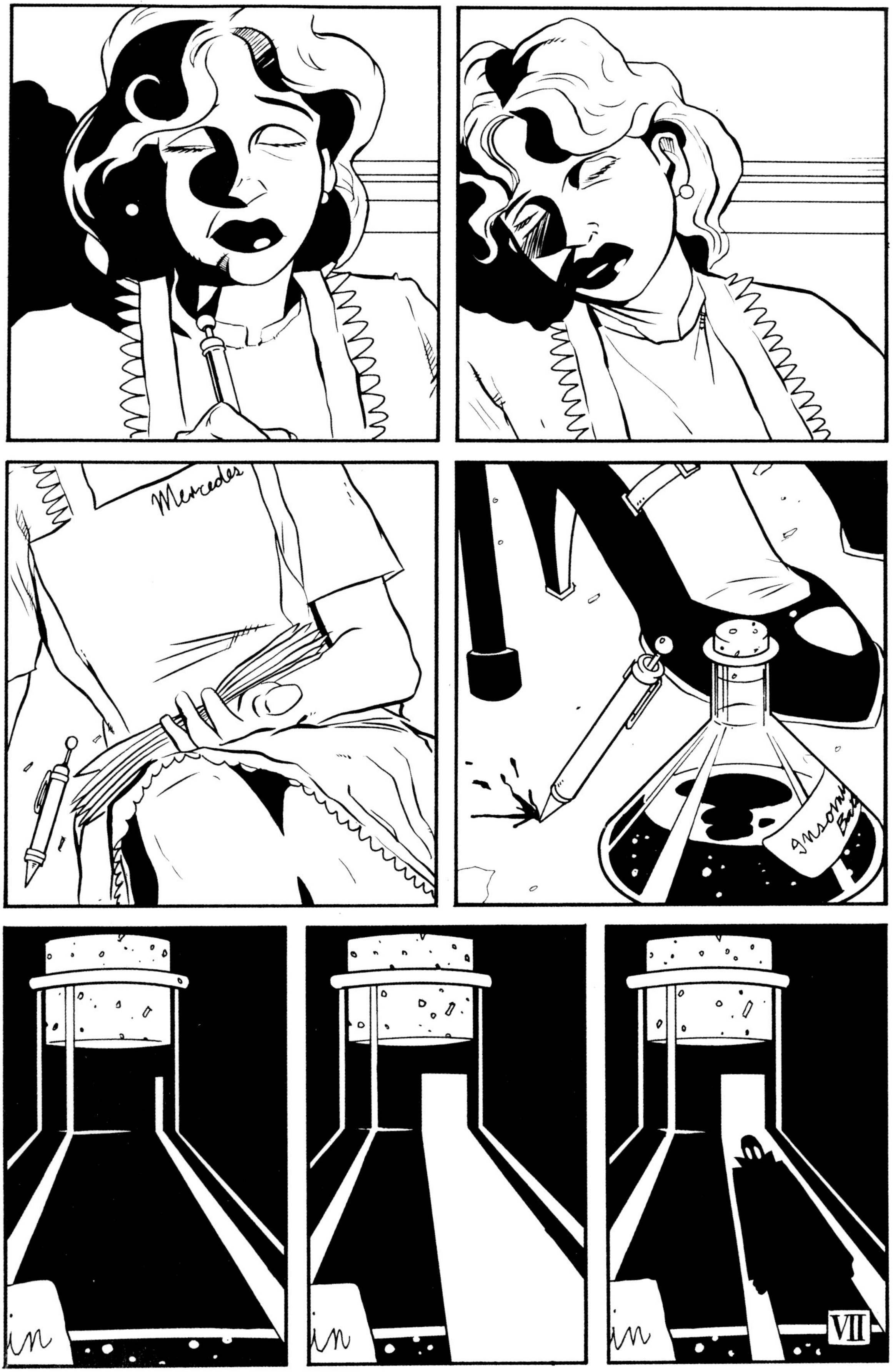
Mercedes
VII

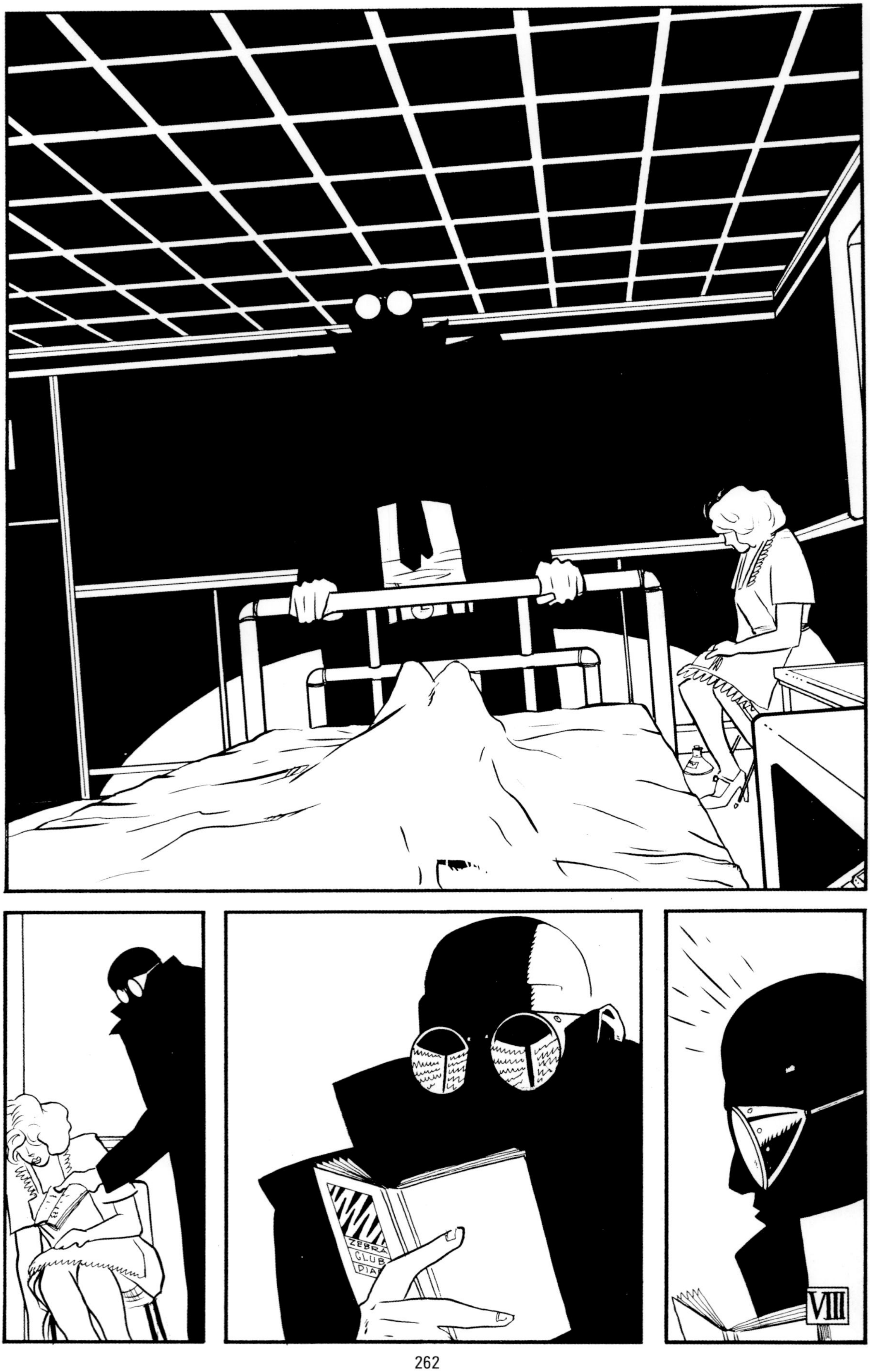
ZEBRA
CLUB
DIA
VIII

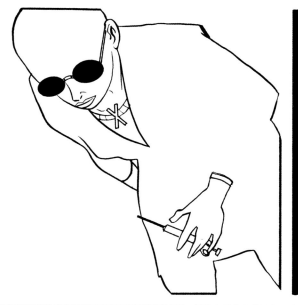

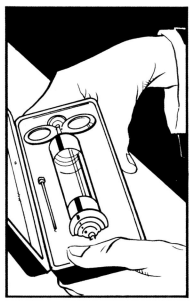
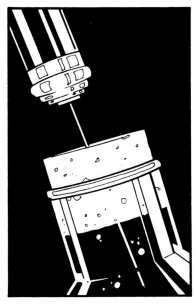
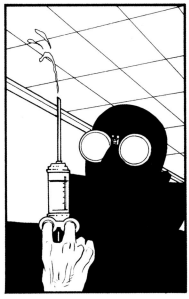
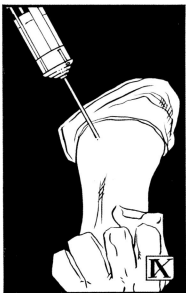

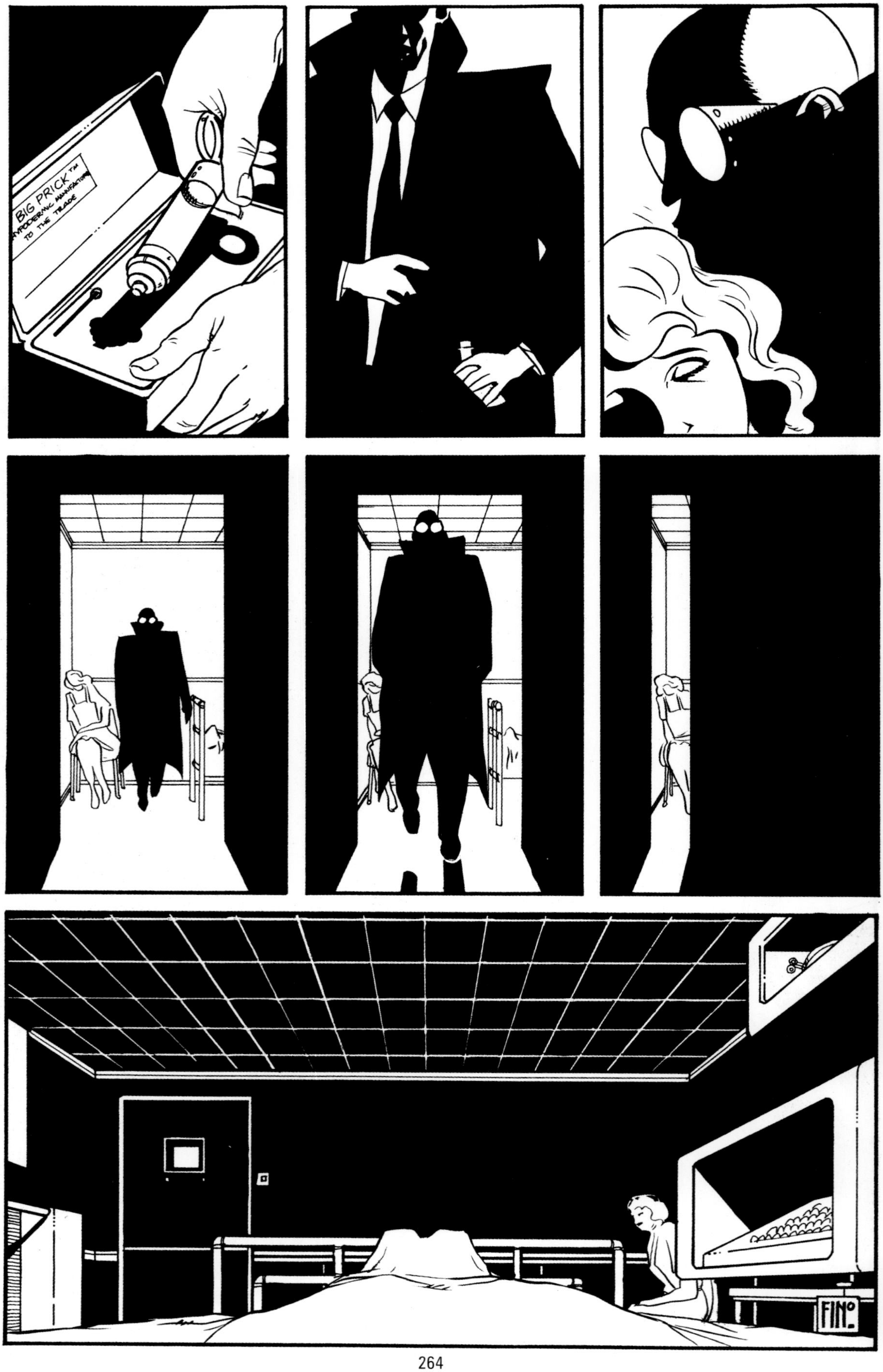
BIG PRICK TM
TO THE TRADE
FIN

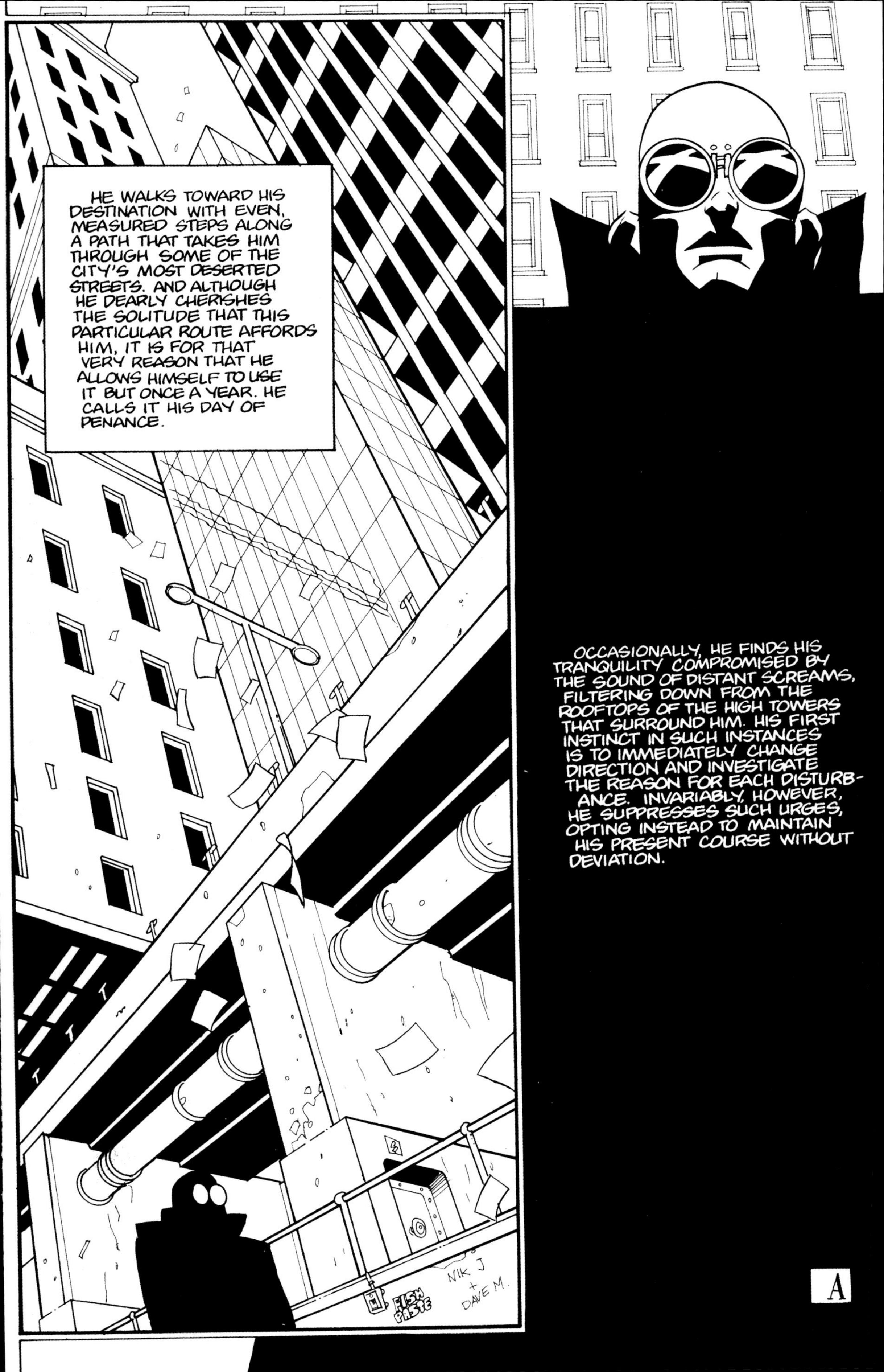
HE WALKS TOWARD HIS DESTINATION WITH EVEN, MEASURED STEPS ALONG A PATH THAT TAKES HIM THROUGH SOME OF THE CITY'S MOST DESERTED STREETS. AND ALTHOUGH HE DEARLY CHERISHES THE SOLITUDE THAT THIS PARTICULAR ROUTE AFFORDS HIM, IT IS FOR THAT VERY REASON THAT HE ALLOWS HIMSELF TO USE IT BUT ONCE A YEAR. HE CALLS IT HIS DAY OF PENANCE.
OCCASIONALLY, HE FINDS HIS TRANQUILITY COMPROMISED BY THE SOUND OF DISTANT SCREAMS, FILTERING DOWN FROM THE ROOFTOPS OF THE HIGH TOWERS THAT SURROUND HIM. HIS FIRST INSTINCT IN SUCH INSTANCES IS TO IMMEDIATELY CHANGE DIRECTION AND INVESTIGATE THE REASON FOR EACH DISTURBANCE. INVARIABLY, HOWEVER, HE SUPPRESSES SUCH URGES, OPTING INSTEAD TO MAINTAIN HIS PRESENT COURSE WITHOUT DEVIATION.
FISH PASTE
NIK J + DAVE M.
A

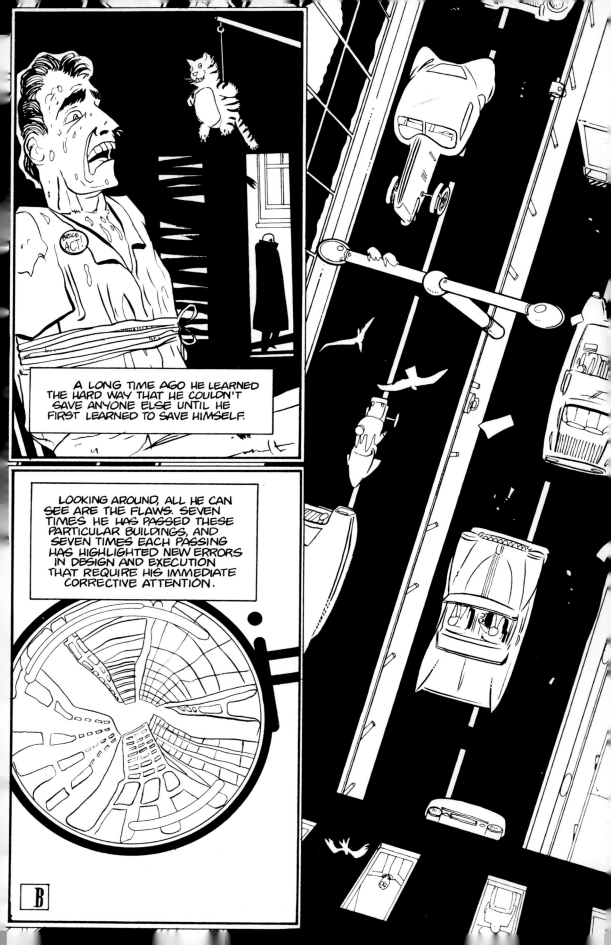

A LONG TIME AGO HE LEARNED THE HARD WAY THAT HE COULDN'T SAVE ANYONE ELSE UNTIL HE FIRST LEARNED TO SAVE HIMSELF.

LOOKING AROUND, ALL HE CAN SEE ARE THE FLAWS. SEVEN TIMES HE HAS PASSED THESE PARTICULAR BUILDINGS, AND SEVEN TIMES EACH PASSING HAS HIGHLIGHTED NEW ERRORS IN DESIGN AND EXECUTION THAT REQUIRE HIS IMMEDIATE CORRECTIVE ATTENTION.

B

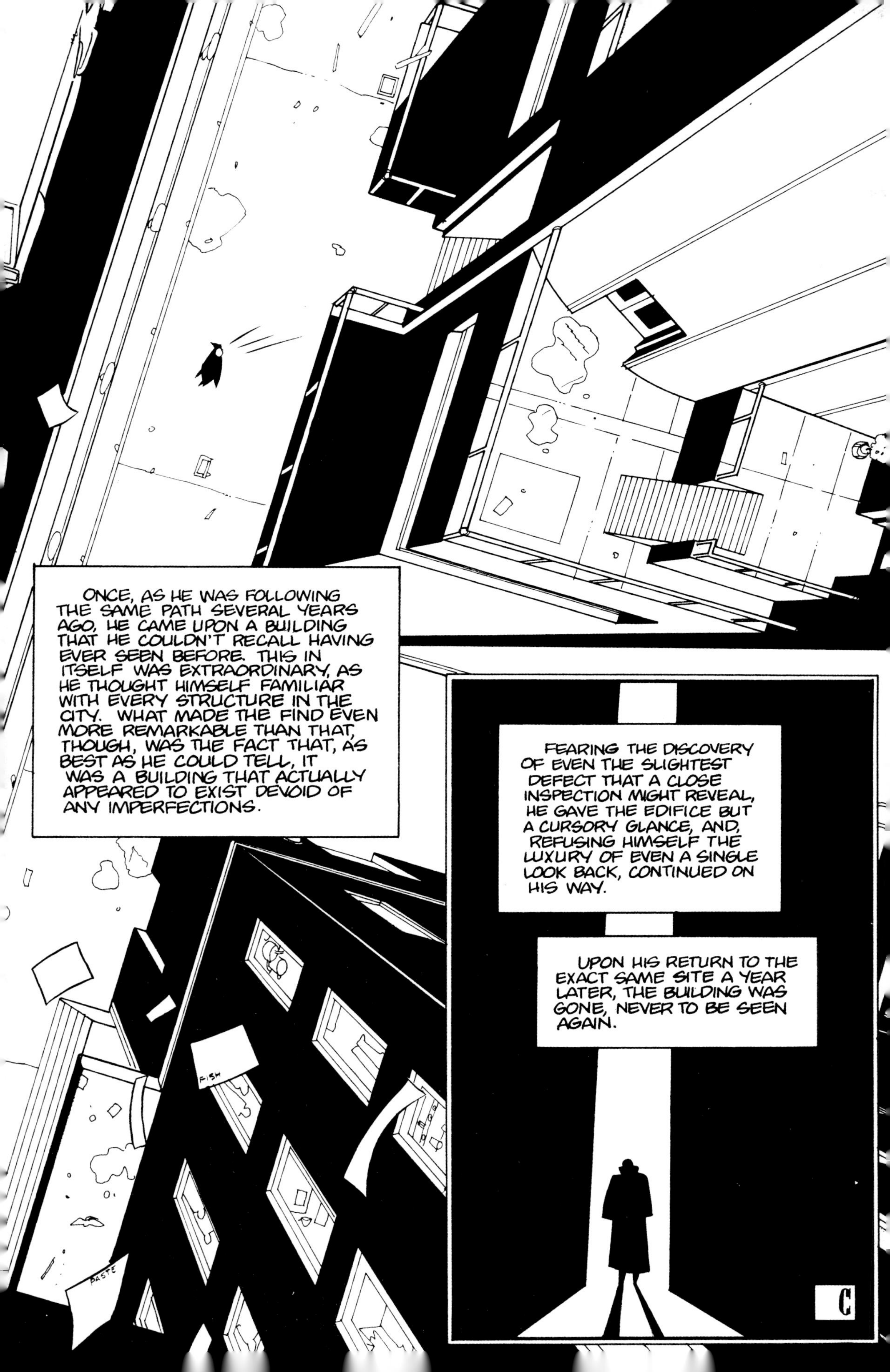
ONCE, AS HE WAS FOLLOWING THE SAME PATH SEVERAL YEARS AGO, HE CAME UPON A BUILDING THAT HE COULDN'T RECALL HAVING EVER SEEN BEFORE. THIS IN ITSELF WAS EXTRAORDINARY, AS HE THOUGHT HIMSELF FAMILIAR WITH EVERY STRUCTURE IN THE CITY. WHAT MADE THE FIND EVEN MORE REMARKABLE THAN THAT, THOUGH, WAS THE FACT THAT, AS BEST AS HE COULD TELL, IT WAS A BUILDING THAT ACTUALLY APPEARED TO EXIST DEVOID OF ANY IMPERFECTIONS.
FISH
PASTE
FEARING THE DISCOVERY OF EVEN THE SLIGHTEST DEFECT THAT A CLOSE INSPECTION MIGHT REVEAL, HE GAVE THE EDIFICE BUT A CURSORY GLANCE, AND, REFUSING HIMSELF THE LUXURY OF EVEN A SINGLE LOOK BACK, CONTINUED ON HIS WAY.
UPON HIS RETURN TO THE EXACT SAME SITE A YEAR LATER, THE BUILDING WAS GONE, NEVER TO BE SEEN AGAIN.
C

NOW HE HEARS ANOTHER CRY, AND THIS TIME HE DOES STOP.

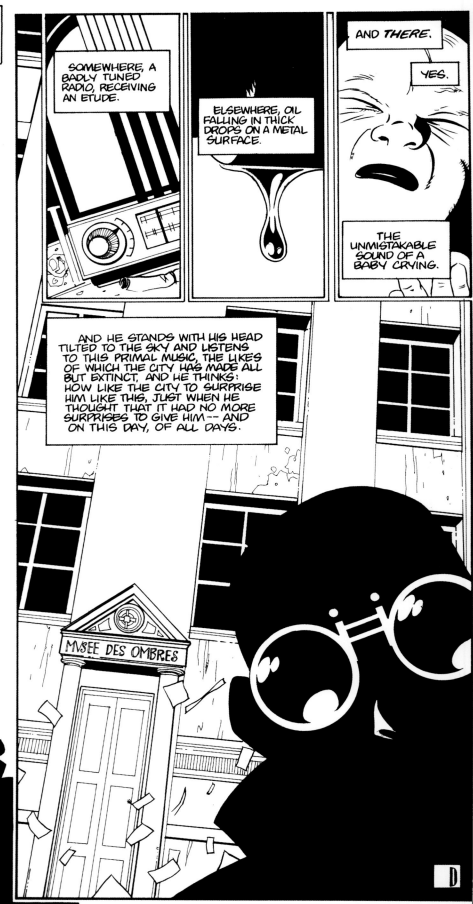

SOMEWHERE, A BADLY TUNED RADIO, RECEIVING AN ETUDE.

ELSEWHERE, OIL FALLING IN THICK DROPS ON A METAL SURFACE.

AND *THERE*.

YES.

THE UNMISTAKABLE SOUND OF A BABY CRYING.

AND HE STANDS WITH HIS HEAD TILTED TO THE SKY AND LISTENS TO THIS PRIMAL MUSIC, THE LIKES OF WHICH THE CITY HAS MADE ALL BUT EXTINCT, AND HE THINKS: HOW LIKE THE CITY TO SURPRISE HIM LIKE THIS, JUST WHEN HE THOUGHT THAT IT HAD NO MORE SURPRISES TO GIVE HIM -- AND ON THIS DAY, OF ALL DAYS.

MVSEE DES OMBRES

D

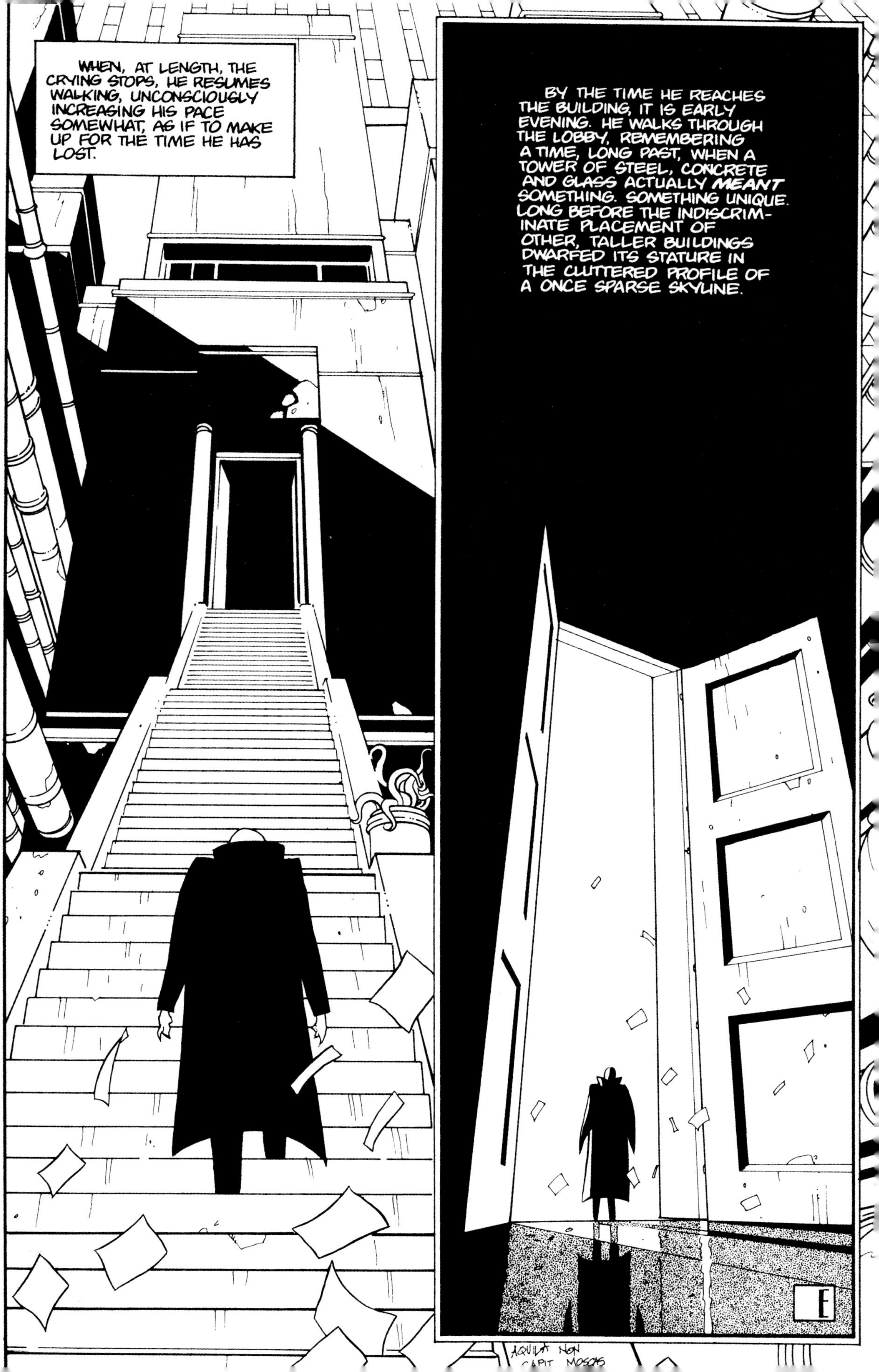
WHEN, AT LENGTH, THE CRYING STOPS, HE RESUMES WALKING, UNCONSCIOUSLY INCREASING HIS PACE SOMEWHAT, AS IF TO MAKE UP FOR THE TIME HE HAS LOST.
BY THE TIME HE REACHES THE BUILDING, IT IS EARLY EVENING. HE WALKS THROUGH THE LOBBY, REMEMBERING A TIME, LONG PAST, WHEN A TOWER OF STEEL, CONCRETE AND GLASS ACTUALLY *MEANT* SOMETHING. SOMETHING UNIQUE. LONG BEFORE THE INDISCRIMINATE PLACEMENT OF OTHER, TALLER BUILDINGS DWARFED ITS STATURE IN THE CLUTTERED PROFILE OF A ONCE SPARSE SKYLINE.
E
AQUILA NON CAPIT MOSCAS

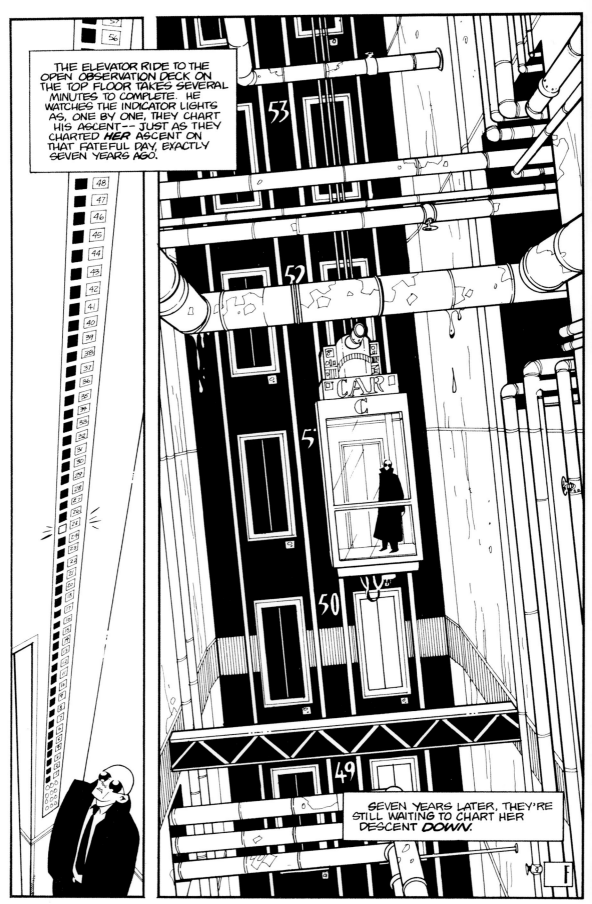

THE ELEVATOR RIDE TO THE OPEN OBSERVATION DECK ON THE TOP FLOOR TAKES SEVERAL MINUTES TO COMPLETE. HE WATCHES THE INDICATOR LIGHTS AS, ONE BY ONE, THEY CHART HIS ASCENT-- JUST AS THEY CHARTED *HER* ASCENT ON THAT FATEFUL DAY, EXACTLY SEVEN YEARS AGO.

SEVEN YEARS LATER, THEY'RE STILL WAITING TO CHART HER DESCENT *DOWN.*

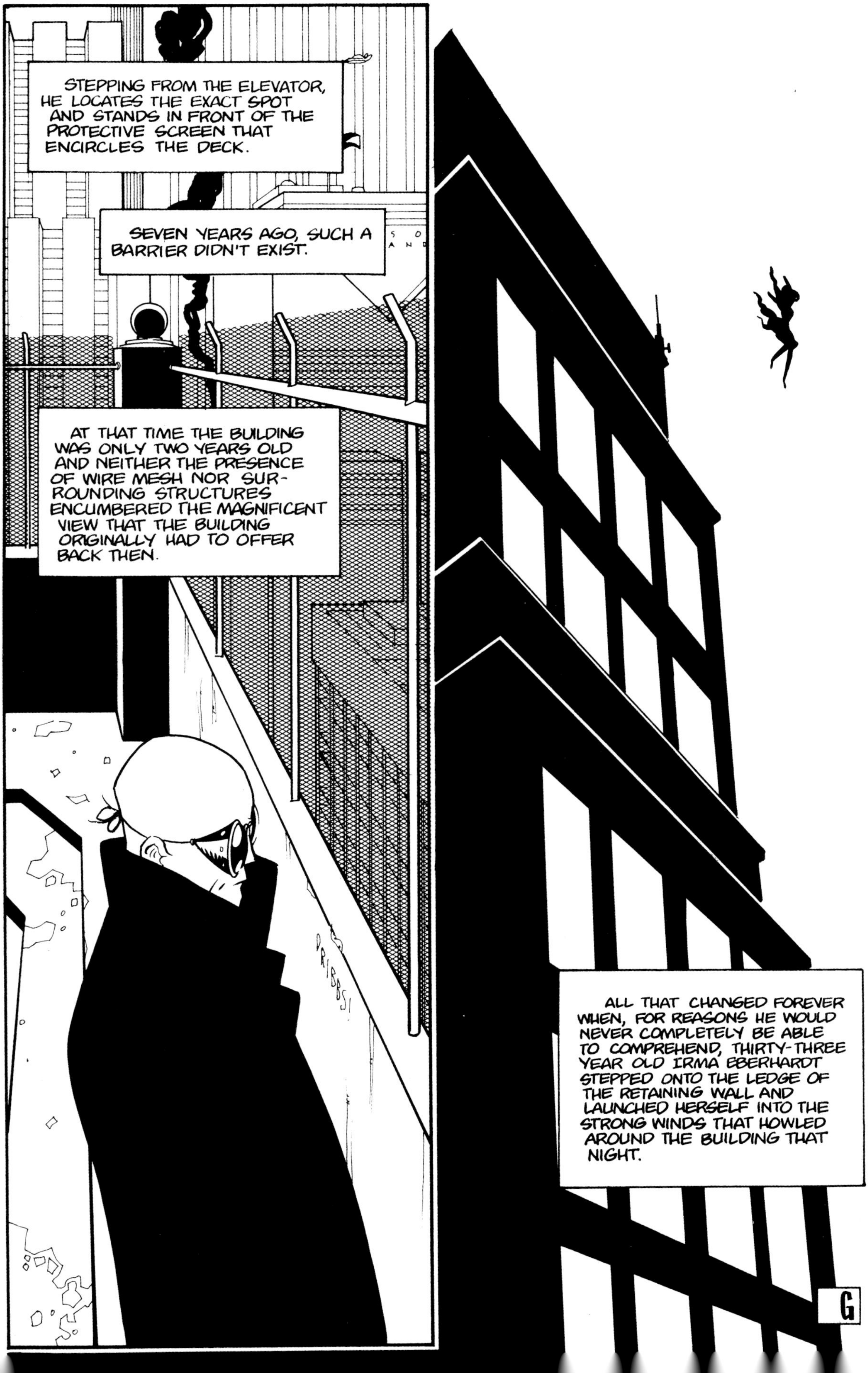
STEPPING FROM THE ELEVATOR, HE LOCATES THE EXACT SPOT AND STANDS IN FRONT OF THE PROTECTIVE SCREEN THAT ENCIRCLES THE DECK.
SEVEN YEARS AGO, SUCH A BARRIER DIDN'T EXIST.
AT THAT TIME THE BUILDING WAS ONLY TWO YEARS OLD AND NEITHER THE PRESENCE OF WIRE MESH NOR SURROUNDING STRUCTURES ENCUMBERED THE MAGNIFICENT VIEW THAT THE BUILDING ORIGINALLY HAD TO OFFER BACK THEN.
ALL THAT CHANGED FOREVER WHEN, FOR REASONS HE WOULD NEVER COMPLETELY BE ABLE TO COMPREHEND, THIRTY-THREE YEAR OLD IRMA EBERHARDT STEPPED ONTO THE LEDGE OF THE RETAINING WALL AND LAUNCHED HERSELF INTO THE STRONG WINDS THAT HOWLED AROUND THE BUILDING THAT NIGHT.
G

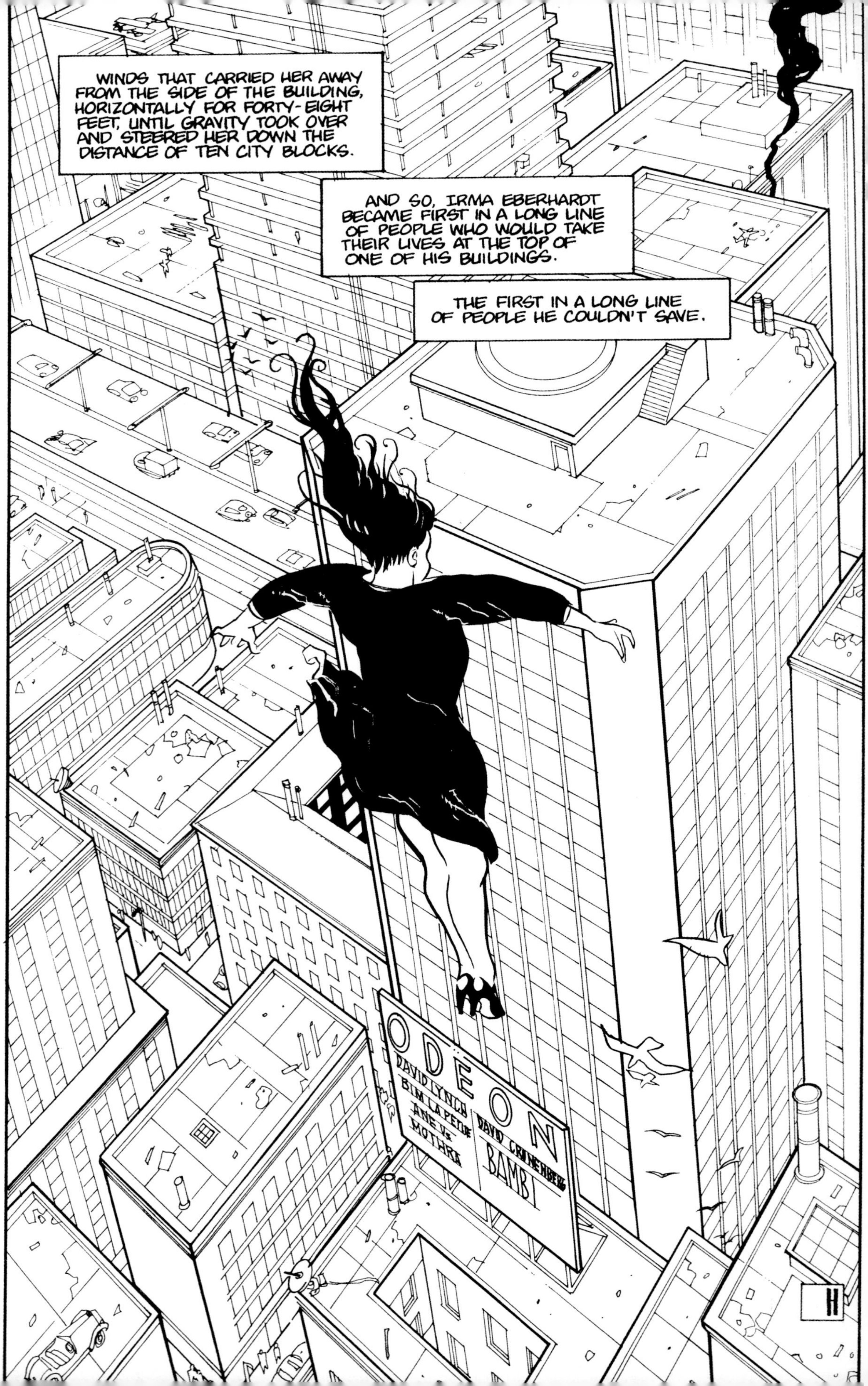
WINDS THAT CARRIED HER AWAY FROM THE SIDE OF THE BUILDING, HORIZONTALLY FOR FORTY-EIGHT FEET, UNTIL GRAVITY TOOK OVER AND STEERED HER DOWN THE DISTANCE OF TEN CITY BLOCKS.
AND SO, IRMA EBERHARDT BECAME FIRST IN A LONG LINE OF PEOPLE WHO WOULD TAKE THEIR LIVES AT THE TOP OF ONE OF HIS BUILDINGS.
THE FIRST IN A LONG LINE OF PEOPLE HE COULDN'T SAVE.
ODEON
DAVID LYNCH
BIM LA PETIE
ANE vs
MOTHRA
DAVID CRONENBERG
BAMBI

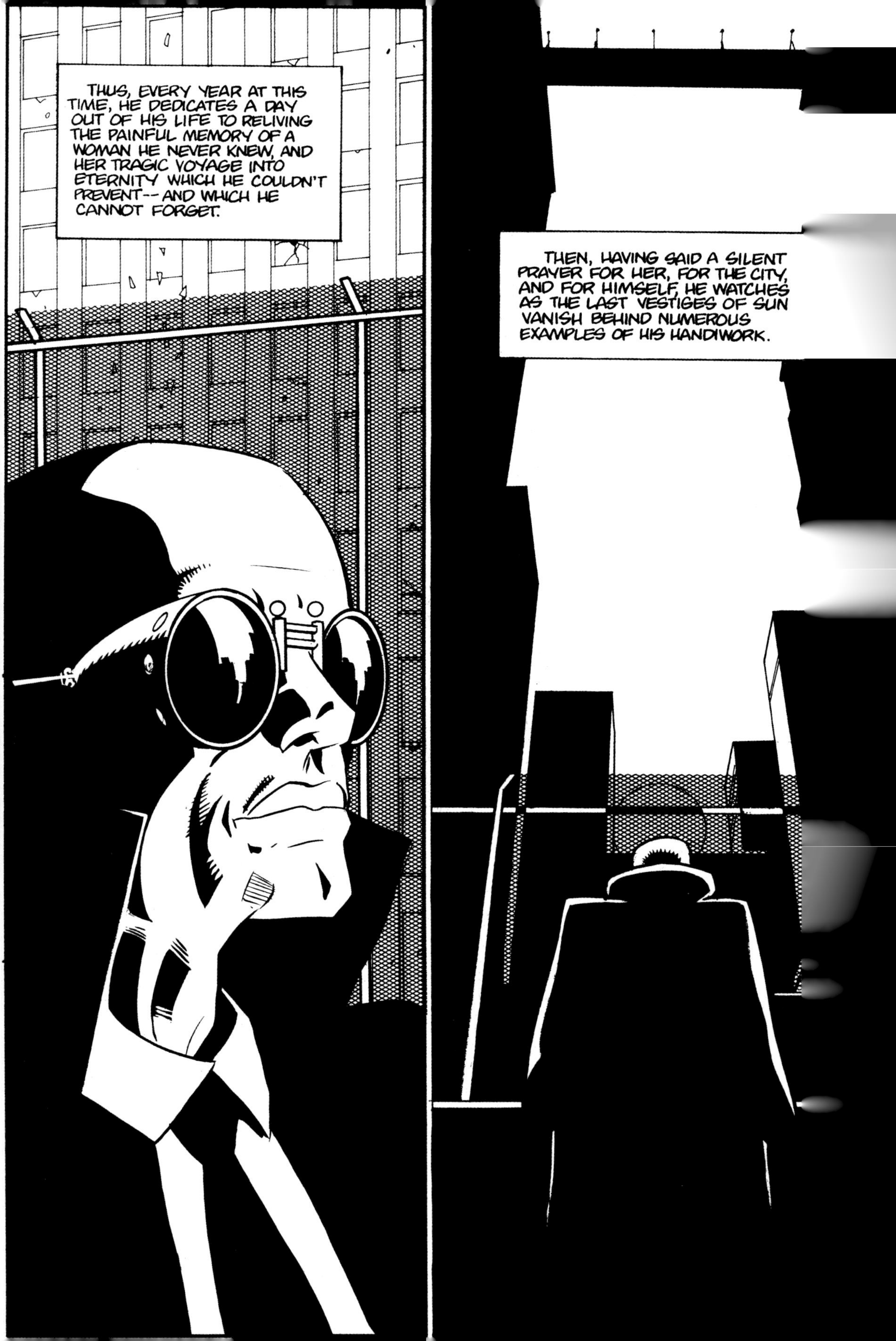
THUS, EVERY YEAR AT THIS TIME, HE DEDICATES A DAY OUT OF HIS LIFE TO RELIVING THE PAINFUL MEMORY OF A WOMAN HE NEVER KNEW, AND HER TRAGIC VOYAGE INTO ETERNITY WHICH HE COULDN'T PREVENT-- AND WHICH HE CANNOT FORGET.
THEN, HAVING SAID A SILENT PRAYER FOR HER, FOR THE CITY, AND FOR HIMSELF, HE WATCHES AS THE LAST VESTIGES OF SUN VANISH BEHIND NUMEROUS EXAMPLES OF HIS HANDIWORK.

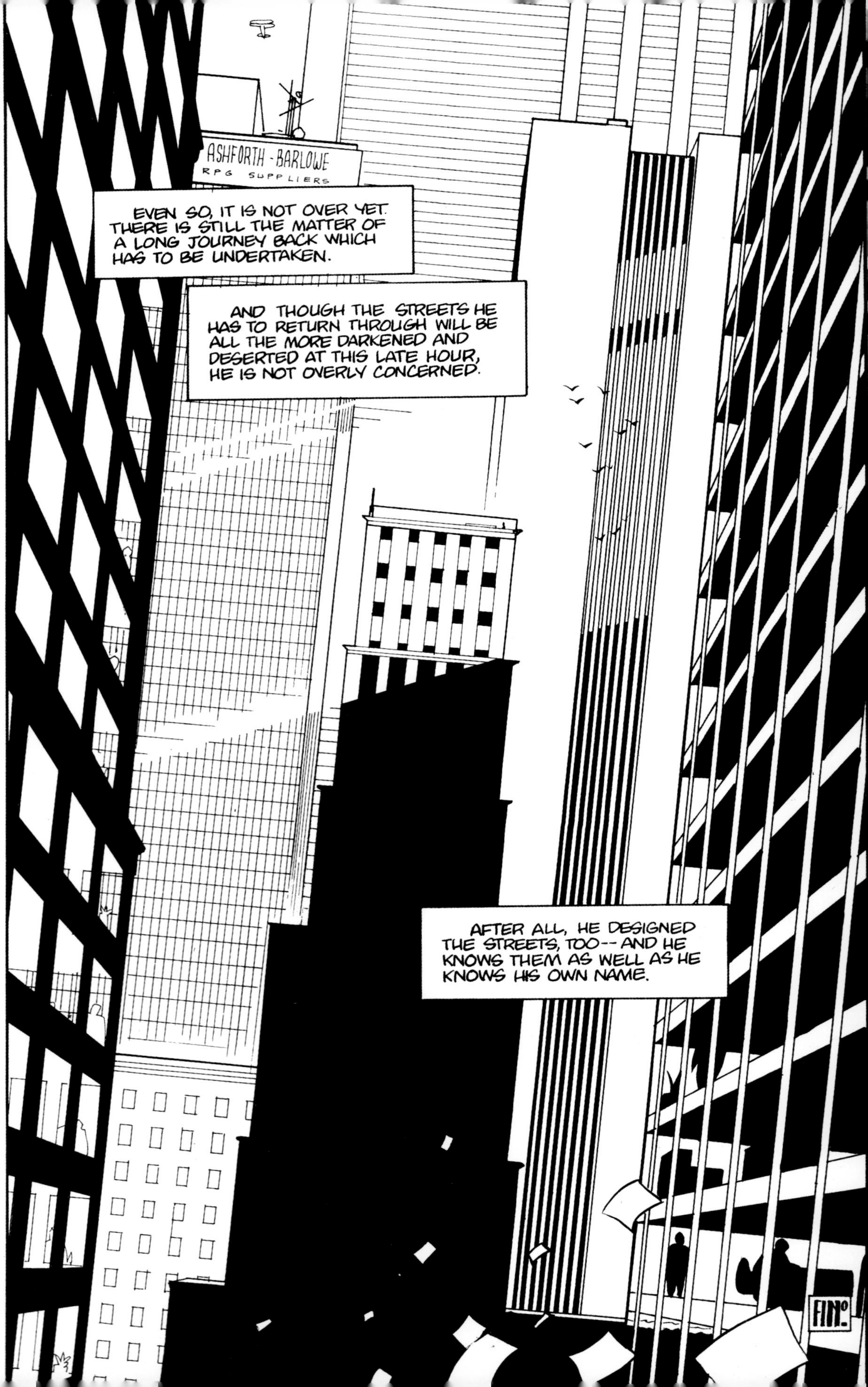
ASHFORTH - BARLOWE
RPG SUPPLIERS
EVEN SO, IT IS NOT OVER YET. THERE IS STILL THE MATTER OF A LONG JOURNEY BACK WHICH HAS TO BE UNDERTAKEN.
AND THOUGH THE STREETS HE HAS TO RETURN THROUGH WILL BE ALL THE MORE DARKENED AND DESERTED AT THIS LATE HOUR, HE IS NOT OVERLY CONCERNED.
AFTER ALL, HE DESIGNED THE STREETS, TOO-- AND HE KNOWS THEM AS WELL AS HE KNOWS HIS OWN NAME.
FIN.

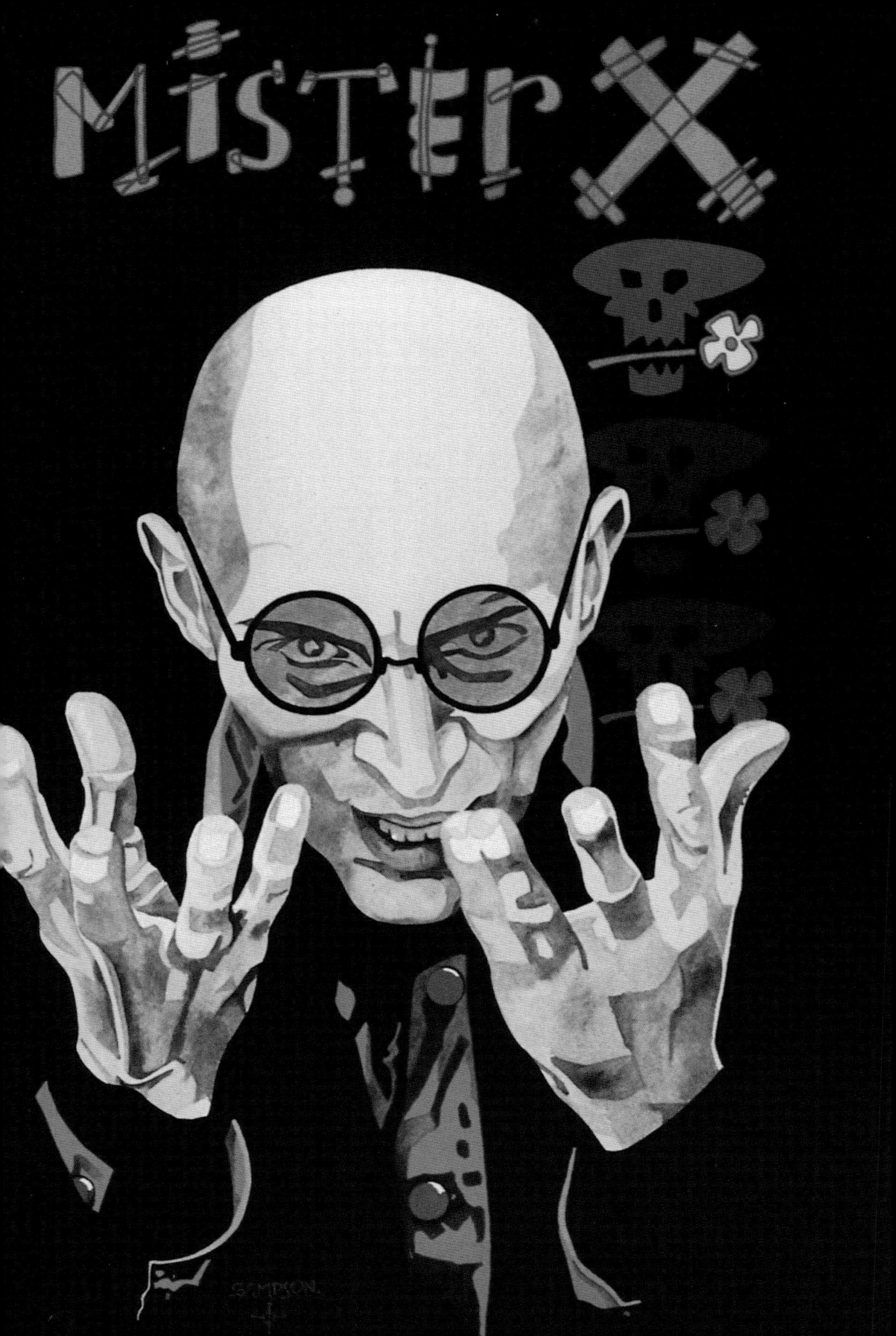
Mister X
SAMPSON

Illustration by **STEVE SAMPSON**

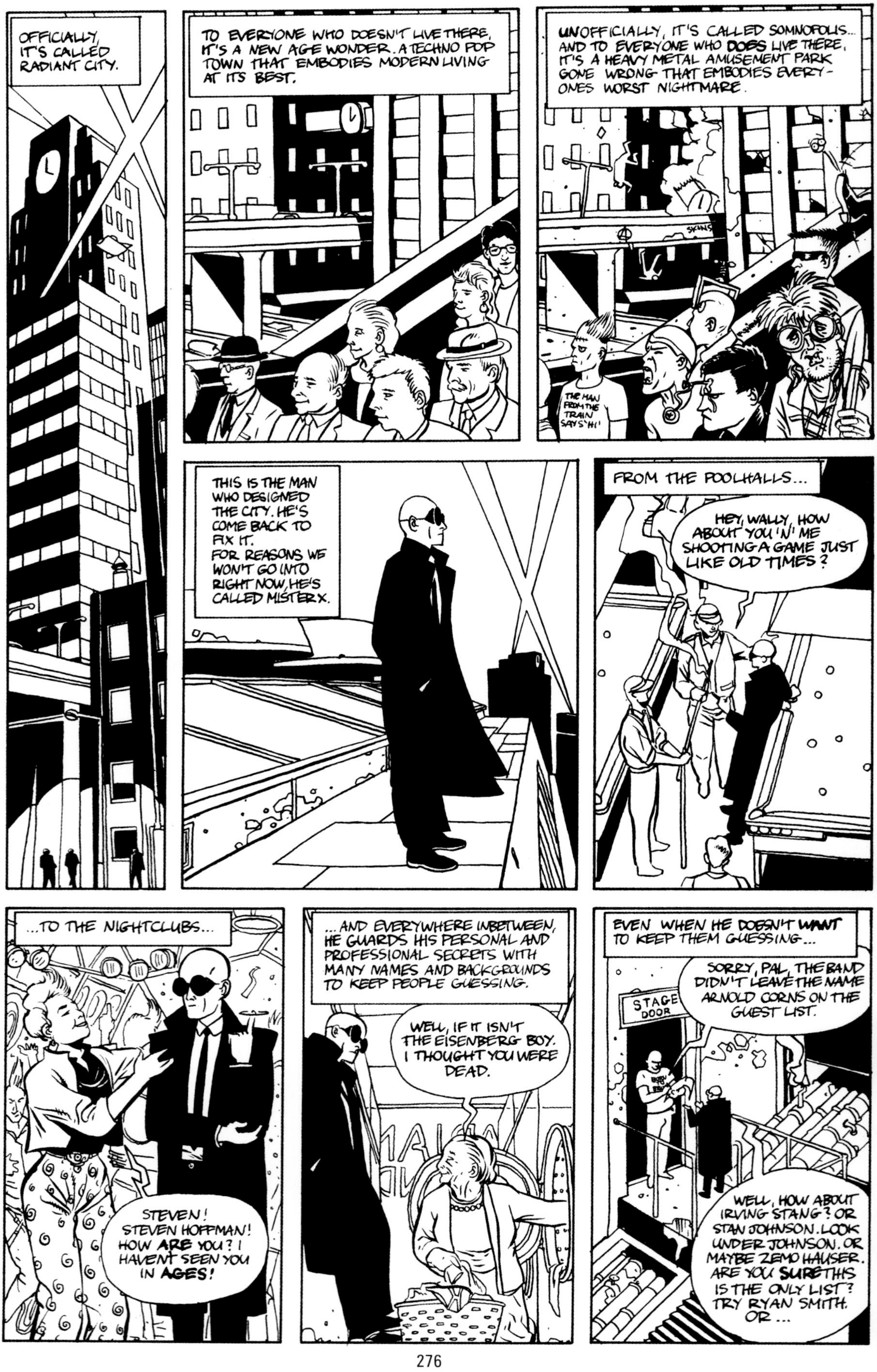
OFFICIALLY, IT'S CALLED RADIANT CITY.
TO EVERYONE WHO DOESN'T LIVE THERE, IT'S A NEW AGE WONDER. A TECHNO POP TOWN THAT EMBODIES MODERN LIVING AT ITS BEST.
UNOFFICIALLY, IT'S CALLED SOMNOPOLIS... AND TO EVERYONE WHO DOES LIVE THERE, IT'S A HEAVY METAL AMUSEMENT PARK GONE WRONG THAT EMBODIES EVERYONES WORST NIGHTMARE.
THE MAN FROM THE TRAIN SAYS 'HI'
THIS IS THE MAN WHO DESIGNED THE CITY. HE'S COME BACK TO FIX IT. FOR REASONS WE WON'T GO INTO RIGHT NOW, HE'S CALLED MISTER X.
FROM THE POOLHALLS...
HEY, WALLY, HOW ABOUT YOU 'N' ME SHOOTING A GAME JUST LIKE OLD TIMES?
...TO THE NIGHTCLUBS...
STEVEN! STEVEN HOFFMAN! HOW ARE YOU? I HAVEN'T SEEN YOU IN AGES!
...AND EVERYWHERE INBETWEEN, HE GUARDS HIS PERSONAL AND PROFESSIONAL SECRETS WITH MANY NAMES AND BACKGROUNDS TO KEEP PEOPLE GUESSING.
WELL, IF IT ISN'T THE EISENBERG BOY. I THOUGHT YOU WERE DEAD.
EVEN WHEN HE DOESN'T WANT TO KEEP THEM GUESSING...
STAGE DOOR
SORRY, PAL, THE BAND DIDN'T LEAVE THE NAME ARNOLD CORNS ON THE GUEST LIST.
WELL, HOW ABOUT IRVING STANG? OR STAN JOHNSON. LOOK UNDER JOHNSON. OR MAYBE ZEMO HAUSER. ARE YOU SURE THIS IS THE ONLY LIST? TRY RYAN SMITH. OR...

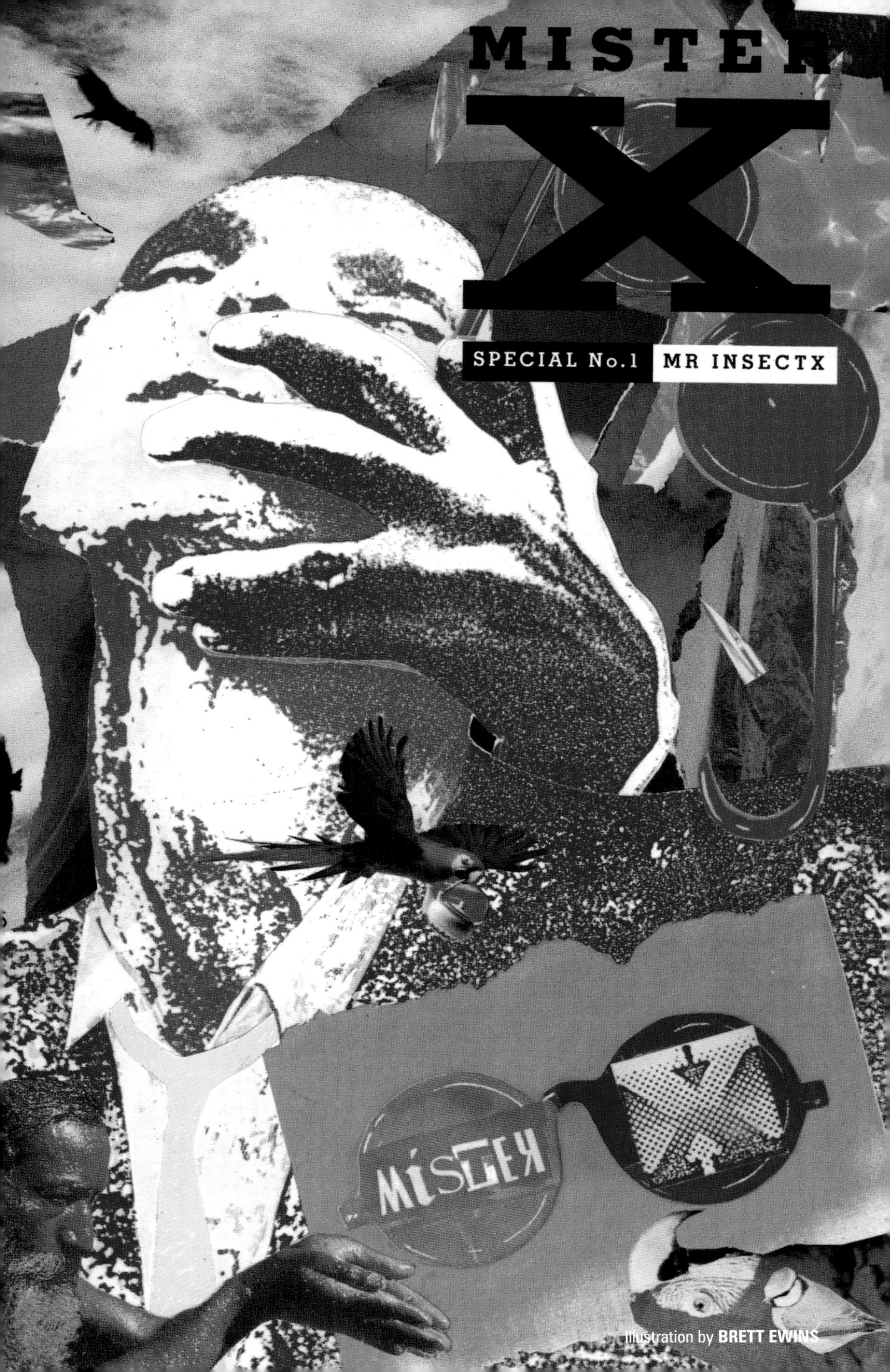
MISTER
X
SPECIAL No.1
MR INSECTX
Illustration by **BRETT EWINS**

MISTER INSECT X

WRITTEN BY **PETER MILLIGAN**
ILLUSTRATED BY **BRETT EWINS**
LETTERED BY **DEBORAH MARKS**

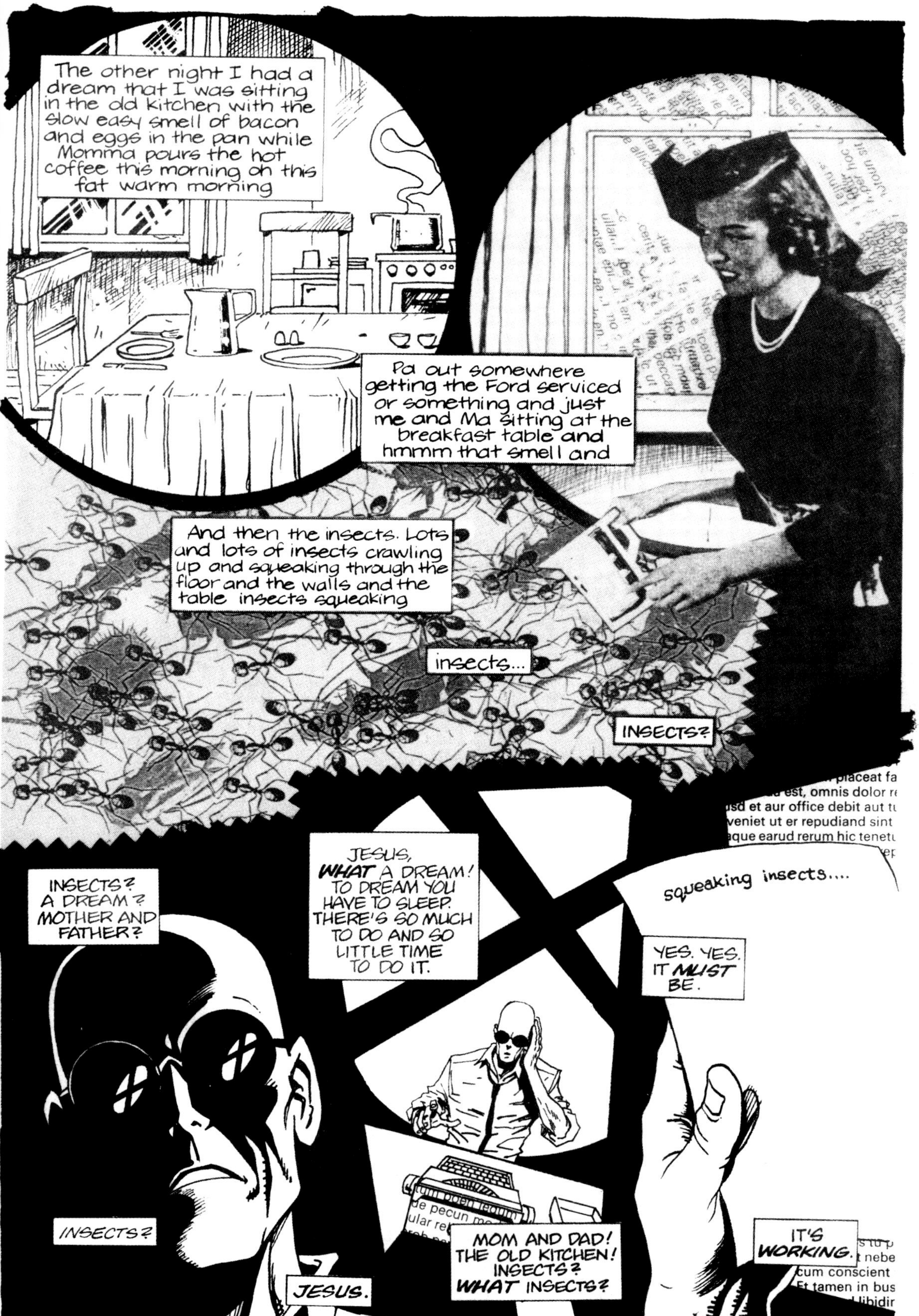
The other night I had a dream that I was sitting in the old kitchen with the slow easy smell of bacon and eggs in the pan while Momma pours the hot coffee this morning oh this fat warm morning
Pa out somewhere getting the Ford serviced or something and just me and Ma sitting at the breakfast table and hmmm that smell and
And then the insects. Lots and lots of insects crawling up and squeaking through the floor and the walls and the table insects squeaking
insects...
INSECTS?
INSECTS? A DREAM? MOTHER AND FATHER?
JESUS, WHAT A DREAM! TO DREAM YOU HAVE TO SLEEP. THERE'S SO MUCH TO DO AND SO LITTLE TIME TO DO IT.
squeaking insects....
YES. YES. IT MUST BE.
INSECTS?
JESUS.
MOM AND DAD! THE OLD KITCHEN! INSECTS? WHAT INSECTS?
IT'S WORKING.

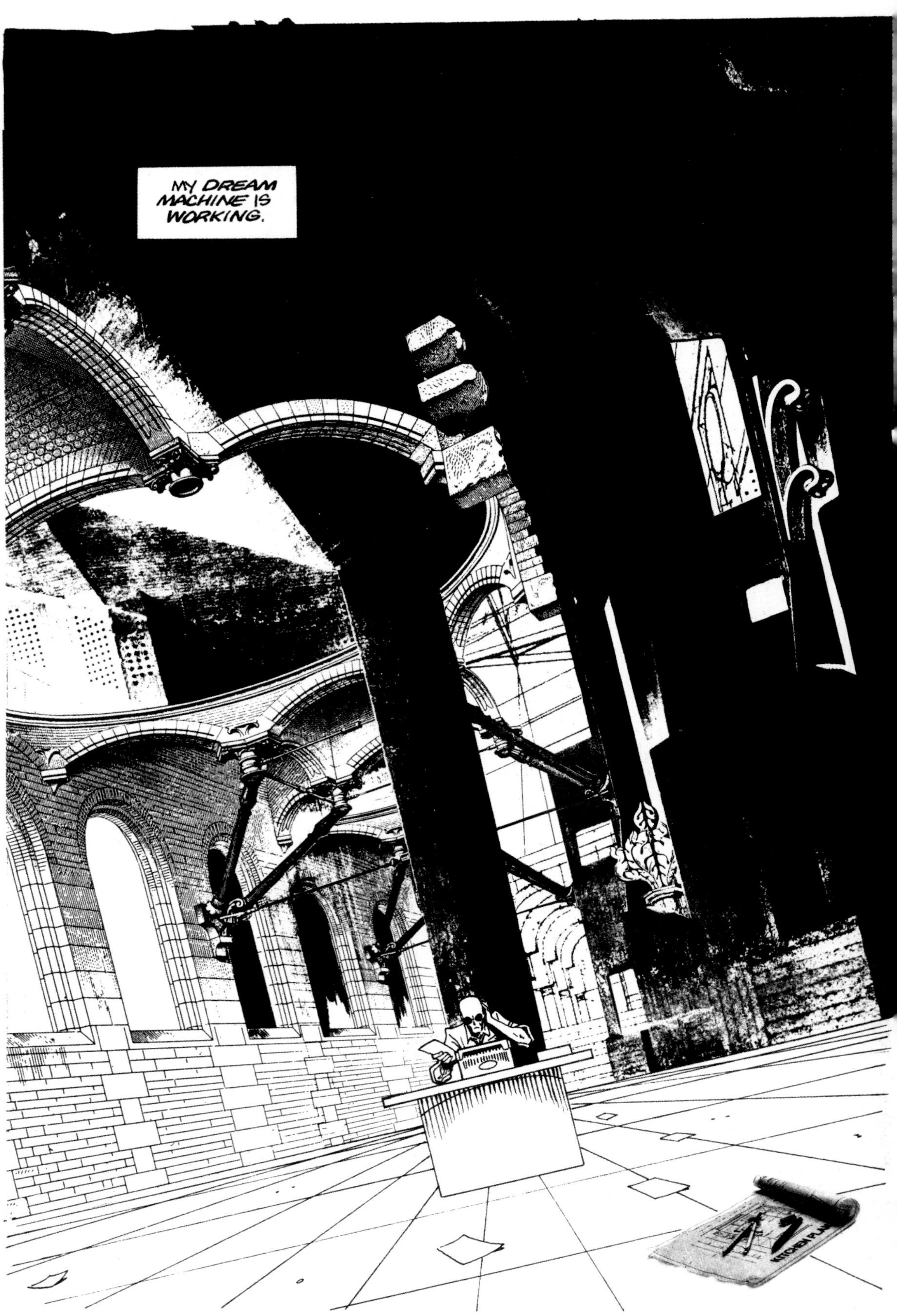
MY DREAM MACHINE IS WORKING.

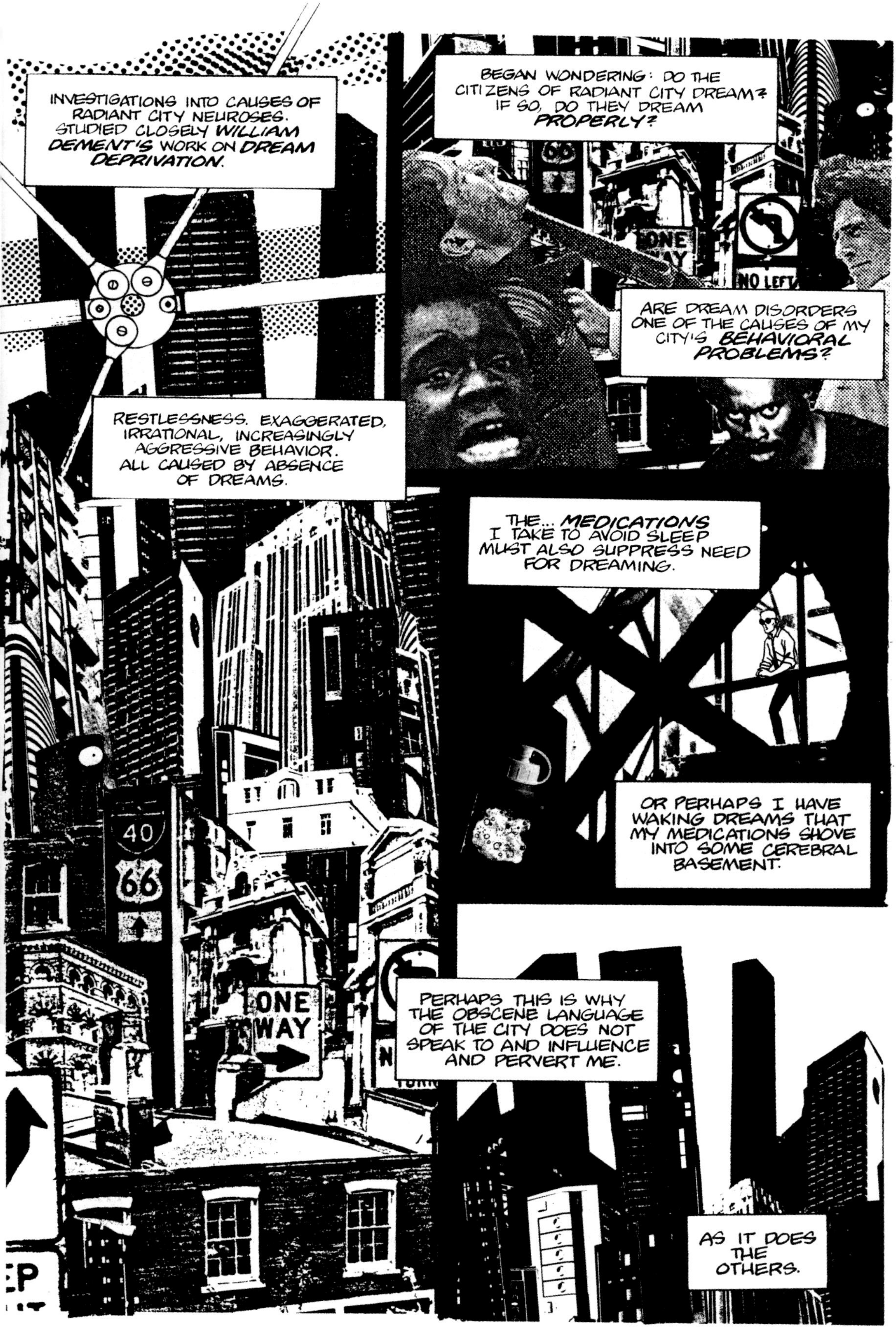
INVESTIGATIONS INTO CAUSES OF RADIANT CITY NEUROSES. STUDIED CLOSELY WILLIAM DEMENT'S WORK ON DREAM DEPRIVATION.
RESTLESSNESS. EXAGGERATED, IRRATIONAL, INCREASINGLY AGGRESSIVE BEHAVIOR. ALL CAUSED BY ABSENCE OF DREAMS.
BEGAN WONDERING: DO THE CITIZENS OF RADIANT CITY DREAM? IF SO, DO THEY DREAM PROPERLY?
ONE WAY
NO LEFT
ARE DREAM DISORDERS ONE OF THE CAUSES OF MY CITY'S BEHAVIORAL PROBLEMS?
THE... MEDICATIONS I TAKE TO AVOID SLEEP MUST ALSO SUPPRESS NEED FOR DREAMING.
OR PERHAPS I HAVE WAKING DREAMS THAT MY MEDICATIONS SHOVE INTO SOME CEREBRAL BASEMENT.
40
66
ONE WAY
PERHAPS THIS IS WHY THE OBSCENE LANGUAGE OF THE CITY DOES NOT SPEAK TO AND INFLUENCE AND PERVERT ME.
AS IT DOES THE OTHERS.

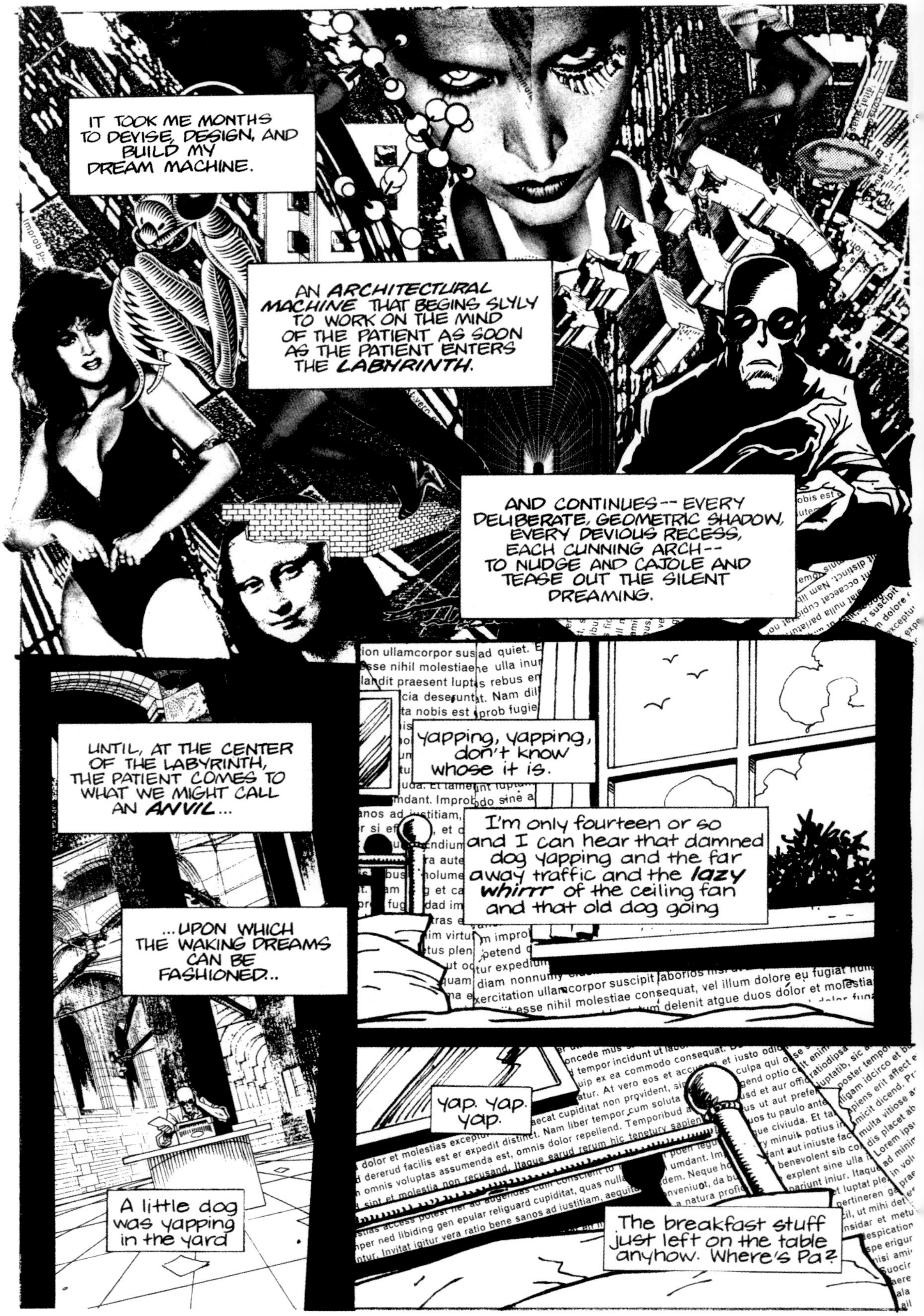
IT TOOK ME MONTHS TO DEVISE, DESIGN, AND BUILD MY DREAM MACHINE.
AN ARCHITECTURAL MACHINE THAT BEGINS SLYLY TO WORK ON THE MIND OF THE PATIENT AS SOON AS THE PATIENT ENTERS THE LABYRINTH.
AND CONTINUES-- EVERY DELIBERATE, GEOMETRIC SHADOW, EVERY DEVIOUS RECESS, EACH CUNNING ARCH-- TO NUDGE AND CAJOLE AND TEASE OUT THE SILENT DREAMING.
UNTIL, AT THE CENTER OF THE LABYRINTH, THE PATIENT COMES TO WHAT WE MIGHT CALL AN ANVIL...
...UPON WHICH THE WAKING DREAMS CAN BE FASHIONED...
A little dog was yapping in the yard
Yapping, yapping, don't know whose it is.
I'm only fourteen or so and I can hear that damned dog yapping and the far away traffic and the lazy whirrr of the ceiling fan and that old dog going
Yap. Yap. Yap.
The breakfast stuff just left on the table anyhow. Where's Pa?

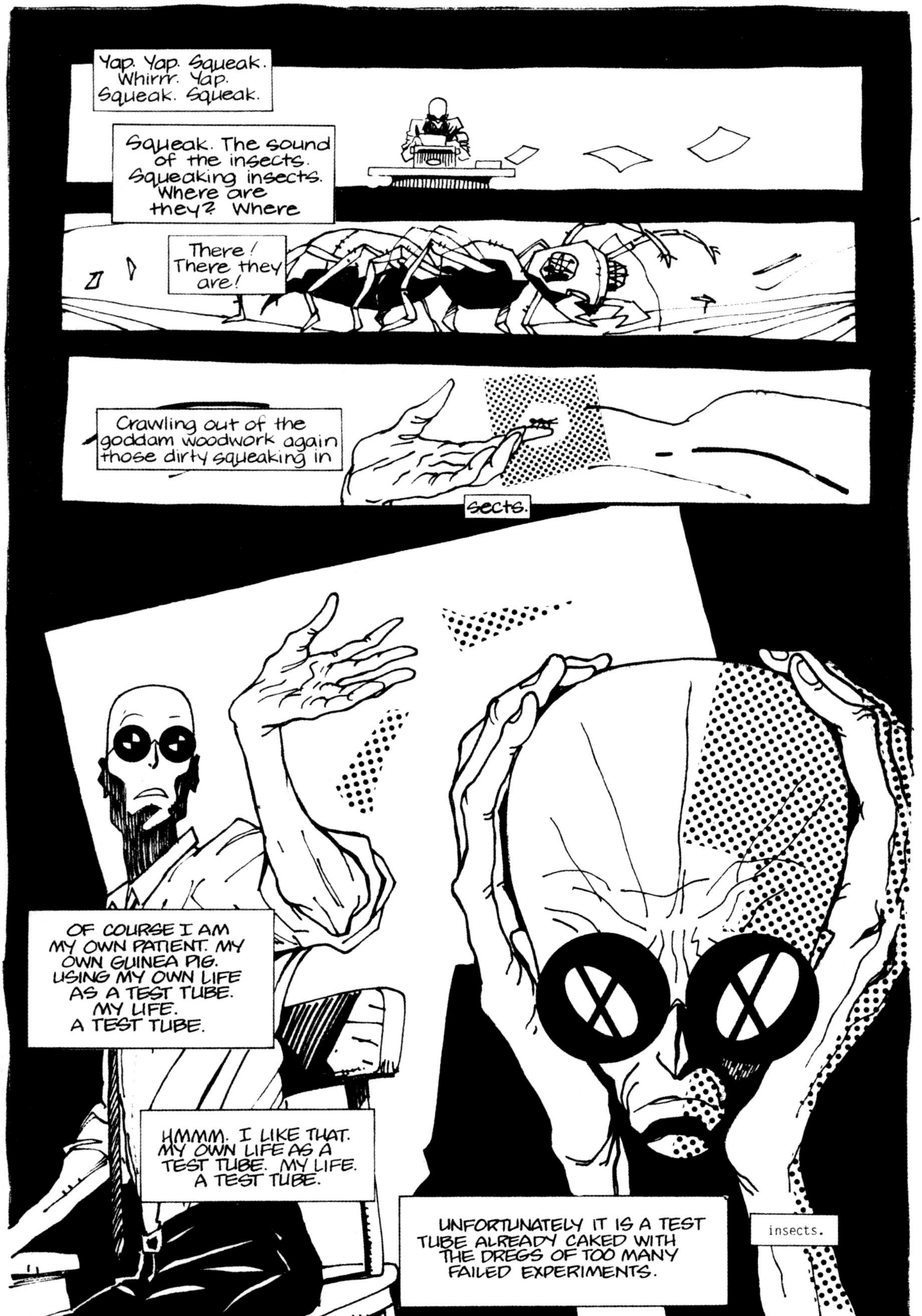

Yap. Yap. Squeak. Whirrr. Yap. Squeak. Squeak.
Squeak. The sound of the insects. Squeaking insects. Where are they? Where
There! There they are!
Crawling out of the goddam woodwork again those dirty squeaking in
sects.
OF COURSE I AM MY OWN PATIENT. MY OWN GUINEA PIG. USING MY OWN LIFE AS A TEST TUBE. MY LIFE. A TEST TUBE.
HMMM. I LIKE THAT. MY OWN LIFE AS A TEST TUBE. MY LIFE. A TEST TUBE.
UNFORTUNATELY IT IS A TEST TUBE ALREADY CAKED WITH THE DREGS OF TOO MANY FAILED EXPERIMENTS.
insects.

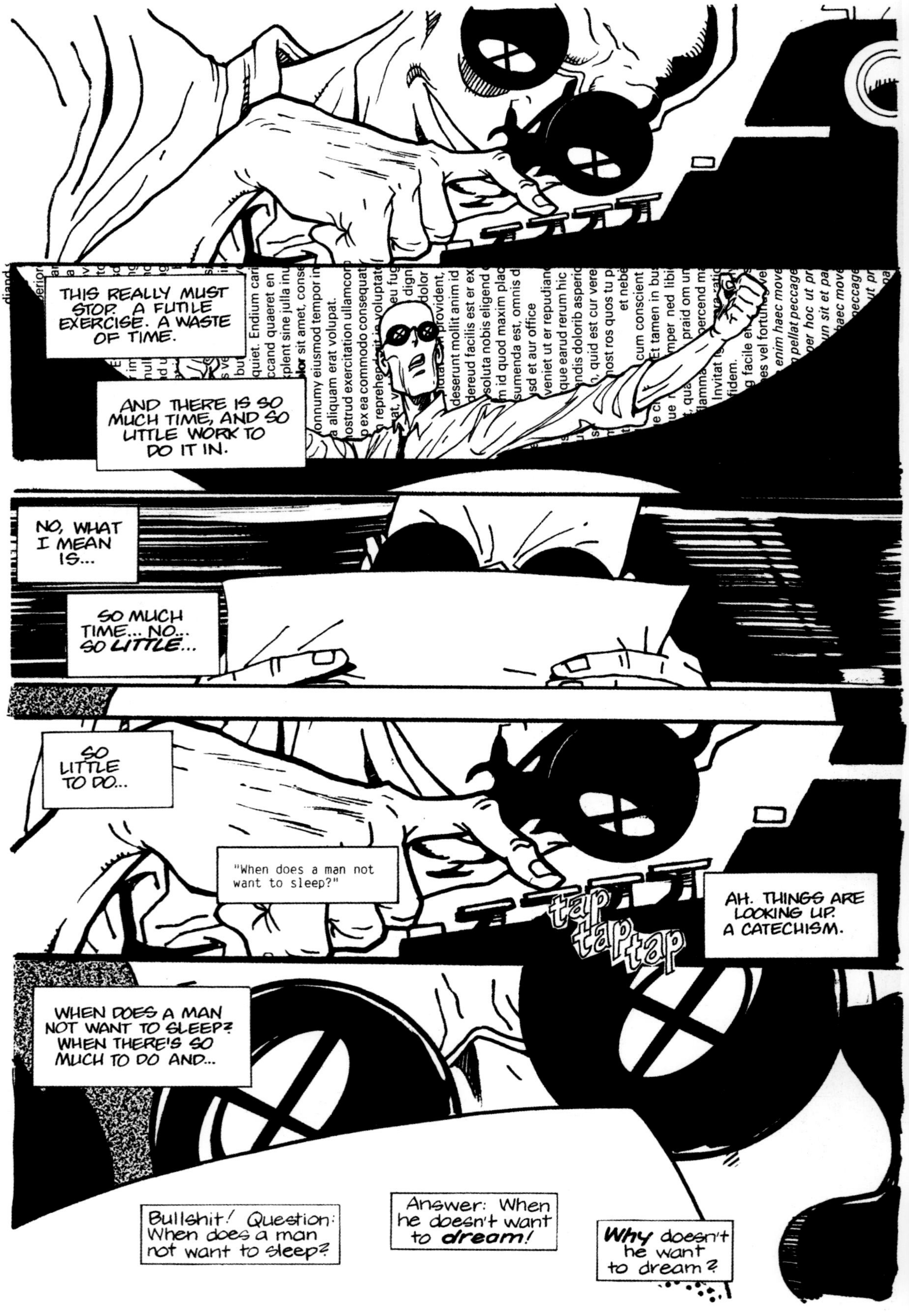
THIS REALLY MUST STOP. A FUTILE EXERCISE. A WASTE OF TIME.
AND THERE IS SO MUCH TIME, AND SO LITTLE WORK TO DO IT IN.
NO, WHAT I MEAN IS...
SO MUCH TIME... NO... SO LITTLE...
SO LITTLE TO DO...
"When does a man not want to sleep?"
tap tap tap
AH. THINGS ARE LOOKING UP. A CATECHISM.
WHEN DOES A MAN NOT WANT TO SLEEP? WHEN THERE'S SO MUCH TO DO AND...
Bullshit! Question: When does a man not want to sleep?
Answer: When he doesn't want to dream!
Why doesn't he want to dream?

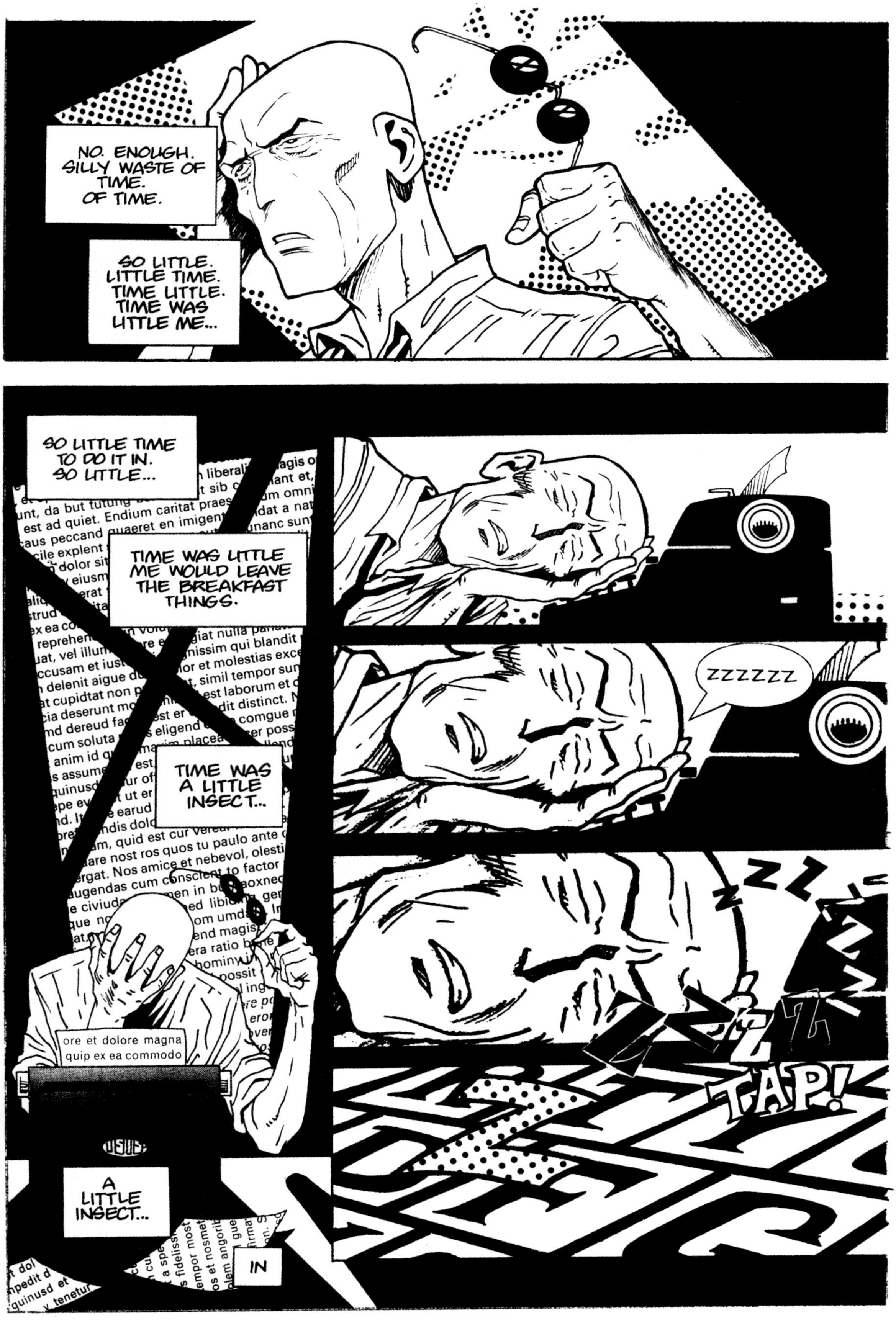

NO. ENOUGH. SILLY WASTE OF TIME. OF TIME.
SO LITTLE. LITTLE TIME. TIME LITTLE. TIME WAS LITTLE ME...
SO LITTLE TIME TO DO IT IN. SO LITTLE...
TIME WAS LITTLE ME WOULD LEAVE THE BREAKFAST THINGS.
TIME WAS A LITTLE INSECT...
ore et dolore magna
quip ex ea commodo
A LITTLE INSECT...
IN
ZZZZZZ
TAP!

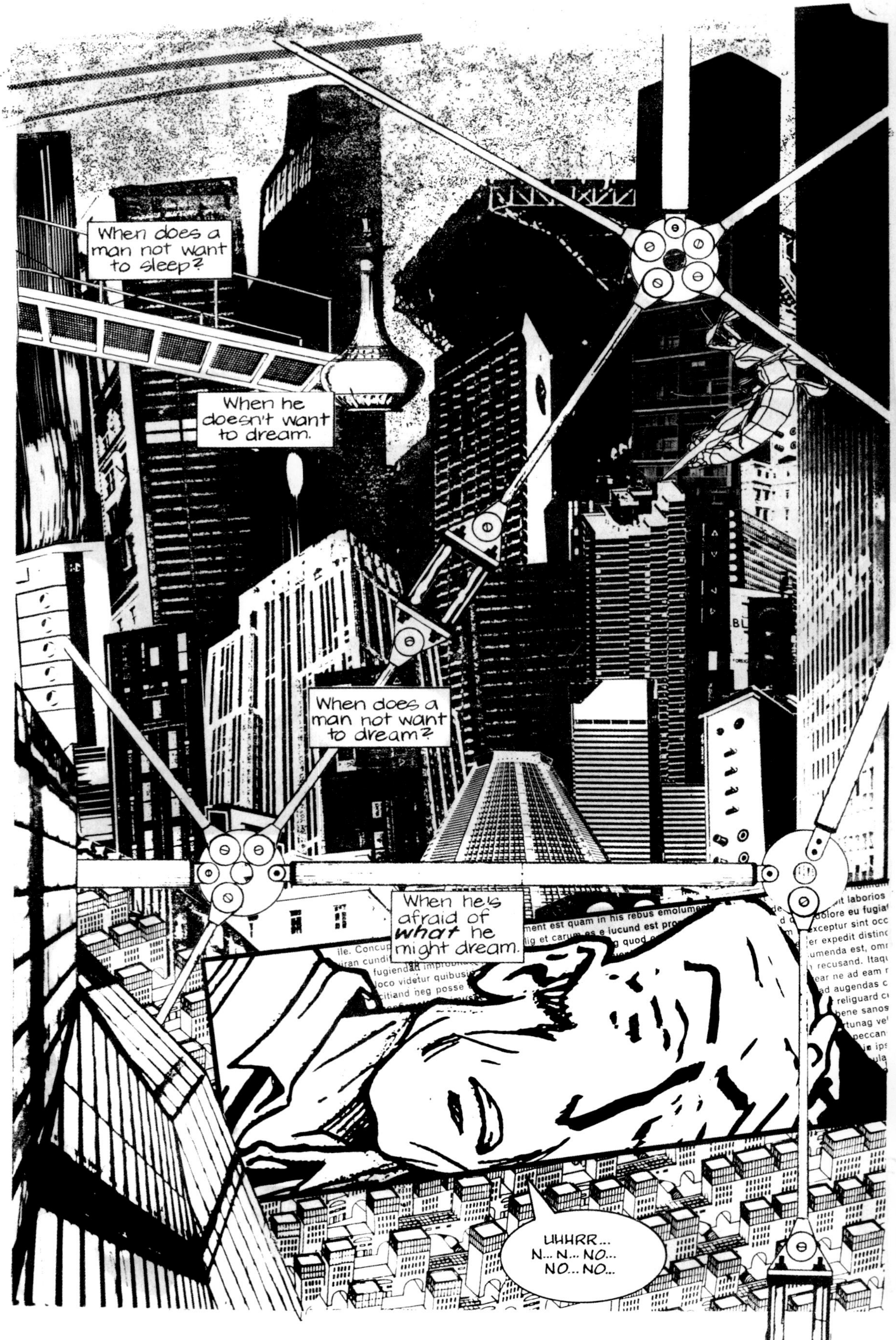
When does a man not want to sleep?
When he doesn't want to dream.
When does a man not want to dream?
When he's afraid of *what* he might dream.
UHHRR... N... N... NO... NO... NO...

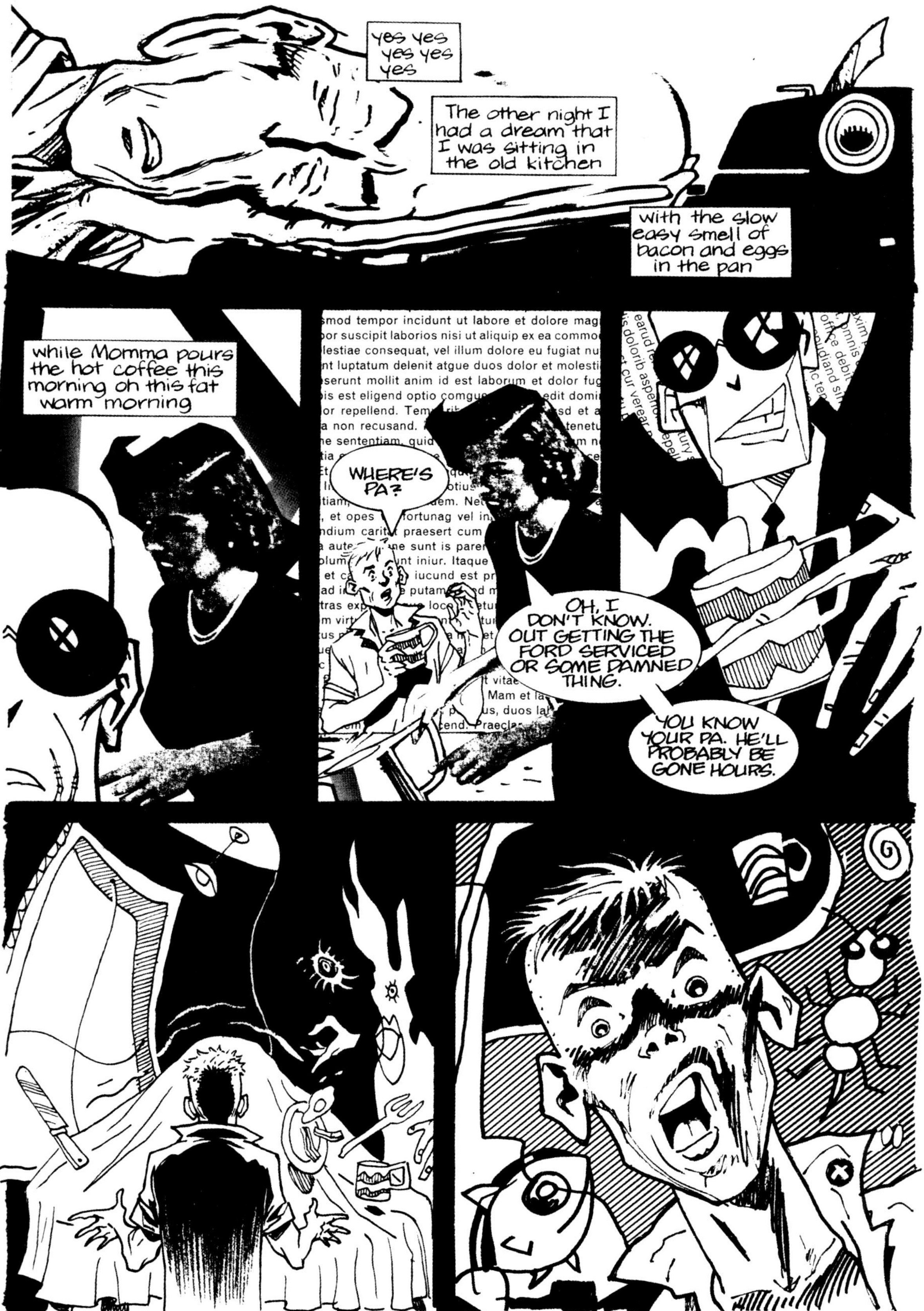
yes yes yes yes yes
The other night I had a dream that I was sitting in the old kitchen
with the slow easy smell of bacon and eggs in the pan
while Momma pours the hot coffee this morning oh this fat warm morning
WHERE'S PA?
OH, I DON'T KNOW. OUT GETTING THE FORD SERVICED OR SOME DAMNED THING.
YOU KNOW YOUR PA. HE'LL PROBABLY BE GONE HOURS.

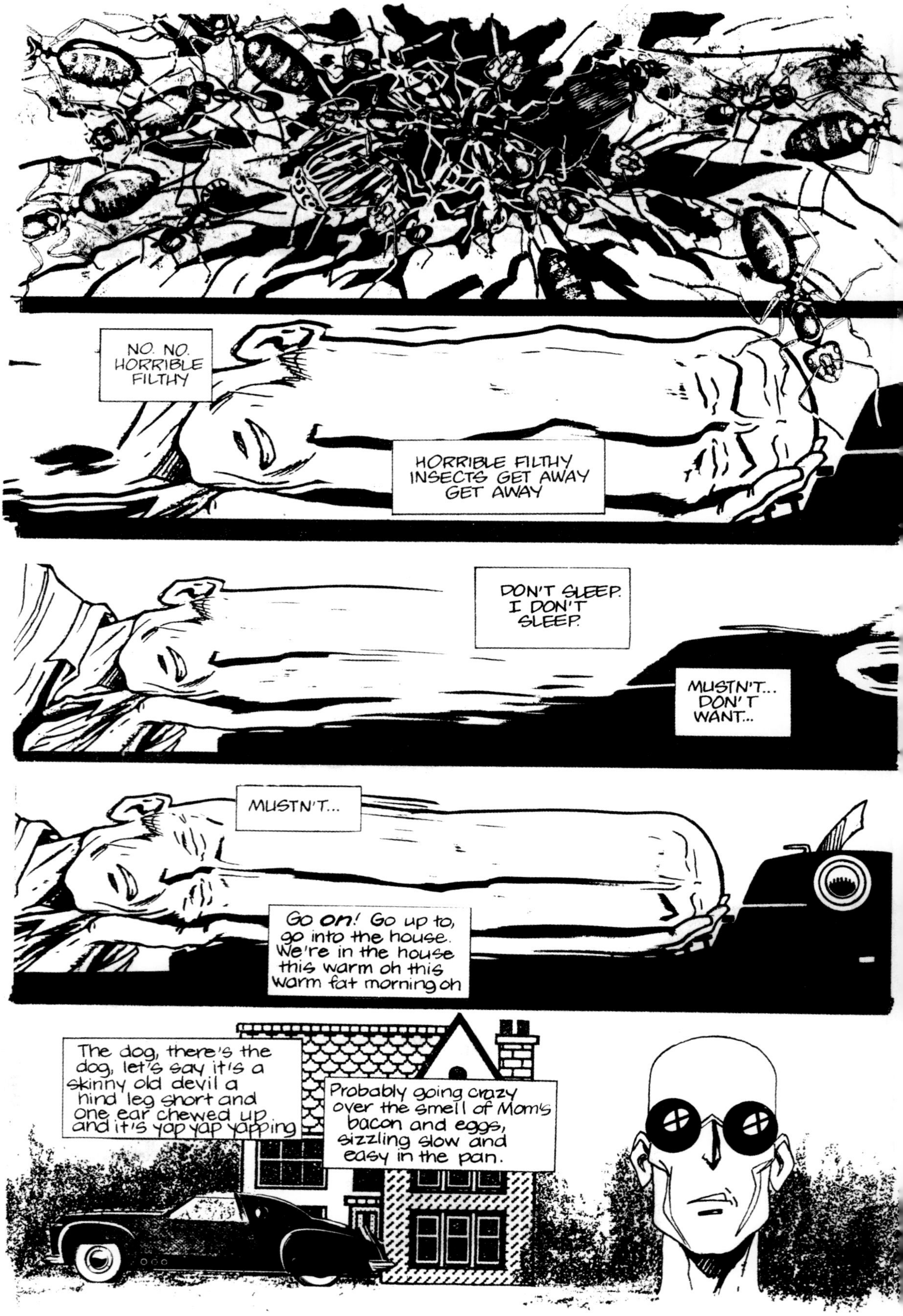
NO. NO. HORRIBLE FILTHY
HORRIBLE FILTHY INSECTS GET AWAY GET AWAY
DON'T SLEEP. I DON'T SLEEP.
MUSTN'T... DON'T WANT...
MUSTN'T...
Go on! Go up to, go into the house. We're in the house this warm oh this warm fat morning oh
The dog, there's the dog, let's say it's a skinny old devil a hind leg short and one ear chewed up and it's yap yap yapping
Probably going crazy over the smell of Mom's bacon and eggs, sizzling slow and easy in the pan.

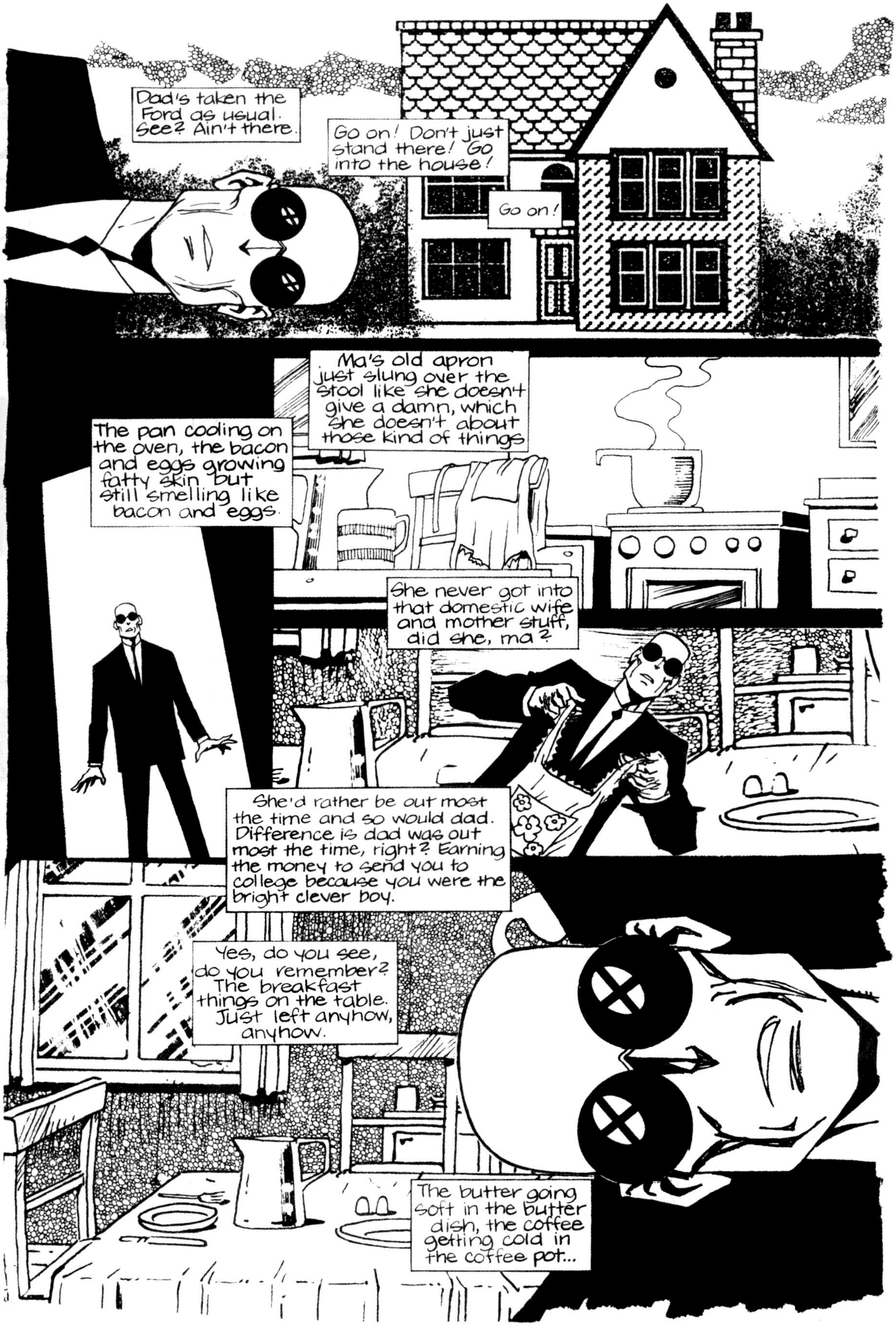
Dad's taken the Ford as usual. See? Ain't there.
Go on! Don't just stand there! Go into the house!
Go on!
Ma's old apron just slung over the stool like she doesn't give a damn, which she doesn't about those kind of things
The pan cooling on the oven, the bacon and eggs growing fatty skin but still smelling like bacon and eggs.
She never got into that domestic wife and mother stuff, did she, ma?
She'd rather be out most the time and so would dad. Difference is dad was out most the time, right? Earning the money to send you to college because you were the bright clever boy.
Yes, do you see, do you remember? The breakfast things on the table. Just left anyhow, anyhow.
The butter going soft in the butter dish, the coffee getting cold in the coffee pot...

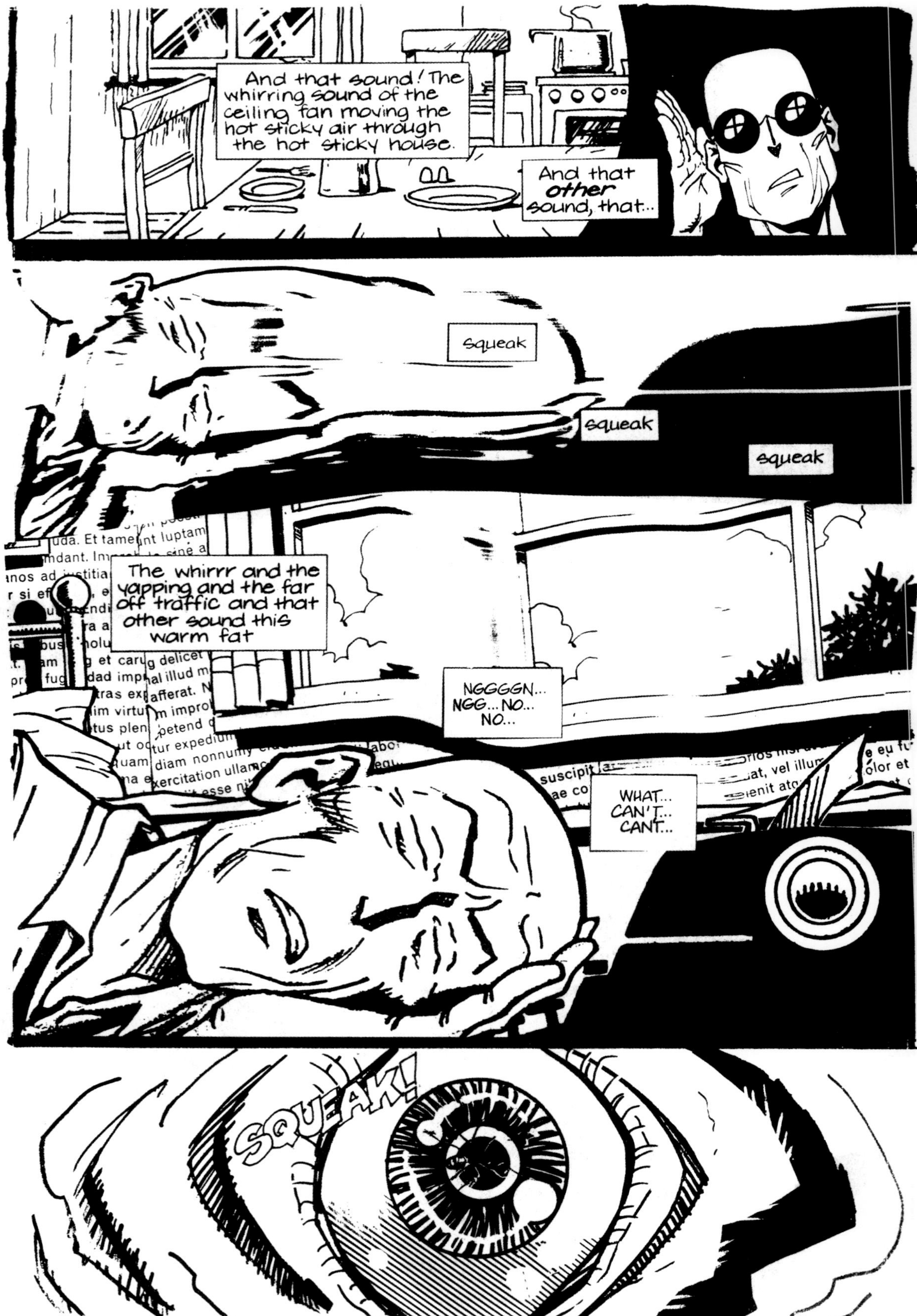
And that sound! The whirring sound of the ceiling fan moving the hot sticky air through the hot sticky house.
And that other sound, that...
squeak
squeak
squeak
The whirrr and the yapping and the far off traffic and that other sound this warm fat
NGGGGN... NGG... NO... NO...
WHAT... CAN'T... CANT...
SQUEAK!

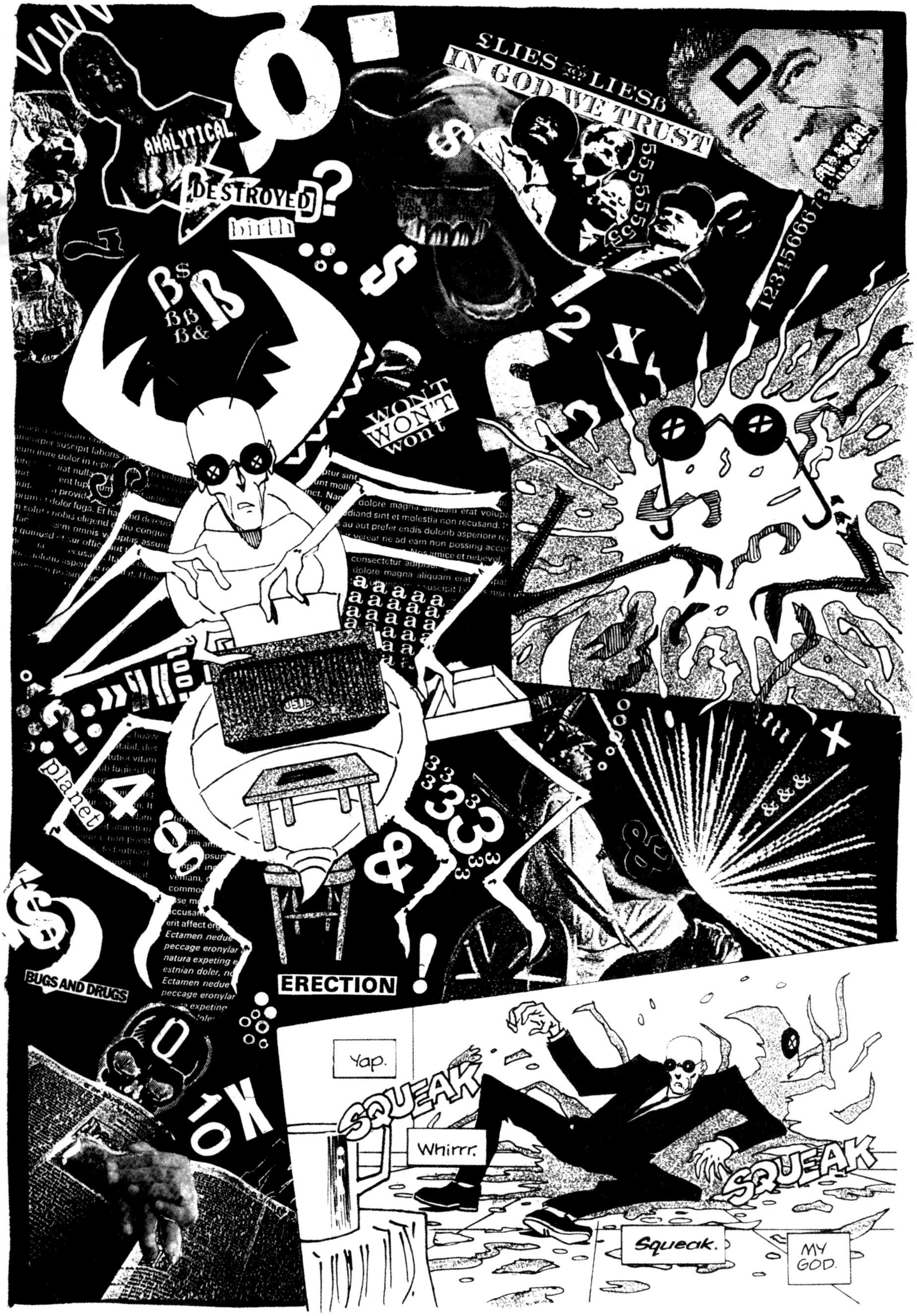
ANALYTICAL
DESTROYED
birth
LIES LIES
IN GOD WE TRUST
WON'T
WON'T
won't
planet
BUGS AND DRUGS
ERECTION
Yap.
SQUEAK
Whirrr.
SQUEAK
Squeak.
MY GOD.

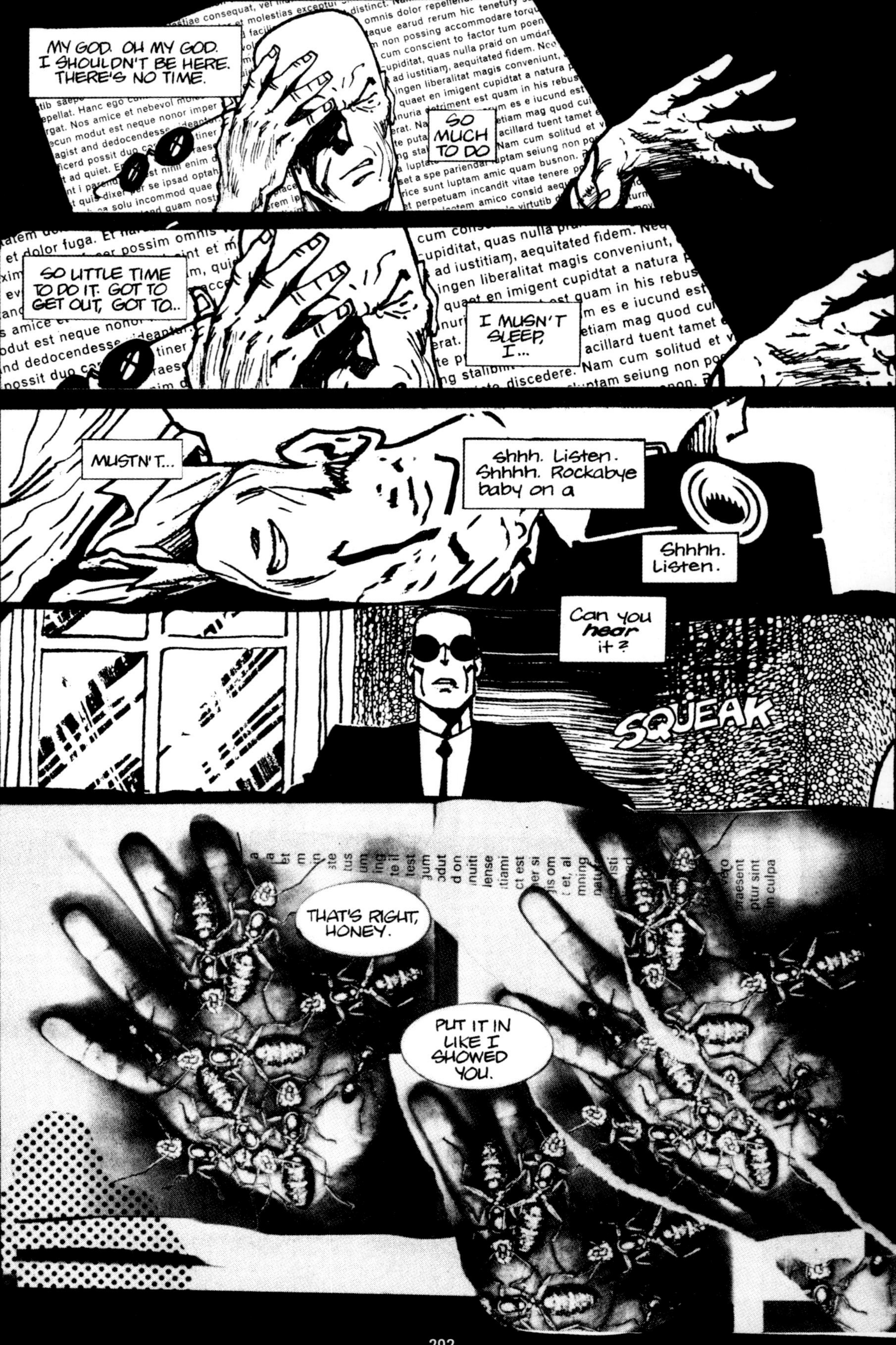
MY GOD. OH MY GOD. I SHOULDN'T BE HERE. THERE'S NO TIME.
SO MUCH TO DO
SO LITTLE TIME TO DO IT. GOT TO GET OUT, GOT TO...
I MUSN'T SLEEP, I...
MUSTN'T...
Shhh. Listen. Shhhh. Rockabye baby on a
Shhhh. Listen.
Can you *hear* it?
SQUEAK
THAT'S RIGHT, HONEY.
PUT IT IN LIKE I SHOWED YOU.

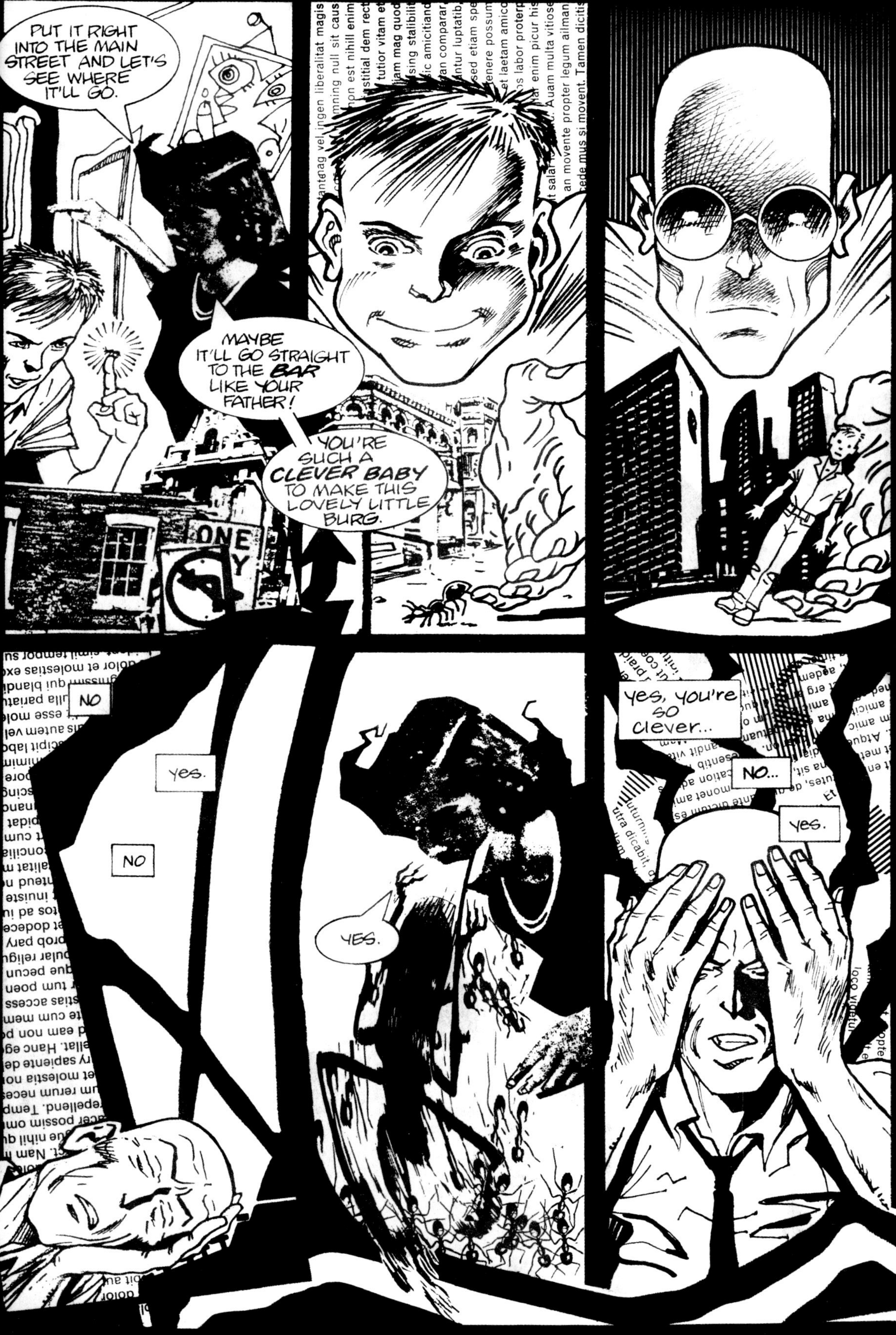
PUT IT RIGHT INTO THE MAIN STREET AND LET'S SEE WHERE IT'LL GO.
MAYBE IT'LL GO STRAIGHT TO THE BAR LIKE YOUR FATHER!
YOU'RE SUCH A CLEVER BABY TO MAKE THIS LOVELY LITTLE BURG.
ONE
NO
YES.
NO
YES.
Yes, you're so clever...
NO...
YES.

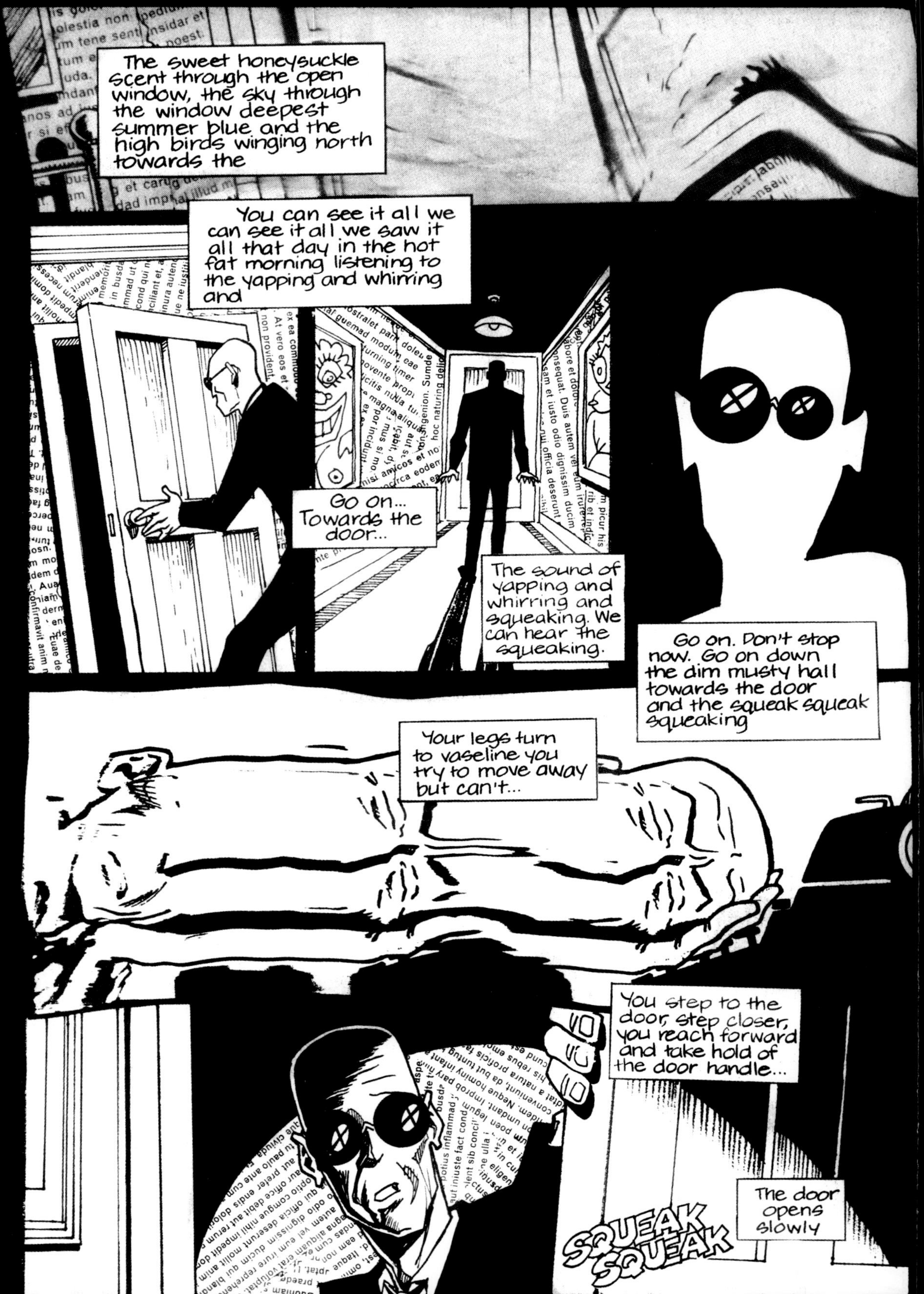

The sweet honeysuckle scent through the open window, the sky through the window deepest summer blue and the high birds winging north towards the
You can see it all we can see it all we saw it all that day in the hot fat morning listening to the yapping and whirring and
Go on... Towards the door...
The sound of yapping and whirring and squeaking. We can hear the squeaking.
Go on. Don't stop now. Go on down the dim musty hall towards the door and the squeak squeak squeaking
Your legs turn to vaseline you try to move away but can't...
You step to the door, step closer, you reach forward and take hold of the door handle...
SQUEAK SQUEAK
The door opens slowly

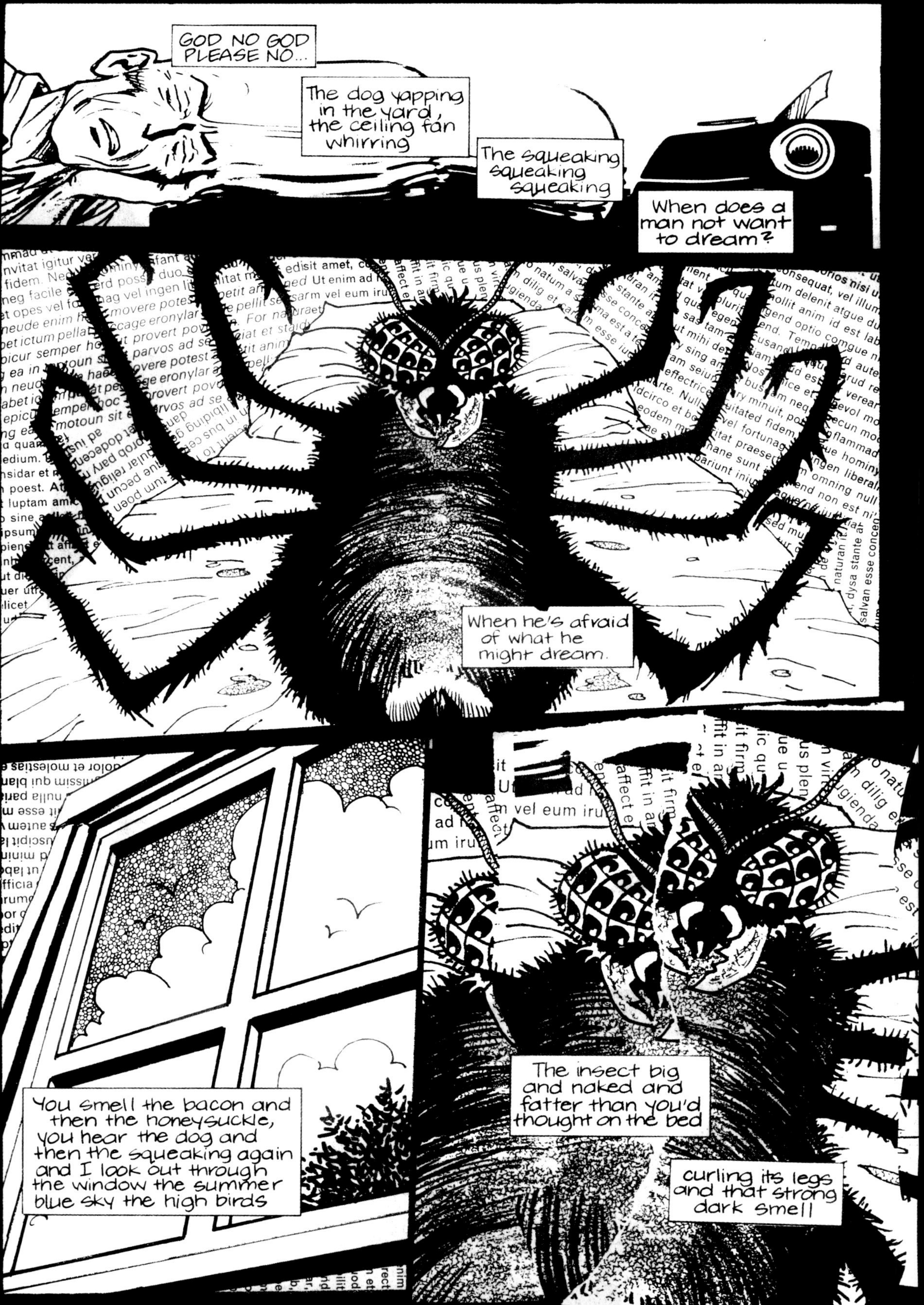
GOD NO GOD PLEASE NO...
The dog yapping in the yard, the ceiling fan whirring
The squeaking squeaking squeaking
When does a man not want to dream?
When he's afraid of what he might dream.
You smell the bacon and then the honeysuckle, you hear the dog and then the squeaking again and I look out through the window the summer blue sky the high birds
The insect big and naked and fatter than you'd thought on the bed
curling its legs and that strong dark smell

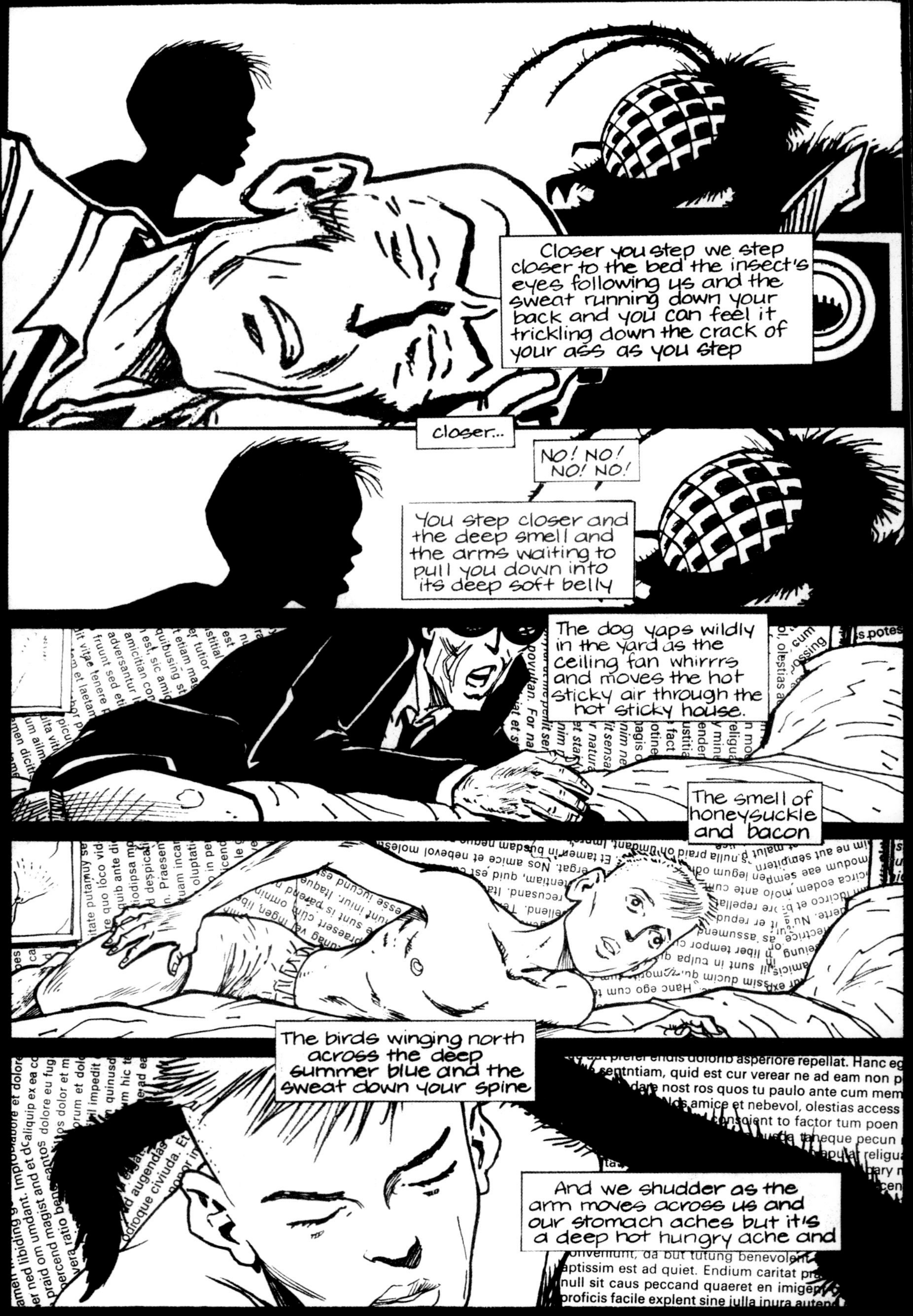
Closer you step we step closer to the bed the insect's eyes following us and the sweat running down your back and you can feel it trickling down the crack of your ass as you step
closer...
NO! NO! NO! NO!
You step closer and the deep smell and the arms waiting to pull you down into its deep soft belly
The dog yaps wildly in the yard as the ceiling fan whirrrs and moves the hot sticky air through the hot sticky house.
The smell of honeysuckle and bacon
The birds winging north across the deep summer blue and the sweat down your spine
And we shudder as the arm moves across us and our stomach aches but it's a deep hot hungry ache and

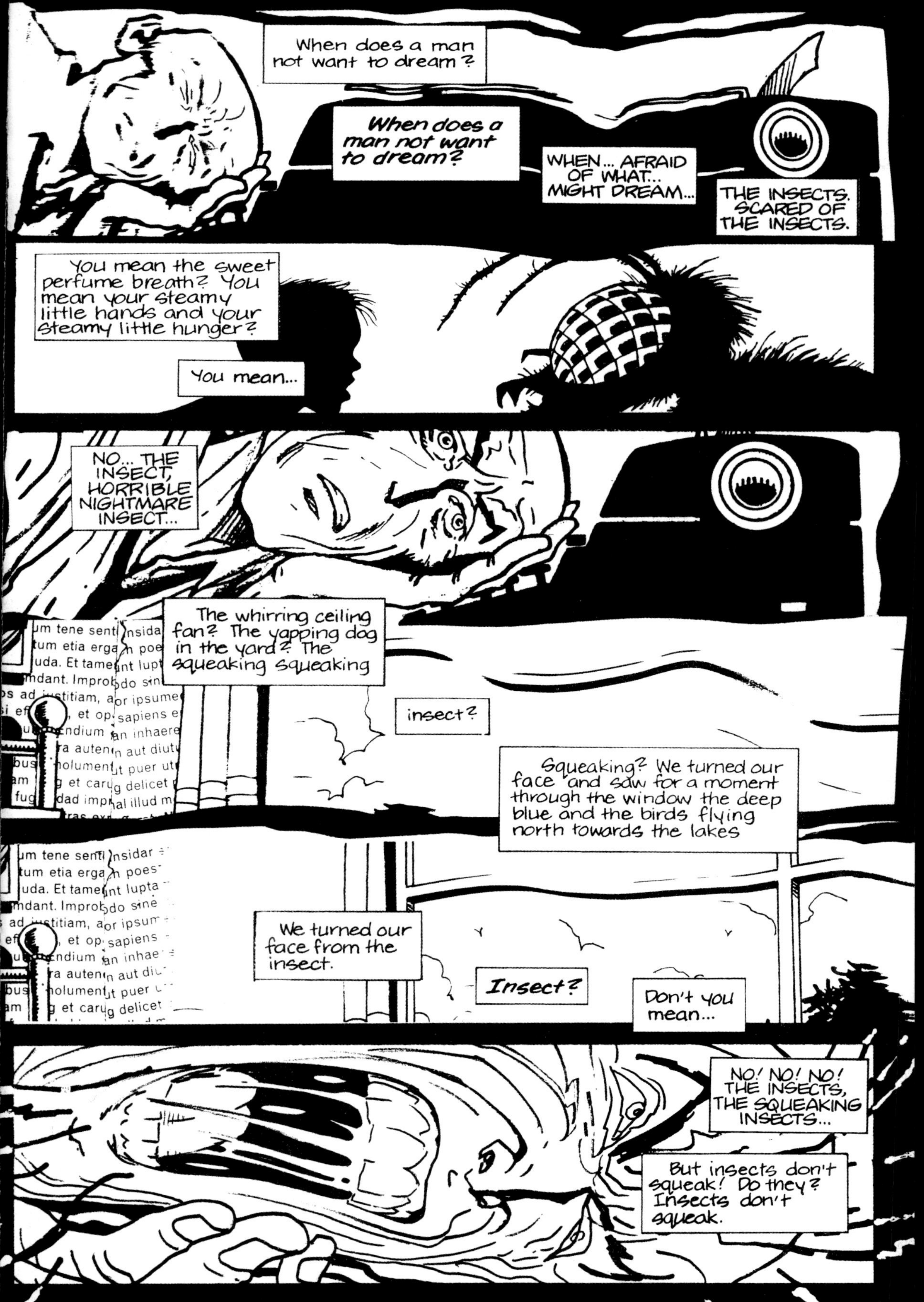
When does a man not want to dream?
When does a man not want to dream?
WHEN... AFRAID OF WHAT... MIGHT DREAM...
THE INSECTS. SCARED OF THE INSECTS.
You mean the sweet perfume breath? You mean your steamy little hands and your steamy little hunger?
You mean...
NO... THE INSECT, HORRIBLE NIGHTMARE INSECT...
The whirring ceiling fan? The yapping dog in the yard? The squeaking squeaking
insect?
Squeaking? We turned our face and saw for a moment through the window the deep blue and the birds flying north towards the lakes
We turned our face from the insect.
Insect?
Don't you mean...
NO! NO! NO! THE INSECTS, THE SQUEAKING INSECTS...
But insects don't squeak! Do they? Insects don't squeak.

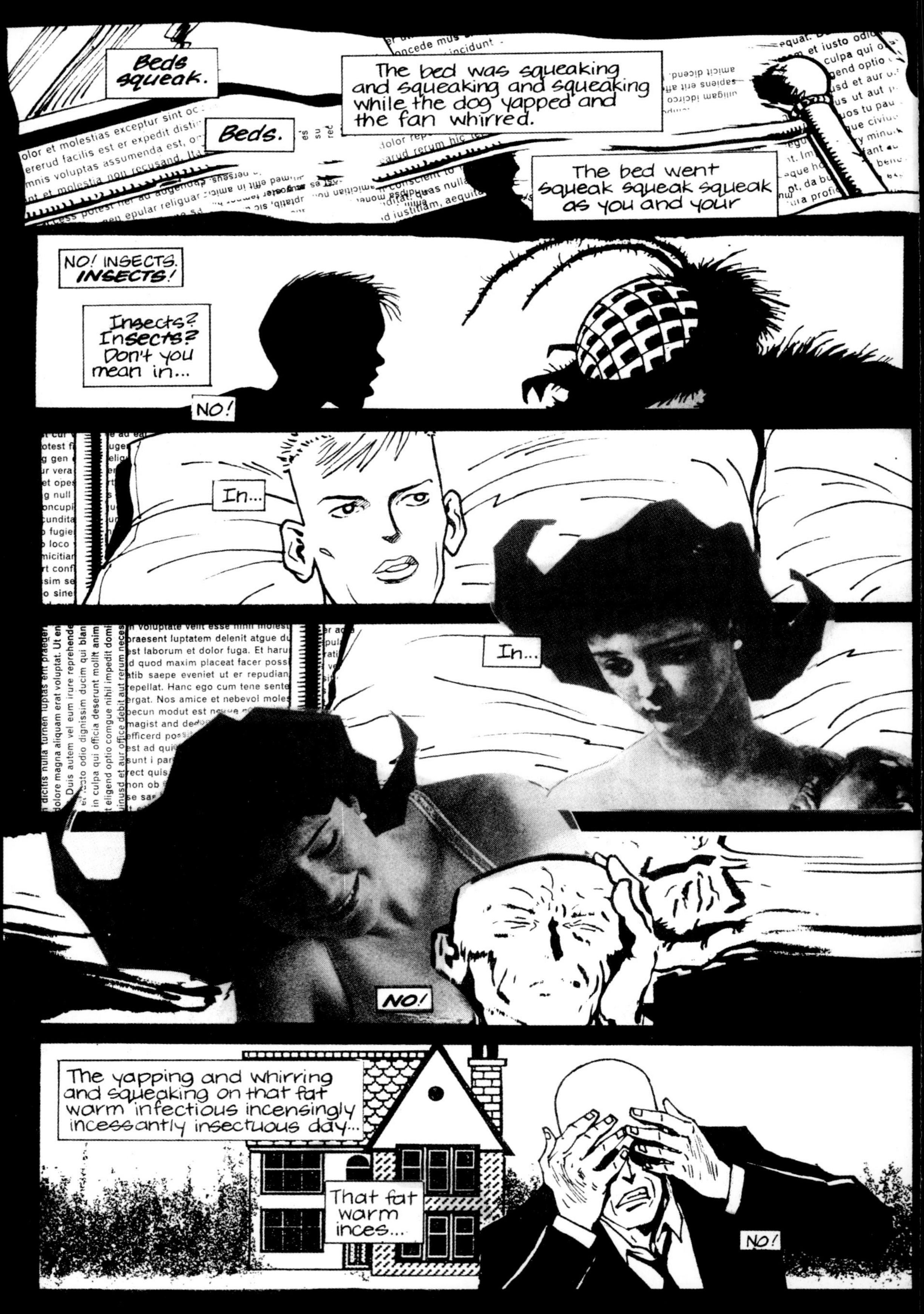

Beds squeak.
Beds.
The bed was squeaking and squeaking and squeaking while the dog yapped and the fan whirred.
The bed went squeak squeak squeak as you and your
NO! INSECTS. INSECTS!
Insects? Insects? Don't you mean in...
NO!
In...
In...
NO!
The yapping and whirring and squeaking on that fat warm infectious incensingly incessantly insectuous day...
That fat warm inces...
NO!

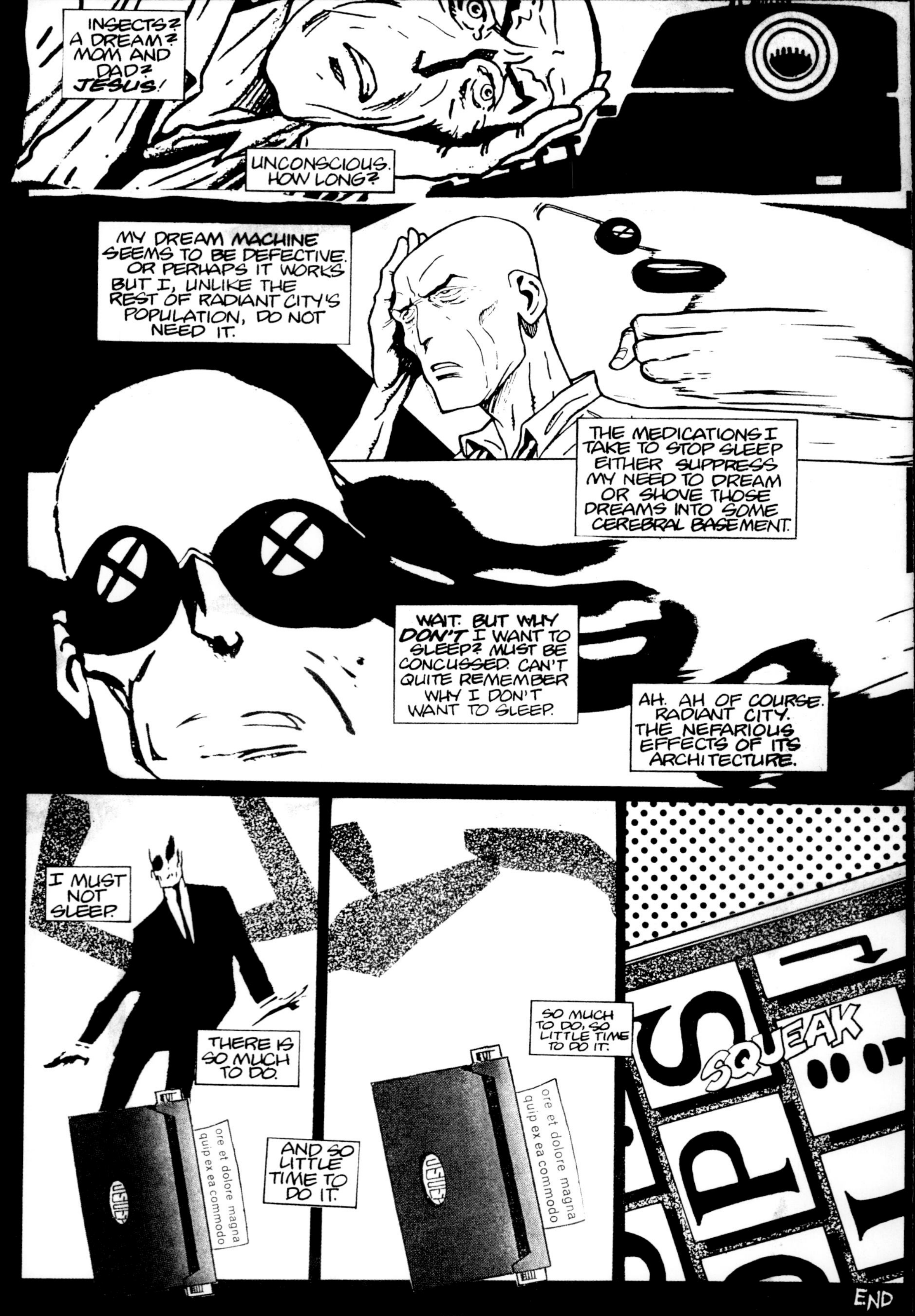
INSECTS? A DREAM? MOM AND DAD? JESUS!
UNCONSCIOUS. HOW LONG?
MY DREAM MACHINE SEEMS TO BE DEFECTIVE. OR PERHAPS IT WORKS BUT I, UNLIKE THE REST OF RADIANT CITY'S POPULATION, DO NOT NEED IT.
THE MEDICATIONS I TAKE TO STOP SLEEP EITHER SUPPRESS MY NEED TO DREAM OR SHOVE THOSE DREAMS INTO SOME CEREBRAL BASEMENT.
WAIT. BUT WHY DON'T I WANT TO SLEEP? MUST BE CONCUSSED. CAN'T QUITE REMEMBER WHY I DON'T WANT TO SLEEP.
AH. AH OF COURSE. RADIANT CITY. THE NEFARIOUS EFFECTS OF ITS ARCHITECTURE.
I MUST NOT SLEEP.
THERE IS SO MUCH TO DO.
AND SO LITTLE TIME TO DO IT.
ore et dolore magna quip ex ea commodo
SO MUCH TO DO, SO LITTLE TIME TO DO IT.
ore et dolore magna quip ex ea commodo
SQUEAK
END

SOMNOPOLIS: CITY OF A THOUSAND FUTILE DREAMS, CITY OF A MILLION UNTOLD NIGHTMARES.

MR. X: WINDOWS

A VIEW OF LIFE THROUGH THE EYES OF A CITY LIVING ON THE EDGE OF FEAR...

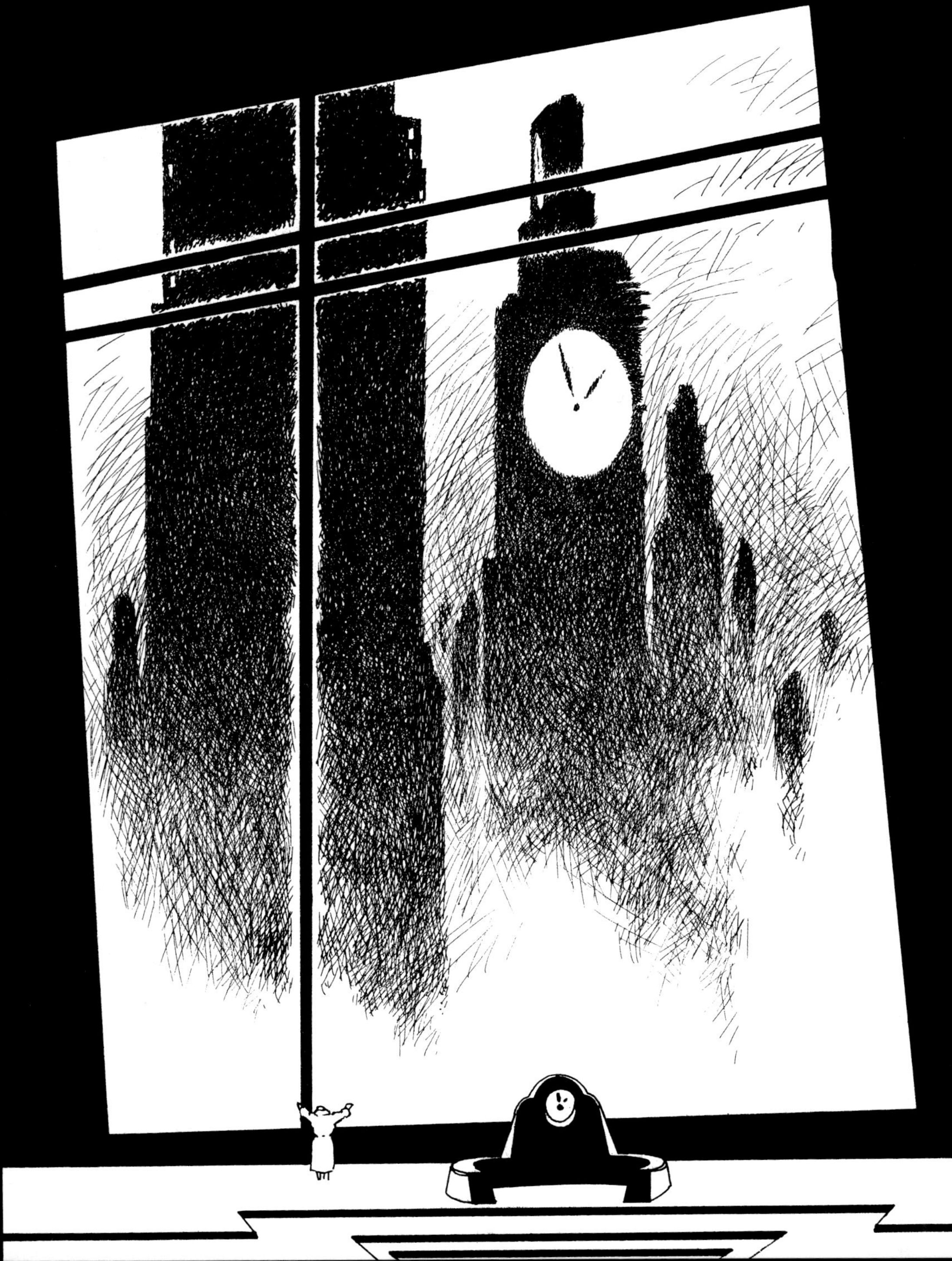

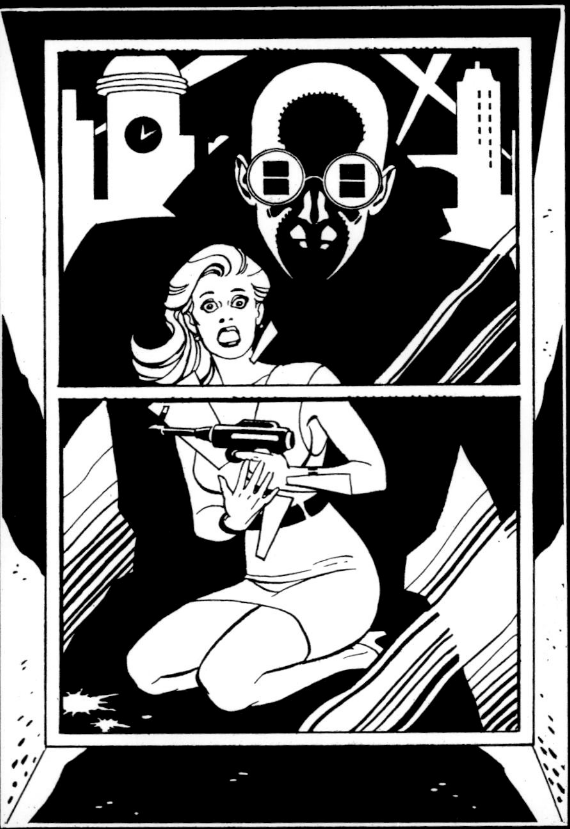

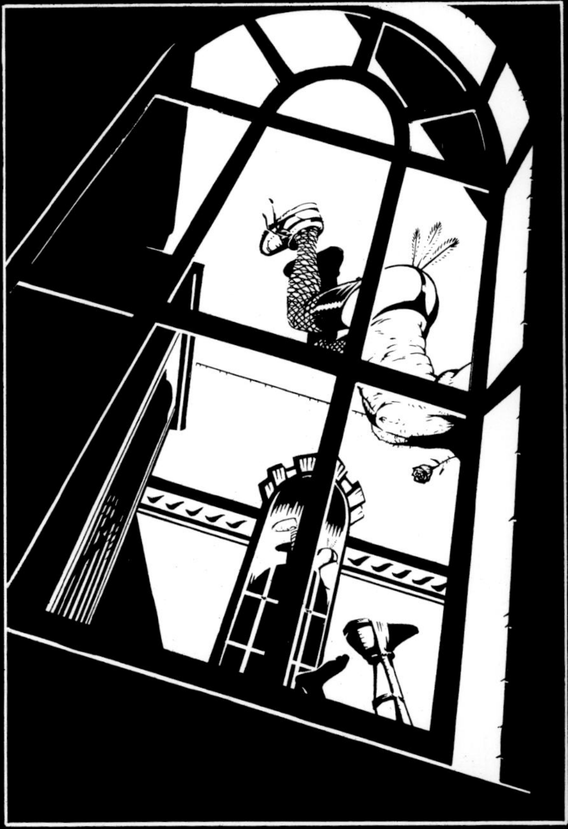

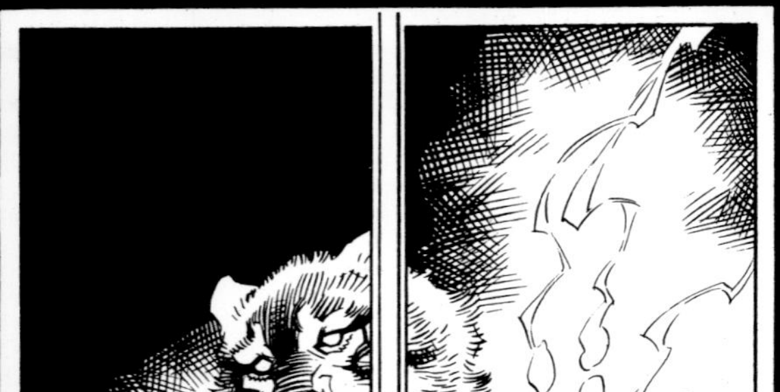
Mignola

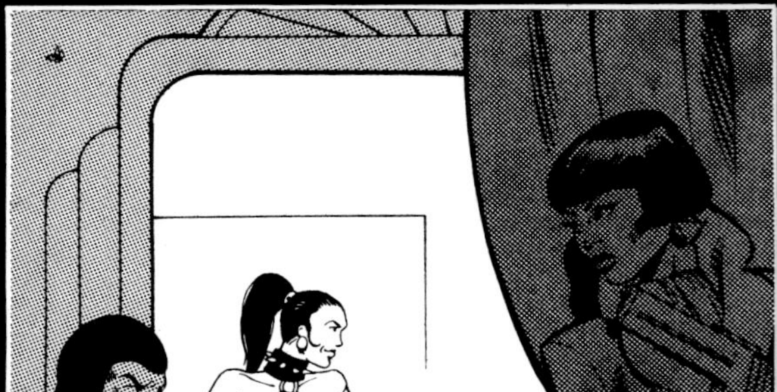

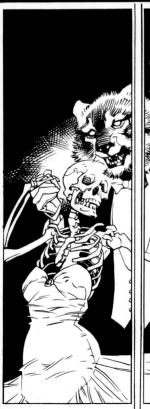

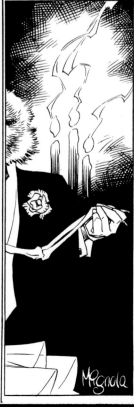

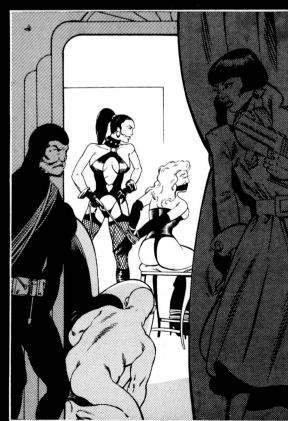

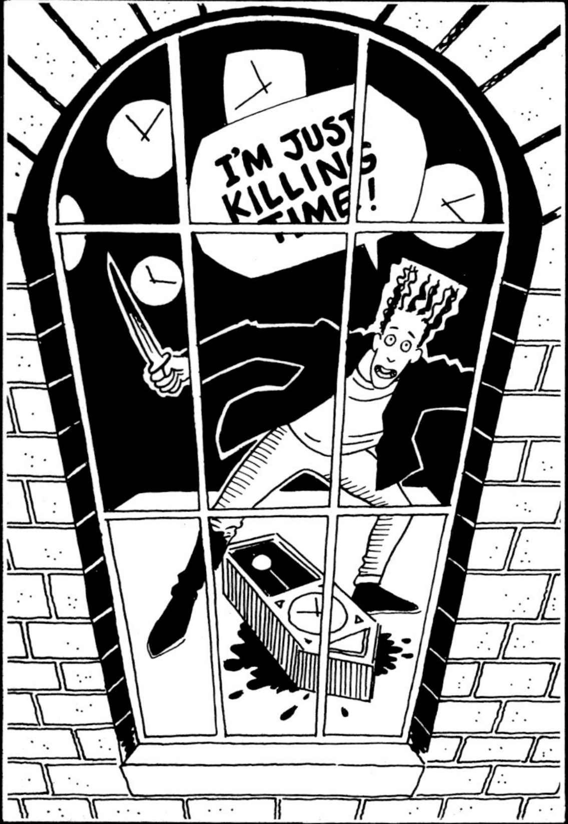
I'M JUST KILLING TIME!

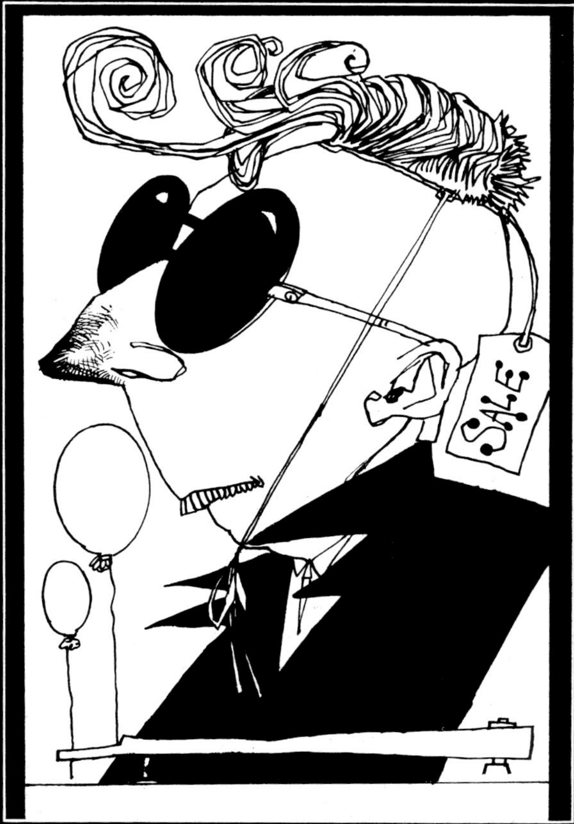
SALE

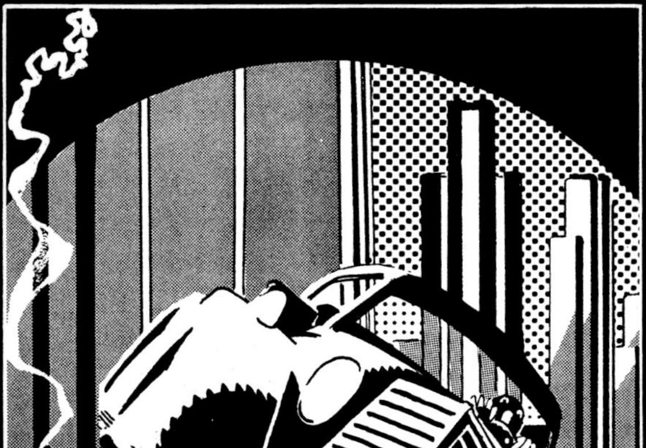
SAME OLD, SAME OLD...
'89

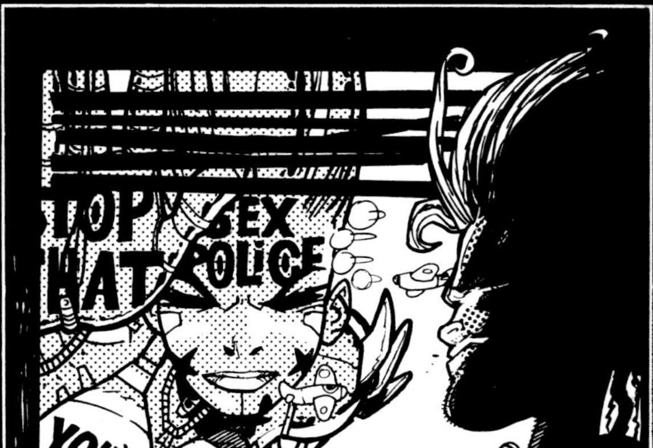
SEX
POLICE
YOU'LL GO

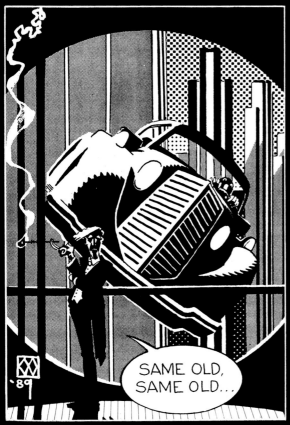

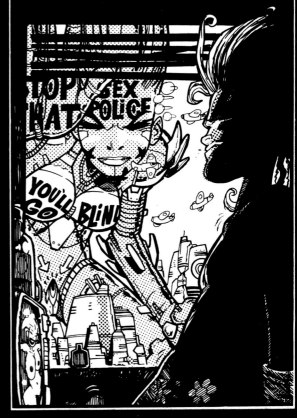

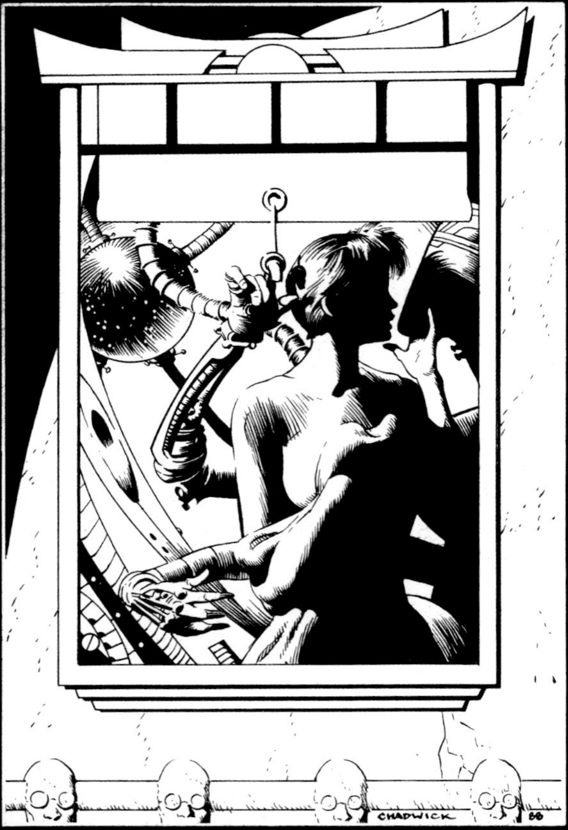
CHADWICK 88

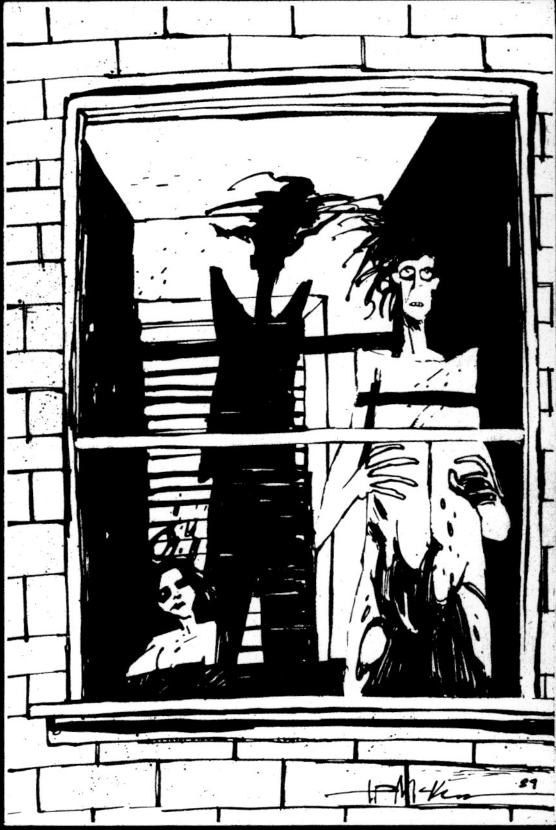

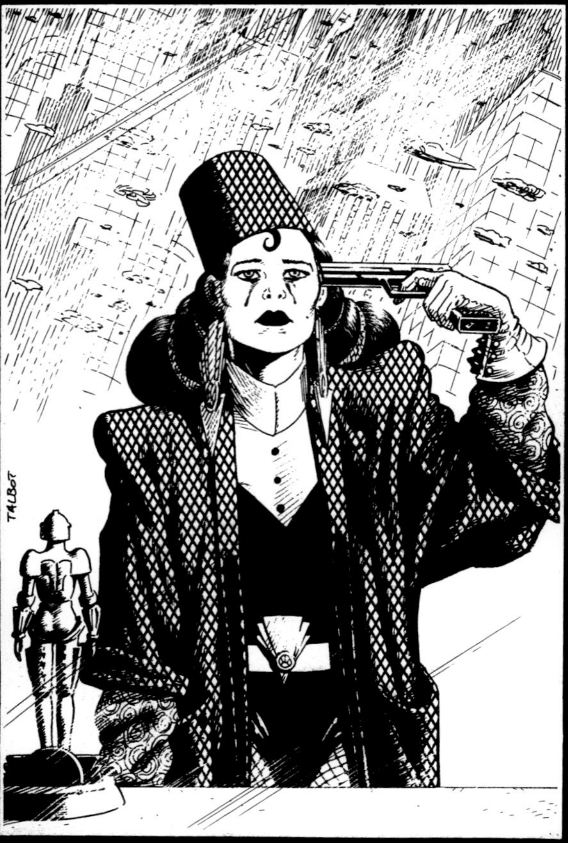
TALBOT

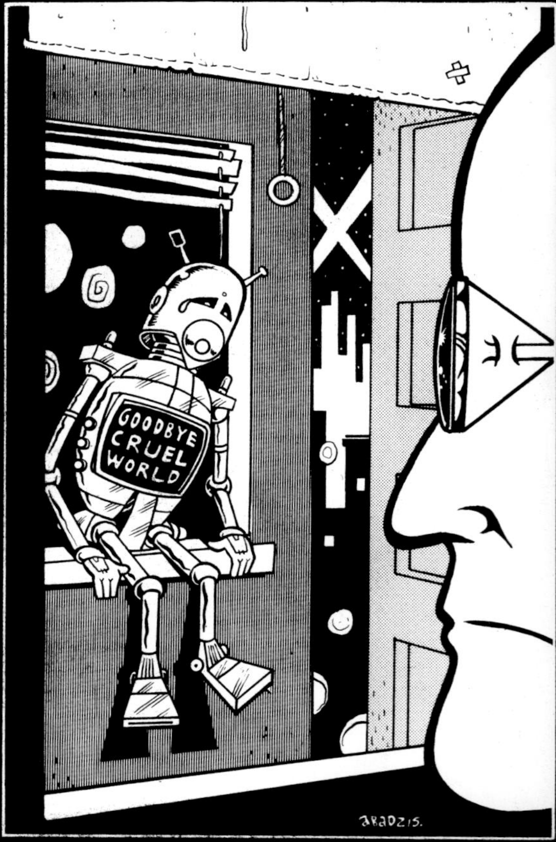
GOODBYE
CRUEL
WORLD

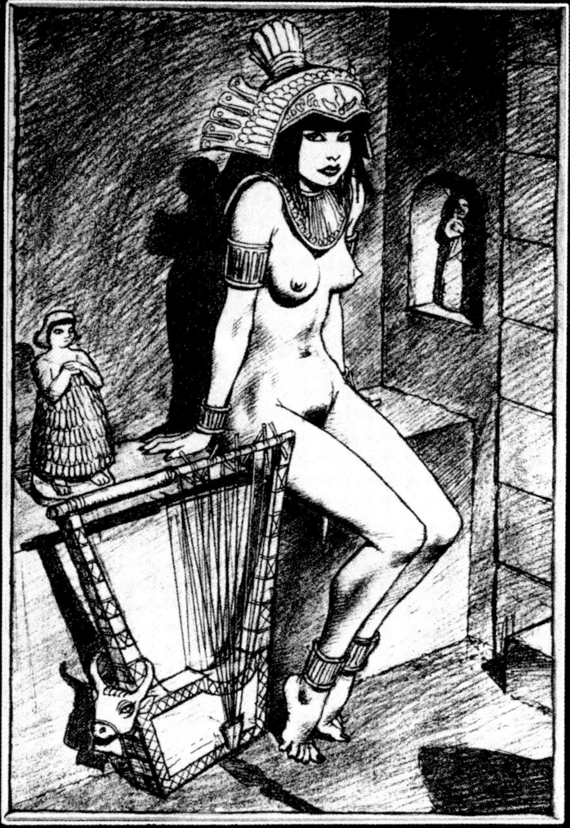

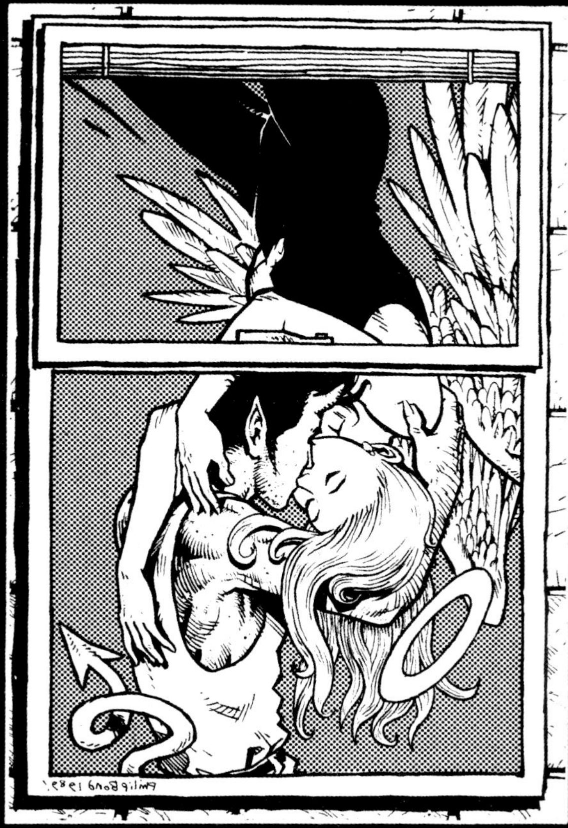
PhilipBond 1989.

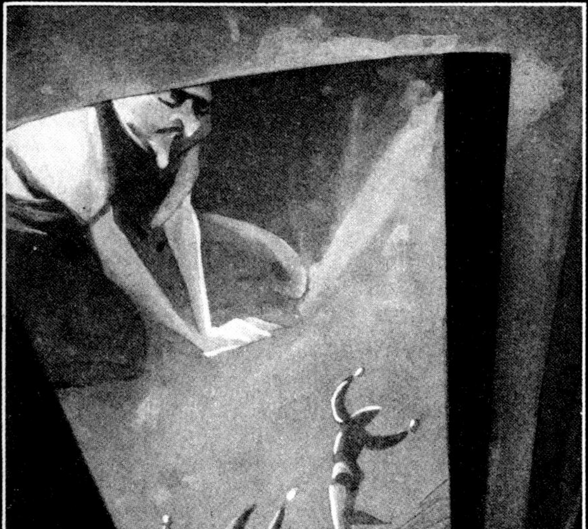

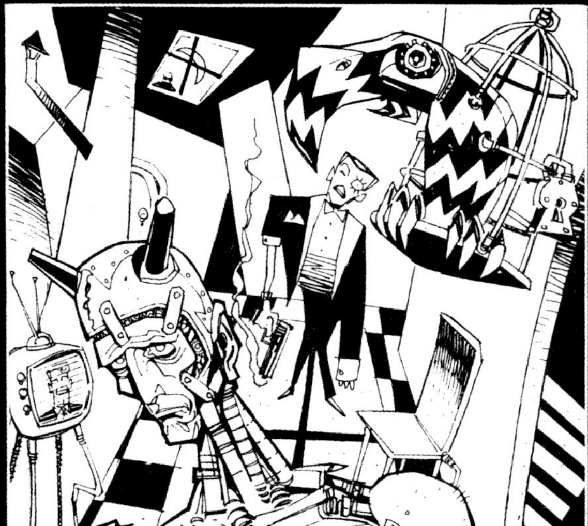
MARKS THE SPOT
REX
K.O.

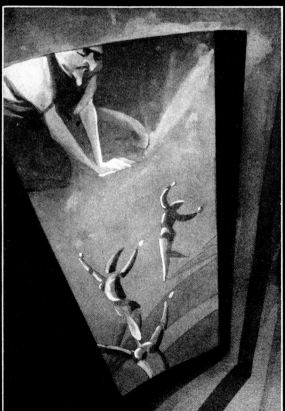

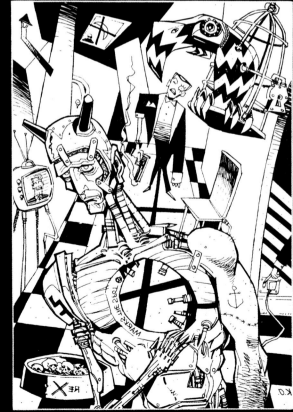

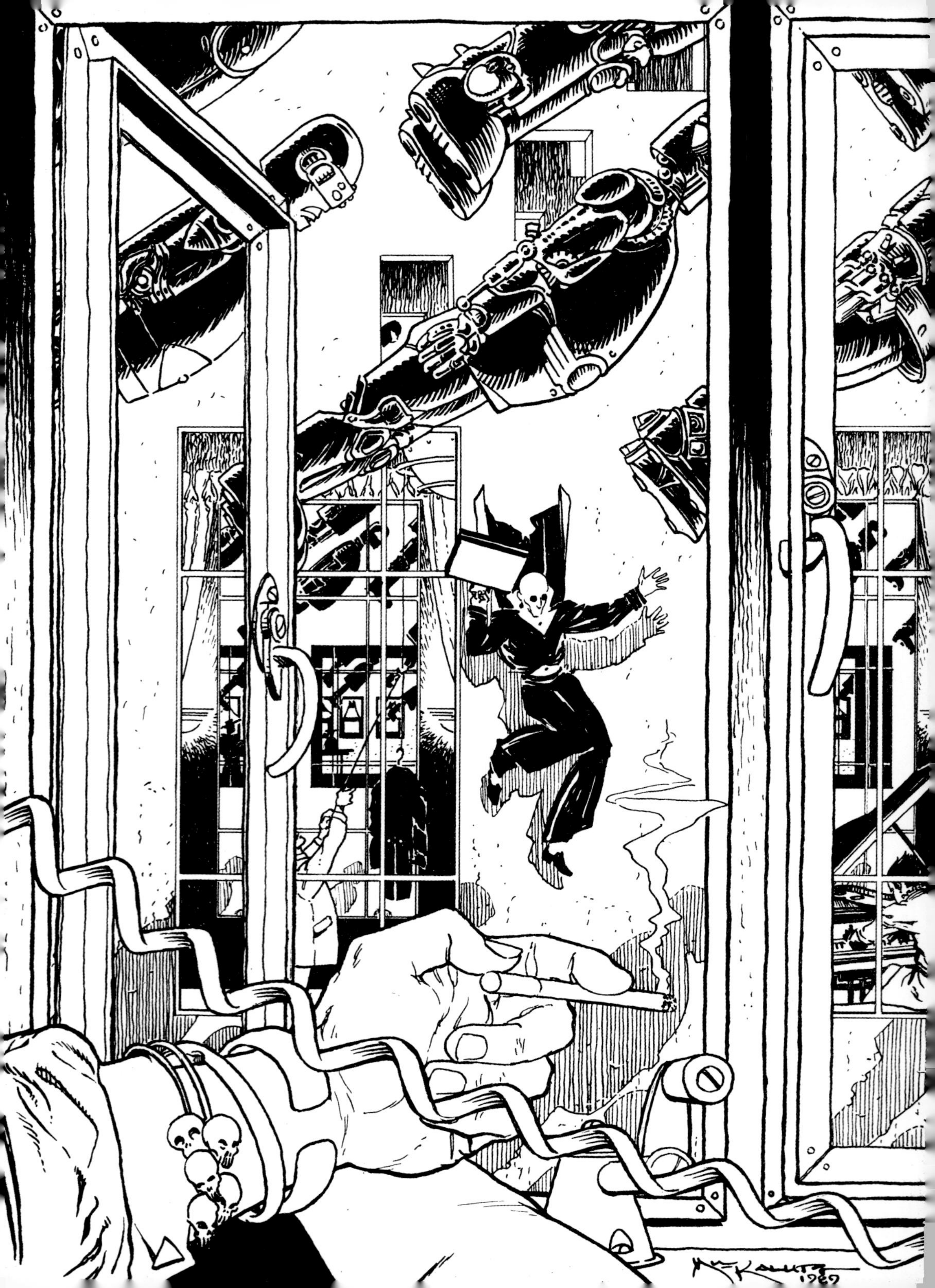

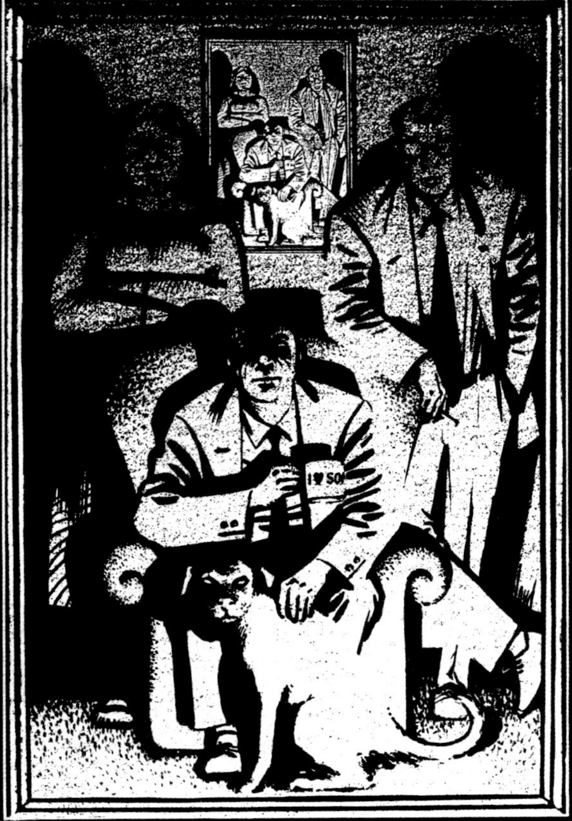

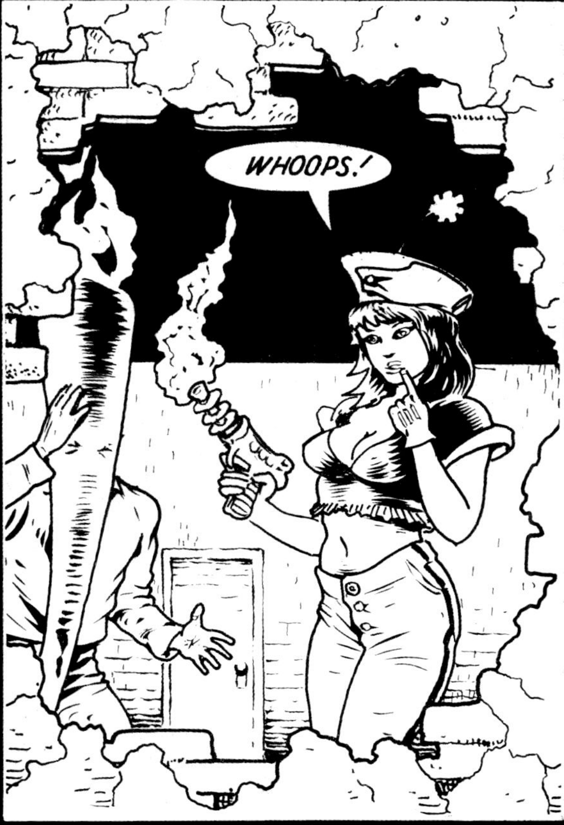
WHOOPS!

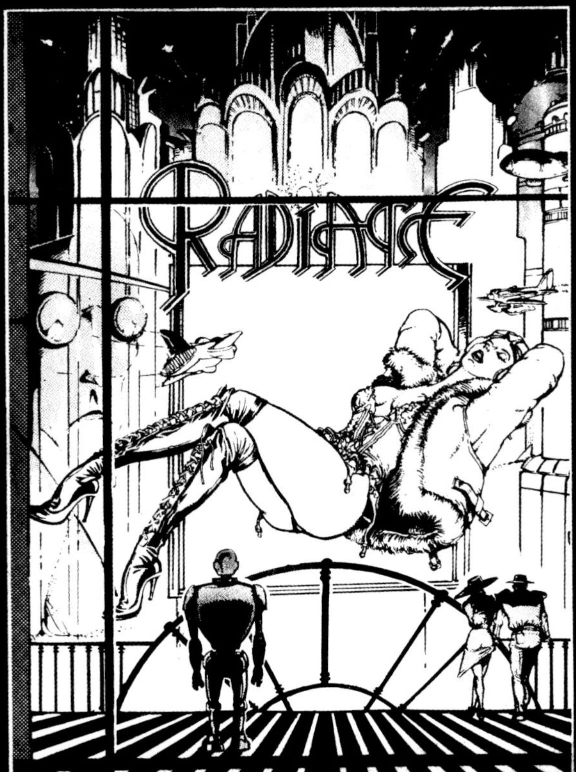
RADIANCE

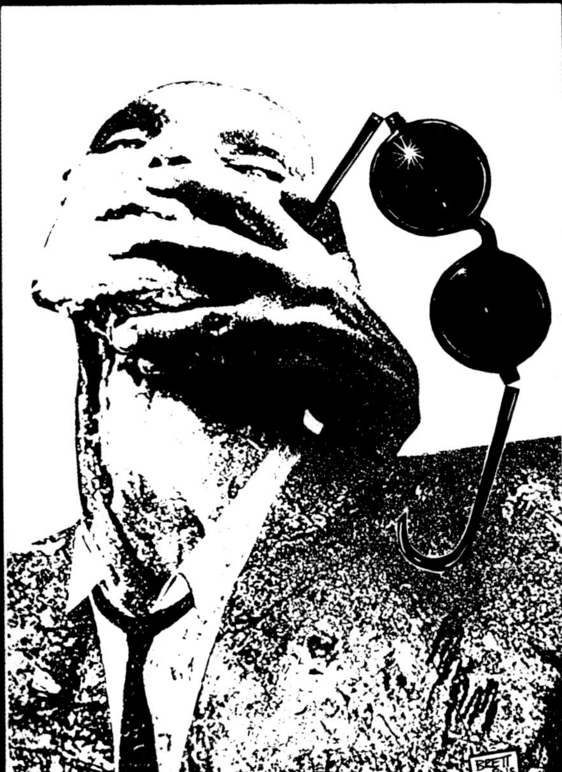
BRETT EWINS

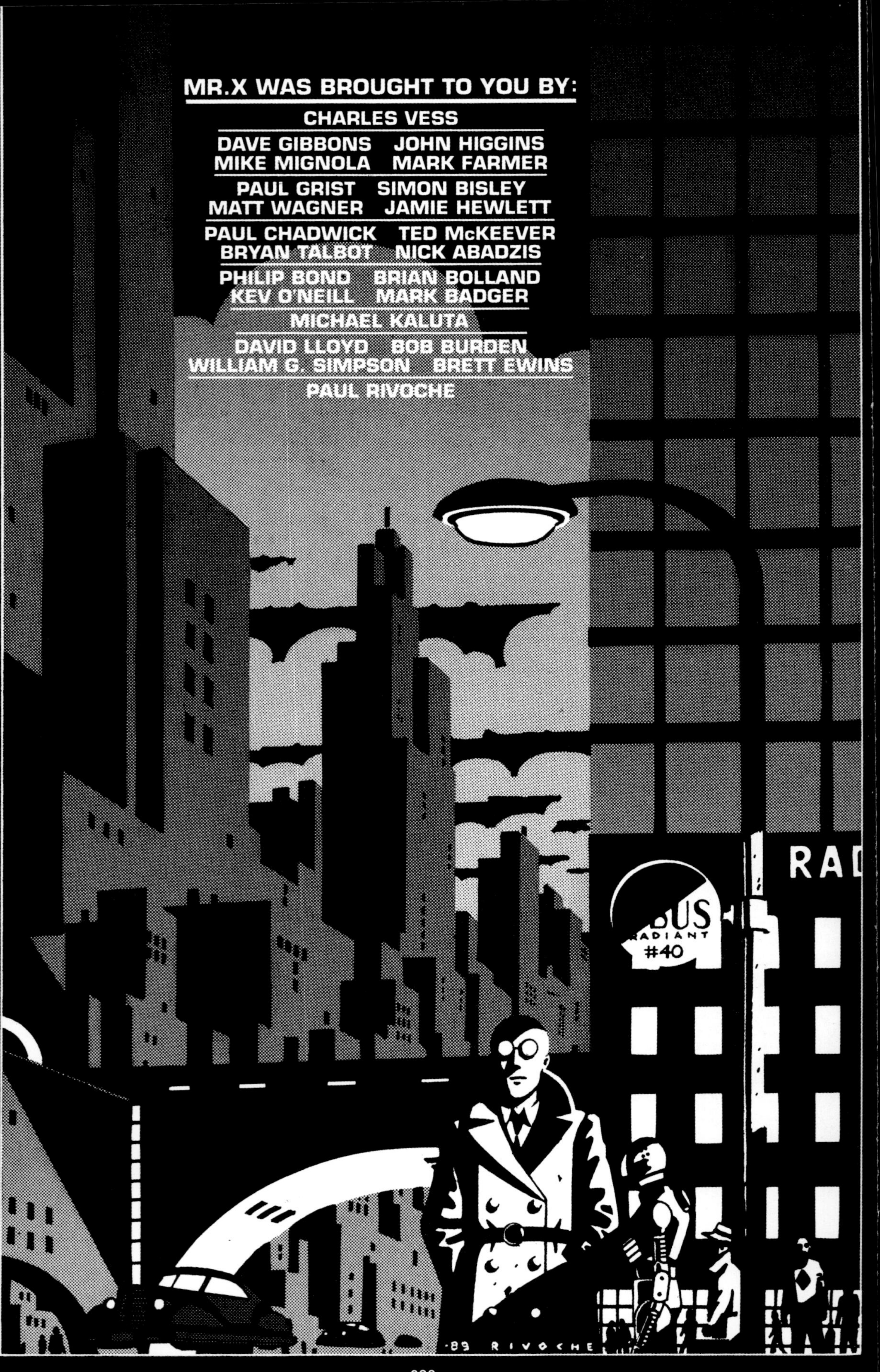
MR.X WAS BROUGHT TO YOU BY:
CHARLES VESS
DAVE GIBBONS JOHN HIGGINS
MIKE MIGNOLA MARK FARMER
PAUL GRIST SIMON BISLEY
MATT WAGNER JAMIE HEWLETT
PAUL CHADWICK TED McKEEVER
BRYAN TALBOT NICK ABADZIS
PHILIP BOND BRIAN BOLLAND
KEV O'NEILL MARK BADGER
MICHAEL KALUTA
DAVID LLOYD BOB BURDEN
WILLIAM G. SIMPSON BRETT EWINS
PAUL RIVOCHE
RA
BUS
RADIANT
#40
'89 RIVOCHE

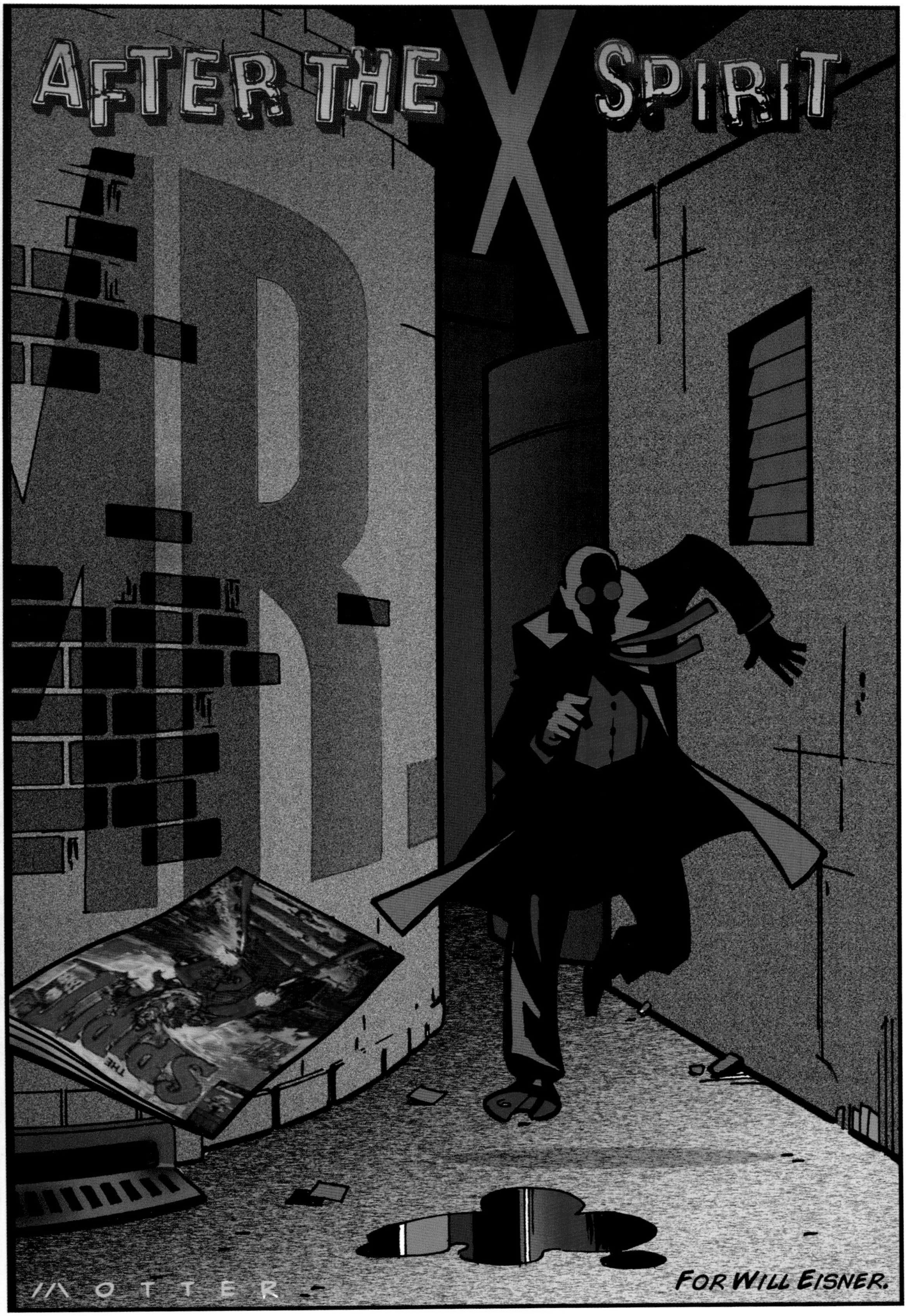
AFTER THE SPIRIT
FOR WILL EISNER.
MOTTER
THE SPIRIT

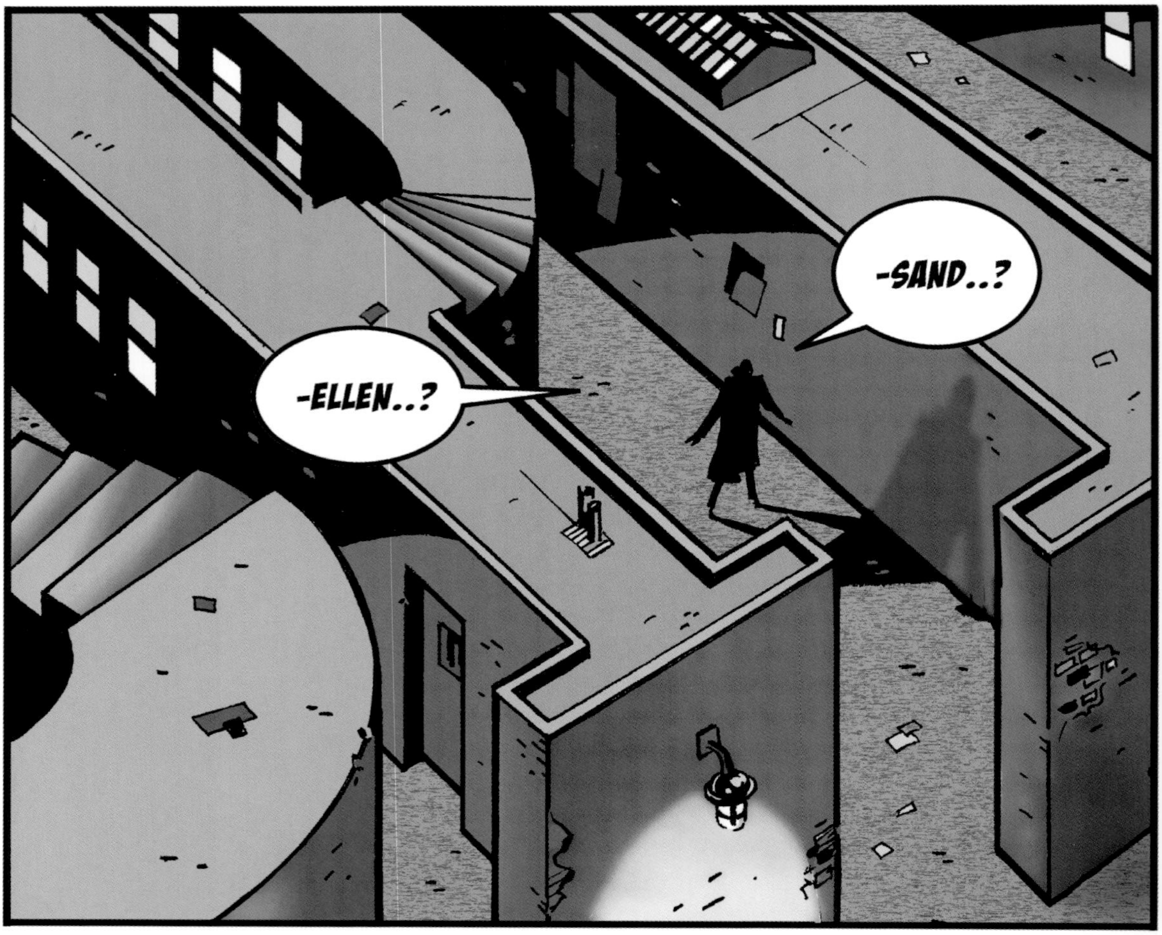
-ELLEN..?
-SAND..?

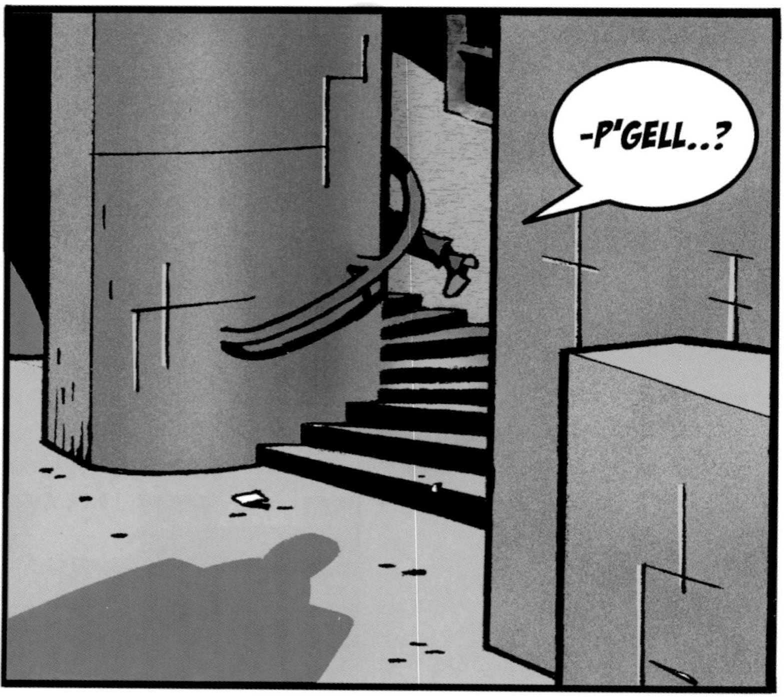
-P'GELL..?

I have been following the man for as long as I can remember. Through the labyrinths of endlessly shifting blind alleys. Through backstreets, both real and imagined.

I have followed his exploits His trials and his heroics.

Like Orpheus calling out for Eurydice, I attempt to summon his muses, hoping he might emerge from the shadows, if only out of curiosity. But, like his namesake he remains fleet and ethereal.

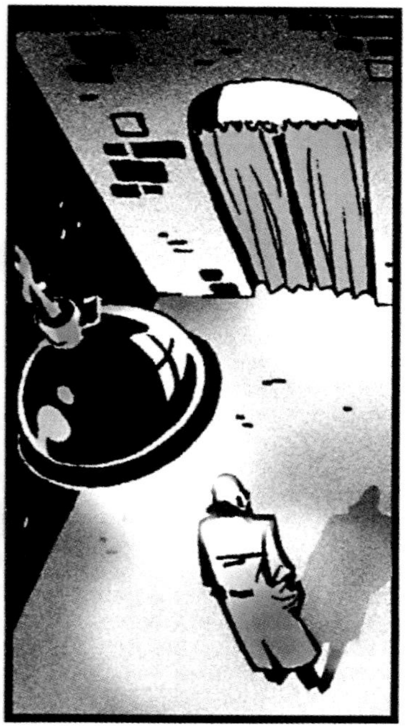

I enter his redoubt, hot on the heels of one of his many chimeras. The path is not difficult. The maze is no Daedalean construct, but nevertheless requires an appetite for endless exploration.

His passageways hold revelations at every turn. And I am unsure just who I might find at work behind the next curtain.

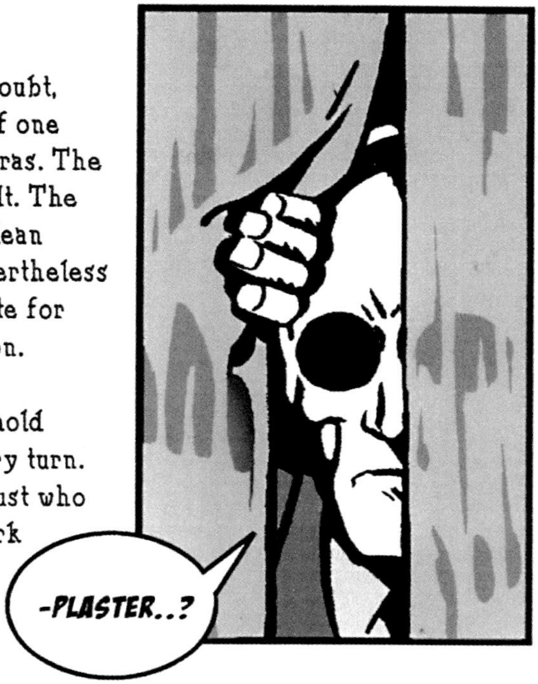
-PLASTER..?

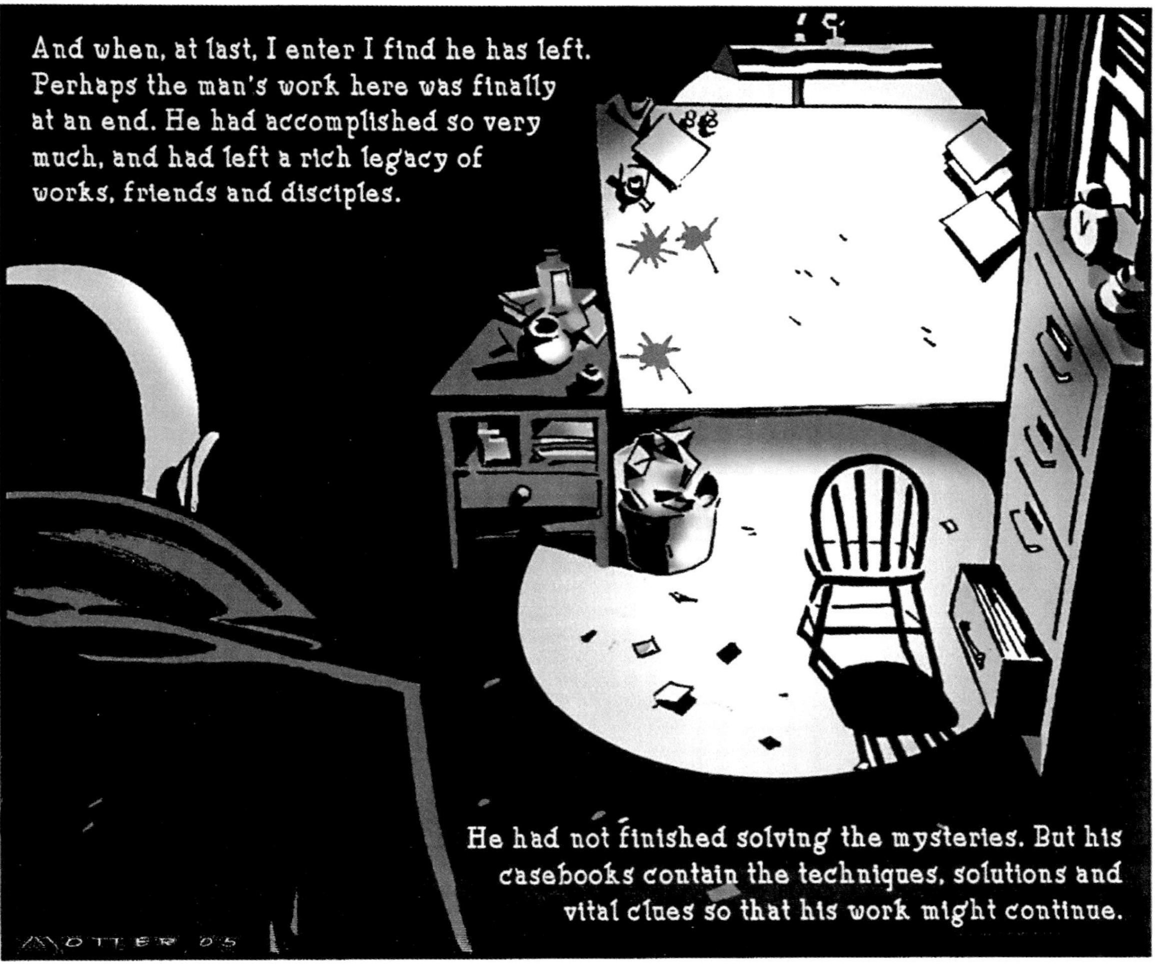
And when, at last, I enter I find he has left. Perhaps the man's work here was finally at an end. He had accomplished so very much, and had left a rich legacy of works, friends and disciples.
He had not finished solving the mysteries. But his casebooks contain the techniques, solutions and vital clues so that his work might continue.
MOTTER 05

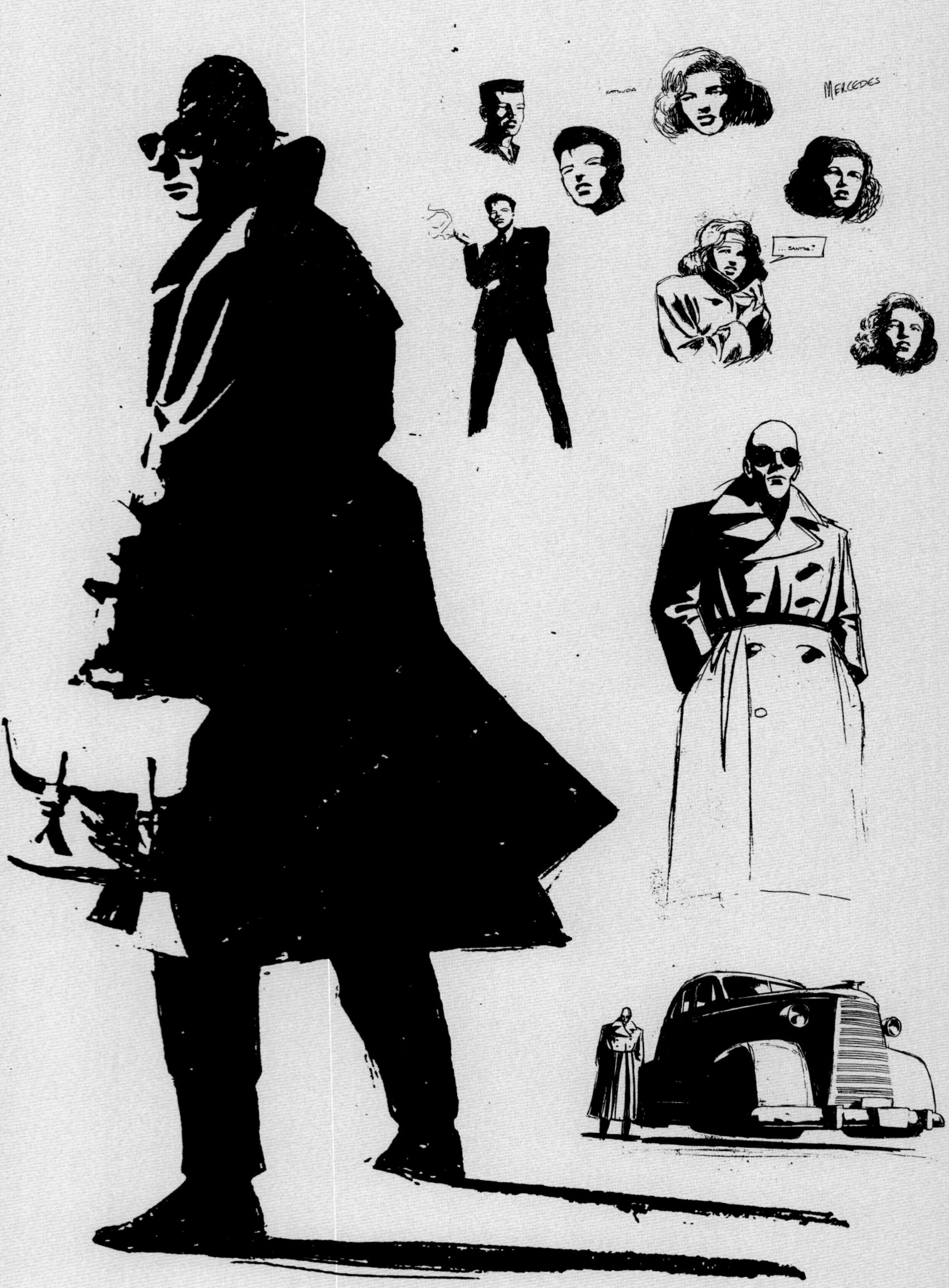
MERCEDES

During the run of issues presented in this volume, Michael Lark auditioned for *Mister X*. I had worked as his editor and art director on *Raymond Chandler's Philip Marlowe: The Little Sister* from Byron Preiss Visual Publications, and always thought he would make a fine contributor for the series. The timing wasn't right, but we later became collaborators on *Terminal City* and *Batman: Nine Lives* for Vertigo and DC. Here is just some of the artwork from Michael's audition.

—DEAN MOTTER

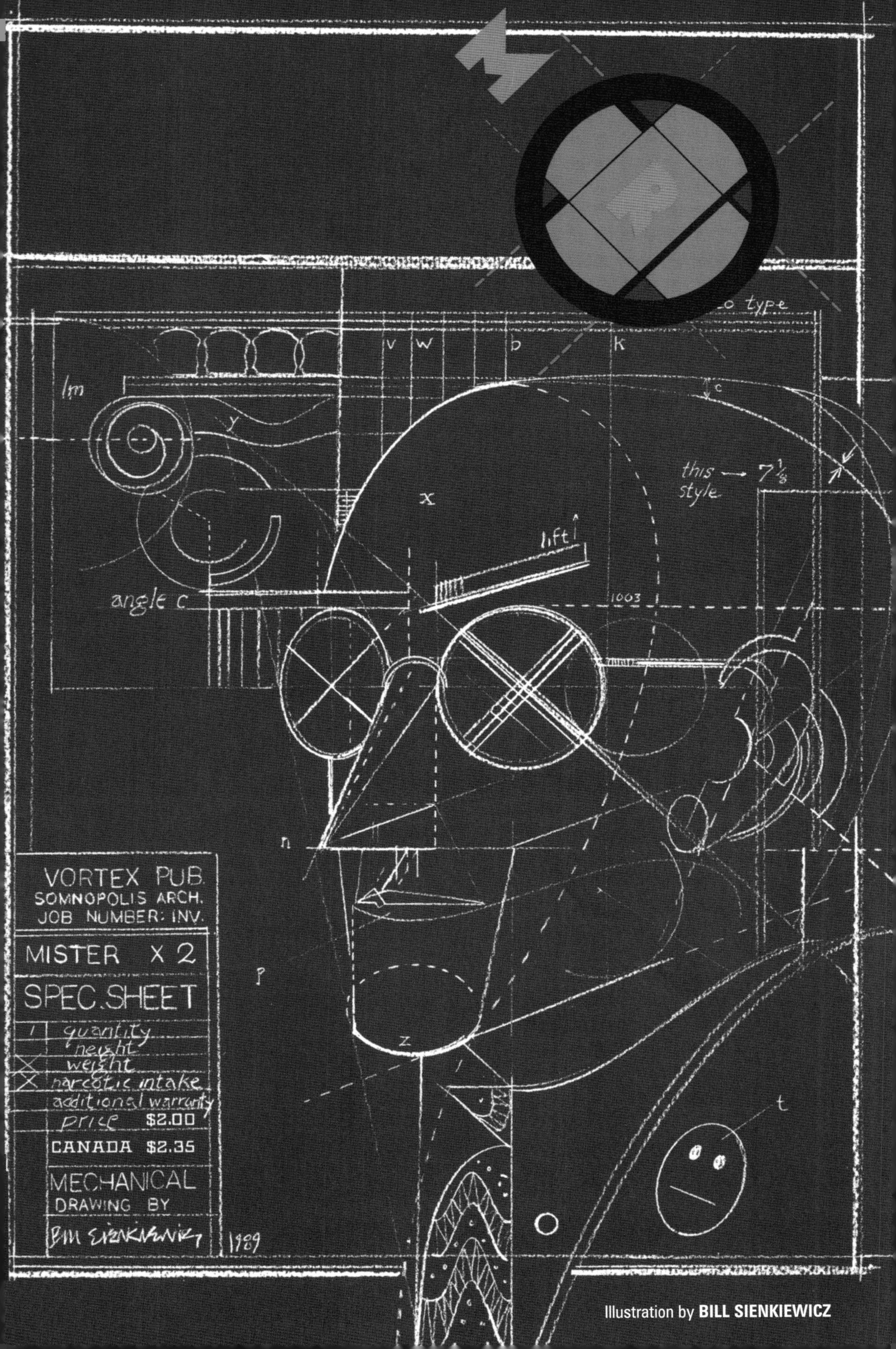

VORTEX PUB.
SOMNOPOLIS ARCH.
JOB NUMBER: INV.
MISTER X 2
SPEC. SHEET
quantity
height
weight
narcotic intake
additional warranty
price $2.00
CANADA $2.35
MECHANICAL
DRAWING BY
1989
this style → 7⅛
lift
angle c

Illustration by **BILL SIENKIEWICZ**

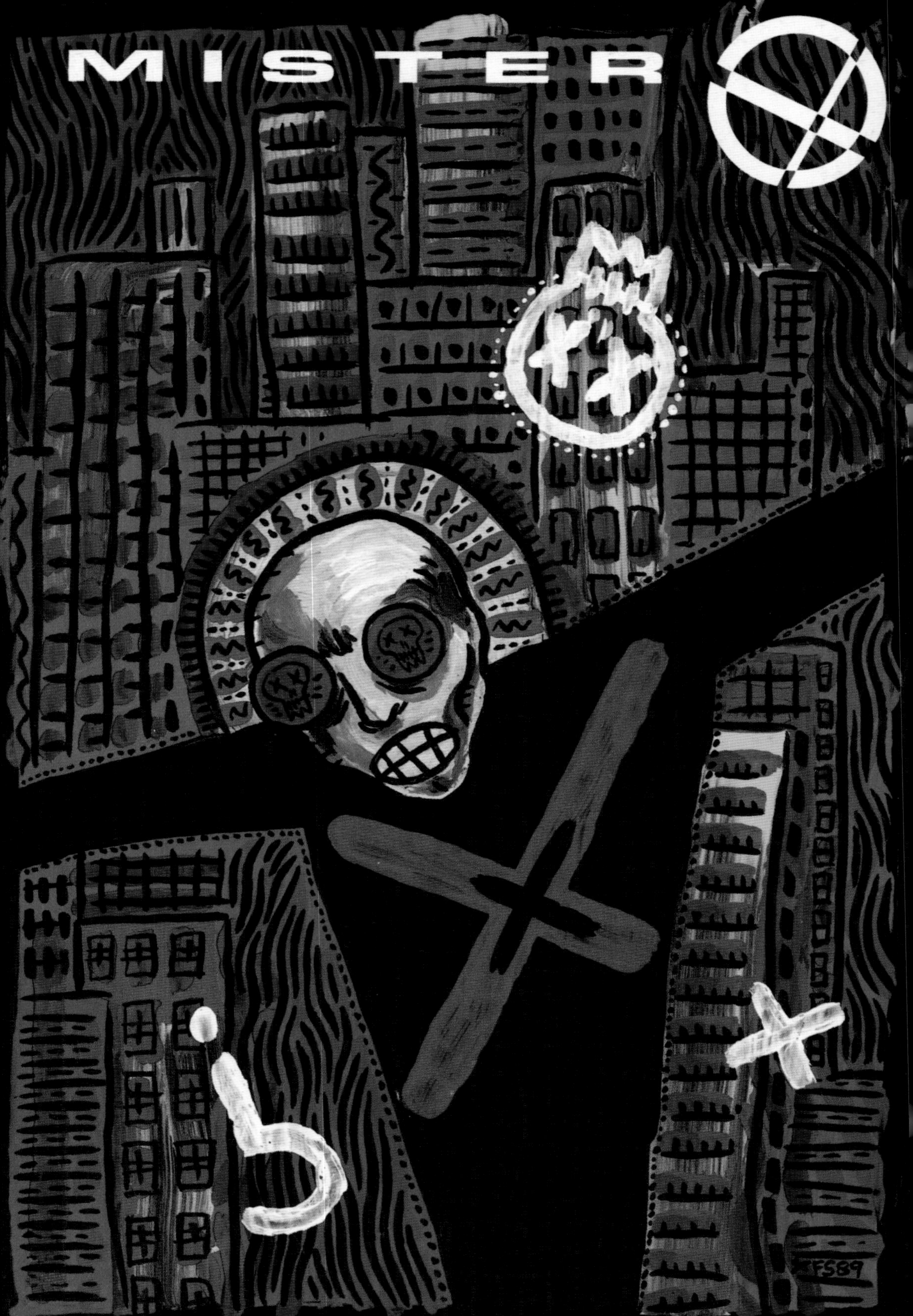
MISTER X
FS89

Illustration by **FIONA SMYTH**

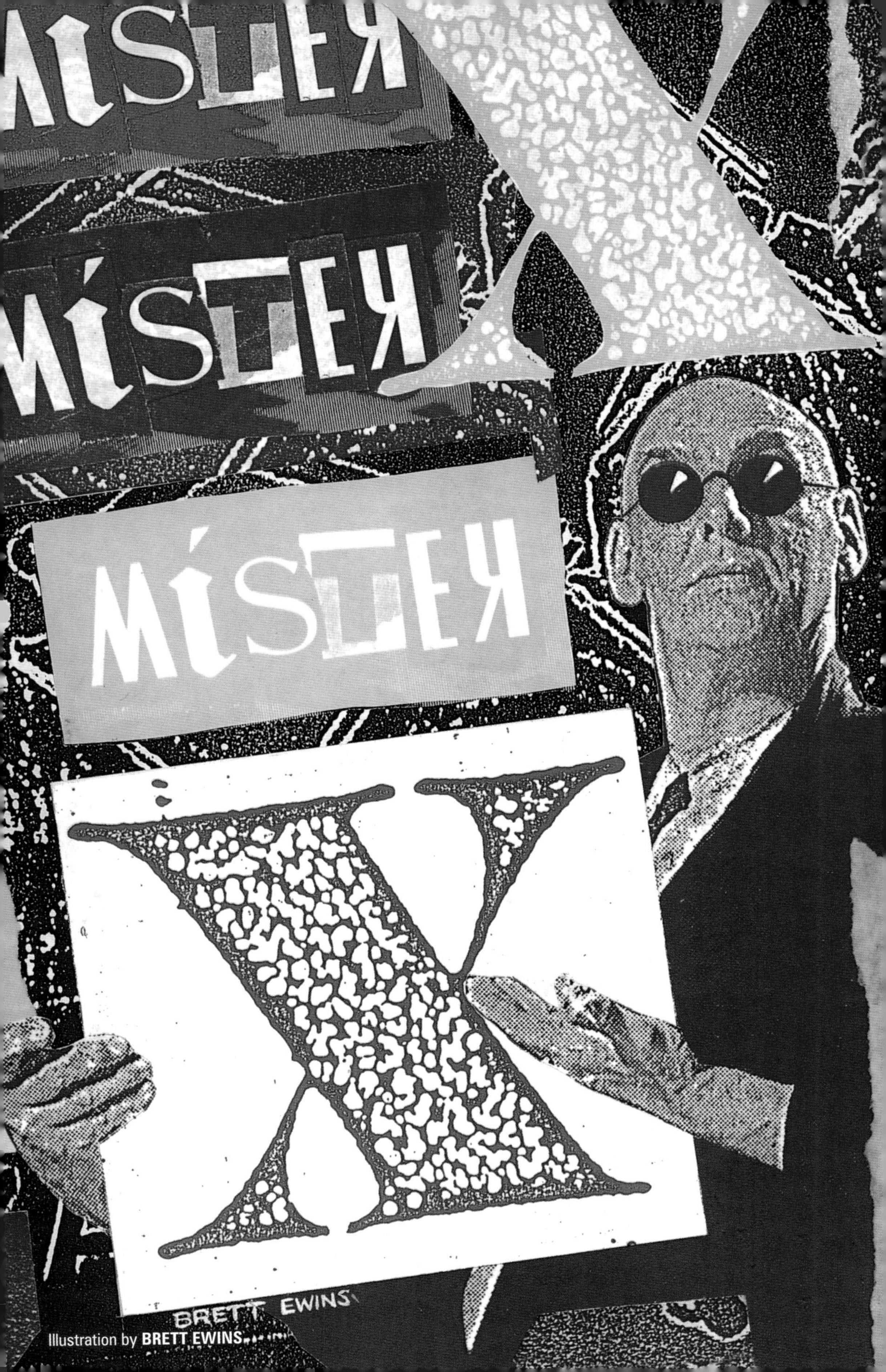

Illustration by **BRETT EWINS**

ISTER

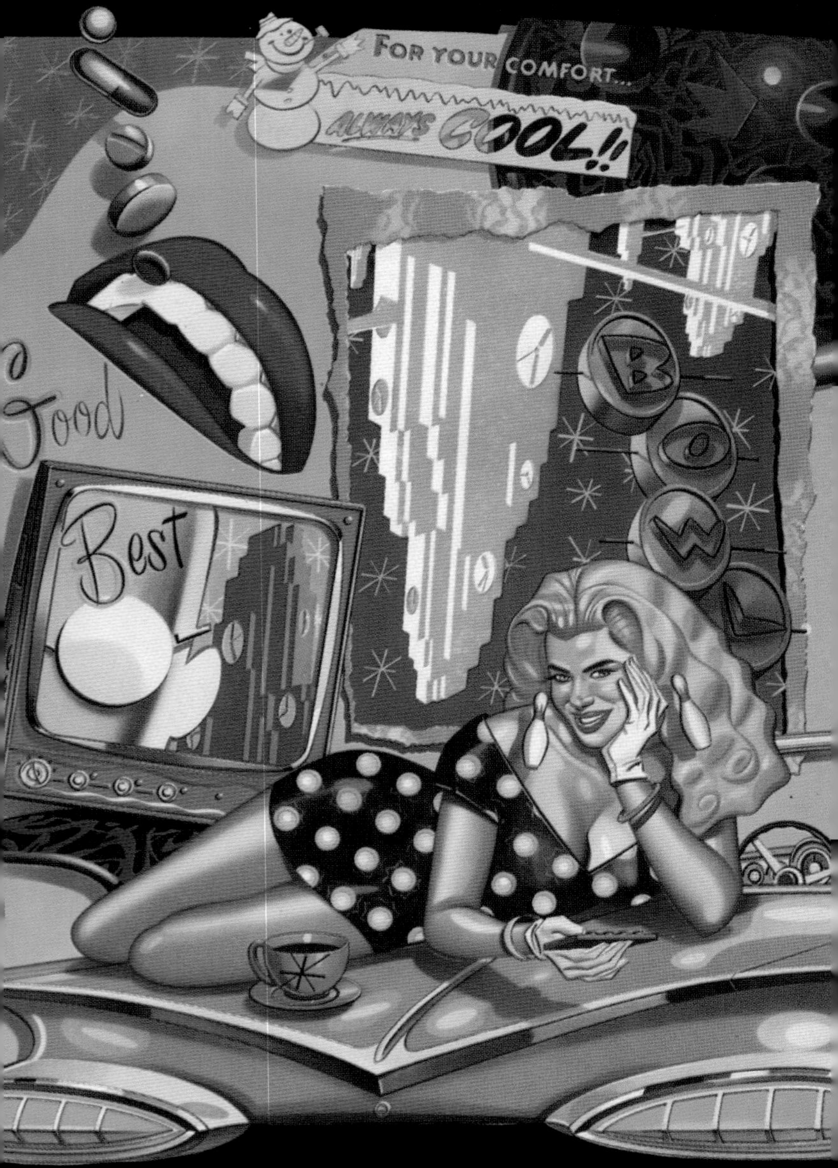

FOR YOUR COMFORT...
ALWAYS COOL!!
Good
Best
BOWL

Illustration by **MITC**

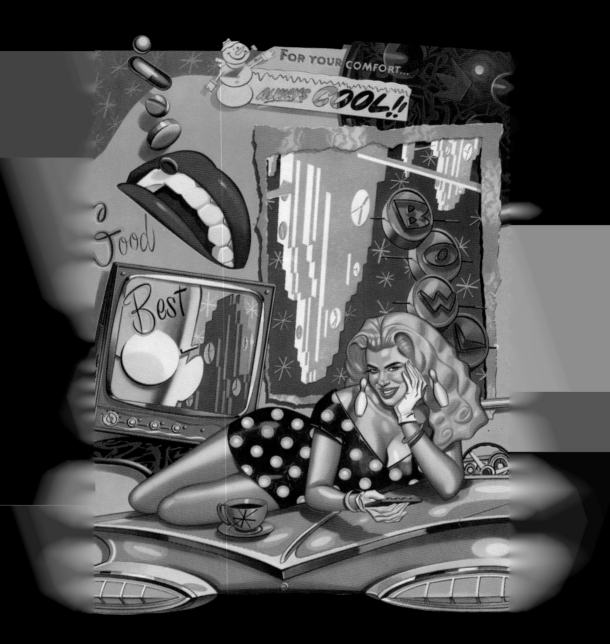

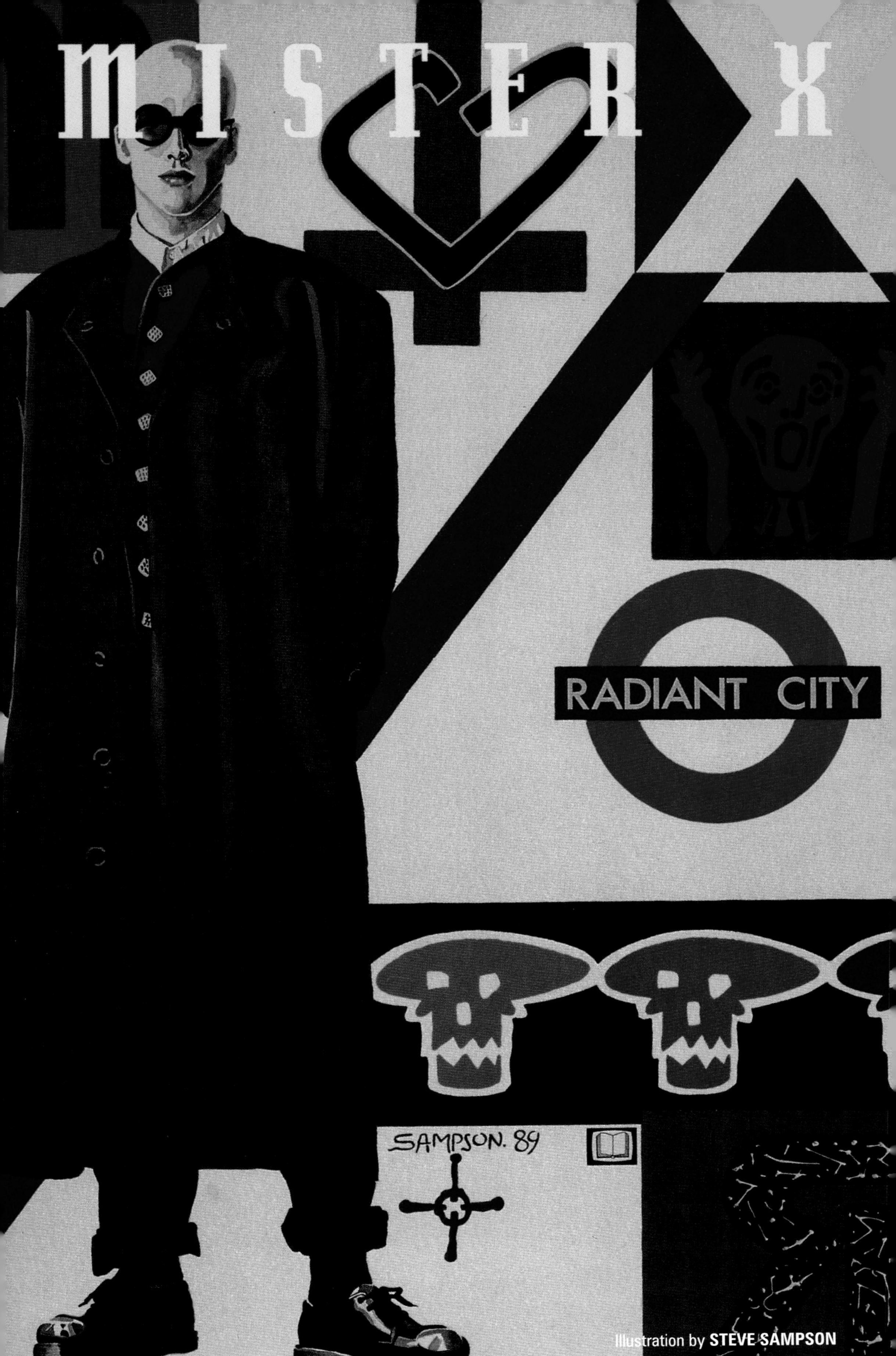
MISTER X
RADIANT CITY
SAMPSON. 89

Illustration by **STEVE SAMPSON**

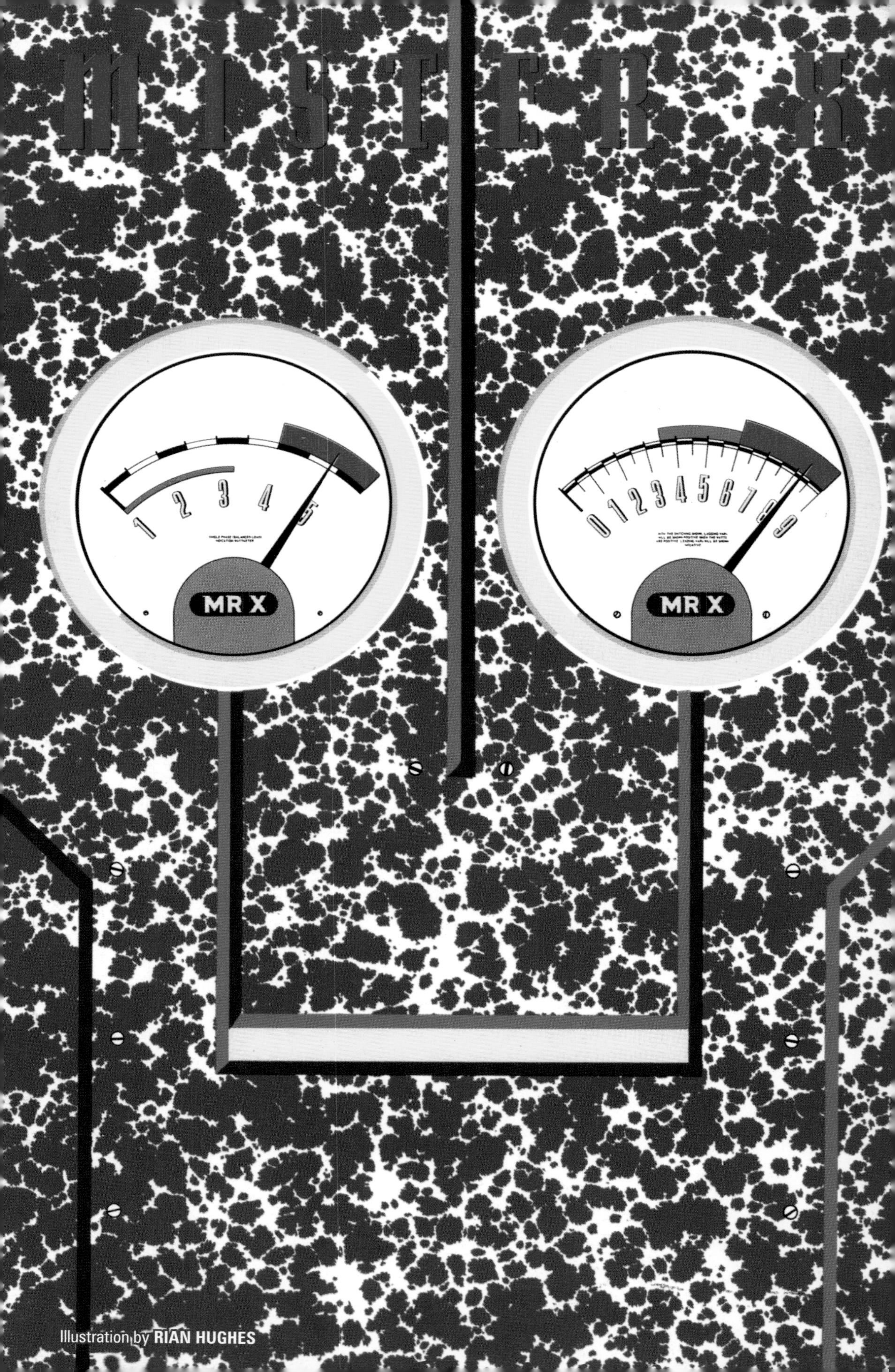
MISTER X
1 2 3 4 5
MR X
0 1 2 3 4 5 6 7 8 9
MR X

Illustration by **RIAN HUGHES**

EXTRO

Stan Lee with Jeffrey Morgan (right) in 1968.

In 1977—seven years before Dean Motter began writing volume 1 of *Mister X* magazine in 1984 and twelve years before I began writing volume 2 of *Mister X* magazine in 1989—Dean and I wrote and recorded an hourlong, sixteen-track ambient electronic avant-garde progressive art rock concept album called *Thrilling Women*.

Admittedly, this record—which is available at BongoBeat.com—is not the official soundtrack to this omnibus. But it very well could be. For although it predates our work on *Mister X* by over half a decade, the extraordinary thing about *Thrilling Women* is that it nevertheless foreshadows many of the themes that we would later go on to develop at length during our respective tenures writing the magazine.

Listen closely between the notes and you'll hear the precognitive ghost roar of future echoes: the shimmering airships, the beckoning metropolis, the lethal women, the unsolved disappearances, the illicit nightclubs, the clandestine romances, the antiquated technology, and, above all else, the vast litany of compulsive obsessions.

Dean's extensive historical liner notes tell the full story of how *Thrilling Women* came to be, but what they *don't* reveal is what happened after we finished recording the album: how I resumed my position as the de facto Canadian editor of *CREEM* "America's Only Rock 'n' Roll Magazine," and became the authorized biographer of both Alice Cooper and the Stooges; and how Dean, never content to let anything lie sleeping, chose instead to remain behind and visually chart the minds-eye environs that his own music had aurally made manifest—the result being the influential odyssey that you can read in Dark Horse's *Mister X: The Archives*.

The twelve issues of *Mister X* which appear in *this* volume under my byline remain an anomaly in my five-decade-long career as a rock critic because, aside from a few early exceptions—most notably in tandem with ace illustrator Ken Steacy for a 1979 cover story in Mike Friedrich's landmark anthology series *Star*Reach*—they represent my entire published output as a comic-book writer.

As such, I'm deeply gratified that Dark Horse has deemed these seldom-seen stories of mine to be worthy of reprint in this deluxe edition. I'm equally indebted to the following five individuals, without whom this book would literally not exist:

Mister X creator Dean Motter, for allowing me to wander around Somnopolis unescorted; Vortex Comics publisher William P. Marks, for printing the tales I came back with; British artists Shane Oakley and D'Israeli for expertly illustrating my words with a suitably unstable style that's *still* decades ahead of its time; and Ken Holewczynski for ably inking their pencils with equally irrational aplomb.

Finally, a few words regarding the current whereabouts of everybody's favorite gun-toting air pirate, Evelyn Mary O'Rilley McBride. Where did Bride go after she left the Ninth Academy? Did she abandon her search for Mr. X? Would she ever resume broadcasting on Radio Crinoline from her iconoclast airship, the *Princess of Hydrogen*? *And what awful fate befell her in the arcane warren of vaults secreted deep beneath Radiant City's hallowed Hall of Heroes?*

Stay tuned to my website for more info!

JEFFREY MORGAN
JeffreyMorgan.info

MORE ADVENTURE AND INTRIGUE IN THE GOOD OLD-FASHIONED FUTURE:

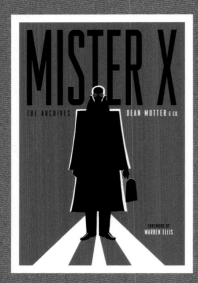

MISTER X: THE ARCHIVES
By Dean Motter, Los Bros. Hernandez, Seth,
Paul Rivoche, and others
ISBN 978-1-59582-184-3 | $79.99 US

MISTER X: CONDEMNED
By Dean Motter
ISBN 978-1-59582-359-5 | $14.99 US

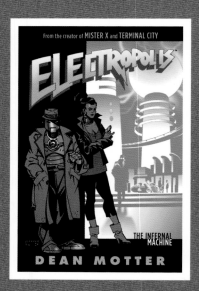

ELECTROPOLIS
By Dean Motter
ISBN 978-1-59582-363-2 | $14.99 US

MYSPACE DARK HORSE PRESENTS VOL. 5
By Sergio Aragonés, Matt Kindt, Dean Motter,
Darick Robertson, Jill Thompson, and others
ISBN 978-1-59582-570-4 | $19.99 US